Norway
Finland
Sweden
Denmark
East Germany
West Germany
Poland
Austria
Czechoslovakia
Hungary
Yugoslavia
Romania
Albania
Bulgaria
Italy
Greece
Turkey
Tunisia
Cyprus
Israel
Syria
Lebanon
Iraq
Iran
Jordan
Kuweit
Bahrein
Qatar
U.A.E.
Oman
AR Yemen
PDR Yemen

Soviet Union
(U.S.S.R.)

Mongolia

China

North Korea
South Korea
Japan

Pacific
Ocean

Afghanistan
Pakistan
Nepal
Bhutan
Bangla-desh
Burma
India
Laos
Taiwan
Hong Kong
Thailand
Vietnam
Kampuchea
Philippines
Sri Lanka
Brunei
Malaysia
Singapore

Libya
Egypt
Saudi Arabia
Niger
Chad
Sudan
Djibuti
Ethiopia
Central African Republic
Cameroon
Gabon
Congo
Rwanda
Uganda
Somalia
Kenya
Zaire
Burundi
Tanzania
Angola
Zambia
Malawi
Mozambique
Zimbabwe
Botswana
Madagascar
Namibia
Swaziland
South Africa
Lesotho

Mauritius

Indonesia
Papua New Guinea
Solomon Islands
Fiji
Vanuatu
New Caledonia
Australia

Indian Ocean

New Zealand

Antarctica

(equatorial scale)
0   2000 miles
0   3000 kilometers

HUMAN GEOGRAPHY

People, Places, and Cultures

HUMAN GEOGRAPHY

SECOND EDITION

PEOPLE, PLACES, AND CULTURES

Robert H. Stoddard
University of Nebraska-Lincoln

David J. Wishart
University of Nebraska-Lincoln

Brian W. Blouet
Texas A & M University

Prentice Hall, Englewood Cliffs, New Jersey 07632

Library of Congress Cataloging-in-Publication Data

Stoddard, Robert H. (date)
    Human geography : people, places, and cultures / Robert H.
Stoddard, David J. Wishart, Brian W. Blouet. —2nd ed.
        p. cm.
    Includes bibliographies and indexes.
    ISBN 0-13-445172-4
    1. Anthropo-geography.   2. Ethnology.   I. Wishart, David J.,
1946-   II. Blouet, Brian W., 1936-   .   III. Title.
    GF41.S76 1989   88-27403
    304—dc19   CIP

Editorial/production supervision: Maria McColligan
Interior and cover design: Kenny Beck
Manufacturing buyer: Paula Massenaro
Cover photo: Courtesy of Sally Stoddard

1989, 1986 by Prentice-Hall, Inc.
A Division of Simon & Schuster
Englewood Cliffs, New Jersey 07632

Printed in the United States of America
10 9 8 7 6 5 4 3 2 1

ISBN 0-13-445172-4

Prentice-Hall International (UK) Limited, *London*
Prentice-Hall of Australia Pty. Limited, *Sydney*
Prentice-Hall Canada Inc., *Toronto*
Prentice-Hall Hispanoamericana, S.A., *Mexico*
Prentice-Hall of India Private Limited, *New Delhi*
Prentice-Hall of Japan, Inc., *Tokyo*
Simon & Schuster Asia Pte. Ltd., *Singapore*
Editora Prentice-Hall do Brasil, Ltda., *Rio de Janeiro*

Captions and Credits for Chapter Opening Photos

Chapter 1: View of the Earth (African Portion) from Space. Photo courtesy of NASA.

Chapter 2: Ruins of Machu Picchu, a Fifteenth Century Inca Settlement. Photo courtesy of Sally Stoddard.

Chapter 3: An American Family Gathering of Two Generations. Photo courtesy of Sally Stoddard.

Chapter 4: Vehicles for Moving Household Belongings. Photo courtesy of Sally Stoddard.

Chapter 5: A Nepalese Family Celebrating a Festival. Photo courtesy of Sally Stoddard.

Chapter 6: Messages on Indian Billboards. Photo courtesy of Sally Stoddard.

Chapter 7: Pilgrims at Altötting, West Germany. Photo courtesy of Sally Stoddard.

Chapter 8: An American Election Office. Photo courtesy of Sally Stoddard.

Chapter 9: Traditional Farming with Animals. Photo courtesy of Sally Stoddard.

Chapter 10: Communication in an Industrial and Service-Oriented Economy. Photo courtesy of Sally Stoddard.

Chapter 11: An Urban Landscape in Hong Kong. Photo courtesy of Sally Stoddard.

Chapter 12: Stream Pollution. Photo courtesy of Sally Stoddard.

Chapter 13: A View of the Future. Photo courtesy of Sally Stoddard.

CONTENTS

5

CULTURE   100

6

LANGUAGE AND COMMUNICATION   142

7

RELIGION   170

8

POLITICAL UNITS   204

LIST OF TABLES

LIST OF BOXES
(with Point Counterpoint)

PREFACE

The purpose of this book is to support introductory courses in human and cultural geography. The inclusion of the changing geographies of the past provides a background for an understanding of contemporary conditions and a basis for predicting future world patterns.

In addition to a broad historical perspective, the text refers to a wide variety of places throughout the world because understanding geographic relationships is enhanced by learning about cultures and activities in many environments. Furthermore, recognizing the global interdependency of people depends on knowing about differences among numerous places.

Both the spatial and ecological components of geography are emphasized. By focussing on spatial characteristics, we hope to help students understand the ways their lives are influenced by their own geographic behavior, which is affected by, and contributes to, the aggregate distributions and interactions of societies in general. To this end, we present information about numerous demographic, cultural, political, and economic forces as they have operated, and continue to operate, in a variety of cultures.

By stressing ecological relationships, we build on students' general awareness that natural features, such as climate and landforms, vary. We emphasize the numerous ways people have produced differences among places in the world by modifying the physical environment, and we discuss ways environmental conditions have affected humans in various cultural settings.

Even though this is an introductory text, we deliberately retain most of the complexity and uncertainty associated with spatial and ecological relationships. The text is interlaced with many other issues that should arouse readers' curiosity about the fascinating world of geography. Controversies about population trends, the future of resource utilization, the convergence or divergence of world cultures, and other geographic issues are presented realistically as complex issues without simple answers. We include several point-counterpoint arguments that can be used to focus on major issues and to generate discussion.

ACKNOWLEDGEMENTS

This book could not have been written without help from many people. Logan Campbell, then of Prentice Hall, originally suggested this text. Since then we have drawn on a wide variety of sources for ideas, examples, and illustrations. We cannot enumerate all the friends and colleagues who have contributed information and photographs, but we especially appreciate the help of a group of reviewers who worked carefully through several drafts of the book and made helpful suggestions. Those who reviewed the text include: Arthur J. Hawley, University of North Carolina-Chapel Hill; Alan Backler, University of Indiana; Peter O. Muller, University of Miami; James W. Scott, Western Washington University; Karl Raitz, University of Kentucky; Olwyn M. Blouet, Texas A & M University; and Sally Stoddard, University of Nebraska-Lincoln. We received valuable advice from the reviewers, who managed to combine suggestions for improvement with sufficient encouragement to keep the authors going during the revision process.

We have benefitted by working with Logan Campbell, David Stirling, Betsy Perry, Nancy Forsyth, Ed Moura, Maria McColligan, and Curt Yehnert at Prentice-Hall.

Of considerable help in preparing the second edition were the reviews of Robert Mitchell, University of Maryland; John Rice, University of Minnesota; Albert Larson, University of Illinois–Chicago; Lynden Williams, Ohio University; Clifton Pannell, University of Georgia; David Stephens, Youngstown State University; and Roland Chardon, Louisianna State University.

At Prentice Hall, Dan Joraanstad initiated the revision and Maria McColligan again offered many suggestions for improving the text.

New maps have been prepared under the direction of Christopher Mueller-Wille and with the assistance of Deborah Partain, Debbie Meier, and Lori Erickson (all at the Cartographics Laboratory, Texas A & M University). We are indebted to Sally Stoddard (University of Nebraska-Lincoln), whose photographic expertise in producing and editing pictures contributed greatly to the visual quality of the text.

The book, of course, stands on a body of geographical literature, part of which we include in the bibliographies. To all the scholars, ancient and modern, whose ideas we have borrowed, modified, and incorporated, we owe a special debt.

R.H.S.
D.J.W.
B.W.B.

HUMAN GEOGRAPHY

People, Places, and Cultures

1 PROLOGUE: WHY GEOGRAPHY?

**The Geographic Viewpoint
Organizational Framework
An Answer**

Imagine a country where the inhabitants, after centuries of isolation, have just been contacted by the rest of the world. Experts rush to learn more about this hitherto unknown land. Anthropologists search for clues to the structure of the society; political scientists examine the system of local government; and botanists identify the flora. In this search for knowledge, geographers can also contribute to an understanding of the land and its people. What would be the geographers' approach and objectives?

THE GEOGRAPHIC VIEWPOINT

Geography is rooted in everyday life. It concerns the diverse ways people live on, and put their mark on, the surface of the earth. One traditional definition of geography, "the study of the earth as the home of humankind," is a valid although insufficient definition. It needs expansion because it doesn't tell enough about the uniqueness of geography.

Geography exists as a separate branch of knowledge because of its distinctive point of view—its way of looking at and generalizing about the earth and its inhabitants. This distinctiveness is not based on any specific set of objects or human activities that geographers study. In this respect, geography contrasts with most other disciplines. Economics, for example, deals primarily with the production, movement, and consumption of goods and services; geology is concerned with the composition of the earth's crust; and demography pertains to the characteristics of human populations. Geography, on the other hand, includes many kinds of phenomena, both tangible and intangible, natural and human-made. Each phenomenon is examined, however, from a distinctive viewpoint—one that is regarded as geographic.

The geographic viewpoint entails two main perspectives; a **spatial perspective** and an **ecological perspective**. Geographers, then, would look at this newly contacted region through two lenses. The first lens is spatial (see Figure 1-1). This means that geographers will try to understand why people and the landscapes they create are arranged as they are. For example, typical questions might involve the economic characteristics of production, consumption, and movement of goods, but such queries would always start with the location of these economic activities.

Initial questions usually include the word *where*. Where are the people located? Where are particular crops grown? Where are the villages situated? And so on.

Geographers generally put such locational information on maps. Maps abstract and simplify reality; they allow us to grasp distributions that often are too complex to understand in their actual occurrence. As an illustration, suppose we wanted to study the geography of the major highways in Brazil. It would be very difficult to describe verbally and remember the location of every highway, especially if we wanted to compare the distribution of highways with those of rivers and cities. In contrast, a map (such as shown by Figure 8-22) can represent all the locations of highways in a way that is easily comprehended.

Maps can show the distributions of many kinds of phenomena, ranging from visible objects, such as grocery stores, to invisible attributes, such as political

Spatial perspective. An emphasis on the locations, patterns, or arrangements of phenomena (see Ecological perspective).

Ecological perspective. An emphasis on the interrelationships between humans and their environments (see Spatial perspective).

3

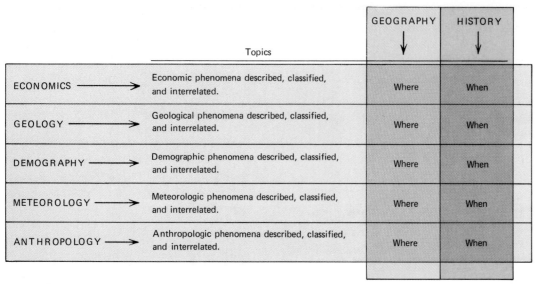

Topics		GEOGRAPHY ↓	HISTORY ↓
ECONOMICS ⟶	Economic phenomena described, classified, and interrelated.	Where	When
GEOLOGY ⟶	Geological phenomena described, classified, and interrelated.	Where	When
DEMOGRAPHY ⟶	Demographic phenomena described, classified, and interrelated.	Where	When
METEOROLOGY ⟶	Meteorologic phenomena described, classified, and interrelated.	Where	When
ANTHROPOLOGY ⟶	Anthropologic phenomena described, classified, and interrelated.	Where	When

Figure 1-1. The Spatial Viewpoint of Geography. Geography is concerned with where economic, geologic, demographic, meteorologic, and anthropologic elements (as well as others not represented here) are located, why they are located there, and how those locations are interrelated.

opinions. They can depict the patterns of the past (e.g., the sites of ancient irrigation works), of the present (such as the location of today's traffic accidents in a large city), or of the future (for instance, the countries predicted to experience high birth rates in 1995). In fact, you are probably already familiar with the large variety of features shown by road maps, topographic sheets, and atlases.

A variety of techniques may be used to represent distributions on a map. One technique is to make a dot or small symbol at each place that corresponds to the actual occurrence on the earth (which is illustrated by Figure 6-11). Another way is to shade all of the areas where a particular kind of feature, activity, or idea exists. For example, all the countries in the world where death rates in 1987 were above 15 per 1000 population can be displayed by a specified shade (as shown by Figure 3-7). The locations can be represented by other techniques (some of which you will discover elsewhere in this book), techniques that can be understood by reading the map legend. Thus the legend (a key that explains what each map symbol represents) is an essential part of a map because it helps the reader understand what is being shown.

The amount of generalization on a map depends largely on its scale. The **map scale** refers to the ratio of map distance to the corresponding earth distance. This ratio can be expressed as a fraction, as a line representing a specified distance, or as a statement of comparative distances (for example, one inch on the map represents one mile on the earth). A large-scale map where, for example, one centimeter on the map represents 650,000 centimeters on the ground can show considerable local detail [see Figure 1-2(a) in Box 1-1]. A small-scale map, on the other hand, of perhaps a scale of one centimeter to 25,000,000 centimeters of real world (1:25,000,000) sacrifices local detail for generalization over a wide area [Figure 1-2(b)]. It is impor-

tant to notice the map scale because it affects the kind of information that can, and cannot, be shown.

Maps are the essential "tools" of geography because the spatial distributions they portray are often the starting point of geographic analysis. That is, maps are an effective way of posing the initial question about locations; but geographic understanding depends on discovering the reasons behind those locations. The reasons might be economic, political, religious, or others; but if they explain spatial distributions, they are also geographic. Knowing something about the reasons for existing patterns of location helps in our general understanding of humans. With such knowledge, geographers can better predict how the inhabitants will use an area in the future. The geographic patterns or distributions of today often form the framework for the spatial behavior of tomorrow. In time, of course, circumstances may change. Some resources may be depleted and others may be discovered, and technological or economic conditions may alter the use of those resources. Nevertheless, the new geographic patterns that emerge will probably reflect those observed now.

The implications of the spatial perspective might be compared with learning the strategies of play in American football. In this game, the purpose of the defensive team is to place players in a pattern that will prevent the opposing team from advancing the ball. Meanwhile, the offensive team notices where the defensive players are located and plans a strategy for outmaneuvering the defenders. Skilled players are able to observe the positions of all other players, analyze those arrangements, predict future patterns, and decide where response moves are most likely to succeed. This concern with the locations—that is, the spatial arrangement—of players is basically geographic, even though it occurs in a small area and under controlled conditions.

BOX 1-1. VARYING GEOGRAPHICAL SCALES

On a large-scale map, the details of Singapore's internal population density can be shown [Figure 1-2(a)].
On a map drawn to a smaller scale but showing a larger portion of Southeast Asia, the population density of Singapore can be represented only as a single, seemingly homogeneous value [Figure 1-2(b)]. On a map of the entire world (see front endpaper), Singapore virtually disappears, so its population density cannot be portrayed.

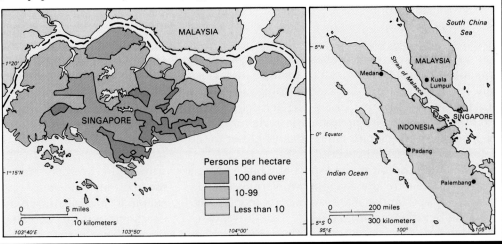

Figure 1-2. Singapore at Contrasting Scales.

The importance of understanding spatial arrangement can be illustrated also by considering the game of chess, especially by noting the difference between **absolute location** and **relative location**. Absolute location is expressed in terms of two dimensions, such as latitude and longitude on the earth (or map) or rank and file on a chess board. For example, Singapore is located at 1°20′ N latitude and 103°50′ E longitude; and the position of a chess piece can be indicated as rank 4 and file K [Figure 1-3(a)].

Although knowing the locations of only one player's chess pieces does not reveal much about the

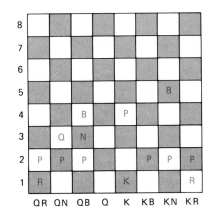

Figure 1-3. The Importance of Position in Chess. (a) The absolute locations of chess pieces can be specified by their rank and file (notations that function like latitude and longitude). (b) These locations are most meaningful, however, in terms of the positions *relative* to the opponent's pieces.

Map scale. The ratio of map distance to the corresponding earth distance. For example, 1:30 means one linear unit (such as an inch or a centimeter) on the map represents 30 of those units on the earth. If a second map has a ratio of 1:3,000,000 then comparatively it has a much *smaller* scale. (See Box 1-1).

Absolute location. A position on the earth that is indicated by a fixed grid (or physical features); for example, the site of Chicago is at 41°49′ N, 87°37′ W (see Relative location).

Relative location. A position on the earth that is indicated in terms of other phenomena. For example, Chicago is situated where rail, water, and highway routes converge (see Absolute location).

probable outcome of the game, if we are able to see where those pieces are relative to those of the opponent, then we can gain insight into the reasons for their locations and will have a basis for predicting the outcome of the game (Figure 1-3(b)). Relative location takes into account the position of a place in terms of other places.

Obviously absolute locations do not change over time. Relative locations, however, do change. For example, the relative locations of Los Angeles, San Francisco, and Seattle have changed in terms of their proximity to major international trade routes. Once they were far from the dominant trading area of the North Atlantic. However, as trading activities in the Pacific have grown in importance in recent decades, the locations of these port cities are now closer to the major trade routes of the world.

Absolute location is one aspect of a place known as its **site.** The term *site* is applied to various characteristics of a particular place such as its topography, soil type, buildings, and land use.

In contrast, the **situation** of a place means essentially the same as its relative position. Take, for example, the case of Singapore. In 1819, Sir Stamford Raffles chose for the site of a new city the low-lying ground on the south side of Singapore island next to the mouth of the Singapore River. This site had disadvantages because it was unprotected from the ocean tides and waves. The situation, however, was ideal for a trading station. Singapore island lay close to the southern end of the Strait of Malacca through which passed most of the ocean traffic moving between the Indian Ocean and the China Sea. As the port of Singapore grew, money was invested to build an offshore breakwater; this protected the harbor from heavy seas and thus modified some of the disadvantages of the original site.

Strategies that depend upon understanding relative locations are encountered frequently in our daily lives. Typical situations are the following: (1) a college student determines where to live during the coming school year; (2) a president of a grocery chain asks a consultant where to build a new store; (3) a family quickly decides where to find protection from an approaching tornado; (4) a manufacturer chooses where to haul toxic wastes; and (5) a farmer ponders on which of his fields to plant wheat during the next season. In all these situations, answers are based on observing the locations of existing phenomena (that is, living quarters, grocery stores, tornado shelters, waste-disposal sites, and arable land), analyzing the locational options, and deciding on the best place. Making such a geographic decision will invariably depend on the relative positions of numerous other features.

The geographers' second lens is ecological. The geographers would seek to explain how the people in our hypothetical country interact with the **natural environment.** Interaction might be expressed by the way the inhabitants recognize and utilize resources and, in the process, how they shape the face of the land. In turn, people may be influenced by various characteristics of the natural environment such as the climate and landforms. This reciprocal relationship between people and the natural environment, each affecting and being affected by the other, has been at the forefront of geographical investigation since the time of the ancient Greeks.

It is important to remember that even today, with our advanced technology, we are still organisms living within the context of nature. In ecological terms, we are members of **ecosystems** and part of the entire **ecosphere.** This means that human actions affect the natural environment in many diverse and complex ways. What we may regard as an "improvement" of the natural conditions (by draining marshland, for example) may also have detrimental effects (such as destroying wildlife and altering the groundwater elsewhere). The "benefits" we gain from using the earth's resources must be weighed against the "costs" of their exhaustion or degradation. These, and numerous other issues concerning the effects that humans and the natural environment have on each other, are central to geographers' interests.

The ultimate objective of the geographers would be to understand this hypothetical country as a place—a portion of the earth's surface. They could go on to show how this place is different from, as well as similar to, other parts of the earth. Given this background of geographic knowledge, it might then be possible to predict how such a formerly isolated land would evolve in contact with the rest of the world.

Geography necessarily is an integrating subject that deals with an extensive range of objects and events. (In this sense, it is similar to history, which integrates activities over time; see Figure 1-1). Integration, or synthesis, is achieved through both perspectives—spatial and ecological. An explanation for the spatial distribution of any one phenomenon must consider the combined locations of many other factors. Likewise, the ecological relationships between humans and their environments usually involve numerous interacting phenomena.

In addition, studying geography requires utilizing an historical approach. Spatial relationships that have occurred under previous circumstances may provide insight into human behavior that is not evident under present conditions. Furthermore, contemporary patterns are greatly influenced by where things were in the past because of **geographical inertia,** that is, the tendency for activities to retain their locations even when conditions change. Similarly, the ways humans affect, and are affected by, their environment at a given time normally result from relationships that have developed over long periods of time. The importance of past patterns and the fact that spatial and ecological relationships continually change mean that time, as well as place, is critical to geographic understanding.

The spatial and ecological perspectives are the central themes of this book. They are woven through each chapter, sometimes on the surface, sometimes in the background, like threads in a carpet. Often historical information supplies the background for a better explanation of current conditions. Moreover, ideas from other disciplines are incorporated into the text to assist readers in understanding the geographic characteristics of humans. The mixture of these conceptual threads forms varying designs, depending on the emphasis of each chapter. First, however, more needs to be said about the objectives and organization of this book because it is better to know where you are going before you embark.

ORGANIZATIONAL FRAMEWORK

The organizational framework of the book can be explained with the use of a diagram (see Figure 1-4). The components of this diagram consist of the entire human population and its divisions into cultural groups, the natural environment, the cultural landscape (or built environment), and several relationships among these elements.

The starting point in this book on **human geography** is world population (see Chapter 2). As geographers, we are interested in where people live and why they live there. The first of three chapters on population is set against a background of the development and spread of agriculture and the beginnings of industrial societies. You may question the relevancy of studying historic, even prehistoric, patterns of population change when it is primarily the contemporary distribution that we ultimately seek to explain. But today's distribution of population did not appear overnight. It is the product of thousands of years of growth and the movement of people to new locations. To examine only the present situation would be like seeing a few seconds in the middle of a movie: you can only surmise how the story developed to that point, and you have an incomplete basis for knowing how it will progress in the future.

The next chapter (Chapter 3) examines the growth of total population (from fewer than 1 billion persons in 1750 to 5 billion in 1987), the contrasting rates of

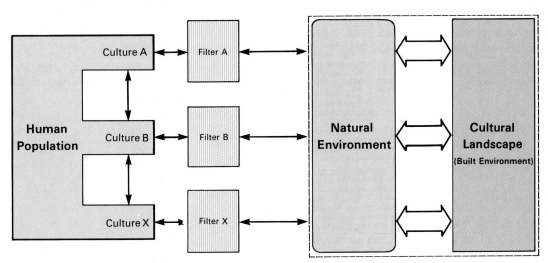

Figure 1-4. Relationships among Cultural Groups, Their Created Landscapes, and the Natural Environment. Culture groups A, B, . . . X affect, and are affected by, the natural environment in varying ways. Likewise, the features built by humans change the natural environment and, in turn, influence people in many ways.

Site. The internal characteristics of a particular place, such as topography, soil types, buildings, and land use (see Situation).

Situation. The position of a place relative to the locations of external features; for example, a town may be situated in the center of a plain and located midway between two major cities (see Site).

Natural environment. The physical elements of the earth, such as landforms, climate, vegetation, and soils (see Cultural landscape).

Ecosystem. The complex of interrelationships that function within an environmental setting.

Ecosphere. The ecosystem that includes the entire earth (see Ecosystem).

Geographic inertia. The tendency for an activity to retain its location even when the conditions that provided initial advantages change.

Human geography. The study of people and their activities from spatial and ecological perspectives.

Figure 1-5. An Area in Western Montana. The low population density in this area affects the kind of features, land values, and human activities here. Contrast this situation with that shown in Figure 1-6. Photo courtesy of Sally Stoddard.

growth in different parts of the world, and changing patterns of population densities. Extreme differences from place to place are evident because a large share of the world's population is concentrated in a few areas, whereas other extensive regions are almost uninhabited. These differences in the numbers of persons in a given area—the **population density**—are important geographically because they influence nearly all human activities. Consider, for example, your choice of destination between either a densely populated metropolitan area or a sparsely settled countryside if you wanted to purchase high-fashion clothing, find a job, attend an opera, go camping, herd sheep, or bury chemical wastes (Figures 1-5 and 1-6).

Populations, of course, are not stationary. People are constantly moving from place to place, either by choice or through coercion. Population migrations, past and present, temporary and permanent, national and international, are discussed in Chapter 4.

Chapters 5, 6, and 7 consider subdivisions of the world population on the basis of **culture.** As explained in Chapter 5, the concept of culture is complex. For the purposes of this introduction, consider cultures as groups of people who are bound together by shared beliefs and values and by their common image of themselves and the world. Because human groups differ in their cultures, the impact they have on the earth's surface is diverse, which contributes to geographic variations.

Cultural groups can be examined at various scales. For example, it is possible to speak of an American culture and recognize ways of life that are distinctly American (Zelinsky 1973). Yet, as you probably realize, the United States consists of a diverse mixture of cultural groups, many of which possess their own distinctive foods, dialects, religions, attitudes, and social networks. At one scale, we can study the geographic differences occurring within the United States, or even within cities. At a contrasting scale, we can look at the United States as part of a larger "Western" culture, which refers to Europeans and people whose ancestry is European. At this level, the Western culture contrasts with non-Western cultures, which include, among others, the Islamic and East Asian cultures.

The connection between world population and cultures at various scales can be clarified through the use of a metaphor that presents world population as the trunk of a tree. The large limbs that spread out from the trunk are the major world cultures, such as Western, Islamic, East Asian, and so on. And the smaller branches, twigs, and leaves are the numerous and varied local groups based on ethnicity, religion, or other cultural components.

Although Figure 1-4 depicts cultural groups as distinct from each other, in reality there are transitional types. For example, according to some criteria, Japanese society is classified as part of the East Asian culture; however, several economic characteristics of Japan resemble the economies of Western nations. The lack of clear and sharp differences separating cultural groups is due to the movement of people, goods, and ideas among the groups. These exchanges (which are represented on the diagram by connecting lines) tend to reduce some of the distinctiveness of cultural groups. The amount of movement between people of differing cultures is affected by many factors, one of which is the geographic distance separating the interacting groups. When movement involves the spreading of people, goods, or ideas outwards from an origin to other areas, it is called spatial **diffusion.**

The geography of culture (as well as other phenomena) can be studied from two approaches. One

Figure 1-6. An Area in Hong Kong. The high population density in this area is associated with the type of features, land values, and human activities that contrast with those shown in Figure 1-5. Photo courtesy of Merlin P. Lawson.

approach is called **regional geography** because it first divides the world into areas or regions. A **region,** which is an area that is considered different from other areas according to specified characteristics, can be identified and mapped on the basis of any phenomenon, including culture. This is illustrated by the map of cultural regions in Chapter 5. After regions are delimited, the geographic characteristics of culture and its subdivisions within each region can be studied.

The other way of organizing geographic information is termed **topical geography** because it commences with culture and its subtopics, such as language and religion, and examines their spatial variations throughout the world.

The two approaches can be compared by looking at the rows and columns in Figure 1-7. Using the regional approach, a geographer considers the locational relationships of many topics such as rainfall, minerals, population density, and language in some specific area, for example, in Japan. The regional geography of Japan, therefore, consists of studying the spatial and ecological facts along the "Japan row." In contrast, when following the topical approach, a geographer examines the spatial and ecological relation-ships of one phenomenon, for instance, language, as it occurs over many regions. The geography of language, then, deals with variations as they occur in a "column" of places, such as Japan, the Chicago urban area, Midwest U.S.A., and the Amazon Basin. The one approach classifies by area, the other by topic. In this text, the basic organization is topical (e.g., population, language, and so on).

Cultural beliefs greatly influence the ways people see themselves in relation to the natural environment. For example, the pragmatic modern American attitude toward the natural environment contrasts with the traditional Native American view (which sees an environment alive with spirits). This is why Figure 1-4 shows perceptual screens, or filters, between the cultures and the natural environment. The natural environment itself is not homogeneous (as simplified in the diagram) but varies in landforms, climates, and a host of other ways. In addition, no two cultures evaluate and use their environments in exactly the same manner. Each culture approaches the earth with different traditions, different hopes, different levels of technology, and different perceptions of what is a "resource." Each reacts in its own particular way to the surrounding environment. These different ecolog-

---

Population density. The number of individuals residing within a specified area divided by the size of that area. For example, if 164,000 persons live in an area of 2000 square kilometers, the population density of that area is 82 persons per square kilometer.

Culture. The phenomenon that binds people together by shared beliefs and values and by a common image of themselves and the world.

Diffusion. The spreading of a phenomenon (such as a group of people, a tool, a disease, an institution, or an idea) over an area of the earth.

Regional geography. An approach that divides the subject of geography according to areas. For example, the geography of tropical Africa is separated from the geography of the grasslands of Asia (see Topical geography).

Region. An area that is differentiated from other areas according to specified criteria (see Box 5-3).

Topical geography. An approach that divides geography according to kinds of subjects (topics). For example, the geography of agriculture is separated from the geography of languages (see Regional geography).

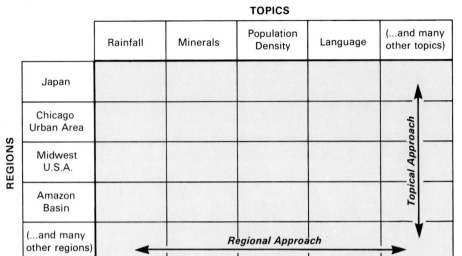

Figure 1-7. Regional and Topical Approaches to Geography. (See text for further explanation.)

ical relationships (which are represented in Figure 1-4 by the two-directional arrows on the lines connecting cultures and the natural environment) contribute to the wide diversity of life.

The varying ways different groups of people interact with the natural environment result in a diversity of **cultural landscapes** (Figure 1-4). These consist of the many structures and features (e.g., houses, temples, roads, statues, canals, fields, junk heaps) that are built or formed by humans. Where natural features are greatly modified by human construction, the setting may be referred to as the **built environment.**

Not only do the features of a particular region reflect the culture of the people occupying that area, but those features in turn influence subsequent geographic decisions. Consequently, groups of people, the cultural landscapes they create, and the part of the natural environment they occupy all are interrelated ecologically and spatially in fascinating ways that invite geographic study.

Variations among people in different areas are often reinforced territorially by the delimitation of sections of the earth into political units. Persons living within a particular political subdivision usually insist that that portion of the earth belongs to them, and they use the boundary of their territory to identify membership in their group. Boundaries may strengthen intragroup cultural characteristics and may also restrict interaction with other groups. Political divisions, therefore, may accentuate differences among groups, both at local scales as well as at the international level.

The evolution of the contemporary world political map is another of the topics examined in Chapter 8. The chapter also deals with the forces that bind political systems together and pull them apart and with the changing concepts about the sources of world power.

The next two chapters (Chapters 9 and 10) emphasize economic forces and conditions that affect geographic patterns and the characteristics of places. On the one hand, trading and marketing encourage movement and communication between places. Such an exchange, which illustrates **spatial interaction,** may reduce the isolation of areas and may diminish differences among groups. On the other hand, at any one time certain places in the world possess economic advantages, such as accessibility to resources. Through time these favored locations often attract humans, who then produce goods and services. This production makes these places even more attractive, which then encourages more producers and generates more economic wealth. This **agglomeration** of numerous activities at a few favorable locations often accentuates differences among places and creates new geographic patterns.

Many human activities and characteristics of populations are closely related to the economic wealth of places, particularly at the international scale. To understand the geography of many aspects of life, therefore, it is useful to differentiate between richer and poorer countries. Although nations are divided into four classes in Chapter 9, only two broad classes— **more developed nations** and **less developed nations**— are mentioned in most chapters.

In contrast to several chapters that deal with differences among countries, Chapter 11 concentrates on smaller regions, including the areas of cities themselves. A large percentage of people, especially in the more developed nations, live in urban areas, so it is appropriate to bring together several geographic themes as they relate to the lives of urban peoples. Chapter 11 utilizes the spatial and ecological perspectives to examine several cultural, political, and economic characteristics of cities and other settlement types, past and present.

Despite its prominent position in Figure 1-4, the

natural environment is not discussed in a separate chapter in this book because that topic is usually studied as "physical geography." Still, even in human geography, the natural environment—the everchanging "stage" for human activities—is never far in the background. This is especially apparent in the final two chapters (Chapters 12 and 13), which concentrate on the past, present, and possible future impact of humankind on the surface of the earth. The picture is one of escalating impact, increasing in scope and intensity over the centuries as populations have expanded and developed the technology for greater dominance over the natural environment. This trend is projected into the future, and several ideas about geographies of tomorrow are explored in the last chapter.

AN ANSWER

This prologue began with the question *Why geography?* Now that some of the contents and goals of the subject have been introduced, it is appropriate to offer a reply.

Geography is intrinsically interesting and worth studying for its own sake. Which of you has not looked at a world map and wondered about those distant places and the people who live there? A course in human geography is no substitute for direct experience because not even the finest teacher nor the most comprehensive textbook can totally evoke the sounds, smells, and sights that contribute to the landscapes of other places. But human geography can tell you much about those places and their inhabitants; it can stimulate your curiosity and imagination and can make you aware of the diversity of life on the earth.

This leads to other practical reasons for studying geography. The subject encourages us to examine the ways we use environments and to understand our spatial and ecological behavior. Such knowledge aids in expanding our perspectives and can serve as a basis for the prediction and rational planning of our lives.

Geography also helps us gain an appreciation of other places and peoples, which breaks down isolationism and shows us that there are many possible and legitimate ways of living on the earth. This is particularly vital in the present era of intense nationalism, when the tendency is for each nation to divide the world's population into "us" and "them" and to ignore the existence of common problems and the reality of global interdependence. Geography gives a global perspective. It raises consciousness above the local and national levels and sheds light on many of the crucial problems facing all humankind.

BIBLIOGRAPHY

Blouet, Brian W., ed., *The Origins of Academic Geography in the United States.* Hamden, Conn.: Shoestring Press, 1981.

Hartshorne, Richard, *Perspective on the Nature of Geography.* Skokie, Ill.: Rand McNally, 1959.

Holt-Jensen, Arild, *Geography: Its History and Concepts.* New York: Barnes & Noble, 1980.

James, Preston, and C. F. Jones, eds., *American Geography: Inventory and Prospect.* Syracuse, N.Y.: Syracuse University Press, 1954.

James, Preston, and Geoffrey J. Martin, *All Possible Worlds: A History of Geographical Ideas.* New York: John Wiley, 1981.

Johnston, R. J., ed., *The Dictionary of Human Geography,* 2nd ed. Oxford, England: Blackwell, 1986.

Taylor, Griffith, ed., *Geography in the Twentieth Century.* New York: Philosophical Library, 1957.

Taylor, Peter J., "The Value of a Geographical Perspective," in R. J. Johnson, ed., *The Future of Geography,* pp. 92–110. London and New York: Methuen, 1985.

Wagner, Philip L., and Marvin W. Mikesell, *Readings in Cultural Geography.* Chicago: University of Chicago Press, 1962.

Zelinsky, Wilbur, *The Cultural Geography of the United States.* Englewood Cliffs, N.J.: Prentice-Hall, 1973.

Cultural landscape. The features constructed by humans that form part of the visible environment (see Natural environment and Built environment).

Built environment. A term that may be used synonymously with cultural landscape but which usually refers to the high density of constructed features in urban places.

Spatial interaction. The exchange that occurs between places that are separated from each other.

Agglomeration. The accumulation of persons and economic activities into a relatively small area; sometimes termed aggregation.

More developed nations. The group of countries that is the richest and most industrialized (see Less developed nations and Box 9-1).

Less developed nations. The group of countries having a wide variety of economic characteristics but generally identified by comparatively low levels of literacy, gross domestic product per capita, and degrees of economic diversification when compared to industrialized countries (see More developed nations and Box 9-1).

2 POPULATION BEFORE THE MODERN ERA

During the last hundred thousand years, the growth of world population accelerated at two distinct times (see Figure 2-1). The first time, commonly believed to have begun about 10,000 years ago, was associated with the domestication of plants and animals and with the development of farming. This radical change is known as the **Agricultural Revolution.** The second time occurred in the late eighteenth century with the harnessing of energy from **fossil fuels** to drive engines and to mechanize many aspects of production. This development is known as the **Industrial Revolution.**

Both events had profound spatial and ecological effects. They are important spatially for two reasons. First, by knowing where they originated, we can form some conclusions about the ways that early societies reacted to and utilized their environments. Second, the increased population growth associated with both the Agricultural and Industrial Revolutions altered population patterns of the world. Even today the distribution of world population is partly explained by where these major events originally occurred.

The Agricultural and Industrial Revolutions are important ecologically because population numbers and densities are at the heart of relationships between humans and the natural environment. If population numbers rise or fall, everything else is liable to change, including land use, settlement forms, the economy, migration patterns, and social mobility.

This chapter is organized around the two significant demographic steps shown in Figure 2-1. They provide a framework for discussing the following topics: pre-farming populations, the Agricultural Revolution, population changes in pre-industrial societies, and the Industrial Revolution.

PRE-FARMING POPULATIONS

Prior to the Agricultural Revolution, human populations consisted of **hunting and gathering societies.** Information about these societies is reconstructed by

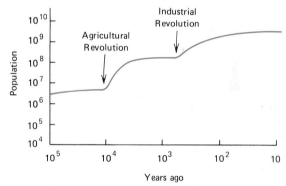

Figure 2-1. Size of World Population Since 100,000 Years Ago (on logarithmic scales). When population size and time are graphed by logarithmic scales, the shape of the line displays two definite "steps" of population increase. (The logarithmic scale is used here because it makes it easy to display the relatively small population changes that occurred during the long period of the past.) After Deevey 1960.

Agricultural Revolution. The relatively abrupt change, which first occurred an estimated 10,000 years ago, involving the domestication of plants and animals. Sometimes the term "agricultural revolution" is also applied to later periods of rapid changes in agricultural methods and production.

Fossil fuels. Earth materials such as peat, lignite, coal, petroleum, and natural gas from which energy can be extracted.

Industrial Revolution. The relatively abrupt change, which first occurred approximately 200 years ago, involving the ways societies utilized energy resources to produce manufactured goods.

Hunting and gathering society. A society whose economy is based primarily on hunting wild animals and gathering food and materials from wild plants (see Agrarian society and Industrial society).

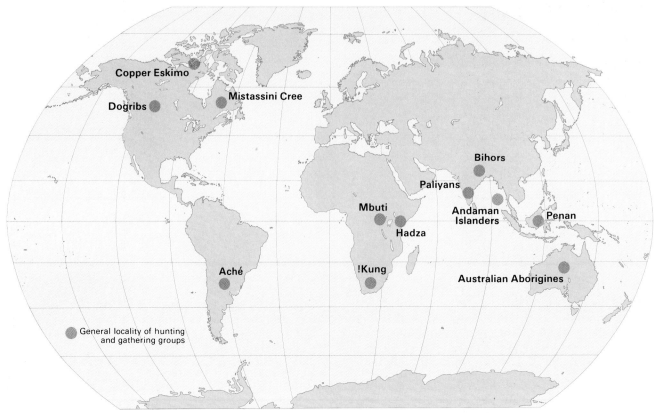

Figure 2-2. Hunters and Gatherers of Today. Those societies usually classified as hunting and gathering now exist in only a few areas of the world.

analogy. A few hunting and gathering societies, remnants of the early pre-agricultural peoples who once occupied almost the entire earth, have survived into the twentieth century in various inaccessible locations (Figure 2-2). Representative of the remaining groups are those living in tropical rainforests, such as in eastern Paraguay where the Aché dwell, in the cold regions, as illustrated by the Eskimo homelands, and in deserts, for example, in the Kalahari of southwestern Africa, where !Kung live (Figure 2-3). Although all have now felt the impact of the outside world, the sparse populations of these societies give us some ideas about the densities that existed in the past.

It is estimated that 10,000 years ago approximately 5 to 10 million people were spread thinly over the surface of the earth (Durand 1973). They lived in bands of fewer than 50 people, the men being primarily hunters, the women providing most of the food through plant gathering. Nowhere on the earth was the population large. Typical densities were about 0.04 persons per square kilometer (4 persons per 100 square kilometers or 39 square miles). There were large uninhabited areas, and each band usually lived in relative isolation from others. Such low densities are not surprising because the economies of bands were based on a form of **extensive land use.** In other words, they obtained their food from large areas without expending much labor per unit of land.

High death rates undoubtedly restricted population growth. It is probable that population growth was also restrained by deliberate control through restricted sexual intercourse, abortion, infanticide, and the use of plants with contraceptive powers. Slow growth for a band meant that its size did not rapidly exceed the **carrying capacity** of the territory being used for hunting and gathering food (Deevey 1960).

The distribution of population prior to the development of agriculture covered parts of most conti-

Figure 2-3. Members of the !Kung Society. Many activities of the !Kung today are similar to those of other hunting and gathering societies that existed several thousand years ago. Photo courtesy of Robert K. Hitchcock.

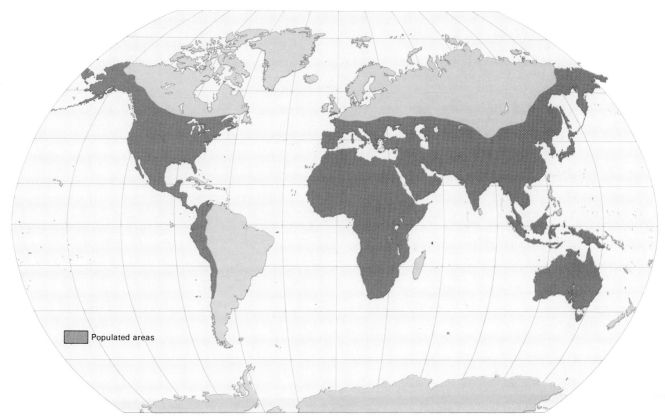

Figure 2-4. Distribution of World Population, 10,000 B.C. It is believed that hunters and gatherers occupied a large portion of the earth's land surface. After Lee and Devore 1968.

nents (Figure 2-4). By 8000 B.C., hunters and gatherers had migrated from Africa throughout Europe and Asia, to Australia, and across the Bering Straits and southward the length of the Americas. Only Antarctica was totally uninhabited by humankind.

The motive behind these migrations, according to Kingsley Davis (1974), was the contrast between exploited territory and virgin territory. Armed with crude but effective weapons, and organized cooperatively, the hunters gradually reduced the game in an area, then moved on. Having possession of fire, skins, shelters, and tools, they were able to adapt to new environmental conditions. Some of these environments were suitable for agriculture.

THE AGRICULTURAL REVOLUTION

Although the Agricultural Revolution refers to a major break with the past, it was not a sudden change but rather a slow evolution over many centuries. In fact, even the generally accepted time of 10,000 years ago is

not certain. Only a small proportion of the earth's land surface has been surveyed archaeologically, and additional findings may reveal new evidence about early populations. Nevertheless, at some time and in some places, groups of people acquired the skills to domesticate plants and animals and, in so doing, to produce food surpluses that could support larger populations.

The Origins of Agriculture

Where did this break with the past take place? The Russian plant geographer N. I. Vavilov was the first scholar to recognize a comprehensive set of **hearth areas**—centers of origin—for domesticated plants (1951). Basing his conclusions on extensive field work, Vavilov argued that the original centers of plant domestication were the areas where there was the greatest number of wild varieties of the plant that eventually became cultivated. According to Vavilov's theory, cultivated plants then diffused from multiple centers of independent origin. Although many aspects of Vavilov's theory have been disproven by subse-

---

Extensive land use. The amount of land that is used for production is large compared to the amounts of labor and capital expended (see Intensive land use).

Carrying capacity. The theoretical upper limit in the number of persons (or, in other cases, animals) that can subsist

adequately on a given area of land under the existing system of technology and land management.

Hearth area. A place of origin of people, technology, or ideas that subsequently spread to other areas.

quent research, his hearth areas have been generally accepted as a framework for understanding the geography of plant domestication (Figure 2-5).

The next question to be asked is: How and in what settings did plant domestication take place? The eminent geographer Carl O. Sauer proposed six basic preconditions for the establishment of settled agriculture (1952):

1. The environmental setting had to provide the existing society of hunters and gatherers with an adequate food supply. Agriculture would be unlikely to originate in an area of chronic food shortage for the simple reason that populations living in the "shadow of famine" would find it difficult to experiment with the sowing and harvesting of potential domesticated plants.
2. Early agriculturalists would have previously acquired skills, such as using plant fibers for a variety of purposes, which predisposed them to experiment with farming.
3. Those hunting and gathering bands that were least nomadic were initially most involved because crops need regular care and protection.
4. Agriculture would probably develop in an area of floral and faunal diversity, possibly in association with a zone of physical contrasts where terrain and climate change markedly.
5. Major river basins were improbable areas of origin because the new farming communities were unlikely to have the resources to construct flood control or irrigation works.
6. A woodland zone was likely. Early cultivators, with limited technology, would find it difficult to break the tough sod of grasslands, but could more easily deaden trees by girdling and then clear the debris with the use of fire.

With these preconditions in mind, Sauer went on to propose that Southeast Asia had been the earliest hearth area of agriculture (1952). He believed that knowledge of farming techniques diffused outward from this point of origin across the Old World. His explanation for the existence of early agricultural societies in several parts of the world at nearly the same time, therefore, was based on the diffusion of farming techniques from groups in Southeast Asia to other receptive societies.

Many of Sauer's ideas about the location of early agriculture have been validated by subsequent archaeological excavation. For example, the diggings at Spirit Cave in Thailand revealed evidence of some

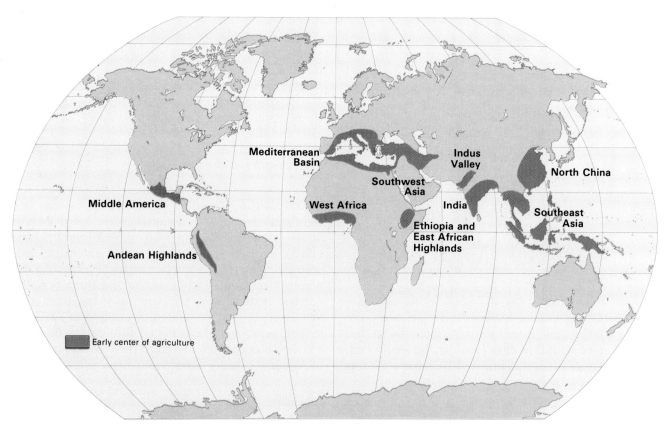

Figure 2-5. Early Centers of Agriculture. During the early phases of the Agricultural Revolution, farming societies existed in only limited areas. Most other lands were occupied by hunting and gathering societies.

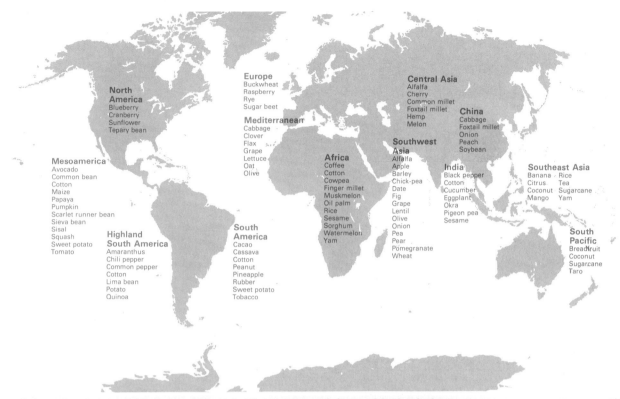

Figure 2-6. Origins of Common Domestic Plants. Many of the world's food plants originated in relatively few areas. Used with permission from Clarissa T. Kimber.

agricultural activity 10,000 years ago. In contrast, some scholars now find Sauer's ideas of diffusion to be too strongly stated. The evidence currently available suggests that agriculture did not develop in only one location and diffuse from this single origin, but evolved independently several times in different parts of the world.

There is no reason to believe that the independent origins and diffusionist arguments are mutually exclusive. It is possible that there were independent centers of origin that subsequently exchanged plants, animals, and techniques with other centers in the same way that ideas diffuse from place to place. Even Sauer conceded the likelihood of independent agricultural development in the New World, but he also believed that there had been many more contacts and exchanges around the Pacific than was generally recognized (1952).

Given the present evidence, there is agreement that farming evolved independently in Southwest Asia, Southeast Asia, and Middle America. But these three regions do not exhaust the possibilities of early farming centers (Figure 2-5). It is not clear whether other centers such as North China, the Indus Valley, and the Andean Highlands of South America were in contact with, and learned from, the experience of the earliest centers or evolved separately. For example, the Indus Valley may have been an independent center or may have been influenced by people, ideas,

and techniques diffusing from Southwest Asia. Some other areas produced their own domesticated plants. For instance, maize and tomatoes were domesticated in Middle America, coffee and sorghum in Africa, and bananas and tea in Southeast Asia (Figure 2-6). Whether or not these domesticates formed the basis of farming systems or were simply cultivated supplements to hunting and gathering has not been fully determined.

Undoubtedly agriculture emerged slowy as humans, crops, and animals became dependent on each other for survival. This is apparent in the region near Mesopotamia in Southwest Asia, an area that contains the sites of many early agricultural villages and, after 4000 B.C., the monuments and cities of the first **civilization.**

The heart of Mesopotamia was the Tigris-Euphrates Valley (Figure 2-7). The valley is flanked on the east by the Zagros Mountains of southwestern Iran, on the north by the Taurus Mountains of southern Turkey, and on the west by the Syrian Desert. The Taurus and Zagros mountains probably received sufficient rain (under current climatic conditions, 50 mm

---

Civilization. A society that usually has, as a minimum, cities, a written language, a literature, a currency, and a division of labor with elites who control the allocation of resources. The word derives from the Latin word *civitas:* "a city."

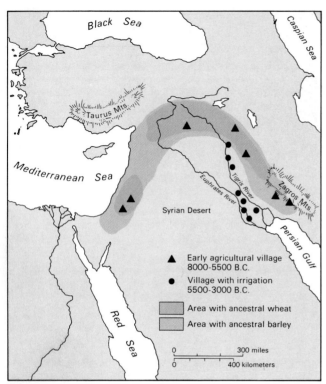

Figure 2-7. Mesopotamia and the Surrounding Uplands. Early forms of agriculture probably commenced on the diverse uplands surrounding the Valley of the Tigris and Euphrates Rivers.

Map legend:
▲ Early agricultural village 8000–5500 B.C.
● Village with irrigation 5500–3000 B.C.
Area with ancestral wheat
Area with ancestral barley

or 20 in. per year) for most crops, whereas most of the Tigris-Euphrates Valley was much drier (with less than 25 mm or 10 in. of precipitation). There was a seasonal supply of water in the major rivers, however.

When the snow melted in the mountains, spring floods extended over the flat alluvial plain close to the main channels of the Tigris and Euphrates rivers. Such land had great agricultural potential once the technology and manpower evolved to control the floods and to manage the irrigation works. But as Sauer pointed out (1952), hunters and gatherers do not possess such technical knowledge. It is more likely that the early agricultural communities developed in the ecologically diverse uplands surrounding the Tigris-Euphrates Valley.

In the Zagros Mountains there were a number of ecological niches providing a wide range of plant and animal species that were used by hunting and gathering groups before the advent of agriculture. The anthropologists Hole and Flannery (1968) outlined a series of three "adaptive eras" for the Zagros Mountains, describing the transition from hunting and gathering to settled farming.

In the first "era," from about 10,000 to 8000 B.C., hunting and gathering groups used a great number of plant and animal resources, including wild grains that yielded highly nutritious crops. Field experiments with stands of wild grain still existing in the Zagros Mountains have shown that a family could harvest all its grain needs for a year in only three weeks!

According to Hole and Flannery, in the second "era," from 8000 to 5500 B.C., the transition to farming was made. The most important cultivated crops were wheat and barley, and goats and sheep were the primary domesticated animals. The people lived in permanent villages and practiced a form of **shifting cultivation.** This farming type involved clearing a

Figure 2-8. Plots of Land in Shifting Cultivation in the Solomon Islands. Shifting cultivation practices today are similar to the methods used during the early development of agriculture. Photo courtesy of Wallace E. Akin.

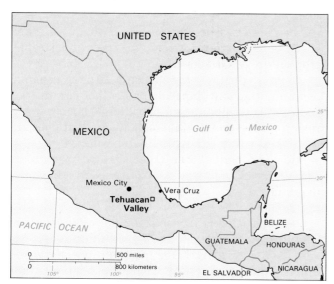

Figure 2-9. Locality of Early Agriculture in Middle America. Former hunting and gathering groups probably began to supplement their diets with domesticated plants in the Tehuacan Valley by 7000 B.C. (Modern names of countries and places added as locational information.)

Irrigation farming was established between 5500 and 3000 B.C. during the third "era." The focus of settlement shifted from the mountains and foothills to the alluvial plain of the Tigris and Euphrates rivers, that is, to the region called Mesopotamia. Here irrigation techniques were utilized to convey water from the rivers to the dry surrounding plains. Irrigation, which involved more **intensive land use** than before, allowed higher population densities and larger agricultural settlements. New crops were introduced, and cattle and pigs were added to the domesticated animals. Eventually, the Sumerian city-states, such as Ur, emerged with tens of thousands of inhabitants, complex religious, political, and military bureaucracies, and extensive trading contacts.

A similar slow evolution of agriculture from hunting and gathering is evident in Middle America (Figure 2-9). In the Tehuacan Valley of Mexico, hunters and gatherers were supplementing their diet with cultivated squashes and chili peppers by 7000 B.C. At first the dependence on such crops was small, probably less than 10 percent; most foods were still provided by hunting and gathering (Figure 2-10).

By 3500 B.C., maize and beans were cultivated, and an estimated 25 percent of the diet came from domesticated plants. By 2000 B.C., settled village life was the rule, and 40 percent of the food base came from cultivated crops. As in Southwest Asia (and probably in the other early centers of domestication), agriculture developed slowly, taking thousands of years to replace hunting and gathering as the main

small area, cropping it for a few years, and then abandoning it (during a long fallow period) and allowing it to recover its natural vegetation (Figure 2-8). Technology was simple. In the region of the Zagros Mountains, implements consisted of hoes and digging sticks, with flint and obsidian sickle blades used to harvest the grain.

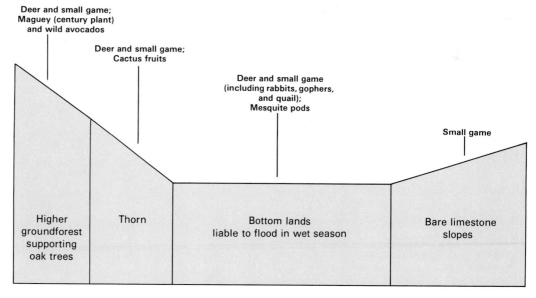

Figure 2-10. Environmental Zones in the Tehuacan Valley, Mexico. Archaeological research reveals that bands of prehistoric hunters and gatherers obtained a variety of resources throughout the year by moving their camps into different microenvironmental zones. After Coe and Flannery 1964.

Shifting cultivation. A type of agriculture that involves clearing the natural vegetation (e.g., forest) from a small area, cropping it for a few years, and then abandoning that area while it reverts to wild vegetation. This type may be subdivided into three subtypes (forest fallow, bush fallow, and short-fallow) based on the length of time the land is not being cultivated. **Intensive land use.** The amounts of labor and/or capital expended are large compared to the amount of land in production (see Extensive land use).

source of food. Also in common with Southwest Asia, the main system of agriculture at this stage was shifting cultivation. Farming first took place on the hillsides and mountain slopes because the heavy valley soils could not be cultivated with only wooden digging sticks.

In Middle America, not until after 900 B.C. (much later than in Mesopotamia) did farming spread onto the valley floor. Irrigation was introduced, productivity increased, surpluses accumulated, and priestly rulers emerged. The decentralized village communities eventually came under the authority of cities and emergent states. For example, Teotihuacan, the "house of the gods" located in a dry valley northeast of present-day Mexico City (Figure 2-11), covered about 20 square kilometers (8 square miles) by A.D. 600 and contained about 100,000 people (Adams 1960).

In addition to questions about where and how agriculture originated, there remains the question of movitation. Why, if hunters and gatherers could provide for their food needs satisfactorily (as the Zagros field experiment demonstrates), did they get involved with the problems of planting, nurturing, and harvesting crops? In general, hunters and gatherers put in less labor to acquire their food than do farmers, or even shifting cultivators. Moreover, because hunters and gatherers utilize a broader variety of plant and animal species, they are not subject to the risk of catastrophic crop failure as farmers are.

A great distinction between a farming economy and a hunting and gathering one is that farming will support higher population densities. It is tempting to rush from this point to the conclusion that overpopulation was the necessity that prompted the "invention" of agriculture. Indeed, some experts see agriculture in prehistoric societies as an adjustment that humans were forced to make because of increasing numbers (Cohen 1977).

A satisfactory answer to the question about the stimulus for the beginning of agriculture is not this simple. To return to Sauer's preconditions, it remains unlikely that people in the "shadow of famine" would be free to invent anything. As time went on, Sauer became increasingly convinced that the domestication of plants and animals was not the result of population increase (1969).

The apparent contradiction of Sauer's and Cohen's views is not necessarily irreconcilable. Several authorities who have offered models of agricultural origins in Southwest Asia combine elements from both viewpoints. They speculate that the process began with the hunters and gatherers living in a semisedentary state, collecting wild grains as an im-

Figure 2-11. The Pyramids of Teotihuacan. The truncated pyramids, located in the center of this earliest city in Middle America, were used for the performance of religious rites. These structures could only have been the creations of a complex society with specialized labor and food surpluses. Photo courtesy of Charles A. Francis.

portant source of their food, and in equilibrium with the resource base. In marginal, particularly semiarid areas, the quantity of available resources fluctuated from year to year. These experts suggest that it was in these environments that efforts were made to extend the size of wild grain stands. Such extension would be a simple matter. Probably women, who were most familiar with the local plants, cleared the land of competing vegetation and planted wild seeds. Eventually, through a long period of selection, the wild plants were modified in their association with humans until, finally, the domesticated plants needed cultivators to survive.

Impact on Population and Society

In the conventional analysis of prehistoric populations, it is assumed that death rates fell with the development of agriculture. The argument is that the increased food supply led to better nutrition, greater resistance to disease, increased longevity of life, and hence a growing population. This may be correct, but we have no conclusive proof that death rates fell. They may even have risen shortly after the advent of agriculture. Disease spreads more rapidly in closely packed communities than in small and relatively isolated hunting and gathering bands. Moreover, as noted above, a total reliance on farming made agricultural communities vulnerable, much more so than the hunting and gathering peoples with their diverse food base. Because of this vulnerability, death rates undoubtedly fluctuated widely in early agricultural societies, reflecting the success or failure of the harvests.

If death rates rose following the transition to agriculture, then evidently birth rates did too because it is known that population increased (Figure 2-12). There may have been a physiological reason for the rising birth rates in agricultural societies. For example, contemporary studies of the !Kung people in the Kalahari Desert suggest that fertility rates are low because their diet, which is based on hunted and collected foodstuffs, produces a low body-fat content. This leads to irregular ovulation and low fecundity (the biological ability to produce children). It is argued, therefore, that the prehistoric shift from hunting and gathering to the cultivation of crops may have influenced fertility by increasing body weight (Coale 1974).

It is also possible that the increase in birth rates, which accompanied the adoption of agriculture, resulted from social changes. Sanctions that had been

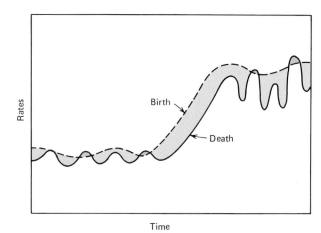

Figure 2-12. Generalized Changes in Birth and Death Rates at the Time of the Agricultural Revolution. Although prehistoric birth and death rates prior to the Agricultural Revolution are difficult to estimate, probably births were controlled and were in some kind of balance with fluctuating death rates. With the development of agriculture, birth rates evidently surged, but death rates also may have risen.

used to keep hunting and gathering bands small and in balance with their resource base may have been relaxed in **agrarian societies** that required more labor to produce food. The sociopolitical changes brought about by the evolution of agriculture are considered in more detail in Chapters 8 and 9, but their relationships to demographic changes are relevant here.

Agriculture permitted the existence not only of higher population densities and settled village life but also of larger-scale cooperative ventures, specialization of labor, development of crafts (such as pottery making), and social stratification. However, the early farming villagers who practiced shifting cultivation were relatively egalitarian, as had been the hunting and gathering bands before them.

The growth of irrigation farming and the emergence of cities concentrated economic power in the hands of numerically small elites, who controlled much of the land and food resources. Such elites, whose positions were often hereditary, were a characteristic of traditional agricultural societies (as they have continued to be in the twentieth century). The great mass of society, however, consisted of **peasants** and laborers who worked the land and produced the food surpluses upon which the entire social structure was built. In the great Mesopotamian cities such as Ur and Babylon, which had arisen by 3000 B.C., 80 percent of the population were farmers who walked to

---

Agrarian society.   A society based largely on agriculture (hence sometimes called an agricultural society); status and power tend to be determined in relation to landholdings (see Hunting and gathering society and Industrial society).

Peasant.   A rural dweller who is part of a family unit that practices small scale agriculture and consumes most of its own production.

the fields each day. They were not influential in political systems, which were controlled by the priesthood, the military, and hereditary royalty. Under these conditions of inequality, families subjected to the demands of the ruling elite probably needed additional labor to produce food surpluses. Therefore peasant families found it advantageous to have more children.

POPULATION CHANGES IN PRE-INDUSTRIAL SOCIETIES

After a lengthy period of development associated with the domestication of plants and animals, the world population increased slowly and with some reversals until fossil fuels were harnessed and industrialization occurred in Western Europe. These years between the Agricultural and Industrial Revolutions were not ones of demographic uniformity; both spatial and temporal variations existed.

By the beginning of the Christian era, there were two main ways of life on the surface of the earth, with all kinds of gradations in between. Large areas were still occupied by hunters and gatherers who continued to live as they had since the dawn of humankind. In select parts of the world, however, a new order had emerged, based on **subsistence farming** and characterized by larger populations and increasingly complex social systems. These agricultural areas coincided with the concentrations of the world's population. Although the estimated total of 300 million persons in the year A.D. 1 has an error margin of possibly 100 million (Durand 1973), the relative densities of specific regions can be noted. The major concentrations of populations were in Europe (particularly southern Europe) with 54 million, in China with between 57 and 74 million, and in India with 100 to 140 million. By this time, the major population regions of the modern world were already emerging (see Figure 3-22 in Chapter 3).

Population growth from A.D. 1 to 1750 reflected a general continuation of past trends. **Life expectancy** (the number of years an infant is expected live; see Box 2-1) remained below 35 years. The **doubling time** (the number of years taken for a population to double in size) for world population was about 1000 years, as it had been before A.D. 1. By 1750, world population had climbed slowly to an estimated total of 791 million (Durand 1967). This was not a steady ascent, however. There were short- and long-term fluctuations reflecting the variations in birth and death rates. There were also dramatic changes in the distribution of population, particularly after 1500 when many Europeans migrated to other parts of the world.

Fluctuating Populations

When the world population for the last 10,000 years is shown on a graph using arithmetic scales, it depicts a low, constant rate of increase to about 1750, then a precipitous rise to the present (Figure 2-13). When population growth before 1750 is examined in greater detail, however, it displays many undulations. In Western Europe, for which data are most readily available, there were periods of growth alternating with periods of decline. It appears that similar conditions existed in China and probably elsewhere (Braudel 1981).

Short-term fluctuations in pre-industrial populations were caused mainly by variations in the death rate. The **crude birth rate** (see Box 2-1) was rarely above 45/1000 or below 15/1000. By comparison, the **crude death rate** (see Box 2-1) often rose as high as 200 or even 400/1000 during times of famine or disease. Population numbers sometimes declined rapidly.

Diseases caused many deaths. At the height of the Black Death, for example, when the bubonic plague swept across Europe in the fourteenth century, extensive areas lost one-third of their population in a single year. Diseases spread rapidly in the crowded, unsanitary conditions that were common in many urban areas. In the Great Plague of 1665, for example, at least a quarter of London's population of 450,000 perished. Such catastrophic population declines from epidemics were common among pre-industrial peoples.

Fluctuations in the death rate were also closely

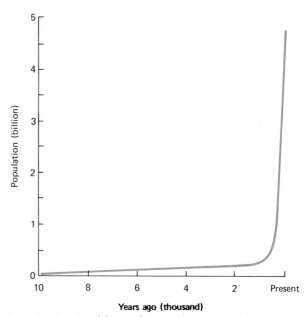

Figure 2-13. World Population Since 10,000 Years Ago (on arithmetic scales). On this graph, the large absolute increase in world population that has occurred during the last 300 years towers over the small population growth during the millennia before the Industrial Revolution.

BOX 2-1. MEASUREMENT OF POPULATION CHARACTERISTICS

The simplest and most commonly used measurements of population change are the crude birth and death rates. The crude birth rate is the ratio of the annual number of births in a population to the total number of persons in that population. This ratio is normally expressed in terms of a base of 1000 persons. Thus, if a region with a population size of 20,000 has a total of 420 births during a particular year, the ratio of births to total population could be given as 0.021. However, this ratio is usually expressed as 21 per 1000 (21/1000) and often written as just 21 because the base of 1000 is understood. The crude death rate is also a ratio with the numerator being the number of deaths occurring in a population during a year and the denominator being the total population. If this region with a population of 20,000 recorded 180 deaths during the year, its crude death rate would be given at 9 (or 9/1000).

The rate of **natural increase,** which excludes all population changes resulting from persons migrating into or out of an area, is the difference between the birth and death rates. This fraction is usually expressed as a percentage (which, of course, has a base of 100). Therefore, the rate of natural increase for our illustrative country can be stated as 21/1000 − 9/1000 =

12/1000, which is the same as 1.2/100 or 1.2%.

As a second illustration, if a country with a population of 5 million has a birth rate of 35 and a death rate of 14, then after one year, 175,000 children will have been born (35/1000 × 5,000,000), and a total of 70,000 deaths will have occurred. The rate of natural increase would be 2.1 percent, and the total population at the end of the year resulting from natural increase (that is, excluding migration) would be 5,105,000.

A comparison of these measurements for two or more countries may be misleading because the age structures of the populations may differ. Costa Rica, for example, has an extremely low crude death rate at the present time (4/1000 in 1987). This rate results not because people live longer than, for example, in the United States, but because a large proportion (35%) of the population is under 15 years of age and, therefore, not at the age when deaths are common.

Another demographic statistic that indicates the rate of growth of a population is the doubling time. This is the number of years it will take for a population to double in size, assuming it will continue to increase at the current rate. The approximate number of years can be calculated by dividing 70 (a mathematical constant used for compounding percentages) by the rate of population increase

(expressed as a percent). For example, the population in the region experiencing a growth rate of 1.2% will double in approximately 58 years (70/1.2 = 58.3); but in the country where the population is growing at the rate of 2.1% per year, the population size will double in slightly more than 33 years (70/2.1 = 33.3).

An alternative way of expressing death rates is by a statistic termed life expectancy at birth. This term refers to the number of years a new-born infant is expected to live, based on the proportion of persons in specified age groups in a population. This concept can be illustrated by looking at the enclosed table. At birth, a child has a life expectancy of 69 years; but those children who survive their first year are expected—on the average—to live 70 more years. On the basis of the current data, those survivors who live to be 70 will then be expected to live another 10 years. Thus, although in a large group some persons will die during infancy and others will live beyond 80, the expectation is that the "average" child will live 69 years.

Age Group	Average Remaining Years
0–1	69
1–2	70
20–21	52
70–71	10
80–81	6

Subsistence farming. A system of agriculture in which the cultivators, and their families, consume most of their own production.

Life expectancy. The number of years a newborn infant is expected to live (see Box 2-1).

Doubling time. The number of years required for a growing population to double in size.

Crude birth rate. The ratio of the number of births per year in a population to the total number of persons in that popula-

tion. Normally the numerator is expressed in terms of a base of 1000 persons (see Box 2-1).

Crude death rate. The ratio of the number of deaths per year in a population to the total number of persons in that population. Normally the numerator is expressed in terms of a base of 1000 persons (see Box 2-1).

Natural increase. The difference between the birth rate and the death rate for a given population, usually expressed as a percentage.

tied to swings in the harvests. Carry-over stocks of food might be sufficient to feed a population during one year of crop failure; but two or three bad harvests would result in hunger, disease, and death for those whose reserves were small (Braudel 1981). Moreover, in an era of poorly developed land transportation, the transfer of food from surplus to deficit areas was difficult. So, at the mercy of the elements and isolated from outside aid, agricultural populations experienced mortality rates that fluctuated in response to food supplies. Deaths were less by outright starvation than by infections, which strike ill-fed and weakened people. Even as recently as 1740–1743, much of Western Europe suffered heavy population losses due to failed harvests.

The impact of crop failure on population size was most severe where the agricultural system tended toward **monoculture,** where most of the land was used for only one crop. An example is the case of the Beauvais region of northern France where crop failure resulted in a tripling of the price of wheat from 1691 to 1694. The death rate rose dramatically in Breteuil and Mouy parishes because these areas practiced a cereal monoculture (Figure 2-14). But the effect of crop failure was felt less harshly in the mixed farming

parish of Auneuil where there were other food supplies, including meat and dairy products, to fall back on. Consequently, the death rate in Auneuil was much lower in 1693–1694 than in the two neighboring parishes (Wrigley 1969).

Periods of high mortality in pre-industrial populations were generally followed by years of lower mortality because the vulnerable members of the population had already died. Moreover, periods of high mortality often prompted higher birth rates. This is because the reduction in population resulted in greater opportunities for those who survived; land and housing, for example, may have become more available. During these more favorable periods, people could marry earlier and produce more children. This demographic cycle is evident in the example of the Beauvais (Figure 2-14).

Combined with these short-term fluctuations were longer periods of population growth, stagnation, and decline. In England and Wales, and in Western Europe as a whole, population grew from A.D. 1000 to the early 1300s. Growth was halted and reversed from that time until the middle of the fifteenth century. Population then increased steadily until the mid-seventeenth century, after which it leveled off until the burst of growth after 1750 (Figure 2-15 and Box 2-2).

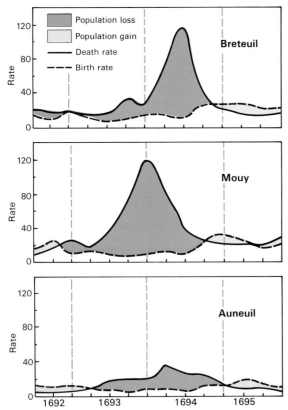

Figure 2-14. Changes in the Number of Births and Deaths for a Region in France, 1693–1695. Diversified farming in Auneuil parish provided a cushion against crop failure and famine. After Wrigley 1969.

BOX 2-2. ESTIMATING EARLY POPULATIONS

The 1086 estimate of population for England and Wales is based largely on the **Domesday Book,** in which approximately 250,000 persons are recorded for England alone. Most of those mentioned were probably heads of households, so we need to multiply the Domesday figure to get a total population. On the assumption that households consisted of 5 persons, the total population would be approximately 1.25 million. Statistics for the fourteenth and fifteenth centuries are derived from tax rolls, again using multipliers to account for the nontaxed population. From the sixteenth century onwards, a variety of sources, including parish records of births and deaths, allow more accurate estimates to be made. The first British census, taken in 1801, counted 9,156,000 persons for England and Wales.

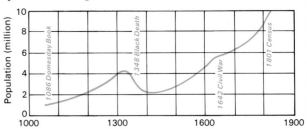

Figure 2-15. Long-Term Population Trends in England and Wales, A.D. 1086–1801.

The causes of the long-term trends are obscure. The population decline after 1340 may have been caused solely by recurring waves of bubonic plague, but climatic change may have also played a role. A period of cooler and wetter summers in Western Europe forced marginal land out of cultivation and reduced yields of the major food and fodder crops. Less food may have led to malnutrition, disease, forced migrations, and rising death rates.

To summarize, pre-industrial agricultural populations experienced the following: high infant mortality, short life expectancy, periodic famine and undernourishment, vulnerability to epidemics, high birth and death rates, and wide fluctuations of death and responding birth rates. The outcome of these conditions was that, although there were sharp periods of population decline, they were followed by short-term revival. The result was a slow, long-term increase in population numbers. It is important to stress that this demographic variability was common to all human groups until after the Industrial Revolution.

World Population Distribution in 1750.

For the post-1750 period, population statistics are more available, and more calculable, than before, so both the total size and the geographical distribution can be estimated with greater accuracy.

Almost two-thirds of the world's population in 1750 lived in Asia (Table 2-1). China and the Indian subcontinent were the world's most populated areas, as they are today. Population in China rose from 65 million in the late fourteenth century, to 150 million in 1600, and to 200 million by 1750. The increase took place despite periods of decline caused by famine, disease, and political disorder. One reason for the increase was the steady improvement of Chinese agriculture after the eleventh century with the development of new crops. The dissemination of early ripening varieties of rice allowed double-cropping of the land, with wheat and other winter crops being sown after the rice was harvested. The new strains of rice also needed less water than older varieties, so that farming was extended from the valleys to the drier margins and hills. The introduction of New World crops (maize, potatoes, and peanuts) to China after 1500 further strengthened the food base. It is probable that food supplies were more assured in China between 1000 and 1750 than in Europe, where important changes in agriculture did not occur until the seventeenth century (see Chapter 9). Certainly the substan-

TABLE 2-1. Estimates of Population for Major Areas, 1750

Area	Population (millions)	Percent of World Total
Asia (not U.S.S.R.)		498	63
China	200	
India[a]	190	
Japan	30	
Indonesia	12	
Remainder of Asia	66	
Europe (not U.S.S.R.)		125	16
U.S.S.R.		42	5
Africa		106	13
North Africa	10	
Remainder of Africa	96	
America		18	2
North America	2	
Middle & South America	16	
Oceania		2	—
World total		791	

[a] Includes present-day Bangladesh and Pakistan.
Source: Durand 1967. Used with permission from American Philosophical Society.

tial population increase in China during that period seems to indicate increased agricultural production.

On the Indian subcontinent, population size rose and fell with such factors as food production, droughts and floods, and the degree of political stability among the various regional groups (Lal 1973). The population may have been as much as 200 million in A.D. 1000, but five centuries later, according to existing evidence, it totaled only 125 million. It probably increased to approximately 190 million by 1750, but it was down to 180 million in 1800.

The other major concentration of world population in 1750 was in Europe, with an estimated 125 million people. This figure, however, does not include the population that lived in western Russia (now U.S.S.R.), which is usually defined as part of Europe.

Africa may have had 106 million people in 1750. This figure is only an estimate because no eighteenth-century statistics, or even written histories, exist for the continent for that period. Some scholars believe Africa's population at this time may have been no more than 25–30 million (Braudel 1981). The eighteenth-century totals possibly were smaller than for earlier times because of the slave trade, but the demographic effects of these forced removals from various parts of the continent are unknown.

By 1750, the population of North and South America consisted of Native Americans, European

---

Monoculture. The practice of growing one crop over a large area of land (see Polyculture).
Domesday Book. A record compiled in 1086 which de-

scribes landholdings for most of England and from which it is possible to reconstruct information concerning farmland, waste areas, woodlands, urban areas, and population.

immigrants, and African slaves. The population estimates are 2 million inhabitants for North America and 16 million for Middle and South America. These numbers are undoubtedly only fractions of the population totals that existed before the European incursions. Some scholars estimate that as many as 100 million people inhabited the Americas at the end of the fifteenth century, before the devastating impact of European diseases and warfare (Dobyns 1976). Other demographic historians believe that figure is far too high (Zambardino 1980). In any case, during the last half of the eighteenth century, settlement by Europeans and Africans increased the population densities along parts of the east coasts and the Caribbean islands of the New World.

THE INDUSTRIAL REVOLUTION

The second major "step" in world population came with the Industrial Revolution (Figure 2-1). The domestication of plants and animals had changed the distribution of people and had increased their power over environments while making larger populations more dependent on these transformed environments. The Industrial Revolution had similar spatial and ecological results. Most of the geographic and demographic effects are considered in subsequent chapters; here the focus is on the characteristics of the change and where the Industrial Revolution occurred.

Characteristics of the Industrial Revolution

An **industrial society** is one in which production has been systematized, mechanized, and energized, so as to develop high output per capita and rapid accumulation of wealth. Many processes had already been mechanized, and some had been organized on a factory basis prior to 1750. The distinguishing feature of the Industrial Revolution was that fossil fuels, primarily coal, provided an energy source other than animal muscles, wind, or water power. The use of fossil fuels allowed productivity to increase rapidly because human effort was supplemented by powered mechanical devices.

The Industrial Revolution as it evolved in countries bordering the North Atlantic in the late eighteenth and early nineteenth centuries had several characteristics in common (Deane 1979):

1. The **primary activities**—farming, fishing, forestry, mining, and quarrying—began to decline in relative, but not absolute, importance. At the same time, **secondary** (manufacturing) and **tertiary** (service) **activities** began to take an increasingly important role in the economic structure. This led to diversity in national economies.
2. Machines were increasingly utilized to supplement or replace human effort. These machines required the application of scientific knowledge to design and maintain them.
3. Economic activity that was organized on a large scale eventually replaced the family as the unit of production.
4. Goods were produced for sale in regional, national, and international markets rather than as items to be bartered in village economies or sold at local marketplaces.
5. Productive activity became increasingly specialized and geographically concentrated, which required more transporting and exchanging of products. It also led to pronounced rural to urban migration.
6. Productivity per capita rose rapidly.

What is meant by the term productivity as used here? Productivity is a way of measuring output against inputs of labor and capital. In short, productivity is a measure of what one "gets out" in terms of what is "put in." Such a measure sounds simple enough. In practice, matters are more complex, and much depends on how the accounts are kept. Account books are easy to keep if one thinks only in terms of direct labor costs like wages and the direct capital costs of factories and machinery. And this is the way accounts were kept in the early phases of the Industrial Revolution.

Now people realize that costs consist of more than the immediate inputs of labor and machinery. There are social and environmental costs. At the time of the Industrial Revolution, urban populations increased rapidly, and living standards in new industrial towns were frequently abysmal, especially for the poorer families. Disease flourished in overcrowded, unsanitary urban settings, and death rates were often catastrophic when cholera contaminated water supplies. Similarly, if manufacturing processes produced wastes that polluted the air, land, and water, humans in general were liable to pay a price.

It took many decades to evolve new forms of social and sanitary administration to deal with the problems of the new urban places. The problems have not been entirely solved to this day. In sum, productivity rose rapidly during the Industrial Revolution, but some of the costs of increased production are still being borne by later generations (see Chapter 12).

The characteristics of an industrial society are not synonymous with those that are regarded as modern. A **modern society** normally has low birth and death rates, high rates of literacy, a well-developed educational system, disease control and health provisions, high per capita earnings, and substantial disposable income (see Chapter 10). Many of these characteristics may not be present in the early phases of industrial revolutions. Certainly the industrialization of Britain was not accompanied by modernization. In Britain the Industrial

Revolution resulted in an uneducated peasantry migrating into the expanding urban centers in the late eighteenth and early nineteenth centuries, but public health acts were not passed by Parliament until the mid-nineteenth century. Universal education, even at the elementary level, was not provided until 1870.

Areas of Early Industrialization

It is impossible to point to a single event, invention, or time period that accounts for the emergence of industrial societies in Western Europe and North America. Certainly the birth of modern science and improved agriculture preceded industrialization. Long-range trade had created business and financial institutions capable of handling more elaborate forms of production. High population densities had developed a general setting that encouraged the search for higher productivity.

As population pressed against the available resources, medieval European society was ready for improved technologies. From the fifteenth century onward, Europeans had sought new sources of wealth. The development of maritime trade and exploration fostered technical advancements, entrepreneurial skills, and the accumulation of financial resources. Speculation about the form of the world and its setting in the universe encouraged scientific inquiry.

It should be noted, however, that these traits relating to trade, exploration, and scientific inquiry were not specifically European. Other civilizations had displayed similar characteristics at earlier times. Between about 200 B.C. and A.D. 1450, the Chinese surpassed the West in acquiring knowledge (Needham 1954). The Chinese invented gunpowder, papermaking, movable type, the compass, earthquake sensors, and numerous other instruments (Figure 2-16). Chinese knowledge of astronomy, acoustics, medicine, optics, silk culture, deep-well drilling techniques, and the making of porcelain was much superior to that of the rest of the world prior to the seventeenth century. By the twelfth and thirteenth centuries, the Chinese were trading with at least 50 countries, which is how

Figure 2-16. An Example of Early Chinese Technology. The apparatus was designed to detect the tremors of earthquakes. Photo courtesy of Robert O. Harding.

Industrial society. A society whose economy depends on manufacturing for the production of many of its needs (see Hunting and gathering society and Agrarian society).

Primary activities. Economic activities that produce goods by "collecting" materials from the natural environment, such as in hunting, fishing, mining, lumbering, and agriculture (see Secondary and Tertiary activities).

Secondary activities. Economic activities that produce goods by remaking materials such as through manufacturing and construction (see Primary and Tertiary activities).

Tertiary activities. Economic activities that produce value through the performance of services (see Primary and Secondary activities).

Modern society. A society whose members have a high per capita income, low birth and death rates, and access to high quality educational and medical services.

the compass, as well as many other ideas and items, reached Europe. The superiority of China over Europe in technology and wealth was so great in the thirteenth century that most Europeans did not believe the reports of Marco Polo when he returned to Venice from his travels in China.

In spite of this head start in technical knowledge, China did not produce the world's first industrial economy. The success of Chinese society, in a sense, led to satisfaction in the status quo. There was very little emphasis on change, either in the structure of society or in the type of economy (see more on Chinese values in Chapter 5). Without strong elements pushing for radical alterations, China did not utilize its knowledge and techniques to create an "industrial revolution."

Innovations also originated elsewhere in Asia. Algebra, a numerical system using zero, and other mathematical concepts began in India. These ideas were later adapted by Arabs; and eventually Europeans used "Arabic numerals" and the accompanying mathematics in subsequent scientific reasoning.

It is apparent that industrialization in Europe benefited partly from the diffusion of knowledge from other areas of the world, but these ideas and techniques were applied by Europeans in new ways. Societal conditions in Europe in the eighteenth century were generally conducive to change. A primary factor for the emergence of industrialization in Europe was this break with the past and an acceptance of change—of new relationships and new ways of doing things.

In the uplands of northern England, where the soil was poor and agricultural yields were low, more and more families began to practice craft industries in the home. The making of simple pieces of hardware and the spinning and weaving of textiles were commonplace. In other areas the exploitation of basic resources such as coal was stepped up, particularly if navigable water was nearby (Figure 2-17).

Frequently one change led to another. For example, after 1733, Kay's flying shuttle speeded up weaving in the cotton industry. Cotton spinners then needed to produce faster in order to meet the demands of the weavers. Hargreaves developed the spinning jenny in 1765 and Arkwright, with his water frame, harnessed water power to the spinning process in 1769. Boulton and Watt started manufacturing steam engines in 1775, and these were used to drive textile machinery in 1785. The overall result was that the cotton textile industry became increasingly productive and efficient. Between 1780 and 1830 the cost of cotton cloth dropped to one-tenth of its former price. The lower price stimulated demand, which helped to create more cotton factories and more manufacturers of cotton-processing machinery.

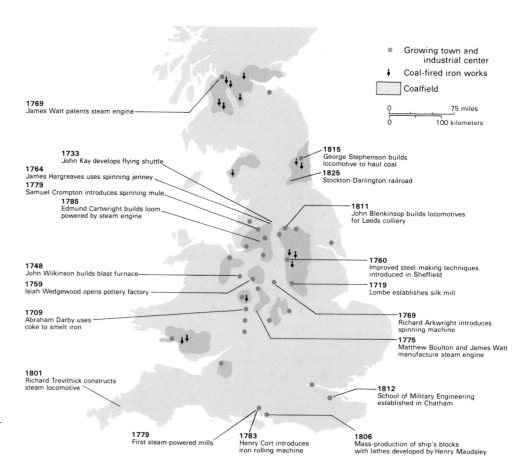

Figure 2-17. Industrial Regions of Britain, 1715–1825. A series of inventions and the existence of coal fields were contributing factors to early industrialization in England.

How widespread were these changes? No one seriously disputes that the first industrial revolution took place in Britain. To recognize certain British industrial regions as early developers, however, is not necessarily the same as claiming that industrialization was a uniquely British process that subsequently diffused to other places. In fact, Belgium's industrialization followed so quickly after the British experiences that the continental activity must have been partially spontaneous and not wholly dependent on English antecedents.

When we look at the origins of industrialization in North America, we come to appreciate the complexities involved. Some industrial processes can be shown to have come directly from Britain. For example, Samuel Slater, frequently described as the founder of the American cotton industry, was born in northern England and worked with Richard Arkwright in developing cotton manufacturing machinery. In 1789, he migrated to the United States, having described himself as a carpenter because the emigration of textile workers was forbidden. Very shortly after his arrival, Slater was successfully involved with companies that were manufacturing textile machinery and promoting its use in the United States.

On the other hand, Eli Whitney, who was American-born, developed a machine in 1793 that solved the problem of separating cotton seeds from cotton fibers. At this stage in his career, Whitney could have had little direct knowledge of British manufacturing techniques. His equipment was designed to solve an American processing problem. His invention of the cotton gin had the effect of stimulating cotton production in the American South and textile manufacturing in New England.

Robert Fulton, who did for river transportation what George Stephenson and Richard Trevithick did for railroads, was born and educated in Pennsylvania. In 1786, he left the United States for Britain and France to develop his career as a civil engineer. On his return to the United States, Fulton built his famous paddle steamer, the *Clermont*, which improved navigation on the Hudson River. The power for the *Clermont* was provided by a Boulton and Watt steam engine imported from Britain. Fulton, then, is an example of a man who fitted easily into industrializing societies on both sides of the Atlantic and who was responsible for transferring ideas in both directions.

One cannot, of course, have a high degree of confidence in conclusions drawn from a small sample. Nevertheless, by the end of the eighteenth century, there were numerous areas around the North Atlantic where many of the preconditions for industrialization had been met, and inventive people could move easily from one region to another and find that their ideas were understood. This leads us to the conclusion that it was not industry that diffused but rather, at an earlier stage, a value system that placed a high priority on inventiveness as the route to increased productivity and increased levels of wealth.

PERSPECTIVES ON POPULATION

It is difficult to see precise relationships between population growth and industrialization. Observing a direct relationship is difficult because a strong upsurge in numbers was apparent in Europe in the eighteenth century before industrial production could have had much impact. Population also increased in agriculturally dependent China at this time. It may well be that the eighteenth century was one of the times of a long-term global upswing in population numbers. Nevertheless, at least in Western Europe, the Industrial Revolution did produce materials that allowed inhabitants to survive longer and eventually to live at a higher standard.

Although the exact effects of industrialization on population growth are not known, the changes in population distributions are quite evident. Prior to industrialization, most workers were farmers, which meant they had to be dispersed in order to utilize land resources. Although farm families may have locally clustered in small communities, the general distribution of population reflected the patterns of fertile land. Even places having crafts and other pre-industrial production were widely dispersed in small towns and rural areas, particularly to take advantage of water power.

The steam engine changed the location of many economic activities. The early engines were inefficient and voracious in their consumption of fuel; they needed to be on or near coal fields if fuel costs were to be minimized. However, compared with earlier sources of power, such as water or wood, the energy output of the steam engine was large. To consume the energy effectively, several factories had to be grouped together to share the power source. The effect of these changes was to concentrate production and people in industrial towns (Figure 2-18).

As industrialization progressed, more and more factories were attracted to the places that already had the power, usable by-products, transportation facilities, and experienced workers. With a multitude of raw materials and finished products to be transported and sold, many people became involved with buying and selling, transporting, and providing numerous related services. Most of these workers were no longer producing their own food, clothing, and shelter, so other people came to the same centers to earn a living by providing such services. In other words, as the economy changed from dependence on primary activities to dependence on secondary and tertiary activities, the forces of agglomeration became very important. With the Industrial Revolution came a major shift in population patterns, a shift from dis-

Figure 2-18. Sunderland, an Early Industrial Center in Britain. In 1842, Sunderland on the River Wear typified an early industrial landscape with its lime kilns, high bridge over a navigable waterway, atmospheric pollution, and cramped housing. Photo courtesy of Olwyn M. Blouet.

persed areas of fertile land to a few centers near concentrated fuel resources and/or places having good transportation (Figure 2-19). By 1851, as people crowded into a few advantageous areas, the percent of population living in English cities rose to 51.

The topic of population growth during and following the Industrial Revolution is expanded in Chapter 3, but here it is appropriate to note the views of some scholars about the population changes in their time. Some commentators pointed to improved agriculture, the growth of trade, and industrial expansion as signs of progress. Others viewed the rising population in Europe with apprehension because they doubted the ability of humankind to support the growing numbers. Foremost among the doubters was Thomas Robert Malthus, who published his famous *Essay on the Principle of Population* in 1798 (Box 2-3).

The *Essay* can be seen as a classic statement of the population problems encountered by pre-industrial societies, which are dependent on agriculture and arable land. Malthus suggested that populations increase faster than the production of food needed for their subsistence. He proposed that population numbers grow geometrically (1, 2, 4, 8, 16), whereas subsistence increases only arithmetically (1, 2, 3, 4, 5). Malthus argued that basic human subsistence regulates the size of a population; therefore, the increase in growth rate cannot go on for long. Increasing population will make food scarce and promote poverty. Population increase tends to overstock an area with people and to make employment and earnings harder to acquire.

Malthus believed that the only permanent improvement in the human condition would come from lowered birth rates. He argued that preventive measures, primarily by delayed marriage, celibacy, and continence, should be used to curb population growth. Otherwise, what he called "positive checks"—warfare, famine, and disease—would hold down numbers. In his 1798 *Essay*, Malthus placed much reliance on the scarcity of food as a control on population numbers. In his enlarged 1803 version, he acknowledged that social forces also played an important part in determining birth rates.

Malthus is sometimes seen as an antiwelfare writer because, in the early nineteenth century, he was very critical of arrangements to support the poor in Britain. He believed that many of the proposed policies made things worse. For example, he declared that providing

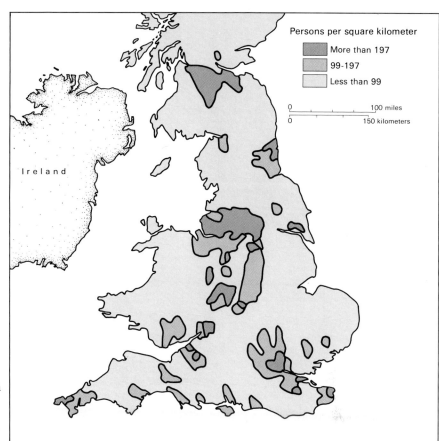

Figure 2-19. Density of Population in England, 1851. As the economy shifted toward industrialization, the population became more concentrated in urban areas. After Lawton 1986.

BOX 2-3. THOMAS ROBERT MALTHUS

Thomas Robert Malthus (1766–1834) was born south of London. Robert, as his family called him, was educated first by his father, who was a believer in the perfectability of man. Then in 1779 Malthus was sent to an academy in northern England. During this time in the north, Malthus may have seen something of the industrialization that had already started in that area of Britain.

In 1784, Malthus entered Jesus College at Cambridge University. He studied history, English, Latin, and Greek, along with his "major" in mathematics. He won an honors degree in the subject in 1788, and took Holy Orders. He then acted as curate at the church in Okewood, Surrey, the county of his birth. Okewood was remarkable for the large number of baptisms and few burials recorded there in the eighteenth century. In 1805, Malthus was appointed Professor of History and Political Economy at the East India College (soon to be named Haileybury College) and helped train young men to be administrators in British India.

The *Essay on the Principle of Population as It Affects the Future Improvement of Society* was published in 1798. In 1799, Malthus undertook field studies in Sweden, Norway, Finland, and Russia and observed how populations seemed to adjust to the availability of land and provisions. He visited France and Switzerland in 1802. In the following year, he published a second edition of the *Essay*. This was really a new book, which incorporated the results of his field work and other studies.

Many references to Malthus place emphasis on his theory, but most of his demographic work was based on field observations combined with his study of statistics. His view of population was at least partially vindicated when, in the years after the Napoleonic Wars, there was a great subsistence crisis in the Northern Hemisphere. The weather deteriorated, harvests were poor, death rates rose, and population numbers were checked.

The *Essay* has had a broad impact in many fields. For example, Charles Darwin had read it before presenting his idea about the struggle for existence and natural selection.

additional monies to allow the poor to buy meat would raise the price of meat and subsequently the price of grain. The outcome would be that "the country would not support the same population . . ." (Malthus, Appleman ed., 1976, p. 37). Eventually every society would have its population numbers checked. It seemed common sense to Malthus that the check:

> should rise from a foresight of the difficulties attending a family and the fear of dependent poverty, [rather] than from the actual pressure of want and sickness. [Malthus, Appleman ed., 1976, p. 41].

As Malthus saw the issue, the only way to improve the lot of the poor was to lower the birth rate so that there would be less labor available. With fewer laborers, workers' wages would go up, relative to foodstuffs, which would permit higher living standards.

As demographic, economic, political, and technological conditions have changed, various writers and speakers have affirmed, criticized, or reinterpreted **Malthusian** concepts. Even persons who dispute his conclusions recognize that his writings have had a continuing influence on the way people think about population issues. You will be able to evaluate further the applicability of the Malthusian thesis to contemporary and future world population after reading the next chapter.

POINT-COUNTERPOINT

Multiple Inventions or Diffusion?

Invention is the creation of a new idea, technique, or device. For an invention to survive, it must be diffused and be adopted by persons other than the inventor. Without diffusion there can be no successful inventions. In this respect, diffusion is a necessary complement to invention.

Some inventions have occurred many times. People do reinvent the wheel. On the other hand, there are inventions that have occurred once and then were diffused so widely that the same idea, technique, or device was not reinvented independently. Papermaking was invented by the Chinese in A.D. 105 and was diffused across Asia through Southwest Asia to

reach Europe in the twelfth century.

The Chinese also invented printing, but this did not diffuse in the same manner. By 1450, the Europeans had invented another system of printing independently.

There has been a long debate about the relative importance of these two contrasting sources of change. The diffusionists contend that major inventions have occurred once and then were diffused over a wide area from one culture group to another. Those who support the idea of independent inventions insist that cultures, as they have evolved through similar stages, have produced roughly similar inventions to solve common

problems. Who is correct? Was agriculture invented in the Zagros Mountains and then diffused to the valleys of the Nile and Indus, or was cultivation invented independently in all these areas? Was industrialization "invented" in Britain and subsequently diffused to other parts of the Western world, or were several industrial innovations developed independently in continental Europe and North America? There are no easy answers to these questions. The discussion continues about the importance of spatial diffusion as a contributor to change.

POINT-COUNTERPOINT

Industrialization: Panacea or Pandora's Box?

From one perspective, industrialization has been seen as the panacea for many of the ills that plagued pre-industrial societies. It has freed humans from the drudgery of traditional agriculture and has created a large variety of occupational choices. This new form of economic activity has also greatly increased the total production of basic necessities, such as food, clothing, and shelter; and it has generated a vast array of new products that make life easier. The accompanying accumulation of

wealth and increased technological knowledge contribute to improved health and universal education and to higher standards of living for nearly all citizens. Because of these many benefits, the goal of all the poorer countries of the world is to become industrialized.

From another perspective, industrialization has not been viewed as the overture to a grand new world. Although many industrialized countries accumulated wealth as a whole, living standards have not

always improved for everyone. In the early stages of industrialization, inhabitants who moved to cities to work in factories often had to endure poor housing and unhealthful living conditions. Even today, many people living in certain sections of industrial cities suffer from poor housing, ill health, and unemployment. For these people, the so-called benefits of industrialization are almost nonexistent. Furthermore, industrialization has introduced new problems, such as creating extensive environmental damage (Chapter 12). Air and water pollution have diminished the quality of health for all humans, rich and poor, living close to the contaminating source and at distant places. The great fear is that, as industrialization increases in more countries of the world, damage to the hydrosphere, biosphere, and atmosphere of the planet will become widespread and will reach intolerable levels. Will the benefits that a few generations of people enjoyed from industrialization eventually be overbalanced by the costs of environmental deterioration?

BIBLIOGRAPHY

Adams, Robert M., "The Origin of Cities," *Scientific American*, 203 (September 1960), 153–68.

Braudel, Fernand, *The Structures of Everyday Life*. New York: Harper & Row, Pub., 1981.

Coale, Ansley J., "The History of Human Population," *Scientific American*, 231 (September 1984), 40–51.

Coe, Michael D., and Kent V. Flannery, "Microenvironments and Mesoamerican Prehistory," *Science*, 143 (February 1964), 650–54.

Cohen, Mark Nathan, *The Food Crisis in Prehistory: Overpopulation and the Origins of Agriculture*. New Haven: Yale University Press, 1977.

Davis, Kingsley, "The Migrations of Human Populations," *Scientific American*, 231 (September 1974), 92–105.

Deane, Phyllis, *The First Industrial Revolution*, 2nd ed. New York: Cambridge University Press, 1979.

Deevey, Edward S., Jr., "The Human Population," *Scientific American*, 203 (September 1960), 104–205.

Dobyns, Henry F., *Native American Historical Demography*. Bloomington, Ind.: Indiana University Press, 1976.

DuPaquier, J., ed., *Malthus Past and Present*. London and New York: Academic Press, 1983.

Durand, John D., "The Modern Expansion of World Population," *Proceedings of the American Philosophical Society*, III (June 1967), 136–63.

———. "A Long-Range View of World Population Growth," in Michael Micklin, ed., *Population, Environment, and Social Organization: Current Issues in Human Ecology*, pp. 92–99. Hinsdale, Ill.: Dryden Press, 1973.

Gilbert, Martin, *British History Atlas*. London: Weidenfeld & Nicolson, 1969.

Grigg, David, "The Growth of World Food Output and Population 1950–1980," *Geography*, 68, pt. 4 (October 1983), 301–6.

Hindle, Brooke, and Steven Luban, *Engines of Change: The American Industrial Revolution, 1790–1860*. Washington, D.C.: Smithsonian Institution Press, 1986.

Ho, Ping-ti, *Studies on the Population of China, 1368–1953*. Cambridge, Mass.: Harvard University Press, 1959.

Hole, F., and K. V. Flannery, "The Prehistory of South-Western Iran: A Preliminary Report," *Proceedings of Prehistoric Society*, 33 (1960).

Hole, Frank, Kent V. Flannery, and James A. Neeley, *Prehistory and Human Ecology of the Deh Furan Plain: An Early Village Sequence from Khirzistan, Iran*. Ann Arbor: University of Michigan, 1969.

Issac, Erich, *Geography of Domestication*. Englewood Cliffs, N.J.: Prentice-Hall, 1970.

James, Patricia, *Population Malthus*. London: Routledge & Kegan Paul, 1979.

Jeremy, David J., *Transatlantic Industrial Revolution: The Diffusion of Textile Technologies between Britain and America 1790–1830*. Oxford, England: Blackwell, 1981.

Kleinman, David S., *Human Adaptation and Population Growth: A Non-Malthusian Perspective*. Montclair, N.J.: Allanheld, Osmun, 1980.

Lal, K. S., *Growth of Muslim Population in Medieval India*. Delhi: Research Publications, 1973.

Lawton, Richard, "Population," in John Langton and R. J. Morris, eds., *Atlas of Industrializing Britain, 1780–1914*, pp. 10–29. London and New York: Methuen, 1986.

Lee, Richard B., and Irven DeVore, eds., *Man the Hunter*. Chicago: Aldine Publishing Co., 1968.

Malthus, Thomas Robert, *An Essay on the Principle of Population*, Phillip Appleman, ed. New York: W. W. Norton & Co., Inc., 1976.

Mathias, Peter, *The First Industrial Nation: An Economic History of Britain 1700–1914*. New York: Charles Scribner's and Sons, 1969.

Needham, Joseph, *Science and Civilization in China*. Cambridge, England: Cambridge University Press, 1954.

Petersen, William, *Malthus*. Cambridge, Mass.: Harvard University Press, 1979.

Roberts, Bryan, *Cities of Peasants*. London: Arnold, 1978.

Sauer, Carl O., *Agricultural Origins and Dispersals*. New York: American Geographical Society, 1952.

———, *Seeds, Hearths, & Herds: The Domestication of Animals and Foodstuffs*. Cambridge, Mass.: M.I.T. Press, 1969.

Ucko, Peter J., and G. W. Dimbleby, *The Domestication and Exploitation of Plants and Animals*. London: Duckworth, 1971.

Vavilov, Nikolai I., *The Origin, Variation, Immunity and Breeding of Cultivated Plants*, trans. by K. Starr Chester, *Chronica Botanica*, 13, nos. 1–6 (1951), 20–43.

White, Leslie A., *The Science of Culture*. New York: Grove Press, Inc., 1949.

Wolf, Eric, *Sons of the Shaking Earth*. Chicago: University of Chicago Press, 1959.

Wrigley, E. A., *Population and History*. New York: McGraw-Hill, 1969.

Wrigley, E. A., and R. S. Schofield, *The Population of England 1541–1871: A Reconstruction*. Cambridge, Mass.: Harvard University Press, 1981.

Zambardino, Rudolph A., "Mexico's Population in the Sixteenth Century: Demographic Anomaly or Mathematical Illusion," *Journal of Interdisciplinary History*, XI, no. 1 (1980). 1–27.

Malthusian. A viewpoint that sees human population numbers as likely to increase faster than the available food supply (see Box 2-3).

3 POPULATION: THE MODERN ERA

A major factor in the geography of humans today is their concentration in a very small proportion of the earth's surface. In addition to being clustered, the people of the world have increased greatly in numbers over the last few centuries. Both of these characteristics influence the ways humans behave spatially and ecologically.

The purpose of this chapter is to describe some of the causes and effects of the demographic changes that have taken place since 1750. Attention is focused first on the European experience because it was there that the break with the past first occurred. The question then arises: Are relationships between the demographic and economic changes that occurred in Europe observable in other countries today? To answer this question, several factors associated with contemporary birth and death rates are discussed. The chapter ends with a look at the major distributional patterns of world population and with some thoughts about future population distribution and ecological relationships.

THE EUROPEAN EXPERIENCE

As explained in the previous chapter, the population changes in eighteenth-century Europe were only one aspect of the social and economic upheavals accompanying the Industrial Revolution. The causal connection between population growth and economic change is controversial. Some argue that the spurt in population growth was stimulated by economic forces: with economic expansion, the demand for labor rose and so there was an increase in population to meet the new demand. Others maintain that population changes were already underway before the Industrial Revolution and that increased population prompted economic growth. A third position is that

neither population growth nor economic change directly "caused" the other. This viewpoint is supported by the fact that population grew in some parts of Europe, like Austria, where industrialization did not develop until much later. These three differing viewpoints demonstrate that no simple cause-and-effect explanation is sufficient.

An understanding of population growth is enhanced by examining the main components of change. Here we focus on the components of mortality and fertility, leaving migration to be dealt with more fully in the following chapter. Both death and birth rates are important because a change in either one affects the difference between the two, which determines growth rates.

Falling mortality rates in parts of the world during the eighteenth and nineteenth centuries were largely responsible for the accelerated rate of population increase. In fact, since 1750 a steadily falling mortality rate has continued to be a significant cause of the growth of world population. This decline is hardly surprising since the vast majority of people are receptive to innovations that will postpone death. In contrast, attitudes toward having children are not so easily changed because they are imbedded in tradition and are affected by diverse social and economic factors. Although death rates can be reduced by general environmental and social reforms (ensuring safe water supplies, for example), birth rates are reduced primarily when individuals decide to limit family size.

Mortality

Before the Industrial Revolution, mortality rates in Europe were high and growth rates low because of recurring famines and epidemic diseases. It was not a matter of death rates being unremittingly high; rather

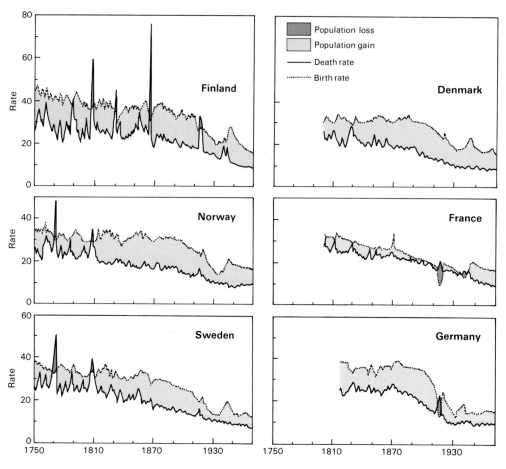

Figure 3-1. Birth and Death Rates in Selected European Countries, 1750–1970. Although death rates declined faster than birth rates, periodic epidemics until 1920 raised the death rate above the birth rate for short periods of time. After Mitchell 1980.

it was a case of periodic crises that pushed the death rates above the birth rates, resulting in temporary population declines. During the Industrial Revolution, the mortality peaks were flattened, except for such events as the deadly outbreaks of cholera. When these rates are graphed, lines of mortality rates are not substantially lower immediately after 1750 than before that date, but they are smoother and show a steadily downward trend (Figure 3-1).

There were a number of factors behind the general decline in the death rate. One main reason for falling mortality was the improvement of general nutrition during the second half of the eighteenth century (Figure 3-2). The European food base was strengthened by the introduction of the potato and, to a lesser extent, of corn from the New World during the seventeenth century. Particularly in the wetter marginal farming areas of Europe—Ireland and Norway, for example—the potato became the main staple of the diet. Even before the advent of the railroads in the second quarter of the nineteenth century, better road systems, new canal networks, and increased coastal shipping had reduced the isolation of places and had allowed the transference of food from surplus to deficit areas. Improved agricultural practices played their part also. Crop rotations, selective animal breed-

ing, manuring, new machinery, and better storage facilities raised productivity and increased the reliability and quality of food supplies. In England these innovations were so important that they created a virtual revolution in agricultural methods (see Chapter 9).

The higher standards of nutrition strengthened resistance to infectious diseases such as dysentery, typhus, smallpox, tuberculosis, and scarlet fever. The downward trend in the death rates was reinforced in the second half of the nineteenth century by major improvements in the quality of the environment, improvements that reduced exposure to infectious diseases. Important advances were the purification of water, better disposal of sewage, and production of higher quality foods (particularly pasteurized milk). Other changes were the increased use of soap in bathing and laundering, which contributed to personal hygiene, and the availability of cheap coal, which permitted better heating.

It is worth stressing that according to this argument it was largely environmental reforms, rather than medical breakthroughs, that were the main reason for the fall in mortality rates during the eighteenth and nineteenth centuries. Although the increased acceptance of immunizations (such as for smallpox)

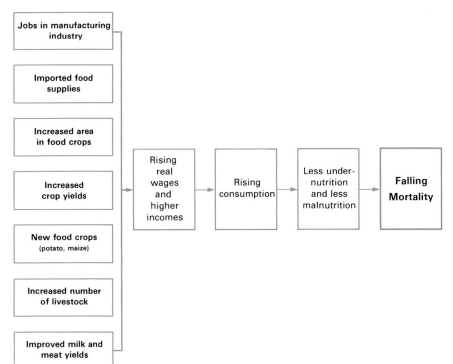

Figure 3-2. Economic Reasons for Falling Mortality in Western Europe After 1750. Changes in many interdependent conditions resulted in the decline of death rates. After Grigg 1982.

in the nineteenth century undoubtedly contributed to decreased mortality rates, it was only after sulfonamides and antibiotics were introduced in the 1930s that medical measures had a widespread impact on national death rates (Omran 1977).

Thus, for a variety of reasons, the mortality rates in several Western European countries declined after 1750. For instance, the crude death rate in England and Wales was approximately 30 (per 1000) in 1750; but by 1900 it had dropped to less than 20. This was typical of the European experience, although the timing of the transition from higher to lower death rates varied from country to country (Figure 3-1).

The rates of mortality also varied from place to place within countries. Particularly in the over-crowded industrial cities of England (vividly portrayed by Charles Dickens), death rates remained high throughout the nineteenth century. It is estimated that, in the worst areas of cities like Liverpool and Manchester, life expectancy at birth was no more than 20 years. Meanwhile, in some affluent rural areas of southern England, average life expectancy was more than 50 years. Although, in general, fluctuations in the death rates declined and the trend of mortality rates was downward, it should be remembered that there were significant variations according to location and social class.

The situation was not so different in "Europe overseas"—as illustrated by the United States. The decline in mortality rates began somewhat later in the United States than in England, and death rates continued to fluctuate widely until the second half of the

nineteenth century (Figure 3-3). Records for Massachusetts suggest a death rate for the white population of about 28 (per 1000) in 1789. The death rate declined steadily to 21 in 1855 and 17 in 1900. By 1950, death rates for the United States as a whole had declined to approximately 10, a level at which they have remained.

Within the United States, mortality rates have varied, and continue to vary, with social class and geographic location. In 1850, life expectancy at birth was 44 years for a white male in Massachusetts, but it was only 21 years for a black male in Baltimore and Charleston (Omran 1977). Meanwhile, as the Anglo-American frontier pushed rapidly across the United States, the Native Americans were decimated by disease, war, and dislocation. From an estimated total of 2–10 million in the seventeenth century, the American Indian population fell to 248,253 by 1890. **Age-specific** death rates (mortality per 1000 population in a designated age group) for infectious diseases like tuberculosis are still higher for nonwhites than for whites (Figure 3-4).

As life expectancy has increased in recent decades, the primary causes of deaths in the industrialized nations have shifted. When medical protection became more efficient after 1935, the major infectious diseases receded. They were replaced as the chief

---

Age-specific death rate. The ratio consisting of (a) the annual number of deaths for a specific age to (b) the total number of persons of that age (see Crude death rate).

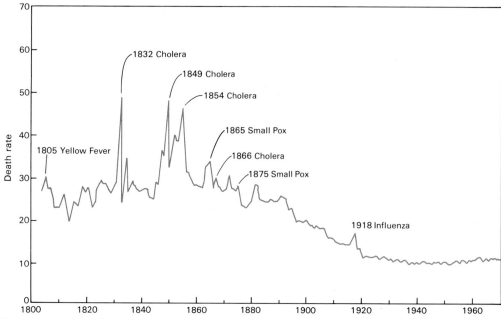

Figure 3-3. Mortality Transition in New York City, 1800–1970. The major decline in death rates in New York City occurred between 1890 and 1920 with the control of disease epidemics. Used with permission from the Population Reference Bureau.

causes of death by degenerative diseases such as heart disease and cancer (Table 3-1). Mounting evidence connects the incidence of various types of cancer to environmental causes, such as air and water pollution, industrial waste, harmful diets, smoking, and, per-

haps, the pressures of high-density urban living. It seems that having controlled the scourge of infectious diseases, more developed societies are now threatened by diseases associated with their affluent, sedentary, and stressful life styles.

Fertility

During the early phases of industrialization, some areas of Europe actually experienced a rise in their birth rates. This was certainly the case in England. The reasons for the increase are complex and may have varied from place to place. One factor appears to have been that when economic conditions were favorable, couples married at a younger age, thus allowing the birth of more children (Wrigley 1983). Also, rural attitudes concerning the importance of children as useful workers may have persisted in urban areas for a time.

The trend of higher birth rates was short-term. Starting in the second half of the nineteenth century (earlier in France where fertility rates declined simultaneously with the mortality rates), birth rates started to fall. They continued to fall during the twentieth century, so today the birth rates in Europe are not much higher than the death rates. Indeed, in some countries—Hungary and West Germany, for example—the birth rate has fallen below the death rate, raising concerns over future populations.

In England and Wales the average number of children per family dropped from more than 6 in the 1860s to around 2 in the 1970s. A similar transition

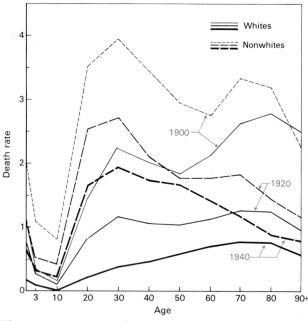

Figure 3-4. Age-Specific Death Rates for Tuberculosis: Whites and Nonwhites in the United States for Selected Years. The incidence of tuberculosis was much higher among nonwhites than among whites, especially ages 20–80, in 1900, 1920, and 1940. Used with permission from the Population Reference Bureau.

Table 3-1. Ten Leading Causes of Death, New York City and the United States, Selected Years

New York City		United States	
Rank	Percentage of Total Deaths	Rank	Percentage of Total Deaths
1866		1900	
1 Tuberculosis	19.8	1 Pneumonia-influenza-bronchitis	14.4
2 Diarrhea & enteritis	15.0	2 Tuberculosis	11.3
3 Cholera	6.4	3 Diarrhea & enteritis	8.1
4 Pneumonia-influenza-bronchitis	6.1	4 Heart disease	8.0
5 Infantile convulsions	5.9	5 Bright's disease (chronic nephritis)	4.7
6 Cerebral hemorrhage	2.7	6 Accidents	4.5
7 Diphtheria & croup	2.7	7 Congestion & brain hemorrhage	4.2
8 Dysentery	2.7	8 Infant diseases	4.2
9 Scarlet fever	2.5	9 Cancer & tumors	3.7
10 Nephritis	2.4	10 Diphtheria	2.3
1965		1970	
1 Heart disease	39.0	1 Heart disease	38.3
2 Cancer	19.9	2 Cancer	17.2
3 Stroke	7.1	3 Stroke	10.8
4 Influenza & pneumonia	3.8	4 Influenza-pneumonia-bronchitis	3.5
5 Accidents (not car)	3.1	5 Accidents (not car)	3.1
6 Infant diseases	3.0	6 Car accidents	2.8
7 Cirrhosis of liver	3.0	7 Infant diseases	2.3
8 Diabetes	2.1	8 Diabetes	2.0
9 Congenital malformation	1.0	9 Arteriosclerosis	1.7
10 Suicide	1.0	10 Cirrhosis of liver	1.6

Source: Omran 1977. Used with permission from Population Reference Bureau.

was experienced in the United States, although the birth rate was initially much higher than in Europe. The higher level was largely because the vast frontiers of the country provided economic opportunities for rural families that required many laborers. In urban areas, children were less of an economic asset, so birth rates in the city declined sooner than in the countryside.

It is much easier to describe these changing fertility rates than to completely explain their causes. A few important factors, however, can be identified. First, the fall in birth rates in the late nineteenth century was not brought about by new contraceptive methods such as modern forms of birth control, which were not used until well into the twentieth century. It was the desire to limit family size that was new, not the means.

Next, although the connection may at first seem obscure, it appears that the falling rate of infant mortality eventually worked to bring the birth rate down. In an era of high death rates, it was necessary to give birth to a large number of children to ensure that some survived to help support the family. When a much higher percentage of children survived to adulthood, that former strategy was no longer necessary; consequently, birth rates fell.

Economic factors were also closely linked to the fall in the birth rate. In an urbanized, industrialized

society where the use of child labor was prohibited, children often became an economic liability rather than an asset. Hence, birth rates tended to fall with urbanization and new social legislation. An example of the relationship between economic factors and family size can demonstrate this. During the mid-nineteenth century in England and Wales, the middle classes enjoyed a period of prosperity. The Industrial Revolution created new habits of consumption and new expectations of rising standards of living. Therefore, when confronted by a period of economic hardship after 1870, the middle classes were reluctant to reduce their standards of living. Consequently, they economized by limiting family size rather than by curtailing consumption (Wrigley 1969). This "economic self-interest" theory is convincing, especially if we examine motivations for limiting family size today.

Lastly, urbanization may have played a role by exposing people to new ideas. Literacy rates generally increased with rates of urbanization and weakened the hold of age-old rural traditions favoring large families. This argument is supported by the fact that large-scale migration from rural areas to cities in Europe and in the United States was accompanied by declining birth rates.

Whatever the forces that combined to persuade people to limit the size of their families, the birth rate would not have fallen if there had not been fundamental changes in attitudes toward the family, the role of women in society, and the acceptability of birth control. Some changes in attitude toward family limitations and social roles were due to the efforts of a few outspoken campaigners for birth control. Geographically, the spread of birth control may be envisaged as a process gathering force in England during the 1870s, spreading to Holland and Germany in the following two decades, and then taking hold in the United States.

It was not just a matter of providing more effective methods of contraception; what was involved was a new ideology that represented a real break with the past. The control of family size became morally acceptable and socially desirable. The decision to have, or not to have, children now rested with the parents, not the state, the church, nor the elders of a closed community. The liberalization of birth control not only aided in bringing fertility rates down but it also freed women from a lifetime of childbearing and child rearing and introduced a new flexibility in the choice of life styles.

The birth rates in more developed nations have continued to decline steadily during the twentieth century. There are many reasons for this, such as the increasing acceptance of birth control and family planning, and more efficient methods of communicating information on birth control, new aspirations and opportunities for women, and doubts about the stability of the traditional family system in countries like the United States and Sweden where over 40 percent of marriages end in divorce. Given the institutional care of elderly persons, the high rates of mobility, and the emphasis on individualism in Western societies, young adults are not expected to look after their parents in old age, which removes yet another reason for having children.

As in the past, lower birth rates reflect changing social and economic forces. For many people, a basic college education is not completed before age 22, professional training can take additional years, and

the establishment of careers for both partners in a marriage involves more time. In these circumstances, the decision to have children is delayed. Furthermore, the high cost of raising and educating children is a continuing incentive to limit family size. In the United States in 1981 it cost an estimated $98,000 to support a child at a moderate level from birth to completion of college. Today the figure would be considerably higher.

The Demographic Transition

The dramatic demographic shift that occurred in Western Europe in the brief span of two centuries has been seen by some as a prototype for population changes in modernizing countries elsewhere in the world. The shift is idealized in the **demographic transition model** (see Figure 3-5). This model generalizes population changes as follows: as a country modernizes, it will pass from a condition of high birth and death rates, and consequently slow population growth, through transitional stages of rapid population growth when the fall in the birth rate lags behind the fall in the death rate, to a condition of low fertility and mortality when population growth is once again slow.

According to some scholars, these demographic changes are associated with—and in complicated ways are prompted by—the transformation from an agrarian into an urban-industrial society. The demographic transition is more than a change in birth and death rates; it expresses a metamorphosis of society. Involved are transitions in population distribution, in the economic organization of society, in literacy and education, in expectations and ambitions, and in mobility.

The demographic transition may be regarded as a time-space model. Although this model is based on the European (particularly the English) experience during the last 200 years, it may be applied to other places and times. Countries could be matched with stages of the transition according to their birth and

Figure 3-5. The Demographic Transition Model. The transition from high birth and death rates to low rates can be divided into five stages:

Stage I. High and fluctuating birth and death rates, and slow population growth.
Stage II. High birth rates and declining death rates, and rapid population growth.
Stage III. Declining birth rates and low death rates, and declining rate of population growth.
Stage IV. Low birth and death rates, and slow population growth.
Stage V. Birth and death rates approximately equal, which in time will result in zero population growth.

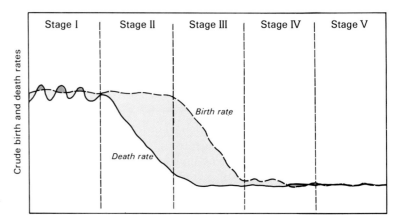

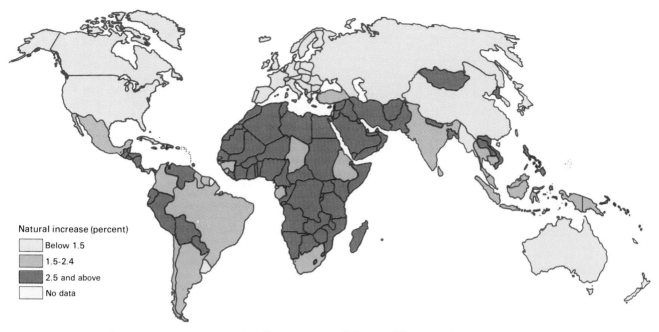

Figure 3-6. Natural Increase in Population for the Countries of the World. Rates of annual change per nation varied in 1987 from 3.9 percent in Kenya to −0.2 percent in West Germany and Hungary.

death rates today. For example, West Germany is in Stage V, with birth rates lower than death rates; the United States, with low birth and death rates, fits Stage IV; China is in the latter part of Stage III; and India is making the transition from Stage II to Stage III. While no country as a whole remains in the initial stage, some may periodically fit Stage I when they face famine (as in Ethiopia in the 1980s) or war (as in Kampuchea in the mid-1970s).

Understanding current trends may be aided by a generalized model of past experiences, but seldom are socio-economic conditions repeated exactly by all countries. So a crucial question is: How relevant is this demographic model to other societies in the late twentieth century?

CONTEMPORARY DEMOGRAPHIC CONDITIONS

An examination of contemporary death and birth statistics for the nations of the world reveals that many countries in Africa, Asia, and South America have rates associated with Stages II and III of the demographic transition model (see Figure 3-5 and Table 3-2). Accordingly, the population growth in these countries is faster than in countries whose demographic characteristics fit Stage IV. Although there are no obvious "breaks" in the continuum of rates of natural increase for the countries of the world, for the purpose of discussion it is worth distinguishing between demographic types. A small group of coun-

tries in Europe now has "zero or negative growth." Another category of countries consists of those where the natural population increase is between 0.1 and 1.4 percent annually. Those countries experiencing increases of 1.5 to 2.4 percent each year fall into the "medium growth" group, and those with an annual increase of more than 2.4 percent may be considered "fast growth" (Figure 3-6). In order to understand the dynamics of these rates of change, it is useful to examine the components—mortality and fertility—separately.

Mortality

As recently as 1945 there was great variation in death rates throughout the world. In most countries—particularly those in Africa, Latin America, and Asia—life expectancy at birth was about 35 years, as it had been in Europe and the United States before 1900. Now the life expectancy in Africa, Latin America, and Asia is 51, 66, and 61 years, respectively. These increased ages reflect a general decline in mortality rates throughout the world during recent times.

Death rates have fallen because the advanced medical and public health technologies of the modernized nations have been transferred to the less

---

Demographic transition model. The generalized decreases in death and then birth rates that European populations experienced beginning in the eighteenth century (see Figure 3–5).

TABLE 3-2. World Population Data, 1987

Country[a]	Population (millions, mid-1987)	Population density (persons per sq. km.)	Population density per cultivated land (sq. km.)	Crude birth rate	Crude death rate	Infant mortality rate	Total fertility rate	Persons under 15 yrs. of age (%)	Population projected to year 2000 (millions)
Afghanistan	14.2	22	176	48	22	182	7.6	46	24.5
Albania	3.1	108	436	26	6	43	3.3	35	3.8
Algeria	23.5	10	316	42	10	81	6.4	46	33.7
Angola	8.0	6	229	47	22	143	6.4	45	11.5
Argentina	31.5	11	88	24	8	35	3.3	31	37.2
Australia	16.2	2	34	16	8	10	2.0	24	17.9
Austria	7.6	91	499	12	12	11	1.5	18	7.5
Bangladesh	107.1	744	1176	44	17	140	6.2	44	144.9
Belgium	9.9	326	1308	12	11	9	1.5	19	9.8
Benin	4.3	38	237	51	20	115	7.1	49	7.1
Bhutan	1.5	32	1500	38	18	142	5.5	40	1.9
Bolivia	6.5	6	192	40	14	127	5.1	43	9.2
Botswana	1.2	2	88	48	14	70	6.7	48	1.8
Brazil	141.5	17	188	29	8	63	3.5	36	179.5
Bulgaria	9.0	81	218	13	12	16	2.0	22	9.4
Burkina Faso	7.3	27	165	48	20	146	6.5	44	10.5
Burma	38.8	57	386	34	13	103	4.4	39	49.8
Burundi	5.0	180	383	47	18	119	6.4	44	7.2
Cameroon	10.3	22	148	43	16	103	5.9	43	14.5
Canada	25.9	3	113	15	7	8	1.7	22	27.9
Cen. African Rep.	2.7	4	136	44	19	142	5.9	43	3.8
Chad	4.6	4	146	43	23	143	5.9	44	6.3
Chile	12.4	16	224	22	6	20	2.4	32	14.8
China	1062.0	111	1053	21	8	61	2.4	28	1200.0
Colombia	29.9	26	525	28	7	48	3.1	36	38.0
Congo	2.1	6	311	47	13	112	6.8	46	3.2
Costa Rica	2.8	55	440	31	4	19	3.5	35	3.7
Cote d'Ivoire	10.8	33	268	46	15	105	6.7	46	17.3
Cuba	10.3	93	318	18	6	17	1.8	27	11.4
Czechoslovakia	15.6	122	302	15	12	14	2.1	24	16.2
Denmark	5.1	118	194	11	11	8	1.4	18	5.0
Dominican Republic	6.5	133	442	33	8	70	4.0	41	8.4
Ecuador	10.0	35	398	35	8	66	4.7	42	13.6
Egypt	51.9	52	2098	37	11	93	5.3	40	71.2
El Salvador	5.3	252	732	36	10	65	4.7	46	7.2

Ethiopia	46.0	38	330	46	23	152	46	6.7	66.5
Finland	4.9	15	210	13	10	7	19	1.7	5.0
France	55.6	102	296	14	10	8	21	1.8	57.3
Gabon	1.2	4	265	34	18	112	35	4.5	1.6
Germany, East	16.7	154	335	14	14	10	19	1.8	16.8
Germany, West	61.0	245	820	10	12	10	15	1.3	58.4
Ghana	13.9	58	493	42	14	94	47	5.8	20.5
Greece	10.0	76	252	12	9	14	22	1.8	10.2
Guatemala	8.4	77	463	41	9	71	46	5.8	12.2
Guinea	6.4	26	406	47	23	153	43	6.2	8.9
Guyana	0.8[b]	4	162	26	6	36	38	3.0	0.8
Haiti	6.2	224	687	36	13	107	39	4.9	7.7
Honduras	4.7	42	264	39	8	69	47	5.6	7.0
Hong Kong	5.6	5385	70,000	14	5	8	24	1.6	6.4
Hungary	10.6	114	200	12	14	20	22	1.8	10.7
Iceland	0.2[b]	2	2500	16	7	6	26	1.9	0.3
India	800.3	243	475	33	12	101	38	4.3	1013.3
Indonesia	174.9	92	839	31	10	88	40	4.2	219.8
Iran	50.4	31	340	45	13	113	44	6.3	73.9
Iraq	17.0	39	312	46	13	80	49	7.2	26.5
Ireland	3.5	50	360	18	9	9	30	2.5	4.2
Israel	4.4	212	1005	23	7	12	33	3.1	5.3
Italy	57.4	191	470	10	10	11	21	1.4	57.5
Jamaica	2.5	227	929	26	5	20	36	3.1	3.0
Japan	122.2	328	2557	12	6	6	22	1.8	126.6
Jordan	3.7	38	892	45	8	54	51	7.4	5.7
Kampuchea	6.5	36	213	39	18	160	35	4.7	8.5
Kenya	22.4	38	959	52	13	76	51	8.0	38.3
Korea, North	21.4	178	926	30	5	33	39	4.0	28.4
Korea, South	42.1	427	1943	20	6	30	31	2.1	48.0
Kuwait	1.9	107	99,107	34	3	19	40	4.4	2.7
Laos	3.8	16	427	41	16	122	43	5.8	5.0
Lebanon	3.3	317	1107	30	8	52	38	3.8	4.1
Lesotho	1.6	53	538	41	15	106	42	5.8	2.3
Liberia	2.4	22	647	48	16	127	47	6.9	3.6
Libya	3.8	2	180	39	9	90	45	5.6	5.6
Madagascar	10.6	18	351	44	16	63	44	6.1	15.6
Malawi	7.4	62	316	53	21	157	47	7.0	11.4
Malaysia	16.1	49	370	31	7	30	39	3.9	20.2
Mali	8.4	7	409	51	22	175	46	6.7	12.3

TABLE 3–2. World Population Data, 1987 (Continued)

Country[a]	Population (millions, mid-1987)	Population density (persons per sq. km.)	Population density per cultivated land (sq. km.)	Crude birth rate	Crude death rate	Infant mortality rate	Total fertility rate	Persons under 15 yrs. of age (%)	Population projected to year 2000 (millions)
Mauritania	2.0	2	1026	50	20	132	6.9	46	3.0
Mauritius	1.1	579	1006	19	7	25	2.3	32	1.3
Mexico	81.9	42	332	31	7	50	4.0	42	104.5
Mongolia	2.0	1	150	37	11	53	5.1	42	2.8
Morocco	24.4	55	293	36	10	90	4.8	42	33.3
Mozambique	14.7	18	477	45	19	147	6.1	46	21.1
Namibia	1.3	2	196	44	11	110	6.4	45	2.0
Nepal	17.8	126	768	42	17	112	6.1	41	24.4
Netherlands	14.6	391	1669	12	9	8	1.5	20	15.0
New Zealand	3.3	12	1170	16	8	11	1.9	24	3.6
Nicaragua	3.5	27	276	43	9	69	5.7	47	5.1
Niger	7.0	6	186	51	22	141	7.1	47	10.6
Nigeria	108.6	118	350	46	18	124	6.6	45	160.9
Norway	4.2	13	491	12	11	8	1.7	20	4.3
Oman	1.3	6	3023	47	14	117	7.1	44	2.0
Pakistan	104.6	130	516	44	15	125	6.6	45	145.3
Panama	2.3	30	408	27	5	25	3.3	38	2.9
Papua New Guinea	3.6	8	957	36	12	100	5.3	42	6.8
Paraguay	4.3	11	222	36	7	45	4.9	41	6.0
Peru	20.7	16	589	35	10	94	4.8	41	28.0
Philippines	61.5	205	544	35	7	50	4.7	41	85.5
Poland	37.8	121	255	18	10	19	2.3	25	40.8
Portugal	10.3	112	290	12	10	17	1.9	24	10.9
Puerto Rico	3.3	371	2519	19	7	16	2.2	30	3.7
Romania	22.9	96	217	16	11	26	2.3	25	24.5
Rwanda	6.8	259	674	53	16	122	8.5	48	11.0
Saudi Arabia	14.8	7	1280	39	7	79	6.9	37	23.2
Senegal	7.1	36	136	46	18	131	6.7	46	10.6
Sierra Leone	3.9	54	220	47	29	176	6.2	41	5.4
Singapore	2.6	4483	11016	17	5	9	1.6	24	2.9
Somalia	7.7	12	722	48	23	150	7.1	45	10.4
South Africa	34.3	28	252	33	10	72	4.6	38	45.3
Spain	39.0	77	190	13	8	11	1.8	23	41.0
Sri Lanka	16.3	248	740	25	7	30	3.7	35	19.4
Sudan	23.5	9	189	45	16	112	6.5	45	33.4

Suriname	0.4[b]	2	27	7	690	33	3.3	37	0.5
Sweden	8.4	19	12	11	280	7	1.7	18	8.3
Switzerland	6.6	160	12	9	1602	7	1.5	18	6.5
Syria	11.3	61	47	9	200	59	7.2	49	17.8
Taiwan	19.6	607	17	5	2528	9	1.8	30	22.3
Tanzania	23.5	25	50	15	300	111	7.1	48	36.6
Thailand	53.6	104	29	8	272	57	3.5	36	65.5
Togo	3.2	56	47	15	224	117	6.6	44	4.9
Trinidad & Tobago	1.3	255	27	7	817	20	3.2	34	1.6
Tunisia	7.6	46	32	7	162	78	4.5	40	9.9
Turkey	51.4	66	30	9	188	92	4.0	36	65.4
Uganda	15.9	67	50	16	244	108	7.0	48	24.7
United Arab Emirates	1.4	17	30	4	9333	38	5.9	30	1.9
United Kingdom	56.8	232	13	12	813	9	1.8	19	57.3
United States	243.8	26	16	9	129	11	1.8	22	268.0
Uruguay	3.1	18	18	10	214	30	2.5	27	3.2
U.S.S.R.	284.	13	19	11	122	26	2.5	26	312.0
Venezuela	18.3	20	32	6	487	38	3.9	40	24.7
Vietnam	62.2	190	34	8	931	55	4.5	40	86.0
Yemen, Arab Rep. (No.)	6.5	33	53	19	481	137	7.8	49	10.0
Yemen, P.D.R. (So.)	2.4	7	47	17	104	135	7.3	48	3.6
Yugoslavia	23.4	91	16	9	302	29	2.1	25	25.0
Zaire	31.8	14	45	15	488	103	6.1	46	47.6
Zambia	7.1	9	50	15	138	84	7.0	47	11.6
Zimbabwe	9.4	24	47	12	350	76	6.5	50	15.1
World	5026.	38	28	10	340	81	3.6	33	6158.

[a] With population over 1 million
[b] Population under 1 million but area over 100,000 sq. km.

Sources: Population Reference Bureau; United Nations, Food and Agriculture Organization.

developed countries. The availability of modern drugs as well as immunizations has reduced mortality from infectious diseases such as tuberculosis, influenza, pneumonia, diphtheria, typhoid, and measles. By one estimation, 21 percent of the mortality decline in Latin America from 1950 to 1973 was associated with increasing control over infectious diseases. Reductions in deaths from diarrhea and respiratory illnesses accounted for another 11 percent and 10 percent, respectively (Palloni 1981). In addition, the control of certain disease carriers has affected death rates. Malaria, long the scourge of tropical areas, has been curtailed by spraying marshlands with DDT. In Sri Lanka, for example, the death rate came down from 20 to 14 in a single year following the 1946 spraying campaign.

Now that mortality rates have declined in most less developed countries, national crude death rates do not vary as much as for some other demographic statistics, such as birth rates (see Table 3-2). This narrowing of differences is because death rates and life expectancy have improved more slowly in the more developed countries in recent years. This is partly because deaths from noninfectious causes (such as heart attacks and cancer) now account for a larger proportion of the total deaths than other causes, and these have proven difficult to reduce. Among the more developed nations, only the Soviet Union has seen an increase in death rates since 1965. This is related to a rising infant mortality rate and inadequate health care, as well as to an aging population (Feshbach 1982).

Another reason for the slow change in crude death rates in more developed countries is their age structure (see Box 2-1 in Chapter 2). In these countries, the percentage of population below 15 years of age is smaller and the percentage of population over 65 years is larger than the world average. Obviously the annual mortality rate among a group of elderly people tends to be relatively high.

Even with the narrowing of worldwide mortality rates, significant differences in death rates do persist (Figure 3-7). As a continent, Africa has the highest crude death rate, with several countries having rates exceeding 20. In contrast, most Latin American countries have relatively low rates; for the region as a whole, the rate is 8. This statistic, which is lower than the death rate of 10 for Europe, illustrates the effects of a country's age structure. Approximately 38 percent of the Latin American population is younger than 15 years of age, while only 21 percent of Europe's population is less than 15 years old. At the other end of the age spectrum, the percentage of people over 65 years of age in Latin America is 4, in marked contrast to a percentage of 13 in Europe.

Reasons for the continued variations in death rates are related to the economic wealth of nations and the extent to which all citizens receive medical services. Many less developed countries have a low ratio of doctors per capita and a limited number of medical facilities (see Chapter 9).

Variations in mortality rates throughout the world are even greater than indicated by a single mortality statistic for each country because there are internal geographical differences. Medical facilities and services in less developed nations tend to be highly

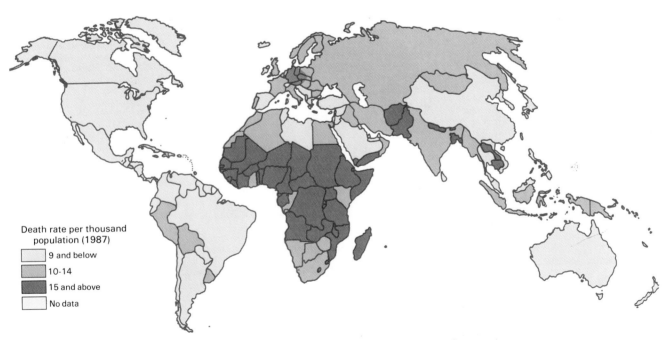

Death rate per thousand population (1987)

9 and below

10-14

15 and above

No data

Figure 3-7. World Distribution of Death Rates. Crude death rates per nation varied in 1987 from 29 in Sierra Leone to 3 in Kuwait.

concentrated in major urban centers, which means lower death rates are similarly restricted. Consequently, in many less developed countries the rate of death among poor families, especially in rural areas, is often much higher than the national average. Future gains in life expectancy will depend not so much on introducing new medical technology as on improving living conditions and diffusing health services throughout each country.

Other differences in death rates within countries may be related to culture. In several cultures (such as Bangladesh), women are expected to serve meals to the male members of the family before they or their daughters eat. If there is a shortage of food, the women and girls are more likely to suffer nutritionally, which then contributes to their higher mortality rates. Malnutrition and lack of medical care are especially critical during pregnancy and childbirth. For example, an East African woman has one chance in 15 of dying during pregnancy (in contrast to one in 6000 for an American woman). The death of a mother, in turn, often means the additional death of children. A study in Bangladesh found that when a mother dies in childbirth, her infant has a 95 percent chance of dying within a year (Chen et al. 1975).

Of particular importance is the rate of deaths among young children, which is normally measured as the **infant mortality rate** (Box 3-1). Modern medical

---

BOX 3-1. ADDITIONAL MEASUREMENTS OF POPULATION CHARACTERISTICS

Several statistics (in addition to those defined in Box 2-1) are useful in describing a population.

The infant mortality rate for a population is calculated by dividing the number of deaths of infants less than one year old by the total number of live births during a particular year. Like the crude death rate, the ratio is expressed in terms of a thousand; but the base figure differs because it is not the total population. To illustrate, a region (such as the one introduced in Box 2-1) that records an annual total of 420 births and 16 deaths of children younger than one year old has an infant mortality rate of 38 per thousand (i.e., 16/420 = 0.038). As a second example, if the country introduced in Box 2-1 has an infant mortality rate of 80, then after one year, 14,000 of the 175,000 infants would have died.

Usually the crude birth rate for a population is lower than the infant mortality rate. When comparing these two statistics, you should remember that the bases for these figures differ, which means the "numerators" cannot be compared directly as absolute numbers. For example, if a nation has a birth rate of 21 and an infant mortality rate of 38, it does not mean that there are more children dying than are being born (as illustrated by the example given above and in Box 2-1).

Specific mortality rates for other age groups, as well as mortality rates for specific causes of death, can be tabulated and compared. The infant age group is commonly reported because it has an important impact on future demographic behavior.

Although the crude birth rate is the most common measurement of fertility, it does not take into account the age structure of the population. For example, two countries with similar crude birth rates may differ in the average number of children born per family because one of the countries may have a larger proportion of women in the childbearing years (generally defined as 15 through 49).

More refined measurements of fertility avoid the complicating factor of age by relating the number of births to women in the childbearing years. The **total fertility rate** is the number of children that a woman would have if she passed through the childbearing years experiencing the average number of births per woman at each age in a specified population.

The **net reproduction rate** refers to the average number of daughters who are born to a woman and who survive through their childbearing years. This is an important fertility measurement because it indicates how a population is being reproduced. A net reproduction rate of 1, for example, means that the current generation of childbearers would be replaced by a generation of the same size. This rate is called the **replacement level.** If a population (without migration change) experiences reproduction at the rate of the replacement level for a generation or two, **zero population growth** will have been attained.

Infant mortality rate. The ratio consisting of (a) the annual number of deaths of infants not over one year old to (b) the total number of live births during that year (see Box 3-1).
Total fertility rate. The number of children that a woman is expected to have during her childbearing years based on the average number of births per woman in a specified population.
Net reproduction rate. The number of girls who would be born to a hypothetical woman who reproduces at the typical rate in a population as she passes through her childbearing years (usually considered to be ages 15–45).
Replacement level. The population growth rate at which the size of one generation is the same as that of the previous generation (see Zero population growth).
Zero population growth. A situation in which the number of births and deaths is equal over a sustained period of time.

services enhance the chances of survival during the first few months of life, so the rate of infant mortality often reflects economic conditions of a nation more precisely than do the death rates of other age groups (Figure 3-8). Therefore, the variation in national infant mortality rates is greater than in total (crude) death rates (Figure 3-8 compared to Figure 3-7).

Like national death rates, infant mortality rates vary greatly within countries according to geographical location and social class. For example, a study of seven Latin American countries in 1970 showed that children of mothers with no schooling were three to five times more likely to die before the age of two than those whose mothers had ten years of education (Merrick 1986). An educated woman is more likely to be aware of appropriate health care and to be located in an urban area where health services are more accessible. Even in the more developed countries there are wide class differentials in infant mortality rates. In fact, a child born to a poor family in an American inner city is as likely to die before the age of one as children born in many less developed countries.

In addition to being a sensitive measure of differences among nations, the rate of infant mortality is important because of its association with other demographic characteristics. As was true in Europe during an earlier period, in many parts of the less developed world today, parents feel obliged to give birth to several children to ensure that some, especially sons, will survive to adulthood. For example, in a country with a high infant mortality rate (above 50 per 1000), parents who want to be 95 percent certain that they will have a son surviving to adulthood must give birth to five children (Heer & Smith 1968).

Another implication of a nation's infant mortality rate is its potential impact on future demographic characteristics. If there is a reduction in the infant mortality rate and if there is not a concurrent decline in the average number of children per family for a generation or two, then more children will live and the age structure of the total population will change. These conditions are revealed by the statistics giving the percentage of a population that is under 15 years of age (see Table 3-2).

Even if each couple, on the average, has *fewer* children than their parents did a generation earlier, a decline in the infant mortality rate still affects future population growth. These additional surviving children subsequently become parents. And even with fewer births per family (than during the previous generation), the larger number of couples normally contributes to a higher number of total births. Major changes in a nation's growth, therefore, tend to lag behind the initial lowering of death and fertility rates because of this "momentum" generated by previous generations. A population with a recent history of rapid growth subsequently experiences, for a few generations, what is called **demographic momentum.**

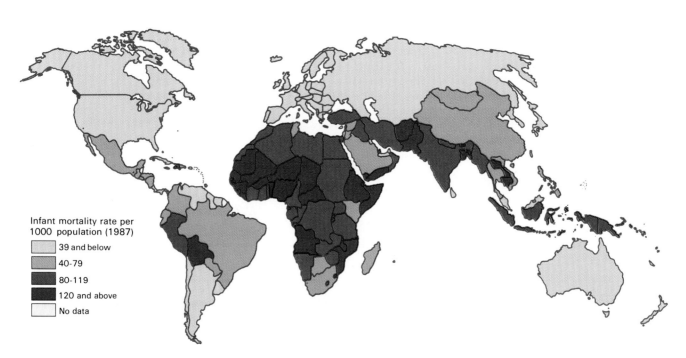

Infant mortality rate per 1000 population (1987)

- 39 and below
- 40-79
- 80-119
- 120 and above
- No data

Figure 3-8. World Distribution of Infant Mortality Rates. The rates of infant mortality per nation varied in 1987 from 182 per 1000 live births in Afghanistan to 6 in Iceland and Japan.

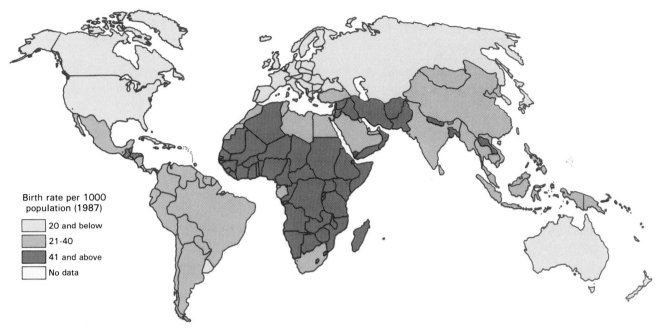

Figure 3-9. World Distribution of Birth Rates. Crude birth rates per nation varied in 1987 from 53 in Malawi, Rwanda, and North Yemen to 10 in West Germany and Italy.

Fertility

Birth rates vary significantly from country to country, from fewer than 12 per 1000 in some European nations to above 50 per 1000 in a few African countries (see Table 3-2 and Figure 3-9). The total fertility rate, another measure of births per area, varies from below 2 (that is, replacement level) in Europe and North America to above 6 in many less developed countries (Box 3-1). These variations are attributable to many of the same factors that existed in Europe when birth rates underwent change as well as to contemporary economic, social, political, and religious conditions.

Economic conditions. One important factor is the economic condition of the family. In an agrarian society where the economic well-being of most families is dependent on their own labor, several children are regarded as an asset. By the time children are ten years old, they are usually contributing more economically than they are consuming. This cost-benefit ratio contrasts very dramatically with the typical situation in the United States where the children seldom return any income to the family unit during most of their childhood but instead incur high costs.

The economic benefits of offspring in most agrarian societies are also apparent when the parents become too old to work vigorously. The adult offspring, especially sons, are expected to care for their elderly parents. In countries that have few institutions for the care and support of elderly citizens, the need for an adult son is critical. Parents expect their offspring to work for them during early years and to care for them during late years. Especially in countries where the probability of infant deaths is high, there is a tendency for birth rates to be high (Box 3-2 and Figure 3-10).

Cultural conditions. Another factor associated with birth rates involves the cultural roles of males and females. In some societies the prestige of men is related to the number of children produced. As an illustration, the Mexican government has recently launched an advertising campaign against *machismo*, the attitude that men must prove their manliness by fathering children. It is difficult to assess how influential *machismo* is; but in Mexico, at least, it is regarded as a serious obstacle to family planning.

In cultures where the role of women is restricted primarily to bearing and rearing children, the birth rate is normally much higher than in those cultures where women have the opportunity to obtain an education and to work outside the home. Consequently the number of children desired by women in

Demographic momentum. The continued effect of a recent history of rapid population change.

BOX 3-2. VARIATIONS IN BIRTH AND INFANT MORTALITY RATES

The points on the **scatter diagram** in Figure 3-10 represent the 1987 rates of birth and mortality for the nations of the world (see Table 3-2). For example, one of the points in the upper right portion indicates a combination of 157 and 53 for the infant mortality and birth rates, respectively, of Malawi; and at the lower part of the graph is a point depicting West Germany's rates of 10 (infant mortality) and 10 (births). The pattern of points as a whole suggests that these two demographic characteristics tend to vary together.

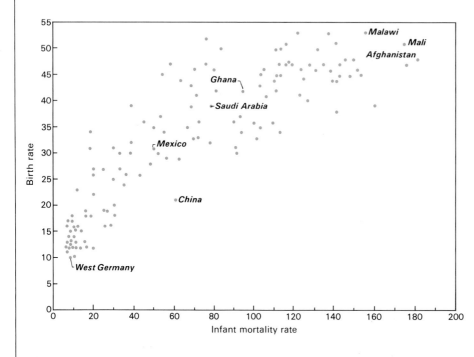

Figure 3-10. Relationship between Birth Rates and Infant Mortality Rates.

various countries usually reflects the contrasting economic and cultural roles of women in those societies (Table 3-3).

The relationship between national birth rates and religious groups is complex. In general, nations where Buddhism is dominant do not necessarily advocate large families, and birth-control measures are commonly used. Hinduism does not discourage birth control, as illustrated by the fact that India, where Hinduism is a major religion, has one of the oldest and largest governmental programs for family planning. Orthodox Hindu parents, however, may want to have enough children to ensure that a son survives to perform religious rituals at the time of their death.

Many people in Islamic countries, following the teachings of the Koran, believe that the primary purpose of marriage is procreation and that Allah should decide the number of children. Even so, at the Population Conference in 1971 (held in Rabat, Morocco), Moslem leaders issued a statement supporting family planning (Bouvier 1975). Today some of the Moslem countries have comprehensive family planning programs, but others do not.

Nations that are dominantly Christian vary considerably in birth rates (see Figures 3-9 and 7-1). Most Protestant denominations have not opposed birth control in recent decades. The Roman Catholic Church has officially remained adamant in its opposition to all forms of birth control except the rhythm method. In most Latin American countries, which are largely Catholic, this religious doctrine has contributed to high fertility. Membership in a religious organization, of course, does not necessarily mean adherence to all official doctrines. Many Mexicans, for example, support the government's program for family planning. In European countries where Roman Catholicism is the major religion and where birth rates are very low (as in France, for example), family size is not greatly influenced by religious doctrine.

Literacy rates. Low literacy rates are associated with high birth rates. If a population is illiterate, it will tend to change slowly and to resist new ideas and innovations. Illiteracy is a form of isolation. It is not surprising, therefore, that the countries with the high-

TABLE 3-3. Desired Family Size, Selected Countries, 1970s

Country	Year of Survey	Average Number of Children Desired by Married Women[a]
Bangladesh	1976	4.1
Colombia	1976	4.1
Costa Rica	1976	4.7
Dominican Republic	1975	4.7
Fiji	1974	4.2
Hungary	1974	2.0
Indonesia	1976	4.2[b]
Japan	1974	2.2
Kenya	1977–1978	6.8
Malaysia	1974	4.4
Mexico	1976	4.4
Nepal	1976	3.9
Pakistan	1975	4.3
Panama	1976	4.2
Peru	1977	3.8
Sri Lanka	1975	3.8
Thailand	1977	3.7
United States	1976	2.7

[a] Women who are now, or once were, married.
[b] Only currently married women.

Source: McFalls, Jr., 1979. Used with permission from Population Reference Bureau.

est rates of illiteracy also have the highest rates of population growth. This is shown by the map in Figure 3-11, where both literacy rates and annual growth rates are divided into two classes. Although there are four possible combinations, most nations have either slow growth with high literacy or fast growth with low literacy. The exceptions include 6 nations in Latin America and Asia that have both a fast growth and high literacy, plus 10 countries (including China) that have a growth rate below 2 percent and a literacy rate below 90 percent.

Literacy rates are particularly low in Africa, where almost 75 percent of the population is unable to read and write, and in rural areas of other less developed countries where education systems are weakly developed. The fact that female illiteracy is generally much higher than male illiteracy is significant because it limits women's access to family-planning information and tends to restrict their role to the traditional one of bearing children.

Age structure. National birth rates, along with crude death rates, are partially influenced by the age structure of the population. Age structure of a population can be represented graphically by means of a **population pyramid**, which displays the age distribution of a population on the vertical axis and the

Figure 3-11. World Distributions of Literacy and Natural Increase in Population. A relationship between literacy and growth rates is indicated by the large number of countries belonging to only two of the four categories mapped here.

Scatter diagram. A graphic display of points, each of which indicates a pair of values by its position relative to two axes.
Population pyramid. A graph showing the percentage of males and females in each of a set of age classes (see Box 3-3).

The age and sex divisions of a population can be shown graphically by a population pyramid. The pyramidal shape results from a graph showing the percentage of males and females (along the horizontal axes) in each of a set of age classes (arranged vertically). For instance, from the graph shown in Figure 3-12(a), we can see that almost 8 percent of the population consists of females 5–9 years old. In contrast, the pyramid formed by graphing a population that is neither growing nor declining approximates a nearly rectangular shape, such as shown in Figure 3-12(b).

The **dependency ratio** for a country is derived by adding the percentages of the population under 15 years and over 64 years and dividing that sum by the percentage of the remaining population. In 1987, 33 percent of the world's population was under 15 years and 6 percent of the population was over 64. This means the world's dependency ratio was 39/61 or 64 percent ($33 + 6 = 39$ and $100 - 39 = 61$).

recent changes in the age (and sex) structure of a population. The transition from a rapidly expanding, high-fertility population with a large proportion of its population in the lower age groups, to a slowly growing, low-fertility population with a relatively equal proportion of the population in each age group can be seen in the changing shape of the United States' pyramid for 1900 and 1980 (Figure 3-13). The pyramid for the later date shows an age and sex structure that has the narrower base of a hypothetically stationary population [Figure 3-12(b)]. The major differences have to do with historical circumstances: the bulge at ages 15–29 is a result of the post-World War II "baby boom," and the constriction in the 40–49 age classes reflects the low birth rates of the depression years of the 1930s. The declining birth rate since 1965 is represented by the pinching at the bottom of the pyramid.

Population pyramids also provide clues about future demographic conditions. For example, the 1980 pyramid for Mexico shows an age structure that is fairly typical of a young and growing population, except for the band for the 0–4 year olds [Figure 3-14(a)]. This age band, which is narrower than for rapidly growing populations, reflects the declining birth rates during the 1970s. The size of this 0–4 age band is expected to shrink even more by 1990 because of a continuing decline in fertility [Figure 3-14(b)]. Accompanying this decrease in fertility rates, however, is the aging of people born prior to 1980, including those of age 15–19 years, which is seen as a wide band on the 1990 population pyramid. By the year 2000, these same persons will be 25–29, the age

proportion of males and females on the horizontal axis (see Box 3-3 and Figure 3-12). Demographic conditions that affect populations can be seen easily by examining the shape of a population pyramid. For example, a population with a large percentage of persons in the 15 to 45 age categories is expected to have a higher birth rate than another population having a large percentage above 65 years of age.

Population pyramids are helpful in detecting

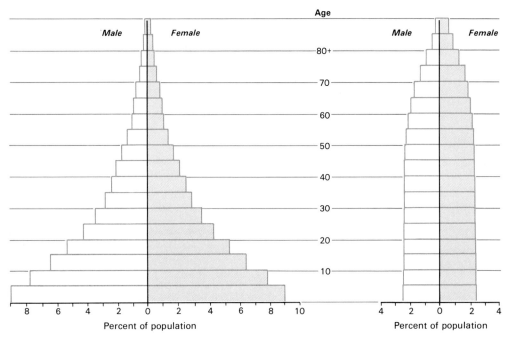

(a) Hypothetical, expanding population   (b) Hypothetical, stationary population

Figure 3-12. Population Pyramids Showing Hypothetical Expanding and Stationary Populations.

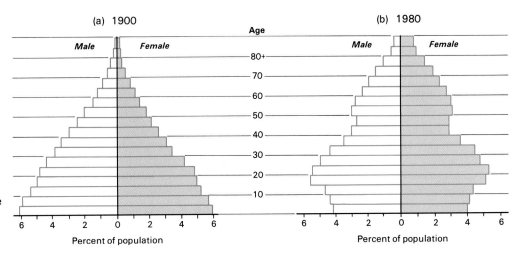

Figure 3-13. Population Pyramids, United States, 1900 and 1980. The population characteristics of the United States in 1980 differed greatly from those in 1900.

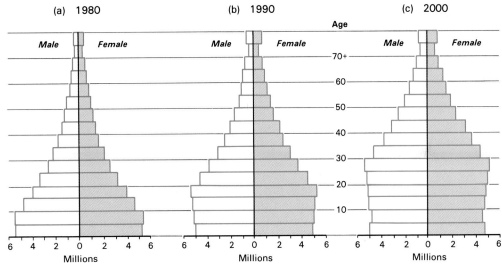

Figure 3-14. Population Pyramids for Mexico. Note the length of the band for persons 5–9 years old in 1980, those 15–19 years old in 1990, and those 25–29 years old in 2000. After Merrick 1986.

of maximum reproduction [Figure 3-14(c)]. Consequently, even if the country's annual growth rate should decline to only 1 percent (through low fertility and some out-migration), a bulge of 0–4 year olds is expected to be partially repeated as an "echo" a generation later.

Policies encouraging population growth. Another factor affecting the national birth rate is governmental policy toward population growth. Policies range from encouragement of high fertility to varying degrees of discouragement. Some of the countries with a policy of **pronatalism** are those in the slow-growth category (Figure 3-9). Twenty-six countries, mostly in Europe, but also including Canada, the United States, the Soviet Union, Australia, Japan, and Singapore, had net reproduction rates (Box 3-1) of less than 1.1 in the early 1980s. This means that their populations are near the replacement level, and the next generation of

children will be about the same size as the parental generation. In several European countries where the birth rate is so low that the total population may actually decline in the near future, a pronatalist sentiment is prevalent.

In France, for example, where in 1987 the rate of natural increase was 0.4 percent, the government has tried to create a favorable atmosphere for children through publicity, the improvement of day-care facilities, and so on. In East Germany, where the birth rate has fallen as low as the death rate, the government has taken stronger measures to encourage larger families. For example, following the birth of a second child, mothers are allowed a year's leave from work at 70 to 80 percent of their salaries. Low interest loans for homes are also available at the time of marriage and when each child is born (Van de Kaa 1987).

Even in the United States, where the birth rate is higher than in most European countries and where a

---

Dependency ratio. The ratio consisting of (a) the percentage of population under 15 years and over 64 years to (b) the percentage of that population which is 15–64 years old.
Pronatalism. A policy that encourages births.

tax allowance is given for each child, there is concern over the implications of a population with a stationary size. Low birth rates combined with low death rates have resulted in an increase in the proportion of elderly people in the population. At the present time, 12 percent of the U.S. population is over 65 years of age, compared to 8 percent in 1950 (Figure 3-15). By the year 2000, it is estimated that 33 million Americans—or 13 percent of the population—will be over 65.

An increase in the proportion of elderly persons has numerous implications. For example, it can affect the future market for various kinds of goods and services, both those sold to young people and those sold to elderly persons. The growing field of gerontology demonstrates this demographic shift. An aging population also enlarges the dependency ratio (see Box 3-3), which, in turn, can affect financial systems such as the Social Security program.

As in the United States and Western Europe, a low birth rate causes concern in the Soviet Union. The low fertility in the 1950s and 1960s is now showing up in the reduced number of youths entering the labor force and the armed forces. This shortage in the labor force has resulted in workers coming from Eastern Europe to take up the slack.

To the leaders of the Soviet government, the problem is not just a matter of totals; it is complicated by the geographical distribution of fertility rates. The Soviet Union, which extends over 8000 kilometers (5000 miles), includes a tremendous diversity of peoples, many of whom are not totally assimilated into the Russian way of life. Ethnic Russians, living mainly in the European part of the Soviet Union (west of the Urals), dominate the political and economic life of the country, yet they constitute barely half of the population (Figure 3-16).

The remainder of the country's population is made up of Ukrainians, Tatars, Uzbeks, and a great variety of other **ethnic groups.** The birth rate has remained high among several of the non-Russian groups, especially Moslems living in the Central Asian republics. In these republics, located along the southern border areas of the Soviet Union (see Figure 6-9), the birth rate is generally above 30, and the rate of natural increase is two or three times that of the ethnic Russians. It is predicted on the basis of current rates of growth that by the year 2000 the ethnic Russians will be a minority, probably accounting for no more than 40 percent of the population. Consequently, the Soviet government is now trying to raise the birth rate in areas of Russians and other Slavic populations through financial incentives and reduced working requirements for women (Feshbach 1982).

Governmental opposition to population control in many African countries (including the Central African Republic, Congo, Guinea, and the Ivory Coast in 1984) is based on the belief that continued population growth is the key to economic development. This view was expressed at the 1974 World Population Conference (held in Bucharest, Romania) by the Guinea delegates who felt that mortality should be lowered and birth rates raised "to give Africa a youthful population ready to develop the continent" (Bouvier 1975, p. 10). This viewpoint conflicts with the efforts of the more developed nations to limit population in countries where it is growing rapidly. Some pronatalist countries, however, regard such outside efforts as a form of neo-imperialism—an attempt to hinder their development. They argue that the United States, for example, did not limit population growth when it was a youthful nation with frontier areas to populate.

Some African countries do not advocate birth

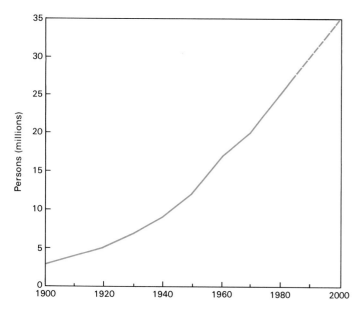

Figure 3-15. Number of Persons Over 65 Years, United States, 1900–2000.

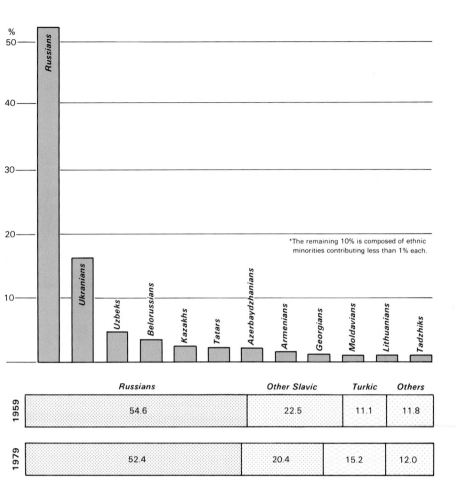

Figure 3-16. Ethnic Composition of the Soviet Union. The percentage of the major ethnic groups is shown in the upper graph. The proportional decline in ethnic Russians since the 1959 census is revealed by comparing the two lower bars.

*The remaining 10% is composed of ethnic minorities contributing less than 1% each.

	Russians	Other Slavic	Turkic	Others
1959	54.6	22.5	11.1	11.8
1979	52.4	20.4	15.2	12.0

control because poor living conditions adversely affect both infant mortality and fertility. In many areas, fecundity is low because of poor nutrition or disease and is considered to be a greater problem than high fertility.

Policies discouraging population growth. In contrast to the countries that are encouraging high birth rates, many other governments are actively discouraging high fertility through programs of family planning. During the last two or three decades, numerous countries have adopted policies aimed at reducing population growth. As late as 1960, only two countries—India and Pakistan—officially supported family planning programs. By 1980, however, over 90 percent of the people living in less developed countries had governments that supported family planning.

The techniques for promoting family planning and birth control vary from supplying contraceptives and information in some nations to much more direct involvement in others. Invariably the promotion involves the communication of new ideas (Figure 3-17).

In this sense, then, family planning programs are concerned with geographic diffusion—the spread of information and services through an area. Generally the strategy is to establish a network of clinics in rural and urban areas to serve as foci for health care and for the distribution of contraceptives and advice, as has occurred in Indonesia.

The Indonesian government, with help from the United Nations, the World Bank, and the World Health Organization, built more than 2000 clinics in Java and Bali between 1967 and 1976. Mass media such as radio, television, and newspapers were, and still are, used to promote the acceptance of the small family and to draw people to the clinics. Particularly in the more remote areas, fieldworkers were paid to locate "acceptors," that is, women who would adopt contraception. In Java and Bali, the first acceptors were older women with many children, but later, as the idea diffused, younger women who wanted to restrict their pregnancies were drawn into the program. The effect in Java and Bali has been a great increase in the number of women practicing contraception and a notable drop in the fertility rate (Hull, Hull, and Singarimbun 1977).

In some countries the government's efforts to reduce the birth rate have moved beyond voluntary family planning into various forms of coercion. In

---

Ethnic group. A term usually applied to a community with cultural characteristics that differ from those of a larger population residing in the same country or general region.

Figure 3-17. Billboard of Family Planning in Nepal. Even in many relatively remote areas of the world, such as in Pokhara in west central Nepal, family planning programs are publicized. Photo courtesy of Sally Stoddard.

Singapore, for example, where space is extremely limited, there have been heavy financial penalties for parents who have had more than two children. Parents have been fined the equivalent of 106 U.S. dollars for the third child, with the size of the fine being doubled, tripled, and quadrupled for the fourth, fifth, and sixth child. On the other hand, parents who have been sterilized after the birth of the second child have been rewarded with guaranteed education and employment for their offspring. As a result of this policy, in combination with a rapid economic development, the total fertility rate fell from 4.9 in 1965 to 1.7 in 1986. The policy has proven to be so successful that the government's Population and Family Planning Board was disbanded in 1986. In fact, because the country's fertility rate is well below replacement level, the Singapore government is now encouraging better educated women to have more children.

Although family planning had been promoted on a voluntary basis by the government of India for many years, a tough sterilization policy that was adopted in 1976–1977 under the administration of Mrs. Gandhi demonstrated that enforced family limitations may encounter opposition. Because India has a democratic form of government and public feelings can be expressed through free elections, objections to the harsher policy became evident soon after it was implemented. Some political analysts believe the incumbent party lost the 1977 election partly because of the widespread belief, particularly on the part of the Moslem minority, that people were being sterilized against their will.

Subsequent Indian administrations returned to less coercive methods of encouraging family planning. These methods include placing health experts in all villages with more than 1000 people, publicizing the merits of small families, and offering financial rewards to parents who accept sterilization after having two children. Many Indian couples now want smaller families, so family planning organizations attempt to provide a variety of contraceptives and other services for them.

During the last three decades, there have been some dramatic decreases in birth rates in parts of India; but fertility rates differ according to region, occupation, and family income. For the country as a whole, the rate of population increase is still 2.1 percent. If this rate continues and if China's rate continues to fall, India could become the most populous country in the world in the twenty-first century.

It is very difficult to understand recent demographic characteristics in the world without some knowledge of what is happening in China. Events in that country merit examination because more than one-fifth of the world's population lives there. Furthermore, one of the greatest reductions in fertility rates through governmental policy has occurred in China within the last decade, so it provides an illustration of the role of public policy in affecting birth rates.

In the 1970s, Chinese leaders declared that, in spite of standard Marxist doctrine relating economic power to a large labor force, the huge annual increase in population was a major handicap to economic development. The government commenced a vigorous program to reduce family size to two children. By 1980, the goal was changed to only one child per family (except for unusual circumstances and for some minority groups). This goal is being achieved through numerous policies (Figure 3-18). One policy is to postpone the age of sexual activity. The marriage age is generally over 24 for women and 26 for men, and premarital sexual relations are uncommon.

Free contraceptives and abortions are available in clinics throughout China. The Communist Party provides the infrastructure for carrying out these policies. From the highest governmental level down to the smallest rural community or urban neighborhood, an organizational network exists for implementing the program. At the local level, peer pressure is particularly effective in achieving conformity. Privacy is limited; women's contraceptive and fertility records are posted at the local health centers so that any deviation from the norm is noticed. Friends and neighbors may strongly, and repeatedly, urge compliance with the one-child policy.

Social and institutional changes have speeded up the decline in fertility. For instance, better health services reduced infant mortality. More available schooling and the accompanying higher literacy of females were instrumental in reducing birth rates (Figure 3-19). Also with the role of women expanding from that of a traditional homemaker to include work in a factory or a profession, fertility rates declined.

In part, the necessity to raise sons for old-age security has diminished. In urban areas, there are retirement pensions for workers. In rural areas, until the early 1980s, the communes guaranteed food, clothing, shelter, medical care, and burial. Now, under the responsibility system (where individuals lease land from the government), many farmers are relatively wealthy, which provides a new form of security (see Chapter 9).

Penalties are assessed against families who have more than one child (again, except under rare circumstances). These penalties vary with local conditions, but they may include ineligibility for better housing, reduced educational opportunities, delayed food rations, fines, and other economic and social sacrifices.

Even so, opposition to the one-child campaign does exist, especially in poor rural areas. Dissatisfaction is indicated by the fact that many couples are having more than one child (see Point-Counterpoint at the end of this chapter).

Although statistics on China are sometimes contradictory, it is evident that the Chinese program is working. In August 1979, the Chinese government announced that the annual rate of increase had fallen from 2.3 percent in 1971 to 1.2 percent in 1978 (Tien 1983). Population growth stayed at this low level until 1985, but rose to 1.4 percent in 1986. Although this rise is explained partly by recent noncompliance with the one-child policy, another reason is that the baby boomers of 1963 and 1964 are now reaching childbearing age.

Because of the demographic momentum from the

Figure 3-18. Billboard of Family Planning in China. Public advertising is one of several policies that encourage parents to limit their family size. Photo courtesy of Population Reference Bureau.

Figure 3-19. Public School in China. Higher rates of literacy, especially among females, are associated with lower birth rates. This is one of several reasons why universal schooling is given importance in China. Photo courtesy of Merlin P. Lawson.

pre-1970 period, the total population of China is predicted to increase for several decades before the current low fertility will effect a total population decline. Nevertheless, this demographic shift will produce a radical change in China's future age structure, even within the next 35 years (Figure 3-20). The aim of present policy is to reduce the country's population to 700 million by 2070 (Jowett 1984; Keyfitz 1984).

China is rapidly moving into the fourth stage of

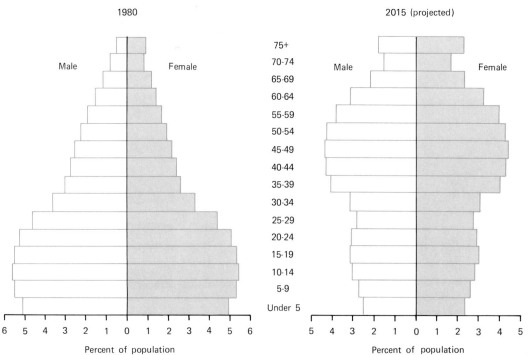

Figure 3-20. China's Age Structure for 1980 and Projected for 2015. The population pyramid for the year 2015 is based on a fertility rate of 1.5 for the 1980–2015 period.

the demographic transition. In contrast to the European experience, this shift is being achieved while still remaining largely rural and agrarian. China has accomplished this by creating a social climate where people do not see themselves as independent individuals but instead identify with the state. In effect, the Chinese are practicing birth control for the country. Obviously a high degree of political organization, as well as social control, economic incentive, and public motivation, is a prerequisite for this kind of program.

Many other nations in the world today are seeking to reduce the rate at which their populations are increasing. Although the goal is clear, there are various ideas about the most effective method of achieving change. At the 1974 World Population Conference there was a fundamental difference of opinion over the form that population policies should take. Many less developed countries argued that "development is the best contraceptive," and they urged the more developed nations to help with economic aid. Most of the richer nations, however, wanted to lower fertility rates directly by concentrating on family planning programs and services.

A decade later, at the World Population Conference in Mexico, there was a partial reversal of these stands. Most less developed countries were committed to population control, while the United States was reducing its support for birth control programs. This position, of course, reflected American domestic politics concerning the role of government in economic and population matters.

Those who contend that economic development is an effective way of accomplishing a reduction in

population growth have evidence to support their position. One item of support is the historic relationship between the demographic transition and the transformation of national economies of Europe. In more recent times, the experiences of South Korea and Taiwan, where economic growth has been rapid and birth rates have fallen to 20 and 17, respectively, may be quoted in support of this opinion.

Another item supporting this contention is the statistical relationship that exists between population growth and economic conditions today. In general, the richer the country, the slower the population growth (Figure 3-21). If this relationship continues to apply through time, then as economic conditions improve within a nation, its population growth rate is expected to decline.

Others are skeptical that a decrease in population growth rates is necessarily dependent on industrialization. Skeptics contend that the European experience is not an appropriate model today because several contemporary conditions contrast with the world of the eighteenth and nineteenth centuries. For one, during the time of the European "population explosion," many families left their homelands and migrated to sparsely settled areas in other parts of the world, especially North and South America (Chapter 4). These out-migrations greatly relieved the pressure on local resources. In contrast, today there is little opportunity for international migration from countries with rapidly growing populations. People living in a country with high population growth cannot seek opportunities in new lands but must remain in their home country, where they continue to compete for

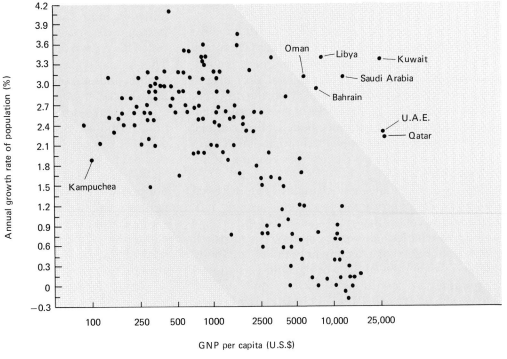

Figure 3-21. Relationship between Natural Population Increase and National Wealth, Mid-1980s. The pattern of points on this scatter diagram indicates an inverse relationship between the wealth of a nation (as measured by gross national product per person) and its rate of population growth. The major exceptions are the "oil-rich" countries.

increasingly scarce food, jobs, housing, and social services.

Another contrast between the historic European experience and the contemporary conditions elsewhere is the difficulty of shifting from an agrarian to an industrial economy. When European nations were becoming industrialized, they enjoyed the benefits of being first with new industrial products. Their shift to industrial production was rewarded with rapidly expanding markets, both domestic and foreign. Today, however, countries attempting to become more industrialized face a world market dominated by products from nations with long-established manufacturing. Unless they can sell to foreign markets, most nonindustrial nations find it difficult to shift their economies. If they can't bring about an economic transformation, according to this viewpoint, they won't be able to change fertility behavior.

Planners who advocate decreasing population growth without necessarily waiting for a rapid change in a nation's economic development stress the speed at which birth rates have been reduced in recent decades. A national birth rate that has dropped to 35 usually signals a change in the country's fertility behavior, and consequently the birth rate usually continues downward to 20 or less. For countries that began a decline in the birth rate before 1830, the decrease to 20 took an average of more than 130 years to accomplish. Countries that began a decline in the birth rate between 1921 and 1950 achieved a birth rate of 20, on the average, in 34 years. Since 1951, most countries undergoing a decline in the birth rate are achieving a rate of 20 in only 21 years (Kirk 1969). Such a rapid change has occurred mostly in Asia (e.g., in China, Singapore, South Korea, and Taiwan) but also in Latin America (e.g., in Cuba).

The faster pace in the decline of fertility results from the advantages of adopting existing technology and from information about birth control as knowledge has spread from the centers of initial change to other parts of the world. As noted above, the diffusion process has been facilitated by the many governmental programs for family planning—policies that contrast with the lack of any governmental promotion of birth control in Europe and the United States during earlier times.

These two strategies—changing the national economy and advocating birth control—are not mutually exclusive. To disregard the role of either may prolong the period of rapid population growth. It might be thought that a decline in population growth, at least in some parts of the world, could be achieved by ignoring the conditions of poverty that produce high death rates. Irrespective of humanitarian issues, such a view denies the observed relationships between mortality and birth rates. As noted above, areas with high rates of death, especially of infants, are associated with high birth rates, and invariably the high birth rates more than compensate for the deaths. Thus, a policy of ignoring requests for aid to prevent deaths would not achieve the goal of reducing population growth. Stated in a positive sense, policies that aid in the economic well-being of population as well as those that encourage the reduction of fertility both contribute to lower rates of population growth.

Most countries concerned about population growth do attempt to combine economic development with the provision of family planning services. Together, economic development and social change provide the motivation to have small families. Reducing infant mortality, expanding education systems, broadening the role of women, and achieving economic growth all have been important catalysts in changing traditional attitudes toward the family, both in European countries in the past and in less developed countries today. Once the motivation is there, family planning services provide the means for bringing the birth rate down.

POPULATION PATTERNS

Most of the comments above deal with the history and conditions of demographic change. It is now appropriate to look at where people are located and explain the reasons for these patterns of distribution (Figure 3-22).

The distribution of people in the world forms neither an extremely clustered pattern nor a perfectly uniform arrangement. Human beings physically take up very little space. The entire population of the world could be packed shoulder to shoulder in roughly the area of metropolitan New York. Even allowing more than shoulder-to-shoulder space per person, we can see that people are not highly concentrated in only one small area of the earth's surface. This is partly because many humans obtain food, shelter, and other needs directly from resources, such as arable land and water, which are widely dispersed.

At the other distributional extreme, population is not distributed uniformly over the earth's surface with exactly the world average of 37 persons on every square kilometer (or 96 per sq mi). Even the resources on which agrarian populations depend are not spread uniformly across the earth. Furthermore, urban populations tend to cluster in small areas where resources are assembled. In reality, approximately half the world's population is clustered on 5 percent of the land, while nearly a third of the total land area is virtually uninhabited.

Major geographic questions arise from this mapped distribution. Why do so many people live in certain areas of the world but not in other places? In what ways does the pattern of population affect the location of other phenomena such as economic activ-

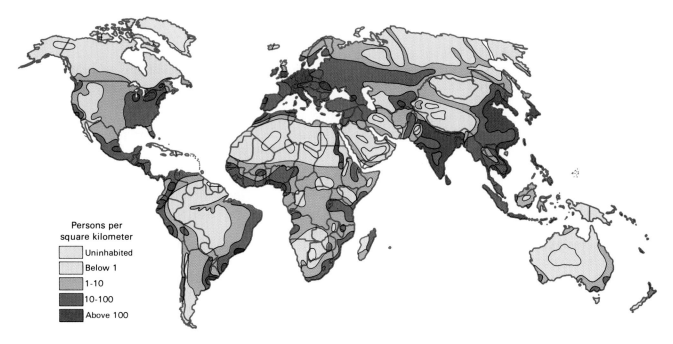

Figure 3-22. World Distribution of Population Densities. The spatial distribution of people, with its great unevenness, constitutes one of the primary patterns that stimulates, and also answers, many questions about the geography of humans.

ities? Answers to these questions make up the contents of the early chapters and they impinge on concepts presented throughout this text on the geography of humans.

Areas of High Density

A map of world population (Figure 3-22) reveals four major concentrations where population density is more than 100 persons per square kilometer (259 persons per sq mi). In generalized terms, these are East Asia, South Asia, Europe, and eastern North America (northeastern United States and southeastern Canada). Approximately one-half of the world's population lives in East and South Asia, which includes the countries of China, Japan, India, Bangladesh, and Pakistan, all of which are among the ten most populated nations of the world (Table 3-2).

Except in Japan, the populations of East and South Asian countries are located primarily in rural areas. Because the people are overwhelmingly rural and agrarian, population distributions in East and South Asia tend to reflect the food-producing potential of the land. Areas that have good soils, gentle slopes, and available water (from surface and groundwater or rainfall) have the highest densities. Arid and semiarid areas, mountainous regions, and some tropical rainforests are characterized by low population densities. Hence in India the greatest densities occur in the middle and lower Ganges Plain and in the

peninsular coastal lowlands of the south. The arid northwest and the slopes of the Himalayas have the lowest densities. The interior of peninsular India with its seasonally dry climate and varying soils and terrain is intermediate between these two extremes.

In contrast to the distributional patterns in most of Asia, the European and North American areas of high population density consist of people in urban places. The concentration of manufacturing and service activities in cities has drawn people from the countryside over the last 200 years so that almost three-fourths of European and American populations live in cities. The highest population densities by country occur not in China or India but in urbanized nations such as Japan, Belgium, the Netherlands, and the United Kingdom (Table 3-2). Within individual cities—London, for example—densities often exceed 40,000 persons per square kilometer (over 100,000 per sq mi). Even the countryside is urbanized, with farming systems geared to the urban market and nonfarming residents commuting as much as 100 kilometers to their place of work in the city.

Of the four regions, only the North American concentration would not have been apparent on a map of world population density in 1750. The early emergence of the other three concentrations is a reflection of the continuity of the Indian, Chinese, and European civilizations. The North American concentration developed as an outlet for the burgeoning European population. By 1750, small numbers of British, Dutch,

German, and French **emigrants** had settled along the northwestern coast of North America. They superseded the Native Americans who were displaced westward and were decimated by war, disease, and other traumatic effects of culture contact. The urbanized seaboard from Boston to Baltimore in the United States and the area along the St. Lawrence in Canada have remained the primary foci of population, economic activity, and political power in North America.

There are a few scattered nuclei of dense population outside the four major concentrations. In Southeast Asia the deltaic lowlands of the Mekong, Menam, and Irrawaddy rivers plus the Indonesian island of Java have high densities. Africa's most densely populated areas include the linear concentration along the Nile Valley in Egypt, the ring of settlement around Lake Victoria, and the populous country of Nigeria. Latin American areas of population concentration include the central part of Mexico, where nearly half the nation's population lives. In central Mexico, rural densities exceed 2600 persons per square kilometer (6700 per sq mi), and Mexico City is a major world metropolis. The coastal areas of Venezuela, Brazil, and Argentina, with cores around the cities of Caracas, Rio de Janeiro, São Paulo, and Buenos Aires, respectively, are also areas of high population density.

Factors of Location

What reasons explain the current distribution of humans? Here we will discuss four general factors: (1) availability of arable land, (2) age of civilization, (3) accessibility of places, and (4) restrictions of national boundaries.

The first factor is availability of **arable land,** which refers to an area having a terrain, soil, and climate that are favorable for the cultivation of crops. Generally people live close to their means of support. Because the majority of the people in the world depend on agriculture for their livelihood, we would expect that places with high agricultural capacity would have high population densities. Indeed, as a first approximation, the distribution of arable land helps explain the distribution of the world's rural population.

This broad generalization might be confirmed by comparing a map of arable land with a map of population to see whether the two distributions are similar. Unfortunately it is difficult to define and measure arability. Arable land might be described as areas that are not topographically rough and neither perpetually cold nor persistently arid. However, this definition is not entirely satisfactory because humans often modify these natural conditions and produce "arable" land by building terraces on mountainsides, heating greenhouses in cold climates, and irrigating deserts. Furthermore, the technology of food production varies greatly according to the economic conditions of producers. Because it is difficult to measure what is potentially arable, we will shift our attention to a map that shows those areas that are presently in agricultural production (Figure 3-23).

Figure 3-23. Agriculturally Productive Regions of the World. A major factor associated with the distribution of the world's population is the availability of land for crop and animal production. (Note that a map at this scale is highly generalized in some areas, such as in Southeast China.)

A comparison of the distribution of agriculturally productive areas and population reveals several similarities. In China, for example, the pattern of population densities resembles that of arable land. And in Egypt, the band of dense population corresponds to the Nile Valley, where irrigation allows farming in what is climatically a desert.

The second factor—age of civilization—refers to the length of time agricultural societies have occupied an area. Generally the longer a place has been continuously used by farmers, the denser is the population. As an illustration, one of the contributing factors to the dense population in eastern China is its long history of a successful civilization based on intensive agriculture. This contrasts, for example, with the Mississippi Valley of the United States, where the arability of the land is similar to that of eastern China, but where the land has not been intensely cultivated over thousands of years.

The third factor—**accessibility** of places—concerns the ease of transporting goods to specific sites. For people living in urban-industrial countries, the arability of land has far less locational significance than does the availability of jobs in the secondary and tertiary sectors. These economic activities, along with all their opportunities for employment, are located in places that are easily accessible. Accessible places are ones that are easily connected by transportation to many other places. Such accessibility is important in an economy dependent on manufacturing and trading. The economic advantages of locations like Rotterdam, Chicago, and Tokyo create employment opportunities that attract large populations. These centers of dense populations grow both by natural demographic increase and by producing the markets that generate even more economic opportunities for additional population. Consequently, these agglomerations where people have been engaged in industrial activities for several generations, such as in most Western European countries, tend to be densely populated.

The last influence on population patterns discussed here—the restrictions imposed by national boundaries—supplements the other three factors of location. Those factors might be summarized by stating that people live close to places where they can work and can produce the necessities of life. In many regions of the world, work consists primarily of using elements of the natural environment in agriculture. In other regions the most productive places are those located at sites accessible for assembling a wide variety of goods and for marketing finished products and related services. In both cases, the length of time that successful socities have existed affects the size of the population. On the world scale, however, these three factors do not adequately explain all population densities because there are some discrepancies between population density and the level of production (compare maps of Figure 3-22 and Figure 9-3). An illustration of a nation having a higher population density than expected based on production is Bangladesh. Conversely, a country with a lower population density than its proportion of the world's production and wealth is the United States. With this imbalance, it might seem likely that many persons from Bangladesh would migrate to the United States so that they could earn a better living. Such international migration is very limited, however, because most nations do not allow a mass influx of new **immigrants.**

This leads to the conclusion that political restrictions to international movements of people constitute a factor helping to explain the current distribution of the world's population. Although major migrations have altered the pattern of the world's population in the past (Chapter 4), such movements have been drastically curtailed in recent decades. Most governments restrict immigration, and several countries control emigration as well. On the international scale, the patterns of population that evolved prior to the twentieth century have become relatively "frozen" (except for the forced displacement of refugees). The contemporary distribution of population is understandable, therefore, only when the practice of restricting massive international migration is included as a factor.

Because national boundaries are important, nations are appropriate units for examining the world distribution of many human phenomena, including demographic characteristics. From this perspective, a cartogram based on national data is useful for visualizing the patterns of world population and for studying human geography (see Figure 3-24).

POPULATION PROSPECTS

Future Distributions

In general, the geography of the past is regarded as an excellent clue to the geography of the future. The distribution of the world's population during the next few decades is expected to remain similar to the present pattern. Some of the reasons for this geographic inertia, besides the political restrictions on international migration, involve the potential for using various sparsely settled environments.

Emigrant. A person who leaves a homeland to settle in another country.

Arable land. Land that is cultivated or cultivatable; literally meaning "plow land."

Accessibility. In its geographic sense, the degree to which a place is connected with, and interacts with, other areas.

Immigrant. A person entering a country for the purpose of living there.

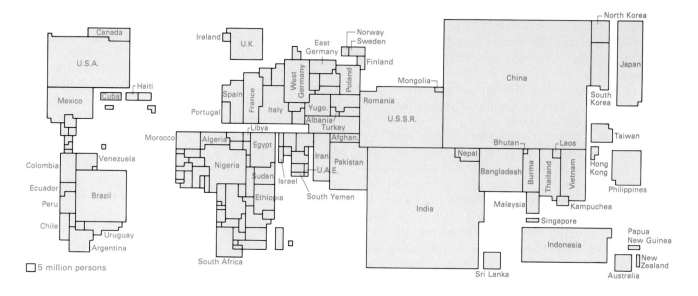

Figure 3-24. Cartogram of World Population by Countries, Mid-1980s. In this *cartogram*, the area of each nation is shown according to its population size instead of its actual geographical shape and extent.

Prospects for the large-scale expansion of population into the cold, arid, or hot and wet climates seem dim. The cold climates with their short growing seasons and long distances from existing commercial regions probably have limited potential for either agriculture or industry. Scattered settlements that may persist will probably include indigenous groups that have adjusted to the harsh conditions over many centuries and the high priority activities of "outsiders" engaged in extracting minerals or fuels, maintaining military facilities, and conducting research.

The greatest problem with the settling of arid lands is, of course, the deficiency of water. Where water is available, agriculture is often successful because desert soils are generally rich in minerals, and in many places the growing season is long. But these areas are few. The irrigated parts of the Sonora Desert in Mexico and the United States, the Nile and Indus valleys, the desert frontiers in Israel, and other scattered oases in Eurasia are the main exceptions to the general condition of barrenness and relative emptiness. As in the cold latitudes, mining settlements have sprung up in deserts around high value resources such as oil in the Sahara.

For the most part, however, the deserts remain uninhabited or else thinly populated by nomadic bands of hunters and gatherers (like the !Kung of the Kalahari) and nomads (such as the Bedouin of the Sahara). It is possible that technological breakthroughs, particularly the desalinization of sea water and the generation of solar energy, may open up desert frontiers for settlement. At the present time, however, areas defined as desert are actually expanding and people are leaving, so the dry areas are being

occupied by an increasingly smaller proportion of the world's population.

A third kind of environment where population density is low is the **tropical rainforest.** These are low latitude areas where precipitation and humidity are high and the natural vegetation consists of dense forests. Topography varies from nearly flat, such as the Amazon Basin of Brazil, to mountainous, as in many parts of Indonesia. Tropical rainforests offer some prospects for future frontier development. One advantage is the proximity to densely populated areas. The Amazon Basin, for example, is envisaged by the Brazilian government as a resettlement frontier for farmers from the drought-ridden and overcrowded northeast corner of the country. Likewise, migration to other Indonesian islands has been seen as a method of reducing the high population density of Java.

Tropical rainforests are not regarded by everyone as reserve areas for subsequent settlement. The skeptics predict that an increased population in these areas will result in a deterioration of the earth's resources. Often forest clearance has led to soil erosion, increased runoff, and siltation of rivers, as well as the decimation of unique plant and animal species. In northern Thailand, where forests are being harvested and cleared as a consequence of government-sponsored frontier development, the resulting disruption of river flow is adversely affecting irrigation works downstream and thus reducing the country's agricultural output. Some experts even believe that destruction of the tropical rainforests will affect the world's climatic balance by reducing the amount of moisture that is returned to the atmosphere by transpiration from the luxuriant vegetation (Chapter 12).

Finally, the development of the tropical rainforests brings modern technological civilizations into contact with hunters and gatherers and shifting cultivators who have survived until today partly because of their isolation. The effect, evidenced in Brazil, is the destruction of these societies through violence, disease, and cultural disorientation.

Another view of the future distribution of population can be obtained by looking at the expected changes in national populations. If we assume that national policies will continue to restrict international migration, then predicting the population of nations consists of comparing expected birth and death rates. Using these data for prediction, however, assumes that they (or their difference, expressed as the rate of natural increase) will remain constant. This assumption is risky because the rates are changing rapidly in several countries, and conditions for change are evident in many other nations (Critchfield 1981). Consequently, it is more difficult to predict population sizes than just projecting the existing growth rates into the future.

Demographers, however, can improve predictions by considering the age structure and age-specific characteristics of a population. By noting the percentage of persons under age 15, for example, experts can account for population momentum by estimating the number of births expected during the next generation. Although demographers may differ in their projections for even a date as close as the year 2000, the data do provide valuable indications of future human numbers (Table 3-2).

As already noted, the nations that have the most rapid population growth and that invariably have a young population tend to be the poorer, less developed countries. It is fairly safe to predict that the areas of greatest increase in the near future will generally occur in the nations that are the poorest.

Future Ecological Relations

A frequently posed question about the future concerns the relationship between total population size and the earth's resources. The basic question is: Will the world population continue to increase until the resources of the earth are no longer adequate to sustain more humans?

Some authorities expect the world's population to keep on growing until eventually it can no longer be supported by the finite resources of the earth (Meadows et al. 1972). These authors predict that pollution, degradation of the natural environment, and the excessive demands for food are some of the conditions that will make it impossible to support more people. Once that situation occurs, any increase in population will result in overpopulation and the subsequent deterioration of living standards. Mortality will then increase to a level that will prevent further population growth. Basically this scenario is the Malthusian thesis that population changes ultimately are determined by the earth's ability to provide subsistence.

This pessimistic scenario is unfortunately more fact than fiction in sub-Saharan Africa today. A 1986 report by the World Bank on sub-Saharan Africa identifies rapid population growth as the major cause of declining living standards and environmental degradation in this part of the continent. By 1982, 15 countries had already exceeded carrying capacity (the ability of the land to support the population under existing agricultural technology; see Figure 3-25). According to this report, an additional 6 countries are expected to be in the same situation by the year 2000 if population growth rates and agricultural production methods remain as they are now.

Others contend that it is misleading to talk about **overpopulation** because there is no agreement on the appropriate measure of the earth's life-sustaining capacity. They ask: What does "overpopulation" mean? *If* it refers to a high population density, then does that mean that the Netherlands is one of the nations closest to becoming "overpopulated"? *If* it deals with the population size compared to the total production of the area, is the poor but sparsely populated country of Nepal approaching "overpopulation"? *If* it pertains to the rate at which the world's resources are being consumed by a particular population, is the United States the most "overpopulated" nation?

Closely related to the problem of identifying an appropriate measure of the earth's resources (i.e., by area, production, or consumption) is the uncertainty about the upper limits of the earth's capacity to support humans. Optimists see evidence of combining improved technology with renewable resources to greatly increase the production of food and energy. According to Colin Clark, a land-use specialist, the earth could support almost 50 billion people at a high standard of living (Clark 1977).

Another consideration deals more directly with the population component of the population-to-resources ratio. Even if a theoretical resource limit is accepted, this does not mean that the world's population will continue to increase until that critical limit threatens the quality of future life. Support for this point of view comes from societies that have maintained stable populations within the context of partic-

---

Tropical rainforest. A vegetational type consisting of forests growing in warm and wet climates.

Overpopulation. A vague but popular term that usually relates number of people to resources of an area.

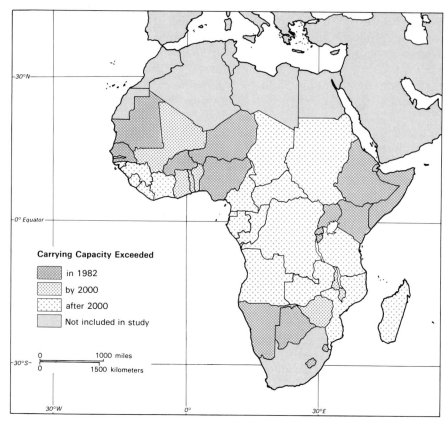

Figure 3-25. Carrying Capacity of Sub-Saharan African Countries. According to the 1986 report by the World Bank, *Population Growth and Policies in Sub-Saharan Africa*, the carrying capacity of several African countries has been exceeded or is expected to be surpassed soon.

Carrying Capacity Exceeded
- in 1982
- by 2000
- after 2000
- Not included in study

BOX 3-4. CHANGES IN RATE OF POPULATION INCREASE

It is important to distinguish between a change in the rate of natural increase and the accompanying change in population size. As demonstrated here (see the data in Table 3-4 and Figure 3-26), the rate of increase may decline while the population size continues to increase. For this hypothetical population of 20 million, the 2 percent rate of natural increase during the first year resulted in 400,000 more persons. Although a decade later the rate of increase was only 1.73 percent, there were 409,143 more persons added to the population.

TABLE 3-4. Changes in Natural Increases

Time	Rate of Increase During the Year (in %)	Size of Population Increase During the Year	Total Population of a Hypothetical Area
Beginning of 1st Year			20,000,000
End of 1st Year	2.00	400,000	20,400,000
End of 2nd Year	1.97	401,880	20,801,880
End of 3rd Year	1.94	403,556	21,205,436
End of 4th Year	1.91	405,024	21,610,460
End of 5th Year	1.88	406,277	22,016,737
End of 6th Year	1.85	407,310	22,424,047
End of 7th Year	1.82	408,118	22,832,165
End of 8th Year	1.79	408,696	23,240,861
End of 9th Year	1.76	409,039	23,649,900
End of 10th Year	1.73	409,143	24,059,043

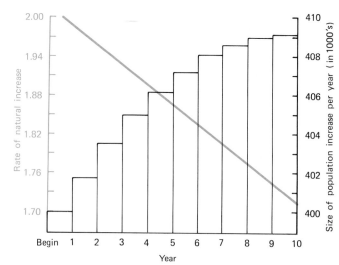

Figure 3-26. Increases in Population Numbers with Declining Rates of Natural Increase.

ular goals, values, and practices. These range from hunting and gathering societies of the past to the modern industrial nations where population size is essentially stationary.

Besides specific societies that have stabilized population, the growth in population for the world as a whole has changed already. The annual rate of population growth two decades ago was faster than 2 percent, but the rate began to decline in the 1970s. This drop in growth rate was a major demographic event because it reversed the trend of past generations. There is now a smaller world population than previously projected would be the case. This important change indicates the possibility of future declines in the growth rates of the world's population.

In the near future, of course, the total number of people in the world will continue to increase because the rates of increase are currently based on progressively larger numbers of people (see Box 3-4, Table 3-4, and Figure 3-26). In 1978, approximately 73 million people were added to the world population, more than 80 million were added each year in the early 1980s, and the population of the world is expected to grow annually by 95 million during the 1990s. Each year for the next several decades, there-fore, the demand for food, water, jobs, housing, and numerous other facilities will increase. And, unless there is a concurrent decline in living standards, these expanded demands will result in the consumption of progressively more earth resources.

It is the more distant future that is difficult to predict. Pessimists and optimists differ greatly in their estimates of future relationships between population and earth resources (as is evident in the Point-Counterpoint discussion at the end of this chapter).

Furthermore there is uncertainty about the future geographic distributions of people who will or will not have easy access to resources. At the present time, consumption levels vary tremendously, with people in some areas of the world enjoying an abundance of resources while others lack many basic necessities of life. Will these patterns of inequality change? The next chapter, which considers the movement of people from place to place, presents additional factors that can help us anticipate the distribution of population in years to come. Subsequent chapters that examine cultural, political, and economic conditions affecting (and being affected by) population patterns will aid in estimating future ecological relationships.

POINT-COUNTERPOINT

Population Growth and Earth Resources

Are the warnings by Malthus that population growth will exceed food production applicable today and for the future? No answer is unanimously accepted, even though the topic is discussed frequently by persons from a variety of backgrounds and responsibilities. Two contrasting responses to the question are given here by the Pessimist and the Optimist.

The Pessimist says that humans in the future will encounter major calamities because food supplies will not be able to keep up with the rapidly increasing world population. Population will continue to grow because:

- The existing trend in world population is a growing one.
- The few societies in which population is not growing rapidly are industrialized, and it is very unlikely that all parts of the world can achieve a similar economic and demographic status, partly because of limited resources.
- Even if a change in fertility rates should occur, population will continue to expand through demographic momentum.

Evidence that food production will be inadequate is the following:

- Many people are hungry now, so the food shortages will certainly be more severe in the future when there are more people.
- The earth's resources are finite, and humans are degrading, contaminating, and depleting them rapidly.
- The few societies with a slow population growth are the very ones that consume the largest shares of the earth's limited resources.

The Optimist does not predict doom but sees the potential for a better world. Observations supporting a prediction that world population will eventually stabilize are these:

- The recent decrease in fertility rates in several countries that are still basically agrarian indicates that slowing population growth is not necessarily dependent on industrialization.
- Prospects for an improvement in the well-being of most societies will lead to a common desire for small families.

- New methods for birth control are being developed, and undoubtedly even more effective techniques will be forthcoming.

The prospect that increased production, including food, can supply the needs of future populations is based on the following:

- Enough food is being produced now to adequately feed the entire world's population, so hunger is not resulting from an insufficient total supply of food.
- Existing agricultural technology and industrial capacity could produce much more food and could fill basic needs for all people.
- Current genetic research indicates that food production, even from lands classified as marginal, can be greatly increased.
- Knowledge about ways of reducing degradation and contamination of earth resources exists, and conservation is being practiced where there is an incentive to do so.

Is China's one-child policy wise? Is it good for the Chinese people? Is it a policy that could benefit, or damage, the well-being of people elsewhere in the world?

The one-child policy is usually justified because of the potentially dire consequences of an increasingly large population. Although Chinese agriculture produces high yields per area and the standard of living has improved throughout the country in recent decades, there are worries about the future. Supporters of the one-child policy believe that continued improvement in living standards can only be achieved by limiting the size of future populations.

In addition, it is contended that the policy is important because what happens in China has an impact on the rest of the world. Since more than 20 percent of the world's population lives in China, the well-being of future populations throughout the world will be affected by the decisions made today about the size of Chinese families.

Backers of the policy insist that, because of the high rates of birth in the 1950s and 60s, Chinese women of childbearing age should have no more than one child today. Although birth rates declined in some communities as a result of programs promoting family planning, attempts to convince families to voluntarily change their previous customs have not been successful as quickly and as universally as desirable. According to this argument, the urgent need to lower the fertility rate justifies maintaining a firm societal control over family decisions through national directives and local enforcement.

The supporters of the policy insist that it is flexible enough to allow exemptions, such as in areas where manual labor is important and in regions of minorities (e.g., the Uighurs and Tibetans). Also, the leaders in a family's work or neighborhood unit may agree that exceptional circumstances warrant an exemption.

Despite these arguments, opposition to the one-child policy exists. From outside of China comes opposition from people who are opposed to most forms of birth control, both for themselves and for others. They disagree with this policy, therefore, because it is highly dependent upon a variety of birth control measures. In the 1980s, for example, these attitudes led to the elimination of American funding of Chinese population control programs.

Some opponents, particularly within China, disagree with any policy that will greatly diminish the number of adults in the next generation. They believe the country will suffer from a shortage of workers and military personnel. They do not favor any policy that will reduce growth rates drastically.

Other opponents do favor a low birth rate, but they regard the strong governmental and societal pressures placed on a family as too high a price to pay for this demographic goal. They give higher priority to individual freedom than to the long-range needs of society in general. From this perspective (which tends to be vocalized more outside of China than within), a low birth rate is desirable, but not when it results from a governmental policy that is forced on citizens.

It has been argued that the goal of the policy cannot be achieved. Defiance of the policy within China has already occurred in a variety of ways. Recent sample surveys have indicated that in some rural provinces fewer than half the births were first children and about 25 percent were third children. Furthermore, birth statistics by gender indicate that female infanticides have occurred in some areas. These statistics seem to reflect a reluctance by some families to abandon the traditions of having several children, especially sons.

Objections have been raised against the policy because of the possible long-range effects of a 1–2–4 age structure (one child, two parents, and four grandparents). Already there are complaints about the excessive amount of pampering that single children receive from parents and doting grandparents. Sociologists speculate that these "spoiled" youngsters, when they become adults, will alter Chinese society unfavorably. At the other end of the age scale, a continuation of the policy will mean that in the future a higher percentage of elderly people will depend on a smaller portion of working adults. This could put severe strains on the economy, especially if it is still highly dependent on agricultural production.

In conclusion, the issue might be stated this way: If a social problem—in this case, rapid population growth—is serious enough, does a government have the right to stipulate such personal matters as the number of children allowed per family?

BIBLIOGRAPHY

Bouvier, Leon F., "Africa and Its Population Growth," *Population Bulletin*, 30, no. 1 (February 1975).

Bouvier, Leon, Elinore Atlee, and Frank McVeigh, "The Elderly in America," *Population Bulletin*, 30, no. 3 (September 1975).

Brewer, Michael F., "The Soviet Peoples: Population Growth and Policy," *Population Bulletin*, 28, no. 5 (1972).

Chen, Lincoln, et al., "Maternal Mortality in Rural Bangladesh," *Studies in Family Planning*, 5, no. 11 (1975), 334–41.

"China's One-Child' Population Future," *Intercom*, 9, no. 8 (August 1981).

Clark, Colin, *Population Growth and Land Use*, 2nd ed. London: Macmillan, 1977.

Critchfield, Richard, *Villages*. Garden City, N.Y.: Anchor Press/Doubleday, 1981.

Day, Lincoln H., "What Will a Zero-Population Growth Society Be Like?" *Population Bulletin*, 33, no. 3 (June 1978).

Espenshade, Thomas J., "The Value and Cost of Children," *Population Bulletin*, 32, no. 1 (April 1977).

Feshbach, Murray, "The Soviet Union: Population Trends and Dilemmas," *Population Bulletin*, 37, no. 3 (August 1982).

Grigg, David, "Modern Population Growth in Historical Perspective," *Geography*, 67, pt. 2 (April 1982), 97–108.

———, "The Growth of World Food Output and Population 1950–1980," *Geography*, 68, pt. 4 (October 1983), 301–6.

———, *The World Food Problem, 1950–80*. Oxford, England: Blackwell, 1985.

Heer, D. M., and D. O. Smith, "Mortality Level, Desired Family Size and Population Growth," *Demography*, 5, no. 1 (1968), 104–21.

Hull, Terence H., Valerie J. Hull, and Masri Singarinbun, "Indonesia's Family Planning Story: Success and Challenge," *Population Bulletin*, 32, no. 6 (November 1977).

Jowett, A. J., "China: Land of the Thousand Million," *Geography*, 69, pt. 3 (June 1984), 252–57.

———, "The Growth of China's Population," *Geographical Journal*, 150, pt. 2 (July 1984), 155–70.

Keyfitz, Nathan, "The Population of China," *Scientific American*, 250, no. 2 (1984), 38–47.

Kirk, D., "Natality in the Developing Countries: Recent Trends and Prospects," in S. Behrman, L. Corsa, and R. Freedman, eds., *Fertility and Family Planning: A World View*. Ann Arbor, Mich.: Univ. of Michigan Press, 1969.

Kleinman, David S., *Human Adaptations and Population Growth: A Non-Malthusian Perspective*. Montclair, N.J.: Allanheld, Osmun, 1980.

McFalls, Joseph A., Jr., "Frustrated Fertility: A Population Paradox," *Population Bulletin*, 34, no. 2 (May 1979).

Meadows, Donella H., et al., *The Limits of Growth: A Report for the Club of Rome's Project on the Predicament of Mankind*. New York: Universe Books, 1972.

Merrick, Thomas W., "World Population in Transition," *Population Bulletin*, 41, no. 2 (April 1986).

———, "Population Pressures in Latin America," *Population Bulletin*, 40, no. 3 (July 1986).

Mitchell, B. R., *European Historical Statistics*, 2nd ed. New York: Facts on File, 1980.

Momsen, Janet Henshall, and Janet G. Townsend, eds., *Geography and Gender in the Third World*. Albany, N.Y.: State University of New York Press, 1987.

Nagel, John S., "Mexico's Population Policy Turnaround," *Population Bulletin*, 33, no. 5 (December 1978).

Newman, James L., and Gordon E. Matzke, *Population: Patterns, Dynamics, and Prospects*. Englewood Cliffs, N.J.: Prentice-Hall, 1984.

Nortman, Dorothy, "Changing Contraceptive Patterns: A Global Perspective," *Population Bulletin*, 32, no. 3 (August 1977).

Omran, Abdel R., "Epidemiologic Transition in the United States." *Population Bulletin*, 32, no. 2 (May 1977).

Palloni, Alberto, "Mortality in Latin America: Emerging Patterns," *Population and Development Review*, 7, no. 4 (December 1981), 623–49.

Population Growth and Policies in Sub-Saharan Africa. Washington, D.C.: World Bank, 1986.

Schumacher, E. F., *Small Is Beautiful*. New York: Harper & Row, Pub., 1973.

Tien, H. Yuan, "China: Demographic Billionaire," *Population Bulletin*, 38, no. 2 (April 1983).

Van de Kaa, Dirk J., "Europe's Second Demographic Transition," *Population Bulletin*, 42, no. 1 (March 1987).

Vander Tak, Jean, Carl Haub, and Elaine Murphy, "Our Population Predicament: A New Look," *Population Bulletin*, 34, no. 5 (December 1979).

Westoff, Charles F., "The Populations of Developed Countries," *Scientific American*, 231, no. 3 (September 1974), 108–21.

Woods, Robert, *Population Analysis in Geography*. London and New York: Longman, 1979.

———, *Theoretical Population Geography*. London and New York: Longman, 1982.

Wrigley, E. A., *Population and History*. New York: McGraw-Hill, 1969.

———, "The Growth of Population in Eighteenth-Century England: A Conundrum Resolved," *Past and Present*, no. 98 (February 1983), 121–50.

4 POPULATION MIGRATIONS

Homo sapiens is a migratory species. From their area of origin (East Africa, in current thinking), humans have spread out and occupied nearly all the continents and environments of the earth's surface. The early bands of hunters and gatherers on the African savannas roamed broad territories in pursuit of game and utilized a variety of environmental **habitats,** partly on a seasoned basis. The organization of these earliest, and simplest, economies facilitated movement to search for new resources.

Millennia later, the development of agriculture brought settled village life, but, paradoxically, the sedentary existence created strong incentives to migrate. Agriculture allowed higher population densities, but when the capacity of the land to support people under these early agricultural systems was reached, changes became necessary. Changes meant that agriculture had to be made more efficient, the birth rate had to be lowered, and/or a portion of the population had to move to a frontier to bring more land into the farming system. In practice, all three strategies were utilized in varying degrees in different parts of the world. In many areas, early farmers chose to migrate.

Virtually all societies have understood the need for members to migrate in order to marry, to spread their religion, to trade, or to gain access to new opportunities. Even though migration has often created tensions and divided loyalties, these disadvantages have not prevented people from moving to new lands. For example, traditionally Chinese farmers have revered the land and the graves of their ancestors, but this did not stop out-migration from China and in-migration into other places where the Chinese often formed minority communities. The delight of the English in their rural landscape has not prevented large numbers of them from becoming expatriates in all parts of the world—sustained by teapots, curious

brands of mustard, and subscriptions to London newspapers. The Irish overseas are prone to sing the glories of the Emerald Isle. Their pride is infectious; for example, they have succeeded in giving the United States an unofficial holiday—St. Patrick's Day. In spite of their pride in Ireland, many more people of Irish stock live overseas than in the homeland.

In this chapter, the concern is with past and present patterns of migration, here defined as a "permanent or semipermanent change of residence." (Short-term movements, especially by urban commuters, are discussed in Chapter 11.) The chapter begins with an overview of some of the reasons why people migrate. Attention then shifts to migration patterns in pre-industrial societies, using England and the United States as primary examples. A separate section deals with migration theories or the attempt to devise generalizations that clarify the characteristics of migration. The chapter then closes with a consideration of international migrations in the contemporary world.

WHY MIGRATE?

Humans migrate for several reasons. For one, humans appear to be equipped with exploratory instincts. Virtually all societies have members who will cross a desert or an ocean, navigate a river, or climb a mountain "because it's there." Knowledge gained from exploratory activity usually creates widespread interest and may well be used to start more permanent movement and settlement.

Another reason why most migrants move is be-

Habitat. The environment of an organism or group of organisms.

cause they perceive an opportunity for betterment, which may involve gaining access to land, raw materials, or employment. When we speak of migrants moving to take advantage of opportunities, it may seem that their motivations are only economic. In the case of many migratory groups—for example, Turkish workers in West Germany or Algerians in France—economic factors are clearly in the forefront. However, there is a social and institutional framework that in many cases primes the migratory pump and facilitates movement. For example, in the 1870s when a second son in a Norwegian family moved to a frontier region in the United States to gain land, his economic motives were intertwined with his society's tradition that the family farm passed to the eldest male.

A primary social reason for a permanent move is marriage because in most societies either the bride or the groom has to move to a new dwelling place. In the United States and several other countries, both the bride and the groom may move.

The migratory process usually combines both social and economic factors. People move to opportunities, but from an existing social system that may well encourage and support movement. Migrants commonly depend on links between the area of origin and area of destination. Families, or institutions, may provide support for the journey and may help with the costs of settling in the new land. This assistance, which helps migrants along the stages of major moves, forms a **migration chain.** Over time, remittances (transmission of money) may flow in either direction. Frequently other members of a family, or community, will follow along the path, which creates a large flow of movers along the same route and thus produces **channelized migration.**

Many who make the journey as migrants from their original social setting return home. Some fail to establish themselves in the new environment. Others move back for family reasons, or like many ardent Puritans in New England, return home when political conditions change. Of those who are successful, a percentage will go back to their place of origin to retire on the wealth they have accumulated. For example, most southern Italian towns have their "Americani"—persons who have been to the United States, made some money, and then returned to enjoy the traditional life styles of their homeland.

People are sometimes forced to migrate. Warfare, famine, persecution, and pogroms can produce massive out-migration from home countries. World War II, the Vietnam War, and conflicts in Southwest Asia have pushed people out of their homes. As the conditions of warfare, famine, or ethnic hatred bring about the collapse of the fabric of life, the normal social processes associated with voluntary migration fail to operate. These conditions sometimes produce a mass exodus, "boat people," and refugee camps.

In fact, since the beginning of the First World War in 1914, the majority of international moves have been by refugees rather than by voluntary migrants. This fact partly reflects the violence of a century that has had two major wars, the rise and fall of totalitarian regimes, and a host of conflicts that have created outflows of refugees. It also reflects the national policies that restrict immigration and that serve as barriers to voluntary international movements.

These introductory comments about reasons for moving provide a backround for examining some specific examples of migration in the past. From these we can draw some general conclusions about human migrations.

MIGRATION PRIOR TO THE TWENTIETH CENTURY

When we imagine the landscape of pre-industrial societies, we tend to envision villages inhabited by peasants whose ancestors had lived on the same territory from time immemorial. We think of immobile societies in which families cultivated the same land, generation after generation. The truth is rather different. While one branch of a family may have worked the ancestral lands, other branches migrated. Although the percentage of migrants in pre-industrial societies was smaller than in modern or modernizing societies, our forerunners were more mobile than is commonly supposed.

It is difficult to trace migratory flows prior to the existence of written records. Historic patterns may be revealed by surviving place names, which often suggest the routes of migrations and the pattern of settlement (Chapter 6). For example, it is known that there were extensive migrations when the Roman Empire collapsed in the fourth and fifth centuries and Germanic tribes such as the Angles and Saxons began to resettle in many parts of Europe. Today every county in eastern England is covered with place names (such as those containing *ing*, *ham*, and *ton*) that indicate the pattern of Anglo-Saxon settlement.

It is important to discover the historical patterns of migration, which give depth to the study of human geographic behavior and provide clues for contemporary population distributions. The following four sections present case studies of historical migrations. First, patterns of migration within medieval England are analyzed. Next, the movements of migrants from England to New England in the seventeenth century are traced. The focus then shifts to European and American migrants on the frontier in the United States. Finally, to give a cross-cultural perspective, historical migrations in China are described.

Migration in Medieval England

By the fourteenth century, a taxation system was well established in England, and through surviving records it is possible to learn something about the inhabitants of the land and their movements. For example, the Lay Subsidy of 1332 gives the names of each taxpayer in every English community that formed a taxation unit. The family names are interesting because they frequently suggest where migrants, or their families, came from. The record contains large numbers of names like John de Lincoln, which indicates that the taxpayer had his origins in Lincoln. This is not the same as having direct information about the migrations of individuals because it is not known whether the taxpayer, his father, or other male ancesters made the original move from the city of Lincoln. Nevethe-less, in a general way, a picture of migration pattern emerges.

As a specific case, consider the names of taxpay-ers in some towns and villages in Lincolnshire, a large county (shire) in eastern England. In 1332, the cathe-dral city of Lincoln had 433 taxpayers, who were usually heads of households. Of the 433 taxpayers, 235 had family names based on a place. Put another way, approximately 54 percent of the taxed heads of households gave an indication of migration by their names. This high figure suggests that the medieval population was fairly mobile.

Lincoln was an important center. Certainly it was in the top ten English cities at the time. Lincoln had markets, a mint, a cathedral, ecclesiastical and crown courts, churches, monasteries, a castle, and merchant and trade guilds (Figure 4-1). Lincoln was a center of

Figure 4-1. The City of Lincoln, England. In the fourteenth century, the busy city of Lincoln was an attractive destination for persons seeking work. Like most pre-industrial cities in Europe, Lincoln was on navigable water, and trade was con-ducted by barges or sailing vessels. "Brayford Pool," painting by John Wilson Carmi-chael. Used with permission from Lincolnshire Recreational Services, Usher Gallery, Lincoln.

Migration chain. The process by which early movers en-courage others to move by providing information and commu-nal assistance.

Channelized migration. The movement of many migrants along a common route connecting the source area to the destination.

Figure 4-2. The Origin of Lincoln's Population, 1332. When all the originating places of migrants to Lincoln are mapped, the distribution forms the city's migration field. The highest density of movers within the migration field was within 55 kilometers (34 miles) of Lincoln. Source of data: 1332 Lay Subsidy, Lincolnshire Record Office.

administration and commerce to which men and women came to find jobs, sell skills, or market produce. Like most important medieval towns, Lincoln was close to navigable water. It was linked by a canalized stream and the Trent River to the coast (Figure 4-2). The city certainly must have been attractive to migrants.

The location of all the place names that were a part of family names cannot be traced, but the indicated origins of most taxpayers in Lincoln in 1332 can be mapped and the distribution examined (Figure 4-2). The area from which the known migrants originated forms what is called the **migration field** for Lincoln. The majority of migrants appear to have come from villages in Lincolnshire, but some had

moved from York, Nottingham, Hull, Norwich, Oxford, Kent, and the West Riding of adjoining Yorkshire.

When family names based on places are examined in the smaller settlements of Lincolnshire, a different pattern is revealed. In general, the villages tended to have less than 20 percent of taxpayers with places mentioned in their names. Analysis reveals that these migrants came predominantly from nearby settlements and travelled only short distances. It is noticeable that poor places, with low tax totals, had few families possessing place names as surnames.

It can be concluded that some of the general migratory tendencies, still operative today, were already apparent in medieval Lincolnshire. Big places were more attractive to migrants than small places; poor settlements were simply unattractive; and distances of most migrations were short.

Some of the conditions that encouraged migrations were accentuated following the Black Death. Within a year or two of its outbreak in 1348, the population of many places was reduced by more than half (Chapter 2). In the short-term, the disease curtailed migration due to the fear of contagion. Over the long-term, the Black Death resulted in job vacancies, which were subsequently filled by immigrants. In York, for example, the migration field expanded after the plague had reduced population numbers, which, in a macabre way, created openings for craftsmen and laborers.

After the great decline of the second half of the fourteenth century, populations recovered. By the end of the sixteenth century, when the English made attempts to establish colonies in North America, the countryside was again relatively densely populated.

English Migration in the Seventeenth Century

Although there were attempts to establish English colonies in the New World in the sixteenth century, the great transatlantic migration of English people did not start until the seventeenth century. Between 1620 and the 1640s, about 40,000 people migrated from England to Plymouth Colony and to the Massachusetts Bay Colonies. There was also settlement in Virginia and Maryland, and in the areas that later became Connecticut and Pennsylvania.

Much has been discovered about the religious, political, and economic backgrounds of the English migrants to America. For instance, the findings of one historian suggest significant regional differences in the motivations for migration (Allen 1981). At the village of Rowley (Yorkshire), the rector was in trouble with his bishop for preaching sermons containing opinions contrary to the canons of the Church of England. When the rector decided to go to the New World, some of his flock, who shared his views, followed him. Here is a case of an influential opinion leader within a community having an effect on the decison to migrate. Such individuals are common in the history of migration. For religious, political, utopian, or economic reasons, leaders have been responsible for many members of a community deciding to move to a new land.

East Anglia, a Puritan stronghold, was a major source of migrants to New England (Figure 4-3). Migration seems to have been related to both eco-

nomic and demographic factors, as well as religious concerns. Population density was high and there was a series of bad harvests in the 1620s and 1630s. In addition, the area was liable to outbreaks of plague, so the desire to find a healthier environment might have contributed to the decision to migrate. Migrants from East Anglia were not poor. In fact, they tended to come from the middle classes. Migration was an expensive undertaking. It required an investment of capital for transportation and other costs of relocation. When the price of moving was high, the majority of migrants had to possess some capital—even if it took the form of training for a job. Migrants who incurred such moving costs judged the long-term economic prospects to be good. Generally in a region with economic problems and a scarcity of land, ambitious people found the prospects of America attractive.

Religious, economic, and demographic considerations do not provide all the answers concerning the decision to migrate. For example, few communities in northwestern England provided migrants, even though Manchester and the surrounding area had plenty of Puritans. People in the northwest undoubtedly heard about the New England colonies from itinerant Puritan preachers, but they were remote from kinship and social networks that had members who had already made the journey to America. They were disconnected from social processes of migration and less likely to be able to attach themselves to a group planning to sail to America. On the other hand, the southwest of England furnished many migrants. The southwest was close to ports like Bristol and Plymouth, and knowledge of transatlantic opportunities diffused relatively easily.

The decision to migrate, like the adoption of any new idea, demonstrates the diffusion of innovations through an area. After the initial appearance of a new idea or practice, knowledge about it is often publicized through media such as itinerant advocates (travelling preachers or salesmen), printed matter, and, in this century, through radio and television. Leaders and venturesome members of a community may then adopt the change. Next, the innovation diffuses more widely as persons interact with, and are influenced by, the leaders and those who have adopted the change. This network of shared information normally is restricted to an identifiable area, or **information field**, where communication among residents is frequent and influential. Thus, the adoption of a new idea, such as migrating to America, tends to be more common in one area than in another because of the geographic extent of a particular information field.

Migration is a selective process because people

Migration field. The area from which a city or other settlement draws migrants.

Information field. An area within which communication among occupants is frequent and influential.

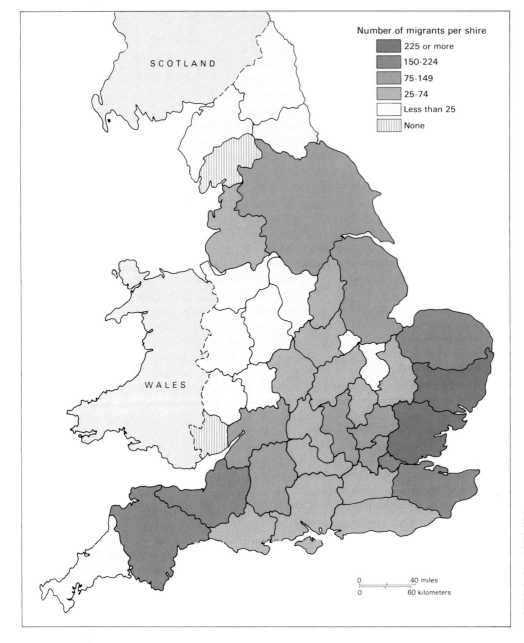

Number of migrants per shire

- ▓ 225 or more
- ▓ 150-224
- ▓ 75-149
- ▓ 25-74
- ☐ Less than 25
- ‖‖ None

SCOTLAND

WALES

0 —— 40 miles
0 —— 60 kilometers

Figure 4-3. Location of English Places Supplying Migrants to New England, 1620–1650. In general, migrants to New England originated in shires located in the south and east of England. Source: Banks 1957.

with certain characteristics are more likely to move than others. What characteristics did the English migrants to America possess? A clue to an answer is provided by the passenger lists of vessels sailing to New England in the period 1620–1640. Hundreds of these lists survive and provide information about the people moving to America. For example, *The Planter* left London on April 10, 1635, and arrived at Boston on June 7th. Aboard were 116 passengers. Of those aboard only about 10 percent were single men and women, apparently travelling alone. Most of the passengers were moving as families or groups that came from the same community. The recorded occupations of the passengers included 12 trades, such as apparel maker, carpenter, and miller. The most common occupations were farmer ("husbandman") and servant.

Only one passenger described himself as a laborer. There were very few unskilled migrants. The 11 servants, who were traveling with groups or families, probably had their passage paid by their employers as an advance on future wages.

The passenger lists provide evidence that families made a decision to migrate, and that they used networks of friends and relatives as exemplars, sources of information, and companions for the journey. Frequently migration chains were set up as the first movers sent back information, which resulted in others from the same community following. This seems clear when passenger lists for a series of years are examined. The same family names, from the same places, particularly in Essex, Norfolk, and Suffolk, reappear again and again.

Settling in New England

In the years after 1635, most immigrants spent little time in the ports of entry like Boston, Plymouth, or Salem. They quickly moved along paths of channelized migration to join communities that were being established away from the coast. If the existing evidence from these inland communities is accurate, migrants to rural New England attempted to replicate many aspects of the landscape of lowland England. The colonists may have changed the forms of religious observance, but they wanted to preserve much of the established social fabric and agricultural practices of the English countryside.

In the seventeenth century, many rural communities in Massachusetts had high rates of **population persistence** because few inhabitants left. For example, in Dedham (Massachusetts), the annual population turnover was only 2 percent, but in Clayworth (Nottinghamshire, England), it was 5 percent. Over a decade this small annual difference created a large contrast in the two levels of population persistence. There are difficulties, of course, in comparing any population statistics for communities in the seventeenth century. The types of records available differ, the units of administration are not the same, and the methods of recording vary. But if the figures are taken at their face value, it seems that the population of lowland England was more mobile than the rural inhabitants of Massachusetts in the early colonial period (Lockridge 1970, p. 64). The stereotype of restless American frontiersmen constantly searching for new lands, as opposed to a village-tied English peasantry, does not stand up for the seventeenth century.

This comparison suggests that, in a **stratified society** (one in which persons are identified as belonging to a hierachy of social classes), there is a constant incentive to move to improve position. England had a stratified society and resources were "closed"; that is, all available land was already claimed and ambitious persons had difficulty acquiring more land. In the New England colonies, however, where resources were plentiful and social stratification less, there was little incentive to move.

In New England, the age of marriage was not significantly lower, and the birth rate was only slightly higher, than in England. The death rate, however, decreased because deaths from disease and malnutrition were fewer than in populations in England. As population grew, communities provided for increased numbers by allocating more land to established land-owning families. It was not until the eighteenth century that pressure on the land began to make it advantageous to seek new resources farther to the west. By this time, mobility was becoming a fundamental characteristic of American life.

General Migration to the United States

In 1790, the date of the first census of the newly independent United States, most citizens who had migrated from Europe came from the British Isles. About 60 percent derived from England, 8 percent from Scotland, and 3 percent from Ireland. The Germans were the leading non-British group, making up 9 percent of the European population. Africans of diverse origins, but mostly from West Africa, accounted for approximately 21 percent of the total population. African migrants, however, arrived through the forced migrations of the slave trade, not through a voluntary movement of people seeking new opportunities.

After 1820, the source areas for migrants to the United States were more diverse than previously. The geographic changes in the origins of migrants were related to industrialization, urbanization, rapid population increase, and the weakening of traditional social structures. In general, the sequence of source areas before 1920 was first from Britain, then from other parts of Western Europe, then from Northern Europe, and finally from Eastern and Southern Europe (Figure 4-4).

Between 1820 and 1860, the Irish were the leading group of immigrants. Germany was the main source area between 1860 and 1890, although many Swedes and Norwegians migrated to the United States during the 1870–1900 period of "American fever" in Scandinavia. By 1900, the main sources of new migrants were Eastern and Southern Europe.

Between the mid-nineteenth century and the 1920s, migrants from overseas provided a considerable proportion of the total population growth of the United States. Altogether, more than 33 million migrants arrived between 1820 and 1920. From 1850 until 1930, migration provided over 20 percent of the annual population increase. In the decade 1880–1890, 35 percent of all population growth was accounted for by immigrants.

In absolute numbers, the first two decades of the

Population persistence.   The degree to which a population continues to reside in one place over a period of time. The persistence is usually expressed as the percentage of remaining population to the total population, and then adjusted for births and deaths.

Stratified society.   A society in which subgroups or classes are recognized and ranked.

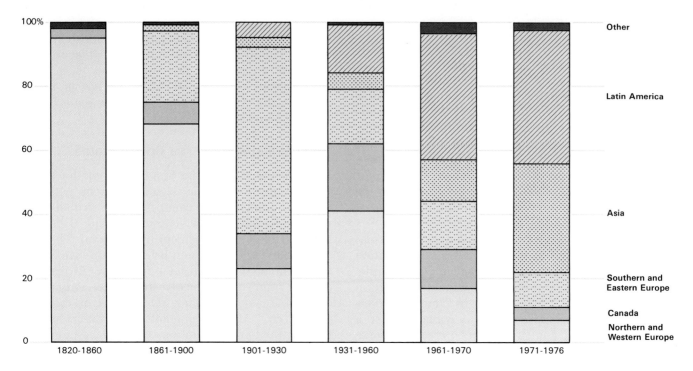

Figure 4-4. U.S. Immigrants by Region of Origin, 1820–1976. The relative importance of source areas has changed through time. Source: Population Reference Bureau.

twentieth century marked the peak of immigration into the United States. Although the American Civil War and the First World War interrupted immigration, these were periods of temporary reductions that were not due to political decisions that barred international movement. Unrestricted immigration was partially curtailed in 1882 with the prohibition of Chinese immigration. In 1917, all Orientals were excluded. Immigration from every country was strictly controlled by legislative acts in 1921 and 1924, and the flow of immigrants was greatly reduced. Not until

after World War II did immigrant numbers again begin to increase (Figure 4-5).

Migration to the American Frontier

Most migrants went directly to the rapidly industrializing cities of northeastern United States. By 1920 (the first census year when more than half the American population lived in cities), almost half of the urban population was foreign-born or of foreign-born parentage (Ward 1971). After 1850, increasing numbers of

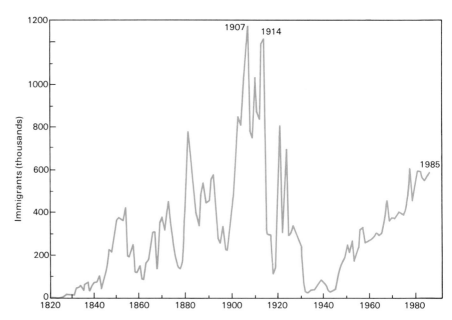

Figure 4-5. Number of Immigrants to the United States, 1820–1985. The number of legal immigrants each year has fluctuated greatly during this period. After Bouvier and Gardner 1986.

BOX 4-1. MIGRANTS TO THE GREAT PLAINS

The following passage, taken from O. E. Rölvaag's novel, *Giants in the Earth, A Saga of the Prairie* (New York: Harper & Row, Pub., 1927, pp. 314–15) vividly describes the gathering momentum of pioneer settlement in southeastern Dakota Territory in the 1870s. Note the frequent comparison between the grasslands of the Great Plains and the ocean.

That summer many land seekers passed through the settlement on their way west. The arrival of a caravan was always an event of the greatest importance. How exciting they were, those little ships of the Great Plain! The prairie schooners, rigged with canvas tops which gleamed whitely in the shimmering light, first became visible as tiny specks against the eastern sky; one might almost imagine them to be sea gulls perched far, far away on an endless green meadow; but as one continued to watch, the white dots grew; they came drifting across the prairie like the day; after long waiting, they gradually floated out of the haze, distinct and clear; then, as they grew near, they proved to be veritable wagons, with horses hitched ahead, with folk and all their possessions inside, and a whole herd of cattle following behind.

The caravan would crawl slowly into the settlement and come to anchor in front of one of the sod houses; the moment it halted, people would swarm down and stretch themselves and begin to look after the teams; cattle would bellow; sheep would bleat as they ran about. Many queer races and costumes were to be seen in these caravans, and a babble of strange tongues shattered the air. Nut-brown youngsters, dressed only in a shirt and a pair of pants, would fly around between the huts, looking for other youngsters; an infant, its mother crooning softly to it, would sit securely perched in the fold of her arm; white-haired old men and women, who should have been living quietly at home, preparing for a different journey, were also to be seen in the group, running about like youngsters; the daily jogging from sky line to sky line had brightened their eyes and quickened their tongues. All were busy; each had a thousand questions to ask; every last one of them was in high spirits, though they knew no other home than the wagon and the blue skies above. . . . The Lord only could tell whence all these people had come and whither they were going!

---

immigrants went to the Midwest, where there was a great demand for unskilled labor. At the beginning of the twentieth century, several of the Midwest states had predominantly foreign-born populations.

The rural settlement of the various ethnic groups in the United States largely reflected the location of available cheap land (and even free land after the Homestead Act of 1862) at the time of their migration. The large numbers of Scandinavians who settled on the northern Great Plains in the 1870s and 1880s, the Ukrainians who homesteaded in Kansas at the same time, and the Slavic peoples who moved to North Dakota and the Prairie Provinces of Canada after 1900 were attracted to the frontier by the prospect of becoming landowners, a status that few had achieved in Europe (Box 4-1). Other settlers in the frontier region were persons who had previously lived in the eastern part of the country (Figure 4-6).

Figure 4-6. Migrants to the Great Plains, 1880s. During the nineteenth century, major migration flows consisted of Native Americans being moved out and Euro-Americans moving into the Great Plains region. Photo courtesy of Nebraska State Historical Society.

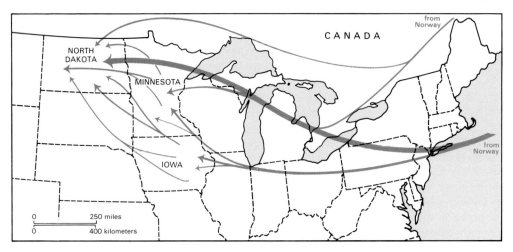

Figure 4-7. Migration Routes of Norwegian-Born North Dakota Pioneers. Norwegians who moved to North Dakota prior to the First World War came directly from their homeland, or stopped en route only temporarily in established Norwegian communities in Iowa and Minnesota. From Hudson 1976. Used with permission from Association of American Geographers.

The immigrants did not come haphazardly to the frontier. They had access to detailed (although sometimes embellished) information about the lands they were to settle. Many were recruited by railroad and land companies, steamship lines, and immigrant agencies, both in Europe and the United States. Information was relayed in letters to friends and relatives in the home country, and through these informal networks migration chains were established.

Channelized migration is illustrated by the movements of Swedes from the Rattvik parish in the Dalarna area of Sweden to Isanti County, Minnesota. As reported by Ostergren (1979, p. 194), the Swedes from Rattvik parish showed

> a remarkable single-mindedness of destination, which seems to have been the result of simply following in the path of those who had gone before them. That path had led them to a cluster of Dalarna settlements in Isanti County, Minnesota. Nearly half of the people who left Rattvik between 1864 and 1885 eventually took up residence there, including the bulk of the family emigration.

Norwegians, too, moved in large numbers to the upper Midwest. By 1910, there were more than 120,000 Norwegians in North Dakota, where they constituted 20 percent of the total inhabitants of the state. Like Swedes, the Norwegians followed well-established migration routes, temporarily stopping with kin or other Norwegians in Minnesota or Iowa before making the final trek to North Dakota (Figure 4-7).

The frontier is frequently portrayed as a restless place with low levels of population persistence. For example, in eastern Kansas, only 26 percent of the people recorded in 1860 were in the same place in 1870. The rapid turnover of the population on the agricultural frontiers of the Midwest and Great Plains suggests that settlers were often less attached to specific places than to the opportunities for speculating on land values. Changing residences also occurred among the nonfarm population. In Sioux City, a town that provided access to the northern plains, 14 percent of the males over 21 left the town each year in the early 1880s (Silag 1982).

Some of the mobility was only seasonal. In North Dakota, for example, farmers frequently supplemented their income as laborers during the harvest time in the Red River Valley (Figure 4-8). In winter many worked in the lumber camps of northern Wisconsin and Minnesota (Figure 4-9).

The foreign-born migrants were much more likely to persist in their homestead than a native-born American. Germans from Russia were legendary for their ability to hold on even in harsh times, although Scandinavians and Bohemians showed some of the same characteristics (Gjerde 1979). Just as the English men and women settled down in the New World in the seventeenth century, so nineteenth-century migrants from Europe tended to take root in their new homesteads.

Voluntary migration affects both the areas of origin and destination because those who choose to move usually possess distinctive characteristics. In the case of migration to the American frontier, both immigrants and the native-born Americans who moved to the frontier were generally young, and often in family groups, but with an abundance of single men (Figure 4-10).

This is evidenced by the population data for newly formed counties in eastern Nebraska after the

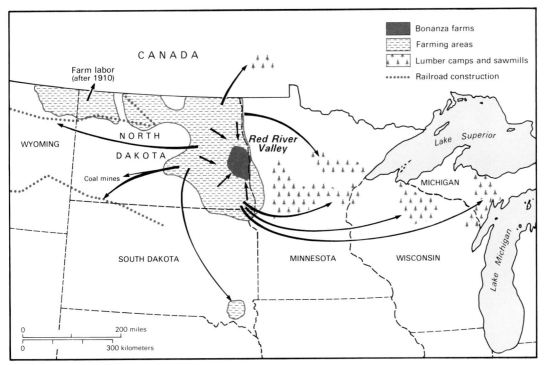

Figure 4-8. Seasonal Labor Migration from North Dakota, 1885–1915. Many farmers worked part of the year in lumber camps, coal mines, or railroad crews during the seasons when farm work was slack. After Hudson 1976.

state was opened for settlement following the Kansas-Nebraska Act of 1854. Along the Missouri River in Richardson and Burt counties, the initial frontier population consisted of young adults, mainly between 20 and 30 years of age, and their children (Figure 4-11). Men were in excess, but certainly not to the extent that occurred in the mining camps of the West or in the lumbering camps of the Great Lakes. Also there were fewer people at the frontier over the age of 40 than in the United States in general. However, within 15 years, the populations of these counties had aged, and the demographic structure was not

Figure 4-9. Seasonal Workers in a Lumber Camp. Some migration flows in the early twentieth century consisted of farmers who left their homes during the winter season to work in nonagricultural jobs. Photo courtesy of Oral History Collection, State Historical Society of North Dakota.

Figure 4-10. An American Frontier Family, 1890. Migrants to the American agricultural frontier in the late nineteenth century tended to be young adults with other members of a generally large family. Photo courtesy of Nebraska State Historical Society.

greatly different from that of the nation as a whole (see Figures 4-12 and 4-13). There were still more men than women in Burt and Richardson counties, possibly because of continued in-migration by single men to fill new job openings in the developing communities (Wishart 1973).

One final point needs to be made about the settlement of the North American interior. The voluntary migration of Europeans and Anglo-Americans westward was preceded and sometimes overlapped by the forced removal of American Indians from the land. By 1871, the end of the treaty-making period, the

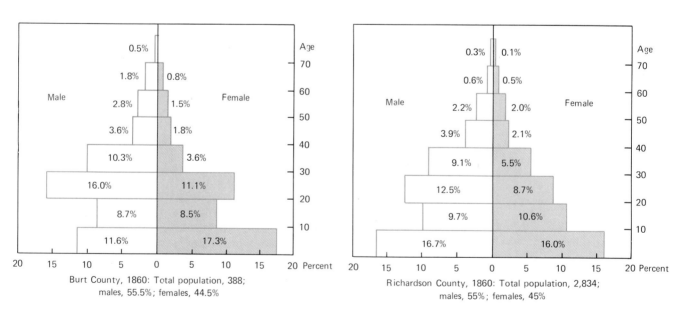

Figure 4-11. Age and Sex Population Structure of Burt and Richardson Counties, Nebraska, 1860. These population pyramids, which reveal a greater proportion of males than females, especially for ages 20–40, are typical of newly settled areas. From Wishart 1973. Used with permission from Nebraska State Historical Society.

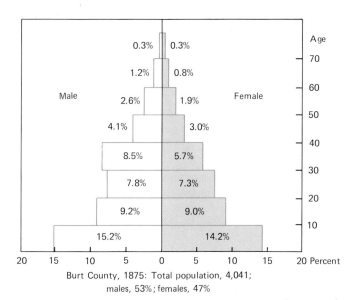

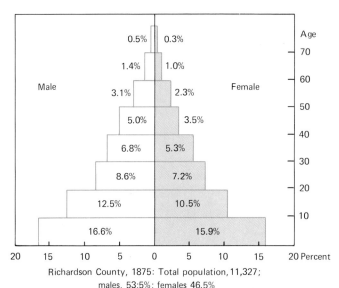

Burt County, 1875: Total population, 4,041;
males, 53%; females, 47%

Richardson County, 1875: Total population, 11,327;
males, 53;5%; females 46.5%

Figure 4-12. Age and Sex Population Structure of Burt and Richardson Counties, Nebraska, 1875. Fifteen years after the major influx of migrants (see Figure 4-11), the population structures of these counties were similar to that of the entire United States (see Figure 4-13). From Wishart 1973. Used with permission from Nebraska State Historical Society.

Native Americans had ceded more than 2 billion acres to the U.S. government and were largely restricted to reservations. A similar process of European expansion at the expense of native peoples also occurred during the nineteenth century in Canada, Australia, South Africa, and Argentina.

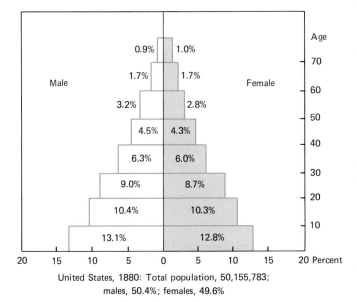

United States, 1880: Total population, 50,155,783;
males, 50.4%; females, 49.6%

Figure 4-13. Age and Sex Population Structure of the United States, 1880. The distinctiveness of populations in specific counties that had experienced recent immigration can be detected by comparing them with the population structure of the country as a whole. From Wishart 1973. Used with permission from Nebraska State Historical Society.

Migration in Non-Western Cultures

The Western world is not unique in having a long and active history of migration. In China, for example, there have been organized schemes since at least 1000 B.C. These schemes were particularly important in the late fourteenth and early fifteenth centuries A.D., when the Ming government moved large numbers of people into strategic border areas. One area was Yunnan Province in southern China, and another was in the far north where migrants formed military and agricultural colonies along and beyond the Great Wall (Figure 4-14).

China also has had a long history of voluntary migrations to farming frontiers (Figure 4-15). The inland province of Sichuan (Szechwan), with fertile soils and abundant water, was the main destination for migrants from 1650 to 1850. Most of the migration took place during the first half of the nineteenth century. In 1786, Sichuan's population was less than 8.5 million; by 1850, the province had more than 44 million people. After 1850, with Sichuan filled up, the main focus of migration shifted to the lower Chang Jiang (Yangtze) Valley, which had been devastated and depopulated in the wars of the early nineteenth century. In the first decades of the twentieth century, the northern frontier of China was extended into the mineral-rich and fertile plains of Manchuria. This extension of settlement was, at least in part, a political response to Russia's ambitions in the region. The movement of more than 20 million Chinese and Korean pioneers into this outlying area is perhaps the

Figure 4-14. The Great Wall of China. Many times in the past, various portions of the Great Wall served as a dividing "line" between agriculturalists and pastoralists. At other times, either nomadic groups or Han Chinese farmers migrated across this partial barrier. Photo courtesy of Merlin P. Lawson.

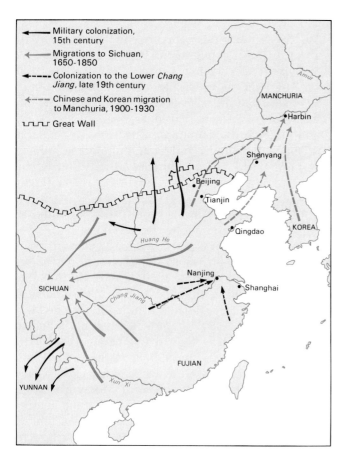

Figure 4-15. Historical Migrations in China. During several periods of Chinese history, large numbers of migrants moved into less populated regions, thus altering the distributional patterns of population.

greatest extension of settlement in the twentieth century (Ho 1959; Lattimore 1932).

Compared to the massive movement of people out of Europe in the nineteenth century, intercontinental migration from Asia was slight before the Second World War. Although Chinese settlers from the southern coastal provinces had colonized Southeast Asian islands as early as the fifteenth century, large-scale migration to Southeast Asia did not occur until about 1860 when emigration from China became legal. The tin mines and rubber plantations of the British colony of Malaya (now Malaysia) were an important destination. The British encouraged this flow of cheap labor, which peaked at more than 349,000 in 1926. The Chinese also settled in large numbers in Thailand, Indonesia, Singapore, Kampuchea (formerly Cambodia), Burma, and the Philippines. In many of these countries, their descendants now are important in industry, commerce, and finance. Today, Singapore is 90 percent Chinese, and more than one-third of Malaysia's population is Chinese.

The Chinese went further than Southeast Asia when they became indentured (contracted) laborers to fill labor needs created by the abolition of slavery in the Western Hemisphere. These migrations produced numerous settlements, most of which were completed by the late nineteenth century. Now there are an estimated 643,000 Chinese in the Americas, as well as 99,000 in Oceania, 94,000 in Africa, and 89,000 in Europe.

The same system of indentured labor took people from India to Guyana (formerly British Guiana), Trinidad, Jamaica, South Africa, eastern Africa, Fiji, and Mauritius. Likewise, Japanese and Filipinos went to Hawaii, and Japanese to Brazil. After the expiration of their contracts (generally 5 years), many of the "temporary workers" settled down in the new countries and engaged in retail trade, farming, and other activities. For these Asian emigrants, just as for the Europeans, the move to an overseas location often served as an opportunity for economic advancement.

By contrast, intercontinental migration from Africa before the twentieth century was not voluntary, nor did it offer opportunities for advancement. Several million Africans were enslaved and shipped to Asia and Europe. The transportation of more than 11 million Africans to the Americas from the sixteenth to nineteenth centuries represents the largest forced migration of all time (Bouvier 1977). These movements of people have had profound effects on the contemporary patterns of populations in many areas of South America, Central America and the Caribbean, and North America.

Even though these case studies do not cover all parts of the world, they provide a basis for developing general principles of migration, which can be useful in understanding migration elsewhere.

THEORIES OF MIGRATION

The first scholar to formulate "laws" of migration was E. G. Ravenstein, who based his generalizations on empirical studies of population movement in Britain, the United States, and Europe (Grigg 1977). Ravenstein's major observations (1885 and 1889) are set out below with a short statement assessing how well they have stood up to the test of time and experience. (Some of his "laws" that contain a repetitive element have been omitted here.)

1. *The majority of migrants move a short distance.* This "law" seems to have been operational at least since medieval times and is still operative today. With the advent of modern transportation, the average distance travelled by migrants may have increased, but relatively short moves are still the most common. For example, the first major concentrations of American black population in northern cities were in Baltimore, Washington, and Philadelphia, all of which are relatively close to the source areas of migrants who left the South in large numbers after 1910 (Morrill and Donaldson 1972).

The tendency for many migrants to move short distances whereas few go long distances produces a relationship termed **distance decay**. This expression, which applies to more human activities than just migration, relates the decline in the amount of some phenomenon with increasing distance from a focal place (see Box 4-2, Table 4-1, and Figure 4-16).

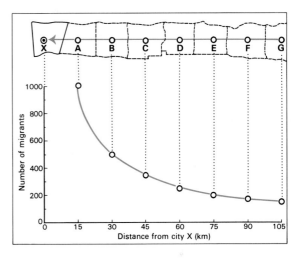
Distance decay. The decline in the amount of any phenomenon with increasing distance from a central node (see Box 4-2).

2. *Migration proceeds step by step.* Ravenstein (1885, p. 199) suggested that

> The inhabitants of the country immediately surrounding a town of rapid growth flock into it; the gaps thus left in the rural population are filled up by migrants from more remote districts, until the attractive force of one of our rapidly growing cities makes its influence felt, step by step, to the most remote corner of the kingdom.

Accordingly, sequential moves extend the effects of migration spatially (Figure 4-17). Such a series of moves was an important feature of migration to the American frontier in the nineteenth century when farmers who wanted to move on to new lands would often sell out to later migrants. On a different scale, a series of step-by-step residential shifts is usually generated in urban areas today when a family moves into a newly built house and thus vacates an older house, which is then reoccupied by another family (which leaves another residential gap and so on).

3. *Migrants going long distances generally move to a major center of commerce or industry.* Again this tendency has been operative since medieval times when London attracted population from all parts of England. The pull of large cities is apparent in the less developed world today where rapid urbanization is occurring.

The effects of a large place on the size of the migration field is expressed by a **gravity model.** This mathematical model states that the number of migrants to a place is directly related to the population size of that place but inversely related to the migratory distance (see Box 4-3 and Figure 4-18).

4. *Each current of migration produces a counter-current of lesser strength.* This statement seems to be true for nearly all migratory streams. Even the slave trade produced a tiny counterflow back to Africa of people who, in one way or another, were able to regain their freedom and to return to their homes. Migrants who choose to move long distances to new places often move back. For example, of the 13 million immigrants to the United States from 1900 to 1914, an estimated 4 million returned to Europe during that same period (Warren and Kraly 1985). In recent years, the proportion of emigrants from the United States has increased relative to the number of immigrants into the country, with the largest numbers returning to Mexico, West Germany, Canada, and the United Kingdom.

5. *The natives of towns are less migratory than those of rural areas.* This observation was related to a stage of economic development in Europe in the nineteenth century when rural-to-urban migration was predominant. In most of the less developed countries today, movement is still mainly from rural to urban places.

At the present time, most of the more developed countries have large urban majorities and relatively small rural populations. Therefore, most migration is interurban or intra-urban and does not consist of rural movers. Furthermore, in the United States in recent decades, there has been a small outflow from urban centers to rural areas. This migration is associated with the decentralization of industrial jobs and the willingness of commuters to travel long distances to their urban places of work.

6. *Females migrate more frequently than males within the country of birth, but males more frequently venture beyond.* This observation was related partly to a stage of economic development and partly to its particular cultural context. At the time Ravenstein was writing, there was a large demand for females as domestic help and factory workers in the cities of Britain. Since women had few employment opportunities in rural areas, they tended to migrate to cities.

Today, the gender of the majority of intranational (domestic) migrants depends on cultural conditions as well as on economic opportunities. In parts of Latin America, women are more likely than men to move to towns where they work as domestic servants or in

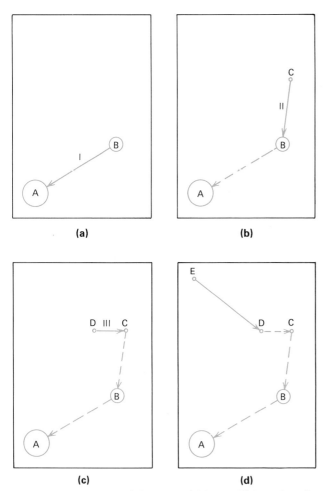

Figure 4-17. A Set of Sequential Moves. This series of figures shows how places, after being vacated, become destinations for other people who move.

BOX 4-3. THE GRAVITY MODEL

The relative influence of a center on surrounding places may be expressed by a gravity model. When applied to the number of persons moving between places, the gravity model indicates that the amount of migration to a specified center is directly related to its population size and inversely related to the distances, or lengths, of migration.

The model presented here, which is the simplest of several different forms, can be represented symbolically as follows:

$$G_i = \frac{P_i}{d_{ij}}$$

where G_i is the "gravitational" attraction of a center i, P_i is the population of this place, and d_{ij} is the distance from some other place j to center i.

As an illustration, consider two cities, A and B (see Figure 4-18). They are located 40 and 60 kilometers, respectively, from region C, and their population sizes are 120,000 and 300,000, respectively. According to the gravity model, the ratio of migrants to A and B, respectively, is expected to be 3000 : 5000 (because $G_A = 120,000/40 = 3000$ and $G_B = 300,000/60 = 5000$). Therefore, if a total of 1600 emigrants leave region C, 600 are expected to go to city A and 1000 to city B (since 3000 : 5000 = 600 : 1000).

The utility of the gravity model is to approximate reality and to serve as a basis for prediction. If there are discrepancies between what the model predicts (e.g., the number of migrants) and what actually occurs, these discrepancies may indicate other conditions (such as topographic and economic) affecting migration.

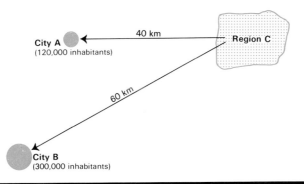

Figure 4-18. Migration from a Region, According to a Gravity Model.

---

light industry. In other less developed countries, such as India, for example, many more males migrate from rural areas to cities than do females. Migration between rural Indian villages, however, is commonly made by females because brides traditionally move at the time of marriage.

Men do seem to be more active in international migration than women, especially in voluntary movements. For example, between 1820 and 1914, at least 55 percent of all immigrants to the United States were male. In over two-thirds of the years, the immigrants were more than 60 percent male; and for 13 years, 70 percent was surpassed. The record high year was 1824, when 80 percent of the immigrants were men. Likewise, among international migrant workers today, men outnumber women three to one.

7. *Most migrants are adults; families rarely migrate out of their country of birth.* This "law" contains two observations. The observation concerning adults is indisputable. In voluntary migrations, the majority of people are adults. The second part of the "law" is more problematic. It is certainly true that families find it more difficult to move than unmarried adults, but as we have seen, families did cross the Atlantic in the past, and many refugees are moving as families today.

8. *Large towns grow more by migration than by natural increase.* It is widely accepted that preindustrial cities grew and prospered because of population influx (Patten 1976). Many nineteenth-century industrial cities and transportation centers also grew largely by migration in their early years. In 1870, for example, more than 35 percent of the population of all the major cities located in the Ohio-Mississippi and Great Lakes region (except Louisville) was foreign-born. When the large number of native-born Americans who had recently moved to these cities is added to the foreign-born, the proportion of migrants in these cities is very large.

Most of the large towns in less developed countries today are growing very rapidly by the in-

---

Gravity model. A mathematical expression which states that the number of migrants or other persons (or objects) attracted to a place is directly related to the population size of the destination and inversely related to the distance between the origin and destination (see Box 4-3).

migration of people from rural areas. In addition to job opportunities (which have always attracted migrants to large cities), today's major cities in less developed countries offer medical, educational, and social enticements (Chapter 11).

9. *The main causes of migration are economic.* This conclusion is widely held, and studies have shown that rates of migration can be correlated with changes in the level of economic activity in the source area, in the receiving area, or in both. It has been argued that international migrants tend to be influenced more by conditions in the area of destination than by pressures at home. The movement of West Indian migrants to Britain, for example, has varied with the cycles of growth and resources in the British economy (Peach 1968). To give another example, the slackening of European migration to the United States in the 1890s was associated with the economic depression that prevailed in the United States during those years.

It is difficult, however, to verify that the major reason for migration is "economic." Human motivations, decisions, and behavior are so complex that it is very difficult to compare the relative importance of economic factors with other considerations. For instance, moving at the time of marriage is not regarded as primarily an economic move in those societies having love marriages (rather than arranged ones). Also, many persons with wealth or large pensions enjoy the flexibility of choosing their residences in areas having an attractive physical and/or social environment (Morrison and Wheeler 1976).

In general, most of Ravenstein's ideas on the nature of migration are accepted as having stood the test of time (Dorigo and Tobler 1983). However, there are many questions Ravenstein did not address, such as the noneconomic causes of migration and the social processes that create migratory streams (White 1980). Other generalizations (or "theories") have been proposed since Ravenstein's time in an effort to explain the process of migration.

The sociologist Everett Lee, who offered an additional theory of migration (1965), grouped factors that enter into the decision to migrate into four categories: (1) factors operating in the area of origin, (2) factors operating at the destination, (3) factors that act as intervening obstacles, and (4) personal factors that are specific to the individual (Figure 4-19). The potential migrant is influenced by positive factors and negative factors associated with both the place of origin and the possible destination. Lee suggested that the potential migrant weighs the known and expected advantages and disadvantages of the destination in comparison with the situation at the place of origin. For a move to result, the attractions of the destination must be great enough to outweigh the advantages of staying and to

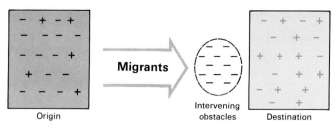

Figure 4-19. Lee's Model of Migration. The decision to migrate involves an evaluation of positive and negative factors at both the origin and destination, as well as the obstacles in the way of moving. After Lee 1965.

overcome any intervening obstacles, such as distance, costs of relocation, and the disruption of established patterns of life.

Personal factors also affect the evaluation process. For example, a family with children in college, or a couple without children, may not consider the quality of public schools at either the point of origin or destination, but schools may be an important factor in the balance sheet of a family with school-age children. Similarly, attachment to place and proximity to family and friends may prevent a potential migrant from moving, even when other factors (such as promotion opportunities) seem attractive.

Another attempt to formulate generalizations about migrations was made by Zelinsky (1971) in what he termed "the mobility transition model." He proposed that changes in migration behavior have been paralleled by the stages of the demographic transition model. Similarity between the two models is not surprising because demographic conditions and migratory decisions are both related to changes involved with the modernization process.

The graphs shown in Figure 4-20 (a to d) show the trends in volume of migration through the five stages of the demographic transition model at four different scales (international, regional, rural to urban, and urban to urban, including intra-urban). In addition, Zelinsky graphed [Figure 4-20(e)] the interrelationships between migration and **circulation** (short-term, generally repetitive movements) over the five stages. The mobility transition, as with the demographic transition model, is primarily a depiction of stages experienced by modernized societies. Nevertheless, it may provide a basis for anticipating some future migration patterns in countries undergoing economic and demographic change.

In the first stage of the mobility transition, when population growth was negligible because high death rates cancelled out high birth rates, little migration occurred at any scale. In India in 1931, for example, only 10 percent of the population lived outside the district of their birth. Life was localized, information on other places was in short supply, and most people

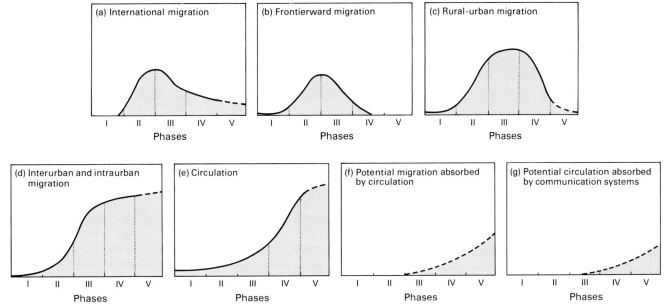

Figure 4-20. Changing Levels of Various Forms of Mobility through Time: A Schematic Representation. Each type of migration is related to particular phases of the demographic and mobility transitions. For example, international migration is most common during the second and third phases, but according to Zelinsky, rural-urban movements are maximum during the third and fourth phases. From Zelinsky 1971. Used with permission from American Geographical Society.

lived and died in the locality of their birth. Some population movements did take place, as the Lincoln study proves (see page 73); but relative to later stages of the demographic transition model, migration was less common. Circulation was mostly daily trips to fields and occasional journeys to markets and festivals.

The second stage, when population increased rapidly because the death rates dropped while the birth rate remained high, was a time of great migration. Mounting population pressure on the land, better transportation systems, and a widening sphere of exploration and trade, bringing knowledge of other places, gave rise in the past to increased population movements at all scales. People migrated from one country to another [Figure 4-20(a)], from settled areas to new frontiers [Figure 4-20(b)], from rural areas to growing cities [Figure 4-20(c)], and from towns to cities [Figure 4-20(d)]. Emigration from Europe and nineteenth-century domestic migration to the American frontier illustrate these conditions.

Zelinsky's third phase is transitional, matching the third stage of the demographic transition model when the birth rate began to fall toward the death rate and population growth rates declined. International migration lessened and agricultural frontiers closed, as in the United States by 1930. But at the same time, rural to urban migrations and movements within and between cities became more important. With the shift to secondary and tertiary occupations, people increased their circulation by commuting to jobs and

travelling to obtain special services (e.g., medical and educational), and so on.

By the fourth and fifth stages, when low birth and death rates brought little population growth to the now developed society, migration was predominantly interurban and intra-urban. Some international movements occurred, particularly of skilled and unskilled workers from the less to the more developed countries, but progressively stricter immigration laws limited the number of people who could cross international boundaries legally. The rural to urban movement virtually ceased because the percentage of farming population, and hence potential movers, was very low.

As would be expected, circulation increased as the societies modernized [Figure 4-20(e)]. The development of the private automobile greatly widened the radius of daily travel. When circulation increased, migration became less imperative. For example, by commuting an hour each way every day, there is an area exceeding 20,000 square kilometers in which to find a job. This increased access to jobs reduces the need to migrate to be near the place of work. Consequently, some potential migration has undoubtedly been "absorbed" by circulation [Figure 4-20(f)].

Current conditions indicate that, in turn, a portion of potential circulation is absorbed by modern

---

Circulation. Movements, usually consisting of short, frequent, and repetitive trips, to and from one's residence.

communication systems [Figure 4-20(g)]. Sophisticated telecommunications are reducing the need to commute because some jobs can be done from home through a computer network. Similarly, the use of home VCRs has cut down on circulation to cinemas.

CONTEMPORARY TRENDS IN MIGRATION

Shifting Patterns of Migration in the United States

No place remains a permanent pole of attraction for migrants. This is evident by noting the movements of people among the census regions of the United States (Figure 4-21). For example, in the late 1970s, the cities of the Northeast and East North Central, once the destination of millions of migrants, experienced net migration losses (that is, they lost more people by out-migration than they gained by in-migration). At the same time, the South and West, especially the portion that is popularly termed the "Sunbelt," enjoyed net in-migration.

From 1970 to 1975, according to a study conducted in the 1970s (Biggar 1979), the Northeast had a net migration loss of 700,000 people, and the North Central experienced a net migration loss of 800,000.

The destination of many interstate migrants was to the 15 states defined, by the study, as the "Sunbelt" (Figure 4-21). In 1970, the 15 states contained almost one-third (61 million) of the population of the United States. By 1977, 85 million, or almost 40 percent of the nation's population, lived in the Sunbelt.

A major cause of migration to the Sunbelt was economic. There was an increase of 432,000 manufacturing jobs in these 15 Sunbelt states, whereas the number of manufacturing jobs in the Northeast declined by 769,000 and in the North Central states by 185,000. The main attractions in the South were the lower labor costs in the less unionized Southern states, the availability of energy in the forms of petroleum and natural gas, and the general economic growth. The first industries to relocate in the South were labor-intensive (such as textiles) and those attracted to oil, gas, chemicals, and other raw materials. Capital-intensive industries (for example, insurance and banking), new growth industries (like electronics), and service activities (such as tourism and real estate) prospered. There was an escalating and agglomerating process of population growth and industrial expansion. The new industries created demands for labor, migration occurred, and new consumers attracted other industries.

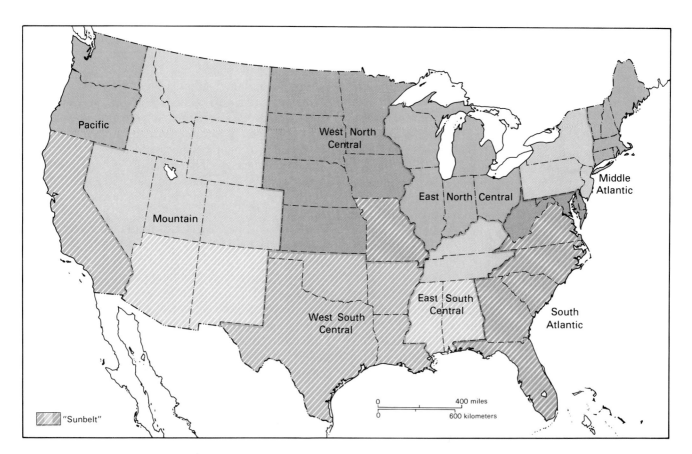

Figure 4-21. Nine U.S. Census Regions and the "Sunbelt." The boundaries of the "Sunbelt," which is not an officially defined region, vary in popular usage.

Affluent people who had the time and money to take advantage of climatic amenities also migrated to some of these Sunbelt states. This group included many who moved after reaching retirement age.

Another group that has recently moved to the South from the cities of the Northeast and North Central states are black Americans. After 1975, there was a net flow of blacks from the Northeast to the South, with New York State alone having a net loss of 80,000 blacks. By 1980, the North Central states were also experiencing a loss of blacks to the South. In historic perspective, this migration illustrates a countercurrent because it is a reversal of the black exodus from the South that occurred after 1910. Many of the migrants moved back primarily for the economic opportunities; but for others—especially the elderly—a major motivation was to return to their original home states (McHugh 1987).

The consequences of migration to the Sunbelt were far-reaching. The cities of the North lost some of their enterprising young population. Most of the migrants were young (although the flow of elderly migrants to retirement areas such as Florida and Arizona was important). The median age (the age that divides the population into two equal halves) of migrants to the Sunbelt during the 1970–1976 period was under 25, whereas the median age for the nation as a whole was above 30.

Politically there were implications because the alterations in population distribution were reflected in the reallocation of seats in the House of Representatives (Table 4-2). Furthermore, the voters who migrated took with them values that altered political balances in the states where they settled.

Migration to the South and West left its mark on the landscape. New housing developments encircled old towns and threatened to envelop outlying communities. Traffic congestion became a major problem in cities like Houston, and rapid growth strained sewer and water systems in many communities (Figure 4-22).

The ability of the South, particularly the West South Central region, to attract industry and migrants diminished when the price of oil collapsed in the early 1980s. In-migration decreased as industrial growth slowed and the regional economy declined. Banks and other financial institutions found they were carrying too many unsound loans and were unable to finance new industries. Meanwhile, financial companies in the Northeast and East North Central (in cities like Boston, Pittsburgh, and Cincinnati) were able to support new economic activity and, consequently, stem the rate of regional out-migration.

It is clear, then, that the migration patterns of the 1980s are significantly different from those of the 1970s. There is no reason to believe that current migration patterns will necessarily persist through the

TABLE 4-2. Members of the U.S. House of Representatives, 1950 and 1988

State	1950	1988
Sunbelt States:		
Alabama	9	7
Arizona	2	5
Arkansas	7	4
California	23	45
Florida	6	19
Mississippi	7	5
Oklahoma	8	6
Texas	21	27
Total	83	118
Non-Sunbelt States:		
Illinois	26	22
Indiana	11	10
Massachusetts	14	11
Minnesota	9	8
New York	45	34
Ohio	22	21
Pennsylvania	33	23
Total	160	129

end of the century. According to a recent report, one-third of all the new jobs in the nation by the year 2000 will be located in only 46 counties, most of which are located in the South and West. The major hubs of this expected economic growth (and, hence, migration flows) include southern California, the arc from Dallas to San Antonio, Texas, eastern Florida from Orlando to Miami, and the Phoenix–Tucson axis. By this account, at least, the "Sunbelt" is not dead.

In addition to the long-distance migrations between regions, many other forms of migration are occurring within the United States. According to a recent study by the U.S. Bureau of the Census, some of the major movements during the 1980s are the following:

1. The majority of migrants move a short distance. Slightly over two-thirds of all migrants only move within their same community. It seems that this migration "law" formulated by Ravenstein a century ago still applies today.
2. Migrants from towns and small cities tend to move to large urban places.
3. The countercurrent from large cities to rural places, which was observed in the 1970s, has decreased in importance.
4. Males are more likely to migrate than females, although the difference is very small.
5. Young adults are the most mobile group. For example, people in their twenties tend to move more than those in their forties.

Figure 4-22. Houston, Texas. Most of the population growth of Houston, which became the fifth largest U.S. city in 1980, resulted from in-migration. Photo courtesy of Houston Chamber of Commerce.

6. A person with a college degree is more likely to move than one with less schooling.
7. Hispanics are more likely to migrate than whites or blacks.
8. The mobility varies from region to region. In 1983–1984, 22 percent of all persons in the West moved, but in the Northeast only 12 percent were migrants.

International Migrations

International migrations in the twentieth century, especially since World War II, differ from earlier movements primarily because governments have become more involved in the regulation and organization of international migration. In the nineteenth century, most Western governments tacitly encouraged or discouraged migration to or from their territories but rarely got involved in detailed regulation. The sick and the indigent were liable to be turned back at international borders, but those with wealth or promised employment moved relatively freely.

This century has seen the passage of restrictive immigration and emigration laws. Some countries such as those in Eastern Europe, the Soviet Union, and China have greatly restricted emigration. Citizens wishing to leave have to apply for exit permits, which are usually difficult to obtain.

More common are the restrictions on immigration. The first major restrictions on migrants coming to the United States, imposed in the Quota Act of 1921 and the Immigration Act of 1924, sought to limit total immigration and to let people in on the basis of ethnic origins. Quotas, based on the composition of the U.S. population in 1890, were established for each ethnic group. That 1890 criterion, of course, favored immi-grants of British, Irish, Scandinavian, and German stock.

A new immigration law was passed in 1965. This act established an annual quota of 120,000 immigrants from the Americas and 170,000 from the rest of the world. No more than 20,000 immigrants a year were allowed from any single country. Preferences were given to relatives of U.S. citizens and to people possessing special needed skills.

In 1980, the immigrant quota was reduced to 280,000 (and subsequently to 270,000); but for the first time, a special quota of 50,000 was established for refugees forced to leave their homelands. This quota was immediately exceeded in 1980, when there was a sudden influx of 125,000 Cubans and the wave of refugees from Southeast Asia crested. Since 1983, the number has dropped again to about 60,000 refugees each year (Bouvier and Gardner 1986).

The United Kingdom is another country that has established increasingly restrictive rules in immigration in recent decades. Traditionally Britain allowed easy access and the inhabitants of Commonwealth countries were assumed to have the right of entry if they wished to work in the United Kingdom. The Commonwealth Immigration Act of 1962 curtailed entry, and further restrictions were imposed in 1971. The result was to markedly decrease the inflow of people from the Caribbean, India, Pakistan, and other Commonwealth countries. The Nationality Act of 1981, which defined who was British, had the effect of curtailing entry rights of persons of British stock who were born outside the United Kingdom, and it limited the entry of families of recent migrants.

Most countries now have stringent immigration rules, which means that international migration contrasts in size and type with that of the previous two or three centuries. From 1950 to 1980, the main destinations of voluntary migrants were, in order, the United States, West Germany, France, Australia, Canada, and New Zealand. In the 1970s, the United States drew over 40 percent of its immigrants from Latin America and about one-third from Asia. Europe, once the primary source of migrants to America, supplied less than 20 percent in the 1970s, mostly from Southern and Eastern Europe (Figure 4-4). By country, Mexico (with 11 percent of all immigrants), the Philippines (9 percent), Korea (6 percent), and Cuba (6 percent) were the main sources of migrants to the United States in 1986.

It is important to realize that these percentages, which apply to the relative size of recent immigrant populations, are based on numbers smaller than the totals for a century earlier. For example, according to the 1980 U.S. Census, the number of American citizens who were born in Mexico was only 2 million. In comparison, nearly 100 million Americans consider their national backgrounds as British or German. Furthermore, of the top five nationalities represented by foreign-born citizens in 1980, three were European and a fourth was Canadian (Table 4-3). Even though the ethnic composition of recent immigrants to the United States has changed in a relative sense, the ethnic background of Americans has not yet changed much in terms of total numbers.

In recent years, the majority of migrants to France (the third main destination for migrants from 1950 to 1980) were from Algeria, Portugal, Italy, and Spain (Table 4-4). Most immigrants in Northern and Western Europe come from North Africa, Southern Europe, and former colonies in Africa, Latin America, and Asia. As a general principle, it can be said that migrants from less developed countries tend to move to nearby more developed countries. For example, Mexicans move to the United States, Greeks to West

TABLE 4-3. Origins of Foreign-Born Americans, 1980

Country of Origin	Number (1000s)	Percentage of Total Foreign-Born
Mexico	2199	15.6
Germany	849	6.0
Canada	843	6.0
Italy	832	5.9
United Kingdom	669	4.8
Cuba	608	4.3
Philippines	501	3.6
Poland	418	3.0
U.S.S.R.	406	2.9
Korea	290	2.0
Others	6465	45.9
Total	14080	

Source: U.S. Census Bureau 1984.

TABLE 4-4. Principal Nationalities of Foreigners in France, 1976

Nationality	Number (1000s)	Percentage of Foreign Population
Algeria	884.3	21.1
Portugal	858.9	20.5
Italy	558.2	13.3
Spain	531.4	12.7
Morocco	322.1	7.7
Tunisia	167.5	4.0
Poland	88.4	2.1
Yugoslavia	77.8	1.8
Others	709.5	16.8

Source: Bouvier 1977. Used with permission from Population Reference Bureau.

Germany, and Spaniards to France. Or, if the migrants move longer distances, it is to more developed countries where there are special ties, as in the case of West Indians moving to Britain (Davis 1974).

Destination countries sometimes encourage "temporary" migrants who are expected to serve as short-term laborers. In the mid-1970s when many European economies were expanding, 11 percent of the French labor force, 10 percent of the West German labor force, and a quarter of the Swiss labor force consisted of foreign workers. During the period of extensive construction in several of the oil-rich but sparsely populated countries of Southwest Asia, many semiskilled workers from South and Southeast Asia were enticed to migrate—but for only a limited number of years (Figure 4-23).

Between 1942 and 1964, the **bracero program** allowed Mexicans to enter the United States on temporary visas. After that program ended, however, many Mexicans continued to enter the United States without visas. Estimates vary on the number of Mexicans who are in the United States today without immigrant documentation, but the number may be over 1 million (Davis, Haub, & Willette 1983). Migration from Mexico is unlikely to slow in the foreseeable future, given the proximity and economic attraction of the United States and the existence of established migration chains.

The impact of undocumented migration is debatable. Arguments often resemble those for and against immigration in general (see the Point-Counterpoint at the end of this chapter). A similar debate centers on the millions of temporary, or "guest," workers who have migrated from Southern Europe and North Africa to the

Bracero program. The authorized migration from 1940 to 1964 of nearly 5 million Mexicans into the United States to serve as temporary workers.

Figure 4-23. Abu Dhabi, United Arab Emirates. Much of the construction of this city in recent years has been accomplished by workers from other countries who came as short-term migrants. Photo courtesy of Robert J. Hall.

cities of Western and Northern Europe. The value of a source of cheap labor is generally appreciated, particularly when jobs are plentiful. In Switzerland in a 1974 referendum, a solid majority of the voters turned down the suggestion calling for the eviction of half the nation's foreign workers over a three-year period (Bouvier 1977). In West Germany in 1982, over 20 percent of all workers in hotels and catering businesses and in foundries were classed as foreigners.

During economic recessions and times of high unemployment, foreign workers often become the target of public resentment and are among the first to lose their jobs. Some citizens in countries that once welcomed short-term workers may express hostility toward the "foreigners." In countries such as the United States and West Germany, debates about the rights to social services and of citizenship for the recent migrants often occur. In countries with small populations, such as Kuwait and the United Arab Emirates, relatively large numbers of worker immigrants may create sizable new ethnic populations.

Even though the migrants from the less developed countries generally have limited occupational skills, they are often better trained than the people who stay at home. Consequently, the source countries suffer the loss of a productive group. In the early 1970s, the number of Greek workers in Germany was equivalent to 8.4 percent of the Greek labor force. Such a loss is tolerated, and may be encouraged, in countries whose governments see emigration as a partial solution to their employment problems. In fact, money sent back to the home country compensates in part for the loss

of young workers. In 1980, Yugoslavia received $4.8 billion in remittances and Portugal received $2.9 billion. The value of workers' remittances received in North Yemen in 1980 was far greater than the value of the country's exports that year.

It is not only unskilled workers who may be allowed to pass through restrictive immigration barriers. Receiving countries may quickly admit potential migrants who possess technical skills that are in demand. For instance, the 1960s and 1970s saw a "brain drain" from many parts of the world to North America, as relatively highly educated individuals sought new opportunities. Every year large numbers of doctors from both more developed and less developed lands entered the United States to practice medicine. In fact, there continues to be a considerable loss of professional and technical skills from less developed countries as people migrate to economically advanced areas like North America and Western Europe. Put in other terms, less developed countries, having paid to train skilled professionals and technicians, then lose their educational investment when experts migrate to more developed countries. Although technicians may move in either direction between rich and poor nations, some scholars believe the outflow from the less developed countries, on balance, hinders the economic development of those lands.

In contrast to the few who are able to move to lucrative jobs in other countries, many others must flee with little hope of a brighter future. An unhappy feature of contemporary international migration is the large number of refugees who have felt compelled to leave their homelands because of famine, environmental catastrophe, war, or political turmoil. Unlike voluntary migrations, forced migrations are not selective by age and sex. They frequently involve the uprooting of entire communities, men and women, young and old. During the twentieth century, some 250 million people have fled from their homelands. In the mid-1980s, it was estimated that there were more than 10 million refugees in the world, the vast majority moving from and between nations in Africa, Latin America, and Asia.

Before 1950, the largest refugee movements occurred in Europe, where the destruction of two world wars and the restructuring of national boundaries resulted in the displacement of large numbers of people. About 20 million Eastern and Central Europeans were uprooted by expulsion, flight, or population transfer during and immediately after World War II. The partition of the Indian subcontinent into India and Pakistan in 1947 also caused the transfer of what suddenly became minority populations. About 7 million Moslems left predominantly Hindu India for the new Islamic state of Pakistan, and as many Hindus and Sikhs fled from Pakistan into India. This mass migration was particularly dramatic because these two streams of migrants moved in opposite directions in less than a year. As is frequently true under conditions that produce refugee movements, many people lost their lives in the process.

In the 1980s, the major refugee movements are taking place in Africa (4 million in 1987) and Asia (6 million). Almost 90 percent of these refugees move between less developed countries. Of the 34 poorest countries in the world, 27 are having to cope with an additional population of refugees (Demko and Wood 1987). Relatively few find asylum in the more developed countries; of the approximately 10 million refugees in the world in 1982, 1.2 million were accepted in Canada and the United States and 0.6 million in Europe. Most refugees are forced to settle in countries whose resources are often already strained and where potential aid may be very limited. For example, the United Nations High Commission for Refugees estimated that in 1983 the proportion of international refugees to the local population was 1 to 7 in Somalia, 1 to 32 in Sudan, and 1 to 34 in Pakistan, but only 1 to 390 in the United Kingdom and 1 to 416 in Sweden.

One serious refugee problem began in the early 1980s in the "horn" of Africa. In 1980, 2 million people fled from Ethiopia, forced to move by the combined crises of drought, famine, political upheaval, and war (Figure 8-16). The refugees lived in makeshift camps in Somalia, Sudan, Djibouti, and Kenya, where they again faced famine (Figure 4-24).

Figure 4-24. Ethiopian Refugees in Somalia. In recent years, millions of persons have migrated across international borders because of calamitous conditions in their homelands. Photo courtesy of Population Reference Bureau.

By 1985, famine conditions became even more widespread and attracted extensive world attention. There is a high probability that conditions forcing people to leave their homes will continue into the future.

Another recent situation creating a large population of refugees has been the war in Afghanistan. By the mid-1980s, an estimated 3 million Afghans had fled into Pakistan and Iran. Likewise, many people in Central America have become refugees as a result of warfare, civil conflicts, and personal threats against their lives. A list of places where events are causing, and are expected to cause, international refugees seems to have no end.

PROSPECTS

It is difficult to predict the course of future migrations, but two points may be made with some certainty. First, specific patterns of migration will change because the relative attractiveness of places is not constant. Second, changes in economic conditions and political decisions will influence the directions of migration.

Migration as a whole will continue as long as there are inequalities in opportunities, particularly economic opportunities, from one part of the world to another. In the 1980s, a major economic inequality exists between the more developed nations and the less developed nations; but the relative differences between nations within each of these broad categories also produce migrations. To the extent that people are allowed to move across international boundaries, migration toward richer countries can be expected in the future.

In 1980, the Independent Commission on International Development Issues recommended that the nations of the world cooperate to establish bilateral and multinational agreements to harmonize policies on emigration and immigration, to protect the rights of migrant workers, and to guarantee the legal protection of refugees (Independent Commission 1980). At the present time, however, most countries are responding individually to the problems of international migration, mainly by intensifying restrictions on entry. If these restrictions continue, the distribution of the world's population in the future will probably not change greatly as a result of international migrations.

In contrast to international restrictions, most governments allow people to move within the boundaries of their country, so intranational migration is expected to continue. As presented in Chapter 9, much of the movement in less developed countries will probably be from rural to urban places. In countries that are already urbanized, residential shifts may continue to reflect changing economic patterns. Other migrations in technological societies are expected to accompany new developments in electronic communications, which permit people to be separated farther from former concentrations of employment.

The New Immigrants—Admit or Restrict?

There has always been anxiety and some opposition on the part of residents of the United States toward new immigrants. The restrictive acts of 1921 and 1924, for example, were the outcome of decades of debate over whether the country should continue a relatively open-door policy or whether immigrants (specifically Eastern and Southern Europeans) should be restricted. The supporters of restricted immigration prevailed at that time.

The debate has continued into the 1980s. According to public opinion polls, the majority of American support a reduction in immigration of all kinds. Much of the controversy is directed toward immigrants from Latin America and Asia, who together comprise more than 80 percent of the total documented immigration. In addition, Latin America, and particularly Mexico, is the source for most of the undocumented immigrants who enter the United States each year.

Opposition to continued high levels of immigration focuses on demographic, economic, and cultural issues. In 1981, about 30 percent of the population increase in the United States came from immigration, both documented and undocumented. This reflects not only the large numbers of immigrants (over a million each year), but also the low birth rate of the nation. It is estimated that if net immigration continues at a rate of one million every year and if the total fertility rate remains at 1.8, then post-1980 immigrants and their children will make up 40 percent of the American population in 100 years.

This argument is countered by the fact that the United States has always been a country of immigrants, and the nation has been built through the efforts of migrants. Moreover, immigrants have often accounted for a large percentage of the population growth. From 1880 to 1889 and again from 1900 to 1909, immigrants contributed 40 percent of the country's population increase. Furthermore, population growth now is more affected by demographic changes in the entire population than by the relatively small proportion of immigrants of recent decades. The demographer Leon Bouvier has pointed out that a small change in fertility rates (say an increase of 10 percent) would have a far greater effect on the size of the future American population than even a 50 percent increase in immigration (1977 and 1983).

Opposition to immigration is particularly intense during hard economic times, when unemployment is high and new immigrants are regarded as competitors for jobs. Immigrants are also perceived as adding costs to the taxpayer by using medical, welfare, and other social services. Moreover, the economic impact of the new immigrants tends to be geographically concentrated in a few areas, such as California, New York, Florida, and Texas, which are the destinations of more than 75 percent of all Latin American immigrants. In response to the argument that immigrants take jobs away from established residents, it is argued that immigrants accept work that other Americans avoid, such as stoop labor in fields. Another counterargument comes from those economists who maintain that more consumers are good for the economy. It is also pointed out that many immigrants, including those who are undocumented, pay more in taxes than they receive in benefits. One study found that 77 percent of apprehended undocumented workers had social security taxes deducted from their paychecks, and 73 percent had federal taxes withheld. In contrast, only 27 percent used medical services provided by public assistance, and fewer than one-half of 1 percent received welfare payments (Murphy and Cancellier 1982).

Finally, immigration, especially Hispanic immigration, is seen by some as a threat to established American culture. Although Hispanics are culturally diverse, they share a common language, which reinforces group identity. This raises the issues of bilingual education and rates of assimilation (see the Point-Counterpoint in Chapter 6).

The difficulties of arriving at a national consensus are illustrated by various Congressional attempts to modify existing immigration laws in the early 1980s. A new bill was finally passed in the fall of 1986. Key provisions included amnesty for aliens who entered the United States before January 1982 and provisions for their eventual acceptance as citizens. The bill imposed penalties (even imprisonment) for employers who knowingly hire aliens not authorized to work in the United States.

This reform bill has not completely satisfied any of the conflicting interests. The U.S. Immigration and Naturalization Service faces an almost impossible task of enforcing the provisions. Meanwhile, American Hispanics and other legal immigrants are concerned about possible discrimination from employers who are continually checking for undocumented workers.

In spite of legislative attempts to provide a satisfactory policy about immigration, the debate continues.

BIBLIOGRAPHY

Allen, David Grayson, *In English Ways: The Movement of Societies and the Transferal of English Local Law and Custom in Massachusetts Bay in the Seventeenth Century*. Chapel Hill, N.C.: University of North Carolina Press, 1981.

Baines, Dudley, *Migration in a Mature Economy: Emigration and Internal Migration in England and Wales, 1861–1900*. New York: Cambridge University Press, 1986.

Banks, Charles Edward, *Topographical Dictionary of 2885 English Emigrants in New England 1620–1650*. Baltimore: Southern Books, 1957.

———, *The Planters of the Commonwealth*. Baltimore: Genealogical Publishing, 1961.

Bernard, Richard M., and Bradley R. Rice, *Sunbelt Cities: Politics and Growth Since World War II*. Austin, Tex.: University of Texas Press, 1983.

Biggar, Jeanne C., "The Sunning of America: Migration to the Sunbelt," *Population Bulletin*, 34, no. 1 (1979).

Bouvier, Leon F., "International Migration: Yesterday, Today, and Tomorrow," *Population Bulletin*, 32, no. 4 (1977).

———, "Human Waves," *Natural History*, 92, no. 8 (August 1983), 6–13.

Bouvier, Leon F., and Robert W. Gardner, "Immigration to the U.S.: The Unfinished Story," *Population Bulletin*, 41, no. 4 (November 1986).

Clark, G. L., "Dynamics of Interstate Labour Migration," *Annals of the Association of American Geographers*, 72 (1982), 297–313.

Clarke, J. J., and L. A. Kosinski, eds., *Redistribution of Population in Africa*. London: Heinemann, 1982.

Cressy, David, *Coming Over: Migration and Communication between England and New England in the Seventeenth Century*. New York: Cambridge University Press, 1987.

Davis, Cary, Carl Haub, and JoAnne Willette, "U.S. Hispanics: Changing the Face of America," *Population Bulletin*, 38, no. 3 (June 1983).

Davis, James E., *Frontier America 1800–1840, A Comparative Demographic Analysis of the Frontier Process*. Glendale, Calif.: Arthur H. Clark, 1977.

Davis, Kingsley, "The Migrations of Human Populations," *Scientific American*, 231, no. 3 (September 1974), 95–105.

Demko, George J., and William B. Wood, "International Refugees: A Geographical Perspective," *Journal of Geography*, 86, no. 5 (September–October 1987), 225–28.

Dorigo, Guido, and Waldo Tobler, "Push-Pull Migration Laws," *Annals of the Association of American Geographers*, 73, no. 1 (March 1983), 1–17.

Fisher, James S., and Ronald L. Mitchelson, "Forces of Change in the American Settlement Patterns," *Geographical Review*, 71 (1981), 298–310.

Gjerde, Jon, "The Effect of Community on Migration: Three Minnesota Townships, 1885–1905," *Journal of Historical Geography*, 5, no. 4 (1979), 403–22.

———, *From Peasants to Farmers: The Migration from Bulestrand, Norway, to the Upper Middle West*. Cambridge, England: Cambridge University Press, 1985.

Greven, Philip J., *Four Generations: Population, Land, and Family in Colonial Andover, Massachusetts*. Ithaca, N.Y.: Cornell University Press, 1970.

Grigg, D. B., "E. G. Ravenstein and the 'Laws of Migration,' " *Journal of Historical Geography*, 3 (1977), 41–54.

Hart, John Fraser, "Population Change in the Upper Lake States," *Annals of the Association of American Geographers*, 74, no. 2 (June 1984), 221–43.

Ho, Ping-ti, *Studies on the Population of China, 1368–1953*. Cambridge, Mass.: Harvard University Press, 1959.

Hudson, John C., "Migration to an American Frontier," *Annals of the Association of American Geographers*, 66 (1976), 242–65.

Independent Commission on International Development Issues, *North-South: A Programme for Survival*. London: Pan Books, 1980.

———, *Common Crisis: North-South Cooperation for World Recovery, The Brandt Commission, 1983*. Cambridge, Mass.: M.I.T. Press, 1983.

Jerome, Harry, *Migration and Business Cycles*. New York: National Bureau of Economic Research, 1926.

Kritz, M. M., C. B. Keely, and S. M. Tomasi, eds., *Global Trends in Migration: Theory and Research on International Population Movement*. New York: Center for Migration Studies, 1981.

Jones, Douglas Lamar, *Village and Seaport: Migration and Society in Eighteenth-Century Massachusetts*. Hanover, N.H. and London, England: University Press of New England, 1981.

Laslett, Peter, *Family Life and Illicit Love in Earlier Generations*. Cambridge, England: Cambridge University Press, 1977.

Lattimore, Owen, "Chinese Colonization in Manchuria," *Geographical Review*, 22, No. 2 (April 1932), 177–95.

Lee, Everett S., "Theory of Migration," *Demography*, 3 (1965), 47–57.

LeMay, Michael C., *From Open Door to Dutch Door: An Analysis of U.S. Immigration Policy Since 1820*. New York: Praeger, 1987.

Lewis, G. J., *Human Migration: A Geographical Perspective*. London: Croom Helm, 1982.

Lockridge, Kenneth A., *A New England Town: The First Hundred Years*. New York: W. W. Norton & Co., 1970.

Lowell, Lindsey B., *Scandinavian Exodus: Demographic and Social Development in Nineteenth-Century Rural Communities*. Boulder, Co.: Westview, 1987.

Luebke, Frederick C., ed., *Ethnicity on the Great Plains*. Lincoln, Nebr.: University of Nebraska Press, 1980.

McClure, Peter, "Patterns of Migration in the Late Middle Ages: The Evidence of English Place-Name Surnames," *Economic History Review*, 2nd series, 22 (1979), 167–82.

McHugh, Kevin E., "Black Migration Reversal in the United States," *Geographical Review*, 77, no. 2 (April 1987), 171–82.

McNeill, W. H., and R. S. Adams, eds., *Human Migrations, Patterns and Policies*. Bloomington, Ind.: Indiana University Press, 1978.

Miller, Kerby A., *Emigrants and Exiles: Ireland and the Irish Exodus to North America*. London: Oxford University Press, 1985.

Morrill, Richard L., and Fred O. Donaldson, "Geographical Perspectives on the History of Black America," *Economic Geography*, 48 (1972), 1–23.

Morrison, Peter A., and Judith P. Wheeler, "Rural Renaissance in America?" *Population Reference Bureau*, 31, no. 3 (October 1976).

Murphy, Elaine M., and Patricia Chancellier, "Immigration: Questions and Answers," Washington, D.C.: Population Reference Bureau, Inc., 1982.

Ogden, P. E., *Migration and Geographical Change*. New York: Cambridge University Press, 1984.

Ostergren, Robert, "A Community Transplanted: The Formative Experience of a Swedish Immigrant Community in the Upper Middle West," *Journal of Historical Geography*, 5 (1979), 189–212.

Patten, John, "Patterns of Migration and Movement of Labour to Three Pre-Industrial East Anglian Towns," *Journal of Historical Geography*, 2 (1976), 111–29.

Peach, Ceri, *West Indian Migration to Britain: A Social Geography*. London: Oxford University Press, 1968.

Plane, David A., "Migration Space: Doubly Constrained Gravity Model Mapping of Relative Interstate Separation," *Annals of the Association of American Geographers*, 74, no. 2 (June 1984), 244–56.

Population Reference Bureau Staff, "U.S. Population: Where We Are; Where We're Going," *Population Bulletin*, 37 (June 1982).

Ravenstein, E. G., "The Laws of Migration," *Journal of the Statistical Society*, 48 (1885), 167–227; 52 (1889), 214–305.

Rogers, A., and J. G. Williamson, "Migration, Urbanization, and Third World Development: An Overview," *Economic Development and Cultural Change*, 30 (1982), 463–82.

Rouse, Irving, *Migration in Prehistory*. New Haven: Yale University Press, 1986.

Silag, William, "Citizens and Strangers: Geographic Mobility in the Sioux City Region, 1860–1900," *Great Plains Quarterly*, 2 (1982), 168–83.

Thomas, Brinley, *Migration and Economic Growth: A Study of Great Britain and the Atlantic Economy*, 2nd ed. Cambridge, England: Cambridge University Press, 1973.

Tien, H. Yuan, "China: Demographic Billionaire," *Population Reference Bureau*, 38, no. 2 (April 1983).

Todaro, Michael P., "Urbanization in Developing Nations: Trends, Prospects, and Policies," *Journal of Geography*, 70, no. 5 (September/October 1980), 164–73.

U.S. Bureau of the Census, *Historical Statistics of the United States, Colonial Times to 1957*. Washington, D.C.: U.S. Govt. Printing Office, 1960.

U.S. Bureau of the Census, Release CB 84–179, October 17, 1984.

Ward, David, *Cities and Immigrants: A Geography of Change in Nineteenth-Century America*. New York: Oxford University Press, 1971.

Warren, Robert, and Ellen Percy Kraly, "The Elusive Exodus: Emigration from the United States," Washington, D.C.: Population Reference Bureau, 1985.

White P., and R. Woods, *The Geographical Impact of Migration*. New York and London: Longman, 1980.

White, Stephen E., "Philosophical Dichotomy in Migration Research," *Professional Geographer*, 32, no. 1 (February 1980), 6–13.

Wishart, David J., "Age and Sex Composition of the Population on the Nebraska Frontier, 1860–1880," *Nebraska History*, 54, no. 1 (Spring 1973), 107–19.

Woods, R. I., *Theoretical Population Geography*. New York and London: Longman, 1982.

Zelinsky, Wilbur, "The Hypothesis of the Mobility Transition," *Geographical Review*, 61 (1971), 219–49.

5 CULTURE

In a particular country at a certain time every year, people rush to grocery stores to buy special foods; most businesses and all schools are closed; and many people travel much farther than they do during their normal daily schedules. All of these events and activities happen because the people in this country follow the custom of celebrating an occasion called Thanksgiving Day.

Such festival activities are but one kind of custom affecting spatial behavior. Normal daily activities such as attending school, working in a business, and purchasing food also follow patterns that are governed by general customs. This chapter emphasizes the role of customs and other components of culture as they affect the geographic behavior of groups.

Because culture works as a guiding force behind much of human behavior, it can be argued that cultural geography and human geography are one and the same. In practice, however, cultural geography is a subset of human geography, just as are population geography and political geography. Cultural geography is concerned with the diverse geographic expressions of culture (such as the distribution of traits like religion and language), the imprint of material culture on the landscape (as in house types or field patterns), and the ways different cultures use, and interact with, the earth (Wagner and Mikesell 1962).

The roots of cultural geography as a discipline are set in the nineteenth century. German geographers pioneered the study of settlement types, plant and animal dispersals, and the impact of culture on the landscape. In the first years of the twentieth century, the French geographer Paul Vidal de la Blache introduced the concept of *genre de vie*, the way of life (i.e., culture) that directs a people's use of their environment. Jean Brunhes, another Frenchman, continued Vidal de la Blache's work by stressing the impact of human groups on the land, particularly the destructive impact. This theme has independent American roots. As early as 1864, George Perkins Marsh was writing about the effects of deforestation and soil erosion in New England (James and Martin 1981).

Cultural geography was given cohesion and direction in the United States in the 1920s by Carl Sauer at the University of California, Berkeley (Sauer 1925). Sauer was familiar with both the German and French schools of geography. In addition, his view of culture was influenced by the Berkeley anthropologists Alfred Kroeber and Robert Lowie. From the 1920s to the 1970s, Sauer's work represented the cutting edge of American cultural geography. He studied the origins and diffusions of peoples, plants, and animals, denounced the destructive impact of humans on the earth (long before concern with environmental degradation was fashionable), and explored the "personalities" of culture areas such as Mexico and the American Midwest (1941).

Until recently, cultural geography was characterized more by continuity than by change. The emphasis was on material culture, especially those aspects that have a tangible impact on the land. Since the 1960s, however, there have been new directions in cultural geography. The traditional emphases have been retained, but there has been more concern with the inner workings of culture. The goal is to reveal the underlying forces that condition human behavior, especially those affecting human relations with the physical environment (Wagner 1975; Mikesell 1978).

This chapter introduces the geographical study of culture (more detailed studies of language and religion appear in Chapters 6 and 7, respectively). Although much of the specialized information is drawn from anthropology, its application here is geographic, with emphasis on how culture influences human spatial behavior and ways of using the environment. The chapter begins with an examination of the concepts and constituents of culture and proceeds with an analysis of the processes of **cultural evolution**. The focus then shifts to **cultural ecology,** the ways different people with specific cultures evaluate and use the physical environment. Cultural landscapes, the visible expressions of cultures on the surface of the earth, and **culture regions,** places that are made distinctive by their continued association with a particular culture, are also emphasized. Running as a common thread through all these themes is the historical approach, which is essential for an understanding of cultural geography because contemporary patterns are only the latest episode in an ongoing story. The chapter ends with a look at some of the changing geographic characteristics of contemporary culture groups and questions whether cultures are converging.

CONCEPTS AND CONSTITUENTS OF CULTURE

Development of the Concept of Culture

Understanding the concept of culture is not easy because culture is so much a part of human existence. As the anthropologist Leslie White stated (1949): "Science will advance and develop in inverse ratio to the significance of phenomena as determinants of human behavior" (p. 69). By this he meant that the most abstract sciences, those farthest removed from human experience and therefore the easiest to study objectively, were the first to develop. The social sciences and the study of culture came much later.

The origin of the word *culture* gives few clues to its present meaning. In Latin, it meant cultivation. This meaning persists in restricted usage as in agriculture or bee culture (apiculture). In English and the Romance languages the word culture denotes social refinement.

It was not until the nineteenth century that the concept of culture was used to mean a set of attributes of human society that conditions behavior. The influence of cultural factors on human behavior was initially recognized in Germany when culture was used to describe the customs or spirit of a people. The English anthropologist E. B. Tylor first defined the concept of culture. In 1874, Tylor wrote that "culture . . . is that complex whole which includes knowledge, belief, art, law, morals, customs, and any other capabilities and habits acquired by man as a member of society" (Vol. 1, p. 1).

Almost 100 years later, anthropologists Alfred Kroeber and Clyde Kluckhohn sifted through 164 definitions of culture (many of them repetitious, others contradictory) and offered the following statement:

Culture consists of patterns, explicit and implicit, of and for behavior acquired and transmitted by symbols, constituting the distinctive achievement of human groups, including their embodiment in artifacts; the essential core of culture consists of traditional (i.e., historically derived and selected) ideas and especially their attached values; culture systems may, on the one hand, be considered as products of action, on the other, as conditioning elements of further action. [1952, p. 181]

This statement needs to be examined clause by clause if we are to appreciate the nature of culture and its influence on human behavior, including geographic behavior. The "patterns, explicit and implicit, of and for behavior" are a society's ways of life, which are embodied in values, practiced in daily activities, and expressed in laws, art, customs, and institutions. These patterns are "acquired and transmitted by symbols," particularly by language, but also through rituals. The use of symbols is the "distinctive achievement of human groups." This restriction to humans is no longer as clear-cut an issue as when Kroeber and Kluckhohn were writing in 1952 because recent studies have shown that chimpanzees can learn vocabularies of 200 words and can form elementary sentences. The preservation of past experience in the transmittal of knowledge from one generation to the next, however, seems to be a distinguishing mark of human societies.

To continue with the examination of the above quote, the "essential core of culture consists of traditional (i.e., historically derived and selected) ideas and especially their attached values." Culture is a continuum, a form of social heredity persisting and changing (generally slowly) over time. We are born into a cultural context of beliefs and customs, just as we are born into a physical habitat of climate, vegetation, and soils. But it is much easier to leave the physical habitat (by migration) than to reject our cultural inheritance. Individuals can, of course, change their cultural beliefs, through religious conversion, for example. But the power of tradition is strong, and most people follow, often unquestioningly and unknowingly, what they see as the "correct" code for behavior. "Culture systems may, on the one hand, be considered as products of action" because they spring from the collective activity of human beings over time. Individuals are both architects and carriers of culture. But culture survives beyond the life span of individuals and continues, through institutions and traditions, to serve as "conditioning elements of further action."

Components of Culture

Culture can be divided into three components—artifacts, sociofacts, and mentifacts. **Artifacts** are tools and physical expressions of human subsistence, shelter, and production. **Sociofacts** refer to the institutions that bind a society together—political, legal, and educational systems, family structures, and religious organizations (but not religious beliefs). **Mentifacts** are the least tangible aspects of culture. They are the ideological underpinnings of a culture: its world view, beliefs, and values, particularly as expressed in art, literature, religion, and nationalism.

This threefold classification is an aid to understanding the meaning of culture. Of course culture is a complex of innumerable parts, and in this sense the divisions between components tend to be artificial. Artifacts, for example, can be much more than just the physical manifestations of a culture. A house is an artifact because it serves as shelter and has material form. It is also related to sociofacts because its size and form reflect the structure of the family system (Box 5-1 and Figures 5-1 through 5-13). The single family dwelling, the most common house-form of American suburbia, is a response to the prevailing American kinship system, the nuclear family. In contrast, the earth lodges of the nineteenth-century horticultural Indians of the eastern Great Plains were designed to house an extended family of as many as 30 people (Figure 5-14).

Moreover, the style and arrangement of houses have mentifactual qualities in that they express the ideology of a cultural group. The Lakota (Sioux) holy man, Black Elk, said that his people's tepees were "round like the nests of birds" and were always set in a circle because "the Power of the World always works in circles." Black Elk, who believed there was "no power in a square," lamented that he had been forced by the Wasichus (whites) to live in a "square box" (Neihardt 1961, pp. 198–200). Whatever the cultural context, a house is more than shelter; it is a "personal and social testament," an etching of culture into the landscape (Lewis 1975, p. 1).

In the broadest sense, sociofacts function to integrate a society, to keep it in order. For nearly all of prehistory, the kinship system was the sole political and social integrating force. When societies became larger and more complex following the domestication of plants and animals, the kinship system no longer sufficed as a binding force, and more formal institutions evolved. The family in its varying forms is still an important sociofact, but it has been supplemented by legal, educational, economic, and political institutions that work to maintain coherence in a society. As the name suggests, sociofacts are designed to socialize individuals into society.

In some societies, such as the United States, institutions leave room for a wide range of individual behavior. In other societies, institutions may strictly define the patterns of life. For example, in India the caste system—a hierarchical ordering of society according to Hindu principles—traditionally permeated every aspect of life. Until recently, in a typical rural village each caste was a distinctive community with its own occupational and social position and residential area. The higher castes occupied the center of the village and owned much of the land, whereas the lower castes and outcastes lived on the outskirts of the village, used separate wells, and were literally kept in their place. In recent decades the caste system has weakened in many parts of India; but culture changes slowly, and the effects of caste on life remain in voting patterns, the selection of marriage partners, and food practices.

A good case can be made for recognizing mentifacts as the "core" of any culture. Mentifacts—basic ideologies and values—are the most resistant to change, whereas sociofacts change more readily, and artifacts are subject to rapid alteration. As an illustration, many Native American societies quickly adopted Anglo-American material products (i.e., artifacts) such as metal pots, guns, and clothing. American Indian social institutions also were rapidly modified, frequently as a result of population loss caused by war and European diseases. Bands merged for protection and villages amalgamated, but the Indians clung tenaciously to their cherished beliefs and customs. Possibly they realized that if these changed, their culture would be virtually dead. For example, even though the Mandan village Indians of the upper Missouri were reduced from approximately 1600 to 150 persons by the smallpox epidemic of 1837, their culture was still intact in the 1860s. They accomplished this cultural preservation by intensifying their religious ceremonies (Bruner 1961).

Cultural evolution. The successive stages of societies, involving the diversification of cultures as they adapt to particular environments (specific evolution) and the progression of all cultures from hunting and gathering to industrial societies (general evolution).

Cultural ecology. The ways different cultures interact with their environments.

Culture region. An area that is distinguished from other areas on the basis of ethnicity, beliefs, or other aspects of culture (i.e., a type of uniform region).

Artifacts. The material evidence of human subsistence, shelter, and production (see Sociofacts and Mentifacts).

Sociofacts. The institutions, such as family structure and educational system, that bind a society together (see Artifacts and Mentifacts).

Mentifacts. The world view, values, and beliefs, such as those expressed in religion and art, that hold a society together (see Artifacts and Sociofacts).

BOX 5-1. VARIATIONS IN DWELLINGS

If, as Pierce Lewis states (1979, p. 12), the cultural landscape is the "autobiography" of a group of people—a visible expression of their values, ambitions, and failures—then houses are surely the main theme of the story. Houses often reflect the local environment, they suggest historical connections and diffusion, and they express the level of technology of their builders. But, as the architect Amos Rapoport writes (1969, p. 47), "What finally decides the form of a dwelling, and molds

the spaces and their relationships, is the vision that people have of the ideal life." In this sense, houses are microcosms of a culture's view of the world.

Take, for example, the American dwellings shown in the following photographic essay. The oldest house type shown, the Cape Cod Cottage, was patterned, like most early American houses, on English precedents. The lavish use of space, both inside and in lot size, could only occur in a place where land

was cheap and abundant. From its American hearth in New England and eastern Long Island, the Cape Cod house diffused and, in modified forms, is found wherever New Englanders settled across New York State and the Midwest (Figure 5-1).

The more recent dwellings show the American penchant for mobility, pragmatism, and individualism. The ranch-style house (Figure 5-2), so common in American suburbia, is dominated by the garage, just as suburban life revolves around the

Figure 5-1. House Built about 1820 in a Style that Combines Features from the Cape Cod Cottage and New England Classic, Cazenovia, New York. Photo courtesy of Peter Hugill.

Figure 5-2. Basic Ranch-Style House with Attached Garage, A Style Common throughout the United States. Photo courtesy of Sally Stoddard.

automobile. The trailer home (Figure 5-3) is even more explicit evidence of the importance of mobility in American society and represents the United States' unique contribution to house types. In both cases, the flimsy prefabricated structures suggest the triumph of pragmatism (rapid, easy construction) over style. Furthermore, although most Americans prefer the single family dwelling, economics and a social system increasingly populated by singles have combined to promote, as throughout the world, condominiums and apartment buildings as homes (Figure 5-4).

Because of the ease of transporting

Figure 5-3. Mobile Home, A Common Form of Residence in America. Photo courtesy of Sally Stoddard.

Figure 5-4. High-Rise Apartments, A Residential Type Common throughout the World. This one is in Medellin, Colombia. Photo courtesy of Sally Stoddard.

BOX 5-1. (CONTINUED)

construction materials, American homes seldom reflect local environmental conditions; they are differentiated by time rather than by place. But in other more isolated parts of the world, dwellings virtually grow out of the local physical environment. Homes of the Masai cattle herders in southwest Kenya, which are located in fortified villages, are partly constructed with cattle dung (Figure 5-5). In the Solomon Islands of the southwest Pacific, house frames are constructed by tying light poles together with coconut fronds, walls are built from bamboo and thatch, and roofs are made with the leaves of the sago palm (Figure 5-6). On the Orkney Islands, off the north coast of Scotland, houses, for many generations, have been constructed from local flagstone. The horizontal layers of flagstone are exposed on the shoreline, and skilled craftsmen cut the large thin slabs that form the roofs (Figure 5-7). Also for centuries, people in the loess region of China have lived in homes carved into the steep bluffs (Figure 5-8). One advantage of these earth homes is the natural moderation of outside seasonal temperatures.

Today, even in isolated areas, new construction materials are often used along with the more traditional ones. The large multiple-family houses of the Toba Butak in Sumatra (Indonesia) are still built with the traditional saddle-shape roofs, the points symbolizing the horns of a water buffalo. But the roof is now corrugated iron (Figure 5-9). Similarly, corrugated iron is replacing thatch as roofing material

Figure 5-5. Home of Masai Cattle-Herders, Southwest Kenya. Photo courtesy of George Tuck.

Figure 5-6. East Kwaio, Malaita, Solomon Islands. Photo courtesy of Wallace E. Akin.

Figure 5-7. House with Flagstone Roof, Westray, Orkney Islands, United Kingdom. Photo courtesy of Sally Stoddard.

Figure 5-8. Cave Home in the Loess Region of China. Photo courtesy of W. Cecil Steward.

Figure 5-9. Toba Batak House, Sumatra, Indonesia. Photo courtesy of Velma Lentz.

BOX 5-1. (CONTINUED)

on some Gurung houses in Nepal, although sometimes metal sheets are used only for a porch roof (Figure 5-10).

In the United States, house types normally do not tell much about a person's occupation (although they clearly reflect income). But in many parts of the world, the form of the house is a direct response to subsistence demands. Among nomadic people, for example, dwellings must be easily erected and disassembled. The brush hut of the bushman of the Kalahari (Figure 5-11) is built by the women in less than an hour. As a home, the shelter is actually less important than the fire, which is the focus of family life. Another illustration is the yurt of nomadic herders in western China,

Figure 5-10. Homes in Pokhara, Nepal. Photo courtesy of Sally Stoddard.

Figure 5-11. Kalahari, Botswana. Photo courtesy of Robert K. Hitchcock.

which is an ancient and efficient dwelling (Figure 5-12). Constructed of willow poles with felt covering, the yurt collapses in sections when the nomads move to a new pasture. In the winter, a double layer of siding is used, and a central fire makes the yurt a shelter from the icy winds.

The yurt, like most, if not all, homes, is a symbol as well as a shelter. The door, which faces east, protects against the prevailing cold winds and represents the direction of rebirth, the source of the rising sun. The fact that Pawnee earth lodges (Figure 5-13) and Navajo hogans also faced their doors in this direction suggests that the symbolic importance of the house transcends individual culture and hints at universal commonalities.

Figure 5-12. Yurt in Xinjiang Uygar Autonomous Region, China. Photo courtesy of Velma Lentz.

Figure 5-13. Pawnee Lodge, Loup Fork, Nebraska, 1870. Dwellings are part of the artifacts that express the culture of a group on the landscape. Photo by W. H. Jackson, courtesy of Nebraska State Historical Society.

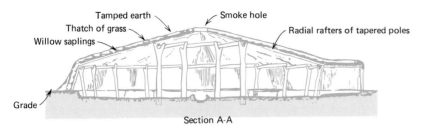

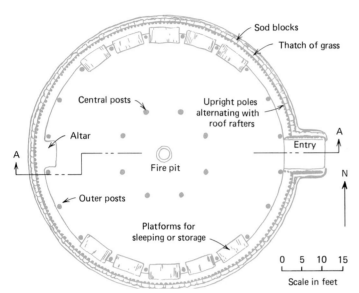

Figure 5-14. Pawnee Earth Lodge. The structure and arrangement of the earth lodge reflect available building materials, the extended family unit, and the Pawnee's view of the world. Reprinted from *The Lost Universe: Pawnee Life and Culture*, by Gene Weltfish, by permission of University of Nebraska Press. Copyright © 1965.

A COMPARISON OF TWO WORLD VIEWS

The importance of mentifacts can be illustrated further by comparing the **world views** of contemporary American and traditional Chinese societies. These comparisons consist of broad generalizations that emphasize major cultural differences. The characterizations do not necessarily apply to those ethnic groups in either the United States or China whose roots are in cultures that differ from the dominant one in each country. Furthermore, general tendencies in each society do not adequately describe the attributes of every individual. It is the overall world view of each society that provides the basis for contrasting these two cultures.

The American World View

Wilbur Zelinsky identified four themes that lie at the core of American culture and greatly affect geographic behavior (1973, pp. 63–64). The first theme recognized by Zelinsky is "an intense, almost anarchistic" *individualism* (p. 40), which de-emphasizes obligations to other members of a family or social group. Zelinsky suggested that this characteristic, which contrasts with the role of persons in many other societies, probably springs in part from the American frontier experience. This value finds geographical

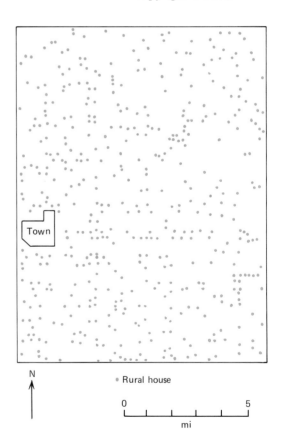

Figure 5-15. Dispersed Farmhouses in Cedar County, Iowa. American preferences for privacy and independence partly explain a rural landscape of dispersed farmsteads.

Figure 5-16. Dispersed Farms in the American Midwest. Photo courtesy of Sally Stoddard.

Figure 5-17. Mobility of a Building. Mobility and change in American society are expressed in many ways. Photo courtesy of Joel Satore.

expression in the primacy of the automobile and the relatively weak development of mass transit systems, in the decentralization of political authority, and in the dispersed nature of rural settlement where houses are located on separate farms, rather than in farm villages (Figures 5-15 and 5-16).

Zelinsky's second theme is the American imperative for *mobility and change* (1973). No other society is so characterized by frequent migrations, restless mobility, and a passion for speed and innovation (Figure 5-17). Zelinsky's third theme is the *mechanistic world vision,* the belief that technology can solve all problems, even the environmental ones that it causes. Finally, there is the theme of *messianic perfectionism,* the assumed superiority of the Ameri-

can way of life and the desire to project it on the rest of the world. For example, the westward movement of population across North America in the nineteenth century was viewed and justified by some as a divine mission to tame the wilderness (see more in Chapters 7 and 8).

In recognizing these four themes, Zelinsky indicated how the world view of a society—the sum of its mentifacts—shapes that society's relationship with the environment and guides its geographical behavior.

World view. The general beliefs held in common by a group which pertain to the universe, the natural environment, and humans.

Of course Zelinsky was generalizing and perhaps overstating some aspects of American life. Many Americans, for example, have a strong commitment to community and, consequently, experience a conflict between the need to nurture community life and the desire to pursue individual goals. In spite of possible overgeneralizations, it is possible to detect differences between the basic ideologies and values of American society and those of some other cultures.

The Chinese World View

For a comparison, consider some characteristics of the traditional Chinese (Han) society. The Chinese culture, or complex of cultures, is the largest in the world in terms of population numbers and is the oldest continuous civilization, extending over 35 centuries from 1500 B.C. Change has occurred, of course, as demonstrated by the establishment of the People's Republic of China in October 1949 and by the increasing openness to Western ideas in the early 1980s. But, as with American society, generalizations can be made about the traditional world view of the Han Chinese.

Many Chinese societal values were based on the philosophy of Confucius (551–479 B.C.). The belief system was not founded on a transcendental god, but was a strict adherence to a way of life. Confucian philosophy stressed a code of conduct designed to create dignity in individuals and harmony in society. Harmony was achieved through recognition and acceptance of the existing social strata, with persons being loyal to their superiors and benevolent to their inferiors. Stratification existed within families and between families. Between families, the educated ruling class stood apart from the farmers and manual laborers and held the power and prestige of political and economic control. Within families, persons were ranked according to sex and age, with males considered superior to females and elders ranked above the younger members. Ranking determined an individual's place in society, and it structured social relations. The eldest male in the family made decisions about the education, marriage, and work of each member, but he also had responsibility for the proper conduct of all members (de Bary 1960; Reischauer and Fairbank 1960).

In contrast to the American tradition, individualism in China was considered selfish and antisocial. It would disrupt the harmony of society and weaken the bonds of the family. Since the family was the most important social unit, any action by an individual that did not promote the goals of the family was regarded as wrong. All behavior was expected to take place harmoniously within a structured family and societal framework. As illustrated by China's current population policies (Chapter 3), individualism is still discouraged.

The traditional Chinese world view was expressed geographically in numerous ways. The emphasis on family and ancestral home created a strong attachment to a place. Succeeding generations of a family often remained in the same farming village and tilled the same fields (Figure 5-18). Expecting future generations of the family to depend on agricultural land, the typical Chinese landowner tried to preserve soil and water resources as much as possible.

The world views of the traditional Han Chinese

Figure 5-18. Chinese Farm Village, Pearl River Delta. Farmers in most of China live in nucleated villages. Photo courtesy of Sally Stoddard.

and contemporary Americans are only two of many cultural types. The wide variety of cultures contributes to the place-to-place differences in human activities and raises many geographic questions. One such question concerns how these differences evolved.

CULTURAL EVOLUTION

The process of cultural evolution involves both the diversification of cultures as they adapt to specific environments and the progression of culture in general through successive stages of development. These two processes are called **specific evolution** and **general evolution,** respectively (Sahlins and Service 1960).

Specific Evolution

Specific evolution is the process of diversification and development of an individual culture as it adapts to its environment, which is composed of the natural environment and other cultures. As a culture ages, it becomes more resistant to change. Internal innovations are less likely to be accepted. This tendency for cultures to become conservative and to resist radical change has been called the "principle of cultural stabilization."

This tendency toward stabilization is understandable at both the individual and group levels. Most individuals follow predictable routines, which are set by cultural traditions and are lived day after day in a fairly habitual manner. At the group level, cultural patterns become so ingrained through customs, ideologies, and institutions that there is an inertia, or built-in resistance to change.

It is important to stress that no culture, even the most isolated one, is entirely static. Change is always occurring to some degree, whether generated internally by invention and innovation, or caused by the infusion of population, products, and ideas from other cultures.

The debate over the relative importance of independent innovations as opposed to the diffusion of inventions and ideas is a continuing one (Chapter 2). Did early centers of agriculture in the Old and New Worlds develop independently as cultures followed parallel evolutionary paths in isolation, or did ideas and tools diffuse from one area to another? It has been suggested that cultural diffusion was less important in the early stages of cultural evolution when societies were often isolated from others than in recent centuries when transportation and communication systems have tied together most parts of the earth.

Internal innovation and cultural diffusion are not exclusive and probably occur in combination to bring about cultural change. The emergence of an "American culture" involved the migration of people and cultural traits from Europe (and to a lesser extent from Africa, Asia, and Latin America) combined with borrowings from the existing American Indians. American culture continued to develop as these groups interacted with each other and with the physical environment and to evolve through cultural exchange with the rest of the world.

A culture, then, is characterized by conservatism on the one hand and by change, often imperceptible change, on the other. There is continuity at the core of any culture, but new elements are constantly being added, while others are being discarded, as the culture reinterprets its physical environment and adjusts to other cultures. Only under great stress—invasion, for example, or maladaptation to the environment—do cultures radically and rapidly change their basic patterns. Cultures may disintegrate altogether, as illustrated by Tasmanian culture, which became virtually extinct by 1840 as a consequence of contact with British settlers.

General Evolution

Unlike specific evolution, which particularizes by referring to individual cultures and their histories, the theory of general evolution tries to explain the stages through which all cultures go. From the perspective of many Western scholars, every culture moves from a "lower" (simpler) to a "higher" (more complex) state of development. Although classifications of these stages vary greatly, most scholars recognize the importance of the Agricultural Revolution and the Industrial Revolution as "acceleration periods" in cultural evolution (Table 5-1).

The mechanisms that move a society from one stage of cultural development to another are diverse and interconnected. Change may be diffused from other cultures, as in the case of the spread of Western technology and ideas through much of the non-Western world in recent decades. Change can also be generated internally, through technological innovations made in an atmosphere of enterprise. Such an atmosphere was created in eighteenth-century Britain on the eve of the Industrial Revolution (Chapter 2).

Cultural change involves a variety of social, po-

Specific evolution. The process of diversification and development of an individual culture as it adapts to its environment (see General evolution).

General evolution. The sequential progression through which all cultures have, or are expected to, develop (see Specific evolution).

TABLE 5-1. Classification of General Evolutionary Development by Various Authors

	White 1959		Beardsley 1956	Bobek 1959	Service 1962	Fried 1967
	Wild food or human energy stage		Free wandering	General food-gathering	Bands	Egalitarian societies
			Restricted wandering	Specialized hunters and gatherers	Bands	
Agricultural Revolution			Central-based wandering	Clan peasantry	Tribes	Rank societies
	Plant and animal domestication stage		Semipermanent sedentary	Feudally or autocratically organized agrarian societies	Chiefdoms	
			Simple nuclear centered		Pre-industrial states	Stratified societies
			Advanced nuclear centered	Early urbanism and rent capitalism		States
Industrial Revolution	Fuel energy stage	Coal	Supra-nuclear integrated	Productive capitalism, industrial society, and modern urbanism	Industrial states	
		Oil and gas				

Source: Modified from Newson 1976.

litical, and economic characteristics (as indicated by the different categories in Table 5-1). A classification of evolutionary development that emphasizes the ecological relationship between humans and the natural environment is that by Leslie White. He interpreted cultural evolution as a process of gaining control over energy resources. He wrote that "culture evolves as the amount of energy harnessed per capita per year increases" (1949, p. 368). This was expressed in the following formula: $E \times T \rightarrow C$, where C is the degree of cultural development, E is the·amount of energy harnessed per capita per year, and T is the quality of the technology employed in the expenditure of the energy.

White divided cultural evolution into three stages (Table 5-1). The first, and longest, was the hunting and gathering stage. Hunters and gatherers hardly tapped the energy resources of the earth. Human energy was the main means of production, supplemented by hand tools, fire, and water flow, which was utilized for transportation. Cultural systems of hunting and gathering societies were, and are, limited in technology and organized around the kinship group and the sharing of food.

The second stage commenced with the gradual domestication of plants and animals in various parts of the world with the advent of the Agricultural Revolution after 8000 B.C. (Chapter 2). Domestication radically changed the human use of the earth and marked a quantum leap in the harnessing of energy. Food surpluses became possible, populations grew, cities developed, and the division of labor became more complex as segments of society were freed from food production. Social organization became more formal, specialized, and coercive in order to keep societies integrated.

After a period of rapid development, reaching a peak in Egypt, Mesopotamia, India, and China before

1000 B.C., and continuing through the civilizations of Greece and Rome in Europe, there was a long pause in cultural evolution. The period from the disintegration of the Roman Empire to the eighteenth century saw many important innovations, including, for example, improvements in navigation and in agricultural technology. Compared to what had gone before and what came afterwards, however, this period was seen by White as a plateau in cultural evolution. According to White, stagnation was caused by the rigid social systems that emerged in the wake of the Agricultural Revolution. Societies became stratified into a small ruling class and a large exploited class. The ruling class had no reason to change this situation because their needs were being met, and the exploited classes had little chance to improve their lot; thus individual enterprise was stifled.

After 1500, however, a number of streams of cultural change—social, psychological, scientific, and technological—combined to initiate the Industrial Revolution that occurred in Europe during the eighteenth and nineteenth centuries. White regarded these changes as the beginning of the third stage of cultural evolution, when societies greatly increased their use of fossil fuels.

The fossil fuel stage can be divided into two overlapping periods. The first period, beginning in England in the eighteenth century and affecting Western Europe and the eastern United States in the early nineteenth century, was based on harnessing coal energy and the development of the steam engine. The second period began in the United States in the early twentieth century and continues to the present. Oil and natural gas became the most important sources of energy; the dynamo (for the generation of electricity) and the internal combustion engine became the new power technology.

The consequences of the fossil fuel revolution were similar to those of the Agricultural Revolution, only at a much larger scale and with greater traumatic effects on the environment. Urbanization was stimulated as industrial development occurred and economic activities became more specialized. Specialization created occupational diversity and new forms of social organization.

The Sociobiological Argument

Another perspective on the evolution of cultures is presented by **sociobiologists.** They suggest that human behavior is in part genetically founded and results from the adaptive processes of gene selection. The evolution of genetic characteristics occurred during the first 2 million years of human evolution when people were organized into small bands of hunters and gatherers. In the sociobiologist's view, cultural evolution, which has occurred since the domestication of plants and animals, has only slightly modified the basic social and biological characteristics that were already ingrained during the first 99 percent of human existence. "The genes hold culture on a leash," dictating relatively few pathways that cultural evolution could follow (Wilson 1978, p. 167).

The sociobiologists maintain that, despite the intricate variation devised by cultures over the last 10,000 years, there are underlying commonalities shared by all cultures. Every culture is characterized by some form of social organization, division of labor, education, food taboos, incest taboos, language, marriage customs, religious rituals, and technology, to name only a few of the common traits. For example, it has been suggested that some of the major sports in the world are only modifications of the natural predisposition of men for hunting. Games that involve running, throwing, and working as a team are essentially imitations of men's primary occupation for thousands of generations.

Sociobiologists emphasize similarities among cultures, rather than the differences that geographers and anthropologists have traditionally studied. Their arguments are controversial, but they merit attention as alternatives to the widely held view that human social and geographic behavior is the result of cultural evolution starting with the domestication of plants and animals in the Agricultural Revolution.

Even if, as the sociobiologists argue, all cultures have basically the same genetic foundations, the variations in lifestyles and beliefs that different cultures have developed over the last 10,000 years are vast. Many studies commence with these existing differences in cultures and then focus on the ways they vary geographically. Of primary interest to geographers, anthropologists, and other social scientists is the relationship between humans and the natural environment, which involves cultural ecology.

CULTURAL ECOLOGY

Relationships between Humans and the Natural Environment

The relationships between humans and the natural environment have been interpreted in several ways. One early interpretation saw human action as a response to environmental controls, particularly climate. This theory, **environmental determinism,** was

---

Sociobiologist. A person who studies the genetic basis of social behavior.
Environmental determinism. The belief that variations in human behavior around the world can be explained by differences in the natural environment (see Possibilism and Box 5-2).

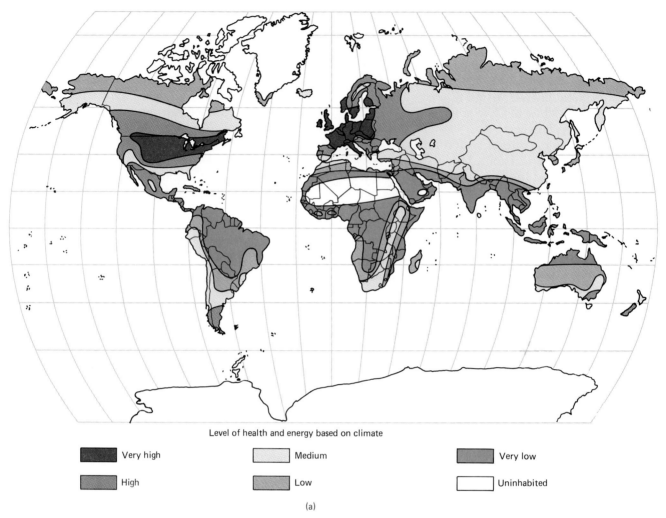

Level of health and energy based on climate

■ Very high   ▨ Medium   ▨ Very low

▨ High   ▨ Low   □ Uninhabited

(a)

Figure 5-19. The Distribution of Civilization, According to Ellsworth Huntington. Huntington, an environmental determinist, categorized the world into various types of health and energy (map a) and by various levels of civilization (map b), which were based on the opinions of 50 experts, 38 of whom were from North America or Europe. From Huntington 1939. Used with permission from Yale University Press.

prevalent in ancient Greece. Aristotle, for example, explained the differences between Northern Europeans and Asians in terms of climatic causes. He argued that the colder climates of Europe produced brave but unintelligent people who were able to maintain their independence but who did not have the capacity to rule others. Aristotle thought that the people inhabiting the warm climates of Asia were intelligent but lacking in spirit and therefore subject to slavery. Because humans often judge their own home as the best place, it is not surprising that Aristotle believed that the middle place, combining the best of all possible worlds, was Greece (Glacken 1967, p. 93).

Environmental explanations, emphasizing climatic controls and human responses, continued in Western thought into the twentieth century. Ellsworth Huntington, a leading American geographer during the first third of the twentieth century, believed that

climate was the fundamental factor in the rise of civilizations (1939). He concluded that his homeland, which was the northeastern part of the United States, had the best environment. He even produced a map, based primarily on the opinions of other North Americans and Europeans, which showed that temperate climates had the highest level of "health and energy" and "civilization" (Figure 5-19). It is obvious that his map is highly subjective and its logic differs little from Aristotle's, except Huntington perceived the world from a different home location.

Environmental determinism is regarded by many people as overly simplistic because it neglects the cultural factors that affect human behavior. Two societies that inhabit areas having similar climates and landforms may be very dissimilar. How could two contrasting societies like the agricultural Hopi and the pastoral Navajo, for example, exist in the same envi-

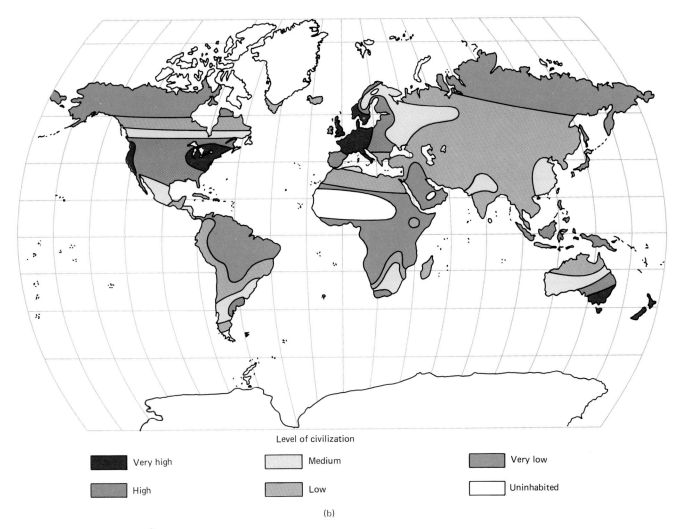

Level of civilization

■	Very high	□	Medium	▨	Very low
▨	High	▨	Low	□	Uninhabited

(b)

Figure 5-19. (continued)

ronment of the southwestern United States if climate dictated the patterns of life?

Reaction to environmental determinism took the form of **possibilism,** the belief that people are not just pawns of the natural environment (Box 5-2). According to this interpretation, the natural environment presents options, the number of which increase as the knowledge and technology of a culture group develop. The emphasis, therefore, was shifted from the natural environment to culture as the dynamic force.

As is often the case when theories are discredited, there was an overreaction. Possibilism tended to exaggerate the role of culture and to neglect the importance of the natural environment. The emphasis of cultural ecology may be seen as an attempt to reestablish a balance between culture and environment as two forces affecting the human use of the earth. This interpretation concerns the way a society utilizes the environment "in culturally prescribed ways" (Steward 1976, p. 37). Culture intervenes between people and the natural environment with values and attitudes that have developed over generations (Figure 1-4). In recent years, cultural ecology has gained strength from the concept of the ecosystem, which views humankind as only one element in an interconnected web of cultural, physical, and biological environments.

The concept of **environmental perception,** the ways a cultural group perceives an environment as a prelude to decision-making and action, has also added a new perspective to cultural ecology. The geographer Harold C. Brookfield has formulated a methodology for the study of cultural ecology based on the concept of environmental perception (1969). According to

---

Possibilism. The belief that the natural environment provides options for human behavior (see Environmental determinism and Box 5-2).

Environmental perception. The way a person or group becomes aware of and comprehends the world (see Perceived environment).

BOX 5-2. ENVIRONMENTAL DETERMINISM AND POSSIBILISM

Determinists believe that most human activity can be explained as a response to the natural environment. Griffith Taylor argued in the 1920s that the limits of agricultural settlement in Australia had been set by factors in the physical environment such as the distribution of rainfall. Taylor's view was most unpopular in Australia at that time, but it has been generally accepted since then. In his 1948 book on Australia, Taylor reaffirmed his basic position:

The best economic program for a country to follow has in large part been determined by Nature, and it is the geographer's duty to interpret this program. Man is able to accelerate, slow, or stop the progress of a country's development. But he should not, if he is wise, depart from directions as indicated by the natural environment. He is like the traffic controller in a large city who alters the *rate* but not the direction of progress. [p. 445]

Other geographers have stressed the range of choices open to humans in any habitat. This point of view was named "possibilism" by Febvre, who wrote:

There are no necessities, but everywhere possibilities; and man as master of these possibilities is the judge of their use. [1925, p. 236]

Brookfield, in order to understand how a cultural group interacts with an environment, it is first necessary to see the land through the eyes of the group. In other words, it is essential to understand the perceptions of the group as well as to know the existing natural conditions. Decisions are not based on the totality of the environment but only on those aspects that are consciously sensed and which then constitute a **perceived environment.** No two cultures evaluate and use an environment in exactly the same way. It has often been said that "natural resources are cultural appraisals," meaning that an element in the natural environment becomes a resource only when recognized as such by the culture group. Oil, for example, was used primarily for medicinal purposes by the American Indians. For people in industrialized economies today, it is an essential source of energy, whereas a century from now it may have only minor importance.

In Brookfield's model, when people arrive in a new area, they assess the environment by filtering it through their own cultural screen and thus create a perceived environment (1969). It is this perceived environment, not the total environment, that first serves as the basis for decision-making. The decisions result in utilizing, through culturally prescribed ways, those parts of the environment that are regarded as resources. With time, the group's perceptions of the environment may change. If there were no significant changes in the actual environment and if people lived in relative isolation from outside contact, a system of cultural ecology would possibly endure for centuries. However, such conditions rarely exist. The environment may undergo changes naturally, as for example through sudden volcanic eruptions or long-term climatic fluctuations. Or the environment is altered by actions of an inhabiting population. Moreover, no culture group is completely isolated from outside

ideas, especially in the twentieth century, so the group may be introduced to, and acquire new attitudes about, resources and other aspects of the environment. Therefore, perceptions of the environment are continually being modified by every culture group (Figure 1-4).

Brookfield applied this model to a study of agriculture and territoriality among the Chimbu, a society that practices intensive sweet-potato farming in the New Guinea Highlands (Figure 5-20). Brookfield, trying to understand the perceived environment of the

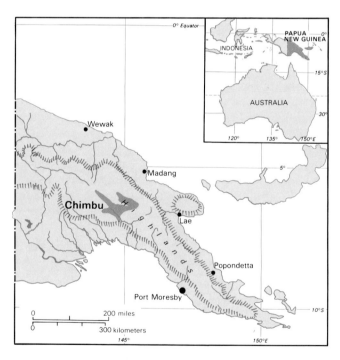

Figure 5-20. The Chimbu Region of Papua New Guinea. The relative isolation of the Chimbu people, who live in a portion of the New Guinea Highlands, provides an excellent opportunity to study several kinds of interactions between humans and the natural environment.

Chimbu people, soon realized that they possessed a well-developed technology for rock, plant, and soil types, as well as an appreciation of local climates. He focused on soil types, believing that the Chimbu use of soils was probably the key to understanding how they valued land. This led him to an initial explanation for the observed patterns of land use.

Later, Brookfield discovered that Chimbu land utilization was not just a simple reflection of soil types. As he candidly admitted, he had previously failed to penetrate some of the hidden dimensions of the environmental perceptions of the Chimbu farmers. He learned that land value was related partly to the closeness of the land to the village, but it was also associated with particular historical events. For example, if the former user of a plot had died from a dreadful disease, then that land became taboo and lost its value. Moreover, Brookfield realized that, even in this relatively isolated society, both the real and perceived environments were constantly changing as the outside world crowded in with new crops, technology, and ideas.

Brookfield's work points out the difficulty in seeing the land through the eyes of other culture groups, but his findings confirm that the effort is worthwhile (1969). The perspectives of cultural ecology can be illustrated further by reference to hunting and gathering societies and to urban-industrial societies, the two extremes of the evolutionary table.

Cultural Ecology of Hunting and Gathering Societies

Many studies of cultural ecology have focused on hunting and gathering societies, partly because the connection between human beings and the natural environment is most direct at this level of subsistence. Everyone in a hunting and gathering group is a food provider and knows the food-yielding capacities of the environment intimately. Furthermore, hunters and gatherers regard themselves as an integral part of nature (Chapter 7). Technology has not intervened, to any great extent, to separate them from the land.

Hunters and gatherers have been depicted as living hard and short lives. Recent research, however, suggests that food obtained by hunting and gathering provides a balanced and adequate diet and that persons who depend on such food often live to a ripe old age. Richard Lee, an anthropologist who lived with the !Kung in the Kalahari during the 1960s, found that 10 percent of the 466 people he surveyed were more than 60 years old (Lee and DeVore 1968, p. 36). This is not so different from the proportion of the aged in contemporary urban-industrial societies. Perhaps the Western bias that equates quality of life with advanced technology and complex socioeconomic organization has obscured the fact that hunting and gathering is a viable ecological system.

Figure 5-21. A !Kung Woman Gathering Tubers. A wide variety of foods can be gathered in desert areas such as in the Kalahari. Photo courtesy of Robert K. Hitchcock.

Like the majority of hunting and gathering peoples, the !Kung derive most of their food from vegetable products (Figure 5-21). Plants are a more dependable source of food than hunting since the occurrence of game is often erratic. Because in the !Kung society the gathering of food from plants is regarded as women's work, women are the main food providers. It is estimated that the !Kung diet provides about 2100 calories a day throughout the year. Famine is rare and much less of a threat to the !Kung than to the Bantu pastoralists (livestock-herders) who occupy the same arid environment. The Bantu economy, being more specialized, is more vulnerable to calamities.

The ratio of labor expenditure to food production in hunting and gathering societies is generally low. Because they have so much leisure time, these people

---

Perceived environment. The portion of the total environment that is consciously sensed and which serves as a basis for decision making (see Environmental perception).

have been called the "original affluent society" (Lee and DeVore 1968, p. 85). In the !Kung society, an adult male spends only about 15 hours a week on subsistence activities, and a woman can collect enough food in one day to feed a family for three days.

Hunting and gathering societies maintain a balance with the environment by spreading subsistence activities over space and by limiting numbers. In the Tehuacan Valley of Mexico, for example, prehistoric bands moved their camps seasonally from the alluvial bottom lands to the mountain slopes and drew on a wide variety of foods so that depletion of their resource base was avoided (Figure 2-10). Similarly, the yearly cycle of the !Kung is characterized by movement, with the distribution of surface water being the key locational factor. The !Kung, like most people, prefer a varied diet, which they achieve by moving from one ecological niche to another (Yellen 1977, pp. 64–84).

Flexibility in spatial patterns is matched by flexibility in social organization; both are mechanisms for adjusting population to food supplies throughout the year. The main social unit in hunting and gathering societies is the band, or group of related families. The size of the band varies according to the time of the year and the nature of the food supply. In the case of the Blackfoot and other nineteenth-century bison hunters on the northern Great Plains, bands amalgamated for the summer hunt, when the bison assembled in huge herds, and divided into smaller family units when the herds fragmented for the winter. The band size of the Shoshoni hunters and gatherers of the Great Basin was small because food sources (mainly seed-bearing grasses) were scattered, so harvesting teams necessarily were small and dispersed.

Hunting and gathering societies traditionally have kept their populations below the carrying capacity of the land (Chapter 2). Abortion, prolonged nursing, sexual abstention, and female infanticide were widely practiced. The !Kung had a population growth of only 0.5 percent a year in the 1960s, which is similar to the rates of more developed nations (Figure 3-6). Richard Lee speculated that the problems of carrying more than one infant during seasonal migrations discouraged the women from raising another child before the previous one could walk (Lee and DeVore 1968). Significantly, as the !Kung have shifted to sedentary agriculture since 1970, their population growth rates have increased dramatically. The increase is related not just to the curtailment of movements but also to a wide range of other cultural changes.

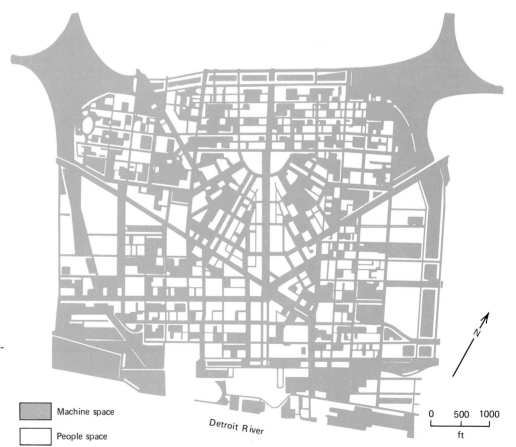

Figure 5-22. Automobile Territory in Detroit. A considerable proportion of valuable space in American cities is devoted to automobiles. From Horvath 1974. Used with permission from American Geographical Society.

Machine space

People space

Detroit River

0   500   1000
ft

Cultural Ecology of Urban-Industrial Societies

Modern urban-industrial societies draw from the entire world for resources, and in turn their environmental impact is global. Whereas it is possible to chart the energy flow in a hunting and gathering band, it would be extremely difficult to estimate accurately the input and output of energy for even a single household in an urban-industrial society.

Despite these difficulties, some generalizations can be made. The Western perception of the environment is characterized generally by feelings of separation from, superiority over, and lack of accountability to nature. For the most part, the natural environment is seen as raw material for human use (see Chapter 7). According to the historian Lynn White, the roots of this **anthropocentric** view that places humans in a dominant position over nature are set in the creation story of Judeo-Christian tradition (1967). The development of technology and urbanization since the Industrial Revolution has reinforced this sense of separation and dominance.

To the extent that modern agricultural environments are created and controlled by humans, they are artificial. In fact, most hybrid crops could not survive without the assistance of humans—they would revert to their genetic predecessors or die out. Agricultural production has generated large food yields, but the system is characterized by high risks. As Roy Rappaport wrote, "In man's quest for higher plant yields he has devised some of the most delicate and unstable ecosystems ever to have appeared on the face of the earth" (1971, p. 130). Disease spreads rapidly through a monoculture. In 1970, for example, a large proportion of the U.S. corn crop was afflicted by corn-leaf blight. In Ceylon (now Sri Lanka) in the mid-nineteenth century, commercial land was in coffee plantations, but a blight ruined most of the trees in the late 1870s. The destruction of this single crop had an immediate effect on the country's economy because the export of coffee had been a major source of earnings.

A major geographical fact concerning urban-industrial societies is that more than two-thirds of their populations live in cities and are engaged in specialized occupations. They obtain their food and many essentials from the activities of others who often live far away. As long as this specialized system functions smoothly, city dwellers are largely insulated from the forces of nature. The occasional snowstorm, for example, is viewed as an intrusion, which only temporarily disrupts the normal operations of the city.

It has become increasingly evident, however, that the concentration of population and technology in limited spaces has drastic repercussions on the quality of the physical and human environments.

Figure 5-23. Vehicles Occupying Urban Space. The importance attached to vehicles by American society is evidenced by the amount of valuable space allotted to them. Photo courtesy of Sally Stoddard.

Technology has become so central to existence in urban-industrial societies that cities are dominated by "machine-space," territories where machines have priority over people (Horvath 1974). Automobile territory, in particular the space devoted to streets, alleys, parking lots, gas stations, business and residential driveways, drive-ins, and garages, consumes large areas of American cities (Figures 5-22 and 5-23). Traffic congestion places a severe friction on movement within modern cities. For example, every workday, 3.4 million people converge on Manhattan in New York City, 1.9 million of them by automobile. Congestion at the bridges and tunnels into Manhattan Island causes delays averaging half an hour each way every day. Emissions from automobiles, along with industrial pollutants, alter

---

Anthropocentric. Interpreting the world from the perspective of human values and experiences.

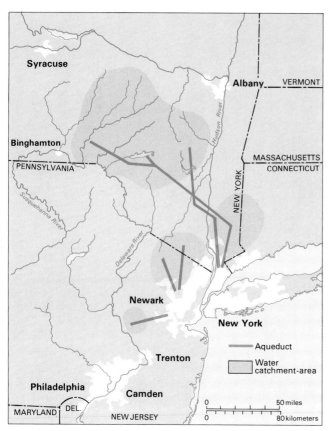

Figure 5-24. Sources of Water for Cities in Northeastern United States. The competition for water supplies in this area is intense.

microclimates, damage vegetation, and can cause respiratory and degenerative diseases.

The urban demand for power and water puts strains on surrounding and distant environments. For example, Philadelphia, New York, and many smaller cities all compete for the water of the Delaware River (Figure 5-24). Decisions made by any one of these cities affect the environment of the Delaware River basin as well as other communities eager to utilize the same water resources. Thus, the decisions made by urban societies have a major effect on the natural environment.

CULTURE REGIONS AND CULTURAL LANDSCAPES

Culture regions and cultural landscapes are sometimes considered separately, but the two are very closely linked. A culture region is a portion of the earth's surface that has a distinctive character, or stamp, created by its inhabitants, who constitute a particular culture. The area may not necessarily be culturally homogeneous. Whatever diversity of individual life styles may exist, however, is less than the shared characteristics that distinguish that area from others. As is true for most regions, the boundary lines that separate culture regions on maps are less clearly defined in life, where transition zones are generally the rule (Box 5-3).

A cultural landscape—the visible imprint of a culture group on the land, most notably in the form of house types, field patterns, and other settlement features—is one criterion for identifying culture regions. Other less visible criteria include diet, dialect, dress, art forms, religious beliefs, and political behavior. But because the cultural landscape is tangible, as well as reflecting mentifactual values, it provides observable clues to the distribution and nature of a cultural group.

BOX 5-3. UNIFORM AND NODAL REGIONS

Regions are areas that are differentiated from each other on the basis of (1) the phenomena being classified and (2) the internal relationships among places within each region. The objects, events, or attributes being classified may be anything that varies from place to place. For example, if we observed that different architectural styles of barns tended to be grouped in various parts of a country, we could regionalize them by drawing lines on a map to show the area where each style was most common. Likewise, a more conceptually complex phenomenon such as culture can be classified into several types, and the locations where each type is common can be shown as regions.

Regions that are differentiated on the basis of the internal relationships among places are divided into uniform and nodal regions. A **uniform region** is identified by noting the locations of all places possessing a specified characteristic. Thus, a uniform region of barn styles would encompass all the places having barns with a particular architectural style. Likewise, a set of cultural regions are also usually uniform regions.

A **nodal region** identifies and delimits on a map all the places that interact with a focal (or nodal) place. What all the places within a region have in common is their functional relationship with the specified node. The migration field of Lincoln in the fourteenth century (Chapter 4) was a nodal region based on the origins of the people who moved to Lincoln. As another example, the area from which people come to shop in a specified town forms a nodal region (which may also be called a **trade area**).

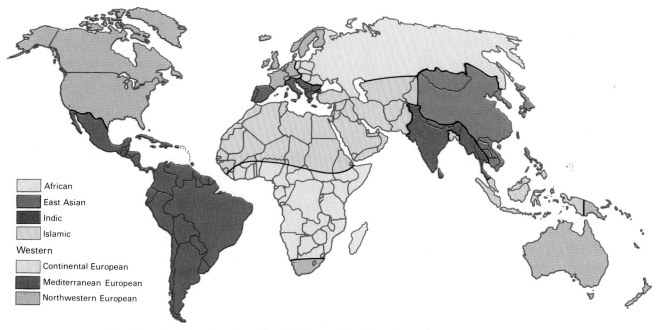

Figure 5-25. World Culture Realms. At a broad scale, five cultural types are shown here; but great cultural variations exist within each of these regions, as illustrated by the three subdivisions of the Western realm.

Legend:
- African
- East Asian
- Indic
- Islamic

Western
- Continental European
- Mediterranean European
- Northwestern European

Culture Regions

Culture regions can be recognized at all scales. At the broadest scale are culture realms (Figure 5-25). According to the very broad regionalization scheme mapped here, there are five major culture realms: the East Asian, Indic, African, Islamic, and Western. Great variation exists within each of the realms. For example, many parts of Latin America where the Indian heritage is strong are not entirely Western. And some areas, such as Southeast Asia, which has been influenced by East Asian, Indic, and Islamic cultures, could be regionalized differently. That area might even be mapped as a sixth region and be called the Southeast Asian culture realm.

The Western, or Occidental, culture realm has a hearth area in Europe and overseas offshoots in the Americas, South Africa, Australia, and New Zealand. This region is recognized as a culture realm because of historical ties, a high dependence on technology, an urbanized population, the dominance of the Christian religion, and common attitudes toward the environment. None of these criteria alone identifies the Western realm; it is a combination of factors that distinguishes that area from the rest of the world.

By subdividing culture realms, greater detail about the geographic diversity of human groups can be revealed. Within the Western realm, for example, the United States and France can be regarded as separate culture regions on the basis of language, history, and world view. Since a similarity in cultural characteristics can define regions at any scale, these national regions can be further subdivided. To illustrate, the United States can be divided into smaller culture regions, one of which may be called the Hispanic borderland (Nostrand 1970). This region, which extends northward from the Mexican border into Texas, New Mexico, Arizona, Colorado, and California, was characterized by Nostrand as the area where many inhabitants are of mixed Spanish-Indian or Mexican descent, speak Spanish as their first language, and are mainly Roman Catholic (Figure 5-26).

At an even more local level, another set of culture regions may be identified. For instance, the Hispanic culture region delimited by Nostrand (1970) can be regarded as consisting of numerous local regions, such as the lower Rio Grande Valley in Texas. Sometimes culture regions at the local scale of generalizations are no larger than various religious communities, such as the Amish and Hutterites living in the Amer-

---

Uniform Region. An area that is differentiated from other areas by the existence of specified characteristics; a classification of earth space based on the distribution of one or more phenomena (see Box 5-3 and Nodal Region).

Nodal Region. An area connected to a common place

(center or node) by lines of communication (see Box 5-3 and Uniform Region).

Trade Area. The region around a city from which buyers and sellers come (i.e., the service area), or the region with which a country exports and imports.

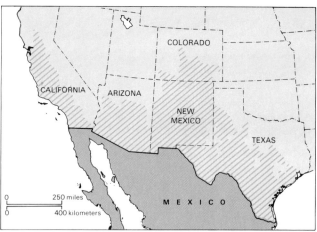

Figure 5-26. Hispanic-American Borderland, 1970. This region, one of several possible subdivisions of American culture regions, is defined on the basis of counties having at least 500 persons and having 5 percent of the population with Spanish surnames. After Nostrand 1970.

ican countryside (Box 5-4), or the ethnic areas of cities (Chapter 11). The distinction between a culture group and an ethnic group is not clear-cut, but in practice, it tends to be one of scale. In the United States, reference to an ethnic group generally implies a smaller entity than a culture group. An ethnic neighborhood might be a small region within a city that is part of a general region identified by its dominant culture group. Irrespective of terminology, we can envisage a hierarchy of regions based on varying levels of shared cultural characteristics. For example, an individual who is part of a Polish community on the northside of Chicago is also a Midwesterner, an American, and a member of the Western culture realm.

Regions may be delineated by a combination of factors, or by the distribution of only one important cultural trait. For example, an American "Bible Belt" was identified by mapping the distribution of adherents to religions that follow a literal interpretation of Biblical scriptures (Heatwole 1978). This region of conservative Protestantism stretches across the South from Virginia to eastern New Mexico (Figure 5-27). Although the Bible Belt was identified by a single criterion, it is only one expression of a cultural outlook that may be characterized by generally conservative attitudes.

It is far more difficult to identify culture regions where many aspects of life combine to give an area a personality. The regionalization of an area by combining several cultural criteria is illustrated by a study of Middle America (Mexico, Central America, and the West Indies) by John Augelli (1962). Although great cultural and physical diversity exists in Middle America, Augelli divided the area into two distinct regions. These are a Mainland, consisting of inland Central America and Mexico, and a Rimland, composed of the

BOX 5-4. THE HUTTERITE CULTURE

The Hutterites are a religiously oriented people who live in approximately 170 rural communities in South Dakota, Montana, North Dakota, Alberta, Manitoba, and Saskatchewan. Their belief system is derived from the Christian Bible, but their ways of daily living differ sharply from most other Christian groups today. Each group of Hutterite families lives in a colony (*Bruderhof*) on a large communally owned farm. The position of the living quarters on the land and the self-sufficiency of Hutterite social life tend to isolate the colonies from the rest of North American society.

Specific types of production vary among the colonies, but all stress modern methods of large-scale agriculture. Economic innovations and adaptations to the changing economies of the United States and Canada through time have produced many financial similarities with other large agricultural enterprises. Marketing of products necessarily involves interaction with non-Hutterites, but these transactions are strictly business.

Socially, however, Hutterite society exhibits a remarkable stability and internal strength. Social relationships are believed to be divinely prescribed, and hence they remain nearly constant through time and differ in many ways from the dominant culture of North America. Child-rearing and socialization practices are very successful in preparing individuals for communal life. Individuals are taught to be obedient, submissive, and dependent on support from other members of the colony. The religious ideology and social structure clearly define the role of each individual within the aspired "colony of heaven."

Two anthropologists, Hostetler and Huntington, summarized the Hutterite culture as follows:

> They do not have illusory ideas that their colony is perfect, but they have acquired some utopian-like characteristics in their social patterns: economy of human effort, elimination of extremely poor or wealthy members, a system of distribution that minimizes privileged position, motivation without the incentive of private gain, and a high degree of security for the individual. All of these characteristics are contained in a communal society without the use of a police force and with an ideology that reasonably satisfies both spiritual and material needs. [1980, p. 1]

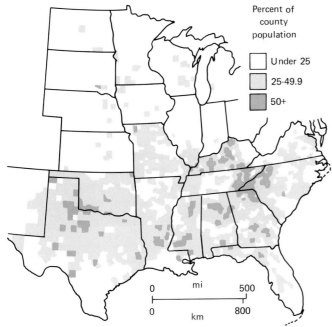

Percent of
county
population

☐ Under 25

▨ 25-49.9

▧ 50+

Figure 5-27. The American Bible Belt. This region is defined by those counties in which more than 25 percent of the population is affiliated with one of the denominations that follows a literal interpretation of the Bible. From Heatwole 1978. Used with permission from National Council for Geographic Education.

Caribbean islands and the Gulf coast of Central America (Figure 5-28).

The population of the area Augelli (1962) defined as the Rimland is largely African in origin, the indigenous (native) population having been devastated by the Spanish, British, French, and Dutch invaders and immigrants. Africans were then imported as slaves to work on the sugar plantations during the sixteenth, seventeenth, eighteenth, and nineteenth centuries. Many aspects of African culture are still a part of land and life in the Rimland: methods of farming; crops such as millets, yams, and okra; systems of land tenure; modes of house construction; and art and

music forms. Moreover, the connection between the Rimland and Africa continues today. For example, the Rhastafari religion, which is particularly strong in Jamaica, seeks to revitalize the African heritage that was suppressed for centuries. The adoption of the late Haile Selassie (once emperor of Ethiopia) as the spiritual leader of the religion emphasizes this connection with Africa.

The Mainland region, in contrast, retains many cultural traits from pre-Columbian Indian cultures and Spanish influences (Augelli 1962). The combination of indigenous and European sources is expressed through the culture of the mestizo population consisting of persons with mixed European and Indian ancestry.

The Mexican part of the Mainland region may be further divided into smaller regions based on more precise cultural differentiation (Figure 5-29). Carl Sauer recognized two cultural components of the "personality of Mexico" that have persisted from pre-Columbian times to the twentieth century (1941). The Mexican South was one of the early independent cultural hearths of the world; later it was quickly (1520–1531) taken over by the Spaniards. Today the area is chiefly mestizo, but strong Indian elements remain, especially in the mountains of Oaxaca and in the Yucatan Peninsula. In contrast, the Mexican North, or Great Chichimeca, was inhabited by groups of hunters and gatherers before 1500. This semiarid environment became the frontier of New Spain in the sixteenth century. Attracted by silver and by grasslands for cattle raising, the Spaniards pushed northward from central Mexico, eliminating the Indians or forcing them to retreat into the western mountains. The area is now settled mostly by mestizos, although families of Spanish heritage are still in evidence.

Even though blurred by twentieth-century developments, the divide between what Sauer called the Mexican South and the Mexican North still exists. In a recent examination of cultural variations in Mexico, Casagrande (1987) also observed regional differences

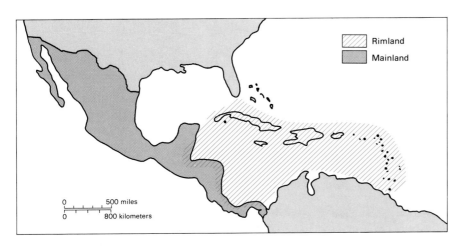

☐ Rimland

▨ Mainland

Figure 5-28. The Mainland and Rimland Culture Regions. According to Augelli, Middle America can be divided into two regions based on cultural characteristics. After Augelli 1962.

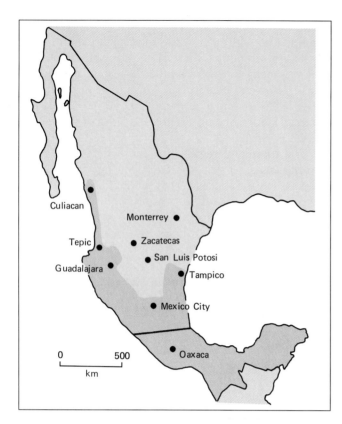

Figure 5-29. Cultural Regions of Mexico. Major cultural divisions of the country are Mexican North or Great Chichimeca, New Spain, and South Mexico. After Sauer 1941 and Casagrande 1987.

between the north and the rest of the country. According to Casagrande, however, the rest of the country should be divided into four regions. He divided Sauer's Mexican South into two major regions (New Spain and South Mexico) and two regions around cities. One of these urban regions is Mexico City and its immediate environs; the other consists of resort enclaves (such as Acapulco, Puerto Escondido, and Cancun).

In the final analysis, a culture region exists not because geographers designate it, but because the inhabitants share a feeling of common identity with a place, as well as with each other. Such a sense of geographic distinctiveness is called **regional consciousness.** In most parts of the world where culture groups have lived in the same area for many centuries, regional consciousness is felt strongly. It may be expressed in a variety of ways, including political affiliations (see Chapter 8).

In the United States, a country with a relatively short history and a mobile population, regional consciousness is less apparent than in many other countries. Nevertheless, people do tend to sense cultural differences between those areas called, for instance, the South, the Midwest, and New England. Joel Garreau, a journalist, believes that regional differences within North America are so great that there are virtually nine different "nations" that "look different, feel different, and sound different from each other"

Figure 5-30. The Midwest, According to Residents. The boundaries of this region were drawn according to the responses of sampled residents living within or adjacent to the delimited area. From Brownell 1960. Used with permission from National Council for Geographic Education.

(Garreau 1981, p. 1). Without going as far as Garreau, other writers have attempted to detect the extent of regional consciousness and to delimit boundaries of American regions.

One geographer, Joseph Brownell, tried to delimit the extent of the Midwest by measuring peoples' feelings of regional identity. He sent a questionnaire to postmasters in communities along several radii extending for hundreds of miles from Chicago, often considered the "capital" of the Midwest. He asked the question: "In your opinion does your community lie in the Midwest?" Brownell discovered that the culture region perceived by its inhabitants to be the Midwest extends over all of Illinois, Wisconsin, Minnesota, Iowa, Missouri, North Dakota, and South Dakota; covers most of Ohio, Indiana, Michigan, Kansas, and Nebraska; and includes small parts of Kentucky, Tennessee, Arkansas, Oklahoma, Texas, and Colorado (Figure 5-30). This is larger than the region most geographers have defined as the Midwest by other criteria because it extends farther westward into the area generally designated as the Great Plains region. The westward position does correspond well, however, with the area perceived to be the Midwest by a recent sample of college students (Shortridge 1985).

In a similar vein, two British geographers (Townsend and Taylor 1975) explored the sense of place and regional identity held by residents in Northeast England. They discovered that a Northeast culture region exists in the minds of its inhabitants because of shared traits and experiences, such as their dialect, support of local soccer teams, and a history of economic problems. These factors have been translated into regional pride. In their discussion of regional consciousness, the authors defined a culture region as:

> one part of a national domain which is geographically and socially sufficiently united to have a true consciousness of its own unity, to feel pride in its own ideals and customs and to possess a sense of distinction from other parts of the country. [Pp. 380–81]

If the area being divided into parts is not restricted to one country, this definition summarizes the nature of culture regions at all scales, from global realms to ethnic neighborhoods.

Cultural Landscapes

A culture region is generally characterized by a distinctive cultural landscape. In other words, a culture group manifests itself on the surface of the earth in building styles, road and field patterns, fence types, and other material forms (Figure 5-31). The landscape is, therefore, a tangible expression and symbol of a culture group. As David Lowenthal and Hugh Prince explain, "Landscapes are founded by landscape tastes. People see their surroundings through preferred and

Figure 5-31. Kashmiri Moslem Shepherd. An informed observer probably could make an accurate guess about this man's home area, religion, and occupation by noticing several cultural clues. Photo courtesy of Sally Stoddard.

accustomed spectacles and tend to make the world over as they see it" (1965, p. 186).

The degree to which people make the world over varies greatly. Temporary shelters of a nomadic group may appear as very insignificant within a vast and sparsely settled grazing land. In contrast, high-rise buildings separated by paved streets and parking lots dominate the landscape of apartment dwellers in large metropolises. In these built environments many natural elements, such as soil and vegetation, may be obscured.

The scarcity of certain natural elements in built environments, however, does not mean a lack of geographic concern about ecological relationships. Geographers, as well as architects and urban planners, are interested in the way people use, perceive, and are

---

Regional consciousness. A feeling held by the inhabitants of an area that "their territory" is distinctive from other places.

affected by built environments. Furthermore, covering the surface of the ground with pavement and buildings has critical effects on natural conditions, such as altering the rate of storm-water runoff and raising air temperature.

Through time, many landscape features are replaced by newer construction as the demands of a society change. The costs of replacement, however, often reduce the extent of rebuilding. City governments will rarely demolish and reconstruct all buildings that line old and narrow streets in order to improve traffic. Likewise, in rural areas, old fences survive even though livestock are no longer being enclosed. Because many features built during previous times persist, cultural landscapes provide evidence of past human activities. The "layers" of features in a landscape are a cumulative record of the historical use of an area by a culture group or a succession of culture groups. So the landscape can be read and its cultural significance discovered. Anyone can detect elements of an area's cultural history because landscapes can be observed and be interpreted as we go about our everyday lives.

Apparently humans have certain landscapes they prefer. Jay Appleton, a British geographer, maintains that our landscape preferences have deeply ingrained origins. He argues that we position ourselves in a landscape in order to "see without being seen" (1975, p. 69). In Appleton's view, this "prospect-refuge" preference goes back to pre-agricultural times, to a period when man was a hunter stalking game. This might partly explain our desire to locate homes on higher ground, so we can "see without being seen." It may be a clue to why new American suburban landscapes often seem so barren to their inhabitants—the

BOX 5-5. A SETTLER'S VIEW OF A LANDSCAPE

Cautiously I slipped from under the buffalo hide, got up on my knees and peered over the side of the wagon. There seemed to be nothing to see; no fences, no creeks or trees, no hills or fields. If there was a road, I could not make it out in the faint starlight. There was nothing but land: not a country at all, but the material out of which countries are made. . . . I had the feeling that the world was left behind, that we had got over the edge of it, and were outside man's jurisdiction. [Willa Cather, *My Antonia*. Boston: Houghton Mifflin, 1918, p. 7]

In this passage from Willa Cather's famous novel about pioneer life on the American Great Plains, a child is expressing a basic concept of human geography: Human groups create cultural landscapes by placing artifacts like fences, fields, roads, and even the trees they plant on the land.

lack of trees gives a sense of exposure, a feeling of nothing to hide behind. It is possible that our landscape preferences are implanted in our childhood years and persist as ideals for the rest of our lives (Box 5-5). Perhaps that early feeling of unity with the environment and of identification with childhood landscapes remain with us as a form of nostalgia.

Every culture group has its symbolic landscapes, those settings that convey special meanings to a people and become part of the national or regional image. Donald Meinig suggested that the United States has three major symbolic landscapes, each represent-

Figure 5-32. A New England Village Landscape. A steepled church is a common element in this type of landscape. Photo courtesy of Robert J. Hall.

Figure 5-33. A Midwest Main-Street Landscape. Businesses related to an agricultural economy are common in the Midwest landscape. Photo courtesy of Sally Stoddard.

ing a type of place: village, town, and suburb (1979). Note that the city is missing from this scheme. This absence is because Meinig believed that Americans are essentially anti-urban in sentiments (although not necessarily in their places of residence).

The symbolic landscape of the village is epitomized by the New England village with white wooden houses and a steepled church set around a central common (Figure 5-32). This "post-card" image, Meinig argues, symbolizes the family-centered, God-fearing, democratic American community (1979).

The symbolic landscape of the town took form in Ohio in the late eighteenth century and spread widely throughout the Midwest and parts of the West. This is "Main Street," a linear business thoroughfare running east-west and lined with buildings having three or four stories, with shops on the ground floor and offices

above (Figure 5-33). Main Street symbolizes the prosperous small town set in agricultural surroundings, a "community of sober, sensible, practical people" (Meinig 1979, p. 167).

Finally, there is the suburb, which has been described as "a failed attempt to flee the city" (Meinig 1979, p. 167). But it is more than that. The suburb developed with the advent of streetcars in the late nineteenth century and expanded with the popularization of automobiles in the twentieth century (see Chapter 11). The process did not begin in southern California, but it reached its fullest development there. As Meinig wrote, "The East built the cars, but California taught us how to live with them" (1979, p. 170). Southern California represents the cultural landscape of the automobile and a way of life based on leisure, individualism, and hedonism (Figure 5-34).

Figure 5-34. A Suburban Landscape: Hollywood from Mt. Olives, 1928. What has evolved as the American suburban landscape was first developed in California. Photo courtesy of Security Pacific National Bank Collection, Los Angeles Public Library.

This life style was projected throughout the United States (and, indeed, much of the world) by Hollywood movies and television, so that it became a standard to strive for. Meinig concluded that "the individual home in the midst of an ample lot, with ready access to a major highway, remains the most prominent element in the landscape of domestic life in America" (p. 184).

Many aspects of American culture, including individualism and mobility, are expressed clearly on the landscape. The "mobile-home" towns of the Southwest and the northern Great Plains, the primary importance of the automobile and its associated drive-ins, and the scarcity of sidewalks in American suburbs all reflect a motorized society. Perhaps more than any other trait, the youthfulness of American culture is written on the landscape (the previous Indian heritage having been largely erased). As Lowenthal put it, this is an unripe landscape that strikes non-American observers as "vast, wild, and empty, formless and unfinished, and subject to violent extremes" (1968, p. 62). Over much of the country, humans seem to have hardly scratched the surface of the land, although this is frequently an illusion because the changes created by human action are often difficult to discern at a glance. Even towns and rural buildings have a temporary feel about them, as if they could be abandoned as quickly as they were established. This is in marked contrast to long-established cultural landscapes like those of Europe and Asia, where layers of history are piled on the land and the detail of ages fills the eye at every view.

It might be expected that, since many European migrants settled in the United States as groups, they would have reproduced the landscapes of their former homelands. Apart from New England, however, few areas experienced sustained attempts to recreate Old World landscapes. The system of land division, acquisition, and hence ownership required living on individual farms rather than clustering in hamlets. A regional or national source for building materials and environmental conditions that were different from those left behind discouraged wholesale transference of "old country" landscapes by ethnic groups. European-style villages laid out irregularly and composed of houses built in folk styles are now more frequently found in recently constructed American resorts than in the long-established areas settled by the early migrants.

Nevertheless, the input of ethnic groups can be read in some landscapes. One example is the imprint of German settlers in the Ozarks. Germans settled in that region in the nineteenth century and have been remarkably persistent. The Ozark landscape has distinctive features that are associated with areas of German homesteading. For example, the Germans frequently established elongated villages (*Strassendorfs*) where farmers lived in houses that abutted the main street and lacked front yards (Figure 5-35). Each village possessed one church, either Lutheran or Catholic, which dominated the settlement architecturally and was a force for social cohesion.

The original German settlers brought with them, as part of the traits of the ethnic group, skills relating to farming and the selection of good farmland. To the present day, "a map showing the distribution of

Figure 5-35. Residence in Westphalia, Missouri. The lack of front yards in this Ozark town provides a clue to its cultural background. Photo courtesy of Russel Gerlach.

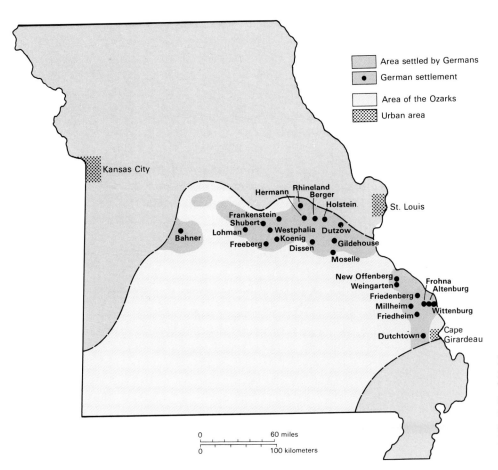

Area settled by Germans

• German settlement

Area of the Ozarks

Urban area

Kansas City

Hermann Rhineland
Berger
Holstein
Frankenstein
Shubert
Lohman • Westphalia Dutzow
Bahner • Koenig Gildehouse
Freeberg • Dissen
Moselle

New Offenberg
Weingarten Frohna
Friedenberg Altenburg
Millheim Wittenburg
Friedheim
Dutchtown Cape
Girardeau

St. Louis

0   60 miles
0   100 kilometers

Figure 5-36. A Region of German Settlement in the Ozarks. The names of towns and numerous landscape features contribute to the distinctiveness of a German culture region in the Missouri Ozarks. After Gerlach 1976.

Germans in the Ozarks can also be a map of the better soils of the region" (Gerlach 1976, p. 107). On farms run by people of German stock, a high percentage of the land is cultivated, especially for grain crops (Figure 5-36). Barns and outbuildings are larger, better maintained, and more numerous than in other areas. Farmers with a German ancestry are more likely to be full-time and to use conservation practices.

Overall, the number of landscape features that were directly transmitted from Germany to the Ozarks is relatively small. The original German settlers, however, had a different perception of the Ozark region than their neighbors. The result was that the German region evolved in a distinctive way. A similar conclusion can be made for many other ethnic groups in various parts of the United States. Usually the early settlers did not reproduce much of their homelands but developed landscape styles in ways that were distinctive from native-born Americans and from other ethnic groups.

An illustration of a distinctive cultural landscape that reflects a religious basis more than a common ethnicity is the region of Mormon culture. Donald Meinig has identified a Mormon culture region with three internal subdivisions based on the evolution of settlement patterns (1965). The inner part, which he called the Core, extends along the eastern edge of the

Great Salt Lake (Figure 5-37). It is the organizational hub, the "capital" of the Church of the Latter-Day Saints, containing 40 percent of the Mormon population of the United States. The second subdivision, the Domain, includes most of Utah and the upper Snake River Valley of Idaho. It is a rural area, with 28 percent of the American Mormon population and some counties that are almost totally Mormon. The Mormon influence is diluted, but remains significant, in the area Meinig called the Sphere and in outlying metropolitan areas, particularly along the Pacific coast.

Another geographer, Richard Francaviglia, used a different approach to define the Mormon culture region (1970). Francaviglia identified several landscape features that are distinctly Mormon. The streets in Mormon towns are wider than is usual elsewhere and often have a dirt or gravel center strip. The roads are generally lined by irrigation ditches, witness to the long Mormon tradition of irrigated farming. Many Mormon settlements are communal, with barns and granaries in the town. Hence the countryside tends to be devoid of buildings, in sharp contrast to the dispersed character of the typical American rural landscape. Farm buildings, whether in town or in the countryside, are often unpainted, as are the fences, which are made from a wide variety of materials. Hay derricks (post and boom structures for loading hay)

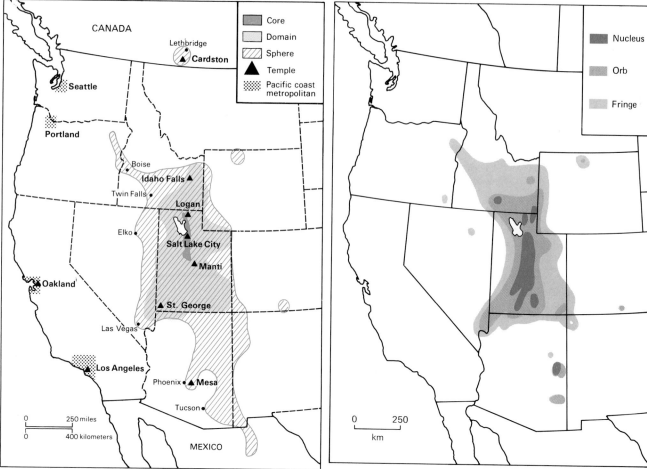

Figure 5-37. A Regionalization of Mormon Culture. This regionalization was based on the evolution of settlement patterns. From Meinig 1965. Used with permission from the Association of American Geographers.

Figure 5-38. A Regionalization of Mormon Landscapes. This regionalization is based on ten observable landscape features. After Francaviglia 1970.

stand in the fields. Mormon towns are characterized by "I-style" homes having one and a half or two stories. The primary building material of brick or stone relates to a religious doctrine: Dwellings in the City of Zion were envisaged as brick and stone. Any doubt that an area is Mormon will be dispelled by the presence of the distinctive brick or stone ward chapel, which stands in the center of Mormon towns.

Using the distributions of these landscape features, Francaviglia mapped a Mormon culture region (1970). Like Meinig, he devised a schema showing a gradation from a central nucleus to a fringe (Figure 5-38). Francaviglia recognized a "visual nucleus" in the agricultural valleys of Utah, parts of Idaho, and the Snowflake area of Arizona where almost all of the specified landscape features were present. Surrounding the nucleus, extending from Utah to Idaho, Nevada, and Arizona, was a "visual orb" where the landscape was predominantly Mormon. Finally, there was the "visual fringe" where Mormon landscape features are intermixed with non-Mormon features. Although there is much correspondence between the

maps of Meinig and Francaviglia, Meinig's Core is only classified as a "visual fringe" by Francaviglia. This is because non-Mormon features in the urbanized area of Ogden, Salt Lake City, and Provo have obliterated many of the traditional Mormon landscapes.

TRENDS IN CULTURAL GROUPINGS

For much of human history, people were born in the same locality as their ancestors, lived their lives within a traditional culture region, and developed a deep attachment to that particular place. The emphasis was on continuity rather than on change, and the relationships between culture groups and specific places endured. This identification with a place makes it relatively easy to construct a map showing regions where members of such cultures existed.

Although traditional culture regions are still the dominant form of cultural groupings in many parts of the world, they are now less meaningful as a way of showing the locations of culture groups. Often the products and values that originated in one culture region may alter the artifacts, sociofacts, and mentifacts of other cultures located in distant places. Also, persons may move from their original home community, yet retain cultural traits through long-distance communication with others in their culture group. For example, foreign students may frequent the periodical sections of university libraries to keep up on the news from home.

In countries with mobile and affluent populations, new forms of cultural groupings can be observed. One form occurs when people are drawn together in particular places to share a common life style. Zelinsky called such a grouping a **voluntary region,** indicating that its existence depends on choice rather than on tradition and accident of birth (1973). For example, people may migrate to certain areas to be with others of a similar age, as in the retirement communities of Florida, Arizona, and southern California. Others seek the atmosphere of areas like Greenwich Village in Manhattan, or university towns like Boulder, Madison, and Berkeley, with life styles that might not be accepted in more conservative parts of the United States. Still others retreat from the pressures of urban life and seek a slower pace in small communities of rural America.

Voluntary regions may resemble those associated with traditional cultures in terms of their internal homogeneity, but they differ in origin (Figure 5-39). They are created when many individuals with kindred personalities, interests, or goals come together in one area by choice—not by birth.

Another new form of cultural grouping is achieved without members necessarily living in close proximity. Devotion to a place is replaced by allegiance to a subgroup. Cohesion comes from sharing political, economic, professional, or recreational interests, beliefs, and viewpoints.

These subgroups can exist, separated in space, because of well-developed communication networks through which members interact. The networks may be maintained through personal modes of communication such as letters, telephone calls, newsletters, underground newspapers, computer networks, and telephone switchboards or "hot lines." The long-distance exchanges may be supplemented periodically by gatherings at some nodal places as illustrated by chess players at meets, political activists at rallies, and railroad buffs at conventions.

This type of cultural grouping fulfills some of the characteristics of a community, even without the element of geographic proximity (Figure 5-39).

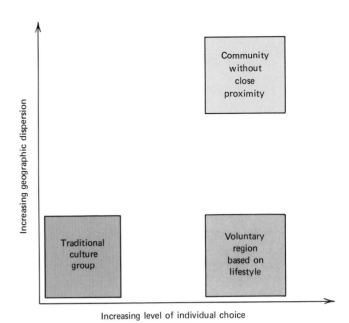

Figure 5-39. Three Types of Cultural Groupings. Cultural groups can be differentiated by the amount of geographic dispersion among members and the level of residential choice by members.

Whereas in traditional societies, cultural unity depends on members being in close proximity, communities maintained by communication networks are formed by persons who, although physically separated, are united by similar views in a world of differing beliefs.

In contrast to these small groups that maintain their distinctiveness through channels of personal communication are large numbers of people that adopt the popularized culture of mass media. A **popular culture** consists of numerous people accepting a set of beliefs and behavior that has been publicized through mass communication. In traditional societies, behavior is shaped by observing and listening to parents and other persons in the community. In most hunting and gathering societies, for example, traditions have been passed on orally from generation to generation, and so the culture has been perpetuated. In popular cultures, on the other hand, behavior is influenced partly by the local environment but also by television, radio, books, records, and other mass media. In the United States, the development of mass communication and mass production has tended to generate a convergence of ideas and ways of life among people with diverse backgrounds. Traditional regional differences still exist, but the same television

---

Voluntary region. A cultural area that is distinctive because people assemble there to be near others having similar preferences.

Popular culture. Those aspects of culture which are widely promoted and maintained through mass media.

programs, interrupted by the same advertising, and consumption of the same mass-marketed foods all seem to produce conformity where diversity once existed.

An illustration of popular culture is rock music. Among many young people, rock is the most influential form of popular culture, affecting hair and clothing styles, self-image, and even politics. As sociologist Simon Frith wrote, "Anglo-American mass music dominates the world more effectively than any other mass medium" (Frith 1981, p. 7).

The roots of rock are deeply set in American folk traditions, particularly in the "blues" music, with its hearth area in the deep South, and in Appalachian country music. Rock-and-roll, which emerged as a form of music for mass consumption in the 1950s, was the outgrowth of interaction between these two traditions. The interaction was made possible by the migration of rural southerners, black and white, to the northern cities. The migrants carried their culture, including musical traditions, to their inner city homes where they blended and merged musical styles into a new urban form: rhythm and blues. The main barrier preventing diffusion to the larger American population was racism because blacks—Chuck Berry, for example—were the main innovators and practitioners of rock music, and they were denied magazine and television space. Widespread diffusion occurred only in the late 1950s when white rockers, mostly southerners like Elvis Presley and Buddy Holly, carried the black music to a larger audience. By that time, radio, international recording companies, rock magazines, and tours made possible the rapid diffusion of rock music to other areas, particularly Europe.

The American dominance of rock music was broken in 1964 when the Beatles spearheaded the first "British invasion." In actuality the British sound was a reinterpretation of American music, particularly black music. The British influence has continued into the 1980s as successive waves of British bands have exerted a major influence on the American music scene and on American popular culture in general.

Although the United States and Britain have been the two most important hearth regions of rock, in recent years many other influences have been incorporated into this cultural form. Since 1972, the year that Bob Marley of Jamaica signed with Island Records, a recording company having a wide distribution, reggae (an indigenous Jamaican music heavily influenced by American black music) has had a growing influence on rock music in the United States and Britain. It has had an important impact, partly as a means of political expression, throughout the Caribbean, Central America, and in many parts of Africa. Today rock music is international. Even in the Soviet Union and Poland, rock bands, once repressed as purveyors of decadent Western ideas, are now allowed considerable freedom of expression. Political barriers to the acceptance of this element of popular culture do exist, as in the case of Iran and other countries adhering to fundamentalist Islam; but there are very few places in the world today where the heroes of rock music are unknown.

The rise and spread of rock music illustrate that, even though mass media can transmit new information over a large area instantaneously, the acceptance of popular culture usually occurs as a type of spatial diffusion. The manner in which elements of a culture spread throughout an area today is similar to ways they diffused in the past—only the rate at which new elements become known has changed with the availability of mass media. In contrast to the rate at which early forms of agriculture diffused during prehistoric time (Chapter 2), the spatial diffusion of ideas and practices today may occur within a short period of time (Box 5-6).

BOX 5-6. THE DIFFUSION OF THE NATIONAL FOOTBALL LEAGUE IN THE UNITED STATES

The distributions of many aspects of culture can be explained partly by the process of diffusion. Diffusion may relate to cultural patterns in traditional societies, and it may help explain the geography of popular cultures. The spread of the National Football League in United States illustrates the diffusion process as it often occurs in modern societies.

In a famous study of spatial diffusion, Hagerstrand (1967) suggested that a successful innovation appears and spreads through three phases. First, the primary phase is when the **innovation** (the adoption of a new idea, technique, or device) originates and receives preliminary acceptance. Second, the main diffusion phase is when the innovation is disseminated from the place of origin. Third, the saturation phase is when there is a slowing down of the diffusion because the innovation has been widely adopted among the available population. If the proportion of adopters is graphed on a time scale,

the three phases appear as an S-shaped (logistics) curve (Figure 5-40). These phases of diffusion can be seen by a historical series of the distribution of the National Football League.

The NFL (originally named the American Professional Football Association) was founded in Canton, Ohio, in July 1919, when representatives of five teams agreed to establish a league. Of the original five teams, four were from Ohio and one from Rochester, New York

(Figure 5-41). The founding of the League represents the primary phase of the diffusion process during which the innovation emerged and was accepted by groups in close proximity to each other.

Shortly after the founding meeting in Canton (now home of the professional football Hall of Fame), the idea of a league diffused to other towns and cities within this same general area. By the time the first season commenced in the fall of 1919, there were 12 teams (Figure 5-42). This expansion illustrates the second phase, when the innovation was rapidly disseminated from the place of origin to surrounding places. Because this form of diffusion results from direct contact between adopters and potential adopters (much like a contagious disease spreads), it is called **contagious diffusion.**

By 1923, there were 19 teams, and the League had spread to many towns and cities south of the Great Lakes (Figure 5-43). The large number of teams within a relatively limited area of the country

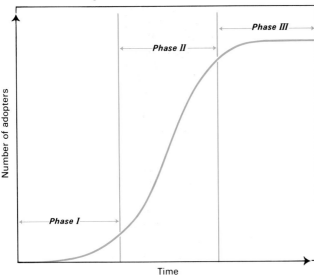

Figure 5-40. The S-Shaped Curve of Diffusion. The relationship between the time since the introduction of an innovation and the number of adopters generally forms an S-shaped (logistics) curve.

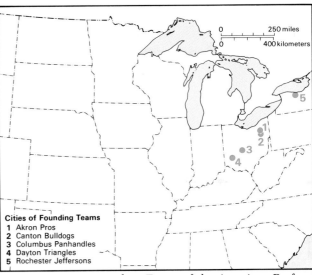

Figure 5-41. Founding Teams of the American Professional Football Association, July 1919. Source: Treat 1972.

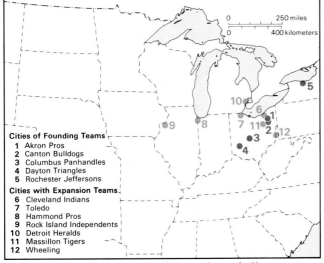

Figure 5-42. American Professional Football Association, Fall 1919.

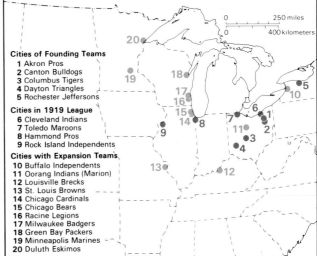

Figure 5-43. National Football League, 1923.

Innovation. The introduction of a new idea, technique, or device.

Contagious diffusion. The type of diffusion that spreads by contact among people who are neighbors or in close proximity (see Diffusion, hierarchical).

BOX 5-6. (CONTINUED)

demonstrates the saturation phase of the diffusion process. Since most potential adopters in a local region had accepted the innovation, the rate of diffusion within that region slowed down.

During the saturation phase, and perhaps because of it, the League spread beyond its region of origin about the Great Lakes and occupied a wider area. This occurred through the process of **hierarchical diffusion,** which refers to diffusion up or down a hierarchy of settlements. Generally, the movement of diffusion is from the originating major cities to other major cities, then down the hierarchy to smaller cities and towns. In hierarchical diffusion, the innovation spreads through channels of communication between places that may be widely separated. The hierarchical diffusion of professional football is evidenced by the addition of several teams in cities far from the Great Lakes region. In 1926, there were 22 teams in the NFL and 9 in the newly formed American Football League (Figure 5-44).

Expansion, however, made the economic success of the league idea vulnerable. With changes in spectator support and in maintenance costs of the teams, a different adoption and retention environment developed. At the end of the 1926 season, the new AFL collapsed and the NFL was reduced to 10 teams. In the retrenchment, most of the teams in the small cities of the original region disappeared, including all the surviving founding members of the NFL (Figure 5-45). Of the earlier teams in small cities, only the Green Bay Packers (founded 1922) survives to the present day.

The emergence of a genuinely national league with teams across the country had to await the 1960s with a large TV audience and easy transportation on jet airliners (Figure 5-46).

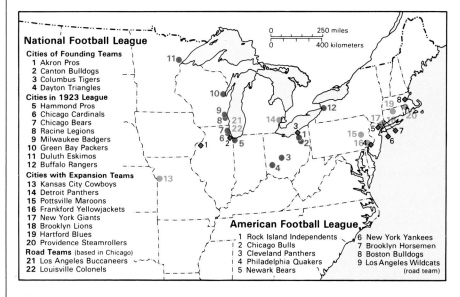

Figure 5-44. National Football League and American Football League, 1926.

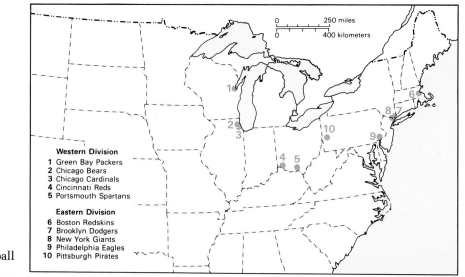

Figure 5-45. National Football League, 1933.

American Conference
1 New England Patriots (Boston)
2 New York Jets
3 Miami Dolphins
4 Buffalo Bills
5 Pittsburgh Steelers
6 Cleveland Browns
7 Cincinnati Bengals
8 Indianapolis Colts
9 Kansas City Chiefs
10 Houston Oilers
11 Denver Broncos
12 San Diego Chargers
13 Los Angeles Raiders
14 Seattle Seahawks

National Conference
1 New York Giants
2 Philadelphia Eagles
3 Washington Redskins
4 Detroit Lions
5 Chicago Bears
6 Green Bay Packers
7 Minnesota Vikings (Minneapolis)
8 Tampa Bay Buccaneers
9 Atlanta Falcons
10 New Orleans Saints
11 Dallas Cowboys
12 Phoenix Cardinals
13 Los Angeles Rams
14 San Francisco 49ers

National Football League, 1988

Figure 5-46. Professional Football Teams, 1988.

THE QUESTION OF CULTURAL CONVERGENCE

For the first 2 million years of human history, cultural uniformity was probably the rule. It is true that early people devised varying methods of adapting to their particular environments as different plants were collected and contrasting species of animals were hunted. In addition, there were differing degrees of specialization. But overall, the differences in hunting and gathering societies were probably less significant than the similarities: lack of permanent leadership and class distinction, integration through the kinship system, low population densities, and rudimentary technology.

With the domestication of plants and animals, cultural diversity became more characteristic of human societies. Gradually knowledge of agriculture spread, giving rise to larger populations and more stratified societies (see Chapter 2). Other societies, however, remained as hunters and gatherers, either because they were isolated from the innovations or because they rejected them. Throughout the world, people continued to make specific adaptions to their environments. As noted earlier in this chapter, the process of specific evolution differentiated people into distinct cultures (Newson 1976). Although there were connections between various parts of the earth, the links were tenuous and ideas spread slowly. The result was **cultural divergence,** the increasing diversity among culture groups.

The relative isolation of cultures changed with the explosive expansion of European societies to overseas areas after 1500. European peoples with their plants, animals, ideas, and technologies spread throughout the world. Missionaries, soldiers, government officials, and teachers sought to replace cultural traits of indigenous peoples with those of Europeans. Their goal often was to **assimilate** the local populations into Western ways of thinking and behaving. In the late nineteenth century, for instance, American Indian children were placed in schools where they were forced to learn English and forbidden to speak their own languages. Europeans generally regarded this spread of Western culture positively, as a "civilizing" process. To an extent, many people agree with this characterization. They note, for example, that the incidence of several diseases in the world was greatly

---

Hierarchical diffusion. The process whereby an idea, technology, or other innovation spreads up or down a hierarchy of settlements (see Diffusion, contagious).
Cultural divergence. The tendency for societies or cultures to become less similar with time (see Cultural convergence).
Assimilation. The process by which nations or communities intermix and become more similar (see Acculturation).

reduced by the introduction of Western medicine and public health. Others, however, describe the spread of European culture in terms of the negative effects of colonization and **imperialism.**

Irrespective of how persons view the effects, Europeans have had a major impact on other cultures. In some places, especially those where colonial governments ruled for several generations, groups within the local population adopted certain European traits. Usually only a small proportion of the population became **acculturated** to the Western ways, but this segment included influential politicians, educators, and professionals. After national independence, elite groups achieved the power to implement policies. The result was a continuation of many Western traits.

In the twentieth century, with the development of rapid global transportation and mass communication systems, the diffusion of European, and particularly American, culture has increased in pace and scope. Most places on the earth now are exposed to American television programs, movies, rock music, and some types of consumption. In 1985, for example, more than 1700 McDonalds outlets were in operation in 30 countries other than the United States, most of them being in Canada, Japan, Australia, and West Germany. In 1987, the largest Kentucky Fried Chicken restaurant in the world opened in Beijing, just outside the gates of the ancient Forbidden City. These "outposts of American culture" affect dining habits, food preferences, and the landscapes of diverse parts of the world. They illustrate the process of **cultural convergence.**

Even though there is considerable evidence of a continuing convergence of cultures, numerous other examples suggest the opposite. The resurgence of Islam in Iran and elsewhere in the late 1970s, for example, has been interpreted as a reaction against Western customs. Emphasis on nationalism and the growth of cultural pride are contributing to political movements that advocate greater regional autonomy in many parts of the world (see more in Chapter 6 on linguistic diversity). Moreover, international communication, which permits the spread of common cultural traits, also aids the forces that perpetuate differences among cultures. Communication networks allow people with unconventional ideas to share a sense of community with like-minded individuals in other areas. In this way, people in widely separated places can become a subculture, united not by proximity, but by common beliefs and behavior. Diversity *between* societies, the norm for most of human history, may be in the process of being replaced by diversity *within* societies.

Are cultures of the world actually converging or not? Answers differ because events and trends display contradictory conclusions. As a student of human geography, you should consider this question and its implications while reading other parts of the text and observing changes in the world.

Imperialism.   The extension of economic, cultural, or political control by a state or power group over other groups of people (see Formal and Informal imperialism).

Acculturation.   The modification of a culture through the adoption of new cultural traits from a society with different traditions (see Assimilation).

Cultural convergence. The tendency for societies or cultures to become more similar with time (see Cultural divergence).

Two Views of the Land

What is the best use of land? Answers to this question usually reflect the cultural perspective of the respondents. This is demonstrated clearly by the contrasting views of the land held by the Native Americans and by encroaching Euro-Americans during the nineteenth century.

The rationale expounded by the Euro-Americans for removing Native Americans from their lands relied on the belief in a "natural law." Believers insisted that a farming society claimed a superior right to the land over a hunting society. On the basis of this premise, the Euro-Americans felt justified in acquiring possession of the land. This action, of course, ignored the fact that many American Indians were actually farmers.

Emmerich de Vattel, a nineteenth-century authority on international law, was particularly influential among American statesmen. His statement illustrates one cultural perspective about the ownership and use of land:

> The whole earth is destined to furnish sustenance for its inhabitants; but it can not do this unless it be cultivated. Every nation is therefore bound by the natural law to cultivate the land which has fallen to its share, and it has no right to extend its boundaries or to obtain help from other Nations except in so far as the land it inhabits can not supply its needs. . . . Those who still pursue this idle [i.e., hunting] mode of life occupy more land than they would have need of under a system of honest labor, and they may not complain if other more industrious Nations, too confined at home, should come and occupy part of their lands. Thus, while the conquest of the civilized Empires of Peru and Mexico was a notorious usurpation, the establishment of various colonies upon the continent of North America might, if done within just limits, has been entirely lawful. The peoples of those vast tracts of land rather roamed over them than inhabited them. [Pearce 1965, pp. 70–71]

John Quincy Adams expressed similar sentiments in 1802:

> The Indian right of possession itself stands, with regard to the greatest part of the country, upon a questionable foundation. Their cultivated fields, their constructed habitations, a space of ample sufficiency for their subsistence, and whatever they had annexed to themselves by personal labor, were undoubtedly by the law of nature theirs. But what is the right of a huntsman to the forest of a thousand miles over which he accidentally ranged in quest of prey? Shall the liberal bounties of Providence to the race of man be monopolized by one of ten thousand for whom they were created? Shall the exuberant bosom of the common mother, amply adequate to the nourishment of millions, be claimed exclusively by a few hundreds of her offspring? [Beal 1963, p. 22]

Those whose ancestors had occupied the land for thousands of years, however, viewed the invasion by foreigners differently. In 1854, Seattle, the Dwamish chief, explained the Indian perspective of the land as follows:

> Every part of this soil is sacred in the estimation of my people. Every hillside, every valley, every plain and grove, has been hallowed by some sad or happy event in days vanished. The very dust upon which you now stand responds more lovingly to their footsteps than to yours, because it is rich with the blood of our ancestors and our bare feet are conscious of the sympathetic touch. Even the little children who lived here and rejoiced here for a brief season will love these somber solitudes and at eventide they greet shadowy returning spirits. [Beal 1963, p. 79]

In addition to being a sacred and cherished part of the group's existence, the Indians believed that the land should not be divided into parcels for the use of only one or a few individuals. From this perspective, land is not a commodity for personal exploitation. This view was stated by Tecumseh, the Shawnee chief, to Governor William Henry Harrison of Indiana Territory in 1810:

> No tribe has the right to sell, even to each other much less to strangers. . . . *Sell a country! Why not sell the air, the great sea, as well as the earth? Did not the Great Spirit make them for the use of his children?* [Armstrong 1971, p. 44]

BIBLIOGRAPHY

Appleton, Jay, *The Experience of Landscape*. New York: John Wiley & Sons, 1975.

Armstrong, Virginia Irving, ed., *I Have Spoken: American History Through the Voices of the Indians*. Chicago: Swallow Press, Inc., 1971.

Augelli, John P., "The Rimland-Mainland Concept of Culture Areas," *Annals of the Association of American Geographers*, 52, no. 2 (June 1962), 119–29.

Beal, Merrill D., *I Will Fight No More Forever," Chief Joseph and the Nez Perce War*. Seattle: University of Washington Press, 1963.

Brookfield, Harold C., "On the Environment as Perceived," *Progress in Geography*, 1 (1969), 51–80.

Brown, Lawrence A., *Innovation Diffusion: A New Perspective*. London: Methuen, 1981.

Brown, Paula, and Harold C. Brookfield, "Chimbu Settlement and Residence: A Study of Patterns, Trends, and Idiosyncracy," *Pacific Viewpoint*, 8, no. 2 (September 1967), 119–51.

Brownell, Joseph W., "The Cultural Midwest," *Journal of Geography*, 49, no. 2 (February 1960), 81–85.

Bruner, Edward M., "Mandan," in Edward H. Spicer, ed., *Perspectives in American Indian Culture Change*, pp. 187–277. Chicago: University of Chicago Press, 1961.

Casagrande, Louis B., "The Five Nations of Mexico," *Focus*, 37, no. 1 (Spring 1987), 2–9.

Coe, Michael D., and Kent V. Flannery, "Microenvironments and Mesoamerican Prehistory," *Science*, 143 (February 1964), 650–54.

Curtis, James R., "McDonald's Abroad: Outposts of American Culture," *Journal of Geography*, 81 (1982), 14–20.

Davis, George A., and O. Fred Donaldson, *Blacks in the United States: A Geographic Perspective*. Boston: Houghton Mifflin, 1975.

de Bary, William T., ed., *Sources of Chinese Tradition*. New York: Columbia University Press, 1960.

Dubos, René, *Man Adapting*. New Haven: Yale University Press, 1965.

Duncan, James S., ed., *Housing and Identity*. London: Croom Helm, 1981.

Febvre, Lucien P. V., *A Geographical Introduction to History*. New York: Alfred A. Knopf, 1925.

Francaviglia, Richard F., "The Mormon Landscape: Definition of an Image in the American West," *Proceedings, Association of American Geographers*, 2 (1970), 59–61.

Frith, Simon, *Sound Effects: Youth, Leisure, and the Politics of Rock*. New York: Pantheon Books, 1981.

Garreau, Joel, *The Nine Nations of North America*. Boston: Houghton Mifflin, 1981.

Gerlach, Russel L., *Immigrants in the Ozarks*. Columbia, Mo.: University of Missouri Press, 1976.

Glacken, Clarence J., *Traces on the Rhodian Shore*. Berkeley, Calif.: University of California Press, 1967.

Hagerstrand, Torsten, *Innovation Diffusion as a Spatial Process*, trans. by Alan Pred. Chicago: University of Chicago Press, 1967.

Heatwole, Charles A., "The Bible Belt: A Problem in Regional Definition," *Journal of Geography*, 77, no. 2 (February 1978), 50–55.

Horvath, Ronald J., "Machine Space," *Geographic Review*, 64, no. 2 (April 1974), 167–88.

Hostetler, John A., and Gertrude Enders Huntington, *The Hutterites in North America*. New York: Holt, Rinehart and Winston, 1980.

Hugill, Peter J., "Houses in Cazenovia: The Effect of Time and Class," *Landscape*, 24, no. 2 (1980), 10–15.

Hugill, Peter J., and D. Bruce Dickson, eds., *The Transfer and Transformation of Ideas and Material Culture*. College Station, Tex.: Texas A&M University Press, 1988.

Huntington, Ellsworth, *Civilization and Climate*. New Haven: Yale University Press, 1939.

Jackson, John Brinkerhoff, *Discovering the Vernacular Landscape*. New Haven: Yale University Press, 1984.

James, Preston E., and Geoffrey J. Martin, *All Possible Worlds: A History of Geographical Ideas*. New York: John Wiley & Sons, 1981.

Kroeber, Alfred L., and Clyde Kluckhohn, "Culture, a Critical Review of Concepts and Definitions," *Papers of the Peabody Museum of American Archaeology and Ethnology*, 47, no. 1 (1952).

Lee, Richard B., and Irven DeVore, eds., *Man the Hunter*. Chicago: Aldine Publishing Co., 1968.

Leighly, John, ed., *Land and Life: A Selection from the Writings of Carl Ortwin Sauer*. Berkeley and Los Angeles: University of California Press, 1967.

Lewis, Oscar, *Village Life in Northern India*. Urbana, Ill.: University of Illinois Press, 1958.

Lewis, Pierce F., "Common Houses, Cultural Spoor," *Landscape*, 19, no. 2 (January 1975), 1–22.

———, "Axioms for Reading the Landscape," in Donald W. Meinig, ed., *The Interpretation of Ordinary Landscapes*, pp. 11–32. New York: Oxford University Press, 1979.

Lowenthal, David, "The American Scene," *Geographical Review*, 58 (1968), 61–88.

Lowenthal, David, and Hugh C. Prince, "English Landscape Tastes," *Geographical Review*, 55, no. 2 (April 1965), 186–222.

Meinig, Donald W., "The Mormon Culture Region: Strategies and Patterns in the Geography of the American West, 1847–1964," *Annals of the Association of American Geographers*, 55, no. 2 (June 1965), 191–220.

———, "Symbolic Landscapes," in Donald W. Meinig, ed., *The Interpretation of Ordinary Landscapes*, pp. 164–94. New York: Oxford University Press, 1979.

Mikesell, Marvin W., "Tradition and Innovation in Cultural Geography," *Annals of the Association of American Geographers*, 68, no. 1 (March 1978), 1–16.

Milgrim, Stanley, "The Experience of Living in Cities," *Science*, 167 (1970), 1461–68.

Neihardt, John G., *Black Elk Speaks*. Lincoln, Nebr.: University of Nebraska Press, 1961.

Newson, Linda, "Cultural Evolution: A Basic Concept for Human and Historical Geography," *Journal of Historical Geography*, 2, no. 3 (1976), 239–55.

Nostrand, Richard, "The Hispanic-American Borderland: Delimitation of an American Culture Region," *Annals of the Association of American Geographers*, 60, no. 4 (December 1970), 638–661.

Pearce, Roy Harvey, *Savagism and Civilization*. Baltimore and London: The Johns Hopkins University Press, 1965.

Rapoport, Amos, *House Form and Culture*. Englewood Cliffs, N.J.: Prentice-Hall, 1969.

Rappaport, Roy A., "The Flow of Energy in an Agricultural Society," *Scientific American*, 225 (September 1971), 117–32.

Reischauer, Edwin O., and John Fairbank, *East Asia: The Great Tradition*. Boston: Houghton Mifflin, 1960.

Sahlins, Marshall D., and Elman R. Service, eds., *Evolution and Culture*. Ann Arbor: University of Michigan Press, 1960.

Sauer, Carl O., "Morphology of Landscape," *University of California Publications in Geography*, 2 (1925), 19–54.

———, "The Personality of Mexico," *Geographical Review*, 31 (July 1941), 353–64.

Shortridge, James R., "The Emergence of 'Middle West' as an American Regional Label," *Annals of the Association of American Geographers*, 74, no. 2 (June 1984), 209–20.

———, "The Vernacular Middle West," *Annals of the Association of American Geographers*, 75, no. 1 (March 1985), 48–57.

Steward, Julian, *Theory of Culture Change*. Urbana, Ill.: University of Illinois Press, 1976.

Stilgoe, John, *Common Landscapes of America, 1580 to 1845*. New Haven: Yale University Press, 1982.

Taylor, Thomas Griffith, *Australia: A Study of Warm Environments and Their Effect on British Settlement*. London: Methuen, 1948.

Tiger, Lionel, and Robin Fox, *The Imperial Animal*. Holt, Rinehart and Winston, 1971.

Tirtha, Ranjit, "Population Problems in India: A Battle with Hydra," *Focus*, 24, no. 9 (May 1974).

Toffler, Alvin, *Future Shock*. New York: Bantam Books, 1971.

———, *The Third Wave*. New York: Morrow, 1980.

Townsend, A. R., and C. C. Taylor, "Regional Culture and Identity in Industrialized Societies: The Case of North-East England," *Regional Studies*, 9 (1975), 379–93.

Treat, Roger, *The Official Encyclopedia of Football*, 10th rev. ed. New York: A. S. Bonds, 1972.

Tuan, Yi-Fu, *Topophilia: A Study of Environmental Perception, Attitudes and Values*. Englewood Cliffs, N.J.: Prentice-Hall, 1974.

———, *Landscapes of Fear*. New York: Pantheon Books, 1981.

Tylor, Edward B., *Primitive Culture*. New York: Henry Holt & Co., 1874.

Wagner, Philip L., "The Themes of Cultural Geography Rethought," *Yearbook of the Association of Pacific Coast Geographers*, 37 (1975), 7–14.

Wagner, Philip L., and Marvin W. Mikesell, eds., *Readings in Cultural Geography*. Chicago: University of Chicago Press, 1962.

Weltfish, Gene, *The Lost Universe*. Lincoln, Nebr.: University of Nebraska Press, 1977.

White, Leslie, *The Science of Culture*. New York: Grove Press, Inc., 1949.

White, Lynn, "The Historical Roots of Our Ecological Crisis," *Science*, 155 (March 1967), 1203–7.

Wilson, Edward O., *On Human Nature*. Cambridge, Mass.: Harvard University Press, 1976.

Wolf, Eric, *Sons of the Shaking Earth*. Chicago: University of Chicago Press, 1959.

Worster, Donald, *Dust Bowl*. New York: Oxford University Press, 1979.

Yellen, John E., *Archaeological Approaches to the Present*. New York: Academic Press, 1977.

Zelinsky, Wilbur, *The Cultural Geography of the United States*. Englewood Cliffs, N.J.: Prentice-Hall, 1973.

6 LANGUAGE AND COMMUNICATION

An essential element in human geography is the communication that binds members of any group together through a network of interaction. Language, either in the written or oral form, is the most common type of communication. As the primary means of transmitting culture from one generation to the next, language is a critical "cultural cement" (Sauer 1944, p. 570). A shared language promotes the transmission of ideas and the functioning of political, economic, and religious systems.

Language is studied by linguists, but the spatial and ecological aspects are studied primarily by geographers. Geographic questions include: Where are the various languages located? How did those spatial distributions develop? How are linguistic variations related to other aspects of human geography such as settlement patterns and national boundaries? And, how do languages reflect human interaction with the physical environment?

DISTRIBUTIONS OF LANGUAGES

Language is so complex and fluid that it is difficult to represent its patterns on a single map. Even detailed maps of word usage and pronunciation cannot adequately portray the various shades of differences and the many ongoing changes. What is often referred to as the "mosaic" of languages, suggesting distinctive units separated by clear boundary lines, is actually a kaleidoscope of shifting boundaries and overlapping regions.

Mapping linguistic variations, as well as analyzing those patterns for their relationships with other aspects of human geography, is difficult. One problem is the lack of a clear definition of what constitutes a language. Other complications are the large number of languages and the continuing changes within them.

Problems of Defining Language

Definitional problems arise partly because the concept of language is almost as complex as the concept of culture. Since the vocalization of an individual constitutes communication only if it is comprehended by other persons, language must be something shared by a group. However, there are innumerable differences in the speech of individual members within a group, no matter how small the group is. The definitional issue is essentially a question about the amount of variation that can exist while still allowing communication to take place. When the linguistic differences between two groups vary in a systematic way but remain mutually intelligible, they are defined as **dialects.** But when speakers of one group cannot be understood by those of another group, the linguistic differences are usually regarded as belonging to two separate languages.

This conceptual differentiation between dialects and languages, however, is not applied consistently when measuring linguistic variations. In the first place, there is no agreement about the percentage or level of "mutually intelligible" meaning that differentiates dialects from languages. Furthermore, other cultural distinctions between groups may affect what is defined as a dialect or a language. For example, although speakers of Serbian and Croatian (as well as Danish and Swedish, or Hindi and Urdu) can be easily comprehended by each other, traditionally it is said they speak distinct languages because religious, national, or other historic factors also separate the groups. Conversely, even though Mandarin, Canto-

---

Dialect. A distinct linguistic form peculiar to a region or social group but which, nevertheless, can be understood by speakers of other forms of the same language.

nese, Hakka, and Wu speakers cannot understand each other, these linguistic differences are considered only dialects of Chinese because the speakers can communicate through the same written symbols.

The problem of defining a language and the lack of comprehensive studies of some small and isolated linguistic communities create uncertainty about the total number of languages in the world. Estimates by linguists range from less than 3000 to nearly 8000 (Fromkin and Rodman 1983, p. 311). Hence, the task of analyzing geographic patterns commences with the disadvantage of an imprecise definition of, and a lack of data about, what is being studied.

Given the large number of languages, it is not surprising that more than one is used in many countries. As a general rule, the greatest linguistic diversity occurs in heterogeneous societies where the extent of most people's communication is restricted to a local area. Often these people are bilingual or multilingual because knowledge of neighboring languages is essential for trade and other social interactions. For example, in Nigeria, which is one-tenth the areal size of the United States, there are about 250 languages. Of the native languages, only Hausa, the main language in the north, is spoken by more than 20 percent of the population. Many of the other languages are limited to a single region or village. In Papua New Guinea, with one-twentieth the size and one-seventieth the population of the United States, approximately 800 languages are spoken.

By contrast, nations that are highly integrated through social, economic, and political systems tend to be characterized by more linguistic uniformity. In Japan and the United States, a single language is spoken by the vast majority of their respective populations. This reflects, as Wagner (1972, p. 13) put it, a "special kind of nationhood" where the people identify with the country as a whole rather than with a region or ethnic group. It needs to be emphasized, however, that linguistic uniformity over extensive areas is the exception in a world where diversity of language is the norm.

Linguistic diversity within a single country is partly a function of its geographic size. Take, for example, the case of India, which is very diverse linguistically, with 15 official languages and more than 150 languages in all, none of them spoken by more than 30 percent of the population. Given the large size of India and its history of political fragmentation, it is not surprising that linguistic diversity is present. Similarly, a large number of languages are spoken in other huge countries like Brazil and the Soviet Union. In contrast, smaller countries are more likely to display linguistic uniformity. The nations of Western Europe, when considered singly, are linguistically homogeneous, with each language prevailing over a relatively small area. (Switzerland and Belgium are the major exceptions to this generalization.) But if Western Europe, which is roughly the same size as India, is considered as a single unit, then it contains as many major languages as India.

Patterns of Major World Languages

Studying linguistic variations can be simplified by concentrating on the largest language groups. Focusing on fewer languages is justified because over 95 percent of the world's population speaks at least one of the most common 100 languages. In fact, nearly half the people on the earth speak at least one of the ten leading languages (see Table 6-1).

The distribution of these ten major languages covers a large part of the earth (Figure 6-1). At least two observations can be made concerning these regional patterns. The first is that the areal sizes of the regions are not consistently proportional to their population sizes. Although Chinese is the first language (or native or **mother tongue**) for more people than any other language, the area where Chinese dominates is much smaller than the combined area making up the English language region. Conversely, although a large area is shown cartographically as the region of the Russian language, the number of native speakers of Russian is smaller than the populations speaking Chinese, English, Spanish, or Hindi.

The second observation is that the regions do not necessarily match national boundaries. Some languages are spoken in more than one country. English, Spanish, or Arabic is the primary language in many countries, and German is dominant in a few countries. The majority of Bengali and Portuguese speakers are in two countries each. At the geographic scale mapped here, Chinese, Russian, or Hindi is the major language in only one country each: China, the Soviet Union, and India, respectively. In each of these three countries, however, other languages are spoken by a large number of people. Of the ten major languages, only

TABLE 6-1. Major Languages of the World

Language	Population size (millions)
Chinese	1015
English	360
Spanish	265
Hindi	230
Russian	210
Arabic	165
Bengali	165
Portuguese	150
Japanese	120
German	100

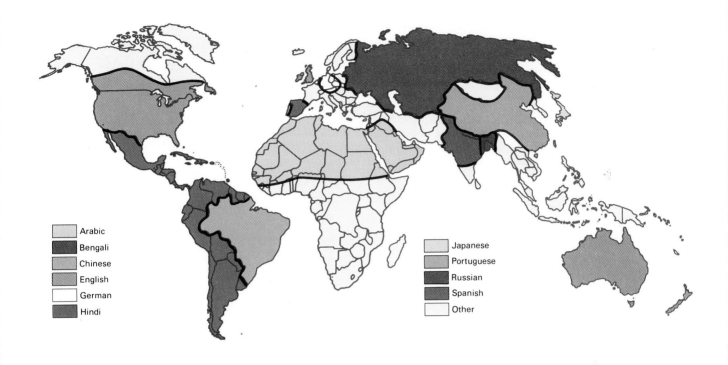

Figure 6-1. The Distribution of the World's Major Languages. Areas without a designated language are either linguistically diverse or the number of speakers of a particular language is less than 100 million.

Japanese is spoken primarily in one country and almost exclusively so.

A map that shows only the major regions where a single language is dominant obscures many details. In the first place, it does not show the people who are fluent in more than their first or native language. For example, English is used as a second language in several areas of the world outside the English linguistic region. The total number of English speakers in India exceeds the total English-speaking population of Australia, and the number of English-speaking people in Nigeria is equal to the English-speaking population of New Zealand. Secondly, most maps showing the entire world cannot clearly depict very small language regions. For instance, Chinese is the major language of many communities in Thailand, Malaysia, Indonesia, Vietnam, Singapore, and the United States. If greater detail is desired, it would be necessary to shift to a different scale of map.

Distribution of Dialects

Mapping and explaining the distributions of specific words, pronunciations, and other linguistic characteristics are the concern of **linguistic geography.** For example, linguists have observed that people in northern Illinois, Indiana, and Ohio use the term *wishbone* to describe a particular chicken bone; but in the southern portions of these states, the term *pully-bone* is commonly used to describe the same bone. The boundary between these linguistic differences can be shown on a map by a line called an **isogloss** (Figure 6-2). Similarly, a linguistic region could be delimited by an isogloss for many other words spoken by the residents of an area.

If the isoglosses for many words nearly coincide, then this bundle of lines displays the boundary of a dialect region. Often a dialect is not a discrete entity having a uniform type of speech, which is separated

---

Mother tongue. A person's native, or first, language.
Linguistic geography. The study of dialects by the mapping of distributions of words, pronunciations, and grammatical characteristics; also called dialectology.

Isogloss. A line on a map showing the areal extent of a linguistic element such as a word, pronunciation, or grammatical characteristic.

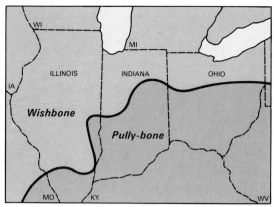

Figure 6-2. Speech Boundaries in the American Midwest, 1940s. The boundary between the areas where *wishbone* and *pully-bone* are commonly used in Illinois, Indiana, and Ohio is shown by the isogloss. After Kuruth 1940.

by a well-defined boundary from other dialect types. Rather, like most linguistic regions, dialect areas take the form of a core having a relatively uniform speech surrounded by transitional zones grading into other dialect areas (Figure 6-3).

In the 1940s, Hans Kurath surveyed the distribution of more than 400 words and expressions and defined three major dialect areas and their regional subdivisions in the eastern United States (Figure 6-4). These dialect areas represented regional patterns of speech that had persisted since Colonial times despite

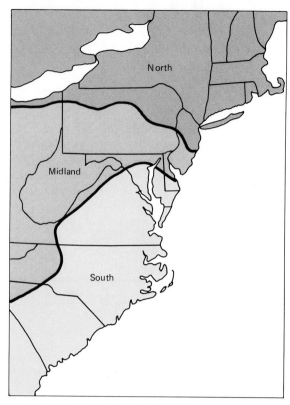

Figure 6-4. Dialect Regions in the Eastern United States, 1940s. On the basis of dialects, the eastern United States has been divided into three linguistic regions. After Kurath 1949.

the blurring of distinctions through population mixing and mass communications. The three major dialect regions—North, Midland, and South—emerged as the early settlers with their distinctive speech patterns radiated out from the original nuclei of settlements around Boston, Philadelphia, and the Chesapeake Bay. The settlers' routes of movement were partly affected by the configurations of topography, streams, and arable land. To a certain degree, therefore, Kurath's distribution map of dialects reflects the ecological relationships of previous periods (1949).

Dialects develop over time as the result of habitual communication among people who form a community, people who in most situations inhabit a specific region. Frequent contact gives rise to similar speech patterns, not only to facilitate communication but also to strengthen the feeling of shared identity. Dialects take hold early in life as an individual's speech is influenced by family and friends. Even if a person learns the nation's standard language, vestiges of the original dialect often remain as a clue to that person's geographic and social origins.

Dialects are most evident when there has been little contact between the community or region and external influences. A frequently cited example is the survival of sixteenth-century Elizabethan speech in

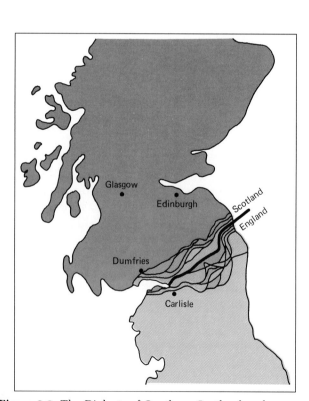

Figure 6-3. The Dialects of Southern Scotland and Northern England. This set of isoglosses displays a zone of transition between dialects. After Speital 1969.

the isolated Appalachian Mountains of the United States long after this speech form had disappeared in England itself. The linguistic effects of mountainous environments that tend to separate groups of people are also illustrated by the diversity of dialects in areas such as in the highlands of Burma and Papua New Guinea.

Dialect contrasts tend to be sharpest in areas where local speech habits have been ingrained over long periods of time. In England, some regional dialects are almost unintelligible to outsiders. Northern dialects may sound like foreign languages to southerners, rather than variations of the same language. These regional dialects are deeply rooted in history and often reflect early ethnic migrations and past political units.

For the most part, regional dialects are less apparent in the United States, where people tend to move frequently and communicate easily over long distances. However, regional dialects do exist in the United States, as in the "Southern drawl" or the "New England twang," but the most dramatic American dialects are related to ethnicity and socio-economic class. The dialects of inner-city blacks, for example, are so distinctive, with their own vocabularies, pronunciations, and sentence structures, that they almost constitute a separate language (Labov 1972).

SOME EXPLANATIONS FOR LINGUISTIC PATTERNS

What are the reasons for the distributions of languages and dialects? First, the geography of a language is a product of the history of its users, including their migrations. Second, languages continually undergo internal changes. Finally, languages, like other aspects of culture, are influenced by external forces that encourage the borrowing of new words from other languages.

Language Change

Languages continually undergo change. The creation of new words for new objects and situations, the introduction of words and phrases from other dialects and languages, and the communal adoption of individual mistakes, distortions, and creative expressions are some of the ways that languages are changed. Linguistic changes are easily seen in English by comparing the King James version of the Bible, Shakespeare's plays, and contemporary writing. Recent changes are observed by noting all the words that are dropped from, added to, or altered by new meanings in each updated edition of a dictionary. Most persons can cite numerous examples of words and grammatical forms that have become archaic or are becoming acceptable.

When the speakers of one community accept linguistic change but do not spread these alterations to other groups from which they are separated, a diversity of dialects emerges. The history of contact and isolation, therefore, is closely related to the development of linguistic groups.

One type of linguistic analysis seeks to trace the development of languages through the common characteristics that are retained. Languages with certain similarities may be grouped together as members of a **language family,** indicating a descent from a common stem in the past in much the same way that a family tree is constructed by tracing the present associations among relatives back to a shared ancestry. Considered in this way, the languages of today are grouped into about 70 language families. Over time, population migrations spread the parent language of each family. With this geographic dispersion came breaks in communication and the gradual development of variations in the original language until new dialects, and finally new subfamilies of languages, emerged. The process of diversification continued, and subfamilies branched out into individual languages that today are related historically but are mutually unintelligible.

The genetic development of languages can be illustrated by reference to the Indo-European family, the most extensive of all linguistic families (Figure 6-5). The various tongues of the Indo-European family (including some of the Indian languages such as Hindi and Bengali and all European languages except for Basque, Finnish, and Hungarian) are spoken by about half of the world's population. The common ancestry of these diverse languages is indicated by the many existing similarities in vocabulary and grammatical structure. For example, the word for *mother* in Greek is *mitar;* in Italian, *madre;* in German, *mutter;* in Hindi, *mata;* and in Russian, *mat.*

The original Indo-European language probably was spoken by prehistoric peoples only in the area north of the Black Sea until about 2500 B.C. Subsequently, the language was carried by migrants and conquerors into other parts of Europe, Southwest Asia, and the Indian subcontinent. As the Indo-European language spread, its accepted forms were altered in each new setting, and gradually a series of subfamilies—Indian, Germanic, Iranian, and so on—evolved. The process of diversification was underway.

One of the subfamilies that developed from this Indo-European root was Italic, from which emerged the language of Latin. Beginning, it is believed, as a local dialect in a community on the Tiber River, Latin spread with the Roman conquests of Italy, Gaul

---

Language family. A group of languages that are related because they evolved from a common ancient language.

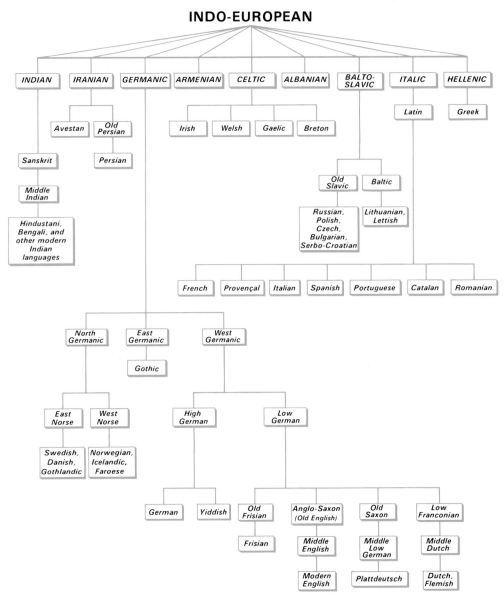

Figure 6-5. The Indo-European Family Tree. Among the major languages of the world (see Table 6-1), English, Spanish, Hindi, Russian, Bengali, Portuguese, and German are members of the Indo-European family.

(France), the Iberian Peninsula (Spain and Portugal), the Balkans, and North Africa. Classical Latin, the standard language, was expressed in the literature of Rome. On the frontiers, however, Roman soldiers, merchants, and settlers used less literary versions of Latin, so from the very beginnings of its diffusion, there were differences between the standard language and the various spoken dialects.

Differentiation increased over time as Latin mixed with pre-Roman tongues. Within a few generations, each Roman province had its own specific pronunciations, vocabulary, and grammatical forms. In general, similarities among the dialects decreased with distance, and widely separated areas had significantly different dialects (Wagner 1972, p. 9). Eventually these divisions led to the emergence of the modern Romance languages: Italian, French, Spanish, Portuguese, and Romanian.

Latin continued to exist as a standard language long after it had been abandoned as the primary form of communication among ordinary people. In particular, the Roman Catholic Church and European universities kept Latin alive, and through the nineteenth century a knowledge of Latin (or Greek) was the mark of an educated person. It is debatable whether or not the European scientific revolution could have taken place without the precision of Latin providing a mode of communication between scientists spread from Poland to Italy. By the twentieth century, however, the use of Latin had declined, even though doctors, lawyers, and scientists continued to utilize selected Latin words.

The descendants of Latin have also been subject to the process of diversification. Spanish, for example, the most widely spoken of the Romance languages, developed from the dialect of the Kingdom of Castile. This Castilian dialect became the form of Spanish that was carried by the conquistadors to Mexico after 1519. The first Castilian grammar was written in 1492 with the express purpose of standardizing Spanish so that it could become the language of an empire. In Mexico during the sixteenth century, this standard form was preserved in the cities by Spanish clergy, administrators, and merchants. In the rural areas, however, remote from the standardizing forces, local variations in vocabulary, pronunciation, and sentence structure developed as Spanish mixed with local languages such as Nahatl and Maya. These geographic variations in Spanish exist today, although regional differences are generally not great enough to make the language unintelligible to speakers from widely separated areas. Yet the process of divergence in separate areas still continues. For example, the migration of Mexicans into the United States has produced a distinctive "Tex-Mex" dialect of Spanish. And the transfer of American English words southward into Mexico has produced such hybrid forms as *jonron* (home run) and *hamburguesa* (hamburger).

Attempts have been made to quantify the rate of change in languages as they separate and evolve independently. This type of study (known as *glottochronology*), is based on two assumptions. One is that the "basic vocabulary" of a language (words for parts of the body, lower numerals, and natural objects such as the sun and the moon) is less subject to change than the other components of vocabulary (i.e., the "cultural vocabulary"). The second assumption is that the rate of loss of basic vocabulary is constant over time. By comparing word lists drawn from the basic vocabulary of different languages, it is possible not only to establish that the languages are related but also to estimate how long they have been separated. The rate of divergence between any two languages established by some glottochronologists is approximately 26 percent per thousand years. That is, if 74 percent of the basic vocabulary is shared by two languages, then the inference is that they have been separated for 1000 years. If the period of separate development is 2000 years, then 55 percent (74 percent of 74 percent) of the basic vocabulary should be the same. According to Eric Wolf, who applied the methods of glottochronology to the history of linguistic growth and change in Middle America (1959, pp. 35–42), the course of language divergence can be measured with a good degree of accuracy as far back in time as 10,000 years ago.

Some linguists doubt the value of glottochronology. They question the criteria used to select basic vocabulary, and the statistical accuracy of the method is also in doubt. In fact, depending on which source is examined, the rate of basic vocabulary retention varies from 74 percent to 81 percent for each 1000 years. The main problem, however, is the assumption that the rate of word loss is constant. There is strong evidence that in this modern era of mass communications and interlocking global economic systems the rates of cultural and linguistic changes differ significantly from those of the past.

Linguistic change is also important to geography because it reflects patterns of social interaction. Human similarities and differences from place to place are affected by the interactions and exchanges between people. If the people in two areas trade and visit with each other frequently, social and linguistic changes in one area will probably diffuse to the other area. Therefore, by studying the kinds of changes in languages and dialects occurring in various parts of the world, geographers can obtain useful clues to other modifications in societies.

Standardization in Languages

Although the forces of change seem to promote linguistic diversity, other conditions act to restrain divergence. One obvious restraint is the fundamental need to communicate. The most effective communication can be achieved when a large number of people share a completely common language. In other words, there is a "centripetal pull" toward including more persons in each linguistic group.

A second factor contributing to linguistic stability is the attempt by governments and other institutions to prescribe a specific dialect as the standard form for a language. In China, an academy of letters (the Hanlin) functioned from A.D. 754 until the nineteenth century as the guide for the correct form of classical Chinese. Both Italy (in 1546) and France (in 1635) established prestigious academies for the purpose of keeping their national languages "pure." Likewise, in the eleventh century, an Iraqi scholar wrote a rulebook (the *Lahn al-Awam*), based entirely on the style, diction, and grammar of the Koran because it was regarded as the approved form for Arabic.

Since a functional language continually changes, attempts to "freeze" usage generally fail to accomplish the goal of maintaining a single linguistic form. For example, Sanskrit scholars were able to prevent change in this classical language of India, but their success led to its demise as an active language (except as one used primarily for religious purposes). Likewise, standardized Latin has failed to survive as a major language. In France, an academy continues to determine what is official and acceptable in the French language, but this action has not prevented hundreds of dialects from persisting throughout the country. Similarly, although classical Arabic based on the Koran still serves as a common language throughout much of North Africa and Southwest Asia, the form of Arabic spoken in the western portions of the Arabic linguistic region is unintelligible to persons in the eastern parts.

Although most contemporary governments do not attempt to officially prescribe a single "pure" language, often one dialect is commonly recognized as the standard or "correct" one. The standard is usually the dialect spoken in the political and cultural center of the country. It is used by scholars, promoted in schools, and taught to nonnative speakers. Most of us in the United States, for example, have been reminded throughout our educational years about the "proper" ways English should be used.

A third factor contributing to the spread of some languages and dialects is mass communication. In recent decades, high rates of literacy and the popularity of public media, especially radio and television, have increased the sizes of interacting communities. The technology that allows people in widely separated locations to communicate and interact with each other makes it possible for large populations to share many characteristics, including linguistic ones.

Contrasting Trends Affecting Linguistic Regions

Linguistic patterns result from the combination of **centrifugal forces** that lead to diversity and **centripetal forces** that tend to encourage convergence. These contrasting forces and influences may produce more complex or simpler patterns, depending on various conditions.

One condition producing apparently contradictory trends concerns the development of pidgin and creole languages. When people of different linguistic groups attempt to communicate, they may create a new language, called **pidgin,** which includes some vocabulary from each of the original languages and the basic structure of one of them. The development of a pidgin language seems to demonstrate the convergence of language forms. If, however, the new language persists and becomes the first language of succeeding generations, it is called a **creole language.** The emergence of a creole language, therefore, produces yet another language (except under rare circumstances when a local language is entirely replaced) and adds to linguistic diversity.

Another situation that can be variously interpreted involves the adoption of a **lingua franca** (Box 6-1). Using a lingua franca, which is a second language spoken by two or more groups whose first languages are different, illustrates both converging and diverging trends. From one perspective, the use of English as a second language by people in many parts of the world demonstrates a trend toward larger groups that can communicate through a common language (Figure 6-6).

From another perspective, as the number of

BOX 6-1. LINGUA FRANCA

Lingua franca literally means "Frankish tongue" and originally referred to a language derived from Italian, French, Spanish, Greek, and Arabic, which served as a means of communication among travellers and traders in the eastern Mediterranean. In this region of great cultural diversity, the lingua franca allowed Greeks, Turks, Arabs, Italians, and Frenchmen to conduct business with each other. The existence of lingua franca meant that itinerant traders needed to learn only one additional language rather than five or six.

Today we use the term *lingua franca* to include any language that allows communication between people who speak or write different mother tongues. For example, Latin provided a means of written communication between European scientists from the fifteenth through the eighteenth centuries. Thus both the Pole, Nicolaus Copernicus, who published *On the Revolution of the Celestial Spheres* in 1543, and the Italian Galileo, who authored *Dialogue Concerning the Two Chief World Systems* (1632), wrote in Latin. Likewise, *Geographia Generalis*, which was written by the German geographer Bernard Varenius in 1650, was written in Latin. The Englishman Isaac Newton read it and produced a revised Latin edition in 1672.

Swahili, consisting of a mixture of Arabic and Bantu words, is used widely in East Africa. Similarly, English functions as a lingua franca in several African countries having multiple linguistic groups, and it also serves as a lingua franca for the international business world.

The recent inauguration of a common language in the People's Republic of China illustrates the role of a lingua franca at the national level. Although over 90 percent of the country's population speaks one of the eight major "dialects" of Chinese, these "dialects" are essentially mutually unintelligible (although they do share a common written language). More than 50 different languages are spoken by the various minority groups (i.e., non-Han people) within China. In an attempt to provide a common communication link for all citizens, the government began a program in the 1970s to make Putonghua the national lingua franca. The goal of the program is not to replace existing "dialects" but to promote Putonghua, which standardizes common speech, as the second language throughout the country.

المؤتمر الثامن لعلماء المسلمين

مؤتمر يتكلم باسم الف مليون مسلم في أنحاء العالم

THE EIGHTH CONFERENCE OF ULEMAS
SPEAKING ON BEHALF OF ONE THOUSAND
MILLION OF MUSLIMS ALL OVER THE WORLD

Figure 6-6. A Sign in Arabic and English. Arabic and English are used as second languages for millions of people whose first language is less international. Photo courtesy of George Tuck.

groups speaking English increases, so too does the number of dialects of that language. Certainly the dialects of English as spoken by Americans, Indians, and Nigerians illustrate linguistic diversity.

Development of Specific Language Distributions

The current distributions of specific languages and dialects have developed as the various factors of linguistic change have operated within the context of historic events. As people moved to new places, sometimes the areal extent of their language region was expanded and sometimes new linguistic forms developed.

Some languages were internationalized during the early periods of extended empires. English, French, Spanish, and Portuguese developed as standard languages in their homelands when a particular dialect, or blending of dialects, was elevated to national prominence and became the language of litera-

ture, trade, and government. These languages were diffused throughout the world after 1500 by European conquerors and colonists, often partially displacing indigenous languages. Portuguese and Spanish now dominate Latin America, although Indian languages such as Maya, Quechua, and Guarani survive. Maya is spoken in various forms in southern Mexico, Guatemala, and Belize; Quechua is the language of several million people in Peru, Ecuador, and Bolivia; and Guarani is widely spoken in Paraguay. Similarly, in North America, English, Spanish, and French largely replaced the more than 100 languages that were spoken by the Native Americans. Today, French and English are used in several former colonies, particularly in Africa, where they are frequently the language of government and education (Figure 6-7).

German, the official state language in West and East Germany, Austria, and Luxembourg, and one of the four official languages of Switzerland, is also commonly spoken in parts of eastern France, northern Italy, eastern Belgium, the Soviet Union, and Roma-

---

Centrifugal forces. Factors that destabilize or lead to the breakup of an existing unit such as a language, a religion, or a nation (see Centripetal forces).

Centripetal forces. Factors that cohere and bind an existing unit such as a language, a religion, or a nation (see Centrifugal forces).

Pidgin. A language with simplified grammatical structure that develops from the attempts of people having different languages to communicate.

Creole language. A language that was originally pidgin but which has become the mother tongue for succeeding generations.

Lingua franca. A language used in common as a second language by people who have different first languages (see Box 6-1).

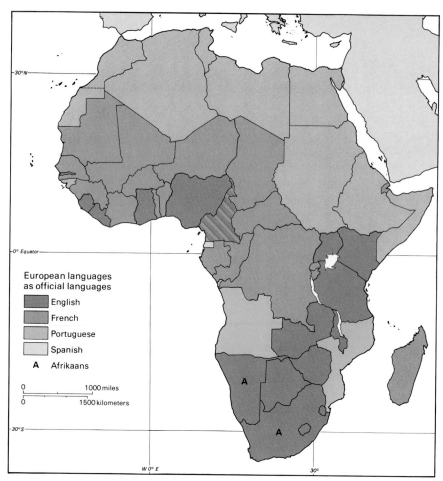

Figure 6-7. African Countries Where an Official Language Is Not the Most Widely Spoken Language. In many countries, French, English, or Portuguese is the one, or shared, official language, even though it is the first language of only a small minority of citizens.

European languages as official languages
- English
- French
- Portuguese
- Spanish
- A Afrikaans

0   1000 miles
0   1500 kilometers

nia. Overseas German-speaking populations, resulting from the migrations of the nineteenth and twentieth centuries, live in the United States, Canada, Argentina, Brazil, and Chile.

The maximum extent of the German language in Europe was attained by 1350, following three centuries of colonization in the Slavic lands of eastern Europe [Figure 6-8 (a) and (b)]. During this period from the tenth to the fourteenth centuries, the western boundary of the linguistic region remained stable, although by 1350 Dutch had emerged as an independent language. The distribution of Germanic peoples and their language remained essentially the same through 1900 [Figure 6-8 (c)]. The German-speaking area diminished in eastern Europe in the aftermath of World War II when millions of Germans were moved westward from what is now Poland [Figure 6-8 (d)]. This was the largest contraction of any European language region in recent history.

The present-day distribution of Arabic likewise traces the extent of a former empire. Confined to the Arabian Peninsula before A.D. 650, Arabic diffused with the Moslem conquests. Within a century, it was spoken from the Indus River in South Asia westward to the Atlantic Ocean. Arabic is now the official language in many countries in Southwest Asia and North Africa (Figure 6-1).

The small regions (too small for the map scale of Figure 6-1) of both Chinese and Hindi that exist outside their core areas result primarily from migrations and not from imperial expansion. Although the ancient empires of China and India, which extended into parts of Southeast Asia, did leave linguistic traces, Chinese and Indian languages were transplanted primarily by more recent migrating workers to several parts of Indochina. Likewise, the Hindi-speaking and Tamil-speaking regions in Surinam, Guyana, and Trinidad began in the second half of the nineteenth century when Indians migrated as indentured workers to fill a labor vacuum on the plantations caused by the emancipation of slaves in those areas.

A study of historical migrations, trade, and political control also aids in explaining linguistic patterns that occur within a country. Because the Soviet Union is a multilinguistic state with 130 recognized languages, it is an interesting case study of the geography of language at a national scale. The current distribution of the Russian language, which is the native language of only 58 percent of the Soviet people, is another illustration of the expansion of a European empire. This linguistic Europeanization was similar to that which carried the English language to North America and the Spanish language to South America after 1500. But whereas the British and Spanish extended their empires overseas, the Russians spread overland from a core around Moscow to cross the vast expanses of Siberia and reach the Pacific Ocean by 1649. During the seventeenth, eighteenth, and nineteenth centuries, the Russian Empire was expanded to the west and south, incorporating Finland and the Baltic States, the Ukraine, the Caucasus, and Central Asia. Over the course of four centuries, the Russian language became dominant over this huge area. During some periods of the Russian Empire, non-Russian ethnic groups were permitted to live their own lives. During other times, the czars tried to force non-Russians into the Russian mold by suppressing their schools and languages. Nevertheless, the ethnic self-consciousness of non-Russians persisted.

When the Soviet state emerged from the Revolution of 1917, the new political order recognized the reality of ethnic diversity by creating separate administrative units for many minority groups. This policy, which continues today, combines a strong centralized government with enough local control to reduce most ethnic demands for autonomy (Clem 1980).

Today the Soviet Union contains a great diversity of non-Russian ethnic groups (see Figure 3-16). The present ethnic and linguistic geography of the Soviet Union consists of a Russian core surrounded by a non-Russian periphery (Figure 6-9). Although the fit is not exact, the language map of the Soviet Union corresponds to the patterns of ethnicity. Each ethnic group (termed *nationality* in the Soviet Union) forms a distinctive speech community. The sizes of these speech communities range from 35 million Ukrainian speakers in the southwest part of the country to fewer than 100 people in northern Siberia who speak Aleut. With some notable exceptions, such as the widely dispersed Jewish population, the non-Russian ethnic people are concentrated in their local administrative units. Since more than 80 percent of the non-Russians marry within their own ethnic group, the geographic

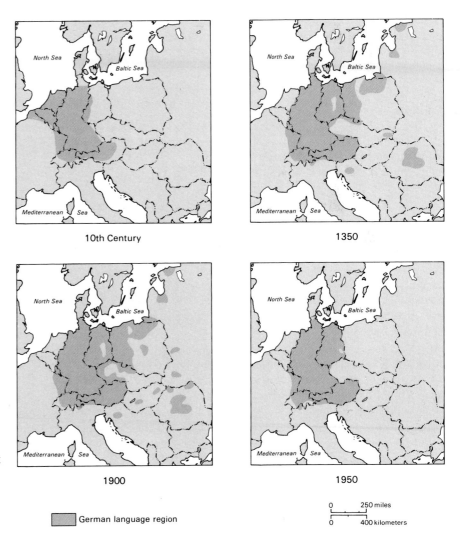

Figure 6-8. The Distribution of the German Language in Central Europe at Four Periods. After the tenth century, the region of German speakers expanded until after World War II, when it was reduced to its current areal extent. After Keller 1978.

10th Century

1350

1900

1950

☐ German language region

0   250 miles
0   400 kilometers

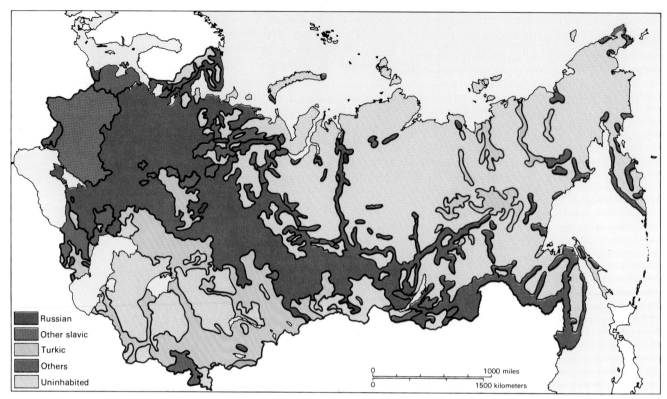

Figure 6-9. The Distribution of Russian and Other Languages in the Soviet Union. The Russian language is not the primary language of many citizens of the Soviet Union. Most of the non-Russian speakers live in peripheral portions of the country.

Legend:
- Russian
- Other slavic
- Turkic
- Others
- Uninhabited

0 ————— 1000 miles
0 ————— 1500 kilometers

patterns of language groups have remained fairly stable.

Two major trends are discernible in the ethnic and linguistic geography of the Soviet Union. On the one hand, the rate of population growth in Soviet Central Asia is swelling the ranks of people who speak Uzbek (9.5 million in 1979), Tartar (5.5 million), Kazakh (6.3 million), and other Turkic languages faster than the growth rate for those who speak Russian. On the other hand, the Russian language, although not officially the national tongue, is gradually becoming the lingua franca of the Soviet Union. Russian is promoted in the lower schools, but without any formal attempt to erase the local languages, and is the main language of higher education, science, trade, politics, and the military. A person who speaks only a minority language is limited in options, whereas a knowledge of Russian opens up opportunities outside the local ethnic area. Consequently, nearly a quarter of the population of the Soviet Union is bilingual. The direction of change is indicated by the fact that whereas more than 42 percent of the non-Russian population claims fluency in Russian, only 3.1 percent of the Russians speak another language of the country. Although the Soviet Union has no official policy of replacing non-Russian languages, it is evident that the country is in the midst of an ongoing process of linguistic assimilation (Comrie 1981).

OTHER PATTERNS RELATED TO LANGUAGE VARIATIONS

The distribution of languages is often a clue to a wide range of other geographic features. As in the Soviet Union, linguistic patterns are frequently similar to the distribution of ethnic groups. In the United States, for example, anthropologists have generally identified traditional American Indian regions on the basis of language rather than on subsistence patterns or other aspects of culture. As described in the following sections, language may be closely related to differences in the natural environment, in stages of settlement, in social classes, and in feelings of nationalism.

Language and the Natural Environment

Is there a relationship between linguistic variations and differences in the natural environment? An affirmative answer is suggested by those distributions of language that resemble the patterns of natural features. For example, the boundaries between linguistic groups in Southeast Asia often coincide with mountain ranges. It is easy to understand why such barriers as mountains have restricted interaction between groups, especially in the past. Topographic barriers tended to limit linguistic exchanges between areas, which means boundaries between language and dialect regions may be located now where physical features have discouraged interaction in the past.

The distribution of creole languages in the world also suggest a relationship with physical features. Almost all creoles occur on isolated tropical littorals or islands (Bickerton 1983). These are areas where slaves and laborers were brought to work in colonial plantations during the last 500 years. Initially the laborers, who were shipped from many different language areas, depended on pidgin to communicate with each other. Among the children and succeeding generations in these communities, however, creole languages developed, which have persisted under conditions of isolation.

Another example of an association between language patterns and natural features is the continuing use of Gullah speech—an English-based creole—in the isolated Sea Islands of Georgia and South Carolina. Gullah, which contains more than 4000 Africanisms (i.e., inflections, syntactic constructions, and words from Africa), is regarded as a good illustration of a culture that survived the forced migration of slaves to North America. Originally brought to work in the rice plantations in the 1700s, West Africans were physically and culturally isolated from the American mainstream. In fact, the first bridges to the Sea Islands were not built until the 1920s. In this setting of isolation, this language form persisted. Even today, beyond the golf courses and marinas of the Sea Islands, there are still about 100,000 Gullah speakers. This survival of speech patterns is paralleled by the existence of other evidence of West African culture such as basketware and foods.

Still another connection between linguistic regions and the natural environment concerns the ways cultural groups perceive their immediate surroundings. If what is observed by people is reflected in the names assigned to things, then language differences should indicate how various groups relate to environmental conditions. For example, the Eskimo language includes numerous words pertaining to varying conditions of snow, indicating that Eskimos are conscious of differences in snow characteristics. In contrast, speakers of English, not having the words that differentiate between various types of snow, will probably not perceive as many differences. Furthermore, the Aztec language has only one word for conditions that can be differentiated as *snow*, *slush*, and *ice* in the English language. It is clear that language is affected by the environmental setting of its speakers and that users perceive their environments partly in terms of their native language.

These ideas that link language with thought suggest what is known as the Sapir-Whorf hypothesis (Whorf 1956). According to this thesis, language has three main functions: (1) to communicate with others, (2) to communicate with oneself (that is, to think), and (3) to mold one's outlook on life. If a particular language spoken by a person affects thinking and outlook, then linguistic terms reflect that person's perceptions of the environment. According to this hypothesis, perceptions of the natural world partly explain differences in languages. Although this concept is controversial, it does imply a close ecological relationship between humans and their natural environment.

Language and Early Settlement

Language is expressed in the landscape by place names or **toponyms,** which often survive as evidence of the early settlement in an area. The prevalence of German place names on the eastern and northern borders of the Missouri Ozarks, for example, is testimony that the Germans were among the first Euro-American settlers in that area (Figure 5-36). If German toponyms are mapped, their distribution identifies a region that is still distinctive in heritage and dialect (Gerlach 1976).

On the Caribbean island of Jamaica, there are at least four "layers" of place names, each a product of a stage of settlement. The first layer has largely disappeared because the indigenous Indians, the Arawaks, were rapidly decimated by the Spanish after 1509. Moreover, the Arawaks had no written language, so most of their words died with them. Still, a few place names such as Aqualta Vale, Liguanea, and Guanaboa are derivatives from Arawak words (Figure 6-10). In fact, the name *Jamaica* itself may be Arawak in origin. Spanish is the second layer. The Spanish dominated Jamaica until they were forced out by the British in the mid-seventeenth century. Spanish names of many towns (Port Antonio, Santa Cruz, Montego Bay) and rivers (Rio Minho, Rio Cobre) remain throughout the island.

The most numerous toponyms in Jamaica are the third layer, consisting of English, Scottish, and Welsh names like Kingston, Glencoe, and Llandovery. Finally, some settlements, particularly in the interior mountains, show the influence of the fourth layer—African. These settlements were established and named by escaped slaves in the eighteenth century and by emancipated slaves after 1838. Wait-a-Bit and Quick Step in the isolated Land of the Look Behind are examples. These lilting names, with English words arranged in Jamaican structures that reveal African influences, are symbols of the varied cultures that have produced the diverse Jamaican society (Cundall 1971).

Place names can also be clues to the history of settlement in an area where no documentary evidence exists. For example, after A.D. 835, the Danes began to

---

Toponym.   The name of a place; place name.

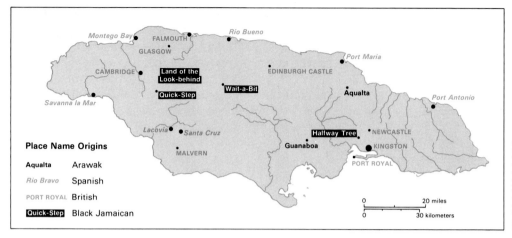

Figure 6-10. Selected Place Names in Jamaica. Names of places in Jamaica developed from the original Arawak people, the Spanish rulers, the British rulers, and the black Jamaican population.

Figure 6-11. Danish Place Names in England. Place names ending in "-by" indicate areas of early Danish settlement.

raid, invade, and eventually settle eastern and northern England. Sources such as the *Anglo-Saxon Chronicle* mention the coming of the Danes but give no precise information about how many settlements the newcomers occupied. However, toponyms give a strong indication of where this settlement took place. The Danish named their settlements in specific ways. Small outlying hamlets frequently had a "thorp" component in their names; larger places often ended in "-by." Towns like Derby and Whitby and the hundreds of other places with "-by" suffixes in England carry an indication of their association with Danish settlement (Figure 6-11). Although names may originate from a variety of sources, a map based on linguistic characteristics provides at least one clue to the distribution of early settlements.

Language and Social Characteristics

Language varies with the distance separating different communication groups. "Distance," however, can be social as well as spatial. Social distance may be related to age, gender, occupation, and class. In Paraguay, for example, where Spanish is the official language but Guarani is the primary language of over 90 percent of the population, many people are bilingual. Usage of the two languages by bilingual speakers varies with social circumstances. There is a tendency for men to use Guarani with other men, but to use Spanish with women who are close friends. Women, on the other hand, tend to use Spanish with both close male and female friends. Children show respect for older persons by speaking in Spanish rather than in Guarani, which they use among their playmates.

In cultures where the contrasts may not be a formal part of the language, word usage may vary, as observed by the differences in informal conversation among males and females or among teen-agers and their grandparents. Many occupations utilize specialized vocabularies, which may be identified as jargon. Some occupational jargon—for example, that associated with computer technology—may actually transcend language boundaries.

Linguistic contrasts are especially evident between social classes, with the language of persons in "upper" classes typically different from that in "lower" classes. Furthermore, because people of a particular social class often cluster together residentially, the "vertical" variations in language based on social status have an accompanying geographical, or "horizontal," dimension (Wagner 1972, p. 14). In Britain, the standard dialect or "correct" form of speech is referred to as **received pronunciation.** This version of the language is spoken by the upper classes (as defined by education, income, profession, and sometimes title) and is perpetuated through the "public" (in Britain, meaning private, fee-paying)

TABLE 6-2. Dialect Variations in the Bradford Area of Yorkshire, England

Social Class	"Aitch"-Dropping (in %)
Upper Middle	12
Lower Middle	28
Upper Working	67
Middle Working	89
Lower Working	93

Source: Data from Petyt in Hughes and Trudgill 1979.

schools. Although the received pronunciation is spoken by only an estimated 3 percent of the population, these speakers are not restricted to a particular region but are widely distributed throughout the country (Hughes and Trudgill 1979).

By contrast, British people further down the social scale (as defined by occupation, income, and education) reveal their geographic origins whenever they speak. In a study of dialects in the Bradford area of Yorkshire, Petyt grouped residents into five social categories: Upper Middle, Lower Middle, Upper Working, Middle Working, and Lower Working (Petyt in Hughes and Trudgill 1979). Petyt observed that the percentage of "aitch" dropping ("house" to "ouse," for example) clearly related to social class (Table 6-2). The speech of the Upper Middle classes in Bradford may not be different from the speech of the Upper Middle classes elsewhere in Britain, but the Lower Working classes in Bradford speak English with an accent that is definitely place-specific (Figure 6-12).

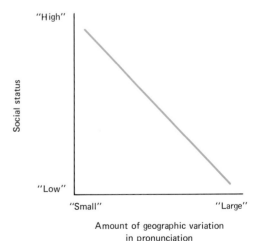

Figure 6-12. Relationship between Social Status and Dialect Variations within England. People of "high" social status tend to have less place-to-place variation in their speech than those of "low" social status.

Received pronunciation. The standard dialect, or "court-correct" form of speech, in Britain.

This contrast between dialects occurs within the smaller areas of cities as well as at the more extensive regional scale. In Britain, the "lower" classes largely inhabit the inner city, with the "upper" classes residing in the suburbs and on the urban fringe. So, in a very generalized way, there is a geographic distinction between the accents of the inner city, which are unique to that region, and the received pronunciation of the suburbs and fringes, which varies less from city to city.

In the United States, a major contrast in spoken dialects exists between black and white populations. Again, this is related to communication networks. Wherever blacks and whites are in daily contact through jobs or residential proximity, there is a mutual influence on speech patterns. In racially segregated American cities, however, the communication networks of blacks and whites rarely intersect. William Labov, an expert on black dialects, discovered that in Philadelphia the differences between white and black dialects are increasing (Labov 1980). Moreover, a similar divergence of dialects between black and white populations has been found in New York, Detroit, Buffalo, and Chicago. So, in terms of speech patterns, the black inner cities of Chicago and Philadelphia, for example, are closer to each other than to their adjacent suburbs. This divergence contradicts the contention that dialects are disappearing under the influence of the mass media.

In addition to differences arising from social characteristics, language is tailored to fit each setting or social situation. The raucous language of a group of men at a boxing match, for example, is not considered suitable for a job interview or for Sunday morning at church. The situational dialect, or **register,** appropriate for a formal occasion contrasts with the slang expressions used in informal settings.

Often linguistic registers are combined with differences in social characteristics. In many societies, not only do males and females occasionally use different linguistic forms, but each gender adjusts its speech when conversing with the other group. The use of different registers is especially apparent in combination with social classes. In Japan, where social conduct within a stratified society is very important, language is carefully prescribed for each occasion. The Japanese language includes 45 words for the first person singular pronoun "I." Some words are restricted to regional dialects, but more than a dozen forms of "I" are represented in the standard version of Japanese that is taught in schools and broadcast through the media. The form that is used depends on the situation: *chin* is used only by the emperor on formal occasions; *baku* and *ore* are spoken only by males; and high-status women use *watashi* whereas women of lower social standing use *atashi*. These variations in speech patterns in Japan reveal and confirm social status by certifying that each person has a niche in the social order.

Many of these linguistic variations associated with social class are not exposed by a map showing broad regions of major world languages (Figure 6-1). At a local scale, however, these differences among social groups are geographically important. Variations in linguistic forms reflect patterns of social groupings and their accompanying networks of interactions. By analyzing linguistic patterns, therefore, one can gain an understanding of existing communities and the geography of their behavior within local areas.

Language and Territoriality

There is a close association between language and the people who share a feeling that a specific area "belongs" to them. This sense of **territoriality** is expressed at many different scales. For large areas, these feelings may reflect attitudes about being a distinct nation of people. In countries like the United States and Japan where a single language dominates, it is easier to forge a feeling of national unity than in countries where a multitude of languages reinforces the fragmentation of the society into discrete communities. Some scholars attribute Japan's economic success, at least in part, to a consensus about national goals. Workers, businesspeople, and government agencies are able to reach agreement more easily than in many other societies because the Japanese work from the same cultural assumptions. This homogeneity of culture is facilitated by the fact that almost the entire population speaks Japanese.

Conversely, in multilanguage countries, such as Nigeria and India, a sense of national unity is often weaker than in single-language nations. National unity is difficult to achieve where there are problems in communicating policies through multiple languages. In addition, linguistic groups, which often coincide with cultural subdivisions, may have differing goals. Furthermore, economic activities function less efficiently where several languages impede a common network of communication. It is not surprising, therefore, that linguistic uniformity within a country is partly related to the country's economic status.

Although a diversity of languages in a country may be related to its economic status, this relationship is not universally evident. When looking at a scatter diagram that shows linguistic diversity and national income per capita for most of the nations of the world (Figure 6-13), it can be concluded that (1) poorer countries include both linguistically homogeneous and heterogeneous populations (e.g., Kampuchea and Chad, respectively), and (2) countries with language uniformity range from rich to poor (e.g., Norway and

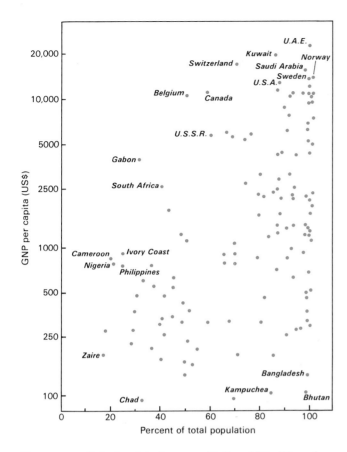

Figure 6-13. Relationship between National Wealth and Linguistic Homogeneity. The horizontal axis shows the size of the largest language community as a percentage of the total population. The vertical axis measures the per capita gross national product. The absence of points in the upper left-hand portion of the graph reveals that richer countries seldom have a high diversity of languages.

Bangladesh). But significantly, there is no rich country that has a great diversity of languages.

Although for many political, social, and economic reasons it may be advantageous for a nation to have a single official language that is spoken by most of the population, a policy that attempts to force minority groups to adopt a new language can be politically dangerous. Since language is a major part of cultural identity, the imposition of a "foreign" language is regarded as especially repressive. One of the main issues that led to the secession of East Pakistan from the rest of the country (resulting in the independent nation of Bangladesh in 1971) was the attempt to impose Urdu, the language of West Pakistan, on the Bengali-speaking people of East Pakistan.

Some nations have attempted to avert potential crises by guaranteeing regional groups the right to their own languages in schools and local governments.

For example, the Basques of northern Spain, the speakers of Catalan in northeastern Spain, and the Kurds of northern Iran have all recently had their languages confirmed as official within their regions (Chapter 8). To the minority people, the recognition of their language affirms their cultural identity and is a measure of political independence; to the controlling government, it may be a form of compromise, which is accepted in hopes of preventing the rise of political separatism (Chapter 8).

Some of the issues relating language to national feelings are exemplified by Canadian history. Since the Durham Report of 1837 and the Confederation of Canada in 1867, both English and French have been recognized as official languages. This agreement to recognize two languages reflects the initial European settlement of Canada. In 1763, when the British took Canada from France, at least 80 percent of the nonnative population was French-speaking. By 1805, as a result of immigration, the British had become the majority group.

In reality, it is more accurate to describe Canada as a multilingual state because in addition to French and English there are large numbers of German, Italian, and Ukrainian speakers. Many American Indian languages are also spoken in Canada, the foremost being Cree, with about 30,000 speakers. The main division, however, and the one with the most serious political implications, is between English-speaking and French-speaking Canadians (Table 6-3).

In 1981, 61 percent of Canada's population claimed English as the language first spoken as a child, whereas, French was reported as the primary language by 26 percent. Most French-speaking Canadians see the preservation of their language as the key to cultural survival. If the French-speaking people were distributed and intermixed throughout Canada, the political problem of linguistic and political separatism might not be as serious as it is today. But the French language and culture are heavily concentrated in the Province of Quebec, where approximately 80 percent of the people report French as their primary

TABLE 6-3. Canadians Whose Mother Tongue Is English or French

Year	English Number (millions)	English Population Share (in %)	French Number (millions)	French Population Share (in %)
1961	10.7	58	5.1	28
1971	13.0	60	5.8	27
1981	14.9	61	6.2	26

Register. A type of speech used for a particular social setting or occasion; also called situation dialect.

Territoriality. The claiming of a specific area by a person or group of people.

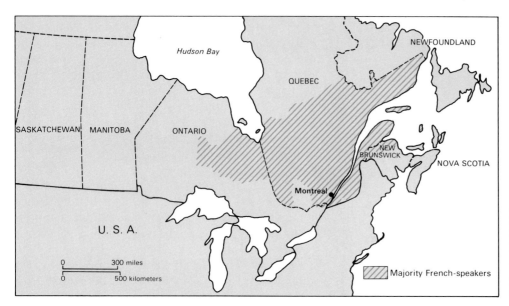

Figure 6-14. The French-Speaking Area of Eastern Canada. Persons who speak French as their primary language live mainly in the Province of Quebec. After Barrett 1975.

language (Figure 6-14). In fact, Montreal is the second largest French-speaking city in the world.

However, the proportion of French speakers in Canada is falling; the current 26 percent is down from 28 percent in 1951. Even in Quebec, there has been a small but significant shift to English. One reason is that the traditionally high French birth rate has declined to lower than the national average. Also important is the fact that new immigrants to Quebec whose language is neither English nor French are much more likely to learn English because it is the dominant language throughout the rest of Canada. Furthermore, English is the working language of most national and international businesses headquartered in Montreal. Despite governmental efforts to promote the use of French, companies regard English as the lingua franca of the international business world. In fact, there has traditionally been a social hierarchy of language use in Quebec, where French speakers who rose in the corporate world were obligated to learn English as they entered an English-dominated environment (Cartwright 1981; Meeker 1982).

The Canadian government, following the advice of the Royal Commission of Bilingualism and Biculturalism in 1963, has promoted bilingualism by requiring schooling in English and French throughout the country, and by affirming the equality of the two languages in all governmental institutions. There is evidence, however, that the bilingual policy is actually contributing to the drift from French to English because the percentage of French Canadians who now know English as a second language is higher than that of English speakers who can use French (Beaujot 1978).

Faced by the threat of gradual incorporation into the British Canadian culture, the French-speaking Canadians have worked tenaciously to preserve their language. In 1977, the government of Quebec passed the "Charter of the French Language," rejecting the policy of bilingualism and promoting French as the language of education and the workplace. This act required physicians, lawyers, and doctors, for example, to pass French tests to obtain professional licenses in Quebec. Minority groups within Quebec, including English, Portuguese, Italian, Haitian, and Chinese speakers, objected to this legislation; and some business headquarters were relocated, particularly from Montreal to Toronto.

In 1980, the Quebec government asked the electorate to give it a mandate to negotiate with the Canadian government for a special sovereignty status within the country. Although this request was defeated by 60 percent of the voters, the issue is far from settled because many Quebecois still favor partial or complete separation from the rest of Canada. It is clear that language, the voice of culture, is at the very heart of Canada's struggle to maintain its present political form.

Even where feelings of distinctiveness are not expressed in terms of national separation, linguistic patterns frequently coincide with some degree of territoriality. For example, in several areas of the United States, especially in the southwest and ethnic areas of cities, the first language of the population is not English. These areas are evident by reading store names and advertising, observing non-English language newspapers and radio stations, and listening to public conversations. Linguistic variations are recognized officially in ways such as in voting instructions and bilingual primary schools. Although most linguistic groups in the United States (with the possible exception of some Native American ones) do not

Figure 6-15. Graffiti in St. Thomas, American Virgin Islands. These wall messages indicate the link between the black people of this Caribbean island and their African roots. Photo courtesy of Sarah Disbrow.

consider themselves as belonging to a separate nation, their ethnic pride may be expressed locally in business organizations, social networks, and political issues.

The connection between language and claimed space may be made explicit at a local scale by graffiti (Figure 6-15). In many areas, these wall-writings are used to announce the territorial claims of street gangs and to demarcate the boundaries of their particular turf. The graffiti, which are "internally supportive and externally aggressive," are more common toward the center of each area of control, but the messages they convey are more aggressive on the margins where rivalries between gangs are intense (Ley and Cybrwsky 1974, p. 501).

MODES OF COMMUNICATION

Networks of communication greatly affect the beliefs and activities of individuals and communities. The extent of this influence differs for several reasons, but the method (or mode) of conveying a message is an important factor. Therefore, understanding the spatial and ecological characteristics of cultures is enhanced by examining various means of communication.

Communication through language occurs in a variety of ways, ranging from direct conversations between individuals to pronouncements that are conveyed to millions of people through public media. One mode of communication consists of written materials; but transmitting information in this way is generally confined to those who are literate (i.e., those who can read and write). The distribution of literate persons, therefore, is an important factor in the geography of human activities. In addition, communication occurs by combining oral and written words with various visual images, which is the second topic that is expanded in the following section.

Patterns of Literacy

Being able to read and write greatly expands the scope of potential communication among individuals. Written words can be duplicated and read by literate persons in diverse locations, and they can be preserved for future readers. The long duration of Chinese civilization is attributed, in part, to the early and continued use of a written language through which literate Chinese, speaking different languages in the various parts of the country, could communicate. The ability to store information in written form, rather than memorizing and repeating it orally from one generation to the next, has contributed immensely to the world's accumulation of knowledge. Building on previous knowledge to produce innovations, as well

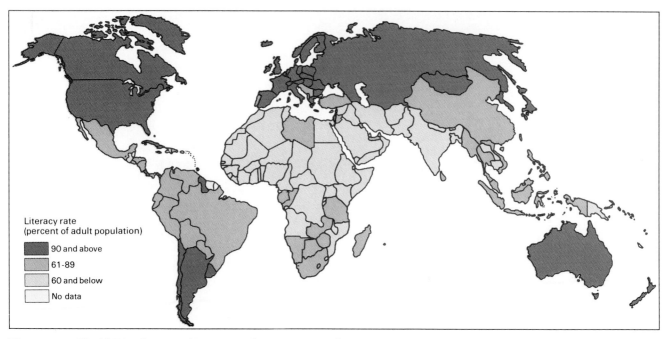

Figure 6-16. World Distribution of Literacy. The percentage of persons over 15 years of age who can read and write varies from 10 in Somalia to almost 100 in several industrialized countries. Source: Sivard 1986.

as transmitting technology to others, is dependent on the ability to read and write.

Levels of literacy vary from person to person. In contrast to the human ability to acquire a spoken language without schooling, becoming literate requires special training. In some populations, most children are taught to read and write; but in others, few have this skill. At the international scale, the percentage of population that is literate varies greatly (Figure 6-16).

As is true for many national statistics, it is difficult to obtain precise figures about literacy rates for every country. The lack of precise statistics results partly from the difficulties of collecting any kind of census data in some countries. Furthermore, national data are not entirely reliable because of the inconsistency in definitions about the level of reading and writing that qualifies a person to be classified as "literate." This is illustrated in the United States, for example, by the large number of persons who have had several years of formal schooling but are still functionally illiterate. When defined by the number of persons who have had five years of schooling, the literacy rate for the United States measures almost 99 percent; but in terms of basic reading ability, the percentage of literate people in this country is in the lower 80s. Despite these difficulties of definition, a map showing the distribution of literacy in the world is useful for the connections it has to many other geographical characteristics.

National literacy rates are closely related to demographic characteristics. As noted previously

(Chapter 3), rates of fertility and infant mortality tend to be high in countries where literacy rates are low. To a great extent, we also know that patterns of fertility and literacy are linked to economic conditions. More developed countries have high literacy and low fertility. In less developed countries, educational opportunities, especially for women, are limited. In cultures where the role of women is primarily to bear and care for children, schooling is considered less important for females. Without the ability to read written instructions, women are less able to combat infant mortality. Babies have a much better chance of surviving, for instance, if mothers can read about simple remedies that treat the dehydration that results from dysentery, a major cause of infant mortality in poor countries.

Literacy rates are closely associated with national wealth (see, for example, Figure 9-9). Rich nations can best pay for the costs of universal schooling, as well as the costs of advanced education in technology and research. In turn, countries with a highly literate population have the human resources to be successful in secondary and tertiary activities, which are the main contributors to national wealth.

Other factors that bear upon the map of literacy are cultural values. Even though poverty may make it difficult for a nation to pay for universal schooling, a few less developed countries give higher priority to funds for education than, say, for new highways. In the East Asian culture realm, education has always been regarded highly, so today's literacy rates tend to reflect this cultural value.

Other Forms of Communication

Visual messages other than written texts, or in conjunction with written texts, are important forms of communication. When words are accompanied by pictorial representations, symbols, or human activities, they may carry stronger messages than those conveyed by words alone. People have conveyed information through images for thousands of years, as evidenced by ancient pictorial artifacts found throughout the world. With the advent of modern electronic modes of recording, transmitting, and displaying visual materials, images have become highly influential. Geographic variations in cultural, economic, and political activities today, whether at the world scale or the local scale, are greatly affected by communication forms that combine language with images.

Drawings, photographs, and computer graphics are commonly used to emphasize and supplement written materials. In different cases, the goals are to instruct, to inspire, to entertain, or to persuade. An illustration of efforts to persuade through written and pictorial forms is the brochures circulated during the late nineteenth century to attract potential migrants to the Great Plains. Such promoters of settlement as railroad companies and state immigration boards bombarded Europe with brochures that proclaimed "wonderful" opportunities for farmers in the frontier territory of the central United States. The promotional literature combined verbal messages, written in the language of a targeted group, with enticing images. Typical views were virgin landscapes waiting to be transformed into fields and factories (Figure 6-17). Although many forces contributed to the rapid settlement of the Great Plains after 1860 (Chapter 4), an important one was this "massive exercise in persuasion" (Emmons 1971, p. 197).

Modern advertising is certainly a "language of persuasion." It is a forceful component of a mass medium that bombards us with messages every day. The messages are frequently "coded" and are designed to influence our thinking about products, candidates, or political issues. Verbal language is involved in advertising, of course. Some researchers are convinced that advertising often conveys a "language within a language" by communicating to us at a level beneath our conscious awareness (Key 1972). Our senses are stimulated by words selected to trigger certain emotions, music chosen to create a mood, and images designed to provoke a particular reaction.

Enormous sums of money are spent on advertising in the belief that it effectively influences purchasing patterns, election results, and numerous other human activities. Its effectiveness, however, depends on accurate information about the language, culture, and other social characteristics of the target group.

Figure 6-17. Land Brochure Distributed by a Railroad Company. Promotional literature distributed in Europe helped convince people to move to the United States in the nineteenth century. Used with permission from Nebraska State Historical Society.

Modifying words, background music, and accompanying pictures may convey a clear and favorable message to one cultural group but may produce a confused or negative reaction in another group. To illustrate, an American-made car did not sell well in Latin America until its original name was changed from Nova because in Spanish, *no va* means "it doesn't go." Large companies that market their products throughout the world certainly have to understand the geography of languages, including all the culturally related attributes of verbal and nonverbal communication (Figure 6-18).

Recent trends in American advertisements and entertainment demonstrate the growing importance of images. Effective communication does not always

Figure 6-18. The Universalizing Language of Advertised Products. Some company emblems are displayed in many parts of the world, such as this one in Guangzhou, China. Photo courtesy of Sally Stoddard.

depend on selecting the most meaningful words; often it is achieved through fast-moving impressions that are flashed on a movie screen, video tape, or TV channel. By creating certain moods and feelings about products and politicians through carefully designed images and accompanying music, those who seek to influence an audience can be effective with a minimum of words. To understand the geography of American culture today requires an awareness of several forms of languages and images.

Images in the form of paintings, photographs, sculptures, and craftwork often portray characteristics of a culture, and they may also reveal how members of a particular group perceive their environment. Landscape paintings, for instance, may show how a people have used or altered the landscape and, in addition, how they have perceived it. In this way, artistic depictions of the American West tell us as much about the American vision as it does about the physical environment (Figure 6-19).

Figure 6-19. "Approaching rain, Salt Valley, 7 May 1988," Painting by Keith Jacobshagen. Landscape painters can often convey the essence of a place more effectively than words. In this painting, the Great Plains region is shown as a horizontal plain dominated by sky. Courtesy of the artist.

Figure 6-20. Public Mural in San Antonio. Communication may occur through words or pictures, or by a combination of the two. Photo courtesy of Daniel D. Arreola.

Visual representations may also be used to mark territory and express pride in belonging to a particular area. Mural art, for example, a striking component of the built environment and an explicit medium of communication, often serves as a window into a local culture, revealing its history and current social concerns. In the United States, exterior wall paintings are common in many Mexican-American communities. This type of mural painting was first evident on the American urban landscape in Chicago in the 1960s. Since that time the art form has diffused widely and is now found in most American cities where there is a sizable Mexican-American population (Arreola 1984).

The main purpose of Mexican-American mural art is the communication of ideas and values that are important to the local community. In fact, the local community often produces the artists. Mural art confirms ethnic identity and is a visual supplement to a history that is largely passed on orally. The major themes include heroes of the Mexican Revolution such as Emiliano Zapata (Figure 6-20) or religious characterizations such as the Virgin of Guadelupe, the patron saint of Mexico. Increasingly, the murals incorporate local landscape features alongside the historical characters, so that cultural memory is firmly anchored in a particular place and community.

Maps, which are visual abstractions, are another form of communication. They are frequently used in television news programs, newspapers, and magazines to provide the geographic context for current political events. Ideally, maps should depict geographic reality clearly and precisely. Often, however,

maps represent reality filtered through the bias of the map-maker and convey messages that leave the reader with a distorted perception of the world (Monmonier 1977).

Some of the most blatant examples of cartographic manipulation are designed to serve the purpose of political propaganda. For example, German geographers working in the 1930s to justify expansionist policies used various devices to communicate the impression that Germany and her allies were surrounded by hostile forces (Figure 6-21).

Generally, the manipulation of the reader is more subtle, involving the use of specific **map projections.** Every map contains some form of distortion (shape, area, distance, or a combination of these) because the curved surface of the earth cannot be represented on a flat surface with complete accuracy. A person wanting to present information on a map must decide which kind of projection is most appropriate. The opportunity for choosing from a variety of projections allows for selecting one that promotes a specific message, such as a political view. Often readers unthinkingly accept a particular projection as if it accurately represented the "real" world.

The Mercator projection, for example, traditionally one of the most popular projections of the world, exaggerates areas toward the poles. For example, it

---

Map projection. A system for representing the sphere of the earth (or globe) on a flat surface. This necessarily involves some distortion.

Figure 6-21. A German Map of Germany during World War I. The map-maker attempted to portray an enemy encirclement of Germany by using concentric circles and a map projection that exaggerates areas away from the map center. After Wirsing 1941.

greatly enlarges the apparent size of the Soviet Union, which has a large proportion of its land area in the high latitudes. The Mercator projection, then, serves as a useful device for those who have an interest in presenting an exaggerated picture of the amount of the earth's surface that is controlled by the Soviet Union [Figure 6-22 (a)]. On the other hand, a map with a projection that is polar can be used to portray the Soviet Union as being surrounded by hostile forces [Figure 6-22 (b)].

PROSPECTS FOR GLOBAL COMMUNICATION

The growing interdependency and interaction among people of the world require effective communication. People from various places must be able to discuss mutual problems and make decisions about global issues, such as the allocation of limited resources and the prevention of worldwide environmental deterioration. The amount of communication that is shared by persons throughout the world will be affected by the availability of information networks and a common language.

Prior to the age of telecommunications, information was relayed from place to place mostly by the direct contact between individuals or through written materials. Even though an event in one part of the world might have a subsequent impact elsewhere, the effect was slow in coming. Today, however, with the achievement of electronic transmission of information, the interdependency of the world's population has increased tremendously. When the financial stock market changes in one city, it has an almost instantaneous effect on the economies of nations throughout the world. Thus, if stocks fall in Tokyo, Hong Kong, or Singapore, declines often occur later in the day in London, Zurich, and New York.

With the rise of greater global interdependency came the necessity for quick access to centers of communication. Just as illiteracy denies individuals many opportunities for acquiring valuable information, the lack of channels to major sources of knowledge is a critical restriction today. In this age of communication, economic and political power are highly dependent on the ability to produce and disseminate information.

In addition to accessibility to communication networks, future communication will be affected by the language used. Even though transmission of information is performed electronically and symbolically, the final mode of communication is through a spoken language. It has long been recognized that a universal language would end the "curse of Babel" and would be a valuable means of communication among diverse peoples. Approximately 700 artificial (or constructed) languages have been devised since the seventeenth century, with Esperanto being the most successful. Esperanto was developed in 1887 by Ludwik Zamenhof, who believed that language differences were the main cause of disunity in the world. His language, based on a simplified derivative of various Romance languages, is spoken today by more than 5 million persons, taught in several hundred schools internationally, and used in more than 10,000 books.

Esperanto has received recent attention in Europe where there is a great demand for multiple translations. The proceedings of the European Parliament, for example, have to be translated into nine languages. These translations can be achieved by using computers, but direct translations among the languages are difficult. Because Esperanto is especially compatible for computer use, translations are made faster and easier by first converting the proceedings into this language then retranslating them into the other languages.

It cannot be said, however, that Esperanto has become the universal language as intended. There are practical difficulties in motivating people to learn a new language, even for use in the United Nations. In a world where many countries are still striving to

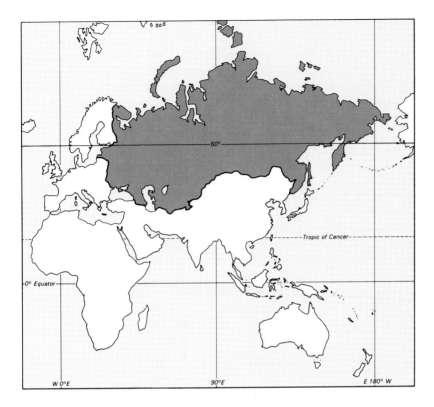

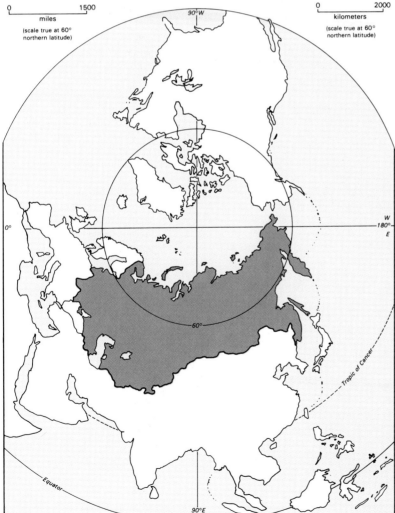

Figure 6-22. The Soviet Union Shown on Two Map Projections. A Mercator map projection (map a) exaggerates the size of areas in high latitudes, which makes the Soviet Union appear larger than its size on a globe of comparable scale. On a polar projection (map b), the size and position of the Soviet Union appear to be very different from the first map.

establish a national language, the concept of a formal international language is probably ahead of its time. Another reason Esperanto has not become a major language is the fact that linguistically it is not a truly universal language. Its Indo-European base, with culturally specific concepts and ways of organizing thoughts, makes it nearly as hard for non-Europeans to learn as any other totally foreign language (Bolinger and Sears 1981, p. 312).

In many respects, English is becoming an international language. In addition to the millions for whom English is the primary language (Table 6-1 and Figure 6-1), there are many more persons throughout the world who use it as a second language. If those who also have a "reasonable competence" in English are included, the total approaches 1 billion English speakers.

English is already the language of air controllers throughout the world, the common language for international shipping, and one of the two official languages of the United Nations. Two-thirds of all scientific papers, three-fourths of telex messages, and 80 percent of all computer data are in English.

In spite of this trend toward the internationalization of English, only a small minority of the world's population can actually use the English language effectively. Also, as discussed earlier, centrifugal forces are continually working in an opposite direction. Newly independent countries, for example, often strive to express their national pride by maintaining their own language rather than adopting one of the major world languages. Furthermore, if a common language were spoken by all people in the world, cultural variations would remain. Different religious beliefs and different political ideologies will still foster diversity. The shared language of Protestants and Catholics in Northern Ireland, for example, has done little to heal the deep cultural rift between the two groups. This topic and many others are considered in the next two chapters, which deal with the geographic dimensions of religion and political organization.

POINT-COUNTERPOINT

Immigration and Language Change

When people migrate to a new country, they expect to make many changes such as eating new foods, purchasing different goods and services, and, in many cases, speaking a foreign language. Often the most critical change involves learning a foreign language. For young children the acquisition of a second language usually has a direct bearing on their early years of schooling. Although educators are generally concerned about providing quality language training, there are disagreements about the pace and methods for teaching a second language.

Differences concerning language training became especially obvious after the U.S. Congress passed the Elementary and Secondary Education Act of 1968. This legislation, passed for the purpose of promoting bilingual education for the approximately 6 million students who lacked English proficiency, allowed children to continue to use their own language in some classes while gaining fluency in English. Even after the enactment of the law, citizens and educators in several communities continued to disagree about its implementation in their schools.

Opponents of bilingual education base their reasons on a variety of factors: (1) They say it is confusing for primary children to struggle with two languages at the same time, so reading skills are delayed. And since learning English must be done sometime, it is best to require the child to learn it immediately. (2) They believe migrants should be willing to give up their old characteristics, including language, just as most of those in the nineteenth century did when they came to America. (3) They contend that, in a pluralistic society like the United States, it is important to emphasize elements of commonality and the English language has always been an element that binds citizens together. (4) Opponents also believe that, by not requiring a total conversion to English, schools are discouraging the assimilation of migrants. This might eventually produce culturally distinct regions where local political allegiance would undermine national unity.

Proponents of bilingual education agree that learning English is essential, but they disagree with the "sink or swim" position of opponents for several reasons: (1) They point out that since language is so much a part of an individual's identity, complete rejection of the first language causes young children to experience personal rejection. (2) They note that the total immersion of a child in a foreign language hinders cognitive development and contributes to a high drop-out rate during later years. (3) They say that it is developmentally important for students to retain their first language while acquiring a second one. Children who know more than one language tend to have language areas distributed more evenly on both sides of the brain. This more even distribution enables the child to integrate more effectively verbal and spatial abilities. (4) Proponents believe that rejection of the child's knowledge of a non-English language destroys a skill that is greatly needed in the United States. The fact that an estimated 75 to 90 percent of the American population cannot use another language handicaps the United States in a world that requires proficiency in more than one language. (5) An associated final point is that the collective American world view is narrowed if children lose the perspectives of their culture and language.

BIBLIOGRAPHY

Arreola, Daniel D., "Mexican American Exterior Murals," *Geographical Review,* 74, no. 4 (October 1984), 409–24.

Barrett, F. A., "The Relative Decline of the French Language in Canada: A Preliminary Report," *Geography,* 60, no. 2 (1975), 125–29.

Beaujot, Roderic P., "Canada's Population: Growth and Dualism," *Population Bulletin,* 33, no. 2 (April 1978).

Bickerton, Derek, "Creole Languages," *Scientific American,* 249, no. 1 (July 1983), 116–22.

Bolinger, Dwight, and Donald A. Sears, *Aspects of Language,* 3rd ed. New York: Holt, Rinehart and Winston, 1981.

Cartwright, Don, "Language Policy and Political Organization of Territory: A Canadian Dilemma," *Canadian Geographer,* 25, no. 3 (1981), 205–24.

Clem, Ralph S., "Russians and Others: Ethnic Tensions in the Soviet Union," *Focus,* 31, no. 1 (September–October 1980).

Comrie, Bernard, *The Languages of the Soviet Union.* Cambridge, England: Cambridge University Press, 1981.

Cooper, Robert L., ed., *Language Spread: Studies in Diffusion and Social Change.* Bloomington, Indiana: Indiana University Press, 1982.

Cundall, Frank, *Historic Jamaica.* New York: Johnson Reprint Corp., 1971.

Emmons, David M., *Garden In the Grasslands: Boomer Literature of the Central Great Plains.* Lincoln: University of Nebraska Press, 1971.

Fromkin, Victoria, and Robert Rodman, *An Introduction to Language,* 3rd ed. New York: Holt, Rinehart and Winston, 1983.

Gelling, Margaret, *Places-Names in the Landscape.* London: Dent, 1984.

Gerlach, Russel L., *Immigrants in the Ozarks: A Study in Ethnic Geography.* Columbia, Missouri: University of Missouri Press, 1976.

Hughes, Arthur, and Peter Trudgill, *English Accents & Dialects.* London: Edward Arnold, 1979.

Katzner, Kenneth, *The Languages of the World.* New York: Funk & Wagnalls, 1975.

Keller, R. E., *The German Language.* London: Faber and Faber, 1978.

Key, Wilson B., *Subliminal Seduction.* Englewood Cliffs, N.J.: Prentice-Hall, 1972.

Klima, Edward S., and Ursula Beliugi, *The Signs of Language.* Cambridge, Mass.: Harvard University Press, 1979.

Kurath, Hans, "Dialect Areas, Settlement Areas, and Culture Areas in the United States," in Caroline F. Ware, ed., *The Cultural Approach to History,* pp. 331–45, New York: Columbia University Press, 1940.

———, *A Word Geography of the Eastern United States.* Ann Arbor, Mich.: University of Michigan Press, 1949.

Labov, William, *Language in the Inner City.* Philadelphia: University of Pennsylvania Press, 1972.

———, "The Social Origins of Sound Change," in William Labov, ed., *Language in Time and Space,* pp. 251–65. New York: Academic Press, 1980.

Ley, David, and Roman Cybrwsky, "Urban Graffiti as Territorial Markers," *Annals of the Association of American Geographers,* 64, no. 4 (December 1974), 492–505.

McCrum, R., William Cran, and Robert MacNeil, *The Story of English.* New York: Penguin Books, 1987.

Meeker, Josephine, "Canada: Path to Constitution," *Focus,* 33, no. 2 (November–December 1982).

Momsen, Janet Hershall, and Janet Townsend, eds., *Geography of Gender in the Third World.* Albany, N.Y.: State University of New York Press, 1987.

Monmonier, Mark S., *Maps, Distortion, and Meaning,* A.A.G. Resource Paper No. 75–4. Washington, D.C.: Association of American Geographers, 1977.

Murray, Jeffrey S., "The Map Is the Message," *The Geographical Magazine,* 59, no. 5 (May 1987), 237–43.

Pool, Jonathan, "National Development and Language Diversity," in Joshua Fishman, ed., *Advances in the Sociology of Languages,* pp. 213–30. The Hague: Moulton, 1972.

Prestwich, Roger, "Maps and the Perception of Space," in David A. Lanegran and Risa Palm, eds. *An Invitation to Geography,* pp. 13–37. New York: McGraw-Hill, 1978.

Sauer, Carl O., "A Geographic Sketch of Early Man in America," *Geographical Review,* 34 (1944), 529–73.

Sivard, Ruth Leger, *World Military and Social Expenditures 1986,* 11th ed. Washington, D.C.: World Priorities, 1986.

Sopher, David E., "The Structuring of Space in Place Names and Words for Place," in David Ley and Marwyn Samuels, eds., *Humanistic Geography: Prospects and Problems,* pp. 251–68. Chicago: Maaroufa Press, 1978.

Speital, Hans-Henning, "An Areal Typology of Isoglosses: Isoglosses near the Scottish-English Border," *Zeitschrift Für Dialektologie und Linguistik,* 31 (July 1969), 50–66.

Thomson, David S., *Languages.* New York: Time Life Books, 1975.

Trudgill, Peter, "Linguistic Geography and Geographical Linguistics," *Progress in Geography,* 7 (1975), 229–52.

———, *On Dialect, Social and Geographical Perspectives.* Oxford, England: Blackwell, 1983.

Wagner, Philip L., "Remarks on the Geography of Language," *Geographical Review,* 48, no. 1 (January 1958), 86–97.

———, *Environments and People.* Englewood Cliffs, N.J.: Prentice-Hall, 1972.

Whorf, Benjamin Lee, *Language, Thought and Reality.* Cambridge, Mass.: M.I.T. Press, 1972.

Wirsing, Giselher, ed., *The War in Maps.* New York: German Library of Information, 1941.

Wolf, Eric, *Sons of the Shaking Earth.* Chicago: University of Chicago Press, 1959.

7 RELIGION

Each year from April through October, almost 5 million visitors from more than 100 different countries converge on Lourdes, a small town located at the foot of the Pyrenees in southwestern France. These are not ordinary tourists; rather they are pilgrims who come to worship at the grotto where, in 1858, a 14-year-old schoolgirl had a vision of the Virgin Mary. More than a century of pilgrimages has transformed the face of Lourdes from an agricultural town into a service center with new hotels, restaurants, and a wide variety of shops selling devotional articles. The landscape, population, and economy have been radically altered by millions of people acting on their religious beliefs (Rinschede 1986).

Not only in Lourdes, but also throughout the world, religion exerts a powerful influence on human spatial and ecological behavior. The purpose of this chapter is to assess this influence. The chapter begins with a classification of religions and a description of their distributions. Subsequent sections deal with the ways that religious beliefs affect the functioning of societies and the shaping of cultural landscapes.

DISTRIBUTIONS OF RELIGION

Problems of Definition and Classification

It is no easier to define religion than to define language or culture in general, and there are probably as many definitions as there are religions in the world. The sociologist Émile Durkheim proposed that religion consists of "a unified system of beliefs and practices relative to sacred things . . . which unite into a single moral community . . . all those who adhere to them" (1915, p. 62). Two aspects of this definition are of direct importance for the study of the geography of religions. First, religion is concerned with "sacred things," the beliefs and symbols that are inspired by a faith in a supernatural divine authority. This distinguishes religions from other societal beliefs, like patriotism or adherence to a political system, which are regarded as inspired by human thoughts only. The distinction is useful, although it should be noted that often religion is so intricately interwoven into everyday life that it is difficult to separate beliefs that are primarily religious from other societal beliefs.

Second, Durkheim's definition indicates the importance of religious beliefs in unifying people into a "single moral community." Probably no other aspect of culture is as important as religion in shaping human value systems. For example, in a 1981 study of values that sway American attitudes and actions, it was discovered that religion was considered to be more influential than age, gender, race, education, economic status, or political stance.

It is impossible to know and describe all the religious beliefs of the more than 5 billion people living today, or even those of a section of the population within a particular country. Consequently, a preliminary task is to classify religious belief systems into a few manageable groups, which can then be used as a framework for observing geographic variations and relationships.

An initial question concerns the criterion to be used to classify individuals into religious groups. One possible criterion is the degree of commitment to a set of religious beliefs and practices. Persons could be categorized into classes that range from the highest degree of religious commitment to the other extreme where religion has no influence whatsoever on patterns of life. By recognizing the degree of religiousness of people, we would have another explanatory factor for human behavior, besides those of income, age, marital status, and other attributes. If we knew the variations in religious commitment, we would be in a better position to interpret and possibly to predict behavior such as the movement of people to holy places (including churches, mosques, and shrines), the avoidance of specific foods, and the support for governmental regulations concerning societal behavior.

A classification based on degree of commitment would be useful also in assessing the varying importance of religion in a society over time. For example, some authorities see a decreasing role of religion in Western Europe today. They cite the relatively insignificant position of the organized Christian church in national governments. There is indeed a great contrast between medieval Europe when religion permeated most aspects of life and the present situation where religious institutions are more peripheral to the economic and political affairs of Western Europe.

In contrast, there are other indications that religious commitment elsewhere is not in retreat. In the United States, the rise of single-issue politics, such as the controversies over abortion or prayer in the public schools, reveals that some voters place what they perceive as religious concerns above all other considerations. In Iran, Pakistan, Malaysia, and several countries in North Africa and Southwest Asia, there has been a resurgence of Islamic influence in governmental policies.

The value of a classification based on degree of religious commitment is undeniable, but unfortunately such a classification is not practical, primarily because of the lack of data. Very little information is available about the religious beliefs of all individuals, much less about their corresponding behavior. Although a few polls provide information about beliefs (such as belief in a Supreme Power) and practices (such as regular attendance at a church), most of these polls fail to provide information that is useful in a geographic way. Therefore, confronted with these practical difficulties, scholars have used alternative classifications of religion.

The most common classification uses the broad groupings of affiliation with a major religion such as Islam. This classification scheme can be applied at various levels of detail and generalization. At the finer level, most major religions can be divided into denominations, sects, or branches. At the broader level, the world's religions are sometimes grouped into universalizing, ethnic, and tribal classes (see Table 7-1).

Universalizing religions, which include the major religions of Buddhism, Christianity, and Islam, are considered by their followers to be appropriate for all humanity. Consequently, admission into universalizing religions is an easy process: baptism and communion in Christianity, recital of doctrine in Islam, and adherence to specified practices in the case of Buddhism. These universalizing religions also have, or have had, active missionary campaigns that attempt to

TABLE 7-1. Major World Religions

Religion	Population	
	Millions	% of Total
Universalizing types:		
Christianity	1619	32.9
Islam	840	17.1
Buddhism	307	6.2
Bahai	5	0.1
Ethnic types:		
Hinduism	648	13.2
Chinese religions	208	4.2
Judaism	18	0.4
Sikhism	16	0.3
Shinto	3	0.1
Jainism	3	0.1
Tribal types:		
Tribal religions	97	2.0
Others:		
Other religions	131	2.7
Atheism and nonreligion	1026	20.8

Source: *Encyclopedia Britannica*, 1987.

spread their beliefs to other people. Given this goal and the mechanisms that promote their diffusion, it is not surprising that universalizing religions have extensive distributions and adherents drawn from diverse nationalities (Sopher 1967).

In contrast, ethnic religions are largely restricted to a single ethnic group or state, and they are strongly tied to specific places. Admission to ethnic religions, other than by birth, is difficult and complex, generally involving the adoption of an entire system of cultural values. Marriage tends to be restricted to other members of the faith. The major ethnic religions are Hinduism, concentrated in India and Nepal, Shinto in Japan, and the complex of religions in China. The Chinese religious complex consists of a religious-philosophical system that incorporates elements of Confucianism, Taoism, and Buddhism. Judaism also may be considered an ethnic religion because, even though Jews are widely dispersed throughout the world, the traditions of Judaism are firmly tied to its region of origin, which since June 1948 has been given explicit recognition as the state of Israel.

The distinctiveness of tribal religions lies in their intimate ties to nature. Because their central focus is the belief in and worship of the gods of nature, these religions are collectively termed **animism.** Objects in nature such as animals, mountains, and trees are seen to possess sacred powers, powers that must be respected and appeased if human life is to function properly. The relative number of persons belonging to tribal religions has decreased over the last few centuries as a result of religious conversions, especially to

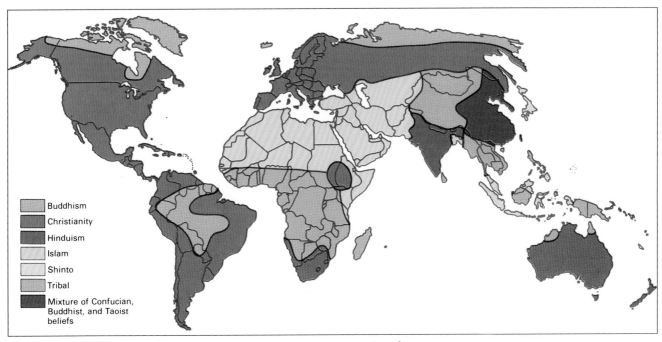

Figure 7-1. Major Religions of the World. Many exceptions exist within these generalized regions.

Legend:
- Buddhism
- Christianity
- Hinduism
- Islam
- Shinto
- Tribal
- Mixture of Confucian, Buddhist, and Taoist beliefs

Christianity and Islam, and because of a slower population growth rate than for other religious groups. Still, an estimated 97 million people practice animistic religions, mainly in remote parts of the world that have remained distant from the impact of other cultures. In the United States, for example, tribal religions persist in traditional Indian communities such as the Hopi Pueblos.

Even this threefold type of classification (universalizing, ethnic, and tribal) suffers from limitations. One problem is the lack of adequate statistics, which means world totals are only very general estimates (Table 7-1). In addition, many nations, including the United States, do not collect official census information about the religious affiliations of citizens.

A second problem is the great variation in beliefs (and resulting behavior) within each major religion. Take, for example, the many subdivisions within Christianity. Some Christians maintain taboos against particular foods and drinks, whereas others have no dietary restrictions; some Christians participate in complex rituals, but others do not; and many Christians engage in wars, but some adhere to pacifism. Similarly, a great degree of diversity exists in the other major religions, so the classification loses some of its differentiating power. In fact, there may well be more similarities among subgroups in different major religions than within each major group. For example, the activities of Buddhist and Christian pacifists may be more alike than the beliefs and practices of different Christian denominations. Likewise, periodic movements to places of worship, for example, are practiced

by some members of every major religion but not by all members of any one religion.

Distribution at a Global Scale

There are many religions in the world, but Christianity, Buddhism, Islam, Hinduism, and the Chinese religions account for a large proportion of the world's religious population and are dominant over a large proportion of the earth's inhabited land (see Figure 7-1). Interpreting this map of major religions, however, requires keeping in mind at least three limitations: (1) As stated previously, each religious category includes many variations of beliefs and practices. Consequently, readers cannot necessarily conclude that each region has a distinct set of religious beliefs and practices that differ from all other regions.

(2) Each region contains more than one religious population. For example, practitioners of tribal religions live in the interior portions of the Australian "Christian region," and Christian congregations reside within the region delineated as "Tribal" in southern Africa. Likewise, more Moslems live in India, which is mapped as a "Hindu region," than in the entire area of the Moslem states of Saudi Arabia, Iran, Iraq, and Syria.

(3) The size of each region is not always an accurate guide to the numerical importance of a

---

Animism. The belief that features in the natural environment have sacred significance and power.

religious population. Contrast, for example, the large population of Moslems in the small area of Bangladesh with the small population of believers in animism that occupy the vast areas of northern Canada.

The largest religious system in the world, in both geographic extent and number of adherents, is Christianity. Europe, North America, Latin America, the Soviet Union (where Christianity is officially discouraged), South Africa, Australia, and some islands of the Pacific fall within the Christian realm.

The most important divisions within Christianity are Protestantism, Roman Catholicism, and Eastern Orthodoxy. In Europe, generally Protestant areas are in the north, the Eastern Orthodox region is in the east, and Catholic countries are in the southern and central parts of the continent. The boundaries between these Christian subsystems are often sharp, nowhere more so than in Ireland where the division between Catholics and Protestants is a cultural cleavage, not just a theological difference.

Just as Christianity began with the teachings of one man, so Islam, another universalizing religion, began with the preachings of the Prophet Mohammed during the seventh century A.D. Faithful Moslems (the adherents to Islam) are commited to the beliefs and prescribed practices recorded in the Koran, the holy book of Islam. The Islamic region now extends across North Africa and Southwest Asia to Pakistan, with important outliers in Indonesia, Malaysia, Bangladesh, and Albania (Figure 7-1). Significant numbers of Moslems live in Soviet Central Asia and in adjacent western China. Within the Islamic region, more than half the population in most countries is Moslem; in many countries, Moslems account for more than 90 percent (Figure 7-2).

There tends to be a greater homogeneity in religious behavior in Islam than in Hinduism, Buddhism, or Christianity. One significant schism does exist, however. The main branch of Islam in terms of numbers of adherents is the Sunni, but in Iran and small areas along the Persian Gulf, the Shiah form of Islam is predominant. Differences between the two groups have religious, political, and economic repercussions. The Shiites, particularly in Iran, have developed a religious hierarchy that owns lands, raises taxes, and wields political power. In Sunni countries, there is no such hierarchy, and the government usually builds the mosques and pays the mullahs, the teachers of Islam.

The third universalizing religion, Buddhism, began as a philosophy of life expounded by Siddhartha Gautama in the sixth century B.C., when he became the enlightened one, the Buddha. Through time, Buddhism spread into many different cultural settings and evolved into a wide variety of religious beliefs and practices. So diverse is Buddhism that some scholars of religion believe that the variations in forms of Buddhism are as great as the total differences that exist within Christianity, Judaism, and Islam combined. Buddhism is the religion of several countries in Southeast Asia and is intermixed in China and Japan with local ethnic religions (Figure 7-1).

Unlike the universalizing religions, Hinduism, the oldest of the major religions, is ethnically less

More than 90% Moslem
50-90% Moslem

Figure 7-2. Distribution of the Moslem Population in the World. In 22 countries, more than 90 percent of the total population is Moslem. Approximately 44 percent of the Moslem population in the world lives in the four countries of Indonesia, Pakistan, Bangladesh, and Malaysia.

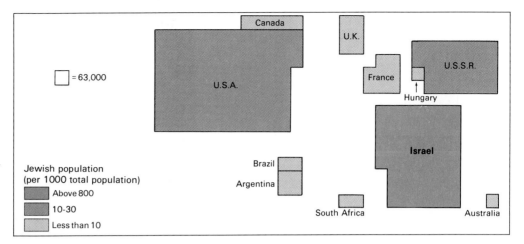

Figure 7-3. Cartogram of the Jewish Population in the World. Approximately 80 percent of the Jewish population lives in the three countries of the United States, the Soviet Union, and Israel.

Jewish population (per 1000 total population)
- Above 800
- 10-30
- Less than 10

= 63,000

diverse. Although there are outliers of Hinduism in Guyana, the Carribbean, parts of Southeast Asia, and other areas where Indians have settled, Hinduism is predominantly the religion of India and Nepal. Hinduism is almost impossible to define in terms of specific beliefs and practices because it forms a varied socio-religious system that has evolved in India over several millennia. Most forms of Hindu philosophy include concepts of moral duty and the individual consequences of fulfilling, or not fulfilling, religious obligations. These same beliefs underlie many aspects of the Indic culture, including the hierarchical arrangement of society (as expressed through caste or *jati*).

These four religions—Christianity, Islam, Buddhism, and Hinduism—account for about 90 percent of the world's population adhering to a religion (Table 7-1). The many other religions have fewer believers, but any one may be dominant within a particular country or in several small areas.

One such religion is Shinto, which is a diverse set of religious practices associated uniquely with Japan. The Shinto religion does not refer to any clearly defined doctrine or to a systematized code of behavior; rather, it is a religion that emphasizes the maintenance of ceremonial traditions for the purpose of communal well-being. Shinto involves personal and communal worship of indigenous deities to celebrate, interpret, and support traditional life in Japan. Its association with the government of Japan was especially close during the century prior to 1945. Since then, Shinto has had a declining role, although it continues to influence Japanese culture (Caldarola 1982).

Judaism is a complex of religious and social ethics. Although an emphasis on morality is common to the various forms of Judaism, no authoritative creed or set of practices clearly separates members of this religion from other faiths. Rather, the factor of being born a Jew is the overriding element that constitutes membership in this religious community. Even after the Diaspora (the dispersion of the Jews following the

Babylonian captivity), the scattered communities of Jews remained in contact, and a literary tradition and intense group spirit served to bind the adherents of Judaism together. Today, Jews are concentrated in the State of Israel, the United States (with more than 40 percent of the Jewish population of the world), and the Soviet Union (Figure 7-3).

Smaller, widely dispersed ethnic religions classified as tribal or animistic are located in the cold high latitudes of North America and Eurasia and in the tropical rainforests and savanna areas of South America, sub-Saharan Africa, and Southeast Asia (Figure 7-1). Most of these groups are small isolated communities, remote from the centers of government, industry, and, in our sense, advanced education. Some outsiders regard these religions as simple, but the belief systems often are complex. Despite variations from place to place, the common element in tribal religions is the holistic belief that every part of the environment is interconnected. Living in close association with the rhythms of nature, these societies perform elaborate rituals and ceremonies to relive their stories of creation and ensure the success of the hunt or the harvest. Although a revival of traditional beliefs is underway in some areas, in many African tribal communities people are converting to Christianity or Islam.

Distribution at a National Scale: The United States

The patterns of religious affiliations, especially at the denominational level, are more complex in the United States than they are in most countries. In this respect, the United States is not a typical illustration; yet it serves to demonstrate the dynamic nature of religion in a migratory and highly individualistic society.

The complexity is partly a result of the wide variety of places from which immigrants came to this country. During the early period of European settlement, various Christian groups from different regions of Europe brought their denominational affiliations to the new land. The interaction of these groups produced conversions and the formation of new religious bodies. Later, other ethnic groups migrated to, and within, the country. Some replaced former residents in older sections of major cities, some settled on newly acquired farmland, and others moved across the country following jobs in construction. The new immigrants often did not abandon their religious affiliations, as they did their language and many other cultural practices. Thus, the history of immigration and internal migrations has contributed to the complexity of religious patterns.

The American emphasis on individualism and the recognition of a pluralistic society have also contributed to change and the rapid formation of new religious bodies. This tendency for change contrasts with the situations in traditional societies where religion is part of the cultural heritage that most members accept and maintain throughout their lives. The history of religion in the United States is full of individual conversions to other established denominations and to new religious bodies. The numerical complexity is documented in a directory that recog-

nized 1275 religious bodies in the United States (Melton 1977, p. xii). All the major religions of the world are presented, with various branches of Hinduism, Buddhism, and Islam showing rapid rates of growth in recent decades.

Given the large number of religious bodies and their complex distributions, it is not easy to summarize the patterns of religious variations in the United States. Two distributions of Christian membership are shown here (see Figures 7-4 and 7-5). One map consists of denominational regions based on the percent of church membership affiliated with one of the five largest groups of churches (Figure 7-4). According to 1980 statistics, church members belonging to one of the Baptist denominational bodies predominate in 1164 counties (Quinn et al. 1982). The number of counties where Catholic, Methodist, Lutheran, and Latter Day Saints (Mormon) denominational bodies predominate are 963, 374, 227, and 74, respectively. Other U.S. counties have a high percentage of church members belonging to another denomination or a high diversity of church membership with no group predominating.

Where several counties having similar membership characteristics are located close together, they

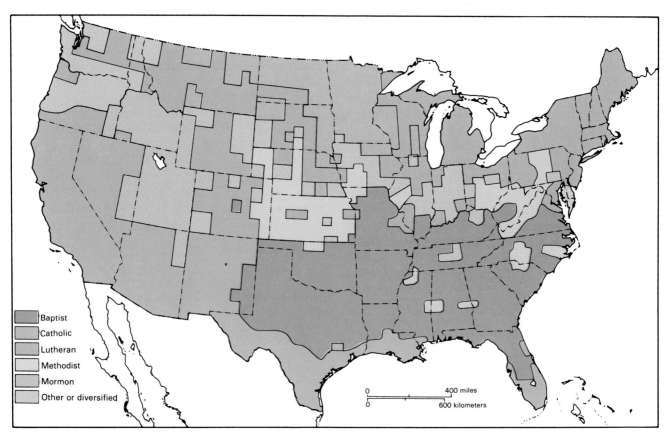

Figure 7-4. Regions of Religious Affiliation in the United States. Based on church membership per county in 1980, this map shows the regional concentration of the largest denominational groups. *Source: Glenmary Research Center.*

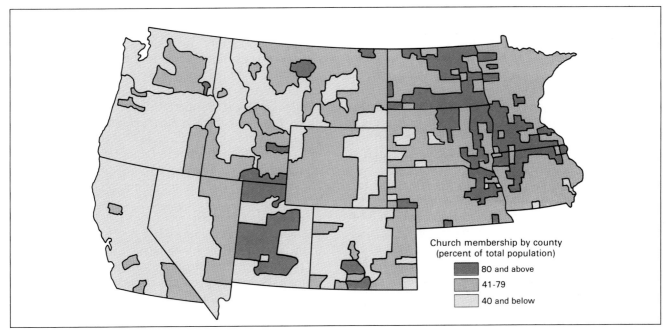

Figure 7-5. Variations in the Church Membership in the Northwest Portion of the United States, 1980. Church membership in the United States is approximately 60 percent of the total population. In most counties of Utah and in many counties in the upper Midwest, however, the percentage exceeds 80, whereas in those along the Pacific Coast the percentage is below 40. *Source:* Glenmary Research Center.

form a denominational region. Most regions actually include one or more counties that are not characteristic of the region as a whole, but at this level of areal generalization, the regional patterns provide an indication of religious variation in the United States.

Areas of relative homogeneity include the Mormon region of Utah and adjoining states, the Baptist region of the South, and the Lutheran region in the north central states. Areas where Catholics are dominant are mainly in the northeast and the southwest, but there are also smaller regions in the northwest and extreme southeast (i.e., southern Florida). Although the number of counties where Methodists predominate is the third largest, those counties tend to be scattered rather than concentrated into a single region. Furthermore, although Methodists are common in most areas throughout the country, typically they are not as numerous as the members of another denomination that is more regionally concentrated. For example, in the South where Baptists predominate, Methodists often rank second in numerical importance.

The second map shows the distribution of church membership by counties for one portion of the country (Figure 7-5). According to the 1987 edition of the *Yearbook of American and Canadian Churches*, about 60 percent of Americans are church members (Jacquet 1987). This statistic may understate the commitment to religion in the United States. For one reason, this figure excludes members of non-Christian religions.

Furthermore, some people who may regard themselves as religious may not be affiliated with a church. On the other hand, the figure may overstate the extent of true religious commitment because some people are members of a church in name only. Others may maintain active membership but do so primarily for social and other nonreligious reasons. However, church membership is probably as close an indicator of religious commitment as is available.

Affiliation with a Christian church varies geographically, from several counties where the percentage of membership is less than 10 to others exceeding 90. Utah and the upper Midwest are the areas with the highest levels of church membership. The former is, of course, the distinctive Mormon region (Chapter 5). The upper Midwest concentration is probably explained by the relative recency of German and Scandinavian migrants who look to the church to bolster ethnic identity.

Another area of high church membership is the South (not shown on Figure 7-5, but see Figure 5-27), where a general attitude of "conservatism" equates church attendance with an affirmation of traditional American ideals. In contrast, the areas of least church affiliation are the west coast and the non-Mormon western interior. These are nonconservative areas where church attendance tends to be low because places lack a strong ethnic identity or the population is sparce so access to churches is difficult (Shortridge 1976).

RELIGIOUS INSTITUTIONS

Territorial Structure

The spatial aspect of religion includes more than the distributions of people with various beliefs (i.e., mentifactual characteristics). It also involves the institutional organization of areas. One facet of religion is its sociofactual expression in the form of institutions. Like other social institutions (political, educational, economic), religious bodies organize areas into territorial units. Doctrine is spread to the adherents of a religion through an information network that has territorial dimensions. Some religions have loosely developed organizational and territorial structures, with many decisions being made at the local level. Sopher referred to these as "locally autonomous systems" (1967). Religions that have elaborate organizations and formal territorial structure are "hierarchical systems."

Many Protestant denominations fall into the category of locally autonomous communities. The Baptists, Disciples of Christ, and other congregational religions decide the details of the form of worship at the local level. Consequently, the spatial linkages of congregational organizations are weakly developed, consisting of a great number of separate groups only loosely associated through national and regional conventions.

Judaism, Sunni Islam, and Hinduism are also characterized by an organization that is essentially local and autonomous. In the case of Judaism, for example, ten adult males are sufficient to constitute a legitimate religious community, and nonspecialists are permitted to perform the rituals. Despite local independence and the absence of a hierarchical structure, the universal importance of the Old Testament and the high degree of contact among widely dispersed Jewish communities have kept the religion intact and relatively uniform. It is worth noting that all three general categories of religion (universalizing, ethnic, and tribal) include some religious subtypes that are locally organized. Indeed, tribal religions, limited to single groups of people and tied to particular places, are by definition local and autonomous.

At the other end of this organizational spectrum are the tightly organized religious systems with complex territorial structures. The Church of the Latter-Day Saints (Mormons), for example, has a well-defined structure, with a "capital" at Salt Lake City, a board and a president who establish policies and doctrines, and a series of grades of membership based on age and aptitude. Mormon territories are organized into stakes and wards. Ideally, each stake has a population of 5000 Mormons and each ward a population of 750. Boundaries of stakes and wards are revised as population changes regionally with time. In the same way that the United States is divided for political purposes into a hierarchy of administrative units (state, county, township), so Mormon society has its own explicit territorial structure.

Another important example of a hierarchical religious system is the Roman Catholic Church. In the words of David Sopher, this is "by far the most extensive—and also the most ancient—spatially organized system in the world today" (1967, p. 64). At the top of the hierarchy is the Pope, whose formal pronouncements on matters of faith and morality are considered to be infallible. Below the Pope, archbishops supervise ecclesiastical provinces, which are made up of several **dioceses,** each headed by a bishop. Each bishopric is composed of parishes, the basic unit of the ecclesiastical spatial structure.

The territorial structure of the Roman Catholic Church is founded on the geographic principle of accessibility to a node. Traditionally, the size of parishes in Europe has been small because the unit was designed to allow everyone to walk to services at the parish church. In Latin America, the parishes are larger, partly because the church may be too poor to support an intensive network.

Despite these regional variations, the Roman Catholic Church attempts to preserve a uniformity in its global territorial structure. When new needs arise, the boundaries of the administrative units are altered to suit the changed conditions. Factors such as population distribution, communications, political boundaries, and linguistic affinities are often taken into account. As the Catholic population grew in the United States over the period from 1900 to 1984, for example, the number of dioceses increased from 90 to 146 (Figure 7-6).

Unity and Disunity

Like linguistic communities and political units, religious systems experience conflicts between centripetal and centrifugal forces. A religion is held together by unifying practices—shared beliefs, formal liturgies, and organizational structures. However, as a religion spreads (which is the explicit aim of a universalizing religion), conflicts often develop between the established form and local variants. Distance is a major centrifugal force, often resulting in breaks in the communication network and the rise of new interpretations that may form the basis for separate religions.

The main divisions in Christianity occurred in the eleventh century, with the schism between the Eastern and Western churches, and in the sixteenth century when most of northern Europe split from the Catholic Church and adopted Protestantism. Subsequently, the Protestants splintered into numerous subdivisions. For example, in the seventeenth century, clergy with Puritan leanings in the Church of England encountered the displeasure of their bishops

Figure 7-6. Dioceses of the Roman Catholic Church in the United States, 1980. The Catholic Church is organized areally into a hierarchy of regional administrative units. *Source:* Glenmary Research Center.

0   400 miles
0   600 kilometers

⊙ Seat of archbishop

○ Seat of bishop

━━━ Boundary of province

─── Boundary of archdiocese/diocese

when they said prayers and preached sermons that did not conform to the practices of the Anglican Church. Such ministers, and members of their congregations, journeyed to America and helped to found communities outside the Church of England, where they could practice what they had preached. The Church of England was separately established in America as the self-governing Episcopalian Church. The Puritans left bishops behind; the Episcopalians, as the name states, retained them.

Even at the present time, when modern communications overcome many of the problems of distance, forces of disintegration and division pull against the unifying practices of religions. In many religions, tensions exist between reformers and defenders of orthodoxy. For example, some Roman Catholic priests in Latin America and Poland differ with the papal directives concerning their level of political activism. Advocating change, however, does not always lead to more disunity, and supporters of ecumenical movements may seek to bring previously separated groups back together again.

RELIGION RELATED TO LAND AND LIFE

Nature and Religion

An important, but often subtle, impact of religion on the land concerns attitudes about the relationships between the deity, humankind, and nature. One gen-

eral viewpoint is that nature is a manifestation of the divine [Figure 7-7(a)]. As a result, humans revere nature and treat the physical environment with the respect due to a divinity. This viewpoint that subordinates human to divine nature is characteristic of tribal societies. For example, the MicMac and Ojibwa Indians of eastern Canada maintained a spiritual contract with nature. The animals that they hunted were seen to possess spiritual powers and were treated by the Indians with a mixture of fear and respect. Hunting was a holy occupation. There were strong sanctions against overkilling game, and these Native Americans believed that the animals could retaliate by inflicting diseases if the hunting rules were ignored (Martin 1978). Similar beliefs were held by tribal societies throughout North America and are still prevalent in tribal societies in northern Asia and Africa today.

A second religious viewpoint maintains that a transcendental god reigns over humankind and nature [Figure 7-7(b)]. Humans and nature are equal and both must abide by the "laws" of the deity. From this perspective, human beings must cooperate with the ecological systems of nature. Farmers, for example, may be legally entrusted with land, but this ownership is regarded as a stewardship that requires them to

---

Diocese. The territory overseen by a bishop.

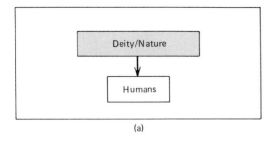

(a)

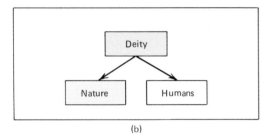

(b)

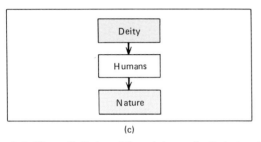

(c)

Figure 7-7. Three Religious Views about the Relationship between Humans and Nature. (a) The deity permeates nature and this spiritual realm reigns over humans. (b) Nature and humans are equals and both are under the reign of the deity. (c) The deity reigns over humans who in turn have dominion over nature.

preserve the land and not disrupt natural systems. This is essentially the religious philosophy of Chinese Taoism. The Taoist seeks to live simply and in harmony with nature, sentiments that are expressed in Taoist poetry and landscape painting (Tuan 1970, p. 122). In Christianity, the Benedictine tradition promotes this attitude, emphasizing careful management of nature with humans working as God's stewards on earth (Dubos 1972).

The dominant Judeo-Christian attitude places God above humankind and humans above nature [Figure 7-7(c)]. Taking its authority from the first chapter of Genesis, this attitude holds that humans have dominion over nature and are free to use land and resources for their maximum benefit. In fact, there is a holy obligation to subdue the untamed forces of nature, and to finish the Creation by bringing order to the physical environment (White 1967).

In the American experience, the wilderness was viewed ambivalently by the Puritans. On the one hand, it was considered the abode of the devil, which

meant it should be subjugated. On the other hand, it was regarded as a refuge from worldly corruption and a place of religious insight (Carroll 1969, pp. 2–3). Americans still retain these conflicting views, but generally subjugation has been the dominant theme.

Although the beliefs and attitudes about nature held by religious groups may not always match these specific viewpoints, the three types outlined above do suggest differences that may affect the use of earth resources. Obviously, economic, political, and other cultural factors also influence the variations in human utilization of the natural environment, but it is helpful to remember that religious philosophies may also underlie ecological decisions.

What about the reverse direction of the ecological relationship? Do environmental differences bring about variations in religions? It is far easier to raise these and related questions than to provide satisfactory answers.

One question might deal with the reasons for the origins of several major religions in only two areas of the world: Christianity and Islam (as well as Judaism and Zoroastrianism) originated in Southwest Asia; and Hinduism and Buddhism (plus Jainism and Sikhism) began in South Asia. Unfortunately our limited knowledge about early civilizations makes it very difficult to reconstruct the environmental and societal relationships that may have contributed to the beginnings of new religions. Most ideas about the locations of religious origins stress the association with early civilizations. Although environmental conditions played a role in the development of ancient civilizations (see Chapter 2), it is difficult to attribute religious origins primarily to elements of the natural environment.

A second question might pertain to the present distributions of religions in relation to the natural environment. The development of religious regions is essentially explained through the history of diffusion based on human migrations and spatial interactions. The generated patterns resemble, to some degree, those of language and other cultural characteristics that resulted from the sequence of human interactions through the ages. Although variations in natural features have partially affected the paths of movement and communication, there is no evidence that religion has been influenced by the physical environment more than have other attributes of culture.

Another set of ecological questions deals with the influence of the natural environment on religious symbols, practices, and similar characteristics. For example, some scholars speculate that the prohibition against eating pork by the "desert religions" of Islam and Judaism originated because of the dangers of disease (trichinosis), which contaminates meat stored in hot climates. In addition, pigs that scavenge garbage (including human fecal matter) transmit parasites like

Figure 7-8. Selling Wedding and Funeral Services. Numerous businesses depend on religiously related activities for marketing their goods and services. Photo courtesy of George Tuck.

tapeworms and roundworms to those who eat improperly cooked pork. The geographer Frederick Simoons, however, is not persuaded by the public health theory of pork prohibition (1967). He thinks that the disdain for pigs and pork developed among pastoral peoples of North Africa and Southwest Asia and later diffused to agriculturalists. He argues that the pig was an unsuitable animal for nomadic herding and that only later did this pragmatic reason for avoiding pork take on religious significance.

An important point about religion needs to be reemphasized here. As an outsider, a person may conclude that certain religious characteristics exist because of their functional relationships. To a believer of a religion being studied, however, scholastic explanations for specific sites, events, and sacred objects may be regarded as irrelevant (if not also irreverent). This outlook follows from the believer's faith that all things exist and are where they are because they manifest the divine will.

Geographic Implications of Rituals and Taboos

Rituals, which are prescribed methods for performing religious ceremonies, often occur in a limited area such as inside a sacred building. Nevertheless, they usually have an economic impact and geographic consequences that extend far beyond the points of their actual occurrence. For one, the performance of rituals requires the provision of goods and services; thus worshippers create a market that is met by suppliers (Figure 7-8). Although numerous rituals use common and relatively cheap items, such as water, fire, and food, the demand may yield a welcome financial boost for suppliers, particularly small entrepreneurs dependent on a local market. Furthermore, some rituals require specific items (for example, burial coffins), which make assessing the economic impact of these rites relatively easy. For example, in the United States, typical funeral costs exceed $2000 (Figure 7-9).

Figure 7-9. A Funeral Procession through a Cemetery. Rituals associated with death are important in virtually all religions. Often these involve active participation by family and friends as well as paying for professional services. Photo courtesy of George Tuck.

Religious activities often alter the amount and timing of economic transactions. In monetary terms, a person participating in religious rites or celebrating a holy day may not be producing goods and services for the marketplace. Therefore, religious events may result in fluctuating trade flows because of the different times that various religions observe holy days. For example, in a large metropolis composed of several religious groups, such as Bombay, retail shops in various sections of the city may be closed Friday, Saturday, or Sunday, thus affecting daily shopping patterns.

Religious rituals generally involve functions performed by priests, who are usually supported by other members of the religious community through contributions of cash or kind. For example, holy men who travel around India while performing religious functions are traditionally provided food and shelter. Similarly, large Christian churches in the United States may employ several persons as religious directors and leaders. So, in addition to creating a market for goods, rituals generate occupations for selected persons in most religious communities.

Religious rituals may also affect the distribution of wealth in a society. In parts of Southeast Asia and the western Pacific, the size of the pig herds is regulated through religious rituals, which aid in the distribution of valuable food (Figure 7-10). In many Native American societies, religious ceremonies were the means of redistributing food and possessions so that no member of the group went without subsistence. Islam traditionally prescribes that individuals who have the means should annually donate 2.5 percent of their net worth to the maintenance of institutions and to support the poor. Members of some Christian groups donate as much as one-tenth (a tithe) of their income to their church.

Persons may make large sacrifices, economic and otherwise, for religious reasons. Examples of self-denial range from ascetics who reject virtually all material possessions to milder forms of self-imposed poverty. The histories of most religions contain examples of the poorer members bearing a heavy financial burden in the construction of large temples. In some traditional agrarian economies today, the costs of special holy foods may consume a large portion of the cash income of the religious population (Stoddard 1976). Even in affluent societies such as the United States, families often accept financial hardships in order to pay for expensive rituals such as weddings and funerals.

Most religions proscribe and prohibit certain activities. The restrictions, or taboos, often involve the avoidance of certain foods and drinks. Prohibitions on drinks generally apply to alcohol, as in Islamic societies; but in some Christian denominations, restrictions include stimulants such as tea and coffee, which are considered injurious to health. In this respect, religious restrictions reinforce "rules for healthy living," such as those contained in the Old Testament.

Dietary taboos may affect the distributions of various animals. In southern Spain and Portugal, both Catholic nations, the pig is an important part of the peasant economies. Only a short distance away, in the similar physical environment of the Atlas Mountains of Morocco and Algeria, few pigs are kept because the area is inhabited primarily by Moslems (see Figure 7-11). Similar contrasts exist between the Christian and Moslem parts of the Philippines and between Chinese and Moslem villages in Malaysia.

Other restrictions prohibit the killing of animals. In some branches of Buddhism, for example, ending the life of any animal is considered wrong. An orthodox Buddhist will not eat any meats, including fish

Figure 7-10. A Kwaio Food Ritual, Solomon Islands. Pigs are prepared for eating during a religious ceremony and can only then be consumed by adult males who have been initiated. Pigs that have not been consecrated may be eaten by anyone. Photo courtesy of Wallace E. Akin.

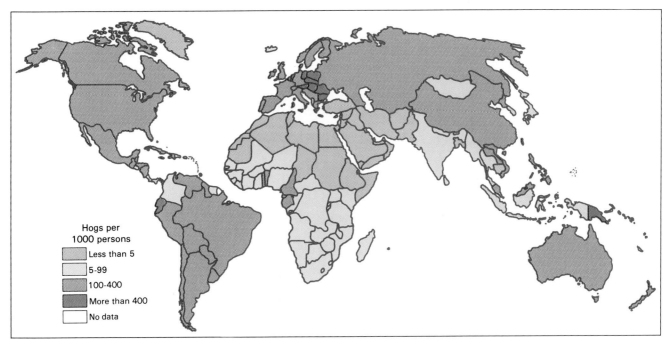

Figure 7-11. World Distribution of Pigs. Jewish and Islamic beliefs that pork is an impure food affect the distribution of pigs in the world.

and either fertilized or unfertilized eggs. Cows are regarded as sacred by orthodox Hindus, which means that killing a cow is a sin and eating the flesh of a murdered cow is abhorrent. The result in a geographical sense is the great concentration of cattle in India (Figure 7-12). Admittedly, the cattle in India, in addition to their sacred significance, provide many benefits such as draft power, milk, and dung (the latter

being an important source of fuel in a country where firewood is scarce and expensive).

Taboos against the eating of human flesh are found in most religions, although cannibalism has not been considered a sin in all societies at all times. In fact, cannibalism had a religious justification in the past, as in the Mayan civilization of the Yucatan Peninsula.

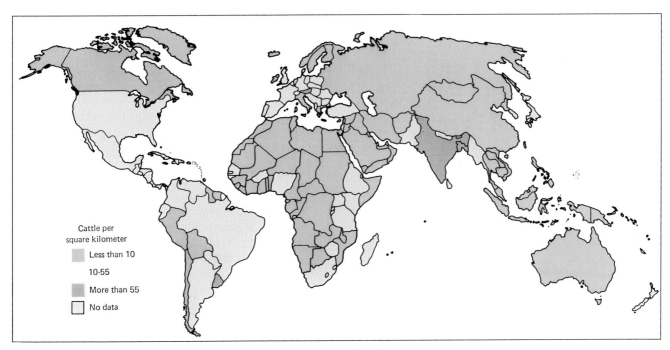

Figure 7-12. World Distribution of Cattle. The Hindu reverence for the cow is one reason for the abundance of cattle in India.

Some religious restrictions apply to a wide variety of "polluted" or "impure" foods, but these prohibitions may be removed after the foods have been sanctified. Only through religious rituals can polluted food (*tref* in Judaism, for example) be transformed into pure food (*kosher*). Some foods may be acceptable under usual conditions but restricted on certain days. Two examples are the traditional avoidance of meat on Fridays in Catholic Europe (which gave a great boost to the fishing industry), and the ban on the sale of alcohol in many American counties and towns on Sundays.

Community conflicts may occur when members of a religious group observe that their nonbelieving neighbors are not recognizing the same food practices. In India, conflicts between Moslems, who have no sanctions on the killing and consumption of cows, and Hindus, who regard this as sacrilege, have sometimes erupted in violence. Transgressions of the ban on alcohol by Europeans working in Islamic countries have resulted in heavy punishments.

Sacred Structures as Part of the Cultural Landscape

Sacred structures are a tangible expression of religion. These include temples (as a generic form) built to house the rituals of worship, public shrines, and many other structures for performing a variety of services sponsored by religious organizations. Of the variety of sacred structures, temples are most impressive because they are often monumental in size and distinctive in their architectural representation of religious beliefs (Figure 7-13).

In general, sacred structures in tribal religions are not very evident on the landscape. Buildings having exclusive religious significance are uncommon because religion permeates all aspects of life. Homes, for example, often are constructed according to divine principles, and many family activities occurring within them have religious meaning, but they are not regarded as primarily religious structures. Furthermore, because many plants, animals, and other features of the natural environment are regarded as sacred and a part of the religious setting, there is no need to maintain separate temples.

The function of sacred structures in some religions is basically to house a god, while in others the temple is constructed to house a congregation (Sopher 1967, p. 26). Hindu temples are primarily houses for gods. As such, they do not enclose large spaces, which are necessary where many people worship together. The architectural style and splendor of the buildings depend on the number and wealth of supporters, time of construction, and regional traditions. The magnificent Minakshi Temple in Madurai, for example, has a

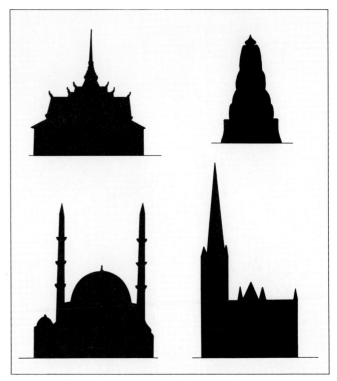

Figure 7-13. Architectural Shapes of Religious Structures. Despite internal architectural variations, certain structural shapes are associated with specific religions, as suggested by these profiles.

south Indian architectural form, in contrast to the regional styles of north India (Figures 7-14 and 7-15). The wealth of the Minakshi Temple is evident in its nine towers, which are adorned with 33 million stone and stucco carvings. At the other end of the scale, most villages have inconspicuous Hindu temples.

Buddhist temples are also places for adherents to keep and display sacred images (that is, their **iconography**) and to assemble individually for prayer. The Jokhang temple in Lhasa, Tibet, for example, contains more than 250 statues plus other forms of religious images in 20 different alcoves and prayer rooms (Figure 7-16). The form and meaning of this single temple, however, do not represent Buddhist architecture in general because styles vary greatly from region to region. Temples in Tibet, which even differ from each other according to sects, contrast with Buddhist structures in Thailand (Figure 7-17); and both of these styles contrast with those in Japan, where the wooden Shinto temples have influenced Buddhist architecture (Figure 7-18).

Mosques, on the other hand, are built specifically to house Moslems assembled for prayer. Interior space for worship is necessary because followers of Islam are required to observe the ritual of prayer five times a day. Although Moslems may lay their prayer rug at any location when it is time to pray, ideally the prayer should take place in a designated place of congrega-

Figure 7-14 (left). South Indian Hindu Temple, Madurai, India. Photo courtesy of Sally Stoddard.

Figure 7-15 (above). North Indian Hindu Temple, Kanpur, India. Photo courtesy of Sally Stoddard.

tion. The Koran expressly forbids any images, including those of the Prophet Mohammed, so no statues adorn mosques. The domes and minarets (the tall towers used for calling the faithful to prayers), like the spires of the Christian church, announce the place of worship and symbolically reach beyond the structure itself. As with the religious structures of other religions, the specific form of mosques varies with region, time of construction, and cultural setting (Figures 7-19 and 7-20).

Sikh temples display some similarity to the sacred structures of both Hinduism and Islam, the two religions on whose traditions Sikhism was founded in the fifteenth century. Like Moslem structures, there are no images and iconography is limited. Like Hindu structures, the area inside Sikh temples is seldom large. Even the famous Golden Temple in Amritsar is modest in size (Figure 7-21).

Christian temples house symbols of the divine and provide a place of congregation. Architecture again varies with time and place (Figures 7-22 and 7-23; also see Figure 4-1), but there is a basic distinction between the magnificent churches and cathedrals of medieval Europe and the simpler churches of more

recent centuries (Figure 7-24). Even those with plainer features range from large buildings with modern designs to small structures with traditional forms (Figure 5-32).

Besides being obvious features on the landscape, sacred structures have often affected the arrangement of other buildings and activities. Towns in traditional societies frequently were organized around a temple or dominant religious structure. In Europe, the major church occupied a prominent position on Italian piazzas, Spanish plazas, and other marketplaces (Figure 7-25). In Islamic towns, a large central mosque served as the focus of city life. The internal arrangement of many Hindu temple towns in India was planned with a complex of religious buildings situated in the focal area, a position which then affected paths of travel, residential districts, and other locations. Even with the many changes that have occurred in cities in recent times, the initial locational emphasis given to religious structures still influences internal urban patterns.

Iconography. The images or symbols associated with, for example, national identity or religious affiliation.

Figure 7-16. Jokhang Tibetan Buddhist Temple, Lhasa, China. Photo courtesy of Sarah Disbrow.

Figure 7-17. Wat Arun, Buddhist Temple, Thailand. Photo courtesy of Velma Lentz.

Figure 7-18. Kinkakuji, Buddhist Temple, Kyoto, Japan. Photo courtesy of Velma Lentz.

Figure 7-19. Mohammad Ali Mosque, Cairo, Egypt. Photo courtesy of George Tuck.

Figure 7-20. Jama Masjid (Mosque), Delhi, India. Photo courtesy of Sally Stoddard.

Figure 7-21 (left). Sikh Golden Temple, Amritsar, India. Photo courtesy of Sally Stoddard.

Figure 7-22 (below). Christian Cathedral, Cologne, West Germany. Photo courtesy of Leslie Hewes.

Figure 7-23 (left). Byzantine Christian Cathedral, Perigueux, France. Photo courtesy of Leslie Hewes.

Figure 7-24 (above). American Midwest Christian Church, Auburn, United States. Photo courtesy of Sally Stoddard.

Figure 7-25 (below). Cathedral Located on an Early Market Square, Salzburg, Austria. Photo courtesy of Sally Stoddard.

The impact of sacred structures is less marked at the center of modern towns, but the growth patterns of North American cities may be influenced by decisions concerning the location of new churches and the associated real estate investments made by religious groups. In the United States, churches, like retail stores, need a minimum population to function successfully. With this in mind, many denominations carefully plan the locations of their churches, taking into account such factors as accessibility and anticipated population growth.

Like other features built by humans, churches persist in places that represent past locational decisions. Large churches in towns of dwindling populations—specifically, declining populations of supporting worshippers—may be relics of previous settlement patterns. A common feature in American central cities is an abandoned church with its boarded-up windows or partial renovations reflecting the building's conversion to a commercial establishment. It may represent the last landscape evidence of a nineteenth-century immigrant group that has since dispersed.

Open-country churches in the Midwest sometimes stand as evidence of larger rural populations that existed before mechanization of agriculture reduced the farming population and before the automobile extended the range of travel. The locations of all rural churches, however, are not relics of previous conditions. Some may reflect the short distances travelled by most church-goers or an ethnic community with a strong attachment to place (Figure 7-26).

In addition to temples, shrines are another landscape feature associated with religion. Public shrines, such as statues, images, and markers, may be distinguished from temples on the basis of size and structure. Temples are generally large enough for worshippers to enter and participate in group rituals, whereas shrines seldom contain any interior space for worship. Most shrines are small (Figure 7-27). As exceptions, Buddhist stupas, which are three-dimensional representations of the religious universe, may be as tall as 70 meters (Figure 7-28).

Shrines are often regularly distributed in areas where the density of believers is fairly uniform. For example, wayside shrines are common features of the landscape in Bavaria, an area of Roman Catholic population. Similarly, the small shrines and images of Hindu deities are common throughout India and Nepal (Figure 7-29).

Figure 7-26. Open-Country Church in the American Midwest. Buildings for worship are a common part of the religious landscape in many parts of the world. Photo courtesy of Sally Stoddard.

Figure 7-27. Roadside Shrine. Shrines along routes of travel are common to many religions in many parts of the world. This one is on a mountain road near the Himalayan city of Darjeeling in India. Photo courtesy of Velma Lentz.

Figure 7-28. Buddhist Stupa in Sri Lanka. Many of the great structures of the ancient world are related to religious activities. Some early stupas near Anuradhapura, Sri Lanka, were built more than 2000 years ago. Photo courtesy of Sally Stoddard.

Figure 7-29. Rural Shrine in the Kathmandu Valley, Nepal. Shrines are located in densely settled urban areas and in the open country. Photo courtesy of Sally Stoddard.

The specific sites of shrines are associated with a variety of factors. In some areas they are located in reference to topographic features such as hilltops and stream confluences. Often they are positioned along travel routes because in most religions they function as protectors for travellers, as illustrated by shrines placed at passes in the Himalayas, Andes, and other mountain ranges (Figure 7-30). Shrines may also commemorate events or individuals who are significant in the religious history of an area.

Other structures associated with religious organizations include hospitals, nurseries, orphanages, retirement homes, rooming houses for transients, recreation halls, and schools at all levels of education. Such buildings are used to provide assistance for persons that have special needs. Examples are a drug rehabilitation center in San Francisco, a retirement home in Copenhagen, a pet cemetery in Tallahassee, and a bird hospital in Delhi (see Figure 7-31). The extent to which such buildings visibly express religious affiliations differs greatly. In some cases, the architecture and attached symbols reveal the building's religious base; in others, there is no visible expression of religious connections.

The locations of many structures associated with organized religion tend to illustrate two contrasting geographic generalizations. First, some buildings, such as parochial elementary schools, are situated according to the distribution of the members of the supporting group. Since they serve the population of supporters, they are positioned at places of easy access for that same population. Second, other types of structures may *not* be close to the supporting religious population because they house a program that represents a mission to nonmembers. For example, Salvation Army rooming houses for transients are

Figure 7-30. Shrine at a High Place in the Peruvian Andes. Shrines are often located in high places where they command attention and provide spiritual protection to travellers. Photo courtesy of Sally Stoddard.

Figure 7-31. Bird Hospital Supported by Jains in India. Members of this austere religion, which originated in India in the sixth century B.C., believe in the sanctity of all forms of life. Photo courtesy of Sally Stoddard.

a type of humanitarian service for needy persons, irrespective of their religious orientations. Consequently, these buildings are located where transients are concentrated and not necessarily close to the people who support the service.

Sacred Places

In most, if not all, societies, certain places are given special significance as locations of sanctity. Sacred places may be dreadful places where evil spirits are believed to reside. Some locations have "always" been regarded as sites of sanctity, whereas others have become sacred as the result of certain events (such as the death of a martyr) or as having been designated a special area (e.g., burial grounds).

The locational relationship between sacred places and topographic features varies from religion to religion, but some natural features take on particular significance. The confluence of two rivers, the source of streams, springs (especially hot springs), peninsulas projecting into the sea, and mountain tops are often assigned sacred importance. The sacred sites of the Pawnee, for example, were located near the waters of the Republican, Loup, and Platte rivers in Nebraska; the Crow hold the Powder River of Wyoming in religious esteem; and the Black Hills are recognized by the Dakota Sioux as a holy place. (See Point-Counterpoint at the end of this chapter.)

In Europe, Christian pilgrims are attracted to thousands of sacred places such as springs, rock formations, and high places. Of the almost two thousand sacred places associated with site features in Western Europe, nearly half are located at high places, a third at springs and other water sites, and most of the rest at groves, rock formations, and grottos (Nolan 1981). In India, the major sacred places of pilgrimage are located mainly on hilltops, along rivers, or at headlands (Figure 7-32). Most are marked by temples and related structures, but some may not be obvious to the uninformed.

The sacred importance of forests varies from place to place and over time. Small groves may be areas of sanctity for the population of nearby settlements, which explains the survival of groves of trees around Nepalese villages in otherwise deforested areas. Elsewhere, forests have been regarded as the

Figure 7-32. Hindu Pilgrimage Sites and Routes in India. Sacred sites in India can be ranked, in a very general sense, according to their level of accepted sanctity and their importance as a destination for pilgrims. This map includes only the major sites and pilgrimage routes.

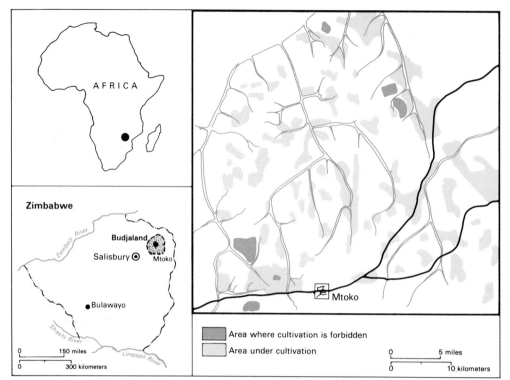

Figure 7-33. Arable Land and Sacred Sites of Budja in Northeastern Zimbabwe. Much of the arable land is cultivated, but Budja people leave some fertile areas uncultivated because they are sacred. From Isaac 1961–1962. Used with permission from *Landscape*.

Figure 7-34. Chinese Cemetery in Singapore. In this urbanized country, burial sites may be located on valuable land in the same way that cemeteries occupy high-value land within American cities. Photo courtesy of Velma Lentz.

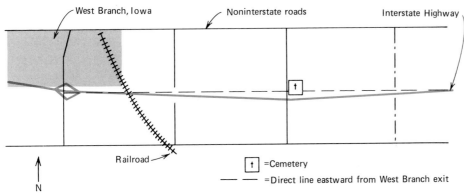

Figure 7-35. The Preservation of Cemetery Land. The route of this interstate highway deviates from a straight line in order to preserve the sacred land of the cemetery.

abode of evil spirits and are considered dangerous. Europeans and their offshoots in colonial America frequently viewed the wilderness as untamed and chaotic space.

The designation of places as sacred may have a significant impact on the landscape and on patterns of life. The Budja, for example, a Shona tribe living in northeastern Zimbabwe, keep certain areas out of use because they are associated with spirits (Isaac 1961–1962). The Budja believe that the spirits of the dead live in these areas and could punish anyone who used the land in an improper manner. These uncultivated places in an agricultural area cannot be explained in economic or topographical terms; they are purely religious in origin (Figure 7-33).

Cemeteries are a major landscape manifestation of sacred space. Many religious persons regard burial land as hallowed territory that should not be used for other purposes. In rural areas of the American Midwest, for example, where most of the available land is cultivated, Christian cemeteries stand out on the landscape as isolated patches of sacred space. In densely settled agricultural areas of Asia, cemeteries may occupy valuable land (Figure 7-34). In China, despite the government's efforts to popularize cremation, the old tradition of burial persists. According to official estimates, an additional 2667 hectares of land in China are devoted to burial sites each year. In contemporary cities of the United States, cemeteries are often the only open spaces in high-rent areas otherwise dominated by buildings and streets. Valuable urban space is not always devoted exclusively to burial grounds, however; in some cities, cemeteries are used also for parks and recreation.

The spiritual nature of cemeteries is evidenced by attitudes about which bodies may be buried in them. For some people, these sacred areas assume special qualities, which are maintained by restricting burial

"admissions." Within the United States, some cemetery owners restrict burials only to people who meet requirements of race, ethnicity, or religion.

The locations of Christian cemeteries in the United States may be associated with a variety of features. In some regions they are situated on hilltops. Often they are close to towns and cities. Because they are likely to remain long after a town has disappeared, they sometimes reveal the sites of previous settlements. The emphasis on retaining land as a cemetery is often strong enough that it may lead to modified locations for other features, as demonstrated by an otherwise straight highway that curves to avoid a cemetery (Figure 7-35).

In some cases, sacred places are so important in the functioning of a religious system that they become major urban centers. Varanasi in northern India, Salt Lake City in Utah, and Mecca in western Saudi Arabia are examples. All are centers of pilgrimages and are major foci for religious activities.

Religious Movements

A form of religious activity that has explicit geographic implications is the travel of worshippers to holy sites. These movements vary in distance, frequency, and purpose—from short daily visits to a local place of worship to long distance pilgrimages undertaken once in a lifetime.

Short trips by many people to a place of worship generate a nodal region that is not much different from those produced by travel to work or to shop. Typically the pattern of movement displays a distance decay because the number of people travelling short distances is larger than the number who journey long distances. Religious movements tend to generate a "steep" decay; that is, fewer persons travel long

Figure 7-36. Religious Procession in Kanpur, India. The occasion for this movement along a sacred route is Moharram, the first month of the Moslem year. Photo courtesy of Sally Stoddard.

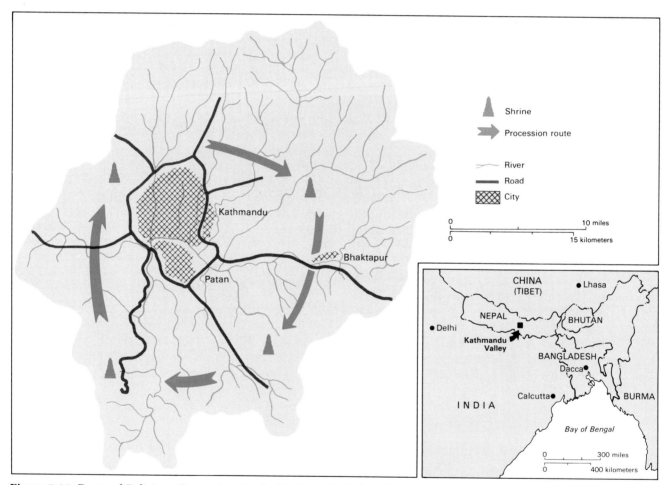

Figure 7-37. Route of Religious Processions in the Kathmandu Valley of Nepal. Some ceremonial routes may be as short as the path around a sacred building; but others may be much longer, such as this 58-kilometer route linking four shrines in the Kathmandu Valley.

Figure 7-38. Buddhist Pilgrims in Nepal. At some holy sites during auspicious occasions, millions of pilgrims may assemble. At other times and places, only a few worshippers may participate in a relatively inconspicuous journey and private worship. Photo courtesy of Sally Stoddard.

distances for religious goals than for many other purposes. For example, in the United States, people generally travel a shorter distance to worship than to attend high school, buy shoes, or watch live theater.

Processions and circumambulation illustrate a type of religious movement that is especially interesting geographically because the role of distance is different from that which produces the pattern of distance decay. Religious processions, which occur in most major religions, often commence and end at the same point. The goal is not to arrive at some destination but rather to achieve a ceremonial objective. The procession may celebrate a holy day, demonstrate the significance of the religion to both believers and nonbelievers, delineate sacred territory, or encourage the faithful to undergo some sacrifice by participating in the procession (Figure 7-36). Examples are the processions by Christians during Holy Week, by Moslems in and around Mecca at the time of the **hajj** (i.e., the pilgrimage to Mecca), and by members of most other religious groups during festivals and celebrations.

An illustration of a longer ceremonial journey is the annual procession that moves in a clockwise direction around four Hindu shrines in the Kathmandu Valley of Nepal (Figure 7-37). Worshippers may commence the processional route at any place, but they proceed from site to site in a clockwise sequence. On the day of the annual procession, participants strive to complete the entire journey to all four sacred sites. The time it takes to walk the entire route (58 km) may require beginning the day before daybreak and continuing well past sunset.

Circumambulation, the walking or moving around an object or place, accentuates the sacrificial objective of movement. The central focus may be a temple (such as the Jokhang in Lhasa), a sacred object or sacred places, such as the city of Varanasi in India and Mount Kailasa in Tibet. The distance of many sacred paths is only the length of a circumambulatory corridor encircling the base of a temple; the length of others is as much as 80 kilometers in circumference and requires several days to complete. In some cases, movement may be undertaken in an arduous manner—for example, by prostrating oneself on the ground and moving only a body's length at a time. Accordingly, circumambulation contrasts with those religious (and other human) movements where distance is a bothersome but inescapable barrier in the way of achieving a particular objective; instead it is a form of worship that utilizes the rigors of travel in a manner that is purposefully sacrificial.

Pilgrimages tend to combine the negative aspects of distance with the positive sacrificial characteristics of processions (Figure 7-38). Many orthodox pilgrims believe the journey to a sacred site should be arduous

---

Hajj. The annual pilgrimage to Mecca that is prescribed as a religious duty of Moslems.

Circumambulation. Walking around a focal point; illustrated by moving around a sacred object or place as a form of worship.

enough to prove that the worshipper is worthy of appearing at the place of the divine. For other pilgrims, the objective is to arrive and worship at the holy place, and the method of getting there is unimportant.

The routes taken by pilgrims also indicate this mixture of motives because they demonstrate at least two types of spatial behavior. One type results from pilgrims who travel to a holy site without regard to a specific route. If the travel routes of thousands of such pilgrims were to be mapped, the combination of all paths would resemble the distance decay pattern formed by travellers going to other types of nodal places. Another type of travel pattern is generated by pilgrims who regard the act of travelling as a form of worship that requires them to follow a specific sacred path to the holy sites (Figure 7-32). The famous 1385-kilometer pilgrimage route linking 88 temples around the island of Shikoku (Japan) illustrates the religious importance of following a specific path.

Many pilgrimages today combine religious objectives with more general travel goals such as tourism. The relative importance of the religious motivation varies with the individual. At a holy site like Varanasi or Rome, there may be pilgrims who have stopped briefly while on vacation, others who are making a tour of religious places, and still others who have made a sacrificial journey to reach that particular destination.

Pilgrimages involve many travellers. In recent years 2 to 4 million Moslems have entered Saudi Arabia annually at the time of the hajj to Mecca. This figure does not include Saudi pilgrims (or those who come at other times of the year). At many Hindu holy sites in India, annual attendance exceeds a million; and 12 million visit the Basilica of the Virgin of Guadalupe on the outskirts of Mexico City every year. Not only do these pilgrimages confirm religious traditions and reinforce beliefs, but they also mix people from different backgrounds. Moreover, the travel facilities, accommodations, and, in many cases, the sale of religious items add an economic dimension to the essentially religious purpose of pilgrimage.

Religion and Territorial Conflicts

Religious beliefs frequently reinforce political feelings about possession of an area. These feelings are partly because religion is often seen as a key to ethnic survival. Religion can function as a cohesive force in both a spiritual and social sense, and it resists acculturation more strongly than other aspects of culture. Certainly the Plains Indians during the nineteenth century, when in the midst of great cultural change, clung to their religions as a mooring in a storm. Similarly, the church is the "guardian of cultural and ethnic identity" among Ukrainian and Hungarian settlers in the Canadian Prairie Provinces, functioning as the center of immigrant culture (Lehr 1982; Degh

Figure 7-39. A Ukranian Orthodox Church in Canada. The church architecture suggests the background of residents in Dauphin, Manitoba, and the size of the building implies its importance in the community.

BOX 7-1. MANIFEST DESTINY

In the nineteenth century, the United States expanded its territory to the west, southwest, and northwest over land already occupied by Native Americans, as well as by Mexico and Britain. This areal expansion was justified by declaring that such action was in accordance with a divine will. This belief was stated by many public leaders; the two statements below are those by the newspaper editor John L. O'Sullivan and Senator T. H. Benton of Missouri, respectively:

Texas has been absorbed into the Union in the inevitable fulfillment of the general law which is rolling our population westward; the connexion of which . . . is too evident to leave us in doubt of the manifest design of Providence in regard to the occupation of this continent. It was disintegrated from Mexico in the natural course of events, by a process perfectly legitimate on its own, blameless on ours; and in which all the censures due to wrong, perfidy and folly, rest on Mexico alone. And . . . incorporation [of Texas] into the Union was not only inevitable, but the most natural, right, and proper thing in the world—and it is only astonishing that there should be any among ourselves to say it nay. [O'Sullivan 1845]

The effect of the arrival of the Caucasian, or White race, on the western coast of America, opposite the eastern coast of Asia, remains to be mentioned among the benefits which the settlement of the Columbia will produce, and that a benefit, not local to us, but general and universal to the human race. Since the dispersion of man upon the earth, I know of no human event, past or present, which promises a greater, and more beneficial change upon the earth than the arrival of the van of the Caucasian race . . . upon the border of the sea which washes the shore of the eastern Asia. . . . It would seem that the White race alone received the divine command, to subdue and replenish the earth! For it is the only race that has obeyed it—the only one that hunts out new and distant lands, and even a New World, to subdue and replenish. Starting from western Asia, taking Europe for their field, and the Sun for their guide, and leaving the Mongolians behind, they arrived, after many ages, on the shores of the Atlantic, which they lit up with the lights of science and religion, and adorned with the useful and the elegant arts. Three and a half centuries ago, this race, in obedience to the great command, arrived in the New World, and found new lands to subdue and replenish. For a long time, it was confined to the border of the new field. . . . The van of the Caucasian race now tops the Rocky Mountains and spreads down to the shores of the Pacific. In a few years a great population will grow up there, luminous with the accumulated lights of European and American civilization. . . . The Red race has disappeared from the Atlantic coast; the tribes that resisted civilization met extinction. This is a cause of lamentation with many. For my part, I cannot murmur at what seems to be the effect of divine law. [Benton 1846]

1980). Even when some religious practices and the architecture of the buildings change, the Ukrainian Orthodox Church still plays a vital role in maintaining ethnic and territorial identity (Figure 7-39). Religion has served as an important cohesive element for many immigrant groups in many other places and times.

When a group or nation attempts to justify territorial control over an area, religion may become more than just an element of cultural distinctiveness. In some societies, especially those in which ideology is emphasized, religious doctrines may be proclaimed to reinforce other reasons presented for ruling over particular lands. Territorial disputes become especially bitter when each of the contending factions believes it is promoting the "true" religion. History is full of events, including wars, in which religion was presented as a strong justification for territorial and cultural expansion. Examples in earlier ages include the religious wars between Catholics and Protestants in seventeenth-century Europe, the Crusades, and the holy wars of Islam. In more recent times, some of the conflicts between Native Americans and the U.S. government resulted from territorial expansion that was justified in the name of **Manifest Destiny** (Box 7-1). According to several nineteenth-century proponents of Manifest Destiny, the United States was thought to have a divine mission to subdue the continent and its original inhabitants.

Religious issues continue to be important in many territorial conflicts today. They range from local disputes over autonomy (such as that sought by some Hindus in primarily Buddhist Sri Lanka), to global attempts to "stop the spread" of "godless" Communism. Two other illustrations are the conflict in Northern Ireland and the war between Iraq and Iran.

In Northern Ireland, religion has been explicitly politicized ever since the North was partitioned from the South in 1921 on the basis of the distribution of Protestants and Catholics. Northern Ireland now has a Catholic minority that is about 37 percent of the population. However, close to the borders of the Irish Republic and in ghettos in Londonderry and Belfast, Catholics comprise more than three-quarters of the population.

Many Catholics and Protestants in Northern Ireland realize that economic and political factors contribute to hostilities, but antagonisms have become

---

Manifest Destiny. The belief that the westward expansion of the United States during the nineteenth century was an expression of divine will (see Box 7-1).

institutionalized along religious lines. Protestants and Catholics tend to live in separate areas, attend different schools, nurture different traditions, praise different heroes, and avoid interfaith marriages. The limited amount of social interaction has created two distinct communities which view each other from their own religiously defined perspectives.

The war between Iraq and Iran, which started in 1980 as a territorial conflict, has been fueled by religious differences. Most Iranians are Shiite Moslems, while Iraq is ruled primarily by Sunni Moslems, although the country has a large Shiite population and contains the holy Shiite shrines of Nejaf and Karbala. Many Iranians and Iraqis believe that it is essential to participate in a holy war to protect their country and religion.

Religion and Governments

The extent to which religion is influential in a society depends partly on the policies and actions of governments, policies and actions that can vary across the entire spectrum from hostility to full support of religion. In most countries where the Communist Party is in control, the government has been hostile to religion

The Communist Party in the Soviet Union, following Lenin's theory that modernization is hampered by religion, works to undermine the influence of religion. Jews, Moslems, and Christians have at times been subjected to particularly harsh treatment because their doctrines are said to threaten the security of the country. In China during the period of the Cultural Revolution (1966-1976), the Communist government was especially hostile to religion and destroyed many historic religious structures.

Although it may curtail some religious activities, persecution does not necessarily destroy beliefs. If a government is too repressive, it may tend to solidify the domestic opposition within a religious institution. In Poland, for example, in the 1980s, the Catholic Church became the symbol of traditional values during times of public opposition to the Communist government. Likewise, a strong belief in Islamic principles and ways of life inspired many Afghans in their opposition to the military presence of the Soviet Union in Afghanistan in the 1980s.

Some national governments maintain a sympathetic view toward religion, but they attempt to retain a neutral position relative to the various religions of citizens. The goal, especially in a pluralistic society where religious differences cut across class and ethnic

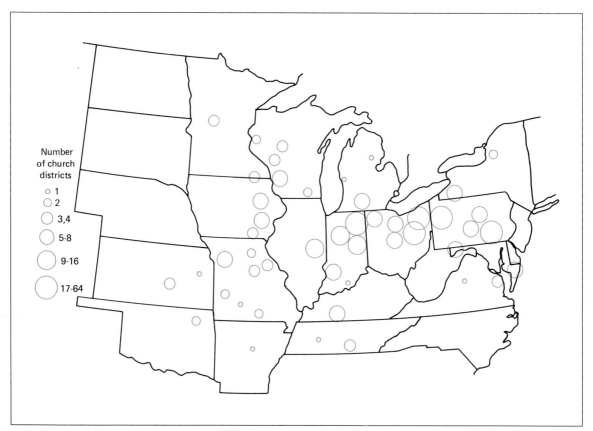

Figure 7-40. Distribution of Old Order Amish Church Districts in the United States. This is not just a map of religion because the Amish also have distinctive farming practices, life styles, dress, and schools. After Hostetler 1980.

lines, is to allow freedom of choice within a framework of responsible toleration of differences.

The objective of religious neutrality is very difficult to accomplish. Questions about what is a religious issue and what is a general societal problem are not easily solved. In India, for example, where freedom of religion is guaranteed by the country's constitution, uncertainties persist about ways to maintain equal treatment for all religious groups. The uncertainties are compounded because it is almost impossible to separate the religion of Hinduism from other aspects of Indian culture. Similarly in the United States, the foundation of many societal values comes from Christianity, a situation that gives rise to debates concerning the separation of church and state.

Questions about the roles of church and state may become quite acute when a religious community seeks to govern itself according to doctrines that may differ from those of the dominant secular society. This situation is illustrated by the Old Order Amish, who live in many rural areas in eastern and midwestern United States (Figure 7-40). The Amish have rejected the high technology and fast pace of American life; they strive instead for self-sufficiency and a simple, pure life in close accord with nature. They make no attempt to convert others, and they hope that in turn others will not interfere in their lives. Yet inevitably the outside society intrudes. One kind of intrusion has been the insistence by public administrators that all children must attend schools that meet specified educational standards. The Amish want their children to attend Amish schools, which offer a curriculum that emphasizes basic skills within a disciplined and religious context. Therefore, for many years preceding the Supreme Court decision of 1972 that upheld the validity of Amish schools, conflicts arose between the Amish and local authorities (Hostetler 1980).

For governments that provide the greatest level of support, the doctrines of a particular religion are equated with the laws of government. In tribal societies, religion and politics are seldom in conflict—political actions are generally consecrated by religious ceremonies. Likewise, in ancient states, the king was often the god of the state religion, and the laws of the nation were frequently a part of religious doctrine. In Japan from 1868 to 1945, the emperor represented a part of the state religion, and nationalism included a belief in Shinto. More recently, the nations of Pakistan and Israel were created on the basis of religion, and each incorporates religious doctrine into its laws. In Pakistan, which has recently undergone a revival of Islamic fervor, the Islamic Ideology Council in the early 1980s began to rewrite the national laws in accordance with a strict and traditional interpretation of the Koran.

In most countries, whether the government is hostile to, neutral toward, or actively supportive of religion, tension between these two institutions exists. Governments invariably have an effect on the spatial and ecological characteristics of religious behavior. Conversely, religion is often an important influence on the political organization of nations. It is only one influence, however. Others are examined in the next chapter.

What Is Sacred Land?

The earth is used in a variety of ways depending on the combined cultural, political, and economic motivations of the occupants of specific areas. Occasionally decisions about the use of a particular parcel of land may be complicated because it has special religious significance for some people but not for others. This raises the questions: What is sacred land? How should it be used?

For believers, sacred land possesses a quality that sets it apart. In some cases, religious groups insist that a sacred place should be reserved exclusively for rituals by adherents to their faith. Desecration would result if nonbelievers altered the land and used the space for secular purposes. Belief is an article of faith, so conclusions and attributes cannot be demonstrated to nonbelievers. What are considered truths by members of a religious group may be regarded as myths and superstitions by outsiders. These differences are expressed geographically when one group declares that a portion of land is sacred, but another group does not regard the same territory as possessing that spiritual quality.

The conflicting claims over the Black Hills illustrate such contrasting perspectives. The legal history commenced in April 1868, when the commissioners of the U.S. government met in council with the chiefs of the bands of the Dakota, or Sioux, at Fort Laramie, Dakota Territory. A declaration of peace was made, Indian lands were sold to the United States, and confirmation was made that the Sioux possessed a reservation covering what is now western South Dakota, including the Black Hills, "as long as the grass should grow."

The Black Hills (or Pahasapa to the Sioux) are a dome of forested mountains, approximately 100 by 200 km (60 × 125 mi) in elliptical dimensions, rising more than 900 m (3000 ft) above the surrounding plains. Like many isolated ranges set in level country, the Black Hills are a sacred place to the native people. To the Sioux they are the "center of the world," a place where the sacred arrows were cut, religious herbs were gathered, and where in the summer young men sought the visions that gave direction to their lives. In addition, the Black Hills were important to the Sioux as rich bison country and as winter camping grounds in the sheltered mountain valleys. The Cheyenne and Crow also claimed the Black Hills as their sacred place, but they had been expelled from the area by the Sioux in the early nineteenth century.

Long-standing rumors of gold in the Black Hills were confirmed in 1874. Miners poured into the area, thus breaking the treaty of 1868. Anglo-Americans justified this occupation of the Black Hills on practical grounds. As explained by the editor of the *Chicago Inter-Ocean* on August 27, 1874:

> It would be a sin against the country and against the world to permit this region, so rich in treasure, to remain unimproved and unoccupied, merely to furnish hunting grounds to savages. We owe the Indians justice and fair play, but we owe it to civilization that such a garden of mineral wealth should be brought into occupation and use.

On February 28, 1877, the Sioux were pressured into selling the Black Hills to the United States. In a strict sense, the treaty was not legal because fewer than 10 percent of the adult males signed, whereas the 1868 Fort Laramie Treaty had stipulated that 75 percent of the Sioux men had to agree to any cession of land. In return for their lands, the Sioux were guaranteed subsistence, and to this end the U.S. government paid them more than $50 million from 1877 to 1953.

In 1980, the U.S. Supreme Court awarded the Sioux an additional $117 million in compensation for the Black Hills in an attempt to end 60 years of litigation. The additional payment was judged to be a fair price for lands that had been taken in 1877 in contradiction of the 1868 treaty. The Sioux refused the offer, insisting instead on the return of their sacred Pahasapa.

Meanwhile, the Black Hills, and particularly Mount Rushmore, have become a symbol of national pride to many other Americans. As a monument, Mount Rushmore has almost become a "sacred place" in a political, if not a religious, sense.

BIBLIOGRAPHY

Barrett, David B., "World Church Membership," in *1987 Britannica Book of the Year*, p. 338. Chicago: Encyclopedia Britannica, Inc., 1987.

Benton, Thomas Hart, "Speech on the Oregon Question: Delivered in the Senate of the United States May 22, 25, and 28, 1846," Washington, D.C., 1846.

Caldarola, Carlo, "Japan: Religious Syncretism in a Secular Society," in Carlo Caldarola, ed., *Religions and Societies: Asia and the Middle East*, pp. 629-59. Berlin: Moulton Publishers, 1982.

Carroll, Peter N., *Puritanism and the Wilderness: The Intellectual Significance of the New England Frontier 1629–1700*. New York: Columbia University Press, 1969.

Compton, Paul A., *Northern Ireland: A Census Atlas*. Dublin: Gill and MacMillan, 1976.

Degh, Linda, "Folk Religion as Ideology for Ethnic Survival: The Hungarians of Kipling, Saskatchewan," in Frederick C. Luebke, ed., *Ethnicity on the Great Plains*, pp. 129–46. Lincoln, Nebr.: University of Nebraska Press, 1980.

Dubos, René, *A God Within*. New York: Charles Scribner's Sons, 1972.

Durkheim, Émile, *The Elementary Forms of the Religious Life*. New York: The Free Press, 1915.

Eliade, Mircea, *Patterns in Comparative Religion*. Cleveland: The World Publishing Co., 1968.

al Faruqi, Ismail Ragi, and David Sopher, eds., *Historical Atlas of the Religions of the World*. New York: Macmillan, 1974.

Finn, James, ed., *Global Economics and Religion*. New Brunswick, N.J.: Transaction Books, 1983.

Gaustad, Edwin Scott, *Historical Atlas of Religion in the United States*. New York: Harper & Row, Pub., 1962.

Hayward, Max, and William C. Fletcher, eds., *Religion and the Soviet State: A Dilemma of Power*. New York: Praeger, 1969.

Highwater, Jamake, *The Primal Mind: Vision and Reality in Indian America*. New York: New American Library, 1981.

Hostetler, John A., *Amish Society*. Baltimore: Johns Hopkins University Press, 1980.

Isaac, Erich, "The Act and the Covenant," *Landscape*, 11, no. 2 (Winter 1961–1962), 12–17.

Ismael, Tareq Y., *Iraq and Iran: Roots of Conflict*. Syracuse, N.Y.: Syracuse University Press, 1982.

Jacquet, Constant H., Jr., ed., *Yearbook of American and Canadian Churches, 1984*. Nashville, Tenn.: Abingdon Press, 1984.

Jennings, Francis. *The Invasion of America: Indians, Colonialism, and the Cant of Conquest*. New York: W.W. Norton & Co., Inc., 1975.

Lehr, John C., "The Landscape of Ukrainian Settlement in the Canadian West," *Great Plains Quarterly*, 2, no. 2 (Spring 1982), 94–105.

Martin, Calvin, *Keepers of the Game: Indian-Animal Relationships and the Fur Trade*. Berkeley, Calif.: University of California Press, 1978.

Mawhinney, Brian and Ronald Wells, *Conflict and Christianity in Northern Ireland*. Grand Rapids, Mich.: William B. Eerdmans Publishing Co., 1975.

Melton, J. Gordon, *A Directory of Religious Bodies in the United States*. New York: Garland Publishing Inc., 1977.

Mitford, Jessica, *The American Way of Death*. Greenwich, Conn.: Fawcett, 1963.

Nielsen, Niels C., et al., *Religions of the World*. New York: St. Martin's Press, 1983.

Nolan, Mary Lee, "Types of Contemporary Western European Pilgrimage Places." Pittsburgh, Pa.: Conference on Pilgrimages: The Human Quest, 1981.

O'Sullivan, John L., "Annexation," *Democratic Review*, 17 (July/August 1845), 5–10.

Pearce, Roy Harvey, *Savagism and Civilization: A Study of the Indian and the American Mind*. Baltimore: Johns Hopkins University Press, 1965.

Quinn, Bernard, Herman Anderson, Martin Bradley, Paul Goetting, and Peggy Shriver, *Churches and Church Membership in the United States 1980*. Atlanta, Ga.: Glenmary Research Center, 1982.

Rinschede, Gisbert, "The Pilgrimage Town of Lourdes," *Journal of Cultural Geography*, 7, no. 1 (Fall/Winter 1986), 21–34.

Sandford, Charles L., *Manifest Destiny and the Imperialism Question*. New York: John Wiley & Sons, 1974.

Shortridge, James R., "Patterns of Religion in the United States," *Geographical Review*, 66, no. 4 (October 1976), 420–34.

Simoons, Frederick J., *Eat Not This Flesh*. Madison, Wis.: University of Wisconsin Press, 1967.

Sopher, David E., *Geography of Religions*. Englewood Cliffs, N.J.: Prentice-Hall, 1967.

Stoddard, Robert H., "Comments on Circulation in an Asian Urban Village," *Great Plains-Rocky Mountain Geographical Journal*, 5, no. 1 (December 1976), 63–70.

Tanaka, Hiroshi, "Geographic Expression of Buddhist Pilgrim Places on Shikoku Island, Japan," *The Canadian Geographer*, 21, no. 1 (Summer 1977), 116–124.

Tuan, Yi-Fu, *China*. Chicago: Aldine Publishing Co., 1970.

Wagner, Philip L., *Environments and Peoples*. Englewood Cliffs, N.J.: Prentice-Hall, 1972.

White, Lynn, Jr., "The Historical Roots of Our Ecologic Crisis," *Science*, 155 (1967), 1203–7.

Zabih, Sepehr, *Iran Since the Revolution*. Baltimore: Johns Hopkins University Press, 1982.

8 POLITICAL UNITS

The surface of the earth is divided into an intricate patchwork of political units. Some units are large, extending over vast areas like the Soviet Union or Canada; others, like American counties, are local in extent and authority. The patchwork is produced by an exact geographic division of the earth for the purpose of ordering and administering societies. In contrast to regions of religion and language, boundaries between political units are precisely defined. Policies, actions, and results often differ greatly from one unit to another, giving rise to different landscapes and different ways of life. Furthermore, political units, particularly at the national level, foster territorial identity, whereby we recognize ourselves as American, Chinese, Egyptian, and so on, each with loyalties rooted in a particular segment of the earth.

This chapter is concerned with the application of spatial and ecological perspectives to the study of political phenomena. The chapter examines the interacting spatial systems at three scales: global, national, and local. First, however, the contemporary political situation is put into a historical context by tracing the evolution of political organization.

EVOLUTION OF POLITICAL ORGANIZATION

Band Societies

For 99 percent of history, until the advent of agriculture about 10,000 years ago, humans were organized politically, socially, and geographically into small hunting and gathering bands, generally no larger than 100 people. Such societies survive today, but only in marginal environments (see Figure 2-2). A defining characteristic of a **band society** is that it is egalitarian (Figure 8-1). That is, there are no formal positions of power, no internal restrictions on access to resources,

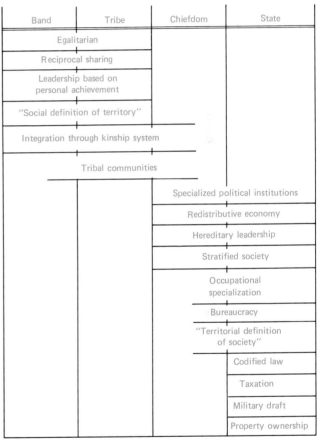

STAGE OF POLITICAL EVOLUTION

Figure 8-1. Evolution of Political Organizations. Various characteristics of political organizations can be arranged sequentially according to their first appearance and persistence (as indicated by the length of the horizontal lines).

Band society. A type of political organization in which members share resources and territory in an egalitarian manner (see Tribal society, Chiefdom, and State).

and no accumulation of individual wealth because of the obligation to share possessions with other members of the group. The bands are formed around the nucleus of the family, which is the primary economic, social, and political unit. Leadership is a position of responsibility and respect, not one of inherited power. Among the former Shoshoni Indians of the Great Basin, for example, the eldest male member of the family was a headman of sorts, but he held no title and had no absolute power over other members of the band.

The nature of territoriality (laying claim to a specific area or territory) in band societies varies greatly; but compared to modern societies (where land is owned and boundaries precisely defined), it is weakly developed. Certain core areas, such as the burial sites of the Australian aborigines, may be jealously protected; and the limits of a band's hunting territory are often identified by landmarks. There is, however, no exclusive claim to a defined territory nor to the resources contained in it. In some Eskimo societies, for example, family bands are associated with particular hunting ranges, but there is no concept of trespass.

Bands do not need to rigidly claim pieces of territory as their own. Usually there are no crops or stock to protect. It makes little sense to divert energy from food procurement to defend an extensive area that might not provide sustenance in hard years.

Significantly, during times of scarcity, territoriality is particularly weak, and food resources may be shared with neighboring bands. The integrity of bands is maintained by establishing elaborate rights of admission into the group; but once outsiders have been accepted, they have equal rights of access to resources. In general, the loose form of territoriality works to preserve a balance between population and resources in these egalitarian societies.

Tribal Societies

The second stage in the evolution of political organization is marked by the development of the **tribal society** (Figure 8-1). Included in this category are most American Indian groups, many African societies, and the peoples of the highlands of Southeast Asia. Although the term *tribe* may be unsuitable, it is often used to describe egalitarian societies that are larger than bands and consist of segments of families related by common descent. The emergence of tribal societies is generally linked to the domestication of plants and animals. The increased food supply and the concentration of population in villages necessitate a more structured political organization than is the case in band societies (Service 1962, p. 101).

Tribes are essentially loose associations of bands. The band remains the main political and economic

unit, but on certain occasions—often in response to an external threat—bands draw together to form a larger tribal entity. Moreover, the tribe is further integrated through fraternal orders, which draw members from all the bands to participate in ceremonies. As in band societies, leadership is transitory. Certain individuals may rise to a higher status by showing courage, generosity, or wisdom. But leadership is not an office, nor is it generally hereditary.

For example, at the beginning of the nineteenth century, the Pawnee of Nebraska were composed of four bands: Chaui, Pitahauerat, Kitkehahki, and Skidi. Each band, particularly the Skidi, was an independent unit. There was trade rivalry, even occasional warfare, between the bands. Yet they cooperated on their biannual bison hunts and in major ceremonies and were united in opposition to their common enemy, the Dakota, or Sioux. Only in the second half of the nineteenth century, when their population was greatly reduced through war and disease, did the Pawnee begin to regard themselves as one people, a tribe, instead of four related bands.

Territoriality in tribal societies is varied, but in general it does not differ greatly from the situation in band societies. The Pawnee, for instance, claimed a core area that contained their villages, ancestral graves, and burial sites. Beyond the core area, the tribal territories graded out until they merged with those of surrounding groups. Within each territory, land and resources were not owned by individuals but were shared by the group as a whole (Figure 8-2).

Chiefdoms

Chiefdoms are transitional between tribal societies and the centralized state. They often emerge in environments where the diverse products of different zones (mountains, valleys, forests) are collected at, and redistributed from, a controlling center. Chiefdoms are more complex and centralized than tribes or bands. Their population density is greater, occupations are specialized, and political activities are institutionalized and explicit (Figure 8-1).

Chiefdoms are characterized by hereditary inequality—that is, members are ranked by birth as either leaders or commoners. The structure of chiefdoms can be visualized as a pyramid with the paramount chief at the apex, below which are the lesser chiefs. The least prestigious members of society form the base of the pyramid. The organizational structure has a spatial dimension, with the upper strata of society residing near the chief at the controlling center of the community.

Chiefdoms probably first emerged as early as 5500 B.C. in Southwest Asia. More recent examples include the Kwakiutl and Nootka chiefdoms of the Pacific

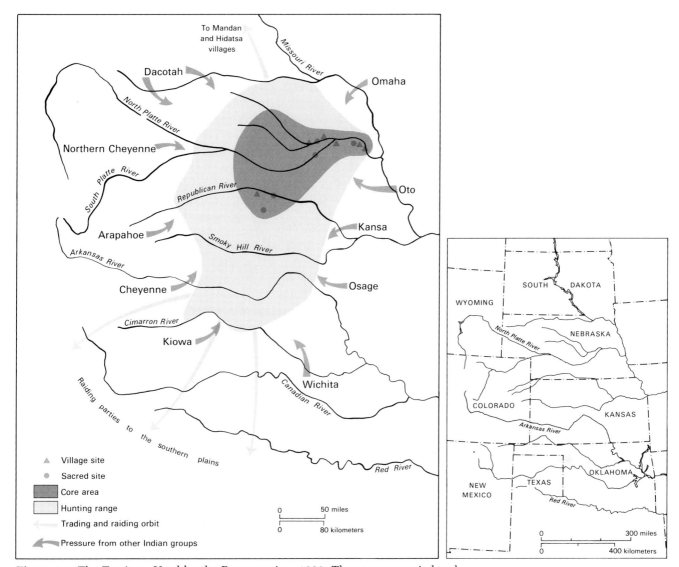

Figure 8-2. The Territory Used by the Pawnee, circa 1830. The areas occupied and used for hunting were generally restricted to those mapped here, but there were no legal or precisely demarcated "boundaries" to these territories. From Wishart 1979. Used with permission from the Association of American Geographers.

Northwest, and the sheikdoms of Arabia. Chiefdoms reached a high state of development in Polynesia, the constellation of islands from New Zealand to Hawaii. In Hawaii, in the late eighteenth century, a single chief had authority over more than 100,000 people; on smaller islands, chiefdoms of 2000 to 3000 people were common. Polynesian chiefs were born into an office of power and claimed the support of the gods. They allocated land and resources among their followers in return for payments of labor or rent. Chiefs accumulated surpluses of wealth, which were redistributed as a means of confirming power and assuring the loyalty of followers. The redistribution of wealth was the supreme political act in Polynesian societies. In a sense, the retinues of followers that the chiefs gathered around them were the forerunners of later state bureaucracies.

Chiefdoms were unstable even before outside colonizing forces disrupted them. They had a tendency to become top-heavy if the chief took in more wealth than he (or occasionally she) distributed. Consequently, they often fragmented and reverted to tribal organization or else made the transition to centralized states.

Tribal society. A type of political organization composed of associated bands (see Band society, Chiefdom, and State).

Chiefdom. A type of political organization in which a hereditary ruler allocates resources to other members (see Band society, Tribal society, and State).

The State

The fourth category of political organizations is the **state** (Box 8-1). With the emergence of the state, territory rather than kinship became the framework for political organization. In other words, the transition was made from a "social definition of territory" to a "territorial definition of society" (Soja 1971, pp. 11–15). Political institutions became more centralized, specialized, and differentiated from other aspects of the social system.

The purpose of political institutions in a state is to exert control over a population and an area. To this end, governments of states are empowered to make laws, wage war, draft citizens, exact taxes, impose tariffs, and conduct foreign policy. In the short run, a state can maintain order by physical force, but no state survives for long unless it has an ideology that binds the population to the political system. Without an integrating ideology, the state loses legitimacy and the people's acceptance of the government.

The state, then, is at the opposite pole from the egalitarian band. It is stratified into socioeconomic classes with a ruling group and a professional bureaucracy that act as agencies of control. The underlying assumption is that the state as a whole, and frequently individuals, can own portions of the earth.

The earliest states emerged about 5000 years ago in Mesopotamia and Egypt, and somewhat later in the Indus River Valley (Pakistan) and the Huang He Valley of China. No single mechanism accounts for the emergence of states from chiefdoms. However, increased population growth, expansion of trade systems, warfare, and the need to manage irrigation works have all been influential at various times (Flannery 1972). Whatever the specific cause, the result was the same: increased economic complexity and the concentration of power in the hands of the state machinery.

Modern states took root in Europe around A.D. 1500 when people began conceiving of places, distances, and areas in a different way. Previously, most humans linked places and their intervening distances with everyday experiences (Sack 1986). As the European view of the world changed with the Age of Discovery, people began thinking in terms of the geometric properties of land areas. The territorial division of the earth's land surface became an important method by which governments identified and controlled specific populations and resources.

Getting people to identify themselves with others within a large territory did not come easily. Newly emergent states (France and England, for example) had to bind together several regions with strong identities and to foster a sense of national purpose. Burgundians, Parisians, and Normans had to become French, just as Northumbrians and Londoners had to become English.

The development of a **nation state,** where the population identified with the state and subscribed to

---

BOX 8-1. COMMENTS ON THE TERMS *STATE* AND *NATION*

Unfortunately, the terms *state* and *nation* have multiple meanings, which cause confusion because the terms may be synonymous in some situations and not in others. Two definitions of *state* are as follows: (1) the legal entity that holds sovereignty over territory and is generally held to have wide administrative powers; and (2) an administrative subdivision of a federated government. According to the first definition, the word can be interchanged with *country* or *nation*. This is the case in the statement:

> The historical growth of the United States illustrates the way a state may expand with the development of land transportation.

The second meaning is exemplified in this sentence:

> Powers not specified by the federal government are reserved for the 50 individual states.

Definitions of the word *nation* include these two: (1) a people, usually occupying a specific territory, who share common cultural traits and subscribe to a set of broadly accepted ideals and objectives; and (2) the legal entity that holds sovereignty over a territory. When the first meaning is applied, it is very close to what is called a *culture group*. Sometimes the expression *nationhood* is employed to convey the feelings of persons in a culture group that constitutes a *nation*. The following sentence illustrates this usage:

> The Kurdish nation exists primarily in an area overlapping the countries of Turkey, Iraq, Iran, Syria, and the Soviet Union.

The second definition of *nation* is convenient because it is easily used as an adjective (e.g., the *national* production of steel). The main misunderstanding comes because the word *nation* can apply to either of the definitions given here. In the following example, the term applies to existing countries:

> The United Nations is a supranational organization composed of more than 150 nations of the world.

The word has a different connotation, however, in the sentence:

> Belgium is a country composed primarily of two nations, the Flemings and Walloons.

It is necessary, therefore, to note the context in which these terms are used.

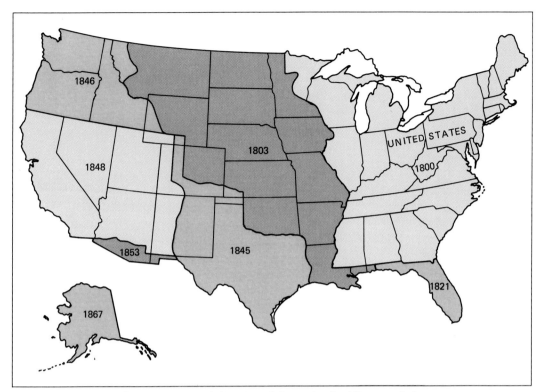

Figure 8-3. Territorial Acquisitions of the United States in the Nineteenth Century. From 1800 to 1870, the United States more than doubled its territory.

its ideals and objectives, was later linked to changes brought about by the Industrial Revolution. The effect of the Industrial Revolution was to provide new mechanisms for communication, making it possible to organize and control larger territories more effectively and to involve populations more fully than before. The development of the railroad after 1825 and the introduction of the telegraph system made it possible to move people and goods and to send instructions quickly, cheaply, and effectively over long distances. For the first time, land transportation of bulk commodities could compete with water transportation. Land resources became more accessible, the reach of governments was extended, and larger states began to emerge.

The United States exemplifies this process well. In the nineteenth century, the U.S. government surveyed, settled, and administered vast areas in the Midwest and West that had formerly been beyond its effective control (Figure 8-3). Associated with this westward movement was the acquisition of territory: Louisiana was bought from France in 1803, Texas annexed in 1845, the Pacific Northwest secured against Great Britain in

1846, the Southwest taken and purchased from Mexico in 1848 and 1853, and Alaska bought from Russia in 1867. The opening of the Union Pacific Railroad in 1869 was both a symbol and a means of continential control. The concept of Manifest Destiny provided an excuse for territorial expansion (see Chapter 7). Although the Indians were recognized as "rightful occupants" of the land, the United States claimed a superior ownership on the grounds that the Native Americans were not using the land to its fullest potential (see the Point-Counterpoint in Chapter 5).

From its point of origin in Western Europe, the idea of the nation state was diffused by colonization and imperialism throughout the world. Today the earth is divided among more than 165 states, each claiming an exclusive territory. Many of these states—particularly in Africa and Asia—have emerged since the Second World War as part of the process of **decolonization** (Figures 8-4 and 8-5).

An important theme to bear in mind is that the Western version of political and territorial organization was superimposed upon a great variety of preexisting social and political systems. In many newly

---

State. A type of political organization that occupies a defined area in which lives a people with an independent political identity (see Box 8-1; also see Band society, Tribal society, and Chiefdom).

Nation state. A political unit with defined boundaries that

encompass a people who share common cultural traits and a sense of identity (see Box 8-1).

Decolonization. The process by which a colonial power withdraws from an overseas territory and hands over political control to an independent successor state.

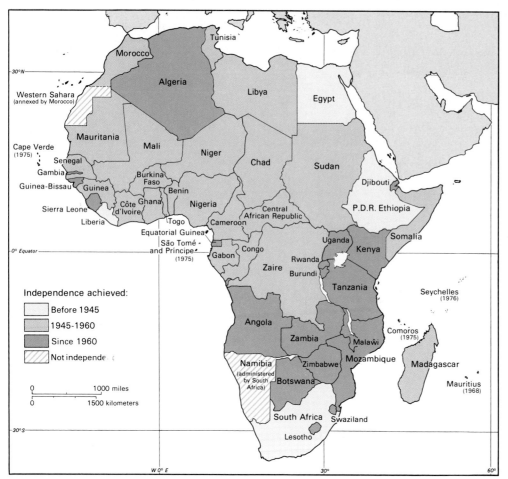

Figure 8-4. Newly Independent Countries in Africa after 1945. Namibia is recognized as an independent country by the United Nations, but in practice it is controlled by South Africa.

Figure 8-5. Newly Independent Countries since 1945. In 1960, 18 countries became independent nations. Most of the countries having large populations (such as India and Indonesia) gained political independence soon after World War II; in contrast, those achieving complete autonomy during the last decade have small populations (e.g., Vanuatu in 1980, Belize in 1981, and Brunei in 1984).

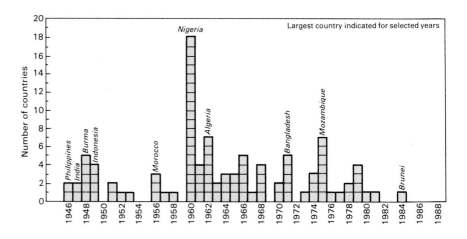

emergent states, especially in Africa, the primary allegiance is not to the country as a whole, but to the band, ethnic group, or region. Although a country may be officially organized as a nation state, some inhabitants within its defined borders may regard themselves primarily as members of a more local group with its own political structure and territory.

THE GLOBAL SCALE

After 1500, when Europeans began to expand their political and economic power overseas, the people of the world became progressively more integrated into a world economy. By the beginning of the twentieth century, this world economy had expanded to encompass the entire globe (Hopkins and Wallerstein 1982). The world economy exerts such a fundamental influence on our lives that some scholars maintain that the global scale is the most important level of investigation for political geography. Peter Taylor (1982), for example, believes that countries are no longer the most important political units in a world where conditions are dictated by economic and political forces operating at the global scale. Although peoples' direct experiences are at the local scale and their ideologies are often expressed at the national scale, in Taylor's view, the controlling forces are those operating at the world scale. Global forces include various forms of imperialism, geostrategic maneuvering, and international economic institutions, all of which affect people in widely separated places.

Imperialism

Imperialism is the extension of economic or political control by a state or power group over other groups of people. It is not a new phenomenon. The term itself derives from Roman times when the Romans extended control over the non-Roman peoples of Europe. The Arabs at their zenith put together an empire that included non-Arabs from Spain and North Africa eastward to central and Southeast Asia. The Han Chinese extended political and economic control over many adjoining areas several times during the last 22 centuries. American, Russian, Australian, and Canadian histories are additional examples of imperialistic expansion at the expense of native peoples.

Imperial activities may be divided into two types—formal and informal—although the two are often connected (Gallagher and Robinson 1953). In **formal imperialism** the imperial power exercises sovereignty and governs over another people's land. The colonial rule of the British in Nigeria and that of the French in Indochina are examples of past formal imperialism. Imperial control over another country, however, does not necessarily mean sending colonists, or even troops, to occupy the land. Where imperial control did not involve colonization, the process of gaining independence meant simply transferring the instruments of government from the imperial power to the successor state. This process occurred in 1957 when Ghana received political independence from the United Kingdom. On the other hand, colonies (such as Algeria) that were occupied by foreign settlers often gained formal independence only after armed conflicts.

Informal imperialism involves the establishment of spheres of influence, trading areas, and zones of capital investment in foreign lands. This type of imperialism went hand in hand with the formal imperialism of the past, but it also occurred where direct political control did not exist. For example, although China was not ruled directly by any European countries in the late nineteenth century, several "treaty ports" functioned as parts of European economic domains (Figure 8-6). Informal imperialism,

Figure 8-6. Chinese "Treaty Port." Canton (now Guangzhou) was one of several Chinese ports where European powers controlled a portion of the city from the mid-nineteenth century until 1949. Photo courtesy of Sally Stoddard.

Formal imperialism. The extension of control by a state over other territories and peoples through political and military power (see Imperialism and Informal imperialism).

Informal imperialism. The extension of economic and political influence by a state over other territories and peoples, but without formal rule; also called neo-imperialism or neo-colonialism (see Imperialism and Formal imperialism).

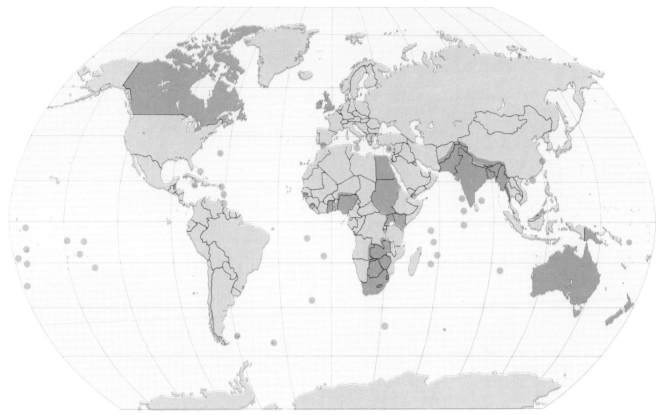

Figure 8-7. The British Empire in the Late Nineteenth Century. Political decisions made in London directly affected people in many areas of the world.

which is the primary type of imperialism today, is often associated with the activities of powerful corporations, which dominate the economies of many less developed countries.

Formal imperialism by Western European countries began in a modest way around 1500, became global in extent in the nineteenth century, and declined rapidly with the decolonization that followed the Second World War. Of all the European imperial structures, none was more widespread than the British Empire (Figure 8-7). By the end of the nineteenth century, the British Empire had the full range of formal and informal imperial attributes. The major imperial possessions were Greater India, Canada, Australia, New Zealand, and South Africa. Many of the colonies provided raw materials and markets, whereas some, such as Hong Kong and Singapore, were primarily trading ports. Control of this far-flung empire was maintained by a navy operating from strategic bases like those in Bermuda, Gibraltar, Malta, Aden, Singapore, and the Falkland Islands.

British informal imperial activities were also widespread. In Argentina, British companies built the rail system, bought huge tracts of land, and constructed the docks. British ships carried grains and meat from the Rio de la Plata to the growing industrial markets of Western Europe. The cultural imperialists were no less active. English private schools were

established, the Church of England was introduced, and prestigious London businesses developed outlets in Argentina. In fact, by the end of the nineteenth century, Argentina was absorbing more British capital than any formal imperial possession.

The British put together an empire for trade, settlement, and strategic purposes; but by the middle of the nineteenth century, the empire had become more than a worldwide business secured by the power of the navy—it had become the "British mission." The British, like most, if not all imperial powers, believed that they were bringing a more civilized life to the subject peoples. They became avowed agents of acculturation, diffusing their language, religion, sports, educational system, and political institutions throughout their empire.

The British Empire, as well as the empires of the French, Dutch, Belgian, and Portuguese, fragmented in the decades after World War II. Three interrelated factors were involved. One was the realignment of world power with the emergence of the United States and the Soviet Union as the new giants. A second factor was the declining ability of the old colonial powers to hold onto their extended empires. The third factor was the rise of independence movements, often given momentum by the diffusion of ideas from Europe about democracy.

The process of decolonization was rapid. When

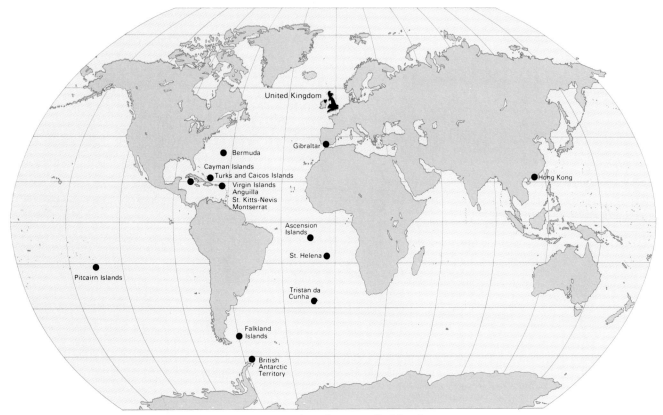

Figure 8-8. The British "Empire" in the 1980s. Areas directly controlled by the British government are much fewer than in the previous century (see Figure 8-7). Moreover, the number of possessions continues to decline. Hong Kong, for example, will return to China in 1997.

the United Nations was established in 1945, there were only 50 member nations. Now there are more than 150 countries in this international organization, with the majority of the additional members being former colonies. Although a few remnants of former empires survive, these areas are small (Figure 8-8). Some countries that were once part of a former empire may maintain special relations with each other. The Commonwealth of Nations, for example, is an association of Britain and former British colonies that promotes ties among members, but affiliation is entirely voluntary. In summary, the large political empires of the past have virtually disappeared.

Informal Imperialism and Economic Dependency

With the decline in formal imperialism, informal methods of imperial activity came to the forefront. Informal imperialism (often called *neo-imperialism* or *neo-colonialism*) was described in the following way by Kwame Nkrumah, former President of Ghana, as a condition in which a state

> is, in theory, independent and has all the outward trappings of international sovereignty. In reality its economic system and thus its political policy are directed from the outside. [1965, p. ix]

The framework for neo-imperialism was partly inherited from the former colonial systems. Cultural and ideological traditions of the British, for example, remained in the former colonies. Moreover, many of the former colonies stayed in the currency zones of their previous rulers, and this perpetuated economic ties. Most important, the dependency of the new states on European nations for development expertise and for markets meant that prior economic structures persisted. France, for example, has been able to maintain a preeminent position in its former West African colonies by preserving financial and economic ties. This can be seen as a generous form of aid, or it can be interpreted as continued exploitation where the wealth of less developed countries is skimmed off by foreign capitalists and local elites (Tunteng 1976). Some people avoid the terms neo-imperialism and neo-colonialism with their historical and emotional connotations and instead use the phrase "economic dependency." Irrespective of terminology, the structure of the world economy tends to be unfavorable for the less developed countries.

Imperialism today involves primarily the influence of the United States and the Soviet Union throughout the world. The United States emerged from World War II as the most powerful nation

Figure 8-9. Military Presence of the Soviet Union and the United States in Other Countries, 1987. The number of military personnel per country varies from a few dozen to several thousand. A few countries (e.g., Cuba) are even occupied by military from both the U.S.S.R. and the United States. In addition to the Soviet Union and United States, more than 30 other countries extend their influence over foreign territories through military personnel and facilities (see Table 8-2).

Legend: Countries with military forces from the: Soviet Union / USA

militarily and economically; and the Soviet Union came out of that war with its sphere of control extended throughout Eastern Europe. Moreover, by 1949, the Soviet Union was also a nuclear power. The two superpowers engage in a rivalry that is global. The priorities of the United States and its allies are to "contain the spread of Communism" and to keep as much of the world as possible within the capitalist system of trade and investment. The Soviet Union, in turn, attempts to extend its influence by supporting anti-capitalist political organizations.

American and Soviet methods of imperialism are similar. Both superpowers have established a network of military bases around the world, and each maintains influence by dispatching advisors, military and economic assistance, and, if necessary, military forces to their client states (Figure 8-9). As the American political expert George F. Kennan has observed, whatever the ideological differences between the United States and the Soviet Union, Moscow's brand of imperialism "resembles too closely our own for us to indulge gracefully in transports of moral indignation" (1982, p. 148).

Central America is one conflict zone where American and Soviet imperialisms collide. In the 1980s, the United States was channeling large amounts of military and economic aid into the area, especially to El Salvador and Honduras (Table 8-1). This was done in the belief that it would prevent the spread of Soviet

influence in an area that American leaders often call "our back yard." In opposition, the Soviet Union was providing, via Cuba, military and economic aid to the same region, particularly to Nicaragua.

The Soviet Union and the United States are the major contemporary practitioners of neo-imperialism, but they are not the only powers involved. The old colonial powers, France and England, play similar but subsidiary roles; and China competes with the Soviet Union for the role of leader of revolutionary socialism. Regional imperialism is practiced by Vietnam in Southeast Asia, by the Republic of South Africa in southern Africa, and by Libya in northern Africa (Table 8-2).

The multinational character of neo-imperialism is well illustrated by the case of Angola, a former colony of Portugal that became independent in 1975. Three guerrilla groups, each with a separate tribal base, competed for power as Portuguese control disintegrated. The FNLA controlled the north and received support from Zaire, France, and the United States. UNITA, supported by an unlikely association of South Africa, China, and Portuguese corporate power, was strong in the south. The MPLA, backed by the Soviet Union and Cuban troops, had its power base in the central part of Angola, near the capital of Luanda. The MPLA came out on top in 1976, and an estimated 20,000 Cuban and Eastern European civilians and soldiers remained in Angola in an effort to maintain

TABLE 8-1. U.S. Aid to Central American Countries (U.S. $ in millions)

Country	Type	1981	1983	1985	1987
Costa Rica					
	Military	0	1.1	9.2	1.7
	Economic	13.3	160.4	201.8	177.7
El Salvador					
	Military	35.5	26.3	128.3	111.5
	Economic	104.5	205.0	313.1	396.2
Guatemala					
	Military	0	0.2	0.3	5.5
	Economic	16.7	38.1	70.2	175.8
Honduras					
	Military	8.9	20.3	62.4	61.2
	Economic	36.1	58.8	134.9	223.7
Nicaragua					
	Military	0	0	0	0
	Economic	59.6	0.3	0	0
Panama					
	Military	0.4	5.5	10.6	3.5
	Economic	10.5	12.3	41.1	8.4

Source: U.S. State Department.

TABLE 8-2. States with Military Forces in Other Countries, 1986

Country	Size of Force[a]	Country	Size of Force
Australia	351	Netherlands (N)	5636
Austria	846	North Korea	1460
Belgium (N)	28,500	Norway (N)	884
Canada (N)	7800	Poland (W)	157
Colombia	500	Portugal (N)	1500
Cuba	36,400	South Africa	21,000
Denmark (N)	482	Spain (N)	21,000
Egypt	700	Sweden	1044
Finland	1913	Syria	12,500
France (N)	60,000	Tanzania	3000
Germany, East (W)	2370	Turkey (N)	23,000
Ghana	690	United Kingdom (N)	93,164
Greece (N)	3700	United States (N)	507,618[c]
Israel	500[b]	U.S.S.R. (W)	219,410
Italy (N)	141	Vietnam	190,000
Libya	5000	Zimbabwe	5000
Morocco	800		

N   Member of N.A.T.O. The other members, West Germany, Iceland, and Luxembourg, report no forces abroad.
W   Member of Warsaw Pact. The other members, Bulgaria, Czechoslovakia, Hungary, and Romania, report no forces abroad.
[a] Figures do not include forces afloat.
[b] Number of Israeli forces in Lebanon fluctuates. Number does not include troops in the occupied territories of Gaza and the West Bank.
[c] 1987 data, quoted in *The Economist*, May 7, 1988, based on Congressional Research Service.

Source: *The Military Balance 1986–87*, International Institute for Strategic Studies.

control. By the mid-1980s, South Africa and the United States were supporting the revived forces of UNITA against the government of Angola.

The complexities of political geography at the global scale can be simplified by applying the concepts of **geostrategy.** From the perspective of geostrategy, conflicts between world political blocs are examined in terms of their relative positions and territorial control of land, sea, and airspace. Usually such concepts emphasize the political strategies of the most powerful countries, with local disputes being considered from the perspectives of major powers. In this context, geostrategic theories are regarded as "spatial models of world power" (Kasperson and Minghi 1969, p. 83).

Geostrategy. The study of the political, economic, psychological, and military value of particular portions of earth space.

Geostrategic Theories

Every age has its own geostrategic perspectives because the relative importance of places shifts with technological innovation, resource discovery and depletion, and political change. As an illustration, in the last 25 years, the dependence of the major industrial powers on the oil-producing nations in Southwest Asia represents a dramatic shift of strategic and political realities.

Any discussion of geostrategic theories necessarily starts with the German scholar Friedrich Ratzel (1844–1904), who is regarded as the founder of modern political geography. Ratzel was the first to attempt to put political geography on a scientific footing by proposing a series of laws, or more accurately, tendencies, to explain the growth of states. Ratzel, who was trained as a biologist and was much influenced by the work of Darwin, described the state as an organism—"a connection between a living population and a fixed earth" (1897, p. 4). Ratzel proposed the concept that organic states are in constant competition for *Lebensraum*, or living space. He believed that the states controlling continental areas such as North America, Eurasia, and Australia would rise to dominate international affairs in the twentieth century.

At the turn of the century, however, conventional geostrategic theory emphasized the importance of oceans. Sea power was seen as the key to world power by most strategists in Britain, the United States, and Germany; consequently all of these nations embarked upon massive programs of naval building. In the 1890s, Captain Alfred T. Mahan of the U.S. Navy and a leading authority on the historical role of sea power, advocated the expansion of the American navy. Mahan believed that the greater flexibility of sea power gave nations like Britain and the United States advantages over land-based powers. He was influential in shaping American expansionist policies in the Caribbean and Pacific.

Mahan was not, however, solely interested in sea power. By 1900 he had turned his attention to what he regarded as the *"Problem of Asia."* He stated:

> Upon a glance at the map one enormous fact immediately obtrudes itself upon the attention—the vast, uninterrupted mass of the Russian Empire. To this element of power—central position—is to be added the wedge-shaped outline of her territorial projection into Central Asia. The Russian centre cannot be broken. It is upon . . . the flanks . . . that restraint, if needed, must come. [*The Problem of Asia*, pp. 24–26]

Here, in rudimentary form, Mahan presented the idea of a Eurasian heartland which someday opposing powers might attempt to "contain."

In a 1904 statement, the British geographer Sir Halford Mackinder predicted that the world was coming to the end of "the Columbian age," when the major powers had controlled the seas. He believed it would be land power, rather than sea power, that would dominate the world scene. Mackinder recognized what he called the "Pivot" area, deep in the heart of Asia, secure from maritime power, where it would be possible to create a foundation from which the world could be dominated (Figure 8-10). Mackinder did not predict which power would control the "Pivot," but he suggested that the balance might shift in favor of the "Pivot" area if Germany were to ally with Russia or if the Chinese, organized by Japan, were to overthrow the Russian empire. He continually stressed the strategic advantages of the "Pivot" irrespective of which power controlled the area.

In 1919, Mackinder published *Democratic Ideals and Reality,* in which he expounded his views on the changed economic and political developments after World War I. The "Pivot" area was renamed the "Heartland" and was expanded to include Tibet, Mongolia, and Eastern Europe. He made it clear that he saw Germany as the major threat and prophesied a battle between that country and the Soviet Union contending for the Heartland. In his famous dictum, he warned:

> Who rules East Europe commands the Heartland,
> Who rules the Heartland commands the World-Island,
> Who rules the World-Island commands the World.
> [Mackinder 1919, p. 150]

This passage defined East Europe as the key strategic region. Just over 20 years after Mackinder made his prediction, East Europe became the battleground for command of the World-Island. In 1939, Germany invaded Poland and, under the terms of a secret pact, allowed forces of the Soviet Union to occupy eastern Poland. Two years later, Germany invaded the Soviet Union but later lost the war. In 1945, Eastern Europe was brought into the Soviet sphere of influence.

Mackinder spent a great part of his political life trying to establish a federated British Empire that might stand up to the Eurasian land power that he feared. In 1943, he still believed his theory was valid because of the rich resources of the Heartland, but by that time he saw that "great power" status had passed from Britain. The country had declined to being only a "forward stronghold" of American power in Europe (Mackinder 1943).

In 1944, Professor Nicholas Spykman modified Mackinder's thesis, believing that Mackinder had underestimated the problems of developing the Heartland. Spykman concluded that the Eurasian coastal lands, which he termed the "Rimland" (Mackinder's "Coastland") were the key to world control because of their dense population, rich resources, and amphibious position between the oceans and the continental interiors. Spykman proposed:

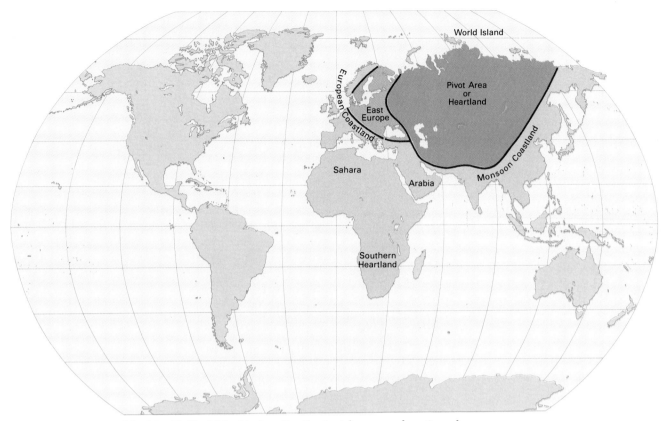

Figure 8-10. The World of Sir Halford Mackinder. See the text for an explanation of Mackinder's geostrategic views. After Mackinder 1904 and 1919.

Who controls the Rimland rules Eurasia,
Who rules Eurasia controls the destinies of the world.
[1944, p. 43]

Spykman's advice was for the United States to prevent a single power from gaining control of the Rimland.

A new dimension to global strategy was added with the advent of air power. The Russian-born American strategist Alexander P. de Seversky believed that the United States or the Soviet Union could achieve world dominance through air supremacy. Writing in the 1950s and early 1960s, de Seversky argued that the United States could only survive with an "aerospace force" that could defeat the growing Soviet air power (1950). His global perspective was depicted on a map projection centered over the North Pole (Figure 8-11). This map shows zones of air dominance of the United States and the Soviet Union, with a zone of overlap (the "area of decision") in North America, Eurasia, North Africa, and Southwest Asia (de Seversky 1950).

The history of the major oceanic powers attempting to prevent the emergence of a strong continental power extends back two centuries. In the Napoleonic Wars (1793–1815), the British worked to prevent the creation of a French empire stretching from the English Channel to the Russian steppes. Later the British and the French became allies to check Russian expansion in the Crimean War (1854–1856). Twice the

British and French, along with the Americans, fought to prevent German domination over the European heartland. After World War II, several European countries and the United States joined in a military alliance (NATO) to contain the Soviet Union. Now some scholars believe that if the Soviet Union were to be destroyed, it would lead "to an unchallenged Chinese domination of the Heartland and of the World Island" (Parker, 1982, p. 211).

It is apparent that the emphasis of geostrategists has been primarily on the size and relative locations of countries. From the perspective of these British and American writers, the goal has been to contain any large state located in the interior of Eurasia, irrespective of its particular ideology.

How well have these geostrategic theories stood the test of time? Today intercontinental nuclear missiles give the United States and the Soviet Union the power to destroy each other in a few minutes. Even though the industrial cores of the two countries are far from one another, each could be struck quickly by nuclear missiles stored on the other's homelands and carried in submarines under international waters. In addition to the danger these two countries pose, the capacity for international destruction is not limited to them, or even to other major powers. Several nations with nuclear technology can devastate their perceived

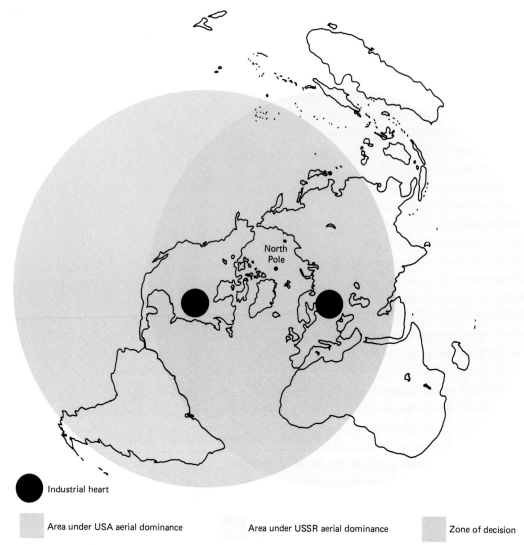

North
Pole

● Industrial heart

▓ Area under USA aerial dominance   ▓ Area under USSR aerial dominance   ▓ Zone of decision

Figure 8-11. The World of Alexander de Seversky, 1950. See the text for an explanation of de Seversky's geostrategic views. After de Seversky 1950.

enemies, including the superpowers (Figure 8-12). From this perspective, Mackinder's Heartland is no more immune from attack than any other area, and the old concepts of geostrategy are no longer applicable.

Some scholars believe that nuclear weapons, because of their enormous destructive power, will not be used again by rational governmental or military leaders. Military planners in both of the major power blocs exclude the role of nuclear weaponry except as "a last resort" (McNamara 1983). According to these assumptions, the views of Mackinder and Spykman may still be meaningful.

We can look at contemporary political regions without necessarily resolving the questions of geostrategic dominance. One such summary of world political patterns has been offered by the geographer, Saul B. Cohen (1973 and 1982). Cohen grouped nations into four regional types: geostrategic regions, geopolitical regions, an independent region, and shatter-

belts. He based these regions on population and power cores and on the political, economic, and ideological bonds between places (Figure 8-13).

Cohen's primary division is into two "geostrategic regions": the Trade-Dependent Maritime World and the Eurasian Continental World. The former has its core in the northeastern United States, with subsidiary cores in Japan and Western Europe. Economic ties and sea transportation are vital to the integration of the Trade-Dependent Maritime World. The Eurasian Continental World is theoretically united by Communism, although ideological rifts exist between the two core areas of the Soviet Union and China. To a much greater extent than in the Trade-Dependent Maritime World, the Eurasian Continental World is held together by military force. Each of the "geostrategic regions" is subdivided into smaller, more homogeneous "geopolitical regions," such as South America and East Asia.

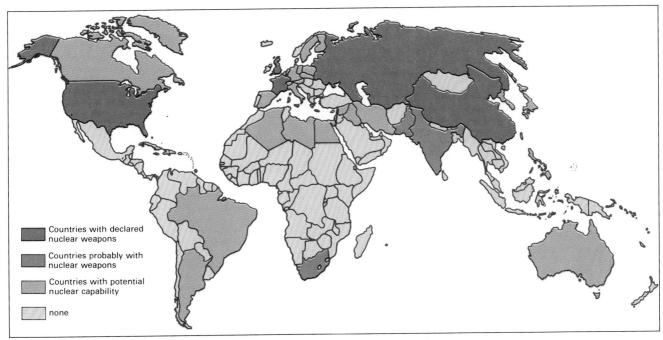

Figure 8-12. Countries with Nuclear Capabilities. Countries classified here as having potential nuclear capability vary from those with advanced nuclear technology but with no declared intentions of developing nuclear weapons to others that are attempting to acquire the materials and technology needed for nuclear weapons.

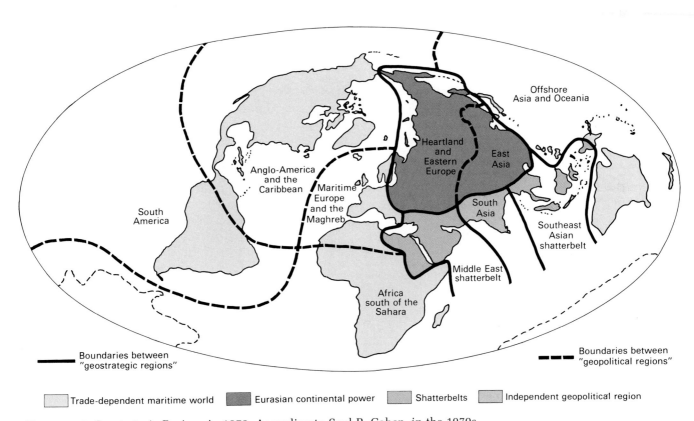

Figure 8-13. Geostrategic Regions in 1973. According to Saul B. Cohen, in the 1970s the world was divided into two major "geostrategic regions," each consisting of smaller "geopolitical" units. "Shatterbelts" existed between the two main regions, and South Asia was recognized as an independent unit. From Cohen 1973. Used with permission from Saul B. Cohen.

Cohen's third component is an independent "geopolitical region," indicating the growing importance and nonalignment of South Asia, especially India. The fourth regional type is represented by two "shatterbelts." In Cohen's original definition (1973, p. 85), a shatterbelt is "a large, strategically located region that is occupied by a number of conflicting states and is caught between the conflicting interests of Great Powers." In 1973, the main shatterbelts were Southeast Asia and "the Middle East" (Southwest Asia).

By the 1980s, a number of significant trends were reshaping these alignments. Regional powers, such as Japan and China (in East Asia) and Maritime Europe, were asserting themselves in and beyond their own areas of the globe without regard for superpower policy. "The Middle East" and Southeast Asia remained shatterbelts; but by the mid-1980s, new shatterbelts were emerging. These included Central America and Sub-Saharan Africa where, either directly or through the use of surrogates, the United States and the Soviet Union were competing for power.

Although the bipolar world of the superpowers was giving way in the 1980s to a multipolar world where regional powers exert more influence (Cohen 1982), the rivalry between the United States and the Soviet Union remains the dominant force in regional alignments. And although people may be most aware of local controversies that affect them directly, these may have less ultimate effect on their lives than the decisions made in Moscow and Washington, D.C. This is not to say that the suffering resulting from localized wars is unimportant to those directly involved, but the impact of localized conflicts on distant places is often much less than actions taken by the superpowers. Furthermore, it is rare that so-called local wars are not supported, at least in part, by the superpowers.

This situation of global superpower rivalry was summarized in 1984 by Peter Jay, former British Ambassador to the United States:

> We live in a world of sovereign nation-states of which two are pre-eminent in military power: the United States and the Soviet Union. Each is condemned by this simple fact to be constantly preoccupied with the potentials and intentions of the other. Ideological differences, though important, are subsidiary to this basic fact of extraordinary and opposed might. Given this duopoly of military power and given the reach of modern technology in communications, travel, and weapons, the theater in which the mutual preoccupation of the United States and the U.S.S.R. is played out is inevitably the whole globe, minus backwaters plus near-space. The part of the drama, whether competitive or cooperative, which is enacted directly between the two protagonists is perforce limited. Like kings on the chessboard they sit almost immobile behind their pawns and subordinates, nearly incapable of direct combat, surveying the whole arena in which their own fate is progressively and indirectly decided. [p. 127]

THE NATIONAL SCALE

This section begins with an overview of the territorial characteristics of states—size, shape, boundaries, and location. However, even more important than a country's physical structure is the inhabitants' emotional identification with the nation. In 1950, the geographer Richard Hartshorne provided a framework for the examination of dynamic aspects of political geography at the national scale by focusing on the centripetal and centrifugal forces affecting countries. These forces, some of which bind a nation together (the centripetal forces) and others that work to tear it apart (the centrifugal ones), are reviewed in the second half of this section.

Territorial Size and Shape

The sizes of countries range from the largest, the Soviet Union, to the microstates that are too small to be shown on a world map. A large land area can be advantageous. As Mackinder implied, there is a strategic value to a continental landmass once the parts are linked by communication and transportation systems. On the basis of size alone, larger nations are likely to contain a greater share of the world's agricultural and mineral resources. Of course, this does not always hold true. Compared to their massive land bases, Canada and the Soviet Union, for example, have relatively small areas suitable for commercial agriculture. Finally, there is the psychological advantage of size. In Australia, Canada, the United States, the Soviet Union, and now Brazil, the existence of a large interior has produced a strong sense of national confidence, along with a belief that their resources are almost limitless.

In many respects, however, a large size brings problems as well as benefits. One problem is the difficulty in binding distant regions to the core. The interior grasslands of Canada, for example, were effectively connected to the more densely populated eastern areas only after the construction of the Canadian Pacific Railroad in the 1880s. Without this connection it is possible that the area would have become part of the United States, which had designs on the prairies. As another example, the Soviet Union feels vulnerable because its far eastern areas are closer to the core of China than to the Russian core centered on Moscow. Transportation advances have overcome some of the problems of integration in large states, but movement over great land distances remains expensive.

At the other extreme, most small nation-states face problems of limited resources and an inability to finance and support many types of economic activities. For example, more than two dozen small countries have a national income (GNP) equivalent to less than a billion U.S. dollars. The implications of this figure are apparent by contrasting it with national incomes exceeding $1000 billion (e.g., the United States, Soviet Union, and Japan), or even $100 billion (e.g., Mexico, China, and India; see others in Table 9-1). For another comparison, the combined national income of the seven small Central American countries (excluding Mexico) is less than one-third the 1986 sales of General Motors (Table 10-1).

The lack of domestic natural resources and a limited financial base are especially apparent in the case of the very small states. Several areally small countries are listed in the tables of national data (Tables 3-1 and 9-1), including Trinidad and Tobago, Singapore, Mauritius, and Hong Kong; but at least each of these has a population exceeding a million. There are numerous other countries, however, that are very small in both area and population (for example, the Bahamas, Bahrain, Barbados, Belize, Brunei, Cape Verde, Grenada, and Luxembourg).

Shape is another characteristic that may affect a country's well-being. Elongated countries like Chile and Italy have the disadvantage of remote extremities, but such a latitudinal spread does mean that they have a diversity of ecological zones. Some countries are compact but contain protrusions, or narrow extensions of territory, which may have strategic significance. The Caprivi Strip, for example, which protrudes from the main part of Namibia eastwards to Zambia, contains military bases used by South Africa in its conflicts with neighboring countries.

Fragmented states, or countries divided into two or more portions, often experience problems in maintaining a sense of unity. The secession of East Pakistan from West Pakistan illustrates territorial fragmentation. The eastern portion of Pakistan, which was formed as a new nation in 1947, was culturally and economically separated from the western part, which dominated the nation's political and economic decisions. The unifying force of a common religion (Islam) was not strong enough to hold the two parts together, and the result was civil war and the emergence of the new country of Bangladesh in 1971.

West Berlin, which is administered as a fragmented part of West Germany, is completely surrounded by East Germany. Travel between the main part of West Germany and this territorial "island" (called an **exclave**) involves the agreement of another nation (East Germany). Conflicts are accentuated because West Berlin is also an exclave of the Trade-Dependent Maritime World (as defined by Cohen, see

Figure 8-13) located within the Eurasian Continental World (i.e., the territory controlled by the Soviet Union).

Boundaries

A national boundary is a line of enclosure and separation. It encloses the area in which a state can exercise sovereignty, and it separates people of the world into different groups. The degree of separation exerted by a particular boundary is largely a function of the relationship between the bordering nations. Some boundaries are relatively open, allowing the movement of people, goods, and ideas. This is partially the case with the boundaries of the nations in the **European Economic Community** (Box 8-2). Other boundaries, such as the Berlin Wall, are hard and fast lines of separation (Figure 8-14).

In the early nineteenth century, there were still many areas of the world occupied, although not necessarily claimed, by band and tribal societies. These areas disappeared when Western powers carved out their empires and imposed sharp boundaries, often in ignorance or disregard of the existing cultural and physical patterns. Today the earth's land surface is almost completely bounded, creating a closed territorial system.

Attempts have even been made to divide the virtually empty land of Antarctica by seven different countries (Figure 8-15). These claims were suspended by the Antarctic Treaty of 1961, which reserved the land for international scientific cooperation. But this treaty is due to expire in 1991, and the future territorial status of Antarctica is undecided.

In the closed territorial system of the world, expansion can take place only at the expense of another country. Consequently, boundaries often become the settings for conflicts between nations. Boundaries are usually delimited first by treatymakers who mark lines on a map. The next step involves demarcating the boundary on the ground, which appears simple enough, but may prove difficult due to inadequate information, poor maps, inaccurate drafting, and/or rugged terrain. A classic example of this problem comes from the 1881 treaty between Argentina and Chile, which stipulated that the boundary should run along the line of the Andean peaks, which divide Pacific drainage from Atlantic drainage. Some streams, however, rise on the east side of the Andes, flow between the highest peaks, and find their way to the Pacific Ocean. It proved impossible to

---

Exclave. A part of a country (or other political unit) that is separated from the main portion by the territory of another country.

European Economic Community. An organization of Western European countries, commonly called the Common Market (see Box 8-2).

BOX 8-2. THE EUROPEAN ECONOMIC COMMUNITY (THE COMMON MARKET)

The European Economic Community (EEC) was established by the treaty of Rome (1957) signed by France, West Germany, Luxembourg, the Netherlands, Belgium, and Italy. The object was to remove all tariffs, dues, and other restrictions on trade and to promote the free flow of goods, labor, and capital among the member states. In addition, the members were to work toward the creation of common business conditions and political unity within the community framework.

By 1968, the EEC had achieved a customs union; that is to say, tariffs on goods originating in the community were no longer charged when products crossed the borders of member states. In addition, a common external tariff was adopted, which means that imports from countries outside the EEC were assessed the same tariff at whichever port they entered. In 1973, Denmark, Ireland, and the United Kingdom entered the Common Market. Greece joined in 1981, and Spain and Portugal joined in 1986.

The advantages of a **common market** are many. Manufacturers operating in the region enjoy an enlarged "home" market. For example, Italian car manufacturers gain access to the markets of Western Europe without having to pay price-inflating tariffs at national boundaries. A large market means the cost of production per unit is normally lower than for a small market, which then allows for a lower selling price.

The enlarged market is attractive to outside investors and may attract new economic activity. For example, many U.S. corporations have invested in plants located in the EEC territory in order to gain access to the markets of Western Europe.

A common market, by removing tariffs on trade between member states, is intended to enhance competition. Competition should promote efficiency and bring prices down. Inefficient producers, no longer sheltered behind national tariff boundaries, must improve or be driven out of business. Furthermore, by having a wider geographic choice, labor and capital are free to move to locations where they are most needed and best rewarded.

The Common Market gives Western Europe a more powerful voice in world affairs because economically the EEC is of the same order of magnitude as the U.S.A.

(Table 8-3). Furthermore, the associated European Parliament with directly elected representatives discusses European problems and may be a stepping stone to a federation of European states. This model of economic and political cooperation, which marks a movement away from purely national considerations, may form a pattern for other regions to follow.

The advantages of joining regions of Europe together into a single administrative unit are not achieved without disadvantages to some people. The members of the common market still regard themselves as separate countries with different economic and political interests. When one area benefits from greater production, another country may suffer. Furthermore, workers in one country may be thrown out of work as a result of competition from a manufacturer in another member country.

Also, differences in economic goals may be manifested politically. People in France, for instance, may be more concerned with the well-being of fellow citizens than with the advantages of a common market that benefits persons in Denmark or Greece.

TABLE 8-3. The Common Market, Compared to Other Regions and Countries, Mid 1980s

Region/Country	Area (1000 sq. km.)	Population (millions)	Total GNP (US$ billions)	Military Expend. (US$ billions)	Education Expend. (US$ billions)	Health Expend. (US$ billions)
Common Market	2122	314	2860	99	139	173
United States	9363	246	4218	217	170	139
Japan	372	123	1561	12	67	61
U.S.S.R.	22402	286	2072	212	87	61
COMECON[a]	990	113	424	19	23	19

[a] Council for Mutual Economic Assistance (COMECON) includes Bulgaria, Czechoslovakia, East Germany, Hungary, Poland, Romania, and the U.S.S.R. In this table, statistics for COMECON exclude the U.S.S.R.

Sources: Population Reference Bureau 1988 and Sivard 1986.

demarcate the boundary in terms of the treaty. Argentina and Chile nearly went to war over the issue, but hostilities were averted by arbitration in 1902. Nevertheless, the Argentina-Chile boundary still continues to give rise to problems.

Other disputes may arise where a boundary dissects the territory of an ethnic group or cuts through a region of newly discovered mineral wealth. The ongoing conflict between Somalia and Ethiopia over the Ogaden Desert in the "Horn of Africa" involves both

Figure 8-14. The Berlin Wall. The Berlin Wall is a dramatic example of a boundary between territorial claims. Photo courtesy of George Tuck.

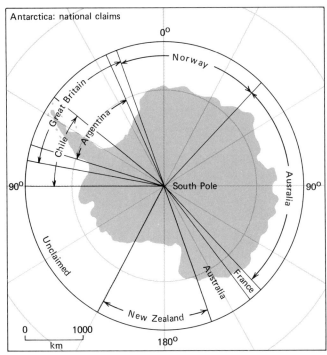

Figure 8-15. National Claims in Antarctica. Although 16 countries (with the agreement of the United Nations) currently maintain the international status of Antarctica, 7 different countries have claimed portions of the continent.

these factors. Somalia claims the Ogaden as part of a "Greater Somalia," which would unite ethnic Somalis presently living in eastern Ethiopia, eastern Kenya, and southern Djibouti (Figure 8-16). The discovery of oil in the Ogaden added new importance to this boundary dispute. In the early 1980s, Ethiopia and Somalia were involved in a sporadic war over the Ogaden, a war made more serious by the Soviet and Cuban presence in Ethiopia and by American support for Somalia.

Boundary disputes are generally only symptoms of wider disagreements. For example, the skirmishes between Soviet and Chinese troops along the Ussuri River in 1969 had more to do with conflicts in general policy than with the three disputed islands. The Chinese-Vietnamese border wars of 1979 and 1986 also involved more than territorial issues. In fact, the boundary is clearly demarcated and offers no grounds for serious dispute (Downing 1980).

Common market. A group of two or more countries that agree (a) to remove tariffs and other restrictions on trade and on the movement of capital and labor between members, and (b) to establish a "common" external tariff on goods imported from outside the single "market" area.

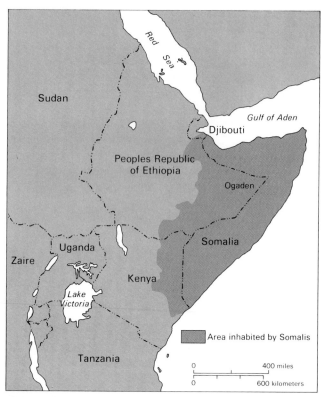

Figure 8-16. A Boundary Dispute between Ethiopia and Somalia. The Ogaden region is claimed by both Ethiopia and Somalia, partly because a portion of Ethiopia is inhabited by Somali people.

With land surfaces completely bounded, some nations have turned to the sea for expansion. Before 1950, most countries claimed that territorial sovereignty extended 3 miles out to sea and that beyond these territorial waters lay the international space of the "high seas." Since 1950, many nations have expanded their maritime boundaries in an effort to secure fishing grounds and offshore mineral deposits, particularly oil and gas. By 1971, a dozen Latin American countries claimed a 200 nautical-mile territorial limit (equivalent to approximately 230 land miles or 370 kilometers), and a complete partitioning of the oceans became a distinct possibility.

In reaction to this rapidly changing situation, the United Nations convened a Conference on the Law of the Sea. After years of discussions, the United Nations adopted a treaty on the Law of the Sea in 1982. The treaty set a territorial limit of 12 nautical miles. It also defined an "exclusive economic zone" that gives the coastal nation jurisdiction over resource exploitation within 200 nautical miles of the shore. In addition, the treaty guaranteed free navigation for naval forces through strategic passages. The United States, along with Turkey, Israel, and Venezuela, opposed the treaty. One point of controversy concerned access to the large deposits of manganese, copper, cobalt, and

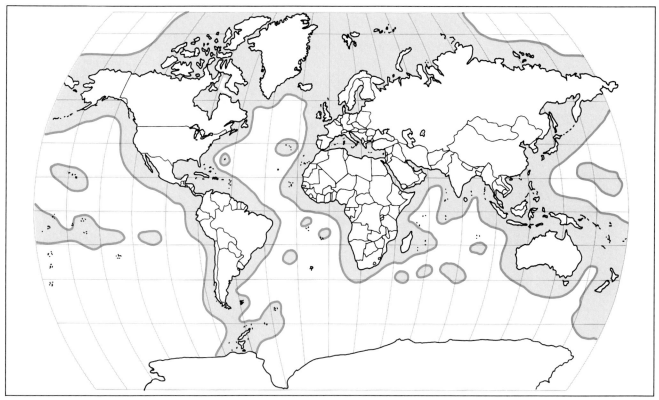

Figure 8-17. Areas of the Seas in "Economic Zones." According to the treaty on the Law of the Sea, 1982, coastal countries have economic jurisdiction over a zone extending 200 nautical miles (370 kilometers) from their coasts.

nickel that lie on the ocean floors. The U.S. government, persuaded by American mining interests, refused to support treaty provisions that would regulate seabed mining and would require all profits from this international space to be shared with nations lacking the technology to participate (McDonald 1982). Whatever the outcome of the dispute over seabed mining, most countries have adopted the 12-mile territorial and 200-mile jurisdictional limits (Figure 8-17). This extension of national jurisdiction, affecting at least one-third of the oceans, is a continuation of the process of partitioning, which is associated with the spread of Western concepts of territoriality.

Boundaries in outer space are also a likely prospect. Although countries do extend their sovereignty to the air space above their land territory, at the present time this jurisdiction extends for an undefined distance. As countries place more and more satellites into outer space, the likelihood increases that they will attempt to establish specific upper boundaries to national territory.

Location

Relative location is the last aspect of the territorial base of nation states considered here. The position of a country is especially significant in comparison with, or related to, the positions of other countries and their activities.

The importance of relative location is well illustrated by buffer states. A **buffer state** is intended to serve as a cushion between competing powers. Although most of the states created in Eastern Europe after World War I were based on a principle of self-determination, they were also intended to serve as buffers between Germany and the Soviet Union.

Another example of a European buffer state is Belgium, which had been ruled at various times by Spain, France, Holland, and Austria. This area became the independent country of Belgium in 1830 when such a status became advantageous to several European powers. The role of buffer was reinforced in the 1839 Treaty of London, which guaranteed Belgium's neutrality by the signatures of Britain, France, Prussia, Russia, and Austria.

Relative locations have a temporal dimension because the advantages of a position may change. For example, Belgium's role as buffer state was first challenged in 1914 when Germany ignored its neutrality in order to attack France. Germany again attacked France through Belgium in World War II. After that war, Belgium abandoned the role of buffer state and

neutral area by joining the other European nations in the military organization of NATO.

A second situation in which the position of a country is important is its location relative to the sea. A nation encounters major locational disadvantages if it is **landlocked,** that is, if it is surrounded by other nations and has no access to an ocean (Figure 8-18). Landlocked nations are isolated from low-cost ocean transportation. They lack the freedom of movement and accessibility to a multitude of places provided by international waters. They are also excluded, by virtue of their position, from developing the resources of the continental shelves. Faced with these disadvantages, landlocked countries have attempted to acquire some kind of connectivity to international waters.

Landlocked nations gain access to the sea by three methods: international rivers, land corridors, and rights of transit through coastal states. The concept of international rivers was developed in the eighteenth century when it was believed that rivers were natural routeways beyond the control of a single country. The Rhine and Danube rivers, which are kept open by international agreement, connect Switzerland, Austria, Czechoslovakia, and Hungary with the sea.

In the first half of the twentieth century, land corridors were used to link landlocked nations to seaports. An historic example is the Polish Corridor, created after the First World War to connect Poland to the Baltic coast. Contemporary examples include Zaire's narrow neck of land to the Atlantic and Israel's extension to the Gulf of Aqaba, which provides a second sea frontage. A corridor is the best method of access because it achieves an extension of sovereignty. But since most nations, including coastal ones, are reluctant to relinquish any territory, it is unlikely that landlocked nations will be able to acquire corridors in the future (except through aggression).

The main contemporary method of access is the right of transit through neighboring nations to a coastal port. This principle has been promoted by international rulings since the Freedom of Transit Conference of 1921. There are no means to force a coastal country to comply with the principle of transit, although it is generally in that country's interest to do so because its ports and railroads profit from the extra business. Nevertheless, in areas of international conflicts, transit rights have often been revoked because of ideological and policy differences.

The plight of landlocked countries is evident in Africa, which contains almost half of the world's landlocked nations. Mali, for example, has relied on transit rights through Burkina Faso and Cote d'Ivoire

---

Buffer state. A country that is regarded as a relatively neutral area because it is located between two, or more, powerful and competing countries.

Landlocked country. A state that has no ocean frontage and thus is completely surrounded by land held by other countries.

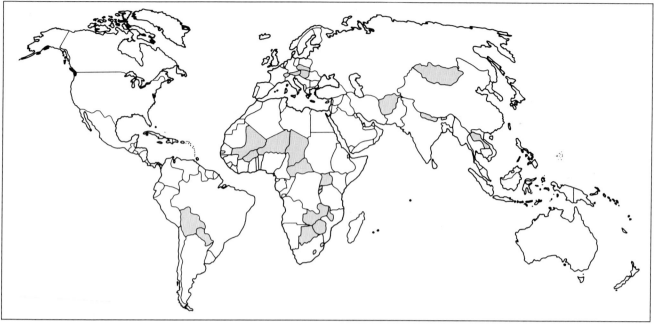

Figure 8-18. Landlocked Countries of the World. Of these 26 landlocked countries, 22 have a per capita GNP below the world mean of $3010. The 4 exceptions are the European countries of Austria, Czechoslovakia, Luxembourg, and Switzerland.

to the port of Abidjan and through Senegal to Dacca for access to the sea (Figure 8-19). These transit rights have frequently been revoked during periods of political dispute (Dale 1968). Even with transit rights guaranteed, the cost of hauling bulky products by road or rail to and from distant ports is a severe burden for less developed nations like Mali. The added costs mean that virtually all landlocked countries (except those surrounded by wealthy states such as those landlocked in Europe) are among the poorest countries of the world.

Integration and Disintegration

A nation state needs more than territory to survive; it also needs organization and a spirit of nationhood, a shared identity. In Western Europe, where states have evolved over centuries, there is generally a strong

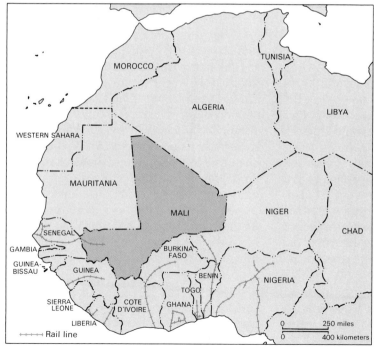

Figure 8-19. The Landlocked Position of Mali. To gain access to the sea, Mali has to obtain agreements with one or more neighboring countries to cross their territories.

feeling of nationhood that is shared by a majority of the population. The newly independent countries in Africa and Asia, on the other hand, often lack spatial and social integration, and their governments face the problem of shaping a nation within a political framework that was inherited from colonial days. With these factors in mind, it is useful to view countries as the setting for the struggle between centripetal forces, which bolster integration, and centrifugal forces, which are the agents of disintegration.

One powerful set of centripetal forces operates at the symbolic level. Most important is the "state idea" or **raison d'être,** which is the underlying rationale for a state's existence. The *raison d'être* for Israel, for example, is Zionism, the force behind the creation of a Jewish homeland in Palestine, the "Promised Land." State ideas are often modified with time as societies change and governments are replaced. For example, the state idea for Iran was dramatically revised in 1978–1979 when the monarchy of the Shah, which had de-emphasized religion in favor of modernization, was swept aside by the tide of Islamic nationalism.

The *raison d'être* is reinforced by state *iconography,* the symbols (e.g., flags, anthems, and national sports teams) that promote a feeling of nationhood (Figure 8-20).

In many respects, capital cities are part of a nation's iconography because they are symbols of national pride, as showcases to the world. Brasilia, the capital of Brazil, was planned to the last detail to proclaim the country's greatness (Figure 8-21). Its location 1000 kilometers (625 miles) inland from the former capital, Rio de Janeiro, is also symbolic, representing the thrust of development into the interior of Brazil (Figure 8-22).

The state idea and associated iconography, together with a selective interpretation of history and politics in the educational system and media, form a state's self-concept or national image. If all citizens of a country share such an image, it is a potent force for integration because it promotes feelings of nationalism and exclusiveness.

There are other, more tangible, forces of integration operating within nation states. If a government is to extend authority throughout its territory, a well-developed transportation network is essential. Otherwise, isolated areas, such as the hills of northern Burma and the interior of northern Zaire, tend to remain outside the control of the national government. To use the example of Brazil again, the recent construction of the Amazonian highway network is an attempt to bind the country together, as well as to open up isolated areas for economic development (Figure 8-22). In fact, construction of this network has been financed partly from what is called a "national integration fund."

A common language, allowing ease of communi-

Figure 8-20. A Display of a National Symbol. A flag symbolizes a nation and instills a sense of patriotism among its citizens. Photo courtesy of Sally Stoddard.

cation, is an important centripetal force in nation building. Although it is true that some countries—Switzerland, for example—have achieved unity despite linguistic diversity, the existence of two or more major languages in a country is likely to separate groups and to obstruct the development of a shared national identity (Figure 6-13). This situation is most common in countries established in recent decades with arbitrarily drawn boundaries, as in the cases of several African states.

In Africa, where there are more than 800 languages, linguistic diversity is a major barrier in the way of creating national identities. Only a few countries (e.g., Burundi, Lesotho, and Somalia) have a single indigenous language that is spoken by almost all the people. Some African governments, in an attempt to increase national communication, are pro-

---

Raison d'être. The "reason for being" or justification for the existence of a state.

Figure 8-21. Brasilia, the Planned Capital of Brazil. Capital cities are often showcases that promote national pride. Photo courtesy of Richard E. Lonsdale.

moting official languages. The problem is which language to choose. The old colonial languages, French and English, have been retained in many former dependencies (Figure 6-7). These European languages have many advantages: they are presitigious—the languages of the educated elite; they are not associated with a single (and hence "favored") internal ethnic group; and they already include an advanced technological and scientific vocabulary that is vital for economic development. In Nigeria, for example, English is used as the lingua franca and is designated as the official language. In Kenya, Swahili is the lingua franca and has been chosen as the official language in an attempt to close the communication gaps among diverse groups. It is possible that if nationalism intensifies, and ethnic loyalties are subordinated to a wider feeling of identification with a nation state, more indigenous languages will attain official status along with, or replacing, former colonial languages (Best and de Blij 1977, pp. 137–40).

National integration is usually promoted by achieving a balance between centralized government and decentralized control. The emphasis of a central government is to promote the interest of all citizens, whereas the role of subsidiary administrative units is to reflect the regional interests of more localized groups. When the regional consciousness of a cultural group is expressed politically as a desire for more autonomy, or even separation from the rest of the country, this is usually called **regionalism.** Regionalism is prevalent in many parts of the world today, as is apparent in numerous political and military conflicts.

The tensions between the forces of nationalism and those of regionalism are illustrated by the increasing number of administrative subdivisions of Nigeria. When Nigeria became independent in 1960, a federal system was adopted in partial recognition of the country's human and physical diversity. Three administrative regions were established, with the national capital in Lagos [Figure 8-23 (a)]. The Northern Region covered four-fifths of the country and contained over half its population, most of whom were Moslem Hausa and Fulani. The Western Region, with 24 percent of the population, was mainly Yoruba country, and the Eastern Region, where the Ibo were the largest group, contained 22 percent of the population. Because representation in Parliament was based on population, the Northern Region was able to dominate the country politically, and tensions grew between the Hausa-Fulani group and the Ibo, the most "Westernized" and schooled segment of Nigeria's population. The Ibo and Yoruba, fearing the dominance of the Northern Region, wanted Nigeria organized into

Figure 8-22. Highways in Brazil. The extent to which a country's transportation network is extensively and intensively developed affects interaction among its citizens and promotes national unity.

more states, an idea supported by minority groups throughout the country.

In 1963, other minority groups were recognized in the creation of a new administrative unit, the Mid-Western Region [Figure 8-23 (b)]. The regional conflicts continued, however, erupting in civil war in 1967 when the Ibo seceded from Nigeria to form the Republic of Biafra. After two years of war and the loss of 2 million lives, Biafra capitulated. Nigeria then commenced a program of reconstruction. In an effort to recognize local ethnic affiliations and interests, the number of administrative regions was increased to 12 and then to 19 [Figures 8-23 (c) and (d)]. To develop a strong sense of identity with national leaders, it was stipulated at the time of the last regional adjustment that an elected president must receive one-quarter of

the votes cast in at least two-thirds of the 19 administrative units.

Many of the forces that help to hold a people together in a local region may promote disintegration for a country as a whole. When a minority cultural group living in one region of a country possesses the *raison d'être*, iconography, and image of a separate nation, these feelings may act as centrifugal forces within the country. In newly independent countries, without the imposed centripetal force of colonial rule, many old stresses reappear as centrifugal forces. Even

---

Regionalism. A feeling held by the inhabitants of an area that "their territory" should be recognized as being a distinct political unit.

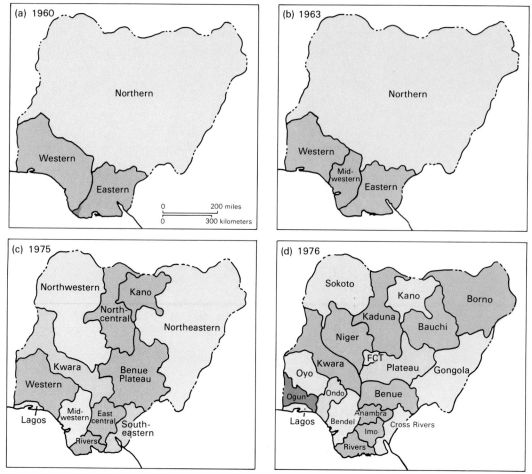

Figure 8-23. The Division of Nigeria into Administrative Regions, 1960, 1963, 1975, and 1976. The country has been divided into several administrative units for the purpose of providing as much ethnic autonomy as possible while preserving national authority.

in older states, an emphasis on ethnicity and regional autonomy may support separatist movements (Figure 8-24). When political allegiance becomes localized and the state loses its "legitimacy" in the eyes of certain segments of the population, the ultimate result can be disintegration.

Figure 8-24. An Indication of Separatist Feelings. Although the voters in Scotland rejected devolution in 1979, not all Scots agree with this decision. Photo courtesy of George Tuck.

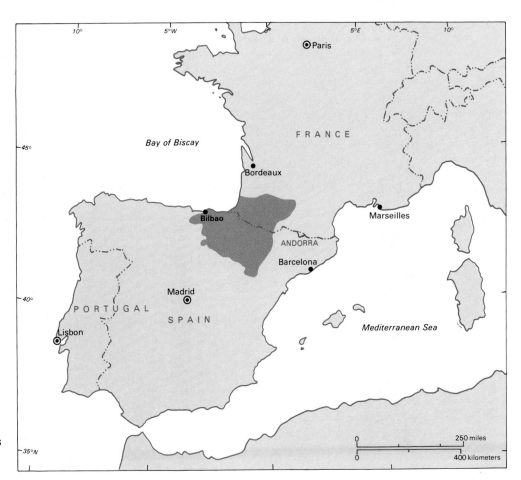

Figure 8-25. The Basque Region. The area where most Basque people live and regard as their "homeland" includes parts of northern Spain and southwestern France.

One of the main centrifugal forces in both old and new nations is the existence of unassimilated minorities, people who identify locally with a region or ethnic group rather than identifying with the nation as a whole. This situation is illustrated by the Basques of Spain. They are a distinctive people whose history predates the Gauls and Iberians. Their culture is largely intact, held together by a language that has no known contemporary relatives. The Basque region spans the French and Spanish boundary, and the people are a minority in both countries (Figure 8-25).

In July 1936, the Basques in Spain were granted a Statute of Autonomy, but this was subsequently withdrawn by the Chief of State, General Franco. In recent years, militant Basque separatists (known as the ETA-m) have been responsible for bombings and assassinations in many parts of Spain. The ETA-m uses the French portion of the Basque region as a sanctuary, so the issue has international repercussions. The Spanish government, in an attempt to defuse the tension, met the moderate Basques' demands for local autonomy in 1980, promising a measure of economic independence for the region and the right to establish their own police force. Basque militants, however, wanted more autonomy, even independence, and they refused the government's proposal; so the strife continues.

The Kurds are another minority group with a sense of nationalism, one that is founded on a strong tribal heritage (Figure 8-26). Kurds living in northwestern Iran are (and have been for many years) beyond the effective control of the Iranian government (Figure 8-27). Moreover, the Kurds are Sunni Moslems, whereas the majority of Iran's leaders are Shiites. In a 1973 manifesto, the Kurds demanded the establishment of an autonomous government of Kurdistan to handle all affairs except foreign policy and economic planning, which would continue to be controlled from Teheran. The Kurds also stipulated that their language, Kurdish, which had been banned in Iran for three decades, should be reinstated in the schools in place of Persian, the official state language. The rulers of Iran have refused to grant Kurdish autonomy, and the conflict continues. The issue is further complicated by the fact that the Kurdish region extends into Turkey, Iraq, Iran, Syria, and the Soviet Union. Thus Kurdish interests often become involved with international relations (such as the war between Iran and Iraq).

Decentralization of political control (sometimes called **devolution** when applied at the national scale)

Devolution. The transfer of some powers from a central government to regional authorities.

Figure 8-26. A Kurdish Village Near Lake Van, Turkey. Kurdish settlements have existed in this area of Southwest Asia for more than 1500 years. Photo courtesy of Cecil Blunn.

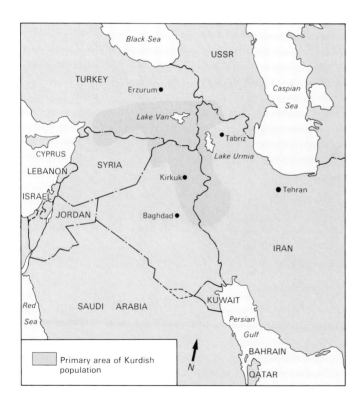

Figure 8-27. The Region of the Kurds. The main area where Kurds live, and which generally they regard as their own territory, extends over parts of Iran, Iraq, Syria, Turkey, and the Soviet Union.

is a significant trend in the contemporary world. Many governments, including Canada, Switzerland, Nigeria, and the United Kingdom, have recognized the need for administrative structures that reflect regional concerns. In all cases, the issue involves the degree of control that a group of people within a specific territory are allowed to exercise over themselves.

THE LOCAL SCALE

Although important political decisions are made at the global and national levels, people experience administrative decisions and territorial delimitations most directly at the local level. Local divisions of land are exemplified by territorial units such as counties, school districts, and private lots in a city (Figure 8-28).

This section looks first at the structure and areal organization of American local governments, then turns to the topic of electoral geography. It concludes with a study of a territorial policy that greatly affects personal lives in the Republic of South Africa.

Local Governments in the United States

The United States has a federal form of government whereby the rights of local governments are guaranteed by constitutional law. The federal government has certain specified powers, but all other functions are reserved for the 50 individual states. The states control the municipalities (incorporated urban areas), counties, townships, and other local governments. The importance of state governments in the American political system is indicated by their expenditures. For example, in recent years, state expenditures average $1.63 for every $1.00 spent by the federal government in the domestic economy (Johnston 1979, p. 31).

The number and areal size of administrative units result from historic conditions combined with geo-graphic inertia. The American political units developed in accordance with land settlement. In the first years of settlement in an area, Congress established an administrative unit called a *territory*. When the population grew, the territory applied for admission as a state. Since the nineteenth century, when most of the states were created, boundaries have not been altered, despite changing patterns of population, transportation, and land values.

Today the trade areas around cities often do not coincide with political boundaries. In other words, the current areal mismatching can be described as the differences between urban nodal regions and the existing administrative units. Consider, for example, all the people who are functionally related to Chicago in their working, shopping, and recreational activities. These same people, however, pay different taxes, obey contrasting laws, and receive dissimilar services because they live in Illinois, Indiana, Wisconsin, or Michigan. A realignment of state boundaries could place the population of Chicago's nodal region into a single state. One geographer, Edzel Pearcy, received considerable attention when he suggested in 1973 that the number of states be reduced to 38 to fit a similar number of urban regions (Figure 8-29). Such a revision is unlikely, however, because the existing pattern is ingrained and the process of changing a state's boundary is difficult.

A major feature of the American political system is its fragmentation. There are more than 3000 counties, 16,000 townships, and 18,000 municipalities in the country. In addition, there are over 20,000 special districts, most of them school districts, but also including authorities for sewage management, water supplies, fire protection, and so on. This fragmentation represents the desire for local control and exemplifies the widely held American distrust of centralized government or even of interstate regional authorities.

Political fragmentation, although laudably demo-

Figure 8-28. Territorial Control over a Small Area. Territorial control may range from vast areas like the Soviet Union or Canada to the small jurisdictions of forecourts and footpaths. Photo courtesy of George Tuck.

Figure 8-29. Proposed 38 States of the United States. The state boundaries suggested by this map match the economic patterns of metropolitan nodal regions better than existing state boundaries. From Pearcy 1973. Used with permission from Plyon Press.

cratic, poses severe problems for the efficient administration of areas that function as larger units. The framework of counties, for example, was largely a product of the "horse and buggy" days when the scale of life was local and the administrative units necessarily small. In the automobile era, however, the county system is often inefficient because of the small population served by units.

Fragmentation of political authority is most extreme in the urban areas, which contain more than three-fourths of the nation's population. Some of the larger units are partitioned into several hundred administrative units. In the New York metropolitan area alone, there are more than 1400 different political entities, including 22 counties. It can be argued that the multiplicity of administrative units is an effective way of meeting local needs, but it limits coordination. Each authority pursues its own objectives, often contradicting the objectives of the others. Fragmentation also means that there may be no single authority to deal with metropolitanwide problems such as flood control, water sources, pollution, and planning in general.

By comparison, metropolitan governments in Canadian and Western European countries tend to be more consolidated. Likewise, numerous countries, such as Italy, often combine many of their small administrative areas for regional planning and development. Regional units encompassing several states, such as the Tennessee Valley Authority and the Appalachian Regional Commission, are less common in the United States.

Bigger is not always better. Small administrative units can usually reflect the needs and wishes of a local population better and faster than the diversity of interests contained in a large area. Having small districts is consistent with the individualism of American culture, which may be expressed in resentment against decisions made by a government perceived to be too distant and too big. Representative government is also enhanced when people can participate in and feel a part of public decisions made at the local level in small administrative units. A recent political trend has been the rise of local community groups. Neighborhood associations (as well as food cooperatives and community action groups) have developed in an attempt to check the power of large government (e.g., "city hall") and centralized businesses (such as national real estate companies and chain retail stores).

Unfortunately, there is disagreement about which political activities are appropriate at the local level and which require the cooperation of people over a larger area. Taxing for military equipment and controlling air pollution are generally accepted as involving the entire country and are therefore considered appropriate for national administration, whereas assessing taxes for a municipal auditorium is normally regarded as a local decision. The answer about who should provide for public education, however, has less agreement in the United States. Some people believe all decisions and funding for education should be accomplished by persons within small school districts. Others insist that many aspects of education concern the entire country and, consequently, should be under the jurisdiction of regional or national political units.

Electoral Geography

Studying electoral behavior in the United States is highly dependent on geographic analysis because voting results are recorded only by areal units. Although "exit polls" and other forms of sampling can provide news reporters, candidates, and political parties with information about the specific characteristics of voters, the official voting results are available only by election districts. By comparing election results with the demographic, economic, and social characteristics of persons living in each election district, geographers and other analysts can form conclusions about preferences of voter groups. At the local level, campaign strategists commonly examine patterns of past elections to determine their relationships with voter characteristics. These relationships form the basis for planning future campaigns.

Similar analyses of voting patterns are done at the state level. For example, the results of presidential elections in the past produced a uniform region sometimes called "the Solid South." For 21 consecutive presidential elections, from 1876 to 1960, four southern states (South Carolina, Georgia, Alabama, and Mississippi) voted Democratic. The one-party domination was broken in 1964 when a conservative Republican (Barry Goldwater) carried five states in the South (Louisiana, Mississippi, Alabama, Georgia, and South Carolina) from the total of six that he won nationally (the other being his home state of Arizona). The political shift was repeated in 1972 when white voters in the South supported the conservative Republican (Richard Nixon) over the liberal Democrat (George McGovern).

In 1976, the South again voted for a Democrat, partly in support of their "native son" (Jimmy Carter), but the same candidate did not hold the region against the Republicans in 1980. In 1984, all of the states in the Solid South went to the Republican presidential candidate (Ronald Reagan). Today, predictions about the outcomes of presidential elections in the South are more difficult than a hundred years ago because of the shifts in party affiliations, the increased participation of blacks, and the in-migration of new voters from the industrial north (Moreland, Baker, and Steed 1982).

In addition to its role in the analysis of election results, geography is important in the operation of representative government. Representation is attempted by specifying areas (election districts) from which voters select persons to present their viewpoints in legislative bodies. Although representative government can be achieved by other methods (such as the quota sytem or proportional system), fair representation is attempted in the United States by dividing citizens into groups of voters according to residential location. The system is based on the assumption that people with distinctive viewpoints tend to live close together. This is a reasonably valid assumption; political values and beliefs in the United States tend to be based on social and economic classes, and such classes are spatially segregated. In other words, the administrative map is also a political map (Johnston 1979, p. 47).

The goal is to draw the boundaries of electoral districts where they divide the population in a manner that provides fair representation. Boundaries should be designated according to at least two criteria. First, the number of people in each district should be virtually the same as the number of people in the other districts, so that the rule of "one-person, one-vote" is accomplished. Failure to achieve this balance creates malapportionment, meaning that all voters do not carry equal weight (see Box 8-3). The criterion of equality of numbers in election districts generally is not difficult to achieve.

The second criterion for fair representation is met when the proportion of elected legislators having a particular viewpoint accurately reflects the percentage of voters with that same viewpoint. Dividing a general area into electoral districts for the purpose of accomplishing fair proportionalities is not always easy. There are innumerable ways of drawing boundaries, and each political party strives to produce a pattern of districts that will maximize its share of the representatives. Manipulating district boundaries for the purpose of political gain is called **gerrymandering.** Gerrymandering is often associated with oddly shaped districts, which seek out isolated pockets of party support, but an odd shape is not necessarily an indication of unfair boundary manipulation (see Box 8-3).

Racial gerrymandering, which deprives a segment of population of fair representation, is not uncommon in the United States. One example involves the gerrymandering of congressional district boundaries in Mississippi in the 1960s and 1970s to the detriment of the black population (O'Loughlin 1982). The black population did form a majority of the population in one of the five districts before 1966, but the blacks had little political effect because very few were registered

---

Gerrymandering. The manipulation of the boundaries of electoral districts for the purpose of maximizing the number of representatives elected from one political party.

BOX 8-3. CHOICES IN DEFINING ELECTORAL DISTRICTS

Map (a) (Figure 8-30) shows the number of voters (expressed to the nearest 10,000) registered for the White Party and the Black Party for each of the 16 small areal units (such as census tracts). Note that the total number of White voters in the hypothetical area is exactly equal to the number of Black voters (300,000 each). Therefore, the general area should be divided in such a way that half the elected legislators express the viewpoint of the White voters and half represent the views of Black voters. If the area is entitled to four legislators, the task is to draw the boundaries of four election districts in a manner that is expected to produce a fair representation.

Map (b) shows one type of areal division that produces four electoral districts. Even though each party is expected to elect two legislators, which is equivalent to each party's fair share of representation, this system is unfair because only 70,000 voters in the northwest district have the same representative weight as 230,000 voters in the southeast district.

In Map (c), this area has been divided into four different districts. They appear moderately compact in shape, and each contains 150,000 voters. The set of four districts as a whole is unfair, however, because White voters are expected to win three of the four legislators. Only in the northeast district is a Black candidate expected to win (by a margin of 13 to 2).

A fourth alternative division is shown by Map (d). Although one of the districts appears rather oddly shaped, the set of boundaries is fair because each district has 150,000 voters and the proportion of representatives for each party (2 of 4) is equivalent to the share of its voters (300,000 of 600,000).

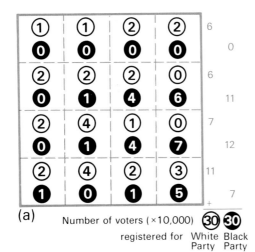

(a)

Number of voters (×10,000) registered for White Party Black Party

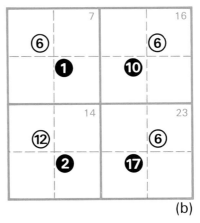

(b)

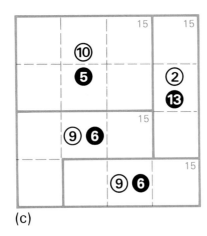

(c)

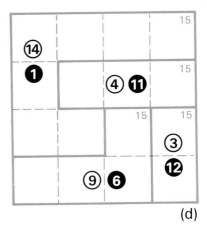

(d)

Figure 8-30. Potential Electoral Districts for a Hypothetical Area.

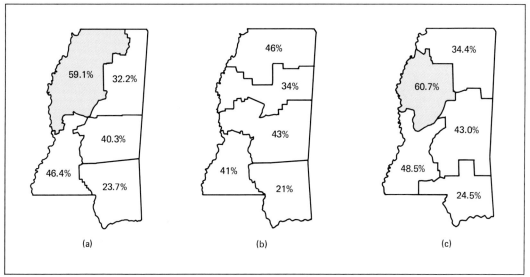

Figure 8-31. Actual and Feasible Congressional Districts in Mississippi, 1960s. The percentage of blacks in each electoral district varies with the arrangements of district boundaries. When district boundaries were changed from those shown in map a to those of map b, the blacks became a minority in all districts. Redistricting according to map c would have guaranteed a majority of blacks in one of the five districts. After O'Loughlin 1982.

to vote [Figure 8-31(a)]. After 1966, however, as more blacks became voters, the districts were redrawn and were shaped to ensure that black voters were a minority in each district [Figure 8-31(b)]. As a result of this gerrymandering, black voters could not be assured of electing even a single representative in spite of the fact that more than one-third of the state's population was black. A fairer set of districts would guarantee that a black population constituted the majority of voters in at least one district [Figures 8-31(a) and (c)].

The Geographic Expression of Policy: The Case of Apartheid

The geographic expression of a national political policy is illustrated by the practice of **apartheid** (officially, "separate racial development") in the Republic of South Africa. In 1984, this multiracial country had a total population of 32.6 million, of which 24.1 million were blacks, 4.8 million were whites, 2.8 million were Coloureds (persons of mixed ancestry), and 0.9 million were Asians. Although the whites comprise only 15 percent of the total population, they are the dominant group in terms of political, economoic, and virtually all other forms of power. The other groups, including the majority group, the blacks, are disenfranchised to varying degrees; they are segregated and subordinated through the policy of apartheid.

Apartheid was officially introduced through the

Group Areas Act of 1950. It is a rigidly segregationist policy, a "tool by which the increasingly outnumbered white ruling group can maintain social distance from, and hegemony over, other groups in South African society" (Western 1981, p. 60). Apartheid has produced physical segregation of races at both a regional and a local scale by designating specific areas for particular groups of people.

At the regional level, the South African government has designated about 14 percent of the area of the country as black "Homelands" or "Bantustans" (Figure 8-32). These Homelands are supposed to form viable economic and cultural bases for separate black development, but they are mostly barren tracts of land with no ports, no industries, and few resources. The poor living conditions for blacks are reflected by an infant mortality rate of 90 per 1000 live births compared to 13 per 1000 for whites (Brewer 1986). Confronted with poverty in their Homelands, black males are forced to sell their labor in the gold and coal mines of the Johannesburg area, the diamond mines of Kimberley, and the ports of Cape Town and Durban. "Pass laws" permit male migrants to go to the cities to work, but they must return to the Homelands each year. Black laborers are needed, but otherwise their presence in the cities is not wanted.

Apartheid. A policy practiced in the Republic of South Africa that separates officially defined racial groups by designating areas in which each must reside.

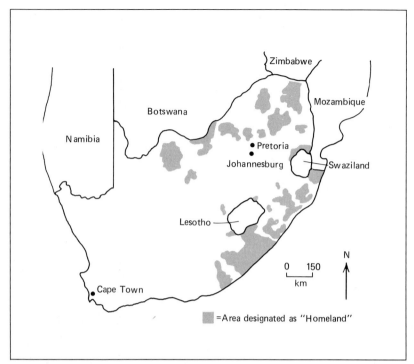

Figure 8-32. Homelands in the Republic of South Africa. Part of the apartheid policy of the government has been to define small areas as the official "homelands" of blacks.

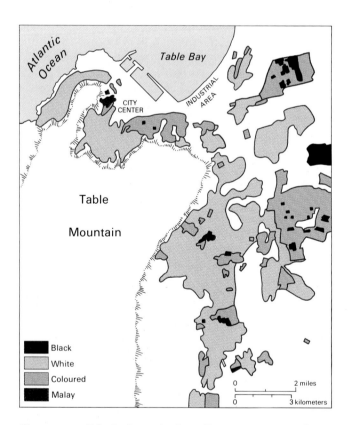

Figure 8-33. Ethnic Areas in Cape Town, 1950–1952. In the early 1950s, residents of this city tended to live in ethnic neighborhoods, arranged in complex patterns similar to those in cities elsewhere in the world. After Scott 1955.

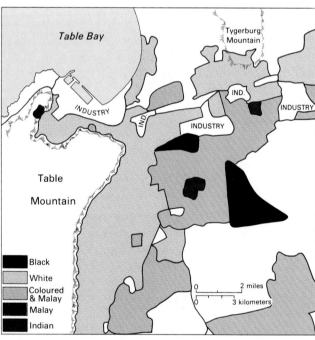

Figure 8-34. Group Areas in Cape Town, 1979. By 1979, many residents had been forced to leave their homes and to move to other areas that had been designated for their particular ethnic group. After Western 1981.

The Homelands policy has taken on a pseudo-international dimension because several of the Bantustans have been declared independent countries by the South African government. By declaring the Homelands as politically independent, the white government in effect has excluded the blacks from most of their own country. No other country in the world, however, has recognized these redefined reserves as sovereign states. Although since 1986 there has been some modification of governmental positions on the Homelands, the basic policy of using territory to control people still remains.

The effects of apartheid at the local level are evident in Cape Town, a city where Coloureds form 60 percent of the population. Cape Town was experiencing some racial segregation before apartheid was legalized and enforced through the Group Areas Act, but much of the city, particularly the working class areas, was multiracial (Figure 8-33). Apartheid changed the geography of Cape Town drastically (Figure 8-34). Separate racial zones were established, and large numbers of Coloureds, blacks, and Asians were uprooted and removed to designated city zones or, in the case of the blacks, to their designated Homelands. Barriers such as railroads, highways, and industrial areas separated the zones. Communities of long-standing were broken up. At the scale of interpersonal experience, apartheid reinforces white dominance through the segregation of buses, beaches, washrooms, and even cemeteries.

As a result of these discriminatory policies, the South African government has faced periodic civil unrest, which has been suppressed by military and civil force. External pressures have been imposed by international sanctions such as restricting trade and banning South African athletes from competing in international sports. Concerned for the country's external image, the government has recently relaxed some of the minor restrictions of apartheid, such as the segregation of post offices and certain hotels. It has also given Coloureds and Asians (but not blacks) a limited role in Parliament. But the essence of apartheid—the shaping of society through the manipulation of space to preserve white control—is intact.

PROSPECTS

Forecasting future political geographies is an uncertain occupation because many political changes cannot be anticipated. The world political map a century from now may bear little resemblance to the present situation, just as today's map is different from that of 100 years ago. Contradictory predictions of continued divisions among nations or of greater international cooperation can both be supported by current conditions.

There is not much evidence that in the near future nations will diminish their disputes over land and sea territories. Furthermore, the forces of nationalism and regionalism seem to be very strong. The desire for a "national" identity and self-rule appears to be universal among cultural groups. These trends and conditions lead to expectations that further divisions will occur among the peoples of the world.

On the other hand, a greater degree of political cooperation at the international level may develop in the future. This is supported partly by the hope that people will act rationally. As they become more aware of their interdependency, they will need to form more global institutions.

Other evidence that more global cooperation may occur in the future is the existence of supranational organizations. The largest is the United Nations with agencies that attempt to solve environmental, demographic, medical, educational, economic, and political problems. Regional bodies include the Organization of American States, the Organization of African Unity, and the European Economic Community (EEC or the Common Market). Except for the EEC (Box 8-2), however, most of the regional supranational organizations have had a limited impact on geographical patterns.

POINT-COUNTERPOINT

Regionalism and Nationalism

Under what circumstances do (or should) people in one region separate from other parts of a country? At one time, a group of people in North America (the 13 colonies) declared that they constituted a new nation and were no longer a part of the British Empire. Less than a century later, that same country fought a civil war when people in one part (i.e., the South) attempted to form another nation by separating from other regions of the United States.

Similar controversies have continued to occur in most countries where groups of people cling to a regional, rather than national, identity. As leaders and citizens of countries have faced this issue, what are some of the choices and hard decisions they have had to make?

In a Utopian world, differences of class, creed, or culture would not prevent citizens of any country from living in harmony. The human variations within each country would contribute to a fuller life for all who shared their traditions and perspectives with others. But Utopia does not exist. Feelings persist among most humans that their particular language, religion, customs, and ways of living are superior to those of other cultures. Even those who do not believe their ways are superior may feel threatened by a majority that seeks domination. Given this situation, hard choices need to be made about how to deal with cultural diversity within a single country.

The feasible options can be identified as absorption, centralized despotism, federalism, and partition. By *absorption*, the dominant culture or political force attempts the assimilation of cultural minorities into a national "melting pot." This may cause extreme hardships among

minority members, as with the Native Americans; but where the minorities have been small, this option has not produced major political conflicts.

Under centralized *despotism*, one group maintains power over other cultural groups and forces state unity through a strong military and police force. Such conditions were illustrated when Adi Amin attempted to force conformity in Uganda during his 1971–1978 reign. The disadvantages of living in a garrison state, which inevitably occurs under despotic rulers, are obvious.

Federalism, as in Switzerland, is a type of compromise between a central government and local administrative units that retain a degree of political autonomy. Keeping a balance between these two levels of government requires considerable trust and self-restraint. Failure to maintain such a balance usually results in conflict and ultimately in having to choose among the other three options.

Partition, which means the division of a country into two (or more) independent countries, is essentially an admission of defeat. Furthermore,

it often results after a destructive civil war and, sometimes, a forced migration of many people to an area newly designated as their new "homeland." The partition of Pakistan in 1971, when the new country of Bangladesh was created, exemplifies this type of political solution.

These four options and how various factions within a country view them can be illustrated by recent events in the island country of Sri Lanka (formerly known as Ceylon).

The population of Sri Lanka prior to the period of European colonization consisted of three main ethnic groups. The Sinhalese, who spoke the Sinhala language and were mostly Buddhists, were the majority. The other two groups, both of which spoke the Tamil language, were the Tamils (mostly Hindus) and the Moors (almost entirely Moslems). A fourth culture group consisting of Tamils from India was brought to the island during the British colonial period to work on plantations. According to the 1981 census, the relative sizes of the four groups were as follows: Sinhalese—74 percent, Sri Lankan

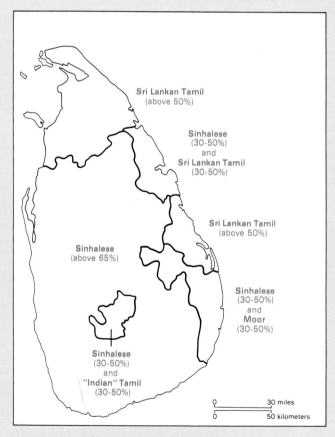

Figure 8-35. Ethnic Regions of Sri Lanka.

Tamil (the early Tamil community)—12.6 percent, Moors—7 percent, and Indian Tamil (the "plantation" Tamils)—5.6 percent. In general, the ethnic groups occupy distinct regions, an arrangement that contributes to feelings of distinctiveness and regionalism (Figure 8-35).

When Ceylon became independent in 1948, a parliamentary democracy was established, a form of government that permitted ethnic feelings to be expressed. For many Sinhalese, it was important to replace the legacy of colonialism—the foreign language of English and religion of Christianity—with Sinhala and Buddhism. After the 1956 elections, in which the two dominant Sinhalese parties vied with each other in promising to restore the importance of Sinhala and Buddhism, the victorious party enacted legislation to achieve the promised linguistic and religious dominance.

At the time of independence, other citizens, especially the more politically active Sri Lankan Tamils, assumed that both Sinhala and Tamil would be recognized as national languages. Furthermore, they expected that the rights of minorities would be recognized in all aspects of life, including university enrollments and access to professional jobs. When political parties were unable to obtain such rights through legislation or peaceful public protests, several Tamil organizations commenced armed protests.

By the mid-1980s, the conflict between the Sinhalese-dominated government and the Sri Lankan Tamil separatists had caused numerous deaths, considerable destruction of property, a slowdown in the country's economic growth, and a climate of continual civil strife. The Tamil separatists, who maintain that their rights will never be fully recognized in a country where the majority is Sinhalese, demand the partition option. That is, they insist on a separate nation consisting of the areas where Sri Lankan Tamils are the majority. In opposition, some Sinhalese leaders have declared that the island is large enough for only one country, a country in which the majority of voters should decide its future. They insist the only viable option is to impose compliance with the government.

Others, including both Sinhalese and Tamil leaders, believe that the most promising prospect for a solution lies in a type of federation in which large administrative areas having a Tamil majority would have greater autonomy. Also, the central government would need to recognize the pluralistic characteristics of the country by giving equal opportunities to persons from the various ethnic, linguistic, and religious communities.

There is no option that is favored by all the factions in Sri Lanka. A similar lack of agreement occurs in many other parts of the world. Controversies about the best way of defining nation states persist.

BIBLIOGRAPHY

Agnew, J. A., "An Excess of 'National Exceptionalism': Towards a New Political Geography of American Foreign Policy," *Political Geography Quarterly*, 2, no. 2 (1982), 151-66.

Archer, J. Clark, and Fred M. Shelley, *American Electoral Mosaics*, Resource Publications in Geography. Washington, D.C.: Association of American Geographers, 1986.

Best, Alan C. G., and Harm J. de Blij, *African Survey*. New York: John Wiley & Sons, 1977.

Bialer, Seweryn, "Poland and the Soviet Imperium," *Foreign Affairs*, 58, no. 3 (1981), 522–39.

Blouet, Brian W., "Sir Halford Mackinder as British High Commissioner to South Russia, 1919–1920," *Geographical Journal*, 142, pt. 2 (July 1976), 228–36.

———, "The Political Career of Halford Mackinder," *Political Geography Quarterly*, 6, no. 4 (October 1987), 355–67.

———, *Halford Mackinder: A Biography*. College Station: Texas A&M Press, 1987.

Blouet, B. W., and O. M. Blouet, *Latin America: An Introductory Survey*. New York: John Wiley & Sons, 1982.

Bohannan, Paul, "The Migration and Expansion of the Tiv," *Africa*, 24 (1954), 2–16.

Brewer, John D., *After Soweto: An Unfinished Journey*. Oxford, England: Clarendon Press, 1986.

Brookfield, H., *Interdependent Development*. Pittsburgh, Pa.: University of Pittsburgh Press, 1975.

Bunge, William W., "The Geography of Human Survival," *Annals of the Association of American Geographers*, 63, no. 3 (September 1973), 275–95.

Chay, John, and Thomas E. Ross, eds., *Buffer States in World Politics*. Boulder, Colo.: Westview Press, 1986.

Cohen, Saul B., *Geography and Politics in a World Divided*. New York: Oxford University Press, 1973.

———, "A New Map of Global Geo-Political Equilibrium: A Development Approach," *Political Geography Quarterly*, 1, no. 2 (1982) 223–41.

Conzen, Michael, "Town into Suburb: Boston's Expanding Fringe," pp. 37–49 in C. Browning, ed., *Population and Urbanized Area Growth in Megalopolis, 1950–1970*. University of North Carolina at Chapel Hill, Department of Geography, Studies in Geography, no. 7, 1974.

Cooper, Allan D., *U.S. Economic Power and Political Influence in Namibia, 1700–1982*. Boulder, Colo.: Westview Press, 1982.

Cox, K. R., and R. J. Johnson, *Conflict, Politics, and the Urban Scene*. London: Longman, 1982.

Cukwurah, A. O., *The Settlement of Boundary Disputes in International Law*. Manchester, England: University Press, 1967.

Dale, Edward H., "Some Geographical Aspects of African Land-Locked States," *Annals of the Association of American Geographers*, 58, no. 3 (September 1968), 485–505.

Downing, David, *An Atlas of Territorial and Border Disputes.* London: New English Library, 1980.

Flannery, Kent V., "The Cultural Evolution of Civilizations," *Annual Review of Ecology and Systematics,* 3 (1972), 329–429.

Fried, Morton H., *The Evolution of Political Society.* New York: Random House, 1967.

Gallagher, John, and Ronald Robinson, "The Imperialism of Free Trade," *The Economic History Review,* 6, no. 1 (1953), 1–15.

Gellner, Ernest, *Nations and Nationalism.* Ithaca, N.Y.: Cornell University Press, 1983.

Gray, Colin S., *Strategic Studies and Public Policy.* Lexington, Ky.: University of Kentucky Press, 1982.

———, *The Geopolitics of Super Power.* Lexington, Ky.: University of Kentucky Press, 1988.

Hartshorne, Richard, "The Functional Approach in Political Geography," *Annals of the Association of American Geographers,* 40, no. 2 (June 1950), 95–130.

Herskovitz, Jean, "Democracy in Nigeria," *Foreign Affairs,* 58, no. 2 (Winter 1979–1980), 314–35.

Hopkins, Terence K., and Immanuel Wallerstein, *World Systems Analysis: Theory and Methodology.* Beverly Hills, Calif.: Sage Publications, 1982.

Immerman, Richard H., *The CIA in Guatemala: The Foreign Policy of Intervention.* Austin, Tex.: University of Texas Press, 1982.

Jay, Peter, "Regionalism as Geopolitics," *Foreign Affairs,* 58, no. 3 (1979), 485–514.

———, *The Crisis for Western Political Economy and Other Essays.* London: Andre Deutsch, 1984.

Johnston, R. J., *Political, Electoral, and Spatial Systems.* Oxford, England: Clarendon, Press, 1979.

———, "Political Geography without Politics," *Progress in Human Geography,* 4, no. 3 (1980), 439–46.

———, *Geography and the State.* London: Macmillan, 1982.

Kaiser, Robert G., "U.S.–Soviet Relations: Goodbye to Détente," *Foreign Affairs,* 59, no. 3 (1980), 500–521.

Kasperson, Roger E., and Julian V. Minghi, *The Structure of Political Geography.* Chicago: Aldine Publishing Co., 1969.

Kennan, George F., *The Nuclear Delusion: Soviet–American Relations in the Atomic Age.* New York: Pantheon Books, 1982.

Ley, David, *A Social Geography of the City.* New York: Harper & Row, Pub., 1983.

Mackinder, Sir Halford J., *Britain and the British Seas.* London: Heineman, 1902.

———, "The Geographical Pivot of History," *Geographical Journal,* 23, no. 4 (April 1904), 421–37.

———, *Democratic Ideals and Reality.* London: Constable, 1919.

———, "The Round World and the Winning of the Peace," *Foreign Affairs,* 21, no. 4 (July 1943), 595–605.

Magdoff, Harry, *Imperialism: From the Colonial Age to the Present.* New York: Monthly Review Press, 1978.

Mahan, Alfred T., *The Influence of Sea Power on History, 1660–1783.* Boston: Little, Brown, 1890.

———, *The Problem of Asia and Its Effect upon International Policies.* Boston: Little, Brown, and Company, 1900.

McDonald, Albert, "Mines in a Lawless Sea," *The Geographical Magazine,* 44, no. 9 (September 1982), 501–3.

McNamara, Robert S., "The Military Role of Nuclear Weapons," *Foreign Affairs,* 62, no. 1 (Fall 1983), 59–80.

Modelski, G., *Long Cycles in World Politics.* Seattle: University of Washington Press, 1987.

Moreland, Laurence W., Todd A. Baker, and Robert P. Steed, eds., *Contemporary Southern Political Attitudes and Behavior.* New York: Praeger, 1982.

Morgan, Dan, *Merchants of Grain.* New York: Penguin, 1980.

Nkrumah, Kwame, *Neo-Colonialism: The Last Stage of Imperialism.* New York: International Publishers, 1965.

"Not Just the Tamils," *The Economist,* 288, no. 7301 (August 6, 1983), 12–13.

O'Loughlin, John, "The Identification and Evaluation of Racial Gerrymandering," *Annals of the Association of American Geographers,* 72, no. 2 (June 1982), 165–84.

Osei-Kwame, Peter, and Peter J. Taylor, "A Politics of Failure: The Political Geography of Ghanaian Elections, 1954–1979," *Annals of the Association of American Geographers,* 74, no. 4 (December 1984), 574–89.

O'Sullivan, Patrick, "A Geographical Analysis of Guerilla Warfare," *Political Geography Quarterly,* 2, no. 2 (1982), 139–50.

———, *Geopolitics.* New York: St. Martin's Press, 1986.

Parker, Geoffrey, *A Political Geography of Community Europe.* London: Butterworth, 1983.

———, *Western Geopolitical Thought in the Twentieth Century.* New York: St. Martin's Press, 1985.

Parker, W. G., *Mackinder: Geography as an Aid to Statecraft.* New York: Oxford University Press, 1982.

Pearcy, G. Etzel, *A Thirty-Eight State USA,* Plyon Monograph Series No. 2. Fullerton, Calif.: Plyon Press, 1973.

Ratzel, Friedrich, *Politische Geographie.* Muchen and Leipzig, Germany: R. Oldebourg, 1897.

Sack, Robert D., *Human Territoriality: Its Theory and History.* New York: Cambridge University Press, 1986.

Scott, Peter, "Cape Town: A Multi-Racial City," *Geographical Journal,* 121, pt. 2 (June 1955), 149–57.

Service, Elman R., *Primitive Social Organization: An Evolutionary Perspective.* New York: Random House, 1962.

de Seversky, Alexander P., *Air Power: Key to Survival.* New York: Simon & Schuster, 1950.

Short, J. R., "Political Geography," *Progress in Human Geography,* 8, no. 1 (1984), 127–30.

Sivard, Ruth Leger, *World Military and Social Expenditures 1986,* 11th ed. Washington, D.C.: World Priorities, 1986.

Soja, Edward W., *The Political Organization of Space.* Washington, D.C.: Association of American Geographers, 1971.

Spykman, Nicholas J., *America's Strategy in World Politics, the United States and the Balance of Power.* New York: Harcourt Brace, 1942.

———, *The Geography of the Peace.* New York: Harcourt Brace, 1944.

Tata, Robert J., "Poor and Small Too: Caribbean Mini-States," *Focus,* 29, no. 2 (November–December 1978), 1–11.

Taylor, Peter J., "A Materialist Framework for Political

Geography," *Transactions, Institute of British Geographers,* New Series, 7 (1982), 15–34.

Tunteng, P-Kiven, "External Influences and Subimperialism in Francophone West Africa," in Peter C. W. Gutkind and Immanuel Wallerstein, *The Political Economy of Contemporary Africa,* pp. 212–31. Beverly Hills, Calif.: Sage Publications, 1976.

Western, John, *Outcast Capetown.* Minneapolis: University of Minnesota Press, 1981.

Wilson, Edward O., *On Human Nature.* Cambridge, Mass.: Harvard University Press, 1978.

Wishart, David J., "The Dispossession of the Pawnee," *Annals of the Association of American Geographers,* 69, no. 3 (September 1979), 382–401.

World Development Report 1987. New York: Oxford University Press, 1987.

Zegarelli, Philip E., "Antarctica," *Focus,* 29, no. 1 (September–October 1978).

9 AGRICULTURAL SOCIETIES

Before the midpoint of the twentieth century, great political changes had taken place. European empires had disintegrated and many former colonies had achieved independence. The United Nations had emerged, and more than half of the inhabitants of the world lived in Communist countries. If the first half of the century was marked by great political change, then the second half can be characterized by rapid economic change.

Changes in economic conditions, in turn, relate to many other aspects of human life, such as demographic characteristics (Chapters 2 and 3), migration (Chapter 4), the creation of cultural landscapes (Chapter 5), and political organization (Chapter 8). Certainly an examination of economic differences from place to place is an important part of human geography.

Here the topic of economic geography is organized partly on the basis of the development of national economies, with Chapter 9 focusing primarily on agricultural societies and Chapter 10 on industrial ones. The economies of countries, however, do not operate independently of each other, which means that an understanding of economic conditions today depends on more than just an appreciation of economic history. Furthermore, because economic activities in most parts of the world have a major impact on the economies of other places, it is necessary to consider several aspects of agricultural and industrial societies almost simultaneously.

After an introductory discussion about the global economy, Chapter 9 examines the economic differences among countries in the world today. Here the terms *more developed countries* and *less developed countries* are given greater emphasis and clarification than previously in the text. Following a definition and clarification of the economic variations of countries of

the world, societies that are, or were, predominantly agricultural are studied. Although the emphasis is on various productive activities, settlement and migration patterns are also included.

THE GLOBAL ECONOMY

We now operate in a global economic system. The system functions within a setting of multiple nation states, yet the political independence of many countries is greatly restricted by the decisions and actions of the superpowers (Chapter 8). Likewise, although there are numerous local markets and national currencies, in most parts of the world these are affected by decisions and actions of the dominant super economies.

The movement toward global economic integration has gone much further than political integration. The common market formed by the countries of Western Europe is more integrated than the political organization of the European Economic Community (Box 8-2). The United States and Canada have been striving to establish free trade, with essentially a single market for goods originating in Anglo-America; but politically the two countries remain distinctive and separate. For most minerals, fuels, and agricultural commodities there is one world market. That is, iron ore, copper, tin, petroleum, cacao, corn, and cotton are bought and sold at a uniform price on international markets. If the United Kingdom, the United Arab Emirates, or the Soviet Union sell oil on world markets, the price is the same at any given time, and it is quoted in dollars.

Most world trade is conducted in a handful of currencies—the dollar, yen, pound, franc, and deutschemark. International currencies are used not only to settle international trade debts but also serve as vehicles for investment and speculation. For example, if the deutschemark is rising against the dollar, many investors sell American currency and buy German. This involves selling off dollars, which drives the price of the dollar down, and buying deutschemarks, thus pushing their price up. International currency markets have become an exchange where speculative bets can be placed on the economic future of nations.

Because the effect of this speculative trading tends to destabilize currency trading, some authorities think it will not be long before a world currency will be used to settle international trade debts (Cooper 1984). Even though no single global currency exists today, it is obvious that what occurs in a few currency markets affects virtually all economies.

Although there is one world market in many commodities and products, the global economy is not perfect and is not equal for all participants. In many ways, the rich, more developed countries function differently from the poor, less developed countries. Although many differences are discussed in greater detail later in this chapter and the next, it is helpful now to have an overview of some contrasts.

The **core** of the present global economic system emerged around the North Atlantic from the fifteenth to nineteenth centuries. Its more recent expansion to the Western Pacific includes primarily Japan, but also Australia, New Zealand, South Korea, Taiwan, Hong Kong, and Singapore.

Core countries, which have undergone industrial revolutions, possess diversified economies, enjoy relatively high standards of living, and engage in world trade as producers, consumers, brokers, and financiers.

Beyond the core of the global economic system is the **periphery,** which consists of the majority of the world's countries and peoples. The economies in the periphery are still dominated by primary production (farming, fishing, forestry, and mining). The living conditions are relatively poor for most inhabitants, and the economies are generally regarded as less developed.

When the less developed countries buy and sell in the global economy, they frequently find that the terms of trade are against them over the long run. The price of agricultural commodities (cotton, palm oil, sugar, coffee, rubber) and minerals (copper, bauxite, tin, iron ore) tend to be cheap compared to the costs of manufactured goods. When several countries, each independently hoping to earn more from increased production, cause a glut on the world market, prices per unit fall even lower. This situation of low prices for primary products is very common because so many poor countries desperately strive for foreign earnings by exporting the few commodities they can produce.

Even if the producing countries cooperate and organize a price **cartel,** they usually fail in the long run. Sometimes this is because the buyer nations have stockpiled commodities (especially minerals) and can break infant cartels by dumping these stored materials on the market. This was the fate of tin when the buying countries released accumulated stockpiles to prevent the few main tin producers of the world from controlling its selling price. Another reason is that potential buyers of many kinds of commodities will avoid paying higher prices by switching to substitutes. As an illustration, buyers of copper may shift to aluminum. Furthermore, even if a cartel is successful in forcing a higher price for a short time, usually other countries outside the cartel soon enter the market, thus creating a production glut and an eventual price drop. The history of world oil prices from the early 1970s to the early 1980s clearly demonstrates this situation.

Less developed countries find they cannot use their own weak currencies for world trade. They must buy and sell in the international currencies (e.g., francs or dollars), and consequently they experience the fluctuations in the values of these currencies. Basically the world economy flows through banks, stock exchanges, commodity dealers, and speculators who operate in major cities in core countries, such as Tokyo, Chicago, Montreal, New York, London, Paris, Brussels, Frankfurt, Amsterdam, and Zurich (Figure 9-1). Thus, if a peripheral country successfully sells its cotton or coffee on the world market, a significant part of the proceeds will remain in core financial institutions. And if there are profits to be invested, they will usually find a home via a bank in one of the major financial centers.

The world economic system is not static. One change is its continual expansion, both in monetary size and geographic distribution. Nearly all the less developed countries are implementing policies aimed at creating more manufacturing and less dependence on the primary sector. More involvement in the world economic system is seen by many countries as a way to diversify their production and to raise living standards.

Economic changes bring about dislocations and hardships as well as benefits. Normally only a small proportion of the population, which is located primarily in the major city of the country, enjoys the benefits of the modern sector. In contrast, general economic conditions in the rural sector frequently do not improve (in fact, they may deteriorate), so inequalities between the richer and poor segments of the society become larger. Several of the implications of such a **dual economy** (the existence of both a modern

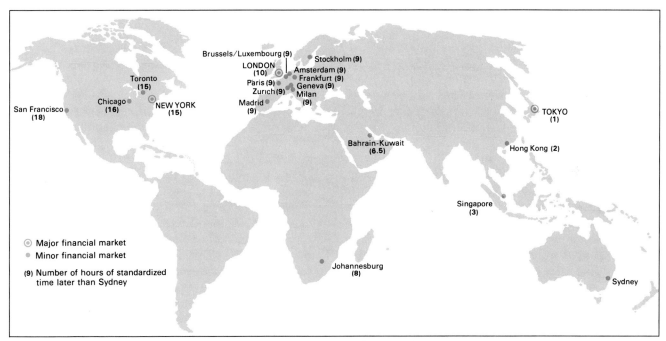

Figure 9-1. Major Exchange Markets of the World. A large share of the world's economy is controlled by monetary decisions made in a few major cities of the world.

economic sector and a traditional economy within a country) are discussed in greater detail in this chapter and the next.

The world economic system is also changing in the relative roles of various countries. Some countries, especially those who have sold petroleum (the one commodity that has been highly valued in the world in recent decades), have become much richer in the last twenty years. For example, in the United Arab Emirates, a tremendous transformation of economic conditions, demographic characteristics, and the urban landscape has occurred during the last two decades. Other countries, such as South Korea, have shifted their economies from being dependent primarily on agriculture to having a more diversified base. In addition to the numerous changes in living conditions within South Korea, this new economic status has affected the country's relationships with other countries, especially Japan and the United States.

As some countries improve their economic status,

the relative strength of others may decline. Even though the United States remains the leading economic power, its dominance has declined since the 1970s (Agnew 1987). Whereas in 1950, the United States produced 40 percent of the world's goods and services (by value), by 1980 its share had dropped to 22 percent. In 1986 West Germany took over as the world's leading exporter (by value).

Although most parts of the world are affected by what happens in the global economy, dividing the world into only core and periphery regions obscures many transitional situations. The world's population is still divided politically into distinct nation-states. Consequently, national policies, as well as environmental, cultural, and historical conditions of countries, also influence the economies of places. A more accurate view of economic variations, therefore, can be obtained by looking at more than just these two broad classes (i.e., more developed and less developed countries).

Core. When applied to a comparison of national economies, the term refers to the more developed countries around the North Atlantic that industrialized and expanded their trading spheres from the fifteenth to nineteenth centuries (see Periphery and Box 9-1).
Periphery. When applied to a comparison of national economies, the term has historically referred to all countries other than those identified as belonging to the "core" (see Core and Box 9-1).

Cartel. A combination of businesses or countries organized to regulate (and control) production, pricing, and marketing of goods.
Dual economy. The existence of both a modern economic sector and a traditional sector within the same country, with the former usually being in a few large cities and the latter in rural areas.

ECONOMIC CLASSIFICATION OF NATIONS

Criteria for Classifying Countries

Nations can be classified according to a variety of socioeconomic characteristics. The classifying criteria often involve a broad combination of factors such as the production of goods and services, national and personal income, levels of consumption, and measurements of material well-being. Because many of these economic factors convey a similar message, it is possible to represent geographic variations by using only a few carefully selected criteria. Furthermore, scholars usually attempt to combine several data into a single index so that the countries can be grouped easily into classes. Here three representative criteria are examined: GNP per capita, percentage of agricultural workers in the work force, and literacy rate.

The first criterion is based on **gross national product** (GNP), which is the total value of goods and services produced in a country during a year. In some respects, the GNP for each country is meaningful by itself because it measures the total economic power of nations. By this measure, the largest economies in the world are the United States, the Soviet Union, Japan, and West Germany (Figure 9-2).

Because the number of persons producing wealth within each country affects the size of the total GNP, a small country, like Switzerland, may have a lower GNP than a country with a large population, like India. Therefore, it is also informative to divide the GNP by the population to obtain a value per person (see Table 9-1). This statistic, GNP per capita, is commonly used as an indicator of the economic standard of living in the world (Figure 9-3). Its merits were demonstrated by Smith (1979) when he found a close correlation between GNP per capita and a composite index of six factors related to living standards for 54 countries (Figure 9-4).

In spite of its general usefulness, a number of limitations are associated with using GNP per capita as a measure of national wealth. First, the GNP does not reveal the distribution of wealth within countries.

Figure 9-2. Cartogram of GNP for Countries, 1986. The economic importance of countries (especially the dominating magnitude of the United States, the Soviet Union, and Japan) is easily seen by comparing their monetary sizes with other nations. Note the differences between this cartogram and the one of world population (Figure 3-24).

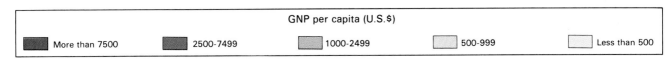

GNP per capita (U.S.$)

More than 7500 | 2500-7499 | 1000-2499 | 500-999 | Less than 500

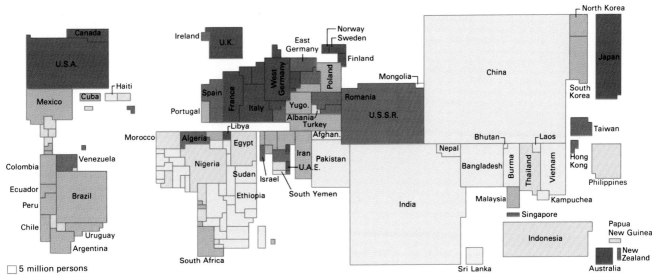

Figure 9-3. GNP per Capita for Countries, 1986. The distribution of GNP per capita is shown (by five classes) on a base cartogram of national population, which provides a visual sense of how much of the world's population lives in a country with a particular income level.

In many nations, a small percentage of the population controls a large share of the wealth, while most of the people are poor. The importance of this factor can be seen by a graphic comparison of income equality with GNP per capita. Inequality, defined here as the ratio of the incomes of the richest 20 percent of the population compared to those of the poorest 40 percent, is plotted on a scatter diagram with 1970 per capita GNP for 54 countries (Figure 9-5).

Figure 9-4. The Relationship between Gross National Product per Capita and a Composite Level-of-Living Index. Except for the poorest countries, there is a fairly close correlation between the single measure of GNP per capita and an index composed of the following six economic factors: life expectancy, per capita animal protein consumed per day, percentage of population age 5–19 in school, newspaper circulation, per capita telephones, and per capita passenger cars. After Smith 1979.

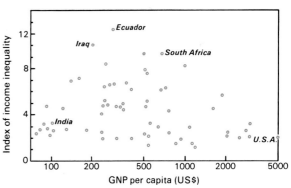

Figure 9-5. The Relationship between Gross National Product per Capita and Income Inequality. This scatter diagram shows that the index of income inequality is not closely related to the total wealth of a country; countries with high, medium, and low GNP per capita may all have low levels of income equality. After Smith 1977.

Gross National Product (GNP). The total value of goods and services produced (and recorded by monetary transactions) in a country during a year.

TABLE 9-1. World Economic Data, Mid-1980s

Country	GNP, 1986, in billion US $	GNP per Capita, 1986	Labor Force in Agriculture, percentage	Labor Force in Industry, percentage	Labor Force in Services, percentage	Commercial Energy Consumption per Capita, 1985, kg. oil equivalent	Population per Physician, 1983	Urban Population, percentage, 1988	Literacy Rate, 1983
Afghanistan	1.8	120^e	—	—	—	73	12,000	15	20
Albania	2.7	900^e	56	26	18	1,267	620	34	75
Algeria	58.6	2,570	31	27	42	1,123	2,560	43	45
Angola	6.5	790^e	74	10	17	207	15,610	25	30
Argentina	73.3	2,350	13	34	53	1,468	500	85	94
Australia	188.2	11,910	7	32	61	5,116	500	86	99
Austria	76.0	10,000	9	41	50	3,217	430	55	99
Bangladesh	16.7	160	75	6	19	43	6,600	16	34
Belgium	91.4	9,230	3	36	61	4,666	360	95	99
Benin	1.1	270	70	7	23	35	14,400	39	28
Bhutan	0.2	160	92	3	5	—	—	5	—
Bolivia	3.5	540	46	20	34	263	1,600	49	70
Botswana	0.9	840	70	13	17	380	8,300	22	62
Brazil	259.4	1810	31	27	42	781	1,150	71	76
Bulgaria	49.5	5,500^e	18	45	37	4,332	370	65	95
Burkina Faso	1.1	150	87	4	9	20	49,300	8	11
Burma	7.5	200	53	19	28	74	3,970	24	70
Burundi	1.2	240	93	2	5	26	45,400	5	27
Cameroon	9.1	910	70	8	22	145	13,680	42	55
Canada	361.0	14,100	5	29	65	9,224	510	76	99
Cen. African Rep.	0.8	290	72	6	21	33	25,200	35	36
Chad	0.6	120^e	83	5	12	—	41,120	27	22
Chile	16.2	1,320	17	25	58	726	1,200	82	96
China	315.0	300	74	14	12	515	1,740	41	69
Colombia	36.9	1,230	34	24	42	755	2,020	65	86
Congo	1.9	1,040	62	12	26	232	5,600	48	62
Costa Rica	3.8	1,420	31	23	46	534	1,250	45	93
Cote d'Ivoire	7.8	740	65	8	27	166	15,940	43	38
Cuba	18.4	1,800^e	24	29	48	1,075	560	71	96
Czechoslovakia	85.3	5,500^e	13	49	37	4,853	340	74	99
Denmark	64.5	12,640	7	32	61	4,001	410	84	99
Dominican Rep.	4.5	710	46	15	39	372	2,700	52	75
Ecuador	11.1	1,160	39	20	42	720	1,300	52	82
Egypt	38.4	760	46	20	34	588	770	45	44
El Salvador	4.2	820	43	19	37	186	2,700	43	66
Ethiopia	5.3	120	80	8	12	17	68,850	10	12
Finland	59.7	12,180	12	35	53	4,587	500	62	100
France	595.0	10,740	9	35	56	3,673	460	73	99
Gabon	3.6	3,020	—	—	—	—	3,070	41	62
Germany, East	121.9	7,300^e	11	50	39	5,680	460	77	99
Germany, West	733.3	12,080	6	44	50	4,451	420	94	99
Ghana	5.3	390	56	18	26	131	6,630	31	50
Greece	36.8	3,680	31	29	40	1,841	360	58	90
Guatemala	8.0	930	57	17	26	176	6,190	33	54
Guinea	2.0	320	81	9	10	53	50,570	22	25
Guyana	0.4	500	—	—	—	—	1,830	32	92
Haiti	1.9	330	70	8	22	55	9,250	25	35
Honduras	3.4	740	61	16	23	201	2,600	40	62
Hong Kong	38.3	6,720	2	51	47	1,264	—	93	—
Hungary	21.3	2,010	18	44	38	2,974	350	58	99

Country	GNP, 1986, in billion US $	GNP per Capita, 1986	Labor Force in Agriculture, percentage	Labor Force in Industry, percentage	Labor Force in Services, percentage	Commercial Energy Consumption per Capita, 1985, kg. oil equivalent	Population per Physician, 1983	Urban Population, percentage, 1988	Literacy Rate, 1983
Iceland	2.7	13,370	—	—	—	—	430	90	99
India	212.0	270	70	13	17	201	2,620	25	42
Indonesia	84.2	500	57	13	30	219	11,000	22	70
Iran	74.6	1,600^e	36	33	31	1,026	2,560	51	47
Iraq	32.0	2,000^e	30	22	48	662	1,790	68	52
Ireland	18.3	5,080	19	34	48	2,627	780	56	98
Israel	26.1	6,210	6	32	62	1,949	350	89	94
Italy	490.2	8,570	12	41	48	2,606	300	72	96
Jamaica	2.0	880	31	16	52	954	2,780	54	92
Japan	1,561.3	12,850	11	34	55	3,116	710	77	99
Jordan	5.7	1,540	10	26	64	771	900	59	70
Kampuchea	0.8	120^e	—	—	—	58	29,400	11	50
Kenya	6.3	300	81	7	12	103	9,070	19	52
Korea, North	23.4	1,140^e	43	30	27	2,118	—	64	95
Korea, South	102.6	2,370	36	27	37	1,241	1,560	65	94
Kuwait	25.0	13,890	2	33	67	4,569	600	80	66
Laos	0.4	120^e	76	7	17	58	17,400	16	46
Lebanon	2.7	1,000^e	—	—	—	777	1,130	80	75
Lesotho	0.7	410	86	4	10	—	14,100	17	70
Liberia	1.0	450	74	9	16	345	8,250	42	30
Libya	29.3	7,500	18	29	53	3,042	630	76	62
Madagascar	2.4	230	81	6	13	33	9,920	22	64
Malawi	1.2	160	83	7	9	39	48,500	12	38
Malaysia	29.2	1,850	42	19	39	826	3,300	35	73
Mali	1.3	170	86	2	13	25	26,210	18	15
Mauritania	0.8	440	69	9	22	127	14,250	35	17
Mauritius	1.2	1,200	28	24	48	311	1,440	42	80
Mexico	151.1	1,850	37	29	35	1,290	1,400	70	88
Mongolia	1.7	900^e	40	21	39	1,313	420	52	93
Morocco	14.0	590	46	25	29	237	16,300	43	23
Mozambique	2.9	210	85	7	8	86	37,490	19	35
Namibia	1.1	1,020	—	—	—	—	5,270	51	68
Nepal	2.8	160	93	1	7	17	27,000	7	20
Netherlands	145.7	10,050	6	32	63	5,138	480	89	99
New Zealand	23.5	7,110	11	33	56	3,823	590	84	99
Nicaragua	2.6	790	47	16	38	259	1,470	57	88
Niger	1.7	260	91	2	7	48	38,600	16	12
Nigeria	67.5	640	68	12	20	165	10,800	28	38
Norway	65.0	15,480	8	29	62	8,920	480	71	100
Oman	6.5	4,990	50	22	28	2,683	1,600	9	50
Pakistan	35.7	350	55	16	30	218	2,800	28	30
Panama	5.1	2,330	32	18	50	634	980	51	87
Papua New Guinea	2.3	690	76	10	14	235	11,600	13	42
Paraguay	3.6	880	49	21	31	281	1,950	43	88
Peru	22.8	1,130	40	18	42	543	1,210	69	84
Philippines	33.1	570	52	16	33	255	6,600	41	88
Poland	77.6	2,070	29	39	33	3,438	530	61	98
Portugal	22.5	2,230	26	37	38	1,312	450	30	82
Puerto Rico	17.1	5,190	19	21	60	—	—	67	—
Romania	68.4	3,000^e	31	44	26	3,453	610	49	97

TABLE 9-1. *(cont.)*

Country	GNP, 1986, in billion US $	GNP per Capita, 1986	Labor Force in Agriculture, percentage	Labor Force in Industry, percentage	Labor Force in Services, percentage	Commercial Energy Consumption per Capita, 1985, kg. oil equivalent	Population per Physician, 1983	Urban Population, percentage, 1988	Literacy Rate, 1983
Rwanda	1.9	290	93	3	4	43	29,400	6	54
Saudi Arabia	79.7	6,930	48	14	37	3,653	2,680	72	30
Senegal	2.9	420	81	6	13	110	13,070	36	25
Sierra Leone	1.1	310	70	14	16	82	17,980	28	25
Singapore	19.3	7,410	2	38	61	2,165	1,000	100	84
Somalia	2.2	280	76	8	16	82	16,630	34	10
South Africa	59.8	1,800	17	35	49	2,184	1,380	56	82
Spain	187.8	4,840	17	37	46	1,932	360	91	94
Sri Lanka	6.6	400	53	14	33	139	8,120	22	85
Sudan	7.3	320	71	8	21	61	8,800	20	28
Suriname	1.0	2,510	—	—	—	—	—	66	—
Sweden	110.6	13,170	6	33	62	6,482	480	83	99
Switzerland	116.0	17,840	6	39	55	3,952	410	61	99
Syria	16.4	1,560	32	32	36	838	2,180	49	56
Taiwan	56.1	2,860[e]	—	—	—	—	1,250	67	85
Tanzania	5.4	240	86	5	10	39	33,930	18	70
Thailand	42.8	810	71	10	19	343	6,370	17	88
Togo	0.8	250	73	10	17	47	18,600	22	36
Trinidad & Tobago	6.1	5,120	10	39	51	3,641	1,280	34	95
Tunisia	8.2	1,140	35	36	29	546	3,700	53	50
Turkey	58.1	1,110	58	17	25	712	1,500	53	67
Uganda	3.5	230[e]	86	4	10	24	23,040	10	54
United Arab Emirates	20.2	14,410	5	38	57	5,102	840	81	68
United Kingdom	504.9	8,920	3	38	59	3,603	600	91	99
United States	4,217.5	17,500	3	28	69	7,278	490	74	99
Uruguay	5.6	1,860	16	29	55	745	510	84	96
U.S.S.R.	2,072.0	7,400	20	39	41	4,885	250	65	99
Venezuela	52.2	2,930	16	28	56	2,409	820	82	86
Vietnam	11.2	180[e]	68	12	21	76	3,970	19	78
Yemen, Arab Rep. (No.)	3.5	550	69	9	22	117	6,480	15	12
Yemen, P.D.R. (So.)	1.1	480	41	18	41	750	6,800	40	35
Yugoslavia	53.4	2,300	32	33	34	1,926	640	47	89
Zaire	5.0	160	72	13	16	73	13,790	34	58
Zambia	2.1	300	73	10	17	412	7,110	43	72
Zimbabwe	5.6	620	73	11	17	427	6,600	24	72
World	14,875.4	3,010	—	—	—	—	1,020	45	71

[e] Estimate   — Data unavailable

Sources: Population Reference Bureau, *World Population Data Sheet, 1986 & 1988*; World Bank, *World Development Report, 1987*; Sivard, *World Military and Social Indicators, 1986*.

People in some nations, such as India, have low per capita GNPs, but the differences between income groups are not extremely large. As might be expected, in the centrally planned economies of Eastern Europe, incomes are relatively equal. But in many countries in the world—Ecuador, Iraq, South Africa, to name only a few—there is a wide gap between the incomes of the majority of the population and those of the small elite class that controls the economy and, generally, the government. In such countries, the GNP per capita is a poor indicator of the actual incomes of most individuals and families.

A second limitation occurs because the GNP statistic depends on recorded monetary exchanges. Using monetary data is valid for a society like the United States where people purchase many goods and services, such as food and entertainment. But in regions where people grow their own food and create their own entertainment, these activities cannot be measured by a statistic dependent on cash transactions. Even in countries where cash is used to obtain most goods and services, underground (illegal and unreported) activities are rarely recorded as part of the total wealth. The production and selling of illegal drugs are among the numerous activities that generate income but are not officially a part of a nation's recorded production. For example, it was estimated in 1987 that the export of cocaine brought about $600 million into Bolivia, compared to $500 million earned from all legal exports.

A third problem in comparing countries according to their GNP per capita results from having to equate various national currencies. Official exchange rates often do not accurately reflect the actual comparative value of goods in two different countries. Also, wild fluctuations in official rates may make comparative data quickly obsolete.

In spite of these limitations in GNP data, as a single indicator, GNP per capita still provides a good approximation of national economic differences. To obtain a more complete view of the variations in countries, however, two other criteria are examined here.

One criterion is the percentage of workers engaged in agriculture (see Table 9-1). The rationale for the inclusion of this measure is the relationship between specialization of production and wealth. A high percentage of agriculturalists in a country indicates that a small proportion of workers are employed in the specialized occupations of manufacturing and services. By contrast, a nation with a small percentage of agricultural workers generally will have a more diversified economy with a wide variety of occupations, many of which generate high incomes. These nonagricultural sectors produce goods, such as machinery and improved seeds, that make it possible for a small proportion of farmers to grow enough food for the entire population.

In general, the wealth of nations is related to the proportion of the labor force engaged in agricultural, manufacturing, and service activities. More specifically, the relationship between the percentage of laborers in agriculture and the GNP per capita is an inverse one (Figure 9-6). In other words, the wealthier countries generally have the lowest percentage of workers in agriculture (Figure 9-7).

As with the GNP, there are problems associated with using agricultural employment as an index of wealth. First, there is a data problem because statistics are not always comparable from country to country. In agrarian societies like India or China, rural children are often important agricultural workers, yet they may not be included in the labor force statistics. Second, laborers that are employed only seasonally may, or may not, be included in the statistics. Third, the migration to cities by underemployed and unemployed people from rural areas in many poor countries may reduce the percentage of workers in agriculture, but it does not necessarily increase the per capita GNP.

The third criterion considered here is the literacy rate, which in turn reflects the development of education. One reason for using this statistic is that a technological and economically diversified society requires an educated population to create, maintain, and utilize complex machines and organizations. Also, the communication of new ideas and techniques is easier when a higher percentage of the population is literate (Chapter 3).

Furthermore, literacy is included because it implies a general availability of several kinds of basic needs, especially clothing, shelter, safe water, and health services. That is, if conditions within a nation are such that most citizens have access to safe water, there is probably also a high rate of literacy because the welfare of all individuals is given developmental importance. The inclusion of a literacy statistic, therefore, measures an aspect of economic development that differs somewhat from those figures that deal primarily with national productivity (for example, GNP).

Literacy rates in the world vary from less than 10 percent to over 95 percent (Table 9-1). As is true with many statistics obtained from national records, there are different definitions of what constitutes literacy and varying ways of gathering data about literate persons, which means that literacy data should be regarded as less precise than the numerical figures imply. Nevertheless, the world pattern of literacy is similar to that of the other two criteria (Figure 6-16).

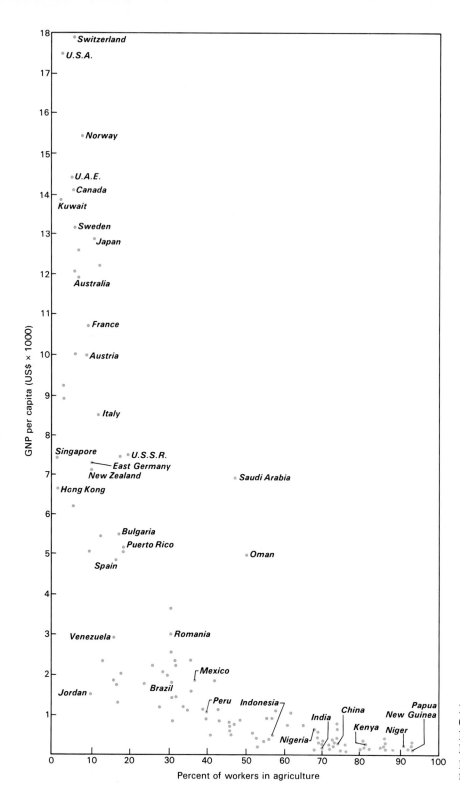

Figure 9-6. The Relationship between Gross National Product per Capita and Percentage of Workers in Agriculture, Mid-1980s. In general, these two phenomena, when measured by national units, are inversely related.

Variations and Interpretations

The national variations in these three indicators—GNP per capita, percentage of agricultural workers, and the literacy rate—can be seen on a scatter diagram (Figure 9-8). Because of the tremendous range in the per-capita GNP values, the units on the vertical axis are logarithmic. The units on the horizontal scale consist of an agricultural-illiteracy index, which is based on the percentages of those two criteria.

As displayed by the scatter diagram, the economic variations among countries do not fall neatly into distinct groups, even though there are large differences between the extremes. For our discussion, the points on the diagram are grouped into four broad categories: those representing countries that are (I)

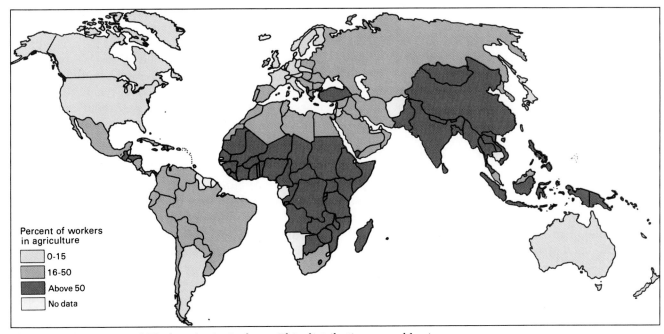

Figure 9-7. Percentage of Workers in Agriculture. This distribution resembles income patterns (see Figure 9-3) and national variations in demographic characteristics (e.g., see Figures 3-6, 3-7, and 3-9).

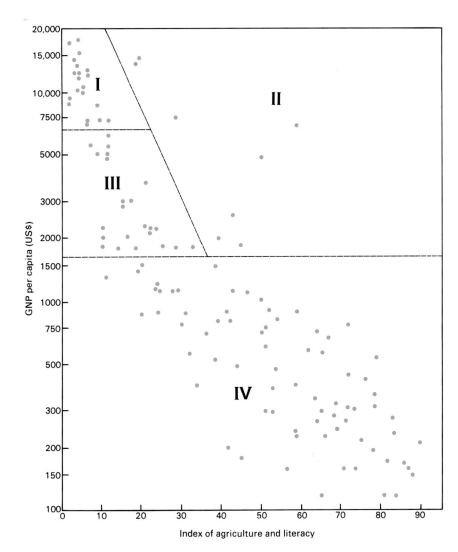

Figure 9-8. Countries Grouped by Selected Economic Criteria. After values based on (1) GNP per capita and (2) an index of agriculture and literacy were plotted on the scatter diagram, the points were divided into four groups (classes). The countries within each group are shown in Figure 9-9.

relatively rich and industrialized, (II) oil-rich, (III) intermediate, and (IV) relatively poor.

The world pattern of these four types displays the geography of national wealth (Figure 9-9), which affects so many human activities. Countries classified as "relatively rich and industrialized" are nearly all the European nations, including the Soviet Union, plus the United States, Canada, Japan, Australia, New Zealand, and Singapore. Most of the "oil-rich" nations are located in Southwest Asia and Northern Africa. The "intermediate" class includes a few countries in Europe (e.g., Portugal, Romania, Yugoslavia), several in Latin America (such as Mexico, Argentina, and Brazil), and some in Asia (Malaysia and South Korea, for example). The main "relatively poor" regions of the world encompass most nations in Africa and much of Asia. The large countries of India and China are both in this category.

It is important to stress that this particular classification is based on criteria that are economic, measurable, and valued by Western cultures. These measures do not differentiate countries by the degree of citizens' happiness or contentment. The classification does not reveal the extent of social harmony within each nation, nor does it measure the quality of value systems in various societies. This particular ranking of countries, therefore, cannot be interpreted to mean that some nations are better than others—it only expresses differences that are economic.

Because these criteria do not measure many aspects of culture, it is not surprising that the world distribution of these economic classes does not match the patterns of religion, language, or other cultural groupings (see Figures 5-25, 6-1, and 7-1). The cross-cultural patterns are illustrated by the Western country of Sweden and the non-Western nation of Japan, both being in the "relatively rich and industrialized class," Arabic Algeria and non-Arabic Iran in the "oil-rich" group, and African Tanzania and non-African Burma in the category called "relatively poor."

Even though national differences are measured here by only three criteria, these statistics do reflect many other conditions that are directly or indirectly economic. Quantity of food consumed, level of schooling, availability of medical services, type of manufactured products, and amount of electricity generated and used (see Table 9-1) are a few examples of other living conditions related to economic status. These quantitative differences may provide a basis for estimating contrasts in the ways economic activities are carried out. For example, not only is a larger proportion of persons in a poor nation engaged in agriculture than in a typical industrial country, but the methods of agricultural production differ too. Also, levels of economic development are related indirectly to demographic factors such as rates of infant mortality and natural increase (Chapter 3). A map showing the levels of national economic development, therefore, provides a good indicator of the spatial distribution of many significant aspects of human life.

Although variations in levels of economic devel-

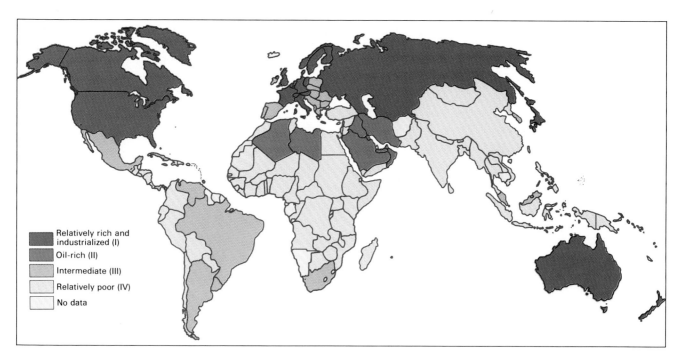

Relatively rich and industrialized (I)

Oil-rich (II)

Intermediate (III)

Relatively poor (IV)

No data

Figure 9-9. World Distribution of Countries Classified by Levels of Economic Development. Countries classified at the same level of economic development tend to be grouped spatially into regions.

BOX 9–1. WHAT'S IN A NAME?

What names can be applied appropriately to the two groups of countries that are highest and lowest on the scale of economic development? In the past, the two extremes were called *developed* and *underdeveloped*, but those terms implied absolute positions rather than comparisons along some continuum of development. The expressions *haves* and *have-nots* suffer from the same weakness. The word *developing* has been used as a replacement for *underdeveloped*, but this terminology only treats one end of the spectrum. The designations used here—*less developed* and *more developed*—represent one of the more common pairs.

Other names have arisen from political relations. Since World War II, the antagonism between the United States with its close allies and the Soviet Union with its affiliated countries has divided most of the world into two blocs (i.e., two "worlds"). The remaining countries, having less political and military power, were called *Third World* countries. In more recent times, the economic differences among nations within the Third World group has led to the addition of the term *Fourth World*. Mixing political alignments with economic conditions, however, causes difficulties in classifying countries that may have the characteristics of two categories (that is, be closely allied with one of the major power blocs but yet be economically poor).

Alternative terms have differentiated between *industrial* and *nonindustrial* countries, but these titles are misleading when countries are industrially important yet economically poor (e.g. China and India) or are rich but not industrial (e.g., Oman and Brunei). Likewise, referring to *North* and *South* countries is confusing because Australia and New Zealand are included in the "north" class, whereas Mongolia and North Korea are considered a part of the "south" group. Similar locational misinterpretations result when *core* and *periphery* are applied because Australia and Japan are far from "the core," whereas Morocco and Albania are close to it. Names that describe the type of economic system as well as wealth (i.e., *technically advanced market economies*, *less developed market economies*, and *centrally controlled economies*) are useful, but these are somewhat awkward when mentioned repeatedly in a discussion.

Reference to a specific set of countries (e.g., those in "the Group 77" of the United Nations or the 24 countries in the Organization for Economic Cooperation and Development) is meaningful, but there is no worldwide system that forms inclusive or mutually exclusive groups.

opment actually constitute a continuum (Figure 9-8), grouping countries into a few classes (such as the four shown here) makes it easy to generalize and map economic differences. Frequently these variations are simplified even more by referring to only two classes, such as the more developed and less developed countries. Even though the names given to these two groups may vary (e.g., rich versus poor, industrial versus agricultural, core versus periphery, and more developed versus less developed), each pair of terms generally means about the same (Box 9-1). The particular terms used to distinguish the two groups are not too critical, but it is very important to realize that the economies of many countries are in a broad zone between the extremes which are implied by such names as "rich" and "poor."

The remainder of this chapter focuses on those parts of the world that are classified as less developed. Since these are the places where most people earn their livelihood by working the land, the emphasis is on societies where agriculture is, and has been, the primary economic activity. Both historic and contemporary examples are described. This provides a background for understanding the current agrarian economies and also those countries that were once rural but later became industrialized.

THE BOSERUP THESIS

Several scholars have argued that the process of agricultural intensification, ranging from occasionally cultivated plots to continuously farmed fields, was brought about by increasing population pressure. One of the best known expositions of this argument was by Esther Boserup in *The Conditions of Agricultural Growth* (1965). Boserup, an economist, suggested that agricultural types changed through time as population increased. Agriculture progressed from extensive types which utilized large amounts of land compared to labor and capital inputs, to intensive farming systems that used much labor and capital per unit of land. Two subtypes of shifting agriculture and three subtypes of traditional agriculture in her scheme are summarized here (Figure 9-10).

Shifting Cultivation

Shifting cultivation is a form of subsistence living that has persisted from the beginnings of agriculture

---

Boserup thesis. The proposal that intensified use of agricultural land is a result of increasing population density.

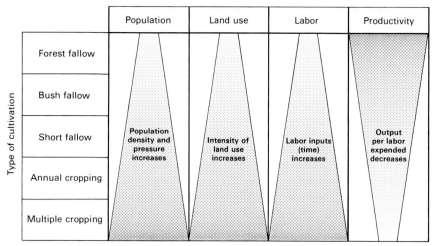

Figure 9-10. Relationships between Cultivation Type and Population, Land Use, Labor, and Productivity, According to Boserup. The five types of cultivation are arranged in terms of increasing inputs and decreasing productivity per labor input.

(Chapter 2) to the present. It is now practiced mainly in tropical rainforests where, to differing degrees of intensity, land is cleared, planted to crops for a few seasons, and then abandoned for several years.

Forest-Fallow Cultivation. The forest-fallow system is a kind of shifting cultivation in which fields are cultivated for a much shorter time than they are left idle or in fallow. Plots are roughly cleared by removing some forest. Crops are grown for 1 or 2 years; then the land is abandoned, and the trees are allowed to reestablish themselves. After a fallow period of 20 to 25 years, which allows for the restoration of soil fertility, the sequence is repeated.

Bush-Fallow Cultivation. This subtype is also a form of shifting cultivation, only the fallow is much shorter, occupying about 6 to 10 years. The forest does not regenerate fully in the fallow time, and the ground becomes covered with small trees and bush. Cultivation is normally for 2 to 5 years, depending on local conditions.

Traditional Agriculture

Traditional agriculture (sometimes called *peasant* farming) refers to producing food, primarily for subsistence, by plowing the soil and planting crops in permanently occupied plots.

Short-Fallow Cultivation. In this least intensive form of traditional agriculture, the fallow lasts for only 1 or 2 years; then the ground may be cultivated again for several years. During the fallow period, the ground is taken over by native grasses, but there is not sufficient time for the reestablishment of shrubs. The **three-field system of agriculture,** which was widely practiced in Western Europe in medieval times, was a form of short-fallow cultivation.

Annual Cropping. The annual cropping system allows a crop to be grown and harvested in a field each year, and the ground lies fallow only between harvest and planting. In the nineteenth century and the early part of the twentieth century, agriculturalists in Europe and North America were able to maintain fertility under this system by practicing crop rotation. For example, a farmer might plant grains for 2 years, followed by alfalfa or clover. In contemporary farming systems, fertility may be maintained by utilizing inputs of chemical fertilizers as well as by rotations.

Multicropping. In tropical and subtropical regions there is no temperature-defined growing season as there is in temperate lands. In many tropical areas, cultivation can be continuous if the soil is kept fertile and adequately watered. Such intensive land use is not practical everywhere, and not all culture groups attempt multicropping. In the heavily populated areas of East Asia, parts of Southeast Asia, and the Indian subcontinent, however, two or more crops are harvested each year. In some areas outside the tropics and subtropics where winters are also mild, two crops are harvested each year. For example, in some temperate areas, a cereal crop may be planted in the fall and harvested in the spring, and then the ground is used to produce a summer vegetable crop.

Boserup argued that increasing population has been responsible for the progressive change from forest-fallow cultivation through multicropping. She stated that if population increases, for example, in an area of forest-fallow cultivation, food production could be stepped up by shortening the fallows and keeping the land in cultivation for longer periods. In this way, forest-fallow evolves into bush-fallow.

There is evidence that bush-fallow was practiced in pre-Roman Europe prior to the development of more intensive agriculture. More recently there have been movements from extensive to intensive land use in many parts of the less developed world. For example, in West Africa, where shifting cultivation was widely employed, agriculturalists now have a tendency to cultivate on a continuous basis. This is particularly the case where cash crops grown for export (e.g., cocoa, palm oil, and rubber) have increased the land values.

A number of points can be made concerning the Boserup thesis. First, the shift from long to short fallows can be ecologically disastrous, resulting in the destruction of vegetation and soils, and hence may hamper efforts to increase food production. Second, Boserup recognized that as people use the land more intensely by increasing their labor inputs, the output per hour of work will probably decline. More labor on the same amount of land will yield a higher total production, but the returns per unit of work will not increase proportionally. For example, traditional Chinese agriculture was very successful in the quantity of foodstuffs it produced by using large amounts of human labor, but gains in production from more labor reached a point of diminishing returns long ago. Third, the relationship between land and labor does not take into account changing technology, such as the introduction of new high-yielding seeds.

Although Boserup's thesis refers particularly to the relationship between population and agriculture in a historical context, she also believed that her analysis could throw light on some modern agricultural development problems. A rapid increase in population growth rates will not necessarily lead to the intensification of agriculture in the less developed world. The reason for this is that more intensive agriculture involves harder toil, and growing rural populations may seek to avoid this by migrating to cities and attempting to find employment in urban labor markets. As a result, many less developed countries have experienced migration from the countryside, urban overcrowding, and high food prices (Boserup, 1965, pp. 118–119). In short, governments that encourage rural population growth in the hope of promoting agricultural intensification may find the policy unsuccessful.

The Boserup thesis, even when restricted in its application to primarily subsistence farming, is only one of several possible explanations for diversity in agricultural systems. You should examine the thesis carefully and compare it with alternative political, social, and economic explanations that are introduced in this text or with those that are familiar to you from other studies. Nevertheless, as an ecological thesis, it

is pertinent to the themes of this text, so the five subtypes are examined in more detail below.

Shifting Cultivation

To observers from industrial societies, shifting agriculture often appears chaotic in a number of ways. Animals run loose; a variety of plants are cultivated as crops; and the apparently haphazard mixture of many crops in a small area creates what appears to be a disorderly landscape. On closer examination, however, it becomes evident that shifting agriculture is an effective cultural adaptation to tropical environments, as long as population densities are low (Netting 1977).

The undisturbed tropical rainforest is one of the most diverse ecosystems in nature. The ecological cycle is rapid and continuous, with vegetation flourishing during a year-round growing season. When plants die, they decompose rapidly and quickly contribute to the organic base of new plants. Because of the continuous heat, organic layers in the soil are often shallow. If the forest is completely cleared, as happens under intensive types of agriculture, the soil is deprived of its constant supply of dying vegetation. When the ground is exposed to heavy rain and direct sunlight, soil nutrients are leached out and the soil becomes infertile.

Given these ecological constraints, shifting cultivation is an effective method of utilizing the biomass of tropic rainforests. Shifting cultivation transforms the natural forest into harvestable vegetation (Geertz 1963, p. 25). A patch of forest is selected, often after careful consideration of soil characteristics. For example, the Hanunoo of Mindoro in the Philippines know 10 basic and 30 derivative soil types. After site selection, the undergrowth is cleared, trees are cut, and vegetation is burned, adding valuable ash to the soil (Figures 9-11 and 9-12). The diversity of the tropical rainforest is then reproduced in the agricultural system. The Hanunoo practice **polyculture** by planting as many as 40 crops in small clearings. The plants are chosen from a repertoire of more than 400 cultivated crops. The crops are interplanted, producing a dense vegetation cover and a mass of roots.

In the plots of the Tsembaga of the New Guinea Highlands in Papua New Guinea, the Kwaio of the Solomon Islands, and numerous other societies in tropical Asia and Oceania, taro and sweet potatoes mature just under the surface of the soil, cassava roots are more deeply set, and yams grow further down

---

Three-field system of agriculture. An agricultural practice in which arable land of a community is divided into three open fields with two fields being cultivated and one field, in rotation, left fallow.

Polyculture. The practice of growing several crops simultaneously within a small area (see Monoculture).

Figure 9-11. Land Cleared by Slashing and Burning. Trees are cleared by using limited tools and fire, a system that preserves much of the organic matter. Photo courtesy of Charles A. Francis.

(Figure 9-13). These crops are not, therefore, competing for the same area or the same moisture. The leaves of yams and sweet potatoes form a protective cover just above the soil; then successive canopies of hibiscus, sugar cane, and banana plants shield the soil from the baking sun and the erosive effects of heavy rains (Rappaport 1971). In addition to the shielding by plants, soil erosion is limited because, within the system of shifting cultivation, plows are not used.

The various crops also draw upon different soil nutrients and therefore minimize the depletion of any one nutrient. For example, legumes, such as peanuts, which replenish nitrogen, may be grown to offset the effects of nutrient exhaustion by maize and cassava. In addition, the variety of crops provides the potential for balanced diets. Food generally does not store well in the hot and humid environments of the tropics, but the gardens yield throughout most of the year because the crops ripen at different times. Food storage is frequently achieved by leaving root crops in the ground until needed.

After a few years of cultivation, fertility declines,

Figure 9-12. New Clearing in a Tropical Forest. Multiple crops planted within a small area tend to duplicate the multiplicity of plants in the natural environment. Photo courtesy of Charles A. Francis.

Figure 9-13. Fenced Plot for Multiple Crops. Kwaio cultivators of the Solomon Islands erect fences to keep pigs and other animals from the fields. Photo courtesy of Wallace E. Akin.

weed infestation becomes a major problem, and yields decrease. At this point, the cultivators allow the plot to revert to forest, move to another area of their territory, and start a new clearing (Figure 9-14). After a long period (e.g., 20 to 30 years) of fallow, the original vegetation and fertility are restored, and the plot may be cultivated again.

Shifting cultivation is not an onerous form of subsistence farming. It is estimated that only 500 to 1000 work hours are expended in a year for clearing, weeding, planting, and harvesting. In a study of the Tsembaga, anthropologist Roy Rappaport (1971) concluded that there is an energy return of 1 : 16. Thus, for each calorie expended in production, 16 calories are generated in food. This is far higher than in modern agricultural systems where the output of energy as food may be less than the input of energy in the form of fuel, fertilizers, pesticides, and human effort (see Chapter 10).

As explained by Boserup, shifting cultivation can be divided into two broad types, depending on the length of the fallow period.

Figure 9-14. Regrowth in an Abandoned Agricultural Plot. In most areas where shifting cultivation is practiced, various types of natural vegetation are reestablished quickly after previously cropped plots are abandoned. Photo courtesy of Wallace E. Akin.

Forest-fallow cultivation. Forest-fallow cultivation is illustrated by the Kuikuru people of central Brazil. This group has a loosely defined territory of approximately 5500 hectares (13,500 acres) located near the Kuluene River, a tributary of the Xingu. They live in clustered settlements with each village containing about 150 persons.

In his study of the Kuikuru, Robert Carneiro (1961) noted that farmers seldom have to walk more than 6 kilometers (4 mi) from the village to cultivate their plots. At any one time, only 40 hectares (95 acres) are in cultivation, which amounts to less than 0.1 percent of the group's territory. Traditionally, the ground was cleared of vegetation with stone axes and the teeth of piranha fish; but in the twentieth century, the use of steel axes and machetes is common. The forest is cut in the dry season and burned just before the onset of the rains.

In the Kuikuru community, men do most of the agricultural work, spending about 2 hours a day in the cultivated plots and another 1 or 2 hours fishing. This division of labor, however, is rare for shifting cultivators in general. In other areas where shifting cultivation is practiced, women do most of the planting, tending, and harvesting. In fact, it is believed that during the thousands of years when this was the dominant way of growing food, women were the primary producers.

Carneiro found that the food supply is always abundant, with an extra margin of production to take care of spoilage and accidental losses. Manioc is the main crop and provides 85 percent of the Kuikuru diet. The remainder is made up largely of corn and fish. Plots are small, but they produce 15 to 17 tons of manioc per hectare each year.

After plots are abandoned, the land is left undisturbed for 25 years. Although cultivated plots are frequently moved, the village has remained in approximately the same location for generations. The population size of the village is constrained, not by agricultural production (with its large surpluses), but by group dynamics. When communities reach a size of approximately 300 people, the potential for discord increases. Fission is likely to take place, and the dissidents leave to form another settlement in the forest.

Carneiro argues that in the Kuikuru system, and in many other areas of shifting cultivation, the exhaustion of the soil is not the major reason for abandoning cultivated plots. He cites studies done in southern Nigeria, Fiji, and the Yucatan Peninsula of Mexico that show little evidence of decrease in soil nutrients over several years of cultivation. Carneiro believes that it is competition from invading weeds that causes yields to decline and necessitates greater labor inputs. He argues that it is easier to move to, and clear, a new plot in the forest than battle the weeds.

Carneiro also holds the view that forest-fallow cultivation is capable of evolving into more intensive types of agriculture. In fact, he anticipated Boserup in suggesting that more intensive agricultural systems arise in response to growing population pressure. He

Figure 9-15. Kwaio Dwellings, Solomon Islands. In some societies that practice shifting cultivation, a cluster of permanent residences may be maintained. Photo courtesy of Wallace E. Akin.

goes further than this and postulates a general theory whereby population pressure on restricted land resources leads not only to more intensive agriculture but, eventually, to a more differentiated society in which some classes gain control of surpluses of labor and production.

Shifting cultivators display a variety of settlement forms that particularly reflect the length of time they have left land fallow. In general, the longer the periods of fallow, the less permanent settlement sites are likely to be. For example, the Campa of the forested eastern slop of the Peruvian Andes allow land to lie fallow for over 10 years. This is possible because population numbers are low, with an estimated density of one person per square kilometer of territory (Denevan 1971).

The Campa live in huts dispersed through the forest. Families may live alone, but groupings of up to six families can be found. Rarely does a settlement contain more than 35 people. The men hunt, and the women tend crops on small clearings where yucca, maize, beans, and a variety of other crops are grown. The plots are cultivated for 1 to 3 years, after which the family or group will move on, build new huts, and clear new plots in the forest. Often the movement is related more to the exhaustion of game than to the depletion of soil fertility (Denevan 1971).

In some regions, shifting cultivators establish temporary secondary residences near the fields while retaining a relatively permanent central village (Figure 9-15). In the case of the Iban, dry rice farmers in the hills of Sarawak (Eastern Malaysia), there are three tiers to their hierarchy of settlement. The largest settlement is the "long house," which is a single fixed building constructed by the entire population and holding as many as 300 people. Nearer the rice fields, satellite settlements called dampa are occupied for periods of 5 to 6 years by small groups of families. These are moved when old areas are abandoned to the forest and new areas are cleared. Finally, at the most dispersed level of the heirarchy, small seasonal huts are built adjacent to each agricultural lot to protect the ripening rice from monkeys, pigs, and other pests. This arrangement of settlements allows the Iban to retain a central village while maintaining the necessary flexibility to settle temporarily near the fields (Carlstein 1982).

Bush-fallow cultivation. If the length of the fallow period is shortened, then forest vegetation does not have time to regenerate fully. In this event, the effect of shifting cultivation may be to alter vegetation patterns and transform woodland into bush or scrubland over wide areas.

Gary Lobb (1982) examined shifting cultivation as practiced by the community of Todos Santos on the slopes of the Sierra de los Cuchumatames in northwestern Guatemala. The population of Todos Santos has grown rapidly in recent decades with the result that great pressure has been placed on resources. Originally the area was covered by tropical forests, locally called montana. Clearings, or roza plots, that were made in the forest were normally cultivated for 3 years (Figure 9-16). Formerly when the land was left uncultivated for several decades, the forest would restore itself to the original form. But in recent times, as the fallows have shortened, the area of the montana has been greatly reduced. Much of the forest has degenerated to bushlands (hautel) or even to tropical grasslands (pajonales) as the result of increasingly frequent cultivation.

At Todos Santos the cycle of cultivation begins in the dry season, from November to February, when the vegetation is cleared, then burned to produce the enriching ash. In the second and third years of cultivation, corn stalks and weeds are collected and burned to provide a second fertilization. Corn (maize) is the major crop, and the simple digging stick is the main tool. When the rains come in late January or early February, the corn germinates and the growing cycle commences. In the first year of cultivation, it is necessary to hoe out the weeds only once, but by the third year as many as four hoeings are needed to keep the plots clean. The harvest is gathered in November when the dry season sets in again.

On roza plots created from montana, yields are twice as great as on plots cultivated in bush or grassland areas. On all plots, yields decline over the years as the advantages gained from burning vegetation and releasing nutrients are lost, and as weed infestation becomes an increasingly intractable problem.

The farmers of Todas Santos, in addition to roza plots, have lands in permanent cultivation close to the habitations of the community. These gardens contain yams, beans, chili peppers, squashes, coffee bushes, and a variety of tree crops, including avocados, bananas, papaya, and mangoes. Gardens around the houses are intensively cultivated and are kept fertile by the application of organic wastes from the household.

This greater intensity of land use by the farmers of Todas Santos is associated with a higher population density. In turn, the number of farm villages and hamlets, the form of settlement for this community, is larger than in most areas where forest-fallow is practiced.

It is probable that many former forests of the world were cleared in a manner similar to that of Todos Santos. For example, it is believed that much of the woodlands in northwest Europe were cleared between the ninth and thirteenth centuries by this system (Darby 1956).

Figure 9-16. *Roza* Plots in Guatemala. The clearing of hillsides for cultivation can expose the soil to erosion and disrupt the natural vegetational cycle. Photo courtesy of C. Gary Lobb.

Traditional Agriculture

Traditional societies are agrarian. The greatest part of the population works the land and depends directly on it for a living. Dependence on the products of the land for family subsistence requires the planting of a wide variety of crops so that several forms of food are available. In a subsistence economy, the growing of many crops (i.e., polyculture) provides several benefits to the agricultural population and helps to preserve the natural environment. Producing food from a variety of plants and animals provides a diverse diet

of energy, vitamins, and proteins. Growing several different plants within a small area tends to maintain soil nutrients better than agricultural systems devoted to a single crop for repeated seasons. Also, pests and diseases are controlled naturally rather than through the application of chemical pesticides. Although peasant agricultural systems do not approximate the conditions of nature as closely as forest-fallow cultivation, generally they do not alter the environment as much as the monocultural systems of modern commercial agriculture.

In traditional agricultural societies, work is done

Figure 9-17. Women Harvesting Tea. Women, as well as men and children, work many hours per day on farming tasks in most agricultural societies. Photo courtesy of Embassy of Mauritius.

by all members of the family, young and old, men and women. Specific tasks, such as planting grains, may be regarded as work appropriate for males in one culture but for females in another (Figure 9-17). Plowing is often performed by males, while many of the other tasks, especially in areas of intensive cultivation, are done by women (Figure 9-18). In Africa as a whole, women produce most of the food crops and do between 70 and 80 percent of the total agricultural work (Boserup 1970). All of the food processing and preparation, 90 percent of the supplying of water, and 80 percent of the acquisition of fuel are done by women (Dixon-Mueller 1985). Certainly in most African societies, the economic and nutritional roles of women are very important.

Wealth, political power, and status are largely determined by land ownership and the degree of access to the land. Note that this contrasts with the situation among hunting and gathering societies and shifting agriculturalists where there is more egalitarian access to land and resources, although private ownership may occur (Herskovitz 1965, pp. 350–70). In traditional societies, landowners form an elite group that characteristically consists of less than 10 percent of the population but controls about 80 percent of the land. Often the majority of the population owns little or no land. Peasants rent land, typically at high rates, or they work as laborers for those landowners who have large holdings. Thus, even though most families depend on agriculture for their livelihood,

Figure 9-18. Farm Workers Transplanting Rice. Within this culture group (located in the Kathmandu Valley of Nepal), men turn the soil in preparation for rice plants, which are then transplanted by women. Photo courtesy of Sally Stoddard.

Figure 9-19. Nucleated Farm Village. This small village of farmers in the Kathmandu Valley of Nepal is typical of the settlement pattern in many societies practicing traditional agriculture. Photo courtesy of Sally Stoddard.

they frequently do not own the resources required to produce more than a minimum subsistence.

Farmers in many agrarian societies live in permanent nucleated villages (Figure 9-19). For persons who live in the United States, where most farmers live on the land they cultivate and are separated from the houses of their neighbors, it is not easy to understand why farmers in traditional societies tend to congregate in villages. It might be thought that, before the advent of modern transportation and equipment, farmers would prefer to live directly on the land they tilled. Dispersed farm settlements, however, are less common than nucleated villages in pre-industrial societies.

Several factors may help explain why farmers in many societies have preferred living in nucleated settlements. It is often suggested that rural populations in the past clustered together in villages for defense. In the hill villages of southern Italy, for example, fear was a factor that prompted the selection of inconvenient, but defensible, sites. However, unless there are fortifications or other evidence that a regular distribution of villages has been distorted in order to locate on defensive sites, the role of fear in producing nucleation can be downplayed (Fossier 1985, p. 40).

Frequently farmers in traditional societies use a variety of land types. For example, they cultivate valley bottom lands, graze livestock on hillsides, and use the woods as a source of fuel. It is convenient to live at a location that gives access to several environments. Examination of the locations of villages will often reveal strings of settlements sited on the line of contact between two environmental zones.

Another reason for nucleated settlements in an agrarian society is the advantage of communal cooperation. For example, well-digging is more easily undertaken on a communal basis. Irrigation projects, especially in dry regions, also illustrate the need for cooperative efforts. Furthermore, once a water supply has been improved, it tends to be a force for agglomeration.

Social factors are important forces of nucleation, especially where land resources are controlled communally. If a peasant gains access to arable land, common grazing areas, and woodlands by being a member of a community, then there are advantages to living close to the point where decisions are made.

The landholding system is also important. In traditional villages, farmers often have scattered plots partly because inheritance laws stipulate the division of land among all the heirs. Living in a centrally located settlement reduces journey time to the several scattered lands.

Furthermore, in pre-industrial Europe, landlords were often opposed to the peasantry dispersing because it was difficult to dispossess peasants who lived on the land they worked. In addition, it was not easy to change land use, such as moving from growing grain to raising livestock, if the land was occupied by peasants claiming they had cultivation rights.

One or more service activities, particularly religious ones, sometimes added an incentive for clustering. In medieval Europe, villagers were called to prayer morning and evening, and Sunday was given over entirely to religious observances. Proximity to the church, standing at the center of the community, was an important motivation for living in the village.

Often several reasons apply. Blok (1969) concluded that nucleated settlements in southern Italy developed in association with low standards of living, high rates of tenancy, and small and scattered landholdings. Where large landholdings existed, farmers tended to live on them rather than in a village.

Only a minority of people in traditional societies are literate, and in general, educational facilities exist only for the benefit of the elite. The educational system, rather than being a means of fostering new ideas, is biased toward perpetuating the existing value system and often has a strong religious component. Most persons in traditional societies have limited knowledge of scientific theory, although some principles may have been worked out in the development of, for example, mechanical devices for irrigation works.

Traditional societies, whether in medieval England or in parts of contemporary Burma, tend to be conservative and resistant to change. This is not necessarily a negative attribute, but represents the perpetuation of economic and social systems that have developed over centuries and often are satisfactory adaptations to the physical environment. There is a lack of social mobility in traditional societies. The possibilities of life are determined to a great degree by one's circumstances of birth, which include gender, birth order within the family, and the family's status within the community. Individual advancement opportunities are limited, although they may exist if a person is prepared to leave the group for seasonal employment, long-distance trading, or settlement in a new territory.

The nonfarming population consists of merchants and traders plus professionals, such as governing officials and religious leaders, who live in market towns and the few cities. Although the service sector of the economy is small, some merchant families accumulate substantial wealth. Secondary activities are mainly the production of home crafts (i.e., cottage industry). The markets served by the producer of crafts are usually local.

Short-fallow agriculture in Medieval England. Short-fallow agriculture, Boserup's third stage of agricultural intensification, existed during the Middle Ages (here defined as the eleventh to the sixteenth centuries) in Europe. This system of agriculture took the form of **open fields** (Darby 1936, pp. 189–213; Dodgshon and Butlin 1978, pp. 81–150).

An open-field village was organized around two or three arable fields in which members of the community enjoyed cultivation rights. Members cultivated individual strips of land, but some tasks, like plowing, were often done communally. In addition to the arable land, the open-field village possessed other resources such as grazing land, woods, and streams. Members were allowed to graze specified numbers of animals on the common pasture, cut timber from the woodland, make hay in the meadowland, cut reeds in the marshland (to use as thatch for roofs or bedding for animals), and graze pigs in the woods. The utilization of resources, however, was not a free-for-all. Access was carefully regulated by the community to prevent overutilization and to allocate land in accordance with ancient rights. Disputes were settled within the community, often by local courts.

The most valuable resource was the arable land. Not every member of the community had the same cultivation rights, and some were entitled to more land than others. Lots were drawn each year for the use of strips of land in the fields. A villager would get access to several strips in different fields. This method of allocation prevented the best pieces of land from being monopolized by one family (Figure 9-20).

The short-fallow system of farming did not employ crop rotations to maintain fertility, so the land had to be rested periodically. In the two-field system, one of the fields lay fallow each year. The three-field system involved cultivating two fields each year and allowing the third to lie fallow. Animals would be put into the fallow field to graze and deposit manure, which would help restore fertility. This field would be brought back into cultivation after a year of rest, at which time another field would be fallowed. A typical pattern of land use might be one field in winter wheat or rye, one field in spring-sown barley or oats, and one field in fallow used as pasture.

The arable land was used for the production of grain crops such as wheat, barley, oats, and rye. Rather than being drilled into rows, seed was broadcast by hand, which was inefficient. Yields were low, with the quantity harvested being only three to four times the amount of grain sown. The varieties of seeds were very low-yielding when compared to modern hybrids.

Livestock consisted of pigs, sheep, and cattle, plus oxen to pull the plows. Numbers were not large, except for sheep, which had the ability to forage year-round. Sheep were valued as a source of wool, hides, milk, cheese, and butter. Pigs scavenged a living around the village and in the woods. Their ability to survive the winter was suspect, and many were killed and the meat salted in the fall. Because the farming system did not produce root crops, and supplies of hay were generally small, there were difficulties in feeding cattle through the winter.

Families owned equipment and planted their own seed, but many agricultural activities were communal. Plowing was a cooperative venture because few villagers could afford, or needed, to exclusively own a team of animals.

Open fields. Large farm areas that are divided into unenclosed strips for the use of individual farmers.

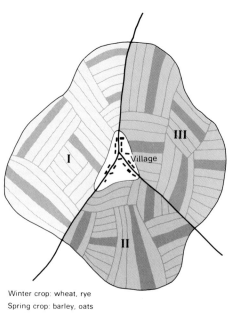

	I	II	III
October	Plough and sow with winter crop	Stubble of winter crop	Stubble of spring crop
March		Plough and sow with spring crop	
June			Plough twice Fallow
August	Reap	Reap	
October	Stubble of winter crop	Stubble of spring crop	Plough and sow with winter crop
March	Plough and sow with spring crop		
June		Plow twice Fallow	
August	Reap		Reap
October	Stubble of spring crop	Plough and sow with winter crop	Stubble of winter crop
March			Plough and sow with spring crop
June	Plough twice Fallow		
August		Reap	Reap
October	(repeat cycle)	(repeat cycle)	(repeat cycle)

Winter crop: wheat, rye
Spring crop: barley, oats

Figure 9-20. The Three-Field System of Medieval Europe. A three-field cycle included a set of fields sown to a winter crop in October (year I), another set sown to a spring crop in March of the second year (year II), and a third set with fields lying fallow after the August harvest of the second year until plowing or sowing time in October of the third year (year III).

The social system associated with medieval England was hierarchical, and social mobility was limited. Spatial mobility was often proscribed by the lords, who legally could, and did, prevent some of their peasants from moving to towns or to areas of new settlement. That does not mean, however, that the system was continually repressive. Villagers were not without rights, and communities did provide some security (Hallam 1981).

The underlying value system in village life was embodied in the role of the Roman Catholic Church (which at that time was the universal Christian church in Europe). Large villages were the center of a parish, which supported a church and a priest. The parish church was endowed with land and took one-tenth (a tithe) of the production from all other lands. Loyalty to the faith was carefully nurtured, and any questioning of the accepted religious tenets could lead to charges of heresy. The church, as an omnipresent institution, played a major role in maintaining conformity and adherence to the value system of society.

The landscape reflected the organization of agriculture and the social system. The village was located at the center of the parish lands, usually at the junction between the open fields. Most of the populace lived in this compact settlement in thatched cottages. Frequently the dwellings were constructed of mud and required periodic rebuilding. Other buildings included the parish church, a water mill to grind grain, and possibly the manor house of the local landlord. Persons who did not have access rights to the open fields lived in cottages on the margins of the woods or marsh, or wherever they were able to establish small plots for cultivation.

This system of agriculture and social organization was successful for a long time in medieval England. From 1086 (the time of the Domesday Survey) until the early fourteenth century, population numbers expanded, woodlands were cleared, marshes were drained, and the area of agricultural land was increased. This was the case in much of Europe. In parts of rural Western Europe, population densities in 1300 were as great as in the mid-nineteenth century (Grigg 1980, p. 65).

The long period of agricultural expansion came to an end in the first decades of the fourteenth century. In England there was growing population pressure on resources, expansion of cultivation into marginal lands, and increased inputs of human labor in an attempt to gain more output from the three-field system. The numbers of livestock decreased as the area of land planted in cereals was expanded in response to population pressure. Climatic conditions worsened, famines occurred, and in 1348 the plague swept across Europe. In many respects, Western Europe seemed to have been caught in a "Malthusian trap" where population growth outpaced food supplies. Viewed in those terms, the plague, which decimated population numbers, could be interpreted as a restoration of a "balance" between population and resources.

The emergence of annual cropping in Western Europe. Under the three-field system, farming in medieval Europe was characterized by low yields and an inability to keep the land in cultivation year after year. By the late sixteenth century, farming practices were much the same as they had been in the thirteenth century (Figure 9-21). At this time the most important way to increase yields was to expand the area under cultivation (Grigg 1980, pp. 90–94). What was needed to raise yields, to improve output of farmers, and to crop fields on an annual basis was a revolution in farming techniques. This came in the seventeenth and eighteenth centuries when Western European farmers, especially the Dutch, introduced improvements that enhanced the efficiency of agriculture.

Dutch agricultural innovations were partly motivated by expanding outlets for farm products. By 1622, almost 50 percent of the country's population lived in towns of 10,000 or more, and the nation was strongly committed to overseas trade. The existence of towns and well-developed trade links gave farmers marketing opportunities. Although part of the increased production came from the reclamation of interior lakes and coastal areas, much of the mid-seventeenth century increase in production came from a series of agricultural improvements. These innovations included the rotation of crops, widespread cultivation of clover to provide fodder and improve soil fertility, selective breeding of livestock, and the development of horticultural zones around cities.

One key to increased productivity was the evolu-

tion of a system of mixed farming. The adoption of crop rotations allowed fallow periods to be reduced, but if yields were to be improved, the ground need manuring. The major source of manure was livestock, but as we have noted, medieval farmers were unable to keep many livestock through the winter because of the lack of feed. The Dutch overcame this problem with the use of clover, root crops such as turnips, and the making of cattle feed cakes from the residues of vegetables like rape that had been pressed to provide oil for cooking and soap. With fodder available, animals could be supported throughout the year. Moreover, the practice of keeping the animals in stalls, at least part of the time, reduced the need for pasture and concentrated the manure, allowing its relatively easy application to arable lands. Animal products—hides, meat, wool, and dairy goods—became the basis of enhanced rural economic activity. In addition to animal manure, "night soil" (a euphemism for human excreta) was brought out by barges from the urban areas and spread on the fields.

The English improved agriculture later than the Dutch, and there is little doubt that ideas were transferred from the Netherlands to England. This is illus-

Figure 9-21. "Harvesting Scene" by Brueghel the Younger. This scene from seventeenth century Netherlands illustrates the large labor inputs required in traditional farming. Photo courtesy of Nelson-Atkins Museum of Art, Kansas City.

trated, for instance, by the fact that in the seventeenth century, the English referred to clover as "Dutch grass." Agricultural specialists went to Holland to gather ideas. Dutchmen saw the opportunity to migrate to England and establish intensive horticulture close to London. Such migrants brought new farming methods with them and established intensive horticulture around several southern and eastern English cities.

Radical changes in English farming came only after 1750 when population was increasing. Crop rotations were adopted. These varied regionally and locally, but some, like the Norfolk system, became well known and were publicized in the literature of the time. A four-course Norfolk rotation might have involved wheat the first year, turnips the second year, barley the third year, and clover the fourth year. Animals, particularly sheep, were grazed on the turnip crop, and the manure enriched the soil. The overall effect was to reduce the area of fallow land, increase livestock numbers, and raise crop yields. Whereas the medieval farmer harvested only four times the amount of what that he sowed, the "improved farmer" of the eighteenth century reaped a tenfold return.

Numerous new mechanical devices such as improved plows, harrows, reapers, and seed drills were introduced into the inventory of farm equipment. Jethro Tull developed a seed drill in 1701 that planted seeds in evenly spaced rows, leaving sufficient space for weeding. The eighteenth century also saw a general interest in animal breeding. Many of the important regional varieties of sheep, pigs, and cattle were developed during this era.

It was believed by some that agricultural productivity could be increased by enclosing open fields and be reallocating fragmented lands into consolidated farms with fenced fields. Although the enclosure of open fields in England had been taking place since the fifteenth century, many open-field villages still remained in the eighteenth century. Farmers continued to go out from their villages each day to cultivate scattered plots. To achieve enclosure, with its wholesale change in the spatial economy of villages, required a separate act of the British Parliament for each open-field community. Between 1750 and 1819, the period of maximum activity, 3828 enclosure acts were passed (Turner 1980, p. 32). Not surprisingly, even after a community had gained the legal right to enclose it, it often took more than 50 years for new farmhouses to be built, fields to be enclosed by fences, and the benefits of the new system to be reflected in increased agricultural output.

Multicropping in China prior to 1950. Boserup's final stage of agricultural intensity is multicropping, where more than one crop is grown successively on the same land each year using labor-intensive techniques of farming. This type of agriculture is characteristic of densely populated areas throughout much of Asia. China will serve as an example.

When the Venetian explorer Marco Polo (1254–1324) visited China in the second half of the thirteenth century, he was astounded at the level of development he saw. On the Chang Jiang (Yangtze River) alone, he saw more shipping and trade than existed in the whole of Europe. He was impressed with the range of manufacturing, the use of paper money, the canal system, and the general level of prosperity. In the thirteenth century, China was well ahead of the Western world economically, as well as in scientific and technological knowledge (Chapter 2).

Agriculture was based on a tenure system, which was, in some ways, similar to that practiced in medieval Europe, but farming methods were more advanced than those in Europe. The Chinese were employing—at least in the more developed agricultural regions—deep tillage, improved equipment, the use of manures, and plant selection to find varieties that were high-yielding, drought-resistant, or fast-maturing. For example, farmers planted the quick-ripening, drought-hardy Champa rice, which had been introduced from Vietnam in the eleventh century. Early ripening rice meant that multicropping of rice, or rice followed by wheat, was possible. In South China, double- or even triple-cropping was widespread. Above all, a superior understanding of hydraulics allowed irrigation works to be constructed, which greatly increased crop yields (Tuan 1970).

In fourteenth-century China, a long phase of expanding production came to an end, just as it did in Western Europe. The causes of the decline are not clear. Waterborne diseases, associated with the enlarged irrigation works, may have been a factor, and climatic deterioration may have played a part. The widespread deforestation of the North China Plain, resulting in floods and soil erosion was certainly a cause of agricultural decline. Population pressure may have been the root cause of the economic decline that began in the fourteenth century and lasted until 1500. During this time, per capita incomes remained low, agricultural surpluses decreased as the population grew, and per capita demands for goods shrank. As a result, according to this hypothesis, profitable agricultural innovations became more and more difficult. The population became increasingly concerned with subsistence, and there was a decreasing amount of capital available to experiment with technical innovations. Stagnation was the result. In short, too much necessity may stifle invention, or at least the acceptance of inventions (Elvin 1973, pp. 204–34).

China is particularly interesting because of the parallels with Western Europe and because the China case illustrates that there are no certainties in the development process. China experienced scientific and agricultural revolutions well before Western Europe, but subsequently went into a long period of stagnation. Instead of continuing to utilize a head start in technological knowledge, China did not progress to a more productive type of economy such as occurred in Europe during later centuries (see Chapter 2).

Information about traditional agricultural practices in China in the 1900s (but prior to the political revolution of 1949) is derived from foreign scholars who lived in the country during this period. One observer, John Lossing Buck, conducted many surveys of Chinese agriculture and rural life styles (1930). Buck, as well as others who studied agriculture in China, was struck by two factors: the intense use of available resources and the large labor inputs.

The first factor—the intensive manner in which resources were utilized—was indicated in several ways. All suitable land was cultivated. In the agriculturally rich regions, only small areas of land were uncultivated, and these often held the graves of ancestors. There was little room for natural fauna and flora. Soils were improved by fertilizers obtained from many "wastes" such as ashes, vegetable matter, canal mud, and domestic animal and human excreta. Crop rotations were practiced, and by careful organization of the agricultural year, it was frequently possible to get several crops from the same plot of ground. It was not uncommon to have two or more distinct crops growing on the same ground at different stages of maturity. After the harvest, the fields were carefully gleaned for all material that could be used as feed, bedding, fuel, and compost (Buck 1930).

Water resources were carefully controlled. In the great river valleys, canals fed water to the fields. Elsewhere, ponds were used to store surface water; well water was drawn for agricultural purposes; and steep slopes were intricately terraced to form benches of level land that retained water (Figure 9-22).

In regard to the second factor, Buck noted the massive quantities of hand labor that were applied to agricultural production. Although peasant farmers used many tools and mechanical devices, much of the motive power was provided by the muscles of the family. Livestock, like water buffalo and oxen, were employed for plowing in some areas, but most labor was done by humans. In fact, livestock were relatively few. Crops were raised for direct human consumption,

Figure 9-22. Ridged Rows and Terraced Fields, North China. The high intensity of land use is evidenced by the ridged rows within fields and the construction of level terraces on slopes. Photo courtesy of Donald Wilhite.

since the peasantry could not afford the luxury of feeding an animal that was likely to consume 10 kilograms of feed for every kilogram of meat produced. Only small, generally rough, areas of land could be used for grazing.

The ratio of arable land to people was low, averaging less than one-third of a hectare per person. The average size of farms examined by Buck was 2.52 hectares (about 6 acres), but his statistics were based on holdings that were larger than the norm. Yields per area were comparatively high. Buck found in the 1920s that wheat yields were about the same as in the United States, and rice yields were twice as high. As F. H. King, another scholar of traditional Chinese farming, observed in 1927, the golden rule of the cultivators was that "whenever an extra hour or day of labor can promise even a little larger return, it must be given, and nothing be permitted to cancel the obligation or defer its execution" (p. 93). Buck's studies reveal just how much effort was given to produce the yields. On an average, farmers put in 117 ten-hour days for every hectare of rice that was grown and harvested. This heavy workload was shared among all family members. As might be expected, the work input figure for wheat was lower, but the crop still required 60 ten-hour days per hectare. In 1921, wheat farmers in the United States put in an average of 2½ ten-hour days per hectare of wheat and received about the same yield per hectare as their Chinese counterparts. Of course, the American farmer used inputs like mechanization and artificial fertilizers, which the Chinese peasant could not afford.

It would be wrong, however, to give the impression that the Chinese agricultural year was filled with unremitting hard labor. Buck found that there were slack times in the year, particularly during the winter months, when there was considerable rural unemployment. In the traditional scheme of things, mechanization would not have helped greatly. Irrigation water could have been lifted more rapidly by gasoline engines than by human pedaling, but basically the population was there to serve the agricultural system, and agriculture provided the predominant means of subsistence. Reducing labor requirements would have created unemployment because alternate forms of employment, in the secondary and tertiary sectors, were uncommon then.

In spite of the commitment that families gave to the agricultural environment and the ingenuity with which soil fertility was maintained, the system was fragile and given to catastrophes. Population numbers were always around the maximum level that could be supported by the traditional agricultural technology and existing economy, so shortfalls in production were liable to result in starvation and malnutrition. Under the economic and political conditions in China during the early twentieth century, there was a perpetual problem of land hunger and an inability to produce sufficient surpluses to provide a cushion against poor harvests, droughts, or floods.

Humans could manage the environment of soils, fields, and canals at the local level, but not the regional patterns of climatic fluctuation that produced too much, or too little, rain. For instance, on the North

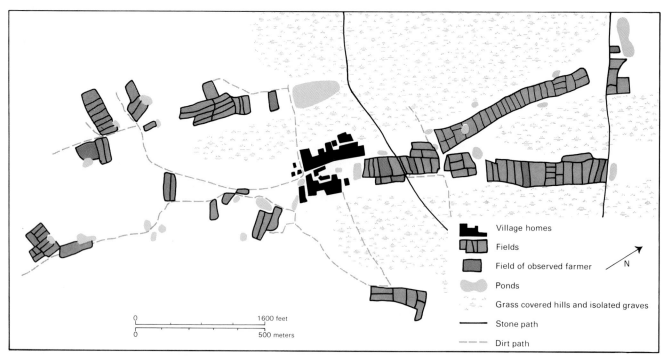

Figure 9-23. Chinese Farm Village, 1928. The farmers lived in the village and worked scattered plots along the valley bottoms. After Buck 1930.

China Plain, rainfall is irregular, and fluctuations are sufficient to produce marked differences in crop yields. On the great river plains, particularly in the delta regions of the Huang He (Hwang Ho) and Chang Jiang, major floods have occurred periodically for thousands of years. Although the use of canals and flood-control works reduced some problems, major inundations still caused havoc in large areas. For example, when the distributaries in the Huang He delta altered their courses in 1852, hundreds of villages were disrupted. And when the river broke its banks in 1877, it killed about one million people.

The landscape of traditional Chinese agriculture was human-made and human-maintained. Terraces covering mountain slopes, complex irrigation schemes, and extensively modified soils display the labor of many generations. It is impossible to describe the innumerable ways that men, women, and children in Chinese farming villages interacted with various environments to create the existing patterns. Nevertheless, an example may help clarify the activities of traditional agriculture. Although the following illustration refers to a rural village in China during the 1920s, some aspects typify millions of villages throughout the world where traditional agriculture is the dominant way of life.

Buck made a detailed study of the village of Tung Chiao in Jiangxi (Kiangsu) Province. One farmer (see Figure 9-23), for example, had ten plots of land scattered around the village territory. Several of the plots lay close to the village, but the farmer also had small parcels of land to the north and southwest of the settlement. Obviously, the farmer and his family spent considerable amounts of time moving from plot to plot and carrying equipment to the scattered landholdings. There were, however, some advantages to this dispersed pattern because not all fields were likely to be equally affected by localized events such as flooding or locust infestations.

The village of Tung Chiao was set in a valley with ridges rising to nearly 120 meters. The ridges were used for graves and grassland, but the valley floor was devoted almost entirely to rice. A significant part of the available ground was covered by ponds, which retained runoff from the ridges for use in irrigation. The rice fields were surrounded by embankments to retain the water. Where gravity feed could not supply the water, endless chains of wooden buckets, propelled by men or cattle, were used to lift water into the fields.

The landscape was arranged for pedestrians. Tracks and hard-surfaced walkways provided access. The narrow tracks and small fields would have made the introduction of machinery difficult, even if the necessary finances had been available. Buck thought it would have been impossible to get threshing machines into the village because of the narrow tracks.

Close to the houses of the village were vegetable plots, the most intensively cultivated lands. In the fields lying further out, the major winter sown crops were wheat and barley. In the spring, relatively large areas were sown with rice and smaller areas with cotton. In summer, soybeans, green beans, sesame, red beans, sweet potatoes, and more rice were planted. In fields suitable for rice, a two-year sequence of crop rotation was common. In the fall of the first year, barley and field peas were planted, and were harvested in the spring; then in the summer, the main rice crop was grown and the fields cleared for the planting of barley and broad beans in the fall. This was followed by rice again the following summer. Beans and peas helped to restore nitrogen to the soil,

Figure 9-24. Paddy Fields in China. Rice, which can yield high amounts of food per area of land, has been an important crop in China for thousands of years. Photo courtesy of Dean S. Rugg.

but the paddy fields also had to be fertilized with organic wastes. On unirrigated lands (i.e., not suitable for rice), a typical crop rotation began with broad beans in the fall, followed by sesame during the first summer, then broad beans and barley in the second fall, followed by sweet potatoes the second summer.

Rice was the major crop in terms of land occupied, and it formed the dietary staple. The rice seeds were thickly sown in heavily fertilized nursery beds. At night the nursery was flooded to hold heat in the ground, and in the morning the water was drained away to allow the soil to be aerated. In three to four weeks, the rice seedlings were about 20 cm (8 in.) in height and ready for transplanting, which was done by hand into a plowed and flooded field (Figure 9-24). Thereafter, the plants were carefully hoed, fertilized, and watered. As the crops ripened, the water was gradually drawn off the paddy (rice) field. Harvesting was done by hand; then the grain was separated from the stalks and stored (Buck 1930).

In summary, over a period of many centuries, the Chinese intensified their use of arable land through increased amounts of human labor. Any change aimed at maintaining production with less labor was bound to involve radical alterations. Some major economic changes did begin when the Communist Party formed the government of the People's Republic of China under the leadership of Mao Zedung in 1949. Since 1950, changes in land ownership, in units of farming, and in governmental policies have altered the characteristics of the Chinese economy in several ways (as described later in this chapter).

Changing Types of Traditional Agriculture

The sequence of the preceding illustrations matches the cultivation types with progressively more intense land utilization. The basic relationship presented by Boserup can be observed also where conditions lead to less intensive agricultural practices. One such illustration was the reversion to bush-fallow cultivation by early European settlers in Colonial America.

The study of agriculture in Colonial America is interesting from two perspectives. First, American agriculture was a blend of European and Indian plants and techniques. The development of Colonial agriculture illustrates the process of culture contact that produced distinctive American institutions. Second, the study of Colonial agriculture reveals the way that farming technology, labor inputs, and land-use intensity were related to the availability of land.

When traditional European agriculturalists were brought into contact with vast supplies of land in North America, where labor was scarce, farmers tended to use land extensively. Frequently, farmers arriving from Europe went from the annual cropping systems, which they had known at home, to bush-

fallow techniques in America. Colonial farmers performed in exactly the way the Boserup thesis suggests: They found they could get a satisfactory return from the land if they farmed less intensively. Later, when population density built up, it became worthwhile to apply more inputs to the land, farm more intensively, and produce more to feed the increased number of inhabitants.

The early settlement of Colonial America was greatly facilitated by the agricultural knowledge that Indian cultures made available to Europeans. At the Plymouth and Massachusetts Bay colonies, virtually all early settlements made use of land that had been cleared and farmed by Indian groups. The ground was available because the indigenous populations had been much reduced by the diseases that spread ahead of the settlers.

In the first planting season of 1621 at Plymouth Colony, the Pilgrims were taught New World farming techniques by two English-speaking Indians. Hobomok had learned English from fishermen on the Maine coast, and Squanto, a native of the Plymouth area, had acquired English while serving on an English ship. Under instruction from Squanto, the Pilgrims cleared weeds from old Indian fields, hoed more than 8 hectares (20 acres), fertilized the soil with herring, and planted maize. Many well-known European plants could not be instantly adapted to the environment of North America, although wheat and barley did become important crops.

In the seventeenth century, New England agriculture was largely unspecialized and had a strong subsistence element. The land was cleared of trees by cutting, girdling, and burning. Usually, the first crop planted after clearing was corn because yields were high and the plant had the ability to do well on lightly prepared ground. Squash and beans, which were adopted from the indigenous inhabitants, were interplanted with corn, the stalks of which provided support for these vine plants.

When the colonies of Maryland, Virginia, Pennsylvania, New York, Connecticut, and Massachusetts were established, ideas concerning the layout of a rural landscape and the structure of a rural society were brought along from the Old World. The most determined attempt to replicate the Old World in the New was made in New England. Communities in the Massachusetts Bay area tried to create open-field villages in an effort to preserve the customary way of life that had existed in England. Not all Massachusetts communities had open fields, but they existed, for example, at Concord, Sudbury, Dedham, Andover, and Rowley. The houses in these farming communities were clustered in villages. By 1650, the Massachusetts countryside appeared remarkably like the traditional English landscape which the colonists sought to recreate (Breen 1980, pp. 27–28).

The open-field village communities flourished for several decades, then declined in the second half of the seventeenth century. Many reasons have been given for this decline, including the rise of individualism, frontier restlessness, and the desire for more land (Trewartha 1946; McManis 1975). An important, but little discussed, cause of decline was the system of open-field agriculture. In most New England open-field communities, the villagers had 8 to 12 hectares (20–30 acres) of arable land allotted in the fields. Farming the small scattered strips of arable land demanded high labor inputs in a situation where labor was scarce and land potentially plentiful. The colonists had insufficient labor to run the relatively intensive open-field system, and yields often failed to reach English standards. After a time the New England farmer took on more land, worked it less intensively, and built a farmhouse on a holding away from the village.

The early immigrants to Maryland, Pennsylvania, and Connecticut also frequently tried to implement traditional English ideas about how to organize a rural society. They failed to make these ideas work, however, and quickly adopted methods more suitable for extensive agriculture. For example, William Penn, like the Puritan leaders of Massachusetts, wished to create "a structured society based upon religion" (Lemon 1972, p. 50). Penn wanted to establish agricultural villages with farmhouses clustered together surrounded by intensively cultivated fields. In fact what occurred was that colonists dispersed their farmsteads on large landholdings, used the land unintensively, and employed bush-fallow techniques.

In Connecticut, where some farm villages were established, most villagers adopted strategies of extensive land use. Daniels concluded that "as long as land was plentiful, clearing new was cheaper than fertilizing old" (1980, p. 431). In Maryland, even a **tenant farmer,** who rented land on the Baltimore manors, typically had a holding in excess of 40 hectares (100 acres) but cultivated only a small portion each year. Earle thinks that the Maryland tobacco growers avoided soil depletion by a system of field rotation that was similar to that employed by shifting cultivators (1975, p. 18).

Were these unsuccessful attempts to establish relatively intensive farming systems in the early phases of settlement unique to the American colonies? Are similar problems recognizable elsewhere? Guelke describes how the Dutch East India Company in 1652 attempted to establish a supply station at the Cape of Good Hope to grow fresh produce for vessels trading with Asia (1982, pp. 73–79). Settlers were given 10 hectares (25 acres), but they had neither the capital nor the labor to farm intensively. These early farmers quickly turned to livestock production where returns were greater and the labor needs less. In short, the effort to transfer the intensive, integrated agriculture of Holland to a colony failed. Similar experiences happened in the early history of farming in Australia and on the Argentine Pampas.

The experience of Colonial agriculture in America illustrates that there is not necessarily a progression from long fallows to a more intensive use of land. American pioneer farmers reverted to longer fallow systems because land was available and because unintensive farming gave them the best return on the labor inputs that could be provided.

CONTEMPORARY CONDITIONS IN AGRICULTURAL SOCIETIES

In the past, traditional agricultural societies tended to operate in relative isolation from other parts of the world. Farming communities were affected largely by the environmental, demographic, cultural, economic, and political conditions of their immediate locality. Later agricultural communities became increasingly affected by forces from distant lands.

Over the last four centuries, many formerly self-sufficient traditional agricultural societies have been greatly altered by contact with European empires and the emergence of a world economy. When European powers acquired territory in Africa, Asia, South America, and the Caribbean, they frequently used these overseas possessions as sources of agricultural commodities. Sugar was grown on **plantations** spread over several West Indian islands (Box 9-2), tea estates were established in India (Figure 9-25) and Ceylon (now Sri Lanka), and rubber was introduced in Malaya (now Malaysia). Where foreign-owned plantations were not created, local peasant farmers were often encouraged, or pressured, into producing palm oil, cacao, coffee, and spices for sale in foreign markets.

The shift to cash crops had far-reaching effects. It meant that rural economies became, at least in part, dependent on selling their farm goods so they could buy the foods they were no longer producing for themselves. The shift from subsistence crops was also accompanied by changes in land ownership as formerly communal lands passed into the hands of individuals and companies. Those who emerged as

---

Tenant farmer. A cultivator who rents land by paying cash, by sharing the crop, or by providing labor services to the landlord.

Plantation. A large agricultural unit that specializes in the growing of a few crops for selling to large, and often foreign, markets (see Box 9-2).

BOX 9-2. PLANTATION AGRICULTURE

Many tropical and subtropical crops are grown on plantations. Plantations are large-scale production units that specialize in the growing of a few crops over extensive areas and selling to large markets. To be successful, plantations have to have cheap land, cheap labor, and access to mass markets. Production is usually concentrated on one crop such as rubber, sugar, palm oil, cotton, bananas, coffee, tea, cacao, or sisal. Partial processing, such as the crushing of sugar cane to produce molasses, is often done at a factory on the plantation. Thus, this form of agriculture also has an industrial component.

North American and Western European companies have developed many plantations in less developed lands. In the past, the Dutch, British, and French all developed sugar plantations on Caribbean islands. Land was taken over, slaves were imported from Africa, and sugar was harvested and processed into molasses, refined sugar, or rum for European markets. In Southeast Asia, the owners and managers of rubber plantations acquired large tracts of land, brought in cheap labor from India and China, and successfully competed with other rubber producers of the world. In Central America, much land was planted to bananas by large American companies.

Plantations are a mix of modern and medieval features. Modernity is reflected in mechanization, capitalization, and long-range marketing. On the other hand, the class system of the plantation is pre-modern. At the top of the social structure are the owners and managers. The bulk of the plantation population, however, is made up of lowly paid laborers (formerly slaves or indentured workers) who live in poor conditions.

Plantations were one of the earlier international institutions that affected people in widely separated places. They helped to establish communication and marketing links between dissimilar parts of the world, which facilitated the flow of cultural and political influences. For people living in wealthier importing countries, plantations provided the crops that could not be economically produced locally. For people in the poor plantation countries, land was taken over, foreign ethnic groups were brought in, and local economies were distorted.

large landowners frequently came to control economic and political power.

When decolonization took place and political independence was achieved, the structure of most economies remained the same. Patterns of crop production and land ownership tended to persist. Families that had gained wealth and power through commercial linkages with foreign markets saw no advantage in returning to a subsistence type of economy. In fact, many newly independent countries tried to increase their exportation of agricultural commodities. This was for the purpose of earning the foreign currency needed to pay for imported manufactured goods.

As a result of these persistent patterns, many less developed countries face conflicting pressures. Some groups insist that land should be used to produce food crops for local consumption; others believe that it is essential to grow cash crops that will earn foreign exchange. Some advocate dividing large farms and plantations into small farms that are available to small-scale farming; others disagree. Many people also differ about the degree to which agriculture should be supported by national investments and price supports.

All of these conflicts have emerged as less devel-

Figure 9-25. Tea Plantation in Darjeeling, India. In some areas, cropping patterns today indicate investments by foreign companies in the past. Photo courtesy of Sally Stoddard.

oped countries try to come to terms with the global economy and the forces of change. Furthermore, if particular ethnic groups within a country feel that their interests are being denied by other groups that are in power, these economic disagreements often become mixed with political and territorial disputes (Chapter 8). These conflicting pressures can be observed in almost any agricultural society today. As illustrations, with contrasting strategies for coping with the problems, El Salvador and China are described here.

Agriculture in El Salvador

An illustration of a less developed country that gains much of its GNP from agriculture is El Salvador. This country is richly endowed by nature for agriculture, with black volcanic soils, fertile valleys, and (despite a dry season from November to March), sufficient moisture for most tropical crops (Figure 9-26). Yet El Salvador is a country where per capita food supplies have fallen since 1950 and where an estimated 60 percent of the population in the late 1970s earned less than the minimum income needed to buy subsistence products (Durham 1979, pp. 22–25). Part of the problem involves El Salvador's rapid population growth, which has reduced the per capita land available for food production. Population growth alone, however, does not account for the extent of poverty and hunger

in El Salvador; an additional cause is the inequality of ownership of land and other resources.

Agriculture is far more important to the economy of El Salvador than to the American economy. Almost half of the economically active population is employed in agriculture, and about one-third of the country's gross national product comes from agriculture. As in many other less developed countries, El Salvador has a relatively small elite that owns a large percentage of the land. Almost 50 percent of the families farm less than one hectare (about 2.5 acres), whereas only 0.3 percent of the farmers own over 28 percent of the farmland. Since wealth is largely determined by land ownership, the poorest 20 percent of El Salvador's population in 1981 earned only 2 percent of the country's total income, whereas the richest 20 percent controlled 66 percent of the national income (Diaz-Briquets 1986, p. 11).

This unequal distribution of land and wealth is related to a series of economic "reforms" that were instituted in 1881–1882. Prior to that time, much of the land was farmed communally, a system that dated back to the Spanish colonial period. After 1882, the land became increasingly concentrated in the hands of a small group of wealthy families who displaced the peasant farmers by converting areas of maize and other food crops into coffee plantations. The peasants were forced onto the thinner soils of the mountain slopes, which led to widespread deforestation and

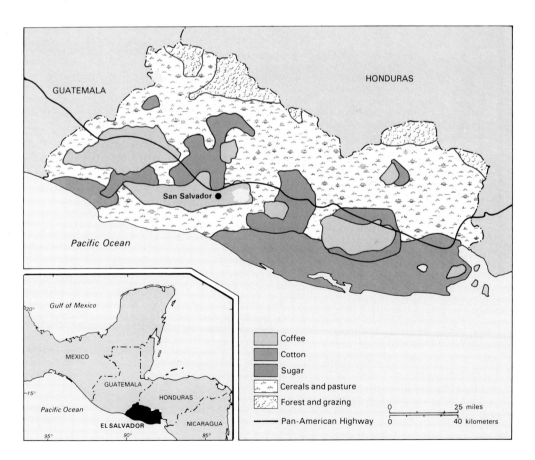

Figure 9-26. Agricultural Regions of El Salvador. A large share of the agricultural land is devoted to export crops. After Browning 1971.

soil erosion. The dispossessed farmers became a source of cheap labor as El Salvador became ruled by a "coffee export oligarchy." After the Second World War, cotton and sugar were added to the group of export crops. Food production stagnated, and the living conditions of more than 75 percent of the population deteriorated (Browning 1971).

For the large landowners in El Salvador, agriculture is a commercial enterprise with goals similar to those of farmers in the United States. Often the landowners can earn a good living by using a large amount of land extensively rather than by using small areas intensively. Frequently part of a landowner's estate is left idle or in pasture. The products (coffee, sugar, and cotton) are sold mainly to world export markets. The reliance of El Salvador's economy on only a few products makes it extremely vulnerable to fluctuations in world prices.

In contrast to the large landowners, the small farmers grow mainly subsistence crops. Coffee may be grown as a small source of income, but maize is the main crop, grown intensively on any patch of land that is available or even marginally suitable. Many of the farmers are tenants, renting or share-cropping land on a year-by-year basis at the discretion of the landowner. As the country's area under export crops has grown, less land is available for the small farmers. If peasants are unable to obtain farmland, they often pass into the ranks of landless laborers.

Landless laborers are unable to grow their own food unless they resort to squatting on the large estates, as many do. Their primary source of income in rural areas is from manual work on the plantations. Such employment pays poorly and is often seasonal. It is estimated that more than 50 percent of the rural labor force is unemployed for more than two-thirds of the year (Simon and Stephens 1981, p. 2). Without a job, or without the land on which they can grow crops, many families experience poverty and hunger.

The food-producing and food-consuming situation in El Salvador illustrates conditions that occur in many parts of the world. Although people may live in agricultural regions and work as farm laborers, they often are too poor to share in the fruits of the harvest. It is a geographic irony that regions where a large share of the population is engaged in agriculture are the areas where malnutrition is most common.

Where many people live on the verge of insuffi-

BOX 9-3. SOME CAUSES OF FAMINE

In his book, *The Geography of Famine*, William Dando stated:

> The primary natural factors creating a crop failure have been droughts, floods, frost, disease and insects; the primary human factors creating a famine have been war, political decisions, internal disruption, cultural restraints, poor communications and inadequate transportation. [1980, p. xi]

Currently enough food is produced in the world to feed the entire population of the planet adequately. Furthermore, in recent years, the rate of increase in food production, for the world as a whole, has been faster than the population growth. These statistics would seem to indicate that famines no longer occur. However, this is obviously not the case.

At the level of individuals or family units, many do not have enough to eat during much of the year. If the meager source of food in a region is greatly curtailed, as during a time of drought, the conditions of hunger may deteriorate to those of starvation.

Famines continue to occur in modern times because of both natural and human factors (as described above by Dando).

Commencing in 1968 and continuing for more than a decade, the precipitation in several parts of Africa (especially in the Sahel or Sub-Saharan area) was much lower than normal. The conditions created by the climatic change, however, were made worse by overgrazing and other agricultural practices that adversely affected pastures, crops, and water supplies. Also, in some countries, government pricing policies discouraged farmers from producing surplus crops for sale. Between 1970 and 1980, when food production for the world as a whole was increasing, the amount of food grown in Africa declined 10 percent. Many people were unable to produce enough food for themselves or to buy food from local sources, and the result was widespread famine.

If humans lived in isolated communities and had no interaction with distant places, the factors discussed in the previous paragraph might adequately explain a famine. The geography of the contemporary world, however, consists of innumerable links between producers and consumers. This interdependency is illustrated by the fact that food consumed by people in the more developed countries is usually obtained from a wide diversity of distant places. In contrast, people who experience starvation are unable to obtain food from other places having an abundance. Their inability to acquire food results from a variety of circumstances. For example, in a civil war or similar political upheaval, one faction may prevent food from being delivered to its opponents. Transportation facilities also may be inadequate to move food to the needed areas. National policies may discourage individual growers from producing and selling surpluses. Frequently several conditions aggravate famine, but invariably among these human factors is widespread poverty.

Figure 9-27. Intercultivation in China. High production per area can be achieved by interplanting crops. Contrast the characteristics of this type of agriculture with that shown in Figure 10-7. Photo courtesy of Merlin P. Lawson.

cient food supplies, a natural disaster such as a drought may accentuate problems of malnutrition and starvation. Likewise, if a political crisis (such as a civil war or conflict with a neighboring country) occurs, the fragile balance between population needs and available food may be completely destroyed (Box 9-3).

Agriculture in China

One of the most successful attempts to achieve a high level of food production for local consumption has occurred in China in recent decades. When the Chinese Communist Party took control of the government in 1949, the feudal land-tenure system was abolished and 50 million hectares of land were allotted to the poorest peasants. Within a few years the land was reorganized into village cooperatives; then in 1958 the 740,000 cooperatives were amalgamated into 24,000 large communes. Combined with the reorganization of land and labor units was a change in the way food was allocated to the population. The goal was to replace the system that had denied food to persons who did not have land or money. In short, the objectives were to restructure agriculture to increase yields and to share the benefits of production more equitably.

Since 1979, the structure of Chinese agriculture has undergone additional changes as part of the national modernization campaign. Although the land is still not owned privately, the communes have been discontinued. Under the new "responsibility system," families farm specified plots of land. The success of the current system is indicated by the dramatic in-

crease in both farm income and agricultural production during the last few years.

Today Chinese agriculture combines the labor-intensive methods of the past with **appropriate technology.** The purpose of appropriate technology is to augment, rather than replace, labor (Schumacher 1973). Using modern genetics, the Chinese developed many kinds of high-yielding seeds, which allow the sequential growth of crops on the same land during the year. The intercultivation of crops is planned carefully to maximize yields per hectare and to produce a diversity of products within a small area (Figure 9-27).

Intercultivation, of course, requires more labor to plant, cultivate, and harvest crops than in agricultural systems using machines. But it produces higher yields and reduces the vulnerability to pests and diseases that attack large areas of a single crop. Multiple-cropping often requires starting seeds in greenhouses or nurseries and transplanting individual plants (Figure 9-28).

Crops and livestock are integrated. A benefit of integration is the availability of organic fertilizers. Ponds in which fish and ducks have been raised are drained and the bottoms dredged for enriched sediments. Hogs are fed on the wastes from noodle-making establishments, and they return manure, which is applied to increase the yields of rice and other crops. This does not mean that chemical fertilizers are not used,

---

Appropriate (or intermediate) technology. The application of relatively unsophisticated procedures and materials that augment, rather than replace, labor.

Figure 9-28. Intensive Cultivation in China. Individual care of plants, such as transplanting, watering, and hoeing, requires much labor, but it can produce high yields. Photo courtesy of Merlin P. Lawson.

but they only supplement a system that recycles what is regarded as waste in some other economies.

Intercultivated crops and integrated production have led to a diversity that allows for considerable regional self-sufficiency. About 80 percent of agricultural products are consumed locally. In fact, the governmental policies stipulate that more than a dozen different types of vegetables must be grown within a designated zone around each of the major cities of China. This policy reduces the cost of hauling goods long distances, and it often forms the basis for local agricultural processing industries. Farmers deliver foodstuffs daily to local urban centers, which eliminates the need for packaging and storage. On return trips, they may haul urban wastes back to the fields for composting.

Rural communities are urged to undertake reclamation programs. Numerous irrigation and reforestation projects have been accomplished by mass labor contributed by all persons in the local communities. The productive capacity of many parts of the Chinese countryside has been improved by using the major available resource—labor—rather than depending on scarce capital.

Some aspects of the Chinese system, especially those that augment abundant labor with appropriate technology, may be suitable for conditions that occur in other less developed countries where population densities are high and labor plentiful. However, few countries could achieve the mass mobilization of people that lies at the heart of the Chinese agricultural system, and many societies do not want to endure the kind of constraints that were imposed by the Mao government from the mid-1950s to the mid-1970s.

Also, many less developed countries are small and lack the environmental diversity of China, so local and national self-sufficiency would be much more difficult to accomplish.

Urbanization in Agricultural Societies

Agricultural societies today differ from those of the past in more ways than just the production of farm products. Not only are the major cities in less developed countries closely tied with the rest of the world, but they affect the neighboring rural areas. These connections bring about a multitude of changes in the lives of the rural population. For example, changes are encouraged by commercial and governmental agents who visit farm villages. This is evidenced by the altered expectations of rural families as medical and educational services have expanded. With increased literacy and the penetration of radio and television into remote regions, more and more people learn about life in other parts of the world and then seek to alter their own conditions.

A common way of attempting to better one's situation is to move. In most agricultural societies, an important cause for rural-to-urban migration is the perception, and sometimes the reality, that opportunities for economic and social advancement are available in the cities. Economic prospects in the rural areas of less developed countries are generally bleak. There is often a surplus of labor, particularly in traditional agricultural systems that are being mechanized. The slow growth of economic opportunities in rural areas is fairly universal. Even in China, where the government has had a commitment to provide jobs in the rural areas, unemployment or underemployment exists in farming regions.

In less developed countries, many young persons turn to the cities as places perceived to have more job opportunities. Indeed, new investments, especially in industries, do tend to focus on the major cities. Manufacturers, both domestic and those affiliated with foreign companies, prefer to locate plants in urban areas where labor, markets, and transportation facilities are best developed. If such urban development contrasts with a relative neglect of investments in rural areas, the imbalance between rural and urban opportunities may widen. Even developmental policies that attempt to aid the farming sector by expanding transportation lines into rural regions may actually facilitate the migration to urban places.

The economic conditions associated with urbanization in less developed countries today are not identical to those that existed previously in countries that are now more developed. The earlier urbanization in Europe and North America took place over a longer period, involved fewer people, and occurred when a greater share of the industries were labor-intensive than currently. Now migrants to the cities of the less developed lands generally find few opportunities for advancement. The supply of workers exceeds the demand, and urban unemployment rates are often very high. In Central America, for example, an estimated 90,000 new urban jobs would have to be created every year just to prevent the present high unemployment rates from rising (Bouvier 1984).

Many new migrants to cities survive by creating their own jobs such as selling trinkets, washing cars, and providing similar services (Figure 9-29). Although this informal sector may contribute to the overall economy of the city, it is not the primary attraction for people to move to the city. Most families regard these low-income service activities as temporary financial sources until someone in the immediate family group is able to obtain a coveted but often illusive position with a reliable employer.

In addition to hopes for employment, rural residents may be motivated to move to urban places because they believe that cities have more accessible water, better schools, better medical facilities, and a greater abundance of other services. In many countries, urban conditions are indeed better than rural ones. But, as migrants stream into the already crowded cities, they strain the existing social services. Schools, sewage disposal, public transportation, utilities, and housing become overburdened.

Frequently new arrivals have little choice but to live in the shantytowns which have proliferated in many cities (Figure 9-30). In the former Brazilian capital of Rio de Janeiro, for example, about one million people live in shanties (*favelas*) immediately adjacent to the downtown section and on the outskirts of the city. Since Indian Independence in 1947, an estimated 4 million persons have moved into Calcutta, many living in shanties (*bustis*).

The demand for expanded urban services becomes urgent, and many governments attempt to meet basic human needs. This may take the form, for example, of new housing complexes. These new facilities, in turn, often attract even more migrants who aspire to "the better life" in the city. Thus, success in

Figure 9-29. Selling Soft Drinks on the Street. Individuals selling items on the street is common in many cities of the world. In some countries where unemployment is high, these activities play an important economic role. Photo courtesy of George Tuck.

Figure 9-30. A Shantytown, Santiago, Chile. Rural migrants to large urban areas in less developed countries often live in shantytowns that have few amenities. Photo courtesy of Population Reference Bureau.

alleviating some of the problems created by migration into cities creates the conditions that attract even more migrants.

Several countries, including Paraguay, Mexico, Brazil, the Philippines, Cuba, and China, are trying to disperse urbanization through the creation, or enlargment, of regional service centers and market towns. China, in particular, has attempted during recent decades to restrict the growth of major cities. In addition to promoting rural industries, policies have involved transforming the more than 2000 county seats, which now have populations between 20,000 and 80,000, into medium-sized cities of 100,000 or more. It is intended that these developments will absorb between 60 and 200 million migrants from the land.

PROSPECTS FOR LESS DEVELOPED COUNTRIES

Predictions about the future of less developed countries vary. Some people see little hope for much change. Their perspective of the world is one in which there will always be rich and poor people, and these differences will tend to exist geographically as a core of wealth surrounded by a periphery of poverty.

Others predict there will be improvements, but only if specific events occur. For some, those events must be primarily demographic. For example, persons with a Malthusian viewpoint (see Chapter 2) believe that poverty will not diminish in a region until the rate of population growth greatly declines. This is a primary reason why planners in many less developed countries are promoting policies designed to reduce population growth.

From yet another perspective, some believe that change will only happen when the political structures of agrarian societies are transformed. Some advocates of this viewpoint may seek a revolutionary restructuring of society; others may work toward slow institutional modifications.

Most scholars believe that a restructuring of global relationships will be necessary before major improvements will occur in the majority of less developed countries. The probability of such worldwide alterations is very uncertain, partly because current trends are difficult to detect (see Point-Counterpoint "Narrowing the Widening Gap" in Chapter 10).

Although no one can predict what economic

changes will actually occur in the future, government leaders and planners in virtually all less developed countries seek to increase national production and to improve living standards. Strategies to achieve these ends vary with concepts about the primary factors that relate to economic development. To further examine the future prospects of less developed countries, therefore, it is worthwhile to study some of the theories of economic development (a topic in the next chapter).

Furthermore, it is very obvious that the economic prospects of all countries, especially the poorer ones, will be greatly affected by what happens within the global economy. The economy of every country is influenced by the economic events in nations elsewhere. Certainly the prospects of less developed countries are contingent on worldwide conditions, particularly those in the industrial countries (the focus of the next chapter).

Green Revolution. The application of chemical fertilizers and irrigation water to genetically improved seeds to produce high yields of wheat and other grains; a practice that commenced in the 1960s.

POINT-COUNTERPOINT

Some Implications of Intensifying Land Use

What are some of the results when people decide to use an area of land more intensively than in the past? Producing more food and raw materials from a plot of land is often equated with progress. More production per area means more people can obtain basic needs, which in a world of increasing population is a vital consideration. If greater production exceeds the rate of population growth, then the average quantity of goods theoretically available to each person is raised. When people can satisfy their basic needs for food, clothing, and shelter easily, they have more time to improve the quality of their lives.

Does intensifying the use of land result in benefits only? Are there social and environmental costs that also need to be considered when evaluating the results of intensified utilization of the earth? Are the methods employed to increase production in ecological balance with the natural environment? If greater production is obtained by depleting resources, such as fertile topsoil, what are the implications for future generations? Does greater production in a particular area (for example, a vegetable field in Denmark) depend on resources (such as petroleum converted to chemical fertilizer) brought from elsewhere? If so, what are the effects, both immediate and long-range, on people living in the regions that export those resources?

Do the methods of production (such as applying pesticides) involve polluting the environment in a manner that affects the health and quality of life of inhabitants? Does an increase in production for an area always mean that everyone dependent on the yields from that area will share equally in the benefits?

The pros and cons of this general issue are illustrated by the conflicting assessments of the Green Revolution. The **Green Revolution,** in its broadest sense, involves transferring to regions of traditional farming the methods of modern agricultural technology— primarily the application of fertilizers and irrigation water to genetically improved seeds. The goal is to increase the yields of wheat, corn, and rice in areas where food production has been low per person and, in some cases, low per unit of land. Using these technological inputs, many less developed countries have greatly increased their yields. Largely as a result of applying the techniques of the Green Revolution, India, for example, moved from importing food to being self-sufficient in basic grains, especially wheat, in the 1970s. This productive accomplishment in India, with its large population and past history of food shortages, has been very beneficial for the nation's economy. Many people concerned about the lack of adequate food in parts of the world have hailed the Green Revolution as a boon.

There are, however, social and ecological problems associated with the Green Revolution. For example, areas suitable for irrigation are limited. Compared to traditional systems, the introduction of a monoculture can increase the risks of economic, ecological, and productive failure. The variety of crops grown under traditional systems provides more insurance against a total loss of food supplies. Furthermore, the costs of inputs, especially fertilizer and irrigation water, are too expensive for many farmers to get started. However, those farmers who do have the initial wealth to utilize the new technology can benefit from high yields. Sales of the bumper crops not only pay for the costly inputs but make it possible to buy or rent additional land and increase production even more. Consequently, in an area where land is scarce, this change in farm ownership (or rental) means that some families that once produced crops may no longer be able to continue farming. As the number of families losing access to land increases in an area, the amount of hunger may also increase.

Have the benefits of increased food production brought about by the Green Revolution been worth the costs? There is no unanimous answer, but rural families that have lost the means by which they could share in this greater production often view the costs as too high.

BIBLIOGRAPHY

Agnew, John, *The United States in the World Economy.* Cambridge, England: Cambridge University Press, 1987.

Boserup, Esther, *The Conditions of Agricultural Growth.* Chicago: Aldine Publishing Co., 1965.

——, *Women's Role in Economic Development.* London & Baltimore: Allen & Unwin, 1970.

Blok, A., "South Italian Agro-Towns," *Comparative Studies in Society and History,* no. 11 (1969), 121–35.

Breen, T. H., *Puritans and Adventurers: Change and Persistence in Early America.* New York: Oxford University Press, 1980.

Brown, Lester R., "World Food Resources and Population: The Narrowing Margin," *Population Bulletin,* 36, no. 5 (December 1981).

Browning, David, *El Salvador: Landscape and Society.* Oxford, England: Clarendon Press, 1971.

Buck, John Lossing, *Chinese Farm Economy.* Shanghai: Willow Press, 1930.

Buultjens, Ralph, "China's Development Efforts and Quest for the Future," *Focus,* 27, no. 4 (March-April 1977), 1–8.

Cantor, Leonard, ed., *The English Medieval Landscape.* Philadelphia: University of Pennsylvania Press, 1982.

Carlstein, Tommy, *Time Resources, Society and Ecology.* Lund Studies in Geography, Series B. Human Geography No. 49. London: George Allen & Unwin, 1982.

Carneiro, Robert, "Slash and Burn Cultivation among the Kuikuru and Its Implications for Cultural Development in the Amazon Basin," in J. Wilbert, ed., *The Evolution of Horticultural Systems in Native South America: Causes and Consequences, A Symposium.* Caracas: Editorial Sucre, 1961.

Chen, Ding, "The Economic Development of China," *Scientific American,* 243, no. 3 (September 1980), 152–65.

Coones, Paul, and John Patten, *The Penguin Guide to the Landscape of England and Wales.* New York: Penguin Books, 1986.

Cooper, Richard N., "A Monetary System for the Future," *Foreign Affairs,* 63, no. 1 (1984), 166–84.

Dando, William A., *The Geography of Famine.* New York: John Wiley & Sons, 1980.

Daniels, Bruce C., "Economic Development in Colonial and Revolutionary Connecticut: An Overview," *William and Mary Quarterly,* 37, no. 3 (1980), 429–50.

Darby, H. C., ed., *An Historical Geography of England before A.D. 1800.* Cambridge, England: Cambridge University Press, 1936.

——, "The Clearing of the Woodland in Europe," in William L. Thomas, Jr., ed., *Man's Role in Changing the Face of the Earth,* pp. 183–216. Chicago: University of Chicago Press, 1956.

Denevan, W. M., "Campa Subsistence in the Gran Pajonal, Eastern Peru, *Geographical Review,* 61, no. 4 (October 1971), 496–518.

Diaz-Briquets, Sergio, "Conflict in Central America: The Demographic Dimension," *Occasional Paper, Population Trends and Public Policy,* no. 10. Population Reference Bureau (Feb. 1986).

Dickinson, J. C., III, "Alternative to Monoculture in the Humid Tropics of Latin America," *Professional Geographer,* 24, no. 3 (1972), 217–32.

Dixon-Mueller, R., *Women's Work in Third World Agriculture.* Geneva: International Labour Office, 1985.

Dodgshon, R. A., and R. A. Butlin, eds., *An Historical Geography of England and Wales.* London: Academic Press, 1978.

Drucker, Peter F., "The Changing World Economy," *Foreign Affairs,* 64, no. 4 (1986), 768–91.

Durham, William H., *Scarcity and Survival in Central America: Ecological Origins of the Soccer War.* Stanford, Calif.: Stanford University Press, 1979.

Earle, Carville, *The Evolution of a Tidewater Settlement System: All Hallows Parish, Maryland 1650–1783.* Chicago: University of Chicago, Department of Geography, 1975.

Elvin, Mark, *The Pattern of the Chinese Past.* Stanford, Calif.: Stanford University Press, 1973.

Eyre, S. R., *The Real Wealth of Nations.* London: Edward Arnold, 1978.

Fossier, Jean Chapelot Robert, *The Village and House in the Middle Ages.* Berkeley and Los Angeles: University of California Press, 1985.

Geertz, Clifford, *Agricultural Involution: The Process of Ecological Change.* Berkeley, Calif.: University of California Press, 1963.

Grigg, David, *Population Growth and Agrarian Change: An Historical Perspective.* Cambridge, England: Cambridge University Press, 1980.

Grove, A. T., "Population Densities and Agriculture in Northern Nigeria," in K. M. Barbour and R. M. Prothero, eds., *Essays on African Population,* pp. 115–36. London: Routledge & Kegan Paul, 1971.

Guelke, Leonard, *Historical Understanding in Geography.* Cambridge, England: Cambridge University Press, 1982.

Hallam, H. E., *Rural England 1066–1348.* Brighton, Sussex, England: The Harvester Press, 1981.

Harris, R. Cole, "The Simplification of Europe Overseas," *Annals of the Association of American Geographers,* 67, no. 4 (December 1977), 469–83.

Herskovits, Melville J., *Economic Anthropology: The Economic Life of Primitive Peoples.* New York: W. W. Norton & Co., Inc., 1965.

Huang, Philip C. C., *The Peasant Economy and Social Change in North China.* Stanford, Calif.: Stanford University Press, 1985.

Jones, E. L., *The European Miracle.* Cambridge, England: Cambridge University Press, 1981.

King, F. H., *Farmers of Forty Centuries.* Emmaus, Pa.: Organic Gardening Press, 1927.

Lappe, Frances Moore, and Joseph Collins, *Food-First: Beyond the Myth of Scarcity.* Boston: Houghton Mifflin, 1977.

Lemon, James T., *The Best Poor Man's Country: A Geographic Study of Early Southeastern Pennsylvania.* Baltimore: Johns Hopkins University Press, 1972.

Lobb, C. Gary, "Agriculture," in Brian W. Blouet and Olwyn M. Blouet, eds., *Latin America: An Introductory Survey,* pp. 150–83. New York: John Wiley & Sons, 1982.

McManis, Douglas R., *Colonial New England: A Historical Geography.* New York: Oxford University Press, 1975.

Netting, Robert McC., *Cultural Ecology*. Menlo Park, Calif.: Cummings, 1977.

Rappaport, Roy A., "The Flow of Energy in an Agricultural System," *Scientific American*, 224, no. 3 (September 1971), 117–32.

Schumacher, E. F. *Small Is Beautiful: Economics as if People Mattered*. New York: Harper & Row, Pub., 1973.

Seager, Joni and Ann Olson, *Women in the World: An International Atlas*. New York: Simon & Schuster, 1986.

Simon, Lawrence R., and James C. Stephens, Jr., *El Salvador Land Reform, 1980–1981: Impact Audit*. Boston: Oxford America, 1981.

Sivard, Ruth Leger, *World Military and Social Expenditures 1986*, 11th ed. Washington D.C.: World Priorities, 1986.

Smith, David M., *Human Geography: A Welfare Approach*. London: Edward Arnold, 1977.

———, *Where the Grass Is Greener: Geographical Perspectives on Inequality*. London: Croom Helm, 1979.

Stross, Randall E., *The Stubborn Earth: American Agricul-turalists on Chinese Soil 1898–1937*. Berkeley and Los Angeles: University of California Press, 1987.

Trewartha, G. T., "Types of Rural Settlement in Colonial America," *Geographical Review*, 36 (1946), 568–96.

Tuan, Yi-Fu, *China*. Chicago: Aldine Publishing Co., 1970.

Turner, B. L., II, Robert Q. Hanham, and Anthony V. Portararo, "Population Pressure and Agricultural Intensity," *Annals of the Association of American Geographers*, 67, no. 3 (September 1977), 384–96.

Turner, Michael, *English Parliamentary Enclosure*. Hamden, Conn.: Archon Books, 1980.

Webb, W. P., *The Great Frontier*. Boston: Houghton Mifflin, 1952.

World Development Report 1987. New York: Oxford University Press, 1987.

"World Population Data Sheet." Population Reference Bureau, Inc., 1986, 1987, 1988.

Yelling, J. A., *Common Field and Enclosure in England 1450–1850*. London: Macmillan, 1977.

10 INDUSTRIAL SOCIETIES

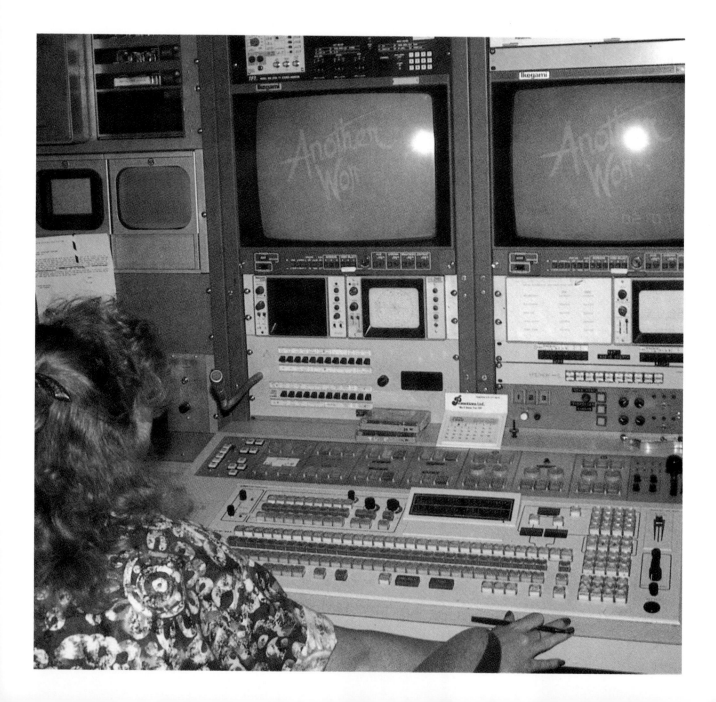

Some countries of the world are rich and others are poor (as measured and discussed in Chapter 9). These national differences affect more than just the amount of goods and services produced and consumed; they are closely related to numerous other conditions of human life. Certainly an understanding of geographic differences and similarities around the world involves learning about landscapes and activities associated with the levels of economic development.

Why are some countries rich and others poor? Several possible explanations are examined in the first portion of this chapter. The remainder of the chapter describes the characteristics of more developed (industrial) countries, which can then be compared with the less developed (agricultural) countries described in Chapter 9. Even though the discussion of these two classes is separated into distinct chapters, it is important to remember that the world economic system links countries in ways that prevent them from operating independently.

FACTORS OF ECONOMIC DEVELOPMENT

It is not easy to isolate the reasons for the unequal distribution of economic wealth in the world. The explanations usually take into account the role of natural resources, the cultural setting, stages of economic development, and global relationships.

Mineral and Inanimate Energy Resources

Industrial economies depend on coal, petroleum, iron ore, bauxite, and other mineral and energy resources. It is tempting to suggest that the possession of these resources provides the main reason why some of these countries are highly industrialized. The role of resources cannot be ignored. Britain and Germany, for example, possessed a good mix of mineral resources in the early stages of industrialization. Even today, several industrialized nations, such as the United States, Canada, Australia, and the Soviet Union, have abundant mineral and energy resources. Conversely, several countries with limited resources (e.g., Bangladesh) are not industrialized.

The possession of abundant resources, however, is not a necessity for industrialization. Some highly industrialized nations, for example, Japan and Switzerland, do not have extensive resource bases (Figure 10-1). Furthermore, still other countries do possess rich mineral deposits, such as Brazil, China, and Zaire, but they are not wealthy countries (see Table 9-1).

Thus it is safe to conclude that the world distribution of mineral and energy resources is not an adequate explanation of why certain countries are industrialized and others are not.

Cultural Setting

Cultural setting refers to the mix of social institutions, belief systems, political organizations, and economic policies that affect national production and consumption. Rigidly stratified societies, with inflexible social systems, may inhibit experimentation, innovations, entrepreneurial activities, and change. Given that most traditional societies were conservative, it is perhaps surprising that humans were ever able to create the social environment out of which industrialization emerged.

The Chinese were close to creating industrialization in the thirteenth and fourteenth centuries but ultimately failed. The Europeans did make the societal breakthrough that generated the Industrial Revolution but not until after the sixteenth century (Chapter 2). Once an industrial revolution occurred in one place, it

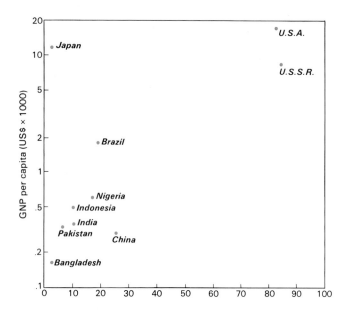

Figure 10-1. Relationship between Wealth and Natural Resources. The values (plotted for the ten most populated countries) represent GNP per capita and an index of natural resources (based on mineral production, coal reserves, petroleum reserves, and arable land per capita). Although the position of the points for the United States and Bangladesh suggests a positive correlation between natural resources and national wealth, the scattering of the other points (especially the one for Japan) indicates the relationship is weak among these major countries.

could be adopted elsewhere. But, the places where it occurred varied politically and economically. For example, the political and economic ideology of the Soviet Union contrasted with that of the United States, and both countries differed from the cultural setting of Japan. Despite the differences, all these countries are industrialized.

Certainly the cultural setting greatly affects the prospects for industrialization. There is no agreement, however, about specific policies that will successfully convert a traditional agricultural society into an industrial one. Stated geographically, there is no particular cultural type that can be mapped and correlated with the industrialized countries of the world today.

Stages of Economic Development

A third explanation focuses on the timing of economic changes. It assumes that a country must go through a series of economic stages to achieve industrialization. According to this explanation, variations in levels of economic development are the result of different stages in an evolutionary process.

The best known classification of economic stages is by W. W. Rostow (1960). He proposed five stages: (1) the traditional society, (2) the preconditions for take-off into economic growth, (3) the take-off into self-sustaining economic growth, (4) the drive to maturity, and (5) the age of high mass consumption.

In the traditional society stage, power is controlled by a land-owning elite, and a majority of the population subsists by laboring in agriculture. The preconditions for take-off (the second stage) include the establishment of transportation networks and financial institutions along with the emergence of an entrepreneurial class. In the stage of take-off (the third stage), investment increases and new industries expand, resulting in new jobs and an increased demand for services. Economic growth begins to feed upon itself and becomes self-sustaining.

In Rostow's fourth stage, the drive to maturity, a country adds more sophisticated industries (such as machine tools, chemicals, and electrical equipment) and becomes heavily involved with international trade. By the time a country reaches the age of high mass consumption (the fifth stage), it has all the characteristics of a more developed nation.

A model of economic development, such as that proposed by Rostow, is helpful in understanding changes that occur when countries industrialize. Furthermore, the model provides a basis for describing economic differences among nations that have begun the process of change. It does not, however, address the issue of why specific countries like Britain and the United States started moving from a traditional society toward the take-off stage earlier than other countries. By itself, the model is not a complete explanation for the geographic patterns of industrialization in the world.

Global Relationships

A fourth explanation for the wide variations in economic development in the world is based on the history of global relationships. This approach builds upon the fact that the first industrial revolution occurred around the North Atlantic and resulted in the creation of a relatively rich and economically diversified core region. With this head start, the core countries were able to achieve political and economic power and to dominate world trade. Consequently, the countries in the periphery became sources of minerals, energy, and agricultural commodities produced by poorly paid laborers.

According to this view, it has been in the interest of the more developed countries to perpetuate a global economic order with large disparities of wealth between the affluent core and the impoverished periphery. From this perspective, the present world economic order is a gigantic neo-colonial system in which the less developed countries produce raw materials cheaply to help sustain lifestyles of high mass consumption in the wealthy nations. Even when capital is exported from the United States, Japan, West

Germany, or Britain to establish manufacturing plants in Mexico, Malaysia, or South Korea, this can be viewed as exploitation of cheap labor in countries with low incomes. With such inherent inequalities in the global system, it is difficult for the nations of the periphery to compete successfully with the more industrialized societies (Blaut 1973).

Even though the relative importance of each of these factors to economic development is unclear, the resulting industrialized societies share some common characteristics. These are examined here by looking at the patterns of manufacturing, agriculture, and service activities.

MANUFACTURING

Assume that economic conditions in a country favor industry and a firm is planning to build a factory. Where are some plausible locations for a manufacturing plant? This geographic question differs from the choice that confronts a farmer who has land and then must decide what to produce. The manufacturer generally begins with a product and then must select a favorable location for a factory.

General Location Factors

Whether in a rich or a poor country, the major factors influencing the location of manufacturing industries are raw materials, power, labor, markets, and transportation. Each of these factors may be affected by government policies and world economic conditions. The relative importance of these elements varies considerably from one context to another. In less developed countries, manufacturing often consists of home-based handicraft industries that utilize family labor and nearby raw materials to produce goods for a local market. In more developed countries, manufacturing takes place primarily in corporately or governmentally owned factories, sometimes employing a large labor force, and raw materials and markets may be distant.

Raw materials, the items to be processed, are essential, but their locations are not always critical in siting an industry. It is true that nations possessing sources of raw materials have assets that potentially benefit manufacturing enterprises. The minerals and agricultural commodities in the United States, Canada, the Soviet Union, and Australia, for example, do reduce the amount of raw materials they must import. The costs of these raw materials, however, are usually relatively low compared to other manufacturing inputs, so this is seldom a critical locational factor. The lack of large quantities of raw materials certainly did not prevent Japan from becoming a major manufacturing nation.

Conversely, many countries possessing large amounts of important minerals (such as Zaire with copper and cobalt and Niger with massive uranium reserves) are not industrial nations. Often they are the sites of extractive industries, which employ few workers and export the raw or partially refined products to the more developed nations.

It should be noted that "raw" materials may include the products of one industry that are used in manufacturing other goods. For example, the cotton cloth produced as a finished product by one factory becomes the basic raw material in a clothing factory. Accordingly, nations with highly developed manufacturing industries create materials that are utilized in other domestic industries. The advantages for interdependent industries to cluster together contribute to the formation of urban-industrial agglomerations.

Power (energy) is now relatively easy to transport, so its source is no longer a major factor in locating manufacturing industries. This was not the case in the past when, in an era of costly and inefficient transportation, a power source such as coal often became the pole of attraction for industrial development (Figure 2-17). Today, with the multiplicity of energy forms and the relative ease of movement by huge tankers, pipelines, and electrical wires, the energy sources have declined as a factor in industrial location. Japan, for example, one of the most industrialized nations in the world, imports about 90 percent of its energy, mostly in the form of oil from Southwest Asia.

The availability of labor does have a number of influences on the location of industries. For example, a highly automated plant, such as an oil refinery, utilizes relatively few skilled workers, and they can be attracted to the factory site if necessary. Since the labor payroll constitutes a small proportion of total costs, locating where wages are lower would not save the owners of the refinery much money. In contrast, factories making clothing or assembling electronic components require many workers, so labor costs are a significant proportion of total costs of production. These industries are attracted to regions and countries where wages are low and labor plentiful. The shift of New England's textile industry to the Piedmont of the Carolinas in the early twentieth century was in large part a move to cheap labor supplies. More recently, American-owned, export-oriented manufacturing plants have been attracted to places such as Taiwan because wages there are low compared to rates in the United States.

Consumers are vital for industrial success, but their importance as a locational factor varies with the type of finished product. Bulky products and low-value goods, such as cement, are often manufactured close to the market. Consequently, the world distribution of cement manufacturing is closely associated with areas of demand. By contrast, high-value items, such as military equipment and easily transported goods (e.g., hand calculators), are often produced for distant markets.

The ability to cheaply transport raw materials, power, and finished products affects the relative importance of other locational factors. Numerous industries seek places that are connected by low-cost transportation routes to many other regions. Especially attractive sites for manufacturers are seaports such as New York, Rotterdam, and Tokyo, where materials are moved from one mode of transportation to another.

In countries with good transportation facilities, factors such as geographic inertia and supportive financial systems are important. Big cities attract new manufacturing activities for these reasons. Overall, manufacturing enterprises are now more strongly influenced by the location of the suitable organizational and entrepreneurial setting than by raw material sources. For instance, Japan can obtain raw materials and power from all over the world and can sell finished goods to a large affluent domestic market as well as to foreign buyers. Thus the existing manufacturing regions and the established supporting services tend to perpetuate industrial locations.

Another important variable affecting industrialization at the national and international scales is the ownership of capital. It takes a large investment in research, equipment, plant, raw materials, power, and labor to start most industrial enterprises, so the people and institutions that control wealth are often the major decision-makers in choosing factory locations.

At the international scale, this means that countries with more wealth have a far greater influence on industrial locations than do the poorer countries. Small firms and governments in less developed countries are generally incapable of raising the capital for large-scale industrialization.

Major Manufacturing Regions of the World

Given the patterns of national development (see Figure 9-9) and the role of the dominant factors of location, it is no surprise that the major manufacturing regions of the world are Western Europe, the United States, the Soviet Union, and Japan (Figure 10-2). The historical evolution of industrialization in each of these regions is discussed below.

The historic factors associated with manufacturing regions in England (described in Chapter 2, especially Figure 2-17) generally apply to other parts of Western Europe as well. For example, the locational influence of coal fields is demonstrated by industrial concentrations in northern France and Belgium and the Ruhr District of Germany. And the industrial attractiveness of ports with their long-distance trade is illustrated by the development of major manufacturing centers at London, Rotterdam, Hamburg, and Marseilles.

The role of geographic inertia is evident in the persistence of several of the early regions of manufacturing. Some original locational factors, such as coal fields, may have little direct importance today, and former heavy industries may have declined. Neverthe-

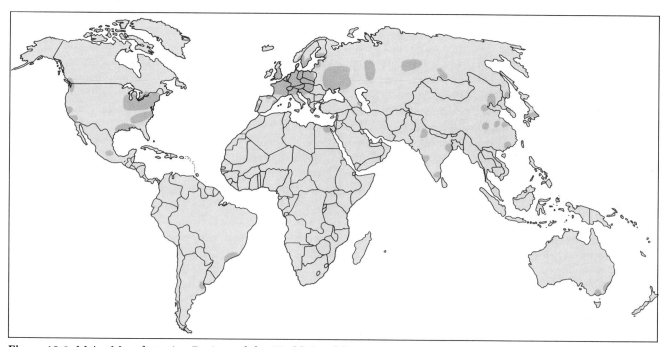

Figure 10-2. Major Manufacturing Regions of the World. In addition to these major regions, manufacturing occurs in many smaller areas (not shown here).

less, large urban areas, with their transportation facilities and concentrated populations continue to attract new manufacturing enterprizes.

The traditional manufacturing "belt" of the United States developed in the Northeast and Great Lakes area of the Midwest. The position of major seaports on the Atlantic Ocean, the existence of penetrating waterways such as the Great Lakes and the Ohio-Mississippi river system, the availability of iron ore and coal, and the major concentration of population all contributed to the emergence of this manufacturing region.

Manufacturing in the South, especially along the Gulf Coast, came later with the rise of petrochemicals and associated industries (Chapter 4). In the Far West, particularly in Southern California, the San Francisco vicinity, and the Pacific Northwest, industrial expansion resulted from the increase in population, the rise of military industries, the boom in computer manufacturing, and the growth of trade with Asia.

Manufacturing in Russia under the czars was very limited and mostly concentrated in the European section of the country. With the change in government after the revolution of 1917 came a policy of planned economic development with an emphasis on heavy industry. Economic planners deliberately built new factories close to sites with raw materials and power even if these places previously lacked industries. Consequently, not only were existing industries of the Ukraine greatly expanded, but new manufacturing centers were purposely developed in the Ural Mountains, in Central Asia, and in the Kuznetsk Basin of southern Siberia (Figure 10-2). Manufacturing was greatly expanded in the Urals and Asian centers during World War II when Germany invaded much of the European part of the Soviet Union.

Patterns of manufacturing in the U.S.S.R. have shifted slightly with the introduction of new technologies and changes in government policies. Furthermore, the discoveries of large fields of petroleum and natural gas in the Volga region and in Western Siberia have altered the map of resources. Nevertheless, the primary manufacturing regions of the Soviet Union have not changed drastically in the last half century.

Shortly after 1868, Japan embarked on a deliberate policy of industrialization. To earn the capital needed to buy textile plants and machinery, the country exported rice, tea, and raw silk. Within a few decades, however, the country was able to export manufactured textiles, particularly silk and cotton goods. The manufacturing of cotton textiles depended entirely on imported raw cotton, which entered the country at a few major ports, so most of the textile plants were located at these same sites.

As the Japanese economy diversified into heavy industries in the 1930s, these seaports continued to grow. Tokyo/Yokohama, Osaka/Kobe, and Nagoya be-

Figure 10-3. Major Manufacturing Regions of Japan. Most manufacturing in the country takes place in these four areas.

came major industrial centers (Figure 10-3). Only the manufacturing and population node situated near the coal fields of northern Kyushu was associated with domestic resources. With the rapid economic growth of the country after 1950, manufacturing has become even more concentrated in these four nodes. Each focuses on a seaport through which imported raw materials and exported manufactured products flow. Each is associated with a large, affluent population that provides the labor, technology, capital, and domestic market for manufacturing.

Although Western Europe, the United States, the Soviet Union, and Japan do not include all the manufacturing centers of the world, in general, they constitute the major industrial core. With a "head start" on other countries, these areas have enjoyed many advantages that have, in turn, attracted new industries. This is partly because the **infrastructure** (transportation, marketing networks, supporting industries) is in place; skilled labor is available; and consumers are at hand.

Infrastructure. The basic framework of a system; a term used especially in reference to transportation, utility facilities, and similar installations that support economic production.

Successful plants that manufacture large quantities of products are able to achieve **internal economies of scale** (savings in unit costs). Such savings allow a manufacturing company to sell a product cheaper than competitors who have only a small volume of production and higher unit costs. The company with the lower priced products then sells more and expands its share of the market.

A company commanding a large share of the market generates enough income to channel funds into the research and development of new products. For small companies, the cost of research and development is a barrier to gaining a larger share of the market. Furthermore, the company that develops a new product before competitors is often able to establish a market that is retained even when latecomers begin to produce similar items. Retention of control permits a continuation of the cycle of product development and market expansion.

The persistence of these core areas is shown by looking at the importance of manufacturing for each of the countries of the world (Figure 10-4). (Here importance is measured by the percentage of the working population engaged in manufacturing, which makes the map comparable to those for workers in agriculture and services; see Figures 9-7 and 10-13.) According to this map (Figure 10-4), countries identified with the core generally have more than 30 percent of their workers in manufacturing (with the United States being an exception; see Services below).

Changing Patterns of Manufacturing

In spite of the geographic inertia associated with the early manufacturing regions, new centers do appear. Conditions of relative advantage change. For example, when new mineral and fuel resources are found, they may attract new industries. Differences in labor costs at one place may rise or decline relative to those in another region. Market demands shift. Transfer of technology makes it possible for new manufacturers to adopt new procedures and equipment and therefore become competitive. Flows of capital may work to the advantage of some places and the disadvantage of others. In short, there are a host of factors in the ever-changing geography of economic activities that alter the map of manufacturing.

Interpreting a map of workers in manufacturing (Figure 10-4) is not easy because many factors affect industrial locations. One complicating element is the fact that factory owners do not necessarily restrict their factories to the home country. A wealthy country may have fewer industrial plants than might be expected because companies have decided to operate plants in

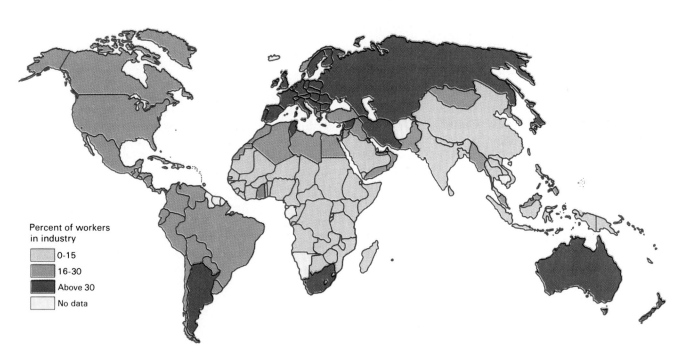

Figure 10-4. Percentage of Workers in Industry. This map is limited by the unavailability of standardized data (i.e., the different ways of defining "industry") and by its focus on percentages (for instance, there are many more industrial workers in China than in Hong Kong, even though their respective percentages are 14 and 51). Also this map should be compared with Figures 9-7 and 10-13 to detect the importance of primary and tertiary sectors, as illustrated by the 49 percent of the workers in Paraguay being in agriculture while 69 percent of the workers in the United States are in services.

foreign lands. For instance, by the mid-1970s, the amount of goods produced by American-owned companies with factories located abroad was four times that of U.S. exports (Coates, Johnston, and Knox 1977, p. 102). On the other hand, some poor countries may have a larger number of manufacturing plants within their boundaries than might be anticipated because of locational decisions made by foreign-based companies. This is exemplified by the siting of labor-intensive American-owned industries in Taiwan, South Korea, the Philippines, Mexico, and elsewhere.

An important trend in recent decades has been the expansion of multinational corporations. Giant economic organizations are nothing new in international trade. For example, they were deeply involved in British imperialism, and American corporations began to move into foreign countries after 1900, following the completion of the continental integration of the United States. But the true **multinational corporation,** with a multidivisional structure covering the entire economic process from research through production to marketing, is largely a development of the period since the Second World War (Hymer 1972).

Although Japan and several western European countries contain the headquarters of some multinationals, the majority of such companies are based in the United States. The annual sales of the largest multinationals, such as General Motors, IBM, and major oil companies, exceed the gross national product of a majority of countries in the world (Table 10-1). More than 200 multinationals have sales in excess of $1 billion, which suggests their potential effect on the world economy. By one recent estimate, multinationals organize between a quarter and a third of all world production and are particularly active in processing and marketing (Independent Commission on International Development Issues 1980, pp. 187–88).

The role of multinational corporations in affecting the lives of people in many parts of the world is typified by Unilever, the British-Dutch consumer-products company. When ranked by sales, it is the seventh largest corporation outside the United States, and it has 500 subsidiaries that employ 192,000 workers in 75 countries (Tagliabue 1983). The bulk of the sales comes from food products and detergents, but Unilever also makes chemicals and packaging materials and operates palm oil and tea plantations in Africa and India. Most of Unilever's sales are in the more developed countries, although the less developed countries are targeted for future sales.

Multinational corporations have a beneficial effect on the economies of the more developed nations

TABLE 10-1. Sales by Multinational Corporations, 1986

Company	Location of Headquarters	Sales (US$ billions)
General Motors	Detroit, USA	102.8
Exxon	New York, USA	69.9
Royal Dutch/ Shell Group	The Hague, Netherlands/ London, UK	64.8
Ford Motor	Dearborn, USA	62.7
I.B.M.	Armonk, USA	51.3
Mobil	New York, USA	44.9
British Petroleum	London, UK	39.9
General Electric	Fairfield, USA	35.2
American T. & T.	New York, USA	34.1
Texaco	White Plains, USA	31.6
IRI	Rome, Italy	31.6
Toyota Motor	Toyota City, Japan	31.6
Daimler-Benz	Stuttgart, W. Germany	30.2
E. I. du Pont	Wilmington, USA	27.1
Matsushita Electric	Osaka, Japan	26.5
Unilever	Rotterdam, Netherlands/ London, UK	25.1
Chevron	San Francisco, USA	24.4
Volkswagen	Wolfsburg, W. Germany	24.3
Hitachi	Tokyo, Japan	22.7
ENI	Rome, Italy	22.5
Chrysler	Highland Park, USA	22.5
Philips' Gloeilampenf'n	Eindhoven, Netherlands	22.5
Nestlé	Vevey, Switzerland	21.2
Philip Morris	New York, USA	20.7
Siemens	Munich, W. Germany	20.3
Nissan Motors	Yokohama, Japan	20.1
Fiat	Turin, Italy	19.7
Bayer	Leverkusen, W. Germany	18.8
BASF	Ludwigshafen, W. Germany	18.6
Amoco	Chicago, USA	18.3

Source: Fortune, August 3, 1987

by providing access to raw materials from all over the world. Several corporations have partial control of oil fields and other mineral deposits. They provide a wide variety of products for potential consumers and are eager to sell their manufactured goods in the largest and most permanent markets, namely, the wealthy countries. Multinational corporations, however, may have the effect of diminishing employment opportunities for some workers in rich nations be-

---

Internal economies of scale. The savings in costs per unit that are achieved by producing large quantities of an item.

Multinational corporation. A business organization with subsidiary companies operating in several countries.

cause they seek out areas of cheap labor for textiles, electronics, and other labor-intensive industries. The impact on a specific community is particularly significant when a factory that formerly employed a large proportion of the work force is relocated overseas in order to cut production costs.

Part of the global impact of industrial societies on other countries of the world occurs through foreign investments. Much of the manufacturing in less developed countries is generated and controlled by multinational corporations, either through subsidiaries or by contracting out to local enterprises. The investment of the multinationals in the less developed countries is geographically uneven. The oil-rich countries of Southwest Asia, Africa, Southeast Asia, and Latin America are a major priority. The bulk of the remainder of the investment goes to the intermediate class of countries in Latin America (Brazil, Argentina) and Southeast Asia (Malaysia). In the poorest countries of the world, multinationals invest mainly in plantations and mining (Independent Commission on International Development Issues 1980, pp. 174–87).

Foreign investment in the less developed countries tends to concentrate in urban areas, often ports or capital cities. In Nigeria, for example, during the 1960s, three-quarters of the capital invested in medium and large scale industry was provided by foreign investors, mainly British. As with most of the less developed countries, Nigerian capital was not available for major industrial development. Foreign firms employed 60,000 people, capitalizing on the abundance of cheap labor in the country. Most of these firms concentrated on the processing of raw materials for the local market, so they were largely located in the major cities of Lagos-Ibadan and Port Harcourt.

The effect of these patterns of investment is to widen spatial inequalities within the less developed countries, focusing industrial development in the cities, while the rural hinterlands remain tied to traditional economies (Coates, Johnston, and Knox 1977, pp. 127–29). These differences between the major urban centers and rural areas often result in considerable internal migration, along with the many economic, social, and political changes that accompany extensive residential and occupational movements (Chapters 4 and 11).

Although multinational corporations have contributed to the diffusion of manufacturing, the recent industrial growth in several less developed countries has been largely internally generated. Often national governments have promoted industrialization directly or through policies that encourage domestic manufacturers. The governments' objectives are to substitute domestically produced goods for imported ones, to encourage exports, to build up the machine-making industries, and to generate jobs. In Latin America, for example, Brazil, Argentina, and Mexico have made considerable progress toward developing domestic high-technology industries.

However, domestic manufacturers in the less developed countries face numerous difficulties in starting and maintaining new industries. Often the supply of capital, the number of skilled workers, and the size of the home market are limited. Unless national policies protect domestic producers through restriction on foreign products for a few years, industrial expansion is usually slow.

Not all attempts to produce manufactured products in less developed countries are failures. Some manufacturers, especially those in which labor costs are a major part of total costs, may be able to produce quality items at lower costs than factories located in industrialized countries. They may have considerable difficulty selling in foreign markets, however, because of protective trade policies. Since the 1960s, most of the more developed countries have increased trade barriers in the form of quotas against products such as shoes, garments, and carpets that are manufactured in less developed nations. Political pressure for such trade restrictions usually comes from domestic producers who cannot compete successfully against imports. In the United States, a 1978 survey of all consumer goods, except food and automobiles, found that imported Latin American and Asian products sold at 16 percent less than American products of the same quality. Demands for national restrictions on trade are mainly from plant workers, owners, and shareholders of companies that have experienced reduced sales because of foreign competition.

Consumers in more developed countries who can obtain imported products for lower prices than charged for domestic products usually do not favor trade restrictions. Furthermore, manufacturers of products that depend on exports, such as autos, robotics, and military equipment, seldom want trade barriers that make it difficult to maintain foreign markets. If the exports of the less developed countries are restricted, resulting in lower foreign earnings, the ability of those countries to import is curtailed. Clearly, patterns of manufacturing, industrial employment, trade, and monetary flows involve global interdependency.

AGRICULTURE

Although manufacturing is regarded as a distinguishing characteristic of industrial societies, this does not mean primary and tertiary activities are absent. The role of agriculture in industrialized societies is minor in terms of the employed workers (see Figure 9-7), but the farming sector continues to be an integral part of the economy. Furthermore, the characteristics of agriculture in more developed countries differ considerably from societies where the raising of crops and livestock is for basic subsistence (Chapter 9).

Agriculture in the United States

The primary goal of agriculture in the United States, as in other countries in the richest group of nations, is to market produce. Virtually all the products of farm enterprises are sold, and the farm owners, managers, operators, and workers generally do not consume the products that they grow. It is important to keep this fact in mind because it is one of the major contrasts with agriculture in the poorer countries, where many food crops are grown for family consumption or for local markets. In economies practicing traditional agriculture, some commodities may be produced for external markets, but these economies are not dependent solely on major national or international markets as are the agribusinesses of industrial nations. Operating as businesses, American farmers and agricultural corporations must minimize production costs and maximize market volume.

To minimize costs, American agriculturalists strive to utilize the optimal mix of production factors, namely, land, labor, and capital. In general, the strategy is to minimize labor inputs, partly because of the high cost of labor in the United States, and to spread equipment costs over large units of production. To reduce the amount of time and the cost of equipment expended per unit of output, most farmers specialize in crop or livestock production. Generally land in the United States has been relatively cheap and plentiful, which has led to large landholdings. During the nineteenth century, federal land was sold at a standard price of $1.25 an acre and, after the 1862 Homestead Act, was virtually free. Although the value of farmland has risen in the last century, it is still lower than in Japan and many European countries.

American farming typically requires large amounts of capital. Capital equipment includes machinery in the form of tractors, harvesters, irrigation systems, and automated feeding equipment. Expenditures are for fuel, fertilizers, pesticides, herbicides, improved seeds, and chemical additives in livestock feeds. In terms of value of all resources committed to agriculture, the share of labor fell sharply from about 40 percent in 1950 to less than 15 percent in 1980. The share of land remained fairly stable at about 20 percent over this period, but the share of capital equipment increased from 25 to 40 percent (Figure 10-5).

One effect of the growing input of capital equipment is that farmers with limited financial resources are hard-hit when interest rates for loans or prices for inputs increase faster than earnings. Many family farms have been forced out of operation (Figure 10-6). From 1950 to 1984, the number of farms in the United

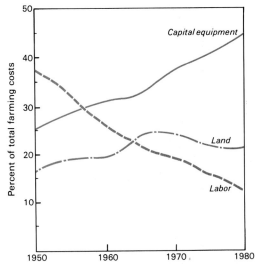

Figure 10-5. Relative Importance of Land, Labor, and Capital Equipment in American Agriculture. As a share of total costs for American farmers, labor has declined, whereas capital equipment has increased in recent decades.

States declined from 5.5 million to 2.3 million, and the average size of the remaining farms increased from 210 to 437 acres. The survivors tend to be the owners with large assets. Many farms are operated by corporate organizations whose interests reach across the spectrum of the economic system.

A major cost is energy. Although the capital-intensive nature of American farming has made it efficient in terms of productivity per worker, food production is inefficient in terms of energy inputs (Perelman 1977). This is not only because of the large amount of inanimate energy consumed for fuel and power but also because three-quarters of the grain is converted into livestock feed. Converting food grains into meats is a less efficient way of obtaining nutritional energy than consuming grains directly. Furthermore, the agricultural system in the United States involves transporting food items long distances from areas of specialized production to marketplaces. Movement requires energy (fuel). Processing and packaging for preservation during shipment and storage require more energy. It is estimated that the total energy used to produce, process, and transport a 1-lb can of sweet corn is 4100 calories. Since the corn contains only 375 calories, the ratio of input of energy to output of food energy is almost 11 to 1. For beef, the system requires an input-output ratio of 77 to 1. In contrast, traditional labor-intensive Chinese wet rice agriculture produces more than 50 calories in the form of food for every calorie of human energy put into farming—an input-output ratio of only 1/50 to 1 (Perelman 1977, p. 12).

When the costs of food production are calculated, usually only the direct monetary outlays are included. Not taken into account are the indirect costs of soil

Figure 10-6. A Farm Sale in the United States, 1984. From 1920 to 1988, the farm population as a percentage of total population declined from 30.2 to 2.2. Photo courtesy of Martha E. Stoddard.

erosion, water pollution, and other modifications of the physical environment that may affect future generations detrimentally. In 1981, the Department of Agriculture reported that the inherent productivity of 34 percent of the U.S. cropland was declining because of the excessive loss of topsoil. However, for an agricultural enterprise attempting to generate profits in the short run or for a small farmer trying to stay on the land, the long-term effects of current farming practices are generally not a top priority.

American farmers and agricultural corporations must be able to sell their products at a price sufficient to cover their direct costs. Often this is difficult. The domestic market, even with its extensive advertising designed to sell more food, is too small to absorb all the huge farm production. Although most persons have adequate diets within the United States, many others are unable to pay for sufficient food. Therefore, American agriculture is partly dependent on exporting to foreign buyers, mostly the richer countries such as Japan, the Soviet Union, and several countries in Europe. Only about one-third of U.S. agricultural exports are purchased by countries in Africa, Latin America, and Asia (excluding Japan), which may have many hungry people but are generally poorer nations.

Like other forms of international interdependency, this reliance on overseas buyers makes agricultural prices vulnerable to fluctuations and uncertainties. Boycotts and direct governmental intervention may prevent exports. The Common Market, Canada, Australia, and similar competing producers may undersell American commodities or otherwise limit prospective world markets. Even the increased domestic production by some less developed countries (such as occurred in India in the late 1970s) may reduce potential markets.

In summary, American agriculture is a major contributor to the world's abundant supply of food. This large output, however, is not necessarily regarded as a favorable outcome by farmers who often are unable to sell their products.

Patterns of Agricultural Production

The patterns of commercial agriculture in the more developed countries tend to differ greatly from those in agrarian societies. In the latter, there is generally a diversity of crops and livestock, especially when the production is consumed by the growers and local buyers (Chapter 9). Because numerous crops are grown within a small area, it is rare that a single crop dominates a region. The exceptions usually indicate a commodity being grown for sale in world markets (coffee in Brazil, for example).

In industrial economies, where agricultural products are grown for sale in distant markets, farmers often produce only a single crop or livestock type (Figure 10-7). When many farms located in close proximity all produce the same crop or animal, the result is an extensive region of agricultural specializa-

Figure 10-7. Milo (Sorghum) Field. Monoculture is a common characteristic of contemporary agriculture in the United States. Photo courtesy of Charles A. Francis.

tion (Figure 10-8). The specific crops and livestock types produced in these regions depend largely on market and transportation conditions. This is not to say that soils, climate, and topography do not affect the distribution of crops, but their influence must be assessed within an economic context.

The importance of transportation on crop patterns in a market economy was expressed more than a century ago by Heinrich von Thünen (1826), an estate owner who farmed in what is now East Germany. Von Thünen speculated about what would be the likely arrangement of land use around a city that was the sole market for agricultural products. To concentrate on the effects of transportation, he considered a hypothetical city that was located at the center of an

isolated plain of uniform characteristics. He assumed an isolated area for the purpose of excluding the influence of imports from adjacent regions, and he assumed the plain to be uniform in soil fertility, climatic conditions, and similar environmental factors that affect land use.

Von Thünen concluded that there would be a decreasing intensity of land use away from the city (Figure 10-9). A series of concentric zones would reflect this pattern of distance decay in land uses. Horticulture and dairying would dominate in the first zone around the city. Land kept in continuous cultivation by crop rotations, but requiring less intensity than horticulture and dairying, would be found in the third zone from the city. The length of fallow periods

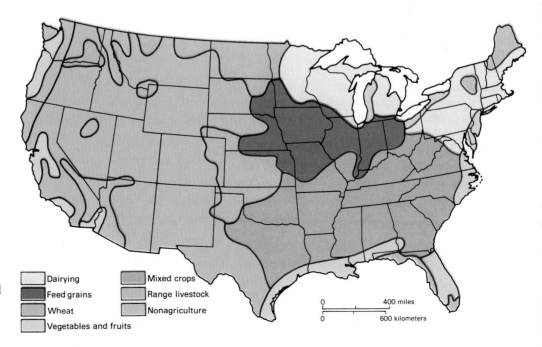

Figure 10-8. Crop and Livestock Regions of the United States. Commercial agriculture tends to create regions having crop and livestock specializations.

Dairying
Feed grains
Wheat
Vegetables and fruits
Mixed crops
Range livestock
Nonagriculture

0   400 miles
0   600 kilometers

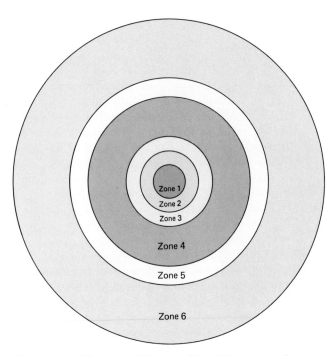

Figure 10-9. Theoretical Zones of Land Use Around a Market Town. According to von Thünen, the variations of land use around a central market form concentric zones, grading outward from most to least intensive. See the text for an explanation of the zones.

would increase with distance from the city (for zones 4 and 5) until finally cultivation would not be undertaken. Beyond the zones of cultivation, grazing would occur (in zone 6) because it is a form of land use with low labor inputs.

One aspect of von Thünen's ideas may suprise the contemporary reader. In the second zone, that is, close to the city, just beyond the horticulture and dairy zone, von Thünen postulated a woodland that would supply building materials and firewood. In the current age of varied construction materials and heavy reliance on fossil fuels, his reference to the woodland may appear strange. Yet, in a pre-industrial society where wood was valuable and difficult to transport, growing trees constituted a high-value use of the land.

Von Thünen adapted his scheme for varying levels of soil fertility and agricultural suitability. In addition, he relaxed the initial assumption that considered only one mode of transportation by examining the effects of varying transport costs. For each of these modifications, von Thünen indicated land use patterns that would differ from the original arrangement of concentric zones.

Von Thünen demonstrated the impact of transportation costs on the patterns of commercial agriculture at a time when the rate of distance decay was very rapid (Figure 10-10). Such conditions still exist in areas having limited transportation facilities and high fuel prices (Figure 10-11). In areas where transporta-

tion costs are relatively low, however, the relationship between crop regions and distance from markets is less obvious.

As the movement of goods becomes easier, the choice of places to sell agricultural commodities increases. Lettuce growers, as an example, may sell their produce to large food companies, which haul the lettuce in bulk quantities to local, national, and international destinations (Figure 10-12). Therefore, U.S. lettuce production is spatially concentrated in Southern California where economic and environmental conditions are favorable. This pattern contrasts with China, for example, where long-distance transportation is more costly. In China, lettuce is grown in many places close to the markets, especially in areas surrounding large cities.

The increased possibility of selling agricultural products in distant places, including foreign markets, has made political policies an important factor in the distribution of crops and livestock at the world scale. Most commercial products are highly affected by prices established in the global market. Moreover, prices are directly related to national policies involving agricultural subsidies for domestic producers and import quotas for foreign producers. The amount of sugar grown in Lousiana, wheat harvested in France, chickens raised in West Germany, and rice produced in Japan are all directly affected by government policies.

For example, rice continues to be grown on the alluvial plains of Japan as it has for centuries. In spite of the extremely high density of population in relation to arable land, Japan is self-sufficient in this basic food grain. In fact, the country produces a surplus of rice. The total production cost of rice in Japan (in 1988),

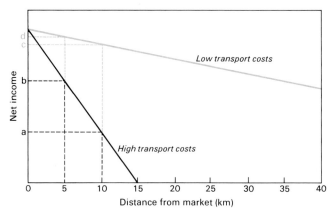

Figure 10-10. A Comparison of Two Rates of Distance Decay Based on Transport Costs. When the rate of hauling goods is high, places 10 km away from the market pay such a large transport bill that their profits (at a) are much less than those farmers who live 5 km from the market (with earnings of b). When the rate of hauling is low, the earnings of sellers located 10 km (c) are not much lower than those located at 5 km from the market (d).

Figure 10-11. Farmers Delivering Milk to the City of Chandigarh, India. As consistent with the von Thünen model, the zone from which farmers make daily deliveries of fresh milk is within a few miles of Chandigarh. Photo courtesy of Sally Stoddard.

however, was eight times that of the world price. If the Japanese national policies were to obtain rice from the cheapest source, the country would buy from Thailand and other rice exporters; and most rice would disappear from the Japanese countryside. Instead, Japan supports rice farmers with incentives and protection against imported grain and thereby ensures that the country will continue to be self-sufficient in this basic food crop.

Government price supports may push up prices within a country and encourage commodity buyers to purchase from abroad. This occurs in the United States, for instance, where large surpluses of wheat and rice are produced. As the grain stocks accumulate, U.S. food companies buy lower-priced wheat and rice from foreign sources. Similarly orange juice can be bought from Brazil at one-third its cost of production in Florida, and processed tomatoes are available from Mexico at a fourth of their cost in Ohio. Such comparative costs of agricultural products have recently led to the situation where more food is imported into the United States than is exported.

The internationalization of agriculture affects farmers in virtually all countries, whether industrialized or agrarian. Farmers in the more developed countries often suffer financial hardships when companies begin to produce the same commodities at a cheaper price in less developed lands. At the same time, small landholders and farm workers in less developed countries may suffer when scarce land is used by large landowners and companies to grow crops and livestock for sale in foreign markets.

Figure 10-12. Long-Distance Hauling. A large share of the food purchased in American grocery stores and supermarkets is transported long distances. Photo courtesy of Sally Stoddard.

SERVICES

In some respects, the term "industrial societies" may be misleading because the role of tertiary activities has become dominant. At least, when measured by percentage of working population, the service sector exceeds manufacturing activities in the more developed countries (see Table 9-1). In the United States, the tertiary sector employs three-fourths of the workers and generates over 70 percent of the GNP. In fact, some scholars refer to such an economy as **post-industrial.**

The tertiary sector generates wealth through a wide variety of activities. It includes the buying and selling (retailing) of consumer goods, wholesale trading, transporting, repairing, banking, accounting, advertising, consulting, governing, doctoring, teaching, preaching, feeding, guarding, entertaining, and a multitude of other services.

Because of the wide diversity of occupations involved with services, a map showing the percentage of workers in tertiary activities tends to obscure economic differences (Figure 10-13). According to these 1980 data, the percentage of service workers exceeds 50 in many countries classified as more developed (such as Canada, Australia, and Sweden), but the percentage is also above 50 in a few less developed countries (for example, Chile and Jordan). Included in an intermediate group of countries, as far as service employment is concerned, are Eastern Europe and the Soviet Union, which have centrally planned economies that de-emphasize consumerism.

There are significant differences, however, between the more developed and less developed countries in the types and characteristics of services available. Some of these contrasts are revealed by considering retailing, labor services, and information services as distinct types of tertiary activities.

Retailing

Selling goods in rich countries frequently occurs in large stores that are part of a chain owned by a corporation. Retailing is done in bulk: supplies are obtained from manufacturing plants, stored in warehouses, transported to outlets, and advertised throughout the marketing region. Goods are placed on display, selections are made directly by the customers, and credit is made available. The goal is to sell a large volume of goods in order to keep the costs of store maintenance, insurance, advertising, and labor low per item sold.

The conditions for selling goods in less developed countries are generally different from those in rich countries. Although supermarkets are increasingly common in major cities of less developed nations, small enterprises engaged in "penny capitalism" are more typical (Figure 10-14). Only small amounts of capital are required to set up a stall in a marketplace or to hawk goods throughout a city. Credit is often available from wholesalers or large traders, generally in the form of merchandise. Inventories are low because sales are made daily in small quantities. More-

Percent of workers in services

- 0-30
- 31-49
- 50 and above
- No data

Figure 10-13. Percentage of Population in Services. The world distribution of service (tertiary) activities differs from the distribution of primary and secondary activities (see Figures 9-7 and 10-4).

Figure 10-14. A Small Shop Selling Convenience Goods. Small shops, owned and operated by families, are a common feature in the cities of many less developed countries. Photo courtesy of Sally Stoddard.

Figure 10-15. A Periodic Market in India. Periodic markets in different regions of the world vary in size, frequency, type of setting, goods, and background of buyers and sellers. Photo courtesy of Sally Stoddard.

over, lack of storage facilities dictates a rapid turnover in perishables such as foodstuffs.

Selling may traditionally be done by one gender or cultural group. In many African societies, sellers are women. Trading may be dominated by ethnic groups, such as Syrians and Lebanese in West Africa, Chinese in Southeast Asia, and Indians in parts of the Caribbean. Profit margins are frequently high, with large markups. Hawkers, in particular, may receive high profits per unit sold (often over 30 percent according to Milton Santos 1979), but because sales are inconsistent, total profits may be small. Wages for workers are seldom paid because most of the trading enterprises are family-run. In some rural places, trad-

ing occurs only periodically because of a low level of demand (Figure 10-15). Markets may be held no more than once a week, or sometimes just once a month.

Irrespective of the retail setting, the products sold may reflect international links. In fact, numerous products sold in market-oriented industrialized countries are manufactured abroad. Clothes from Hong Kong, toys from China, and electronic goods from Japan are now a part of American lifestyles. Availability, price, and brand choice of products are all highly

---

Post-industrial economy. An economy that has shifted its productive emphasis from manufacturing to service activities.

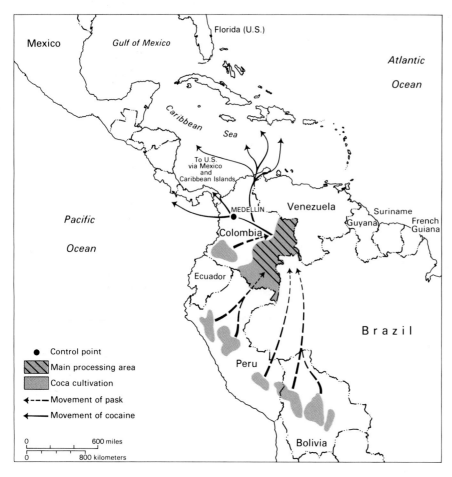

Figure 10-16. Source Areas of Cocaine in South America. Cocaine moves from the fields in Bolivia, Peru, and Colombia through the control point at Medellin to the streets of the United States.

influenced by the existence of international linkages.

Even in less developed countries, foreign trade may have far-reaching effects. For example, the penetration of soft drinks, jeans, and other items of Western culture into previously isolated societies may prompt significant economic and social changes (Chapter 5). Furthermore, if specific items collected or produced in agrarian countries become popular in foreign markets, the resulting inflow of new wealth to a few individuals may alter the traditional structure of society.

The economic demand for illicit drugs in the rich countries is one illustration of an international chain of buying and selling having far-reaching effects. The patterns of production, movement, and consumption of drugs are necessarily different from those of legal commodities like coffee and tea. Whereas legal commodities are often grown in environmentally suitable areas that have easy access to transportation lines and markets, illegal narcotics are produced in physically remote areas. For example, virtually all of the estimated 60 metric tons of cocaine that reach the U.S. market each year are derived from coca leaves grown on the isolated eastern slopes of the Andes in Bolivia, Peru, and Colombia (Figure 10-16). Much of the growing area lies outside the scope of effective government control.

For the local farmers, the coca plant is the best option for a cash crop. The plant is hardy, has a life span of 30 years, and yields three harvests a year. In regions where $50 a month is a good wage, one harvest of 500 kilograms of coca leaves can yield $1000 for the farmer (Hudson 1985).

The crop is converted into a small-volume, high-value product that can be easily transported to the market. Coca leaves grown in Peru and Bolivia are reduced to paste in makeshift "factories" near the production areas. After processing, 500 kilograms of leaves make about 2.5 kilograms of paste, with the value of about $4000. The paste is then moved to isolated factories in eastern Colombia where it is refined to form 1 kilogram of cocaine, worth at least $20,000.

The transportation networks of illegal drugs are circuitous, rather than direct, because of the need of concealment. Furthermore, the specific routes of trade change frequently in response to the efforts of law officers to control the movement of drugs. Latin American cocaine is shipped by air, land, and sea through points in Central America and the Caribbean Islands to the United States, which buys more than three-quarters of the world's total production. The major areas of entry are Florida, the Gulf Coast, and the border with Mexico.

On the streets of the United States, one kilogram of pure cocaine is diluted with other products, which usually makes its final market value as high as $1,000,000. Because cocaine is addictive, a market is virtually assured. If law enforcement is successful in limiting the amount of cocaine that reaches customers, the street price rises and encourages additional entrepreneurs to become involved.

The drug trade has effects all along the route from production to consumption areas. For example, the economic well-being of farmers in areas of production is greatly affected by the extent that drug control officers are able to destroy their crops. Local and national officials are subject to bribes, harassment, and threats if they attempt to curtail illegal drug activities. The high value of drug products in the market areas also has considerable influence on individual hustlers, street gangs, crime organizations, and the "laundered" investments by crime syndicates.

Labor Services

Providing labor services often resembles working in the primary and secondary sectors. Many farm workers, miners, and factory laborers are paid mainly for the physical tasks they perform. Wages for such workers vary internationally according to the wealth of the nation in which they work, but generally rates tend to be lower than for other kinds of work. The same is true for those services in which the principal input by the worker is a physical task that does not require much skill. Such tasks are the cleaning of homes, offices, stores, hotel rooms, and streets, the caring for institutionalized patients, the driving of taxis, buses, and delivery trucks, and the preparing and serving of food in restaurants, fast-food outlets, and institutions (Figure 10-17).

Labor services vary greatly in the levels of skill required by workers. Some services can be performed satisfactorily by a person after a few hours of instruction; others may be practiced only after extensive training. Nevertheless, this broad category of labor services is the economic sector that continues to employ a large share of new workers in most industrialized countries. In the United States, for example, the largest categories of new jobs in 1990 are expected to be secretaries, medical aides, and janitors (Table 10-2).

Usually labor services are performed where the consumers of the service are located. In general, the

Figure 10-17. Working in the Service Sector. A large share of employment opportunities in the United States is in services that require very little specialized training. Photo courtesy of Sally Stoddard.

TABLE 10-2. New Jobs Expected in the United States, 1990

Occupation	Number of New Jobs
Secretary	700,000
Nurse's aide or orderly	508,000
Janitor	501,000
Salesclerk	479,000
Cashier	452,000
Nurse	437,000
Truckdriver	415,000
Food service worker	400,000
General office clerk	377,000
Waiter/waitress	360,000
Stock clerk	262,000
Elementary school teacher	251,000
Kitchen helper	231,000
Accountant or auditor	221,000
Trades' helper	212,000
Automotive mechanic	206,000
Worker supervisor	206,000

Source: "The Myth of High-Tech Jobs," *Harper's*, 269, no. 1611, August, 1984, p. 24.

major urban areas have the largest number of service employees, as well as the greatest variety of labor services. Thus, a detailed map of population usually also displays the distribution of labor-intensive services.

A partial exception to the rule that services tend to congregate in urban centers are those associated with tourist destinations. When the attraction is a natural site occurring far from a city, the consumers (the tourists) must travel to the site (Figure 10-18). In these cases, small centers may generate a major source of their income as they lodge, feed, and entertain tourists. The development of ski resorts in the White Mountains of New Hampshire, for example, has led to increased population, new affluence, and hence a stimulated demand for services.

In a broad sense, tourism encompasses all travelers to another place, whether they are convention-goers, sports fans, pilgrims, or vacationers. Many tourist attractions tend to occur in large cities, so in many cases the patterns of tourist services are not distinct from services in general.

Figure 10-18. Niagara Falls, a Popular Tourist Site. An attractive tourist site may provide the economic base for many service jobs in a nearby community. Photo courtesy of Sally Stoddard.

Some countries, such as Spain and Nepal, derive a sizable share of their national income from tourist spending. Irrespective of whether tourists are attracted to isolated natural and archaeological features, museums and festivals in metropolitan centers, or tours that combine many places, the cumulative effect is that a high percentage of workers at tourist destinations are engaged in service activities.

Information Services

Those economic activities that produce value from knowledge or communication are sometimes called **quaternary activities.** Scholars may regard them as a type of tertiary activity (as in this text) or as a fourth economic class (i.e., in addition to the primary, secondary, and tertiary classes). In any case, services involving the collection, organization, and communication of information possess distinguishing functions and characteristics.

Many quaternary activities, such as teaching, personal counseling, brokering, advertising, and managing, have been around a long time. Nevertheless, there has been a rapid growth in this sector in most industrialized nations in the last few decades. In the United States, for example, information services have grown rapidly in the last thirty years (Table 10-3).

Part of the quaternary growth is associated with

Figure 10-19. Research Triangle Park, North Carolina. This area has grown rapidly in recent years, largely because of its proximity to universities and research laboratories that provide producers' services. Photo courtesy of Sally Stoddard.

the increase in size and complexity of large corporations, which require more planning and coordination to handle the volume of information. Some of the growth arises from the internationalization of businesses and the need to transmit information globally.

In some cases, the apparent growth reflects a shift in the affiliation of a service worker. In the past, if a small manufacturing business directly employed accountants, attorneys, and marketing experts, they were counted as part of the working population engaged in a secondary activity. Now the same business may find it cheaper to buy services from specialists. It can purchase computer and financial services from an accounting firm, legal expertise from another firm, and marketing and advertising recommendations from yet a third firm.

Like services in general, information services are attracted to urban areas where their clients are located. Agglomerations of quaternary services can, in turn, be an attractive force for other industries. Firms that provide services for other businesses (and therefore are called **producers' services**) are the driving force behind much economic growth today. In the race among corporations for new products and markets, techniques of effective management are critical. Thus, many industries are attracted to urban centers with universities, research laboratories, and service firms that can deliver high quality producers' services (Figure 10-19).

TABLE 10-3. Growth Rates of Workers in the United States by Sectors, 1960–1984

Sector	Compound Annual Growth Rate, 1960–1984 (%)
Agriculture, Forestry, Fisheries	2.8
Manufacturing	3.5
Construction	0.7
Mining	2.1
Services	4.0
Communication/Information	7.1
Finance, Insurance, Real Estate	4.0
Public Utilities	3.9
Transportation	2.1
Wholesale and Retail	3.9
Other Services	4.1

Source: U.S. Commerce Department, 1985.

Quaternary activities. Economic activities that produce value by performing communication and information services; sometimes included within the general category of tertiary activities.

Producers' services. Services that are provided for other businesses rather than directly for consumers.

PROSPECTS

In the last three decades, spatial patterns of economic activities have changed markedly. As industrialization has diffused, some basic forms of manufacturing have emerged in countries which previously had little industry. Textile production, shoe-making, and the assembly of electronic equipment are now conducted in several less developed countries. The larger countries, such as India and China, are among the top twenty countries of the world in terms of total manufactured products. Steel produced in Brazil competes in the world export markets while, significantly, the steel industry has declined in North America and Western Europe. New producers of ships have emerged in countries like Poland and South Korea to take the place of traditional builders in the United States, Britain, Japan, and Sweden. The global distribution of heavy manufacturing and assembly industries appears to be in a phase of major change.

The patterns of several types of service industries are also changing. Tourism has become more widespread than previously as the affluent inhabitants of rich countries seek new vacation places in what they regard as exotic environments. Likewise, although industries providing financial services have generally remained concentrated in the more developed countries, a few places—Panama, Bahamas, Cayman Islands, Singapore, and Hong Kong—have become international banking centers (and tax havens).

These changing patterns raise questions about future distributions. Will the current economic differences between the nations of the world be reduced? (See additional comments on this question in the Point-Counterpoint at the end of this chapter.) Will international trade and business linkages decrease the role of domestic economies? Some believe that the electronic linkage of the global economy "has created a world no longer effectively composed of individual national economic entities" (Blumenthal 1988, p. 545).

Another factor associated with economic trends concerns the general expansion of production throughout the world. Whether the earth's environmental systems will be able to absorb the impact of some of these changes, especially the spread of industrial activity, remains to be seen (see Chapter 12).

BIBLIOGRAPHY

Blaut, J. M., "The Theory of Development," *Antipode* 5, no. 2 (May 1973), 22–26.

Blumenthal, Michael W., "The World Economy and Technological Change," *Foreign Affairs*, 66, no. 3 (1988), 529–50.

Brewer, Michael, "The Changing U.S. Farmland Scene," *Population Bulletin*, 36, no. 5 (December 1981).

Brookfield, Harold, *Interdependent Development*. London: Methuen, 1975.

Chisholm, Michael, *Modern World Development*. New York: Barnes & Noble, 1982.

Coates, B. E., R. J. Johnston, and P. L. Knox, *Geography and Inequality*. London: Oxford University Press, 1977.

Cole, J. P., *The Development Gap: A Spatial Analysis of World Poverty and Inequality*. New York; John Wiley & Sons, 1981.

"The Fortune 500," *Fortune*, August 3, 1987.

House, John W., *United States Public Policy: A Geographical View*. Oxford, England: Clarendon Press, 1983.

Hudson, Tim, "A Geography of Cocaine," *Focus*, 35, no. 1 (January 1985), 22–29.

Hymer, Stephen, "The Multinational Corporation and the Law of Uneven Development," in Jagdish N. Bhagwati, ed., *Economics and World Order*, pp. 113–40. London: Macmillan, 1972.

Independent Commission on International Development Issues, *North-South: A Programme for Survival*. London: Pan Books, 1980.

Jumper, Sidney R., Thomas L. Bell, and Bruce A. Ralston, *Economic Growth and Disparities: A World View*. Englewood Cliffs, N.J.: Prentice-Hall, 1980.

Kahn, Herman, *World Economic Development: 1979 and Beyond*. Boulder, Colo.: Westview Press, 1979.

Kidron, Michael, and Ronald Segal. *The New State of the World Atlas*. New York: Simon & Schuster, 1984.

Myrdal, Gunnar, *Rich Lands and Poor: The Road to World Prosperity*. New York, Harper & Row, Pub., 1958.

Perelman, Michael, *Farming for Profit in a Hungry World*. Montclair, N.J.: Allanheld, Osmun, 1977.

Santos, Milton, *The Shared Space*. London and New York: Methuen, 1979.

Smith, Everett G., Jr., "America's Richest Farms and Ranches," *Annals of the Association of American Geographers*, 70, no. 4 (December 1980), 528–41.

Tagliabue, John, "Unilever: Big, Plodding, Safe," *New York Times*, January 4, 1983.

Taylor, Michael, "Industrial Geography," *Progress in Geography*, 8, no. 2 (1984), 263–74.

United Nations Department of Economic and Social Affairs, *Multinational Corporations in World Development*. New York: Praeger, 1974.

von Thünen, J. H., *Der Isolierte Staat in Beziehung auf Landwirtschaft und Nationalökonomie*, 1826. Trans. by Carla M. Wartenberg, *von Thünen's Isolated State: An English Version of "Der Isolierte Staat."* New York: Pergamon Press, 1966.

Wallerstein, Immanuel, *The Capitalist World-Economy*. Cambridge, England: Cambridge University Press, 1977.

Narrowing the Widening Gap

The rich get richer and the poor get poorer, according to an adage. The gap, in terms of GNP per capita, is widening between the economically more developed countries and the less developed nations. This is the conventional view, and for decades after World War II, it appeared to be true.

In a famous book, *Rich Lands and Poor* (1958), Gunnar Myrdal pointed out that all the economic advantages seemed to lie with the rich and industrialized countries. Poorer countries, lacking capital, infrastructure, and skills, were ill-equipped to compete. Some less developed countries had prospered in World War II; but after the end of the Korean War in 1953, the international terms of trade moved against countries that produced raw materials in favor of those that manufactured goods. The prices for minerals and agricultural commodities remained static, or fell, while the cost of industrial products rose. Poor countries found that their income from iron ore, oil, or bananas did not rise, but they paid more for imported machinery and trucks. The rich definitely were getting richer.

In the 1970s, new trends emerged.

The economies of North America and Western Europe "overheated." Inflation accelerated, and the demand for raw materials and oil became so strong that it strained the world supply. Excess demand pushed up prices. The price of oil, for example, went from $3 a barrel to $30 between 1973 and 1979. As a result, a group of oil-rich countries emerged (such as Saudi Arabia; see Figure 9-8).

Other forces improved the prospects of countries attempting to industrialize. In the 1970s, inflation pushed up production costs in the more developed countries and created a situation in which it was possible for some less developed countries to start manufacturing. The products of these less developed countries then penetrated world export markets. Some of these newly industrialized countries in Asia, such as Hong Kong, Singapore, Taiwan, and South Korea, had become so successful that they were no longer granted a favored tariff status after 1989 by the United States.

A group of Latin American countries, including Argentina, Brazil, and Mexico, also increased the pace of their industrialization in the 1970s and 1980s. Brazil entered world export markets with steel, planes, and vehicles. The northern borderland of Mexico became a manufacturing zone that exported heavily into U.S. markets. Unfortunately, much of the expansion had been financed with badly conceived loans that were difficult to repay when world commodity prices slumped in the late 1980s. Nevertheless, the whole base of Latin American manufacturing has been broadened in recent years.

Furthermore, increased industrial production by a particular country does not automatically mean higher income for everyone. In terms of total production, both of the world's population giants, China and India, have joined the ranks of the top 20 industrial countries of the world. Yet, the value of national production per capita remains low in both countries.

Whether the gap is widening or not between rich and poor countries depends on the statistics and trends one emphasizes. What is certain is that the old economic order in which a few rich industrialized countries completely dominated the economies of less developed countries is changing. What do you see as the direction of change? Is the general trend of the gap between rich and poor widening or narrowing?

11 URBAN PLACES

"Cities are places of excitement and opportunity; they are where the economic and social action is!" "Cities are congested, polluted, and dangerous; they are artificial environments where people live divorced from the beauties of the nature." These two views express the contradictory opinions that people have about urban places and activities associated with them.

Irrespective of one's perception of cities, their importance to human geography cannot be denied. More than 2 billion people (i.e., over 40 percent of the world's total population) live in cities now, and the size of the urban population is increasing rapidly. Cities are also the hubs of industrial and service activities, as described in Chapters 9 and 10. Furthermore, as discussed in previous chapters, cities tend to be associated with distinctive social characteristics, such as lower birth rates and higher literacy rates than rural places.

The geography of cities is examined here at two scales. At one scale, cities can be regarded as points in a network of settlements. From this perspective, which is the emphasis in the first half of the chapter, cities are discussed in terms of their locations and connections with other cities and the rural areas which surround them. At another scale, cities can be studied as geographic areas within which spatial variations occur. From this perspective, which is the focus of the second half of the chapter, the internal structure and distributional patterns are the most important factors.

URBAN CENTERS

Pre-Industrial Cities

Even though the percentage of people living in urban areas was small prior to the Industrial Revolution, cities are as old as civilizations. In fact, civilizations and cities began at the same time, as indicated by the common Latin root (*civitas*) for the terms *civilization* and *city*. Early hunter-gatherers and shifting cultivators did not agglomerate in urban places, but with the development of sedentary agriculture and stratified societies, cities began to emerge. In stratified societies, cities functioned as points from which the elite groups exerted control over the predominantly agricultural population.

Ancient cities, such as the Sumerian cities of Mesopotamia, developed in agricultural societies that produced a surplus of food, so these cities often functioned partly as places for the storage of grains. These food supplies were collected and controlled by the ruling elite of kings and religious leaders. Accumulations of food in granaries, along with the wealth in temples and palaces, tempted raiders from elsewhere. Thus, cities had to function also as centers of defense, which meant they were walled and protected by a warrior class. These administrative, defensive, and religious functions of the cities further stratified the initial class inequities of the agricultural society (see Chapter 2).

The central portions of early cities were dominated by governmental and religious buildings, with the latter often being the most imposing. The privileged elite resided near the city center in the most accessible zone and close to the institutions of social control. The more numerous lower classes lived away from the city core and were often segregated into occupational groups in distinct patterns. Inhabitants of the very lowest class and those pursuing subordinate trades, such as tanning, lived outside the city walls.

In spite of social segregation by class and occupation, land uses were mixed within the city. Markets lay close to temples, and shops occupied the street level of buildings that otherwise served as residences. As urban populations grew in numbers but remained

Figure 11-1. Richmond Castle, England. Like many medieval towns, Richmond commanded a valley routeway and stood at a crossing point on a river. The marketplace of the town lay in the shadow of a Norman castle. Photo courtesy of Olwyn M. Blouet.

confined within the city walls, the majority of people lived in conditions where wastes accumulated, diseases spread rapidly, and fires threatened.

In many societies, the city was a place where traders and craft workers operated. Persons who engaged in business, however, occupied a low social status. Power and prestige were based on the ownership of land. As in any agriculturally based society, the control of this basic resource sustained the elite in their position.

The role that cities played in early societies affected their locations. They were often located at defensive sites, as well as at places where adequate water was available. The most important cities were almost always on navigable waterways. Also, because cities were the centers of religious and political administration of an agrarian population, they usually were situated in a central position relative to the agricultural area.

Later, when trade with other regions became more important, cities that were situated along routes traveled by merchants and traders grew more rapidly than the more isolated centers (Figure 11-1). The rise of Baghdad (in present-day Iraq) in the eighth century illustrates the importance of interaction with other areas. Its location on the Tigris River provided water transportation both north and south. To the north were the products of Syria and the Black Sea vicinity; to the south were the Persian Gulf and sea trade with Asia. Baghdad was also on many east-west caravan routes.

By the fourteenth century, Venice, located on the east coast of Italy, was a major trade center. Its commercial shipping network dominated the eastern Mediterranean Sea and linked the land routes of Southwest Asia to the markets of Europe. Although the low-lying marshy islands were not an ideal site for a city, Venice thrived because of its location relative to distant places with which it traded. In other words, it was not the local site but the general geographic situation that sustained Venice's growth.

Cities as Industrial Centers

Although cities were a part of past civilizations, it was rare for more than 10 percent of any country's population to live in urban places. Except for minor city-states, it was not until after the Industrial Revolution that a major country had an **urban majority,** that is, more than 50 percent of its population living in a city. For example, England did not achieve an urban majority until 1851, and it was 1920 before more than half of the population of the United States lived in cities. Even today, the percentage of urban population in a country is an indication of its degree of industrialization (see Table 9-1).

The major growth in cities came with industrialization, when nonagricultural production, especially manufacturing, occurred at a few advantageous sites (Chapters 9 and 10). Cities grew rapidly at places that possessed earth resources, especially coal. In the early stages of industrialization, when land transportation was still difficult and costly, many factories were situated close to their source of energy, which was usually coal. Thus many of the English cities that grew rapidly in the nineteenth century were located on coal fields (Figures 2-17 and 2-19).

For the assembling of raw materials and the marketing of finished products, manufacturing requires connections with other places. Transportation

Figure 11-2. Manchester, England, in 1840. The Industrial Revolution produced cities that expanded into previously rural landscapes. Photo courtesy of Olwyn M. Blouet.

nodes, therefore, were also important manufacturing centers. Cities like London that were already trade centers continued to grow as factories, warehouses, and the other facilities associated with industrialization became increasingly important to the economy.

Most early industries were labor-intensive, so they attracted migrants from rural areas. Even though the living conditions of factory workers were poor in industrial cities of the eighteenth and nineteenth centuries, many people who were experiencing economic hardship in rural regions flocked to the cities. Through this process of rural-urban migration, urbanization transformed the economic, demographic, and social characteristics of life in newly industrialized cities of Western Europe and North America (Figure 11-2).

The Development of Major Cities in the United States

The importance of transportation routes and accessible locations is demonstrated well by the development of major cities in the United States. Some cities, such as Youngstown and Rochester, grew because they were close to coal or falling water (Figure 11-3). However, most major cities of the United States developed as trade centers at places accessible to long-distance commerce.

The first urban centers in North America, which were at coastal locations, functioned largely as collecting and exporting points for staples, such as timber and furs, which were sent to Europe. These centers were also the destination for goods imported from Europe. Later, as settlers moved inland, other cities developed, usually within the **hinterland** of one of the coastal cities.

James Vance (1970) argued that it was long-distance trade that led to the emergence of the major cities of the United States. He generalized the historical evolution of the urban system in a **mercantile model,** a modification of which is the basis for the four phases presented here.

1. *The Colonial Era (Prior to 1776).* During the seventeenth century, the English, French, and Dutch established colonies in North America. These colonies, such as Virginia, were often regarded as "investments in trade" and formed part of the mercantilist systems of European governments. Although people in the colonies were primarily concerned with self-sufficiency, they did export high-value resources such as tobacco, lumber, furs, and fish (Figure 11-4). This trans-Atlantic trading contributed to the growth of towns that were ports, whether located on the seacoast or on inland waterways.

None of the early urban places in the American colonies was large. By 1700, Boston had 6700 inhabitants. New York and Philadelphia had populations of

---

Urban majority. A situation in which more than 50 percent of the population of a country or region lives in cities.
Hinterland. A trade area, especially the region situated inland from a seaport.

Mercantile model. An explanation for the location of cities in North America in terms of long-range trade and wholesaling functions.

Figure 11-3. Rochester, New York, on the Genesee River. In the nineteenth century, the city used the waterfall on the Genesee River as a source of power for grain mills and other factories. Photo courtesy of Olwyn M. Blouet.

Figure 11-4. Fisherman's Wharf, Boston. Ports through which high-value resources were exported grew rapidly during the Colonial period and the nineteenth century. Photo courtesy of National Archives, Washington, D.C.

about 5000 each, and Charles Town (Charleston) had 2000 inhabitants. The early French towns, located on the St. Lawrence River, were even smaller.

2. *Independence and Expansion (1776–1850).* When the newly independent United States took its first census in 1790, slightly over 5 percent of the population lived in places with more than 2500 inhabitants. The new country was still essentially rural, and all the major towns were East Coast ports.

New towns were beginning to emerge in the Ohio Valley as Americans began the process of westward expansion. Cincinnati, Louisville, Pittsburgh, and Knoxville were all created as river towns to open up trade in the interior of the continent. Land routes were difficult and expensive, particularly for the transportation of bulky products, but water transportation was comparatively easy and cheap. Therefore, as Americans expanded westward, towns that were located on waterways grew rapidly.

Trade on the Ohio and Mississippi rivers depended, to a considerable degree, on the ability to navigate freely downstream and on the use of the ports the French had established on the lower Mississippi. In 1803, the United States purchased the Louisiana Territory, and the former French ports were brought into the American urban system. These ports included New Orleans (founded 1718), Natchez, Baton Rouge, and St. Louis (founded 1764). The introduction of steam navigation in the second decade of the nineteenth century greatly enhanced trade on the Mississippi.

The other major route into the interior was the Great Lakes. Like the Mississippi, this route had been pioneered by the French from towns on the St. Lawrence River. The expansion of the Great Lakes trade routes and the settlement of the Upper Midwest were speeded by the construction of the Erie Canal (1825), which linked the Hudson River with Lake Erie. Four years later, the Welland Canal was constructed to connect Lake Erie to Lake Ontario, which gave access to the St. Lawrence River. Lakeshore towns like Detroit, Buffalo, Cleveland, and Toledo prospered in the first half of the nineteenth century. The main beneficiary of the linking of the lakes to the Hudson River, however, was New York City. By 1830, New York, with a population exceeding 200,000, had outstripped Philadelphia and eclipsed Boston and Baltimore. From this time on, New York was the leading wholesaling, trading, banking, and port city.

By 1850, the basic pattern of towns in the eastern half of United States was established (Figure 11-5). Other towns, such as those in Utah, New Mexico, California, and Oregon, had not been integrated into the national urban system at this time. Although

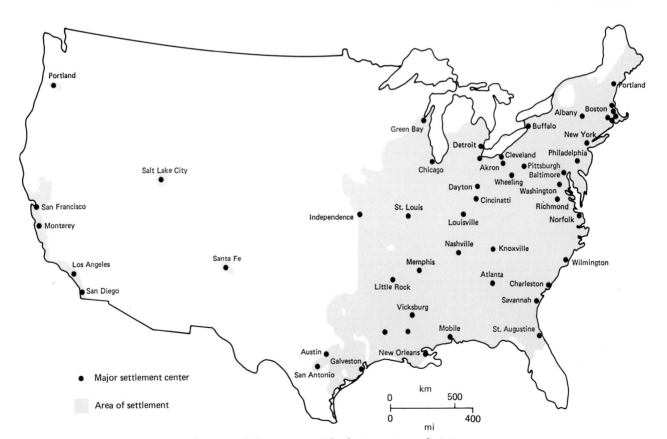

Figure 11-5. Major Settlements in the United States, 1850. The basic pattern of cities in eastern United States had developed by the middle of the nineteenth century.

Figure 11-6. Chicago Railway Station, 1890. During the second half of the nineteenth century, cities located at railroad foci grew rapidly. Photo courtesy of National Archives, Washington, D.C.

towns and cities were vital to the economy, only 15 percent of the total population resided in urban places.

3. *Railroads and Industrialization (1850–1900)*. Although the railroad era started in the United States with the opening of the Baltimore-Ohio line in 1830, it was 1852 before the tracks reached the Ohio River at Wheeling. Also in 1852, the Philadelphia to Pittsburgh line was completed, and railroads from the East reached Chicago. The early rail lines sought to link the major existing urban places; and those places, after being connected by this new form of transportation, grew rapidly and became even more important.

After the Civil War, with the opening of transcontinental rail routes, the railroads created many towns and markedly altered the fortunes of others. Cities at nodal positions in the rail network, such as Chicago, grew dramatically (Figure 11-6). Other places, like St. Louis, that had experienced economic prosperity as a result of river traffic, declined.

Prior to the Civil War, most cities were centers of trade and transport. After the Civil War, large-scale manufacturing became an increasingly important urban function and contributed to city growth. Also, railroads gave access to an expanding national market for goods produced in cities like Cleveland, Buffalo, Pittsburgh, Detroit, and Chicago.

By 1900, the rail network had been largely completed, and the pattern of major cities had been established. The United States had become the world's major industrial power and the largest producer of steel, railroad and shipping equipment, and manufactured goods. Cities that were a part of this national economy were prosperous and expanding.

4. *Metropolitan Expansion (The Twentieth Century)*. The basic pattern of major cities in the United States, which was largely complete by the beginning of the twentieth century, remains today. Cities generally have persisted in their locations even after the primary factors that accounted for their beginnings have changed. The very existence of a city attracts other activities that are logically located where there are large populations; thus the momentum of the past is perpetuated.

Furthermore, most large cities now possess diverse economies, so they are less influenced by changes in one sector than were cities in earlier periods. This is illustrated by New York City, which lost most of its trade with the Great Lakes region when the St. Lawrence Seaway was opened in 1959 and goods could pass directly to the Atlantic via this water route. The impact on the economic life of New York City, however, was minimal because the city was already highly diversified and no longer depended heavily on port functions.

Although their locations remain the same, the major cities have changed greatly in recent decades by increasing in size. This is partly because the entire national population has grown (from 76 million in 1900 to over 244 million in 1988). Urban growth has also resulted from continued urbanization (i.e., migration to cities). In 1900, 40 percent of the U.S. population lived in urban places, but by 1988 the urban percentage exceeded 75.

The growth of cities has produced several **metropolitan areas,** consisting of clusters of urbanized places. Although the political boundaries of the original cities may not have expanded greatly in recent decades, extensive suburban areas have formed around the cores to create metropolises. In 1910, when the U.S. Census Bureau first identified metropolitan areas, there were 25 cities with populations in excess of 200,000. Today there are more than 70 urbanized areas with populations exceeding 200,000.

The comparative growth of metropolitan areas is still affected by their situation relative to transportation networks and levels of industrial production. Other factors, however, are increasingly influential in metropolitan growth. The vital role of services, especially information services, in the United States economy has a direct bearing on the growth of urban areas (Chapter 10).

The role of amenities is also an important consideration for businesses and workers when they ponder a move to another city. Amenities include all the conditions and facilities that people see as enhancing their lives. For some, this may mean the existence of a golf course, a large sports stadium, and low property taxes. For others, amenities may take the form of good schools, limited street crime, and a municipal symphony, even if supported by higher taxes. Combinations of features attract people differently, as indicated by the various rankings of cities that appear occasionally. Nevertheless, some metropolises grow simply because they are regarded as "better places to live."

The geography of major cities today is closely related to past and present human decisions and actions. Conditions that attract service industries are often the result of conscious decisions in the past, such as the establishment of a university or a research laboratory. The amenities of metropolitan places result from a variety of public and private decisions about what to build and which services to provide. In other words, the vitality of urban places today depends more on the location of built environments than on natural sites, such as earth resources, harbors, or inland waterways.

Cities as Central Places

The mercantile model helps explain the distribution of major cities in the United States. Understanding the pattern of the entire urban system also requires looking at the smaller cities scattered across the country. Many of these are not located at a site where an earth resource is concentrated nor at a major transportation node; instead, they are situated in areas where environmental conditions may be fairly homogeneous. The factor that is important to the location of each town or city is its accessibility to people living nearby.

Cities that are primarily related to their surrounding areas tend to be distributed fairly regularly. This was the case of early market towns that traded goods and services for farm products. The spacing of these

centers was affected by the evolution of viable trade areas. That is, if towns were too close, the excess number tended to be reduced through competition. If market places were too far apart and thus beyond the travelling range of some potential customers, additional towns often arose to serve the unmet demand.

There have been attempts to give theoretical precision to the observed distributional regularities of marketplaces. The sociologist Charles Galpin, in a 1915 study of small towns in Walworth County, Wisconsin, showed that there were service areas (or trade areas) for banking, trade, and education around each community. Galpin suggested that these service areas, which formed nodal regions based on trade between dispersed farmers and townspeople, were circular.

Nearly two decades later (in 1933), the German geographer Walter Christaller published a well-known theoretical study concerning the distribution of service centers (central places). He examined the pattern that would result where rural residents behaved in a specified manner as they traded with a **central place** or settlement providing goods and services.

To focus on the relationships between functions and patterns of central places, Christaller assumed that the service centers were located on a uniform plain. Like most spatial models, Christaller's model holds conditions of the natural environment constant so that the factors of distance and relative position can be isolated. Christaller argued that a **threshold of demand** (i.e., a lower limit of total purchases) had to be reached before a good or service could be provided profitably in a settlement. Smaller places would offer only basic goods and services (for example, food goods and postal services) because of the limited number of consumers. Larger places would provide a greater range of products and activities. Hence, a hierarchy of central places would develop over time based on population sizes and the ranges of particular goods and services.

Christaller assumed that consumers would follow the principle of least effort and therefore minimize their travel time and transportation costs by going to the nearest central place. The inhabitants on the hypothetical plain would travel to small places for their most basic and frequent needs but would go farther to larger central places for specialized goods and services. Under these theoretical conditions, the nodal regions of movement would form hexagonal trade areas (Figure 11-7). The largest service center would be located where it would be accessible to the

---

Metropolitan area. A region consisting of several urbanized places, usually around a core city, that operates as an economic unit.

Central place. A settlement (village, town, city) that provides

goods and services to people in a surrounding trade area.

Threshold of demand. The minimum number of purchases required to make it feasible to offer a good or service.

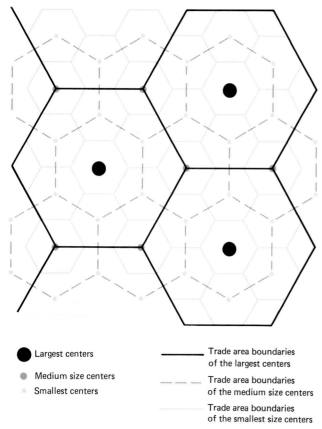

Largest centers

Medium size centers

Smallest centers

Trade area boundaries
of the largest centers

Trade area boundaries
of the medium size centers

Trade area boundaries
of the smallest size centers

Figure 11-7. Theoretical Trade Areas Around Central Places, According to Christaller. Based on the concepts of central place theory, the trade areas for three levels (sizes) of marketplaces are hexagonal in shape and the smaller regions nest within the larger ones. After Christaller 1933.

central places. The hexagonal hinterlands or trade areas of Christaller's central places would divide the territory more efficiently than Galpin's circles because they would neither overlap nor leave some areas unserved.

There are problems, however, with this particular form of central place theory. Even though the service centers are situated on a uniform plain, all centers of the same size do not have the same locational advantages. For example, a low-ranked place close to the large central city can anticipate more through-traffic than a place located in an outlying position. In fact, in another model (not shown here), Christaller did recognize the effects of transportation routes on the arrangement of trade areas.

It is difficult to know the effects of some of the initial assumptions of the model. In the real world, it is rare to find uniform plains covered with an even network of central places. Consequently, there are few opportunities to determine whether the irregularity in pattern results from the differences in the natural environment or from weaknesses in the theory itself. Not all consumers, for example, travel to the nearest settlement to obtain goods and services. For various reasons, such as family connections or personal preferences, some people will choose to make a slightly longer journey to an alternative center that they find more congenial or efficient.

Since central places are highly dependent on customers in the local vicinity, population changes affect their vitality. If the number of residents in a trade area declines, many businesses in the trade center will not survive. As prime businesses close, the town becomes less able to hold customers who then decide to travel farther to other towns or cities that have a wider choice of goods and services. Unless such a declining town can attract an alternative eco-

greatest number of people. Places of lesser rank would lie around the central city, so that the entire plain would be in the trade area of hierarchically ranked

Figure 11-8. A Declining American Town. Numerous landscape features may suggest that a town is losing, or has lost, its former economic base. Photo courtesy of Sally Stoddard.

nomic activity (e.g., a factory or service firm) that is not entirely dependent on local support, it may eventually cease to be a viable central place. Many small towns in the United States have declined in this way during the last half century, particularly because the farm population has dwindled (Figure 11-8).

Cities of the World

The distribution of the major cities of the world today (Figure 11-9) can be explained in terms of the same general locational factors that operate in the United States: resource sites, central places, and transportation routes and nodes. The association with resource sites is most evident in the persistence of places that were established at an earlier time near coal fields, such as Birmingham (England), Essen (Germany), and Krakow (Poland). Now these metropolises possess a broad range of functions.

Most of the world's major cities that function as central places are capitals, such as Paris (France), Delhi (India), and Mexico City (Mexico). The many services that are attracted to the administrative core of a country invariably create the conditions that bring more secondary and tertiary activities and hence a variety of urban functions.

The importance of transportation and wholesale trading functions is illustrated by the large number of major world cities that are seaports. Most seaports in the more developed countries became metropolises as the countries industrialized. Rotterdam (the Netherlands), London (UK), New York City (USA), and Tokyo (Japan) typify this group.

The origins of several other major world seaports are associated with colonialism. As industrializing European countries expanded their economic and political control to distant lands, they created conditions that encouraged the growth of port cities in their nonindustrialized colonies. Jakarta (Indonesia), Singapore (Singapore), Bombay (India), and Lagos (Nigeria) were developed as centers for the export of raw materials. Even in nominally independent countries like China, economic penetration by industrial countries promoted the growth of such ports as Shanghai, Canton (now Guangzhou), and Tianjin.

These major seaports in formerly colonial states have grown very rapidly in recent decades. Most serve as the points of attachment to the global economic system, as illustrated by the recent growth of Manila (the Philippines) and Dar es Salaam (Tanzania). They are the ports through which primary commodities are shipped; they are the centers in which multinationals invest; and they are often the foci for domestic industrialization, especially if the major seaport is also the capital.

The growth of cities in less developed countries is not restricted to just seaports; all the largest cities are increasing in population size, partly from natural increase but mainly because of rapid urbanization (Chapter 9). For example, from 1950 to 1975, while the more developed countries as a group experienced an urban population increase of 71 percent, the size of the urban population of the less developed nations swelled nearly 200 percent. The percentage increases in Africa were 222, in Latin America 191, and in Asia 179. In absolute numbers, Africa's urban population increased by 71 million between 1950 and 1975. In

Figure 11-9. Major Cities of the World. Many of the largest metropolises are seaports and/or capitals.

the same period, Latin America added 130 million people to its urban population, and Asia's urban population grew by 315 million.

One result of the rapid urbanization in the less developed countries and the slowing of the rate of urbanization in Europe, North America, and Japan is a dramatic rearrangement in the order of the largest cities (Table 11-1). In 1950, the largest three cities in the world were in the United States and Europe. According to the accepted population figures, no European city is within the top ten now (but note the

TABLE 11-1. World's Ten Largest Urban Agglomerations, 1950, 1985, and projected to 2035.

1950

Rank	Urban Area	Population (millions)
1	New York metro. area	12.3
2	London	10.4
3	Rhein-Ruhr	6.9
4	Tokyo/Yokohama	6.7
5	Shanghai	5.8
6	Paris	5.5
7	Buenos Aires	5.3
8	Chicago	4.9
9	Moscow	4.8
10	Calcutta	4.4

1985

Rank	Urban Area	Population (millions)
1	Tokyo/Yokohama	21.3
2	Mexico City	18.8
3	New York metro. area	18.2
4	Shanghai	17.0
5	Sao Paulo	14.5
6	Beijing	14.1
7	Los Angeles metro. area	10.8
8	Buenos Aires	10.7
9	Rio de Janeiro	10.4
10	Seoul	10.3

2035

Rank	Urban Area	Projected Population (millions)
1	Mexico City	39.1
2	Shanghai	38.8
3	Beijing	34.5
4	Sao Paulo	32.4
5	Bombay	30.6
6	Dacca	29.2
7	Calcutta	28.9
8	Jakarta	26.8
9	Madras	23.3
10	Tokyo/Yokohama	19.3

BOX 11-1. MEASURING THE SIZES OF METROPOLITAN AREAS

Comparing the sizes of cities is complicated because of varying definitions of what constitutes a city's boundaries and its resident population. In many cases, the core city of a metropolis is much smaller than the entire urbanized area [Figure 11-10 (a)]. For example, the size of Chicago proper is far smaller than the entire metropolitan area bordering Lake Michigan all the way from the Wisconsin state line, through Illinois, and into Indiana. Conversely, the boundaries of some cities, such as Beijing [Figure 11-10 (b)], are defined to include the nearby surrounding countryside. Consequently, the population statistic used in comparisons depends on whether the figure includes just residents of the political unit carrying the city's name or whether it includes the residents of the entire metropolitan area.

The number of people belonging to a city also depends on when they are counted. During a business day, huge numbers of workers occupy office buildings, factories, and stores within the main part of the city. When the day ends, many of these daytime residents leave for their homes in suburbs and outlying communities. White-collar workers of New York, Tokyo, and Paris frequently spend hours in transit between home and office each day. In Tokyo, 15 of 16 workers in the business district live elsewhere. Thus, in official census, people are normally reported according to the location of their residences. This difference in daytime and nighttime locations affects the statistical results. Officially the populations of cities like New York and London may be recorded as decreasing, while in fact the populations of their commuting regions are increasing.

Figure 11-10 (opposite). A Comparison of the Urbanized Areas and Political Boundaries for Chicago and Beijing. The urbanized area of metropolitan Chicago greatly exceeds the city's political boundaries (map a). The urbanized area of Beijing is smaller than its administrative region (map b).

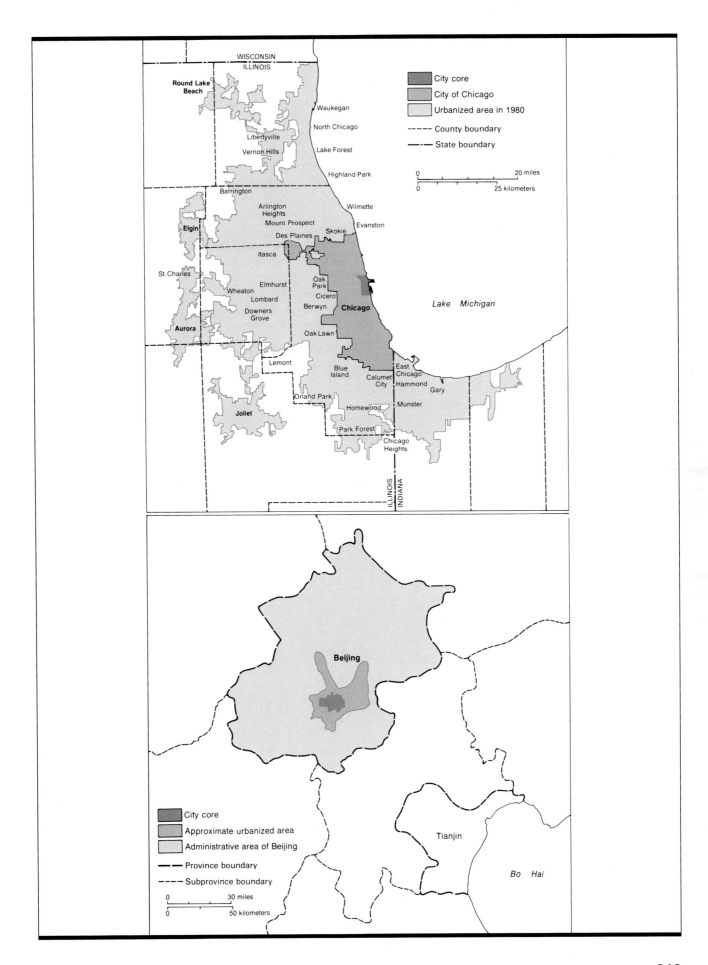

City core
City of Chicago
Urbanized area in 1980
County boundary
State boundary

0   20 miles
0   25 kilometers

WISCONSIN
ILLINOIS

Round Lake
Beach

Waukegan

North Chicago

Libertyville

Lake Forest

Vernon Hills

Highland Park

Barrington

Wilmette

Arlington
Heights

Mount Prospect

Evanston

Des Plaines

Skokie

Elgin

Itasca

St. Charles

Oak
Park

Elmhurst

Wheaton

Cicero

Chicago

Lombard

Berwyn

Downers
Grove

Lake   Michigan

Aurora

Oak Lawn

Lemont

Blue
Island

East
Chicago

Calumet
City

Hammond

Orland Park

Munster

Gary

Joliet

Homewood

Park Forest

Chicago
Heights

ILLINOIS
INDIANA

Beijing

Tianjin

Bo   Hai

City core
Approximate urbanized area
Administrative area of Beijing
Province boundary
Subprovince boundary

0   30 miles
0   50 kilometers

problems of measuring the sizes of cities; Box 11-1). If the present urbanization trend continues for the next half century, by the year 2035 none of the top ten cities will be in the United States or Europe.

The Comparative Sizes of Cities within Countries

The sizes of cities can also be compared within each country. In a national framework, such a comparison provides information about the **urban hierarchy.** The existence of a ranking of urban places is indicated by the names we apply to them: town, city, and metropolis. Also, according to the central theory, a hierarchy is formed by the sizes of trade areas and the distances between service centers. Other characteristics of a settlement hierarchy can be examined by ranking the places in a country on the basis of their population sizes.

In many of the more developed countries, an interesting relationship emerges if cities are ranked by population size. The largest city is often approximately twice as big as the second most populous place, three times the size of the third ranked center, and four times the fourth largest city. This type of relationship has been called the **rank-size rule.**

The top cities in the United States tended to conform to the rank-size rule in 1970. For example, the population of Philadelphia, the fourth largest city, was 1.95 million. If Philadelphia had been exactly one-fourth the size of New York (7.90 million), its population would have been 1.93 million (Table 11-2).

Since the populations of places do not change uniformly within a country, the rank-size relationship does not remain constant. As people migrate to new regions, the relative sizes of cities change, as illustrated by relationships among U.S. cities in 1980 (Table 11-2). Sunbelt cities like Houston and Dallas moved up in the rankings, and population declined within the boundaries of older places like Chicago and Detroit. In 1980, Chicago and Los Angeles were ranked second and third, but their populations were nearly the same and therefore both could not fit the sizes expected by the rank-size rule.

The rank-size rule seldom applies to less developed countries, where often the leading city is tremendously larger than all others. In this case, the major city is referred to as the **primate city.** Primacy occurs when one area establishes economic dominance over the rest of the country. In Mexico, for example, the primate place is Mexico City, with 19 million people. The next most populous city is Guadalajara with 3.4 million inhabitants—which is considerably less than half of 19 million. Bamako, the capital and largest city in Mali, is more than six times the size of the second ranked city (Segou).

In the less developed countries today, a primate city often indicates a situation in which essentially two economies are operating. One economy consists of the traditional sector, which is prevalent in rural areas. For this economic sector, the primate city may function as the largest central place in the country by providing many governmental, educational, and financial functions. Otherwise it may be regarded by many rural residents as quite separated from their daily lives.

The primate city may also be a part of the global economy as a result of its linkage to other major cities of the world through industrial and marketing organizations. For example, primate cities (like Buenos Aires, Bangkok, Jakarta, and Dar es Salaam) are frequently the places where multinational corporations

TABLE 11-2. Population of Largest U.S. Cities, 1970 and 1980, in Reference to the Rank-Size Rule

		1970				1980	
Rank	City	Population (millions)	"Expected"[a] Population	Rank	City	Population (millions)	"Expected"[a] Population
1	New York	7.90	(7.90)	1	New York	7.07	(7.07)
2	Chicago	3.37	3.95	2	Chicago	3.01	3.54
3	Los Angeles[b]	2.81	2.63	3	Los Angeles[b]	2.97	2.36
4	Philadelphia	1.95	1.93	4	Philadelphia	1.69	1.77
5	Detroit	1.51	1.58	5	Houston[b]	1.60	1.41
6	Houston[b]	1.23	1.32	6	Detroit	1.20	1.18
7	Baltimore	.91	1.13	7	Dallas[b]	.90	1.01
8	Dallas[b]	.84	.97	8	San Diego[b]	.88	.88
9	Washington	.76	.88	9	Phoenix[b]	.79	.79
10	Cleveland	.75	.79	10	Baltimore	.79	.71

[a] = Expected according to the rank-size rule.
[b] = Sunbelt city.

Source: U.S. Census

place their investments in the less developed countries.

The comparative sizes of cities within countries do not always match either the rank-size or primacy conditions. This is partly because nations range in their economic characteristics and do not fit neatly into only the two classes of more developed and less developed (Figure 9-8). Countries that are changing their economic characteristics by industrializing may show changes in the comparative sizes of their cities. It has also been observed that cities in the older civilizations of China and India display neither primacy nor the rank-size rule.

URBAN AREAS

For the remainder of the chapter, the scale of examination shifts from cities as places (such as illustrated by the points on a world map like Figure 11-9) to cities as areas. At this latter scale, geographic variations in land use, ethnicity, and movement within urbanized areas are examined.

General Patterns of Structure

One of the basic factors affecting and reflecting differences within cities is the arrangement of features of the built environment such as streets, plazas, warehouses, shopping malls, apartments, and single-family housing. In many small cities, one or two features may dominate the form and structure (or **morphology**). One distinctive form is the town built along a main thoroughfare. The effects of this transportation strip are conspicuous in societies where private cars are common. The most active area in many small towns in America is the street (strip) bordered by drive-ins and other automobile-oriented businesses.

Another prominent morphological form is the relatively open central area (Figure 11-11). Such areas may serve as marketplaces with temporary stalls, as gathering arenas for public events, or as symbolic spaces that accentuate government buildings (Figure 11-12). In America, the courthouse square in many small towns and cities has all these functions.

The morphology of cities may be more related to

Figure 11-11. Morpeth Marketplace (circa 1830). In this north English town, which was typical of pre-industrial market towns, stalls displaying pottery, hardware, clothing, and foodstuffs were erected in the town square during the weekly market day. Photo courtesy of Olwyn M. Blouet.

Urban hierarchy. The ranking of towns, cities, and metropolises by size and function.

Rank-size rule. The regularity in the population sizes of cities in a country or region such that the largest city is twice the size of the second largest place, three times as big as the third-ranked urban center, and four times greater than the fourth largest city.

Primate city. The major city that is many times greater in population size and number of economic activities than any other urban place in a given country (see Rank-size rule).

Morphology. The study of form and structure.

Figure 11-12. Open Area by Government Buildings, Eichstätt, West Germany. Open spaces within crowded city centers often serve economic and aesthetic purposes. Photo courtesy of Sally Stoddard.

historic functions than to current ones. For example, the port functions of early American cities on the Great Lakes and the Ohio River are still reflected in the street patterns that are aligned to water transportation. The T-towns of the Great Plains normally began as settlements associated with railroads. The streets were laid out on a grid pattern with the main street being perpendicular to the railroad (Figures 11-13 and 11-14). Bismarck, Cheyenne, and, to a certain extent, Topeka are T-towns (Hudson 1979).

Although the original street pattern may remain in the older sections of large cities, many of the earlier structures may have become obscured. The rebuilding of a large portion of the urban core, the construction of multiple-laned highways through and around urban areas, and the addition of numerous suburban centers have all made the structural patterns of metropolitan areas much more complex than in the past.

In spite of the complexity of urban features and activities, general patterns of land use are common. This is demonstrated when a person visits another city, especially one within the visitor's home country or culture. For example, a person from Cleveland who arrives in Atlanta for the first time is soon able to figure out the business center, the areas of wealthy residents, and so forth. Likewise, if you were to make a map showing the median family income per census tract for a particular American city, you would probably see a general spatial pattern that would resemble the arrangement of family wealth mapped for other cities of the United States.

Attempts to generalize the spatial forms of American cities have produced several different models of urban structure. These models vary in the ways they generalize the internal variations in cities, so they are not necessarily mutually exclusive. Each provides some insight into certain kinds of spatial regularities found within cities.

Concentric Zones. One model of urban patterns was proposed by a group of University of Chicago sociol-

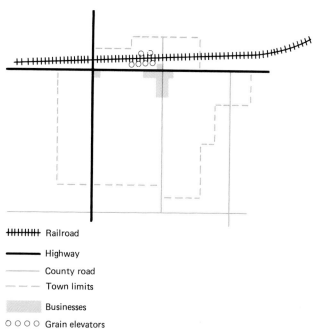

⊢⊬⊬⊬⊬⊢	Railroad
———	Highway
———	County road
– – –	Town limits
▨	Businesses
○ ○ ○ ○	Grain elevators

Figure 11-13. T-Pattern Morphology of Midwest Towns. In the town plan commonly used in the Great Plains, especially after the late 1880s, the main business street was approximately perpendicular to the railroad line. After Hudson 1979.

ogists headed by Ernest Burgess. According to the Burgess model, the core of the American city, the **central business district (CBD),** contains shops and offices providing goods and services (Figure 11-15). The central business district is surrounded by a series of concentric rings or zones. The first ring (Zone II) is a zone of transition where older and deteriorating housing is occupied by immigrants or other people with limited income. With time, however, this zone is invaded by commercial uses as the CBD expands in a growing city.

In this model of concentric rings, successive zones outward consist of the housing of low-income workers (Zone III), residences of higher-income families (Zone IV), and finally a commuter zone on the fringe of the city (Zone V). Burgess suggested that each zone invaded the next outer zone as the city expanded. For example, he inferred that as immigrants move up the socioeconomic ladder, they move outward in the city and vacate housing as the next wave of immigrants arrives (Park, Burgess, and McKenzie 1925).

Radiating Sectors. Homer Hoyt (1939), a land economist, offered an alternative model of land use and urban expansion. Constructing his argument from an analysis of patterns in more than 100 American cities, Hoyt proposed that different land uses form wedges or

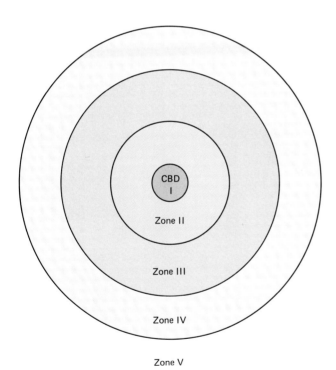

I Central business district

II Zone of transition

III Zone of housing of low-income workers

IV Zone of housing of higher income workers

V Commuter zone

Figure 11-15. Burgess's Model of Land Uses. According to Burgess, patterns of land use in urban areas occur as concentric rings. After Park, Burgess, and McKenzie 1925.

Central Business District (CBD). The centrally located core of an urban area containing concentrations of shops, offices, and financial institutions.

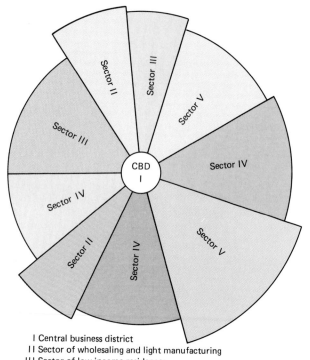

I Central business district
II Sector of wholesaling and light manufacturing
III Sector of low-income residences
IV Sector of higher income residences
V Sector of highest income residents

Figure 11-16. Hoyt's Model of Land Uses. According to Hoyt, patterns of land use in urban areas occur as sectors. After Hoyt 1939.

sectors radiating outwards from the CBD (Figure 11-16). As a city grows, similar land uses tend to follow railroad lines, high or low ground (togography), and other linear features. In Hoyt's model, for example, the residential districts of high income families, once established in particular sectors, such as in an area of high elevations, extend along the same direction from the center of the city to the outskirts of the city.

Multiple Nuclei. A third model, the multiple nuclei model, was proposed by Chauncy Harris and Edward Ullman in 1945. They suggested that contemporary cities do not focus on a single core but instead have several areas that serve as nodes of attraction. In addition to the CBD, suburban business districts, industrial regions, and large shopping malls each may attract distinctive populations and activities. The distribution of land uses in a metropolitan area, therefore, does not form a regular geometric pattern; instead it is a coalescence of distinct clusters (Figure 11-17).

Because large cities have expanded into metropolises that encompass numerous suburban cities, the multiple nucleii model seems to be even more applicable than when it was first proposed several decades ago. Certainly the urbanized Los Angeles basin, with more than 10 million people and 122 incorporated cities all connected by over 1000 miles of freeway, exemplifies the multiple nuclei model.

Social Areas. A fourth model of cities, which was developed after computers became available for analyzing large amounts of data, generalizes the variations in residential characteristics. When many facts about inhabitants in each census tract are statistically grouped according to common attributes, three distinct types of characteristics emerge. One type, termed *economic status,* reflects the income, the value of the home, the educational level, and the occupation of families. *Family status,* a second type, includes statistics on the size of the family unit, the median age of family, and other indicators of a family's life cycle. The third type, *ethnic status,* is essentially an indication of ethnicity.

When these three types are mapped by urban census tracts, they display the patterns of the social areas model. Even though the distributions of the three types may differ in details from city to city, the general patterns are similar for all North American cities.

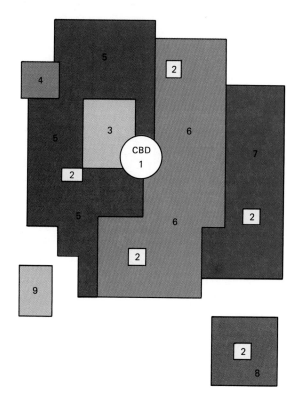

1. Central business district
2. Outlying business district
3. Wholesaling and light manufacturing
4. Heavy manufacturing
5. District of low-income residences
6. District of higher income residences
7. District of highest income residences
8. Residential suburb
9. Industrial suburb

Figure 11-17. Harris's and Ullman's Model of Land Uses. According to Harris and Ullman, patterns of land use in urban areas are irregular but are related to various nuclei. After Harris and Ullman 1945.

Differences in economic status are arranged in sectors; that is, if the values for economic status of a city are divided into, say, three classes, such as High (H), Medium (M), and Low (L), then the mapped result will appear as alternating sectors radiating outwards from the core.

A map of family status, however, shows concentric differences. The ring with the oldest median age will be closest to the center of the city, and rings of families with younger members will be farther out.

Suppose the differences in family status are classified into three groups labeled I (inner ring), II (middle ring), and III (outer ring). If these two maps are combined, nine combinations of economic and family status will occur: H-I, H-II, H-III, M-I, M-II, M-III, L-I, L-II, and L-III (Figure 11-18).

In this fourth model of urban structure, the differences in ethnic status do not display a geometric pattern that is applicable to all cities. The locations of ethnic areas depend upon patterns of past migrations and other factors that are distinctive for each specific city. Sometimes an ethnic district is confined primarily to a single zone or sector; in other cases, it may overlap more than one zone-sector.

Growth and Transportation. A fifth model summarizes the major changes in size and shapes of cities as they have evolved through time. This model incorporates the technology of transportation, which—along with economic, political, and sociological conditions—greatly influences the internal structure of cities. The dynamic aspects of this model are

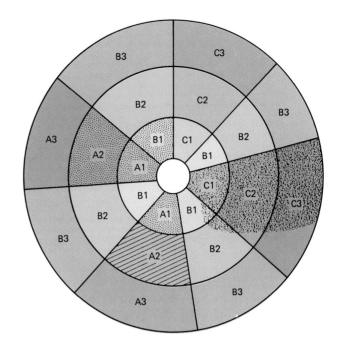

1,2,3   Concentric zones of family status

A, B, C   Sectors of economic status

          Districts of ethnic status

Figure 11-18. Model of Residential Land Use Based on Social Areas. In most American cities, the distributions of many population characteristics display a pattern that combines sectors, concentric rings, and multiple nuclei.

displayed by considering four periods of transportation technology (Figure 11-19).

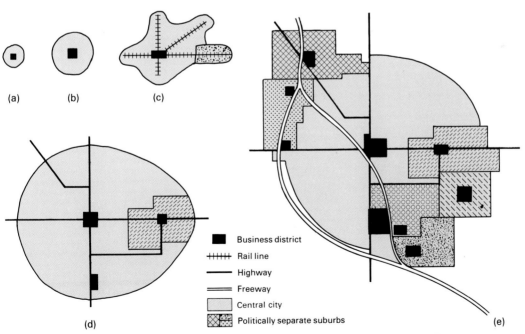

Business district
Rail line
Highway
Freeway
Central city
Politically separate suburbs

Figure 11-19. Model of Urban Growth with Transportation Changes. During the last two centuries, cities have changed in both size and shape as various forms of transportation have evolved.

From colonial times until the nineteenth century, urban morphology was shaped by pedestrians. Towns were compact, reflecting the constraints of distance associated with pedestrian travel [Figure 11-19 (a)]. The development of the horse-drawn tram around 1850 permitted the growth of outlying neighborhoods, but this areal expansion did not alter the shape of most cities [Figure 11-19 (b)].

In 1887, the electric streetcar was inaugurated, and by 1900, approximately 200 cities had this form of transportation. In the largest places, railroad lines served outlying areas and facilitated suburbanization. For example, Harlem, that part of Manhattan between Central Park and Washington Heights, was linked to the densely populated southern portion of the island by three steam railroads in 1880. By 1900, Harlem, which was then inhabited mostly by German, Irish, and Jewish populations, was a full-fledged suburb of New York City. Suburbs, however, did not extend uniformly around the core of cities but were located along the lines that provided the rapid transportation [Figure 11-19 (c)].

After 1920, private automobiles and motor buses gave greater flexibility in the choice of residential locations (Figure 11-20). Both the city itself and the surrounding suburbs grew rapidly [Figure 11-19 (d)]. As the urbanized areas grew, new shopping centers were built in more peripheral parts of the city.

The construction of freeways and similar highways having limited access encouraged even more urban expansion [Figure 11-19 (e)]. Freeways, which greatly affected the relative accessibility of places within large cities, became an important influence on the arrangement of many urban activities and land uses.

These five models are primarily generalizations about arrangements within American cities. This does not mean that parts of one or more of these models do not represent patterns occurring in cities elsewhere in the world. Nevertheless, conditions in many societies tend to produce general patterns that differ from those in American cities.

In European countries where land-use planning is an important factor in locational decisions, regulations tend to restrict the extent that cities can sprawl into the surrounding countryside. Consequently, urban areas are more compact and have greater population densities than cities in the United States. Also, because of the desire to preserve the historic core of most European cities, the central portions are not so heavily rebuilt with tall office buildings as those in American cities. (See additional comments about rebuilding in the core of U.S. cities in the Point-Counterpoint at the end of this chapter.)

Eastern European cities, many of which had large sections destroyed during World War II, have been rebuilt according to strict governmental policies. Likewise, most of the expansion of cities in the Soviet Union during the last half century has conformed to the policies of a planned economy. The resulting patterns create a "Socialist urban landscape," marked by monolithic government buildings and monotonous public housing.

Several cities in Asia that were developed by colonial rulers in the eighteenth or nineteenth centuries retain sections that reflect previous land uses. These

Figure 11-20. Traffic in Washington, D.C., 1937. Because of the greater ease in moving from residence to work and shopping places, the private automobile relieved much of the previous housing congestion in cities; but soon the cars themselves produced a new form of congestion, as expressed by traffic jams. Photo courtesy of National Archives, Washington, D.C.

Figure 11-21. Queen Victoria Memorial, Karachi, Pakistan. Features and patterns of land use in central Karachi still reflect those created during the earlier period of British colonial rule. Photo courtesy of Sally Stoddard.

may include a section near the center of the city (such as "the fort" area of Colombo, Sri Lanka) where governmental and military offices as well as colonial businesses were located. These cities also contain a "cantonment" that once consisted of scattered residences of the colonial population. Although the colonial functions disappeared with national independence, current urban patterns are affected by such historic roots (Figure 11-21).

In many less developed countries, the patterns of urban residences contrast with those of American cities. In general, a larger share of people with low incomes live on the outer fringes of large cities than in the United States. Although in many metropolises in less developed countries there are areas where people are crowded into poor quality shacks and tents located near the city center, there are also many squatters' sections on the urban periphery (see Figure 9-30).

In summary, although cities vary with national and cultural settings, their internal patterns generally display considerable spatial regularity. These patterns change over time, however, which means that understanding urban geography also depends on studying processes of change.

Changing Forms and Functions

In American cities, the central business district remains the core of the city, but the managers of only certain kinds of urban functions now regard it as a prime location. For example, the head offices of banks and financial institutions are most likely to stay in central business districts. Sensing changes in the prices of stocks, commodities, and currencies requires first-hand contact, and bankers and brokers cluster in centralized financial districts. Other activities in the CBD include several forms of specialized retailing plus those establishments that serve the daytime population which is working, visiting, or shopping in the central district.

In recent decades, many forms of retailing have decreased in the central business district as stores have relocated in accessible malls with easy automobile parking. By the 1970s, approximately 75 percent of the regional retail trade was carried out in the suburbs of metropolises. In addition, many manufacturing activities have moved from the highly taxed and congested areas in central parts of cities. Industrial parks conveniently located on ringroads, such as Highway 128 around Boston, provide attractive sites for manufacturers.

Why did urban areas sprawl out, disperse population, and create new concentrations of economic activity in peripheral parts of the city and in suburbs? When urban populations grew in the last century, cities could either expand at the fringes or accommodate higher densities at the core. In American cities, several factors have encouraged expansion outward. First, changing transportation technology has allowed people to live further from their place of work without a great sacrifice in travel costs and time.

Second, modern transportation has improved the accessibility to outlying cheaper land. As explained by von Thünen (Figure 10-9), the further from the city, the cheaper is the value of land. Because the cost of land is a significant part of housing expenses, the relatively low land prices on the fringes of cities create an incentive to build outwards rather than redevelop existing core areas.

Third, urban expansion creates distance between centrally located services and residential areas. In terms of central place theory, we would predict that, once distances from the CBD exceed a few kilometers, new centers will arise to provide basic goods and services to residential areas. The effect is, initially, to create outlets for many convenience goods and services in suburban locations. These new outlets then begin to intercept consumers who previously shopped in the central business district.

Fourth, zoning laws and other political decisions have not discouraged urban sprawl. In Western Europe tough zoning regulations have prevented the proliferation of outlying shopping malls. In the United States, however, the growth of large malls and industrial parks in the suburbs has not been seriously impeded by zoning. In effect, cities have partially turned themselves inside out. Many functions that formerly occurred in the central part of cities are now located in the suburbs.

These centrifugal forces have not emptied the urban core, as attested by the gleaming towers of city centers. The heart of the city still remains attractive, but some of the expressions have changed. In many cities, the central district has undergone considerable renovation (as described in the Point-Counterpoint at the end of this chapter). Even the shopping mall, which so typifies retailing in the suburbs, has returned to the downtown of some American metropolises. Because of the higher value of land in the city center, these malls are usually smaller than the suburban ones, and their associated parking facilities may be multistoried; but nevertheless, they represent changing patterns in retail activities.

Although the predominant shift of population is

Figure 11-22. Gentrification in Baltimore. Recent renovation of buildings and improvements in the street are indicated by trim surfaces and young trees. Photo courtesy of Albert J. Larsen.

still from the inner city to the suburbs, a significant counterstream movement has been taking place involving the resettlement and revitalization of housing in areas around the central business district (CBD). This process has been called **gentrification.** In the United States, gentrification was apparent in large cities like New York, San Francisco, and Washington by 1970. Five years later, according to a study by the Urban Land Institute (1976), almost half of the cities in the United States with more than 50,000 people were experiencing rehabilitation of inner city housing. In the 1980s, gentrification is even more widespread in the United States, and the trend is also evident in Canadian, European, and Australian cities.

A major cause of gentrification is the growth of white-collar employment associated with financial institutions in the downtown area. An associated asset is proximity to the social amenities of the city core. The people attracted to inner city living tend to be young, professional, well-educated, well paid, predominantly single, or if married, generally childless. The first wave of urban resettlement focused on high-rise apartments—the "Gold Coast" of cities like Chicago. More recently the urban "pioneers" have moved into townhouses that have been remodeled from older, often decrepit, housing (Figure 11-22). Even old warehouses have been converted to attractive apartments.

Gentrification occurs incrementally, spreading block by block from an initial node of development into working-class neighborhoods and blighted areas. In New York City, for example, gentrification was flourishing in the southern and western parts of Manhattan (Soho, Tribeca, Lower East Side, and Upper West Side) by 1970; now, in the late 1980s, the process is taking hold in Harlem (Schaffer and Smith 1986). As the renovated housing rises in value, it affects the market values and rents of nearby residences. This causes displacement of the previous inhabitants, many of whom have low incomes and cannot afford the increased rent. As the available supply of low-rent housing is decreased, former residents are often forced from their neighborhood.

Population displacement aside, gentrification is generally beneficial to the inner city. The movement to the downtown district of high wage earners invigorates the city's tax base, reduces commuting, preserves historic buildings, and establishes new commercial enterprises (often elegant restaurants, bars, and specialty shops).

Changes in Social Areas

Ethnic neighborhoods, like other areas of cities, display the locational persistence of past patterns as well as the shifts associated with urban change. Urban ethnic areas usually emerge through the process of migration and settlement. After an initial enclave is established by a few members, the group becomes a neighborhood as later migrants from the same ethnic background settle nearby. The newcomers are attracted because they can rely on the established members for temporary housing and help in finding jobs. The ethnic neighborhood serves as "a halfway house between the new land and the old country" allowing a continuation of traditions, such as language and diet, and shielding the immigrants from severe culture shock (Ley 1983, p. 58).

The degree to which ethnic areas survive in American cities is tied to the rate of assimilation of the minority groups into the mainstream of urban life. In general, the greater the social distance of a minority group from the dominant culture, the slower the rate of assimilation. By 1930, for example, many early immigrants to Chicago (Germans, Irish, and Swedes) had experienced upward social and outward spatial mobility. In contrast, later immigrants (Czechs, Poles, Italians, and Jews), who were perceived as being very different by the majority culture, remained in the inner city and adjacent districts.

Even when members of one group are assimilated and move away from a former ethnic neighborhood, this does not necessarily mean the disappearance of an area of ethnic distinctiveness. This is because the moves by members of the first ethnic group may open up low-rent housing that is affordable for new immigrants. For example, some of the traditional European ethnic neighborhoods of Chicago now house recent Asian immigrants. Some areas may undergo several such "invasion-succession" sequences.

Movement away from the inner city usually leads to the social dispersion of most ethnic groups as their identity merges with that of the majority. In contrast, some ethnic groups (Jews, for example) tend to remain cohesive even after they decentralize. In these cases, social networks generate spatial interaction as members assemble periodically for religious meetings, school, and recreational gatherings.

Despite the tendency for geographic dispersion and cultural assimilation, many American cities are still enriched by ethnic neighborhoods (Figures 11-23 and 11-24). In Chicago, for example, a patchwork of ethnic communities persists, consisting of long-established groups—Poles, Italians, and Irish—as well as more recent arrivals, such as Asians and Hispanics. Often these miniature culture regions are associated with a church or similar landscape feature that focuses ethnic identity and preserves links with the past.

In addition to the practical and psychological advantages of ethnic aggregation (i.e., voluntarily liv-

---

Gentrification. The process by which housing in deteriorated inner city areas is taken over by middle and high income groups and refurbished.

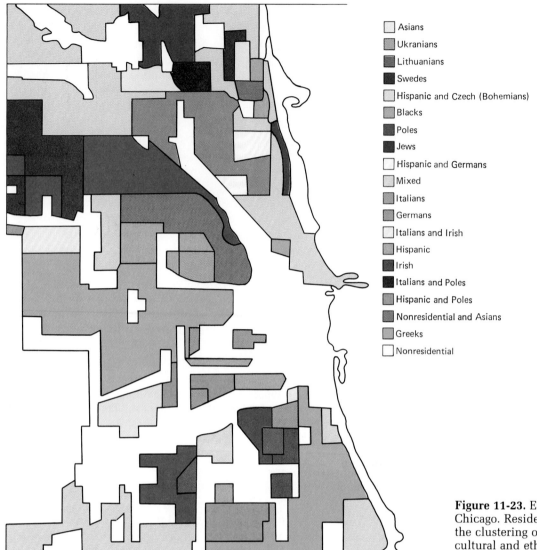

- ☐ Asians
- ▨ Ukranians
- ▨ Lithuanians
- ■ Swedes
- ☐ Hispanic and Czech (Bohemians)
- ▨ Blacks
- ▨ Poles
- ■ Jews
- ☐ Hispanic and Germans
- ☐ Mixed
- ▨ Italians
- ▨ Germans
- ☐ Italians and Irish
- ▨ Hispanic
- ■ Irish
- ■ Italians and Poles
- ▨ Hispanic and Poles
- ▨ Nonresidential and Asians
- ▨ Greeks
- ☐ Nonresidential

Figure 11-23. Ethnic Areas in Chicago. Residential patterns reflect the clustering of people with similar cultural and ethnic backgrounds. Based on a map by Ron Grossman.

Figure 11-24. Mexican American Area in Los Angeles. Landscape features often provide clues to the ethnicity of urban neighborhoods. Photo courtesy of Daniel D. Arreola.

ing in close proximity), there are the disadvantages of segregation which separates residents into distinct regions. Income constraints frequently oblige new immigrants to seek areas of cheap but poor quality housing, generally in the inner city. Social discrimination often restricts newcomers to areas of lower value. In the late 1960s, for example, newly arrived Appalachian migrants in Cincinnati sought the companionship of friends and relatives who had arrived earlier, but they also experienced pressures of segregation that excluded them from other areas. They clustered near the city center in a spatially restricted area where they attempted to replicate the social networks of their rural and small-town origins (Hyland 1970).

The establishment and growth of New York's Chinatown furnish an example of how an ethnic area grows through migration and persists as a result of both aggregating and segregating forces. The kernel of Chinatown was established in 1840 when the tea merchant Quimpo Appo located on Doyer Street and Soon Wo Kee opened a general store on Mott Street (Figure 11-25). Because of strict laws preventing Chinese immigration into the United States during the 1883 to 1965 period, the community grew slowly. Many of the early residents migrated from California where anti-Chinese sentiments had become intense. This early population consisted predominantly of males who found an economic niche in the restaurant and laundry businesses, which required little capital investment and involved little competition from established enterprises. The ethnic area grew by accretion on the fringes to include the entire district between Chatham Square and Baxter Street by 1898 (Figure 11-25). Until 1965, this remained the core of Chinatown, a fairly homogeneous neighborhood of people who spoke the same dialect from southern China.

This situation changed rapidly after 1965 when the Chinese, like all other national groups, became eligible for entry into United States under a new immigration policy (Chapter 4). Chinatown's population increased rapidly, to at least 75,000 in the 1980s, and the boundaries of the community expanded across Canal Street into Little Italy and along East Broadway to claim portions of the Lower East Side (Figure 11-25). Immigrants now come from diverse parts of China, as well as from Taiwan and Hong Kong. Sex ratios have equalized and educational standards approximate the national average. Although many men and women are still employed in the more than 450 garment factories and 300 or so restaurants of Chinatown, some residents have amassed fortunes from buying and selling real estate (Kleinfield 1986).

Chinatown is bound together internally by a mesh of social networks: kinship societies which reach back to specific Chinese villages, trade associations, and the secret organizations of the Tongs. Nine Chinese

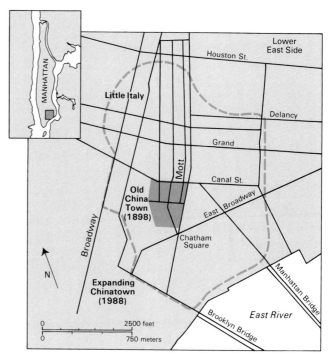

Figure 11-25. Chinatown, New York City. The area called "Chinatown" emerged around Mott Street in lower Manhattan in the second half of the nineteenth century. Since 1965, its boundaries have expanded to include the district from Little Italy to the East River. After Wong 1982 and Kleinfield 1986.

language newspapers reinforce identity and actively campaign against assimilation. Festivals such as the Chinese New Year (when the area is cordoned off for celebrations) maintain age-old customs.

These institutions provide a form of social security for the residents, and they protect against the threats of outside forces. Most outside hostility has been expressed through discriminatory housing and limited occupational opportunities. For example, only in the last 20 years has it become possible for an educated Chinese to buy a home and practice a profession outside this ethnic enclave (Wong 1982).

The relative isolation of the Chinese community complicates solving social problems. For example, Chinese street gangs and organized crime, both of which have increased rapidly in recent years, have not been successfully controlled. Municipal and federal law enforcement personnel who do not understand the Chinese language and culture have difficulty obtaining information about the criminal organizations. Individual law-abiding citizens and merchants have no more power against organized crime than do people anywhere else. In fact, because of the long history of kinship associations and obligations, the Chinese community finds it particularly difficult to withstand these powerful crime organizations.

Despite the inner-looking nature of the community, living in Chinatown is also living in the United

Figure 11-26. Chinese American Area in New York City. Neighborhood businesses are often clues of ethnicity. Photo courtesy of John Disbrow.

States. Public schools, social agencies, churches, mass media, and the political system all intervene as forces of acculturation. Racial discrimination has decreased relative to the period before 1950, and some Chinatown residents have suburbanized. In the 1980s, more than 70,000 of New York's Chinese Americans live outside of Chinatown, scattered throughout Queens, Brooklyn, and Upper Manhattan. For many of these acculturated Chinese, Chinatown has become a shopping center and a place for social gatherings rather than a confining ethnic sanctuary where they are obliged to live (Figure 11-26).

Race, often a main determinant of ethnicity, has been, and is, the greatest barrier to assimilation, so it is not surprising that black and Asian neighborhoods are strongly segregated. Perhaps the most striking demographic characteristic of American cities is their dual nature, where the central city is populated by black and other minority groups and the surrounding suburbs are inhabited by predominantly white populations with European ancestry.

The rise of a black **ghetto** (an area of involuntary segregation) in a typical American city is mainly a phenomenon of the twentieth century. In 1910, 90 percent of the American blacks lived in the South, and about 75 percent were in rural areas. This distribution reflected the blacks' historic ties, first as slaves, then as tenant farmers, to the Southern plantation system. Blacks began to leave the South in large numbers during World War I, attracted by industrial jobs in northern cities and pushed by a diminishing demand for agricultural labor and by discrimination. By 1980, approximately 80 percent of the black population lived in metropolitan areas, compared to 73 percent of the nonblack population. At this time, about half of the blacks lived outside the South, with a third of all American blacks residing in seven cities—New York, Chicago, Detroit, Philadelphia, Washington, Los Angeles, and Baltimore.

Within a typical metropolitan area, blacks tend to be concentrated in the central city rather than in the attached suburban cities or other political subdivisions. With increased suburbanization by whites beyond the legal limits of the city and the continued segregation of blacks, there are now nine central cities exceeding a population of 100,000 in which blacks account for more than half the urban population (Table 11-3). The increase in the percentage of blacks living in the suburbs from 1960 to 1980 (Figure 11-27) is more an indication of the expansion of the ghetto beyond the central city than an expression of increasing integration. In spite of legislation aimed at prohibiting segregation, it is declining very slowly in American cities (Rose and Christian 1982).

Many social, political, and economic forces combine to maintain black districts in the typical American city. The dominant forces are segregative. Blacks, like other recent migrants, moved into the dilapidated neighborhoods of the inner city as former migrants moved outward into newer housing. Although black populations grew rapidly because of in-migration and natural increase, there was not a similar areal expansion throughout the city. Numerous institutional practices, combined with culturally biased perceptions of who "belongs" in particular territories, has restricted black citizens from moving to certain parts of metropolitan areas.

To a lesser extent, black ghettos are maintained also by aggregative forces. Spatial concentration gives a degree of power and political advantages to blacks.

TABLE 11-3. Largest U.S. Central Cities with Black Majorities, 1960 and 1980

	1960		1980	
City	Black Population (% of Urban Total)	City		Black Population (% of Urban Total)
Washington, D.C.	53.9	Gary, Ind.		70.8
		Washington, D.C.		70.3
		Atlanta, Ga.		66.6
		Detroit, Mich.		63.6
		Newark, N.J.		58.2
		Birmingham, Ala.		55.6
		New Orleans, La.		55.3
		Baltimore, Md.		54.8
		Richmond, Va.		51.3

Source: Reid 1982

In 1988, for example, three of the nation's largest cities (Los Angeles, Chicago, and Philadelphia) had black mayors.

For the most part, however, the spatial segregation of blacks in the inner cities has meant economic hardship. Despite progress since the 1960s when the Civil Rights Movement and governmental assistance programs were activated, about one-third of all black families remain below the poverty level. Rather than finding the cities a gateway into the mainstream of American society, blacks have been left with all the problems associated with the decaying districts of urban areas.

Segregation of ethnic groups is not, of course, limited to North American cities. In Northern Ireland, since 1969 when the most recent outbreak of ethnic strife began, Protestant and Catholic areas have become increasingly segregated as members of both groups retreated into the haven of their religious heartlands (Chapter 7). In Indonesia, the Chinese historically have been grouped in specified quarters of the cities. Even since the abandonment of segregative laws they have tended to remain concentrated in ghettos near the city centers. In South Africa, the nonwhite populations are strictly segregated by law through the practice of apartheid (Chapter 8).

Patterns of Urban Activity

Inside the shell of the city formed by the built environment of roads and structures, people live their daily lives of work and leisure. Daily activities tend to be repetitive, with routines centered around home, work, school, and friends. These routines, as David Ley pointed out, "consolidate a lifestyle or a subculture . . . [involving] repeated interactions with persons, places, and objects that are well-known and have a meaning to people over and above their objective features" (1983, p. 102). The neighborhood bar, the local church, and the union hall are among the focal points of peoples' experience of, and attachment to, the city.

The patterns of movement during a specified period of time forms each individual's personal region

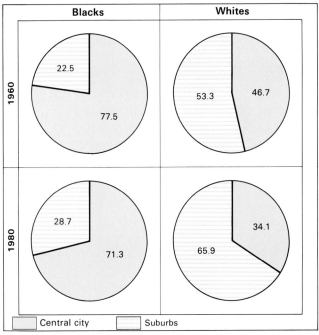

Figure 11-27. Proportion of Metropolitan Population Living in Central Cities, Blacks and Whites, 1960 and 1980. The contrasting percentages reveal that residential segregation persists in most American metropolises. After Reid 1982.

Ghetto. A residential area largely occupied by one ethnic group. Originally the term referred to sections of European towns to which Jews were restricted. The term usually implies segregation of a group experiencing discrimination.

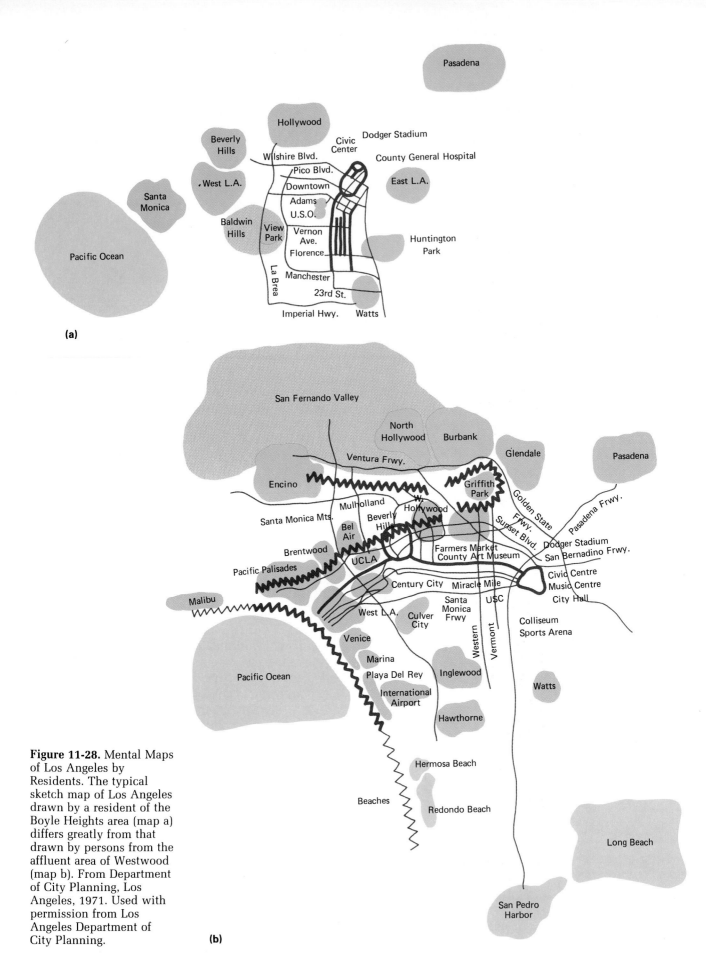

Figure 11-28. Mental Maps of Los Angeles by Residents. The typical sketch map of Los Angeles drawn by a resident of the Boyle Heights area (map a) differs greatly from that drawn by persons from the affluent area of Westwood (map b). From Department of City Planning, Los Angeles, 1971. Used with permission from Los Angeles Department of City Planning.

334   **CHAPTER 11: URBAN PLACES**

or **activity space.** The configuration, or geographic shape, of urban activity spaces varies greatly from one segment of the population to another. Traditionally, the location of the workplace away from home and the necessity of travelling to it have dominated male activities, whereas the location of the workplace in the home has governed female activities. As women have changed their place of work from the home to outside places of employment, the differences in activity areas based on gender have lessened. Nevertheless, contrasting patterns have persisted to the degree that many jobs remain gender-specific.

Income and education also influence the range of urban activities. Distance is a problem for the poor, many of whom are without automobiles or the means to pay for other transportation. Consequently, the orbit of activities tends to be smaller for the poor than for the affluent, whose social networks may extend across the city.

Patterns of urban activity are closely related to **mental maps** or geographic images of the city that people carry in their heads. Mental maps are largely a product of our experience of the environment (natural and built). Generally groups whose ranges of activities are limited have less comprehensive images of the city than the images of those groups who travel widely across it.

In a study of Los Angeles conducted by the City Planning Commission in 1971, the ''upper class'' respondents from Westwood (near the UCLA campus) had an extensive knowledge of the city. Residents in the poor, Spanish-speaking area of Boyle Heights had a view restricted to their local inner-city neighborhood (Figure 11-28). The Westwood residents, however, knew very little about Boyle Heights, demonstrating in a dramatic way the different worlds that exist within the bounds of a city (Orleans 1973).

The world of the downtown elderly is an invisible land to most Americans. The residents of the Golden West Hotel in downtown San Diego, for example, live in a tightly circumscribed world. Located in the midst of a skid row, with its landscape of pawnshops and tattoo parlors, the hotel was home for 400 residents in 1974, predominantly men with a median age ''around 70.'' A majority of the residents were nonwelfare poor, living alone, and close to the margin of subsistence (Stutz 1976).

Activity patterns were similar and repetitive. Most journeys were short and made on foot to obtain food and drink. Longer trips, to the San Diego Zoo, for example, were by bus, although transportation costs tended to limit the number of such outings. Most time was spent in a small activity space adjacent to the hotel (Figure 11-29). The core of activity space was

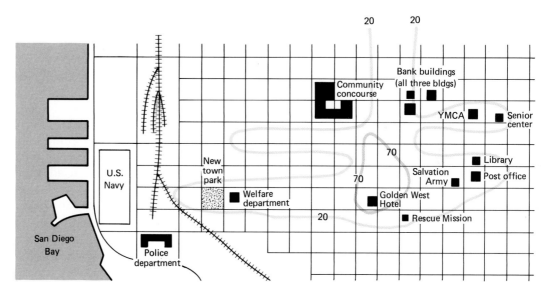

Outer boundary of activity space for 20 percent of residents during typical one week

Outer boundary of activity space for 70 percent of residents during typical one week

Figure 11-29. Activity Space of Elderly Residents in San Diego. The area of movement during a typical week in 1974 for 70 percent of the residents of Golden West Hotel was limited to only two or three blocks to the north. After Stutz 1976.

Activity space. The territory in which a person or group lives and travels.

Mental map. The locational knowledge or mental images

that a person has about the positions and characteristics of specific places.

bounded on the south by warehouses and a black residential area, which were regarded as dangerous. To the north were the Horton Plaza redevelopment project and the white-collar business district, where the old men felt out of place. Newtown Park and the Welfare Department drew residents to the west, but the United States Naval Supply Center blocked direct access to San Diego Bay. To the east, the Public Library, Post Office, YMCA, and Senior Center were visited regularly, but 11th Avenue, a busy arterial connected to an expressway, hindered any wider circulation in this direction.

In 1974 when Stutz made his survey, this pattern of existence was facing traumatic change. Urban renewal near the Horton Plaza was removing many of the cheap eating establishments that the residents of the Golden West Hotel depended on. The residents' voices were not heard in the formulation of the development project, although in many ways they were most affected by it. The old people stayed in the Golden West Hotel, living poorly in an area of expensive restaurants and stores.

THE FUTURE OF URBAN AREAS

It is difficult to project the geography of human activities very far into the future. Undoubtedly the residents of Peking a hundred years ago did not visualize the large contemporary metropolis of Beijing. Even in their wildest dreams, the traders and fishermen of Jeddah, Saudi Arabia, could not anticipate the modern urban settlement that exists there now.

Americans in the 1880s could hardly have anticipated the form, size, and functions that characterize cities of the United States a hundred years later. They would have been astonished to know that their pedestrian-oriented settlements, having radii not exceeding 6 or 7 kilometers, would someday become centers of commuting networks in which people would travel daily 100 kilometers each way to and from work. They probably would not have expected that the large cities in the Northeast would lose population in the 1970s, while the cities in southern states from Florida to California would account for five of the nation's top ten cities in 1980 (Table 11-2).

The development of American cities is difficult to predict, even for the near future, because of the many economic, political, technological, and social forces influencing urban change. If gasoline prices were to rise enormously, for example, commuting over large distances might be greatly curtailed, and the decentralization of urban populations might be reversed. On the other hand, telecommunications might make it unnecessary for many workers to live within commutable distance of large cities because many tasks could be accomplished by connections with home computers. Even today, numerous consultants and technicians who provide informational services operate from their homes. In the future many people may be able to live in environments of their choice, far from the crowds and problems of urban places.

Despite the revival of nonmetropolitan growth in the 1970s and 1980s, the United States will undoubtedly continue to be a country with an urban majority. Without question, the role of cities as centers of education, administration, and performing arts will persist (Gottmann 1983).

It is likely that urbanized places will become more diffused and spread out over wider areas. If several cities coalesce, they may form an urbanized region like the area called **Megalopolis.** This term was first used by Jean Gottmann (1961) when he described the continuous urban area stretching from Massachusetts Bay to the Potomac, which contained Boston, New York, Philadelphia, and Washington. Gottman noted that, while the suburbs were expanding in megalopolis the population of the established central cities was already showing symptoms of decline.

Other urban areas in the United States are developing in a similar way. Metropolitan areas are coalescing and diffusing widely over surrounding areas and forming megalopolislike regions. The Commission of Population Growth and the American Future (1970) envisaged 25 large urban clusters by the year 2000 (Figure 11-30). These clusters could cover one-sixth of the land area and contain five-sixths of the population of the United States.

The most dramatic change in world settlement is expected to be the continued urbanization in less developed countries. In the last two decades of the twentieth century, an additional 1.3 billion people will probably reside in urban areas, with more than 1 billion of them living in less developed countries. In many nations, such as Nigeria and Burma, the degree of primacy may increase as the largest city grows faster than other cities. In other cases where there are already several large urban centers, such as in India and China, migrants from rural areas are expected to be attracted to more than just the largest metropolis.

It is predicted that by the year 2000 more than half of the world's population will live in cities. In the more developed countries, where urban percentages already exceed 50, growth will probably continue to be associated with a decline in inner cities and an expansion of urban forms over the surrounding land. In the less developed countries, rapid urbanization

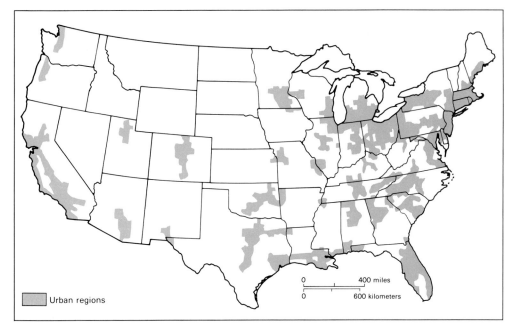

Figure 11-30. Urban Regions in the United States, Predicted for the Year 2000. It is expected that over 80 percent of the U.S. population will live in these metropolitan regions by the end of the century. From the Commission of Population Growth 1973.

will further test the ability of cities to provide basic needs (safe water, health services, electricity) to the millions of new urban dwellers.

As a higher percentage of the world's population clusters into urban places, geographic relations will certainly change. One of the implications of a more urbanized world population may be an increased feeling of separation from the natural environment. This theme, along with other ecological relationships, is discussed in the next chapter.

The Future of Urban Cores

In the past, the downtown area of a city was the focal point that produced an urban agglomeration of people and economic activities. In recent decades, however, many American cities have been partially turned inside out as numerous urban functions have moved to peripheral areas. What is the future of the downtown section of American cities?

Various policies and projects have attempted to maintain or revitalize the core of a city. One type of effort involves urban renewal. As economic activities left downtown areas, the tax base and property values were undermined. The drop in certain types of property values made it feasible to buy deteriorating blocks and to start comprehensive urban renewal projects. Frequently, city governments encouraged this process by exercising powers of eminent domain to facilitate the acquisition of substantial areas of downtown property. City governments wanted to prevent further decay of existing property, and they wanted the enhanced tax revenues that large high-rise development would bring.

The cumulative effect of these forces was to produce some spectacular renewal schemes, which altered the built environment of the city center, as illustrated by the Renaissance Center in Detroit (Figure 11-31).

The results of urban renewal have been mixed. On the one hand, the new hotels, convention centers, and office blocks have created new employment. On the other hand, redevelopment has removed certain types of businesses, with their associated employment, from the center of the city. When blocks of

Megalopolis. Originally defined as the nearly continuous urban area stretching from Massachusetts Bay to the Potomac River; the term is often applied to any urbanized area that consists of coalescing large cities.

low-story shops and offices are knocked down, many businesses are forced to relocate. Usually the small businesses cannot afford the rents charged in the new developments. Even if operators are able to pay higher rents, many family restaurants, movie theaters, and stores are pushed out of central locations because redevelopment schemes do not include suitable accommodations for them.

At the time of the earlier development projects, the perception was that shopping had been declining already in central locations so the displacement of stores by high-rise office buildings was only part of an inevitable change. The replacements, of course, accelerated the retreat of consumers who found a redeveloped city center lacking the variety that suburban shopping malls provide.

Dissatisfaction with the results of some of the earlier urban renewal projects resulted in a new emphasis in later attempts to revitalize downtown areas. It was realized that small businesses, which had previously provided a vital function in the centers of cities, needed to be included in development plans. Later urban renewal projects, therefore, encouraged the building of shopping complexes composed of many small units. Some included preservation and restoration schemes, like Larimer Square and the Sixteenth Street Mall in Denver (Figure 11-32); others renovated several buildings within a designated district and connected them with a network of enclosed skywalks (Figure 11-33) or footpaths and walkways (Figure 11-34).

What is the future of urban cores? Will the urban renewal projects that include facilities for numerous small businesses create the social environments that will produce revitalized city cores? Will they produce the vibrant social life associated with people shopping, strolling, eating, and talking during the day and evening (as found in many world cities outside the United States)? Or, are the cores of American cities doomed? Will the attempts to restore the vitality of downtown areas soon fail?

Figure 11-31 (opposite, top). Renaissance Center, Detroit. The Renaissance Center towers above the surrounding land, which is mostly in highways, parking lots, and other automobile space. Photo courtesy of Sally Stoddard.

Figure 11-32 (opposite, middle). Sixteenth Street Mall, Denver. This renovated section of downtown Denver includes pedestrian malls lined with many small shops. Photo courtesy of Sally Stoddard.

Figure 11-33 (opposite, bottom). Enclosed Shopping Mall, Lincoln. Malls and connecting skywalks often represent the attempt to preserve retail shopping in the downtown portion of cities. Photo courtesy of Sally Stoddard.

Figure 11-34 (above). The River Walk, San Antonio. Aesthetic spaces within urban cores are a type of amenity that attracts businesses, shoppers, and visitors. Photo courtesy of Sally Stoddard.

BIBLIOGRAPHY

Adams, John S., "The Meaning of Housing in America," *Annals of the Association of American Geographers*, 74, no. 4 (1984), 515–26.

———, "Residential Structure of Midwestern Cities," *Annals of the Association of American Geographers*, 60 (1970), 37–62.

Berry, Brian J. L., and Frank E. Horton, *Geographic Perspectives on Urban Systems*. Englewood Cliffs, N.J.: Prentice-Hall, 1970.

Binford, Henry C., *The First Suburbs: Residential Communities on the Boston Periphery 1815–1860*. Chicago: University of Chicago Press, 1985.

Borchert, John R., "American Metropolitan Evolution," *Geographical Review*, 57 (1967), 301–32.

Bouvier, Leon F., "Planet Earth 1984–2034: A Demographic Vision," *Population Bulletin*, 39, no. 1 (February, 1984).

Brunn, Stanley D., "Cities of the Future," in Stanley D. Brunn and Jack F. Williams, *Cities of the World*, pp. 453–89. New York: Harper & Row, Pub., 1983.

Bunce, Michael, *Rural Settlement in an Urban World*. London: Croom Helm, 1982.

Bunge, William, "Detroit Humanly Viewed: The American Urban Present," in Ronald Abler et al., eds., *Human Geography in a Shrinking World*, pp. 149–81. N. Scituate, Mass.: Duxbury Press, 1975.

Carlstein, Tommy, *Time Resources, Society and Ecology*. Lund Studies in Geography, Series B. Human Geography, no. 49. London: George Allen & Unwin, 1982.

Chisholm, Michael, *Rural Settlement and Land Use*. London: Hutchinson & Co., 1962.

Christaller, Walter, *Die Zentralen Orte in Suddeutschland*. Jena: Gustav Fisher, 1933. Trans. by C. W. Baskin, *Central Places in Southern Germany*. Englewood Cliffs, N.J.: Prentice-Hall, 1966.

Commission on Population Growth, *Population Growth and the American Future*. Washington, D.C.: U.S. Govt. Printing Office, 1973.

Conzen, Michael P., "American Cities in Profound Transition: The New City Geography of the 1980s," *Journal of Geography*, 82, no. 3 (1983), 94–102.

Department of City Planning, *The Visual Environment of Los Angeles*. Los Angeles, 1971.

Galpin, Charles, J., *The Social Anatomy of an Agricultural Community*. Madison, Wis.: Agricultural Experiment Station, University of Wisconsin, 1915.

Gottmann, Jean, *Megalopolis: The Urbanized Northeastern Seaboard of the United States*. New York: Twentieth Century Fund, 1961.

———, The Coming of the Transactional City. College Park: University of Maryland, Institute for Urban Studies, 1983.

Harris, C. D., and E. L. Ullman, "The Nature of Cities," *Annals of the Academy of Political and Social Science*, 242 (1945), 7–17.

Harris, Richard, "A Political Chameleon: Class Segregation in Kingston, Ontario, 1961–1976," *Annals of the Association of American Geographers*, 74, no. 3 (1984), 454–76.

———, "Residential Segregation and Class Formation in the Capitalist City," *Progress in Human Geography*, 8, no. 1 (1984), 26–49.

Hoyt, Homer, *The Structure and Growth of Residential Neighborhoods in American Cities*. Washington, D.C.: U.S. Govt. Printing Office, 1939.

Hudson, John C., "The Plains Country Town," in B. W. Blouet and F. C. Luebke, eds., *The Great Plains: Environment and Culture*, pp. 99–118. Lincoln, Nebr.: University of Nebraska Press, 1979.

———, Plains Country Towns. Minneapolis, Minn.: University of Minnesota Press, 1985.

Hyland, Gerald A., "Social Interaction and Urban Opportunity: The Appalachian In-Migrant in the Cincinnati Central City," *Antipode*, 2, no. 2 (December 1970), 68–83.

Johnson, E. A. J., *The Organization of Space in Developing Countries*. Cambridge, Mass.: Harvard University Press, 1970.

Johnson, R. J., *The American Urban System, A Geographical Perspective*. New York: St. Martin's Press, 1982.

Kellerman, A., "Telecommunications and the Geography of Metropolitan Areas," *Progress in Human Geography*, 8, no. 2 (1984), 222–46.

Kleinfield, N. R., "Mining Chinatown's Mountain of Gold," *New York Times*, June 1, 1986, Sec. 3, pp. 1, 8.

Ley, David, *A Social Geography of the City*. New York: Harper & Row, Pub., 1983.

Lösch, August, *The Economics of Location*, trans. by W. H. Woglom and W. F. Stolper. New Haven, Conn.: Yale University Press, 1954.

Lynch, Kevin, *The Image of the City*. Cambridge, Mass.: M.I.T. Press, 1960.

Mayer, Harold M., and Richard W. Wade, *Chicago: Growth of a Metropolis*. Chicago: University of Chicago Press, 1969.

Mellor, Rosemary, "The Urbanization of Britain—A Review," *International Journal of Urban and Regional Research*, 7, no. 3 (September 1983), 380–403.

Muller, Peter O., *Contemporary Suburban America*. Englewood Cliffs, N.J.: Prentice-Hall, 1981.

Murdie, Robert, *The Factorial Ecology of Metropolitan Toronto, 1951–1961: An Essay on the Social Geography of the City*. Chicago: University of Chicago, Department of Geography, 1968.

Murphey, Rhoads, "The City as a Center of Change: Western Europe and China," *Annals of the Association of American Geographers*, 44, no. 4 (1954), 349–62.

Orleans, Peter, "Differential Cognition of Urban Residents: Effects of Social Scale on Mapping," in Roger M. Downs and David Stea, eds., *Image and Environment*, pp. 131–47. Chicago: Aldine Publishing Co., 1973.

Palm, Risa, *The Geography of American Cities*. New York: Oxford University Press, 1981.

Park, R. E., E. W. Burgess, and R. D. McKenzie, *The City*. Chicago: University of Chicago Press, 1925.

Reid, J., "Black America in the 1980s," *Population Bulletin*, vol. 37, no. 4 (December 1982).

Rose, Harold, *The Black Ghetto: A Spatial Behavioral Perspective*. New York: McGraw-Hill, 1971.

Rose, Harold, and Charles M. Christian, "Race and Ethnicity," in Charles M. Christian and Robert A. Harper, eds., *Modern Metropolitan Systems*, pp. 362–89. Columbus, Ohio: Charles Merrill, 1982.

Schaffer, Richard, and Neil Smith, "The Gentrification of Harlem," *Annals of the Association of American Geographers*, 76, no. 3 (1986), 347–65.

Sjoberg, Gideon, *The Preindustrial City*. Glencoe, Ill.: The Free Press, 1960.

Sturdy, David, "Correlation of Evidence of Medieval Urban Communities," in Peter J. Ucko, Ruth Tringham, and G. W. Dimbleby, eds., *Man, Settlement and Urbanism*, pp. 863–65. Cambridge, Mass.: Schenkman, 1972.

Stutz, Frederick P., "Adjustment and Mobility of Elderly Poor Amid Downtown Renewal," *Geographical Review*, 66, no. 4 (October 1976), 391–400.

Tien, H. Yuan, "China: Demographic Billionaire," *Population Bulletin*, vol. 38, no. 2 (April 1983).

Todaro, Michael P., "Urbanization in Developing Nations: Trends, Prospects, and Policies," *Journal of Geography*, 79, no. 5 (September–October 1980), 164–73.

Urban Land Institute, *New Opportunities for Residential Development in Central Cities*. Report no. 25. Washington, D.C.: Urban Land Institute, 1976.

Vance, James, *The Merchant's World: The Geography of Wholesaling*. Englewood Cliffs, N.J.: Prentice-Hall, 1970.

Wade, Richard, *The Urban Frontier*. Chicago: University of Chicago Press, 1959.

Wong, Bernard P., *Chinatown: Economic Adaptation and Ethnic Identity of the Chinese*. New York: Holt, Rinehart & Winston, 1982.

Zelinsky, Wilbur, and David F. Sly, "Personal Gasoline Consumption, Population Patterns, and Metropolitan Structure: The United States, 1960–1970," *Annals of the Association of American Geographers*, 74, no. 2 (1984), 257–78.

12 THE HUMAN IMPACT ON THE ENVIRONMENT

Environmental Changes in the Past
Contemporary Environmental Issues
Trends Involving Humans and the Natural Environment

In one sense, the title of this chapter is misleading. It suggests that humans are separate from the environment that surrounds and supports us. This is an illusion fostered by Western traditions and by the effects of living in urbanized societies where nature is pushed into the background. This feeling of separateness from nature is dangerous because it leads to the belief that we are free agents on the earth, immune from the repercussions of our actions. It is increasingly obvious that this is not the case. The linking of high rates of cancer to the dumping of chemical wastes in the Love Canal area of New York State is evidence that we reap what we sow in our interactions with the environment (Brown 1979).

It is useful, however, to temporarily consider the human component as separate from the rest of the biological and physical environment, so that the human impact can be understood. Unlike most organisms, human beings affect every ecosystem, directly or indirectly. For example, DDT residue is found in birds thousands of miles from the point of application to the land. Radioactive fallout from nuclear bomb testing in the Pacific during the 1950s and 1960s had a worldwide distribution. Therefore, the impact of humans on the environment needs to be singled out because of its spatial scope and general intensity. This impact, at first slight and areally limited, then increasing in force and extent as population and technology developed, is the subject of this chapter.

ENVIRONMENTAL CHANGES IN THE PAST

Changes by Prehistoric Hunters and Gatherers

For almost 2 million years, humans lived by hunting game and collecting plant products. Population densities were low and technology rudimentary, so the human impact on the environment was limited. Never-

theless, hunters and gatherers left their mark on the earth in the form of diminished numbers of animal species and altered vegetation.

It is possible that overhunting resulted in the extinction of numerous species of large animals such as the mammoth at the end of the glacial period 10,000–15,000 years ago. The theory of prehistoric overkill, first advanced by A. R. Wallace in 1911 and more recently supported by Paul Martin, maintains that widespread extinction of large animals was unknown before the advent of hunters. Extinctions had taken place in earlier periods, but then the life forms that died out were replaced by related species. In contrast, the ecological niches that were suddenly emptied in the late Pleistocene were not refilled by large animals. In Martin's words, it was "extinction without replacement" (Martin and Wright 1967, p. 78). Armed with increasingly efficient hunting equipment—the thrusting spear, missile spear, spear thrower, and bow—and techniques such as fire drives, prehistoric people probably decimated the population of large herbivores, including the mammoth and mastodon. Predators, such as the saber-toothed cats, lost their food base and also perished.

Martin charted the progression of prehistoric overkill, starting in Africa and South Asia, affecting the Americas, Europe, northern Asia, and Australia during the late Pleistocene (the main period of extinction), and occurring most recently in the islands of the West Indies, Madagascar, and New Zealand. In New Zealand, the extinction of the moa, a large flightless bird, is directly linked to the arrival of Polynesian settlers after A.D. 800.

The overkill theory is persuasive, but the evidence is thin and the ideas are hypothetical. Standing against the theory is the knowledge that contemporary hunters and gatherers do not hunt their game to extinction.

Fire was the most important force that hunters and gatherers used to control the environment. Hunters used fire to drive game to convenient places for the kill, to clear forests, and to reduce pasturage so that potential prey could be kept within restricted areas. Food gatherers used fire as a form of land management, to improve the quality and yields of grasses. The ecological effect of burning, whether by humans or other agents such as lightning, is to eliminate long-lived perennials like trees and shrubs, which cannot sustain damage to their above-ground parts, and to encourage the establishment of grasses, which quickly recover from fire and so take control. It is possible that many of the grasslands of the world (the North American prairie, Australian grasslands, Argentinian pampas, and Russian steppes) were not the **climax vegetation** but were the result of periodic burning during thousands of years. The theory gains strength from the accounts of Euro-American settlers in the American Midwest in the mid-nineteenth century where it was noted that woody vegetation quickly revived when the land was fenced and Indian burning was prevented.

It is impossible to know the attitudes the prehistoric peoples held toward the environment; there was surely great variation from place to place and time to time. Yet it is important to get some idea of their view of nature because, in theory at least, this affected the way they used the environment. The best estimate can be made by examining hunting and gathering societies of today.

Aborigines have occupied the continent of Australia for at least 13,000 years, subsisting by hunting and gathering and using Stone Age tools and equipment. To the aborigine, nature is animate—alive with the spirits of plants, animals, and ancestors (Chapter 7). The aborigines believe that the "Ancestral Beings" created the continent from nothing, filled it with animals, plants, and water, and arranged for a continuing ecological balance by establishing strict rules controlling the exploitation of the environment and the consumption of food. The Australian anthropologist Norman Tindale suggested that these ideas of creation developed from the accumulated experience of trial and error operating over thousands of years to produce a workable view of the limits of the environment. Consequently, the aborigines' beliefs contributed to their survival (1959, pp. 36–51).

This is not to say that the aborigines (or all other hunting and gathering societies) have lived in complete harmony with nature. In every society there are discrepancies between beliefs and practices. Tindale (1959) believed that the early aborigines altered vast areas of vegetation by burning and eliminated numerous animal species by overhunting. But eventually the aborigines had to come to an accommodation with the environment. Each band was tied to a specific (but imprecisely bounded) territory by deep-rooted attachments, particularly to their sacred sites. These tribal areas functioned as ecological survival units, proportioning population to food supplies. If too many animals were killed or too many plants collected in any one year, then the results could be future famine for the group that overexploited its territory. Aborigines, and other hunting and gathering societies that relied on a small number of ecosystems, were conservationists by necessity.

Environmental Alterations in Ancient Civilizations

The domestication of plants and animals revolutionized human relations with the environment. The Agricultural Revolution lifted humans into a dominant position in the ecosystem, changing their role from hunters and gatherers to manipulators of the environment. The transition took place in diverse places at different times (Chapter 2), but the ecological results were probably similar.

Even the simple tools and techniques of shifting cultivation used by early farmers had a powerful impact on the environment. Pollen analysis (a method of dating that identifies each period by its prevailing vegetation) reveals that extensive areas of European forests were cleared by farmers using stone axes and fire as tools. Danish archaeologists have shown that clearing large areas of forest is possible with stone axes and fire. Working in a mixed-oak woodland similar to the original vegetation, the archaeologists cleared a two-acre plot using axes to cut the trees and fire to remove the undergrowth. It is reasoned that once the mantle of forest was removed, grazing by cattle, sheep, goats, and pigs hindered regeneration.

In a discontinuous belt from the lower Nile through Mesopotamia to the Indus Valley, technological advances made agriculture more complex. The development of large irrigation systems and the invention of the plow increased agricultural production. These changes were accompanied by the stratification of society (Chapter 8) and the emergence of the first urban civilizations.

The irrigation civilizations, with their large concentrations of population, placed great pressure on local, and even distant, ecosystems. For example, the cedars of Lebanon were seriously depleted at an early date by Egyptians and Mesopotamians who valued the tall straight trees for construction. In the case of the Mesopotamian and Indus Valley civilizations, the eventual decline of the society may have been associated with ecological collapse. As population grew, the agricultural systems were strained: soil fertility was decreased by shortened fallow periods, marginal land was plowed up, and vegetation was damaged by

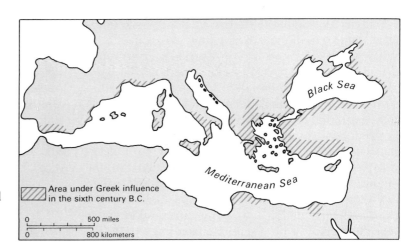

Figure 12-1. The Extent of Ancient Greek Influence. Greek methods of using the physical environment affected many coastal areas around the Mediterranean Sea and Black Sea by the sixth century B.C.

enlarged herds of sheep and goats. The results were rapid runoff, floods, increased soil erosion, and the silting-up of the irrigation channels. Centuries of irrigation without adequate drainage left the soils saline, and agricultural areas were abandoned. According to this ecological thesis, the cities of Mesopotamia and the Indus declined because of excessive demands on the natural environment. In contrast, the Nile Valley, with its yearly rejuvenating flood adding fresh alluvium to the soil, escaped ecological disaster and continued to be a grain-exporting area through Roman times.

The manner and extent to which various early civilizations exploited the natural environment resulted from a variety of societal conditions, including their belief systems (Chapter 7). Prehistoric farmers and herdsmen believed in the tangible presence of good and evil forces in nature. Relations with the environment were ritualized. Agricultural activities were guided by ceremonies aimed at encouraging nature to be beneficent, to provide rains, and to nurture the crops to maturity.

The first people who are known to have broken from the concept of unity with nature were the Mesopotamians, who waged a "war" against the natural environment. The Mesopotamian attitude was expressed in their cultural mentifacts where nature was depicted as a terrible, threatening chaos, which had to be brought under control by human labor with the assistance of the gods. The grid pattern of the streets of Babylon and the canal network symbolized the attempt to impose order on the land. It is no coincidence that the feeling of separation from nature initially appeared in the first urban societies where a portion of the population was separated from working the land and where the works of humans seemed to overshadow the works of nature.

In contrast, the early Greeks glorified nature. Their poetry, drama, and architecture were filled with imageries of nature. To a great extent their religion was the worship of nature. They believed that the

earth was designed by a divine force and that there existed a harmony between nature and humankind. The Greeks thought that the human role was to oversee the creation of the earth and to improve on nature. Agriculture, irrigation works, and cities were evidence of this finishing process. Yet, because widespread deforestation, soil erosion, and wildlife depletion were there for all to see, it was obvious that not all the changes made by the Greeks to the environment were beneficial.

By 200 B.C., the forests of Greece had been destroyed in all but the most remote areas to provide construction lumber, fuel, pitch, tar, and resin for waterproofing. In many parts of the peninsula the only surviving trees were sacred groves. The inevitable result of deforestation was soil erosion. According to Plato, the hills of Attica were like the "skeleton of a sick man [with] all the fat and soft earth having wasted away, and only the bare framework of the land being left" (quoted in Glacken 1967, p. 121). Unable to carry heavy loads of eroded materials, the rivers silted up and marshland formed. The large areas of stagnant water became breeding grounds for mosquitoes, and malaria was a serious problem by the fourth century B.C.

The Greeks tried to devise agricultural systems that preserved the fertility of the soil. Crop rotations, fallowing, terracing, plant breeding, manuring, and the use of legumes were all known and employed. As population grew, however, marginal land was plowed up, leading to soil erosion and environmental deterioration. Minerals were depleted as demands increased, forcing the Greeks to reach far afield, to Italy and Spain, for supplies. The influence of the Greeks on the environment was not localized. By 600 B.C., the Greeks had colonized many coastal areas of the Mediterranean and Black Sea (Figure 12-1). Three hundred

---

Climax vegetation. The stage in which a community of plants becomes stable and begins to perpetuate itself.

years later, Alexander the Great extended Greek influence south into Egypt and as far east as India.

The early Romans, like the Greeks, were an agrarian people with ties to nature and a great love for land. Not surprisingly, then, their religion contained a strong element of animism, and the agricultural cycle was controlled by elaborate rituals. In the late stages of the Roman Empire, however, respect for nature was replaced by an exploitive attitude toward the environment. The changes that the Romans made in the environment were more sweeping and enduring than any of the Western civilizations that had preceded them and, indeed, than most of the European societies that followed in the centuries leading up to the Industrial Revolution. These changes were regarded as great achievements. The landscapes of Europe, North Africa, and Southwest Asia were stamped with the distinctive marks of Roman organization: towering aqueducts (some of which still survive); straight, well-constructed roads that reached to the frontiers of the empire; forts that became the nuclei of towns, particularly in Western Europe; and the centurion system of land allotment that divided the countryside into a checkerboard of 125-acre squares.

In addition to these achievements, the Romans left a legacy of environmental damage. One severe environmental impact was deforestation. The accessible forests of Italy were depleted to meet the demand for charcoal and construction timber. Specialty timber for masts was brought from as far away as the Black Sea coastlands and Lebanon. As in Greece, the results of deforestation were soil erosion, river silting and flooding, and the formation of marshes. Silt clogged the harbors of major Roman ports such as Ostia and Ravenna, and the large areas of stagnant water made malaria a widespread disease by the second century A.D.

Roman mines scarred the landscapes of what are now Italy, Spain, Greece, Britain, and France (Figure 12-2). Engineers stripped the surface deposits first, using open-pit methods, which removed hillsides, caused soil erosion, and silted and poisoned streams. Later, they worked in underground shafts until mineral veins were exhausted. For example, the tin mines of Spain were worked out by the third century, forcing greater extraction of tin ores in England.

The Romans did try to preserve the fertility of agricultural land, using manuring, crop rotations, terracing, irrigation, and drainage. But because of deforestation, overgrazing, warfare, and the fragile nature of the Mediterranean ecosystem, the land deteriorated. By the second century A.D., there were chronic food shortages and a declining population. There is even evidence that ecological conditions

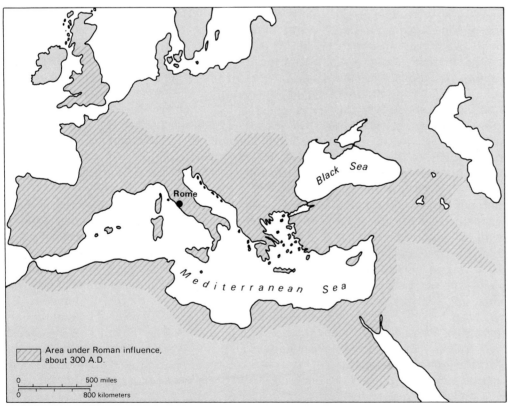

Figure 12-2. The Extent of Roman Influence, circa A.D. 300. Roman attitudes about the natural environment shaped the landscape of large portions of Western Europe, Southwest Asia, and North Africa.

should be considered, as well as social and economic factors, as reasons for the decline of the Roman Empire (Hughes 1975).

Environmental Changes in Europe Prior to Industrialization

The Middle Ages, particularly the period from the eleventh through the thirteenth centuries, was a time of active environmental change in Europe, characterized by the expansion of arable land and settlement and the retreat of forest and marsh. These activities all took place within the framework of Christian philosophy. Although Christianity contained both the themes of stewardship of, and human domination over, nature (Chapter 7), the latter was the stronger emphasis. According to the historian Lynn White, Christianity separated humans from nature and gave them a license to exploit it. White argued:

> In Antiquity every tree, every spring, every stream, every hill had its own ... guardian spirit.... Before one cut a tree, mined a mountain, or dammed a brook, it was important to placate the spirit in charge of that particular situation. By destroying pagan animism, Christianity made it possible to exploit nature in a mood of indifference to the feelings of natural objects. [1967, p. 1206]

Once again, the most immediate impact of human activity on the environment was deforestation. With the disintegration of the Roman Empire, the forest had crept back over the land that had once been cleared for settlement and agriculture. But after 1050, during the great age of reclamation, many forested areas were again cleared (Figure 12-3). The effect was to change the face and economy of Europe. The lowlands were cleared for agriculture, and only the uplands remained as "great wooded islands in a sea of cultivation" (Darby 1956, p. 195).

The process of deforestation and agricultural expansion was accomplished faster than during previous times because of technological advances. The hydraulic saw diffused through Europe during the Middle Ages and allowed timber to be more widely used as a building material. The invention of the horse-collar, replacing the noose, increased the efficiency of the horse as a source of power. The heavy plow, equipped with a vertical knife to cut the furrow, a horizontal plowshare to slice the sod, and a moldboard to turn it over, all permitted the advance of settlement into areas of heavy soils that could not have been farmed with the light scratch plow that was used on the thin soils of the Mediterranean lands.

After 1500, Europeans thrust out from their tiny peninsula of Eurasia to trade and settle throughout the world. As is often true of conquering people, they carried with them a belief of their own superiority over the native peoples they encountered. Europeans

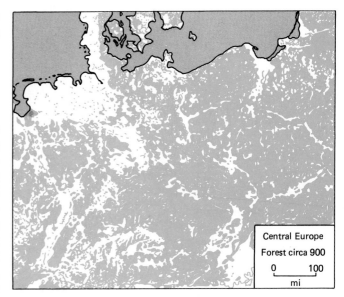

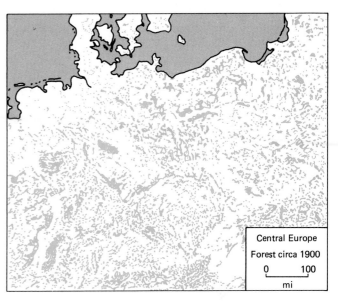

Figure 12-3. Deforestation of Europe from A.D. 900 to 1900. Much of the European forest was cut after A.D. 1050 to create agricultural land. After Schlüter and Darby 1956.

were convinced that they had a divine mission to subdue the wilderness of sparsely settled areas and to bring greater productivity to "underutilized" areas.

The sixteenth century saw much environmental destruction (Sauer 1966). In 1519, the Spanish conquistadors led by Hernando Cortez landed on the mainland of Middle America. They came to search for gold and to save souls in the name of Roman Catholicism. By 1521, they had captured the Aztec capital of Tenochtitlan and had started the process of exploration and conquest that extended Spanish control northward to New Mexico by the end of the century. Middle America became a source of raw materials (gold, silver, sugar, cacao, indigo, leather, and tallow) for Spain.

Figure 12-4. Ruins at the Guanajuato Silver Mine. This mine began extracting silver in 1548. Photo courtesy of Leslie Hewes.

After the accessible surface deposits of gold and silver were exhausted, the Spaniards started to work large and deep veins around Zacatecas (1546), Guanajuato (1548), and Durango (1555) (Figure 12-4). The demand for timber and fuel for the mines led to deforestation. Zacatecas, once the site of the richest silver mines in the world, was situated in the midst of an oak and pine forest in colonial times. Now it sits on open barren ground (Figure 12-5). On the semiarid uplands of the north, sheep and cattle (imported from Spain) overgrazed the land.

Environmental destruction was also common in England's North American colonies. The English never came to ecological terms with the American South, a region quite different from their homeland in climate, vegetation, and soils. Plantation crops like cotton and tobacco were sown in rows, leaving soil exposed to the rain, and were grown year after year

Figure 12-5. The Landscape Near Zacatecas, Mexico. Zacatecas was once surrounded by an oak and pine forest. Photo courtesy of Leslie Hewes.

until the land was exhausted. The planters then moved on, leaving behind eroded slopes and silted channels. In Virginia, Maryland, and North Carolina, the late eighteenth-century shift of tobacco cultivation from the tidewater locations inland to the Piedmont region was partially prompted by the exhaustion of the soil. In some places the land has never recovered from the damage of colonial agriculture.

These comments on the impact of agricultural societies on the natural environment are concentrated on Western culture because, with the diffusion of European peoples and culture after 1500, the European approach to the environment was transmitted throughout the world. European culture became the model for change and economic development in many non-Western countries, even in those that opposed Western political domination.

Even though European views of nature have been influential in many parts of the world, other cultural approaches to the environment were dominant in numerous areas for centuries. For example, in contrast to the Christian tradition of Western culture, Taoist and Buddhist philosophies stress the importance of working in harmonious cooperation with the environment (Chapter 7). This concept of stewardship proved to be rewarding because, for many centuries up to 1850, China was probably the most productive agricultural area in the world (Murphey 1967).

There were discrepancies, however, between Chinese beliefs and practices. Ever since ancient times, deforestation and soil erosion plagued northern China, and extensive areas were overgrazed by sheep and goats. Paradoxically, one of the main agents of environmental destruction in China was associated with Buddhism (Tuan 1970). The most severely overgrazed land occurred around the Buddhist monasteries where monks pastured large herds. The Buddhists were also responsible for introducing the practice of cremation into China, which contributed to deforestation in the southern coastal provinces from the tenth to the fourteenth centuries. In neighboring Japan in the seventeenth century, the Buddhists were responsible for a large percentage of the nation's timber consumption.

It is obvious that environmental destruction was not confined to Western culture and the Christian tradition alone. Even in societies where the people revered nature, some environmental damage was inevitably associated with the process of exacting a living from the land.

Transformations of the Environment by Industrialized Societies

The advent of industrialization represented a major change in the relationships between humans and the natural environment (Chapter 2). Manufacturing required a wide variety of resources, especially those providing inanimate energy. Many industrial operations created by-products and wastes that were capable of polluting the environment. Basic heavy industries like metal smelting resulted in spoil heaps, air pollution, and often toxic conditions where few plants and animals could live. The associated concentrations of people overburdened water supplies and created problems of sewage. Natural settings were transformed into the built environments of the early industrial cities.

Much environmental destruction in the nineteenth century took place in the "new lands" settled by Europeans. In Carl Sauer's opinion, "The free booters of Europe . . . did more damage to the earth in a few generations than in all of human history preceding" (1967, p. 147).

Nowhere was this transformation of the environment more evident than in the United States. The forests of New York and New England were depleted by 1840, and the timber companies moved on to the woodlands of the Great Lakes. The heyday of the Great Lakes timber industry was in the 1870s and 1880s; but by the end of the century, the forest resources of this area were exhausted. The last stand of white pine, the most prized of all commercial species, had been cut by the time of the First World War, and secondary growth covered the area, aptly described as the "cutover region."

There was no real understanding of how fragile many soils in the United States were. As late as 1909, the U.S. Bureau of Soils regarded soil as a resource that could not be exhausted. The major problem area was in the South where soil erosion was already widespread by the time of the Civil War. Like tobacco, cotton is a clean-cultivated crop that leaves the soil exposed to erosion. By 1850, as the core of the cotton belt shifted westward from the Piedmont of the Carolinas and Georgia to Alabama and Mississippi, it left behind impoverished soils and slopes scarred by gullies, some of them 45 meters deep. Only after 1930, when cotton acreage was reduced and leguminous crops like peanuts and soybeans were introduced, did the soils of the South begin to recover from the centuries of abuse.

The Great Plains region was second only to the South as an area of serious soil erosion in the early twentieth century (Figure 12-6). Difficulties commenced during the last few decades of the nineteenth century when the technological advances of the Industrial Revolution encouraged the extension of commercial farming into the drylands of the Great Plains. Improved transportation systems, particularly the railroad, diminished isolation. New agricultural machinery allowed large-scale production. But technological changes were not necessarily accompanied by cultural changes. Most Anglo-Americans were used to

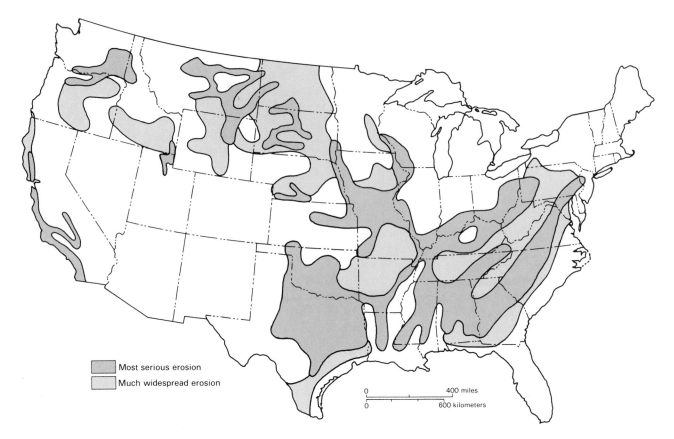

Figure 12-6. Soil Erosion in the United States in the Early Twentieth Century. The Great Plains and South stand out as the areas of greatest soil erosion. *Source:* U.S. Department of Agriculture, 1933.

the forested environments of humid climates, and they had great difficulty adjusting to the semiarid grasslands of the Great Plains. The climatic hazards, particularly drought, were compounded by unsuitable land laws and harmful agricultural practices, such as overgrazing pastures and devoting cropland to wheat monoculture (Worster 1979). Decades of environmental mismanagment, combined with severe drought, produced the "Dust Bowl" of the 1930s when the topsoil of extensive areas was carried away by the wind (Figure 12-7).

Although agricultural practices have improved since the days of the Dust Bowl, soil erosion is still a problem on the Great Plains. For example, in the early 1980s, Nebraska lost more topsoil to wind and water erosion than at any time during the 1930s. Compared to an annual rate loss of 5 tons of soil per acre, which can be replaced by natural processes, several areas in corn are now losing as much as 100 tons per acre per year.

When the Europeans arrived on the shores of North America, they found a continent teeming with wildlife. Since then several species of wildlife have been destroyed for a variety of reasons, including sport and profit. It is true that many species of animals were introduced to the continent by Europeans; but,

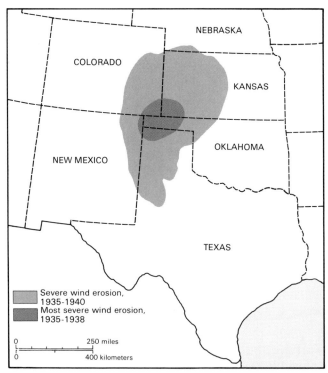

Figure 12-7. The Dust Bowl of the 1930s. The heart of the Dust Bowl was over the panhandle of Oklahoma and the adjoining parts of Kansas, Colorado, New Mexico, and Texas. After Worster 1979.

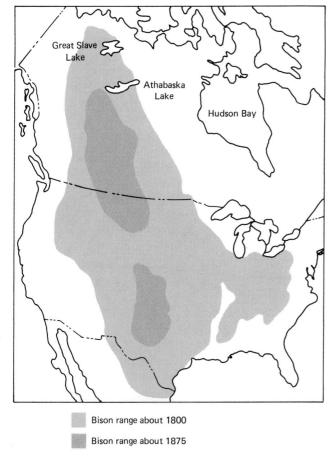

Bison range about 1800

Bison range about 1875

Figure 12-8. The Depletion of Bison in North America. From 1800 to 1875, the size and range of bison herds were greatly reduced by overhunting. After Brown 1948.

in balance, European settlement in North America was accompanied by a rapid decrease in species diversity. The auk, Labrador duck, Carolina parakeet, and passenger pigeon (which had numbered 3 to 5 billion in the early nineteenth century) were hunted to extinction.

The bison were saved from a similar fate only at the last moment. In the early nineteenth century, the bison range stretched from the Gulf of Mexico to the Great Slave Lake in Canada and from the Appalachians to the deserts of the Great Basin (Figure 12-8). Hunting by the Indians for the fur trade, as well as for their own direct use, and by Euro-Americans for hides and sport reduced the bison population to 10 million by 1865. In the 1870s, when railroads gave better access to the bison range and rapid-fire rifles increased hunting efficiency, the slaughter began in earnest. By 1890, only 1000 bison survived as a remnant of the once great herds.

Although the nineteenth century in the United States was a period of resource depletion and environmental exploitation, it was also the century that saw the birth of the conservation movement. The intellectual seeds of this movement were sown in Europe, but they took root and matured in the United States.

The Rise of the Conservation Movement

The conservation movement was greatly influenced by George Perkins Marsh's widely read book, *Man and Nature* (1864). Marsh, a Vermont politician and scholar, argued for forest preservation to prevent floods, erosion, and unfavorable climatic change. Likewise, the ideas of the historian Frederick Jackson Turner were influential (1893). Writing in the 1890s, Turner argued that the American national character had been shaped by the confrontation with the wilderness on repeated frontiers, which fostered individualism and democracy. Turner saw that the frontier was closing and proposed that the American ideals might not be sustained when the wilderness ceased to exist. Turner's **Frontier Thesis** prompted many Americans to reevaluate their traditional feeling of antipathy toward the wilderness, which now became something to protect rather than overcome.

The first National Park, Yellowstone, was established in 1870. The most persuasive advocate of creating more parks was John Muir. Even though his father was a Calvinist intent on subduing the wilderness on the family farm in Wisconsin, Muir took to nature study. After graduating from the University of Wisconsin in 1863, he walked to Florida. On the way he jotted down the thought that nature's object in creating plants and animals was the happiness of each species, not its subservience to "the needs of man" (1901). From Florida, Muir went to California where he became a shepherd in the Sierra Nevada. He recognized the damage sheep were doing and referred to his flocks as "hoofed locusts."

Muir became a powerful force in establishing Yosemite National Park in 1890. He talked about the necessity of wilderness as a place where members of industrial societies could recharge the "fountains of life." It is no coincidence that his arguments had great effect at just the time urban dwellers were becoming aware of their environmental problems (Melosie 1982). In 1891, the Forest Reserve Act was passed, which Teddy Roosevelt used during his administration to greatly increase the size of the national forests.

Concern for the natural environment was expressed from a variety of perspectives, even within the conservationist movement. Those who advocated preservation insisted that wilderness areas should be

---

Frontier Thesis. The proposal by Frederick Jackson Turner that American characteristics, such as individualism, independence, and democracy, were a product of readily available land at the edge of settlement (i.e., the frontier).

retained in their "natural" state. The preservationists, who were influenced partly by Thoreau and Emerson, believed in the value of unaltered nature to offset "the corruption of urban civilization."

Another position was expressed by conservationists who accepted the continued use of resources but advocated using them carefully and in a manner that did not cause rapid exhaustion. Aldo Leopold introduced the idea of an "ecological conscience," which referred to the need to view the environment as a whole, not just as a collection of raw materials to be consumed by humans (1969). Thus, as American industrial society grew, so did a spectrum of concerns about the natural environment (Nash 1967).

CONTEMPORARY ENVIRONMENTAL ISSUES

More stress has been placed on the global ecosystem during the twentieth century than in all preceding human history. This stress is caused by an increasing population and by growing rates of resource consumption per person. The rapid development of technology has magnified the human capacity to manipulate nature and has given us the power, in the form of nuclear weapons, to destroy ourselves and the ecosphere in its present form.

Ecosystems, by nature, are adaptable; but the accumulating evidence of environmental degradation from all over the world suggests that the present level of stress cannot be tolerated for a long period of time. Some well-known scholars fear that our present course is "suicidal" (Boulding 1966b, p. 234). The Council on Environmental Quality in its 1980 report on the future of the global ecosystem expressed grave concern about trends such as deteriorating quality of agricultural land, diminishing amounts of easily extractable oil, accelerating extinction of species, continuing deforestation, and increasing air pollution.

The dimensions of the human impact on the environment in the second half of the twentieth century can be gauged by examining three major areas of concern: resource depletion, environmental pollution, and warfare.

In addition, a fourth area of concern focuses on natural hazards. This topic is relevant because the relationships between humans and the natural environment are not restricted to only those in which nature suffers from human activities. Humans and the natural environment both affect, and are affected by, each other (Figure 1-3).

Resource Depletion

The future of agricultural land is critical to the world's families that support themselves directly by farming, as well as to nonrural people who depend on arable land for their food supply. Demands for improved productivity of farming will continue to increase as the population grows.

On the surface, the prospects for increasing world food production are good. At the World Population Conference held in Bucharest in 1974, it was estimated that if yields comparable to those achieved by Iowa farmers were attained globally on all existing available land, 7.6 billion people could be supported on a subsistence diet of 2500 calories a day. Furthermore, if the problems of utilizing land in the humid tropics could be overcome, the prediction continued, then 38 to 48 billion people could feast on well-balanced diets of 4000 to 5000 calories a day.

Some scholars believe that these higher predictions are pipe dreams or technological illusions. Even if political and economic barriers to achieving these goals are ignored (Chapters 8 and 9), there are serious ecological obstacles. According to Lester Brown (1981), an expert on world agricultural systems, most of the productive land is already grazed or in crops, and extension of farming into marginal areas like the humid tropics or semiarid regions will result in falling productivity and accelerated soil erosion.

The alternative to increasing the area of land devoted to farming is to increase agricultural production from the existing acreage. One way to do this is to apply the techniques of scientific farming, including specialized machinery, genetically improved crops, inorganic fertilizers, and synthetic pesticides. This technology has raised the productivity of agriculture dramatically in the United States, but it has also caused many environmental problems.

The dominant American system of farming is monoculture. Viewed ecologically, rather than just economically, extensive growing of a single crop can be destructive. One of the axioms of ecological theory is that a complex ecosystem is a stable system because energy flows through it in many channels. If one species in a tropical rainforest, for example, is destroyed, the ecosystem will continue to function because the interacting relationships among the other species still continue. But when a diverse ecosystem is replaced by a specialized single crop, the ecosystem is simplified to the point where it becomes vulnerable. The entire vegetation of such an ecosystem could be destroyed by disease, such as happened in the Irish potato famine in the 1840s.

Monoculture takes a heavy toll on the soil. Under natural conditions, nitrogen accumulates in the soil through the constant breakdown of plant and animal wastes by bacteria. When the land is repeatedly planted to crops like corn or wheat, the nitrogen stock is depleted. In the American corn belt there has been a steady decline in the natural store of nitrogen since farming began. In its place, nitrates are added to the soil in the form of fertilizers. These fertilizers contribute to high yields, but they can be an environmental hazard by polluting water supplies. In areas of Illinois and California (the two leading agricultural states in the United States), concentrated levels of nitrates in the water have been linked to high levels of mortality among female babies. Monoculture usually depends on the application of chemicals to control weeds and pests. In addition to potentially causing damage to the health of humans and other life, toxic herbicides and pesticides may be hazardous to the soil because they destroy the bacteria that are responsible for nitrogen fixation. Moreover, in the long run, pesticides are not effective. By 1984, 447 species, including most of the world's major pests, had acquired a genetic resistance to pesticides.

These agricultural methods are not restricted to the United States; they are common in other more developed countries. Furthermore, in recent years, many less developed countries have adopted some of the same farming techniques by planting genetically improved seeds and applying heavy amounts of fertilizer and irrigation water to produce the high yields associated with the Green Revolution (Chapter 9). In several countries where food production had previously been insufficient to meet the national demand for food, the increase in wheat and rice production was generally welcomed. Nevertheless, these productive benefits were accompanied by some of the same environmental problems experienced by American agriculture. In the Punjab region of India, for instance, the spectacular increase in wheat production that resulted from using the techniques of the Green Revolution has been accompanied by an expansion of saline soils on irrigated land and an accumulation of nitrates in areas of heavy fertilization.

The typical methods used by farmers in America and elsewhere to produce high yields are not the only alternatives. Some farmers in the United States apply only organic fertilizers and avoid chemical pesticides and herbicides but still employ scientific knowledge to achieve high yields. For example, Old Order Amish dairy farmers in Pennsylvania produce as much milk per unit of area as neighbors who use "modern" methods and who consume greater energy inputs (Johnson, Stoltzfas, Craumer 1977). In several less developed countries where attempts are being made to increase crop yields through improved methods, there remains an emphasis on the continued use of indigenous strains of crops, planted in combinations that are environmentally sound and thus sustainable for the future.

Knowledge and farming techniques exist that can greatly curtail the depletion of agricultural resources. The extent to which conservation is practiced, however, depends on the cultural, political, and economic setting in which individual farmers decide on the use of land. Preventing environmental depletion and con-

tamination is only one of several objectives. The American farmer who is threatened by financial failure attempts to utilize resources as cheaply as possible to achieve a profit. The costs of conservation may seem too high under current financial conditions, whereas the amount of soil damage per year is perceived to be minor. Similarly, in a less developed country, a farmer who rents a small plot of land and produces barely enough to meet family food requirements usually gives priority to immediate necessities. Although most farmers are aware of the long-range effects of resource deterioration, they feel their current problems leave them little choice but to produce food and other agricultural commodities as cheaply as possible.

Overgrazing, soil erosion, and deforestation are the main types of deterioration in many of the relatively poor countries (Eckholm 1976). Environmental destruction is frequently accentuated by the desperate need to produce food on land that is marginal for agriculture. Problems generally begin when an increase in rural population forces farmers to cut down forests to make room for crops. Deforestation then leads to soil erosion, flooding, and silting of irrigation systems, as it did during the times of the Greeks and Romans.

The problem of climatic aridity is often aggravated by overgrazing and by the extension of farming into dry environments. Expanding **desertification** is as much a product of human damage to the environment as it is a result of climatic change. This is demonstrated by the southward expansion of the Sahara Desert and by similar desertification in several other areas of the world (Figure 12-9).

Forests are also cut to provide firewood for cooking and heating because wood is the primary source of energy in many agrarian nations (Figure 12-10). In Niamey, Niger, for example, the average manual laborer's family spends one-quarter of its income on firewood. The Council on Environmental Quality (1980) estimates that per capita supplies of wood will fall by 47 percent by the year 2000. The impact will be most traumatic in the less developed countries, where an estimated 90 percent of the energy used in homes comes from wood, crop residues, and dung. The shortage of firewood is probably the most critical energy problem in the world when measured by the number of people affected.

Some of the forces leading to resource depletion are illustrated by the deforestation currently taking place in Nepal. Until recent decades, a large share of the country was forested, especially on the slopes of

---

Desertification. The spread of aridlike conditions, which may be caused by climatic change, by human activities, or by both.

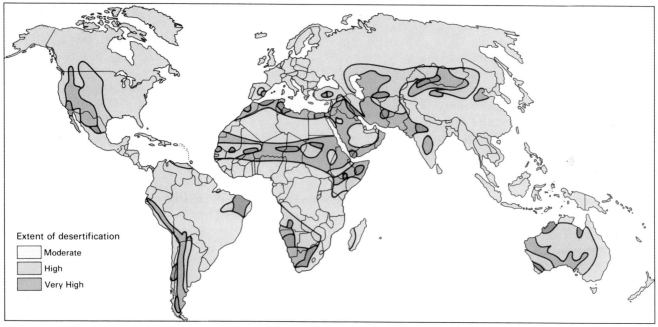

Figure 12-9. Desertification in Dry Areas. The expansion of deserts is caused both by decreasing annual precipitation and increasing stress from human use. *Source:* United Nations 1977.

Extent of desertification

☐ Moderate
▨ High
▓ Very High

the Himalaya Mountains and in the malarial lowlands bordering India. After a political change in the early 1950s, the new government attempted to improve the life of its citizens through economic development and associated benefits in housing, health, and education. By applying pesticides in the malarial zone, health was improved and the land was made suitable for settlement. The lowland forests were cut to clear the land for agriculture and to gain capital from timber. As is true in many less developed countries (especially those in tropical regions), deforestation results

partly from the need for development capital that can be acquired by exporting forest products.

With improved health, the population of Nepal is increasing at a faster rate than prior to 1950. Because the country's economy is still based primarily on agriculture, the population increase creates a demand for more arable land. To make room for crops in the mountainous regions, people cut trees that occupy mountainsides. Furthermore, more people require additional firewood, which is often acquired from the forested slopes.

Figure 12-10. Women Carrying Firewood, Kathmandu, Nepal. Throughout much of the world, women spend many hours collecting and carrying firewood for cooking and other daily needs. Photo courtesy of Sally Stoddard.

Attempts to expand economic opportunities in the mountains may also produce detrimental pressure on forest resources. For example, tourists who hike in the Himalayas offer attractive pay for wood for their campfires.

In summary, forests are cut because farmers need more land to grow food, the general population requires firewood, and those enterprises depending on tourism want to provide the facilities demanded by hikers.

Clearing trees from the rugged slopes of the Himalayas, which receive very heavy rains during the monsoon season, causes several forms of environmental damage. Without trees to retain some of the precipitation, runoff is increased. On exposed slopes, even those that have been painstakingly terraced, soil is easily eroded (Figure 12-11). The resulting landslides may destroy fields, roads, and entire villages. Downstream the eroded soils and debris clog hydroelectric dams. On the lowlands of Nepal and northern India, the added runoff floods extensive areas. Coarse gravels accumulate over the cropland near the base of the mountains, and valuable fine soil is carried to the Bay of Bengal.

People in Nepal know about the destruction caused by deforestation. Nevertheless, they (like others around the world) often make decisions about the use of a specific earth resource within the context of immediate needs. Consequently, they often give a lower priority to choices that may affect future generations than those options satisfying current demands.

To many people, resource depletion suggests the exploitation of the world's oil. Under present technology, industrial economies are heavily reliant on petroleum products. The United States, which uses approximately a third of the world's annual consumption of oil, is particularly vulnerable to future shortages. Since petroleum is a nonrenewable resource, any consumption constitutes a depletion of the world's total reserves. The impact of depletion, however, is difficult to assess because neither the existing amount remaining in the earth nor the future rate of usage is known. Estimates of the total amount of oil in the earth are revised whenever new oil fields are discovered. Likewise, estimates of recoverable oil vary with changing extractive techniques and fluctuating oil prices. Thus, it is impossible to predict when total exhaustion will occur or, more likely, when

Figure 12-11. Terraced Cropland on Mountain Slopes in Nepal. Nearby residents cut trees to obtain firewood and to clear the land for farming. Photo courtesy of Sally Stoddard.

extreme scarcity will make the remaining reserves too expensive to use. Although there is a finite quantity of oil that exists and ultimately it will be consumed if exploitation continues at the current rate, no one knows when exhaustion will occur.

Even harder to predict is the rate of future world consumption, which will reflect the number of consumers and the feasibility of using alternative forms of energy. The number of consumers is expected to increase as the world's population grows. With the growing acceptance of agricultural techniques that depend on chemical fertilizers and mechanically pumped irrigation water, more petroleum will probably be needed. If countries presently classified as less developed become more industrialized, the demand for oil will grow. These predictions, however, exclude the possibilities of changing technologies. If, for instance, genetic characteristics of plants are developed so nitrogen fertilizers and large quantities of water do not need to be added to achieve bumper yields, then the adoption of highly productive agricultural methods will not necessarily require additional oil.

Other elements of uncertainty about future rates of oil consumption are the availability and comparative costs of alternative sources of energy. It has been predicted that by the year 2050, the mix of energy resources will be markedly different from the present. According to one prediction (Figure 12-12), petroleum will have little importance as a source of energy. Coal, fuels from oil shales and tar sands, solar converters, and nuclear generators are expected to provide an increasingly greater share of the world's energy requirements. In many other predictions nuclear power is given less importance. Virtually all predictions, however, anticipate a diminished dependence on petroleum.

A shift to alternate sources of power will not eliminate environmental problems. The hazards of nuclear energy have been widely publicized. The explosion of a nuclear reactor at Chernobyl in the Soviet Union on April 26, 1986, spread radiation over a large area, which resulted in widespread opposition to nuclear power. For example, a 1987 Italian vote to curb construction of nuclear plants was undoubtedly prompted by the heavy doses of radioactive fallout from the Chernobyl explosion which were deposited on the northern parts of Italy.

The hazards of coal, tar sands, and oil shale conversion have been given less attention than nuclear ones, but they too pose serious threats to the natural environment and to the health of workers and residents in production areas. For example, the incidence of skin cancer at a pilot coal-conversion plant in West Virginia in the 1950s was between 16 and 37 percent higher than the incidence in a similar population outside the plant.

As E. F. Schumacher argued, we have not solved

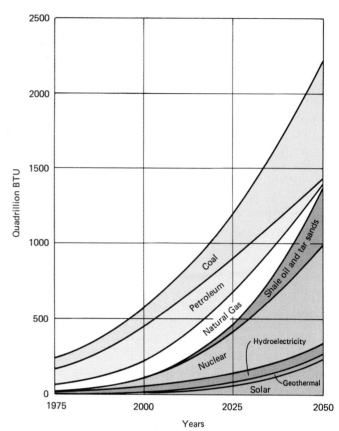

Figure 12-12. Source of World Energy—Proportions Consumed in 1975 and Predicted for Future Dates. Some scholars predict that the relative importance of petroleum and natural gas as sources of energy will decline after the year 2025. From Rudker and Cecelski 1979. Used with permission from Population Reference Bureau.

"the problem of production" (1973). Technological changes, such as the conversion of coal into liquid fuel or the development of nuclear fission to generate electricity from uranium, only give us an illusion of unlimited power. According to Schumacher, we fail to apply the basic economic distinction between income and capital to our relations with the environment. We use resources as if they were a regenerating income when in fact they are irreplaceable capital. If we recognized fossil fuels, for example, as capital, then we would be more concerned about conservation, we would try to minimize the rate of exploitation, and we would continue to search for energy sources that are more compatible with the natural environment.

Solar energy is an "income" resource because the sun continually supplies huge amounts of energy (Figure 12-13). Some experts believe that with a relatively small amount of research and development, solar energy could be used to supply a large proportion of residential and commercial requirements for space and water heating (Figure 12-14). Eventually it should be economic to convert solar energy into

Areas with most hours of sunlight per year

Areas with moderate number of hours of sunlight

Areas with fewest hours of sunlight per year

Figure 12-13. The World Sunbelt. Most places on the earth receive abundant amounts of solar energy that could be harnessed for human use.

Figure 12-14. Residential Use of Solar Energy. Both passive and active solar systems are being used in many parts of United States. Photo courtesy of Sally Stoddard.

electrical energy using photovoltaic cells and even to utilize solar energy as a combustible fuel in the form of hydrogen. Many agree with Commoner that solar energy is an "almost perfect energy source" (1976, p. 151).

In the world of politics and economics, some of the advantages of solar energy have become barriers to its development. Unlike coal, oil, or uranium, its supply cannot be controlled by a few giant corporations. As a source of energy ideally suited to small-scale local development, solar energy is a financial threat to companies that have dominated the production of power.

Environmental Pollution

In natural ecosystems, there is no such thing as waste; organic material is channeled back into the environment where it is taken up by other organisms as food. For example, a respiratory by-product of animals is carbon dioxide, which is used as a nutrient by green plants. Plants, in turn, release oxygen for use by animals. Animal excreta are broken down by bacteria into inorganic materials like nitrate and phosphate,

and so on. Basically, everything must go somewhere. The problem is that "wastes" produced by humans have increased to such an extent that natural ecosystems are unable to handle them. Some forms of waste are toxic, and they can accumulate in the air, soil, and water as pollutants.

Air pollution is not unique to the twentieth century; it was a problem in ancient Babylon and in seventeenth-century London. However, with the rapid growth of population and industrial production in the twentieth century, air pollution has become an ever greater environmental hazard (Figure 12-15). Contamination of the air has global implications because winds carry pollutants long distances, and acid rain and similar problems may occur far from the source areas.

The main causes of air pollution in the industrial world are automobiles, power plants, industry, and residential heating. The major pollutants are carbon dioxide, carbon monoxide, sulfur oxides, hydrocarbons, and particulate matter. Carbon dioxide is discharged into the atmosphere through the combustion of fossil fuels. In earlier times, all the carbon dioxide was taken up by the oceans and the terrestrial biomass

Figure 12-15. Air Pollution. Air is polluted by gases and particulates from a wide variety of sources. Photo courtesy of George Tuck.

and so presented no danger. Today, however, because the use of fossil fuels is increasing and because deforestation is reducing the amount of the biomass, carbon dioxide is accumulating in the atmosphere. For instance, in 1860, the concentration of carbon dioxide in the atmosphere was 290 parts per million; by 1960, it had increased to 320 parts per million.

The long-term global effects of increased atmospheric carbon dioxide are unknown. One possible effect could be a significant increase in the temperature of the earth. The accumulation of carbon dioxide in the atmosphere could create a "greenhouse effect" and would reduce the loss of heat energy from the earth. According to some models, this could raise the earth's average global temperature by 1.5° to 3.0° Celsius, resulting in the dislocation of the earth's climatic and vegetation belts. Eventually polar ice-caps would melt and raise the level of oceans, which would flood low-lying coastal lands. This scenario is countered, however, by those who argue that other pollutants are blocking incoming heat and may reduce earth temperatures.

Another alarming development of global proportions is the depletion of the ozone layer, the oxygen screen which shields the earth from harmful ultraviolet light. In 1985, British scientists discovered that ozone levels over Antarctica were 50 percent lower than they had been a decade earlier. This depletion was even more severe by the summer of 1987. The thinning of the protective shield may be attributed to specific weather conditions over Antarctica that interact with atmospheric chemistry to destroy the ozone. The evidence is mounting, however, that human-made chlorofluorocarbons (used as ingredients in aerosols and as coolants) are also to blame. In response to this threat, 24 nations signed an accord in Montreal in 1987 to halve production of ozone-depleting chemicals by 1999.

At the local scale, the current results of atmospheric contamination are well known. Air pollution had become part of the way of life in Los Angeles, Denver, and most large urban areas in the world. The main culprit is the automobile, which emits hydrocarbons and carbon monoxide. Other pollutants in urban areas include sulfur dioxide, which is produced mainly from the burning of fossil fuels containing sulfur. Sulfur pollutants have more than a local impact because the acidity of rain elsewhere is attributed to them. Industrial cities located south of the Great Lakes, for example, may be the prime contributors to acid rain that is being deposited in Canada. Likewise, the acid rain occurring in Scandinavian countries is attributed to industrial pollutants created by British factories. Also of concern to residents in many urban areas are asbestos particles from automobile brake linings and building materials, mercury vapor released by chemical industries, and nitrogen dioxide,

another product of automobile and power plant combustion, which reduces visibility and is highly toxic to vegetation.

Although it is difficult to prove that a particular pollutant is the specific cause of a disease, statistics do show that people living in polluted business environments experience more health problems, particularly respiratory diseases, than inhabitants of less polluted rural areas. Certainly the quality of life is reduced in cities such as Los Angeles and Beijing where smog frequently hangs over the landscape.

The United States, Japan, and several European countries have striven with some success to reduce levels of air pollution. For example, carbon monoxide levels declined significantly in the United States following the Clean Air Act of 1970 and the enforcement of automobile emission controls. In London, the transition from soft coal (which produced soot and smoke) to smokeless solid fuel, gas, and electricity transformed the city environment. The famous London fog is now a rare occurrence; sulfur dioxide levels have been reduced by 40 percent; and the number of bird species has doubled over the last two decades.

Another form of environmental pollution is the contamination connected with the storage of highly toxic chemical wastes and radioactive materials. The inadequacy of regulations for the disposal of chemical wastes is illustrated by the case of Love Canal. That abandoned hydroelectric canal in a residential district of the city of Niagara Falls was used as a dump for at least 22,000 tons of chemical wastes in the late 1930s and early 1940s. The stored residues, which included highly toxic PCBs and tetradioxin, were covered with a thin layer of dirt. Later, houses were located within 10 meters (30 ft) of the earth-covered ditch, and children played on the filled dump. By the 1950s, residents were complaining of noxious odors in the air and chemical sludges in their basements. By the 1970s, it was obvious that these were not just inconveniences, but real dangers. The health of the inhabitants deteriorated; they were afflicted with ear infections and deafness, nervous disorders and headaches, and there was a high incidence of miscarriages and birth defects (Brown 1979). Eventually, in 1978, Love Canal was declared a national disaster area. During the following two years, the residents were evacuated and relocated. Although in 1982 the Environmental Protection Agency (EPA) declared that Love Canal had been cleaned up and the area was habitable, for several years it had been, in effect, a poisoned place.

Love Canal is not an isolated case. A 1982 report by the EPA showed New York, Pennsylvania, Michigan, Ohio, Indiana, and New Jersey as the states most seriously affected by toxic landfills (Figure 12-16). The areas with the smallest number of industrial storage, treatment, and disposal sites are the western

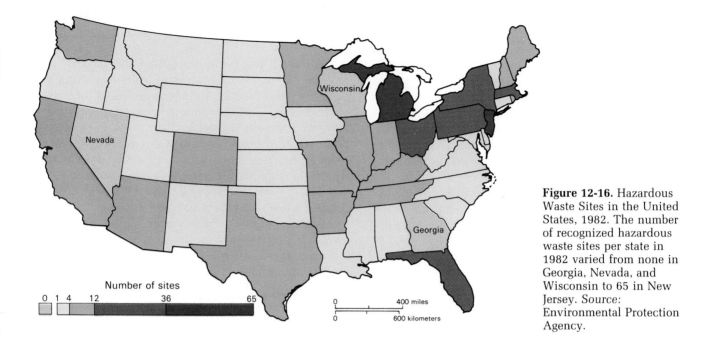

Figure 12-16. Hazardous Waste Sites in the United States, 1982. The number of recognized hazardous waste sites per state in 1982 varied from none in Georgia, Nevada, and Wisconsin to 65 in New Jersey. *Source:* Environmental Protection Agency.

Number of sites

Midwest, the Rocky Mountains, and northern New England. However, even rural states like Iowa have contaminated areas where toxic chemicals that were stored in shallow pits have seeped into underground water. Furthermore, the hazards of chemical wastes are not going to diminish in the foreseeable future unless drastic changes are brought about. These hazards are a by-product of industrial societies. Only now—some two hundred years after the start of industrialization—are we fully recognizing this fact.

The disposal of waste is complicated when the materials are hazardous for very long periods, such as with radioactive wastes. Burial in the ground is the most common way of storing wastes with low levels of radiation. Selecting the most appropriate sites requires geographic analysis about where not to locate the long-lived wastes. Ideal sites are those that avoid areas where people live and work as well as places that might be disturbed by geologic or hydrologic conditions. In practice, many storage sites have been close to places of production and hence close to areas of high population density.

The problem of what to do with the most dangerous wastes has not been solved. In the United States, numerous nuclear reactors and plants manufacturing nuclear weapons generate large amounts of radioac-

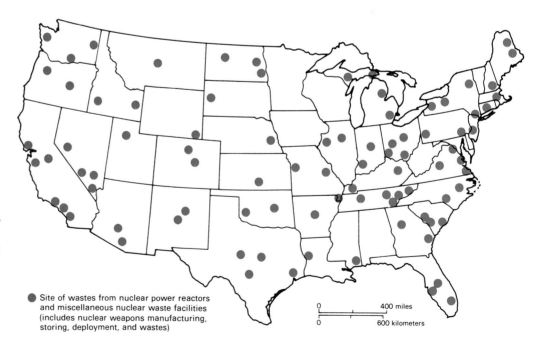

Figure 12-17. U.S. Nuclear Waste Facilities. Sites for manufacturing and storing nuclear weapons, nuclear power reactors, and for disposing of nuclear wastes are distributed in many parts of United States.

● Site of wastes from nuclear power reactors and miscellaneous nuclear waste facilities (includes nuclear weapons manufacturing, storing, deployment, and wastes)

tive wastes annually (Figure 12-17). A dangerous by-product of nuclear fission is Plutonium 239, which lasts 24,000 years before it is reduced to half potency. Studies at the Maxey Flats disposal site in Kentucky and the Rocky Flats nuclear weapons plant in Colorado have shown that buried radioactive waste does infiltrate the water, soil, and atmosphere. In both studies there was evidence that high incidences of cancer were connected with exposure to the wastes. After thousands of studies of disposal of wastes, no guaranteed solution has been found. Plans to melt the wastes through polar icecaps, to ship them toward the sun, to dump them in the oceans, and to bury them in deep caverns in salt mines are all judged to be either ecologically unsound or economically unfeasible.

The difficulty of finding suitable places to store toxic wastes is such that industrialized countries are seeking to export their wastes to less developed lands. In the United States, for example, the number of applications received by the Environmental Protection Agency for permission to ship hazardous wastes overseas to other countries jumped from 30 in 1980 to more than 400 in 1987. Likewise, in 1988, Dutch companies were seeking permission to dump toxic wastes in Suriname, a former Dutch colony in South America. In poor countries, payments for accepting the wastes appear attractive, and often there is little public opposition to toxic dumping. Nevertheless, the legacy that the less developed nations could inherit is one they might regret in the long run.

The use of contaminating poisons illustrates the contradictory objectives facing humans as they modify the natural environment. For example, the application of insecticides to control malaria has improved the health of people throughout the world and has resulted in dramatic declines in infant mortality in several countries (Chapter 3). The dangerous residues from many forms of insecticides, however, have affected wildlife and humans in many undesired ways. Furthermore, decisions about utilizing contaminants often have an impact on more places and people than just those who made the decisions. As demonstrated by the production and use of pesticides, the effects may have detrimental consequences in distant places. Although pesticides are manufactured in several countries, the international characteristics of their use can be illustrated by describing some of their effects in the United States.

Public concern over the long-range effects of pesticides in the United States has led to legislation banning the use of many products. Although legislation has not totally eliminated the dangers from the surreptitious use of illegal pesticides or the excessive application of approved forms, regulatory attempts have been made to protect the food of American consumers. The legal restrictions that apply to the use of pesticides in the United States, however, do not eliminate the potential contamination of food eaten by Americans because of international trading with countries where such pesticides are not banned. For example, at least a quarter of American-exported pesticides involve products that are banned, tightly restricted, or not registered for use within the United States (Weir and Schapiro 1981, p. 4).

These exports may then affect people in the importing country and, subsequently, in the United States. In the importing country, farm workers can become contaminated because they are not aware of the dangers, or because they may be too desperate for work to object to the decision by farm owners or managers to use potentially harmful pesticides. Consequently, the rate of pesticide poisoning in some less developed countries has been estimated to be more than 13 times that in the United States. In addition, farm produce that is consumed locally may contain the poisonous residues. For example, people in Nicaragua and Guatemala have 31 times more DDT in their blood than inhabitants of the United States, where this product has been banned since 1970 (Weir and Schapiro 1981, pp. 11, 13). It has been estimated that 1.5–2.0 million people in less developed countries suffer from acute pesticide poisoning (Pearson 1985).

As mentioned above, the potential for indirect pesticide poisoning of Americans results from the global trade patterns. That is, the effects of pesticides are spread farther than just the boundaries of a country where they are purchased and used. When foodstuffs are imported into the United States from countries using U.S.-banned pesticides, the poisonous residues may return to the country of their origin. According to samples of the U.S. Food and Drug Administration, in recent years more than half the imported fruits and vegetables and nearly half of the imported coffee beans contain residues of pesticides that are now banned for use in the United States.

Environmental Destruction by War

Resource depletion and environmental pollution are detrimental side effects, not the calculated objectives, of the ways we use the earth. Warfare, on the other hand, is generally an organized and premeditated destruction of the enemy's population, built environment, and natural environment. Warfare has always tended to be harmful to natural environments as well as to humans and their cultural landscapes, but in recent decades the capacity for destruction has increased manyfold.

In the Second World War a major strategy was to destroy the built environments of enemy countries. As industrial plants, transportation facilities, and entire cities were razed to the ground, the result was essentially "place annihilation" (Hewitt 1983). During the

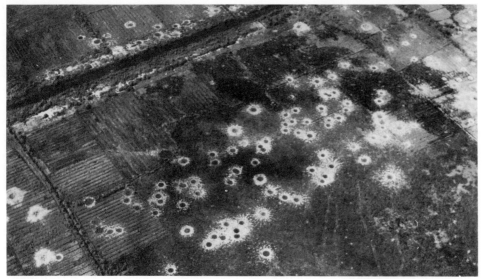

Figure 12-18. Cratered Area, South Vietnam. Bombing of Vietnam during the late 1960s and early 1970s greatly damaged formerly arable land. Photo courtesy of Gordon H. Orians.

London blitz of 1940, German bombing was so effective that on occasions it created fires stretching miles into the atmosphere. In return, British and American bombing devastated over 50 percent of the built-up area of more than 40 German cities. American bomb-

ing of Japan removed 25 percent of the nation's housing.

The American military involvement in Vietnam from 1964 to 1973 has been characterized as a "war against the land" (Westing and Pfeiffer 1972). From

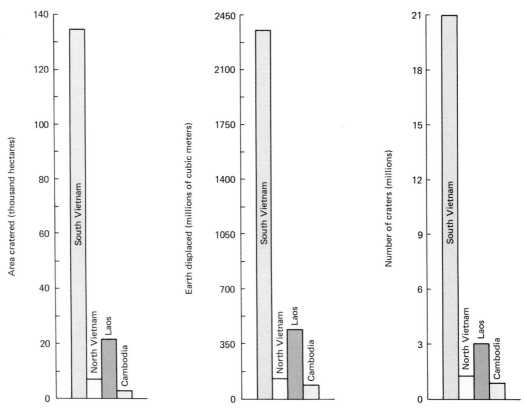

Figure 12-19. The Environmental Impact of Bombing in Indochina, 1965 to 1971. Bombing damaged the land of South Vietnam and, to a lesser extent, other parts of Indochina. After Westling and Pfeiffer 1972.

1961 to 1971, the United States dropped 13 million tons of bombs (i.e., twice the tonnage dropped by the country during the entire Second World War) on Indochina, an area slightly larger than the State of Texas. According to some experts (e.g., Karnow 1983), only 5 to 8 percent of the bombing was aimed at tactical targets. The rest was "area bombing" calculated to deprive the enemy of its support base by stripping the forest cover and forcing the peasants into government-controlled areas. The impact on the environment was traumatic. Large areas of productive land were left in craters and made immediately useless (Figures 12-18 and 12-19). In addition, some of the environmental destruction was caused by the direct application of herbicides that defoliated and destroyed 12 million hectares of forest and cropland by 1971.

More recently, the Soviet Union has intensively bombed many areas in Afghanistan. The immediate goal has been to destroy the food base of their Afghan opponents, but the devastation of the natural environment will have long-term effects.

The capacity for destroying or modifying the physical environment over all the earth was increased greatly with the advent of nuclear weapons. To date, major damage has been confined primarily to two large Japanese cities, which were razed during the Second World War, and to some atolls and desert areas that were contaminated during the testing of nuclear weapons. It is recognized that the potential exists for destroying the entire landscape of the earth, even though the ecological consequences of detonating thousands of nuclear weapons cannot be fully predicted.

There is concern that the fire balls created by the weapons, and subsidiary burning, would put so much smoke and dust into the atmosphere that incoming sunlight would be shut out. There would be a "nuclear winter" in which temperatures, in the Northern Hemisphere at least, would drop below freezing for many months, even in the summer. In addition to the impacts of nuclear blast, flash, and fallout, the climate of a darkened world would be altered. Many forms of life would become extinct, farming would be impossible, and all humans would perish in the Northern Hemisphere. Regeneration from the disaster would be slow, and the new ecosystems would not replicate the forms prior to a nuclear war (Ehrlich 1984).

Natural Hazards

Even though humans have the power to severely damage the ecosphere, this does not mean that people completely dominate the natural environment. Floods, earthquakes, tornadoes, hurricanes, volcanic eruptions, blizzards, and numerous other hazardous natural events clearly demonstrate the potential ef-fects of the environment on humans. The extent of human suffering from natural hazards varies (1) with the severity, areal extent, and frequency of environmental hazards, (2) with the degree to which natural disasters are accurately predicted, and (3) with the amount of public support available to victims after calamities occur. Also affecting the extent of damage from natural hazards are the perceptions that humans have about the environment (Chapter 5).

Human perceptions about environmental hazards are flawed. There is a tendency to underestimate risks and to indulge in wishful thinking. We hope the city along the coast will not be hit by a hurricane; we choose to believe the dormant volcano will remain at rest; and we assume that the floodplain on which we live will not be inundated by water overflowing the banks of a river.

Why do we occupy sites that carry long-term risks? In part it is because the areas are advantageous for certain types of activities. Floodplains may provide arable land for agriculture and suitable construction sites for buildings; the soils near some types of volcanoes are fertile; and many coastal locations provide good accessibility for trade. Even if people knew the probabilities of a flood, tornado, or earthquake causing damage to them or their properties, often they choose to take a chance and to live within the danger zone because of economic, social, and political advantages.

In many cases, sites that carry risks of natural hazards are occupied because of geographic inertia. People continue to reside in cities in hazardous locations long after dangers are revealed by events or additional research. San Francisco was rebuilt even after the 1906 earthquake demonstrated the dangers of the faultlines. Galveston was reconstructed after the hurricane of 1900 (Box 12-1).

When faced with the powerful geographic attraction that specific places possess, individuals are prone to dismiss the dangers of what they perceive to be rare events. Imagine the career prospects of executives who refuse to move to San Francisco on the grounds that it might be hazardous to the health of their families. Consider the future of persons in Bangladesh that give up their farmland because it might be flooded during a tropical storm in the Bay of Bengal.

Unfortunately, willingness to accept a location that is necessary for making a living may affect perceptions about the danger from other environmental hazards. Living within a region subject to tornadoes, for example, does not mean people must also construct houses on unstable coastal cliffs, in floodplains downstream from faulty dams, or in other locations that carry high risks of damage. In many cases, catastrophic events are largely the result of people's failure to understand the ecological relationships between humans and the natural environment.

BOX 12-1. THE GALVESTON FLOOD OF 1900

The city of Galveston was established in 1836 on a barrier island lying between mainland Texas and the Gulf of Mexico. At its highest point, Galveston Island is just over 2.5 meters (8 ft) above sea level; much of the land is less than half that high. The sheltered anchorage that lies on the landward side of the island provided an excellent transhipment point for goods entering Texas and for cotton being exported. In 1859, a rail line was built along a causeway linking Galveston Island to the mainland.

However, Galveston had disadvantages. In the early days, yellow fever was a problem. And, occasionally a tropical storm would produce high tides that overflowed the island and damaged property. Nevertheless, inhabitants accepted the overflows as part of the risk of doing business in Galveston.

In September of 1900, a powerful storm came over Cuba, touched Florida, and then, instead of curling out into the Atlantic as most storms do, it travelled westward to the Texas shore. The effect of the storm's direction was to pile up water on the Gulf Coast and create very high tides and strong storm surges. By the evening of September 7th, the low-lying parts of Galveston Island were flooded, but there was no concerted attempt by inhabitants to evacuate. The established residents had lived through storms and overflows before. They believed that overflows produced property damage but little loss of life. This mentality created the disaster.

By mid-morning September 8th, trains could no longer cross the causeway from the island to the mainland, and the seas were too rough for boats to navigate Galveston Bay to Houston. The residents were now trapped. Soon waves 20 feet high had demolished the greatest part of town and had drowned many of the inhabitants (Figures 12-20 and 12-21). The number of deaths was never accurately reported because many bodies were washed out to sea. From a population of 30,000, at least 6000 died in the storm.

After the disaster, a seawall was built and the level of the island was raised. The economy of Galveston, however, never recovered. Houston took over as the main Texas port when the Houston ship canal was opened in 1916. Today Galveston is a pleasant Gulf Coast resort.

Figure 12-20. Devastation from the Galveston Flood of 1900. Photo courtesy of the Rosenberg Library, Galveston.

Figure 12-21. Destruction Around Bishop's Palace, Galveston, 1900. Photo courtesy of the Rosenberg Library, Galveston.

TRENDS INVOLVING HUMANS AND THE NATURAL ENVIRONMENT

Human beings have been an ecological dominant since their first emergence on the earth. Although the locations of oceans, mountains, soils, and climates remain generally as they were thousands of years ago, the quality of the natural environment has been altered by societies in a variety of ways. These alterations have changed the geography of places and have, in turn, affected subsequent ecological and spatial behavior of populations. In general terms and on a worldwide scale, the impact of humans can be summarized by a few major trends.

One of these trends has been an increase in population (Chapters 2 and 3). Concurrent with the greater number of persons has been a trend toward a more intense use of earth resources (Chapters 9 and 10). Population growth and resource utilization are closely interrelated. As the population grew, the number of people that had to be supported per area increased. By utilizing new techniques and intensifying the use of the land, workers produced more food, which resulted in fewer childhood deaths, longer lives, and hence larger populations.

An accompanying trend was the increasing impact of humans on the natural environment. In early times, most changes in vegetational types and animal populations happened during prolonged periods of human occupancy of an area. After the Industrial Revolution, however, people could transform landscapes quickly by using machines powered by inanimate energy. Now a few humans can alter the entire ecosphere (i.e., the global ecosystem) within a few hours by releasing the power of nuclear weapons. As power has increased, larger areas have been changed by human actions. Early societies tended to affect only their localized territories, but now many kinds of human activities in one part of the world can alter the environments and lives of people in distant places.

These major changes have produced benefits in improved living conditions, but they have also inflicted costs, some of which have not been immediately obvious. Decisions about the relative costs and benefits differ because they are made within the context of cultural values (Chapters 5–7). Even within the context of each culture, what benefits one or a few individuals may harm others. Furthermore, the impact of decisions varies with the number of persons making similar decisions and the relative influence of the decision-makers. For example, the decision by a tribesman to cut a tree for a dugout canoe has less impact than a decision by a company president to cut a large forest for lumber. To an individual, the benefits of driving a car powered by leaded gasoline may outweigh the disadvantages of alternative transportation; but when a similar decision is made daily by thousands of travellers in an urban area, damages by lead poisoning may produce high environmental costs.

Assessing the impact of trends is so complex that predictions range all the way from being pessimistic to optimistic. The pessimists suggest that the earth is like a spaceship with finite resources. Some resources have already been exhausted, and the current rate of depletion jeopardizes the limited supply of other nonrenewable forms. Elements of the environment are being contaminated by the pollutants and wastes generated by humans. These conditions are expected to become more critical in the future because world population and consumption per person are continuing to increase.

Optimists view the human utilization of the environment as a historical trend of progressive improvement. Even though certain resources have been almost exhausted in the past, substitutes and new practices have replaced the old. Optimists realize that the natural environment can be ecologically stressed, but they have faith that future technology and social institutions will provide the means to adjust to the natural ecosystem and to improve the lives of all people.

There are, of course, other interpretations about what has happened in the past, what is occurring today, and what may transpire in the future. As an additional aid to understanding the implications of human actions and environmental conditions, some possible scenarios are presented in the following chapter.

BIBLIOGRAPHY

Boulding, Kenneth E., "The Economics of the Coming Spaceship Earth," in H. Jarrett, ed., *Environmental Quality in a Growing Economy*, pp. 3–14. Baltimore: Johns Hopkins University Press, 1966.

———, "Economics and Ecology," in F. F. Darling and J. P. Milton, eds., *Future Environments of North America*, pp. 225–34. Garden City, N.Y.: Natural History Press, 1966*b*.

Brown, Lester R., "Food Resources and Population: The Narrowing Margin," *Population Bulletin*, 36, no. 3 (September 1981).

Brown, Michael H., *Laying Waste*. New York: Pantheon, 1979.

Brown, Ralph H., *Historical Geography of the United States*. New York: Harcourt Brace, 1948.

Commoner, Barry, *The Closing Circle; Nature, Man and Technology*. New York: Knopf, 1971.

———, *The Poverty of Power: Energy and the Economic Crisis*. New York: Knopf, 1976.

Council on Environmental Quality, *The Global 2000 Report to the President*. Washington, D.C.: U.S. Govt. Printing Office, 1980.

Crosby, Alfred W., *Ecological Imperialism: The Biological*

The Nation's Forests—Exploitation, Preservation, or Multiple Use?

Since the late nineteenth century, when concern over the disappearance of America's wilderness gave rise to a public outcry, there has been a three-way split among advocates of unrestricted exploitation, supporters of total preservation, and proponents of limited use of forests. Those advocating exploitation, mainly timber companies, had virtually a free hand during the first century of U.S. development. Areas of secondary growth, such as the cut-over region of the upper Great Lakes, are their legacy. By the 1890s, however, the "exploiters" were opposed by men like John Muir of the Sierra Club, who succeeded in preventing development in areas of wilderness (e.g., Yosemite Valley), and Gifford Pinchot of the U.S. Forestry Commission, who pioneered the principle of multiple use. Pinchot advocated combining timber cutting with watershed and wildlife protection.

These differences over the proper use of the nation's forests are still prevalent in the 1980s, as illustrated at McKenzie Bridge, Oregon, which is in the heart of the Willamette National Forest. Ancient Douglas firs, towering hundreds of feet above the ground, are at the center of the controversy between those advocating immediate exploitation on the one hand and the conservationists and wilderness groups on the other. The Douglas firs are a remnant of an original forest that once stretched from the Cascades to the Pacific. Only about 10 percent of that virgin forest remains.

The federal administration in Washington during the 1980s urged the removal of the Douglas firs to make way for faster growing trees. This position was consistent with a program designed to generate more economic activity on federal lands by opening up their resources to private industry. Timber companies, arguing that jobs were at stake, supported this policy. Some citizens in the vicinity of McKenzie Bridge, especially those who were unemployed, agreed that the need for jobs should be a deciding factor.

Conservationists, including many who hunt and fish, opposed rapid exploitation on the grounds that the previously accepted concept of multiple usage was being ignored. Not only would rapid removal of the Douglas firs impair the aesthetic qualities of the forest, they argued, but it would also lead to increased soil erosion and the elimination of endangered species such as the spotted owl and the flying squirrel.

Preservationists wanted to prohibit all commercial use of the virgin forest. They believed the Willamette National Forest should be added to the nearly 36 million hectares of public wilderness lands in the United States.

The controversy at Mckenzie Bridge directly involves the national policy about forests and reflects basic differences in attitudes about the environment. Should forests be used primarily to generate jobs and revenue from lumbering? Should they be placed aside as virgin sanctuaries for the benefit of future generations? Should they be utilized in a closely regulated manner that combines sustained-yield cutting with environmental protection?

Expansion of Europe, 900–1900. Cambridge, England: Cambridge University Press, 1986.

Darby, Henry C., "The Clearing of the Woodland in Europe," in William L. Thomas, ed., *Man's Role in Changing the Face of the Earth,* pp. 183–216. Chicago: University of Chicago Press, 1956.

Eckholm, Erik P., *Losing Ground.* New York: W. W. Norton & Co., Inc., 1976.

Ehrlich, Paul. R., "North America After the War," *Natural History,* 93, no. 3 (March 1984), 4–8.

Ehrlich, Paul R., J. P. Holdren, and R. W. Holm, *Man and the Ecosphere.* San Francisco: W. H. Freeman & Co., 1971.

Ehrlich, Paul R., and John P. Holdren, *Cassandra Conference, Resources and the Human Predicament.* College Station, Tex.: Texas A & M University Press, 1988.

Flavin, Christopher, "Italian Voters Reject Nuclear Power," *World Watch,* 1, no. 1 (January-February 1988), 7–8.

French, Hilary F., "Toxic Wastes Crossing Borders," *World Watch,* 1, no. 1 (January-February 1988), 7–8.

Glacken, Clarence, *Traces on the Rhodian Shore.* Berkeley, Calif.: University of California Press, 1967.

Goudie, Andrew, *The Human Impact.* Boston, Mass.: M.I.T. Press, 1986.

Heathcote, R. L., *The Arid Lands: Their Use and Abuse.* London & New York: Longman, 1983.

Hewitt, Kenneth, "Place Annihilation: Area Bombing and the Fate of Urban Places," *Annals of the Association of American Geographers,* 73, no 2 (June 1983), 257–84.

Hughes, J. Donald, *Ecology in Ancient Civilizations.* Albuquerque, N. Mex.: University of New Mexico Press, 1975.

Jackson, Barbara (Ward), and Réné Dubos, *Only One Earth: The Care and Maintenance of a Small Planet.* New York: W. W. Norton & Co., Inc., 1972.

Johnson, Warren A., Victor Stoltzfas, and Peter Craumer, "Energy Conservation in Amish Agriculture," *Science,* 198, no. 4315 (October 1977), 373–78.

Karnow, Stanley, *Vietnam: A History.* New York: Viking Press, 1983.

Lacoste, Yves, "An Illustration of Geographical Warfare: Bombing of the Dikes on the Red River, North Vietnam," *Antipode,* 5, no. 2 (May 1973), 1–13.

Leopold, Aldo, *A Sand County Almanac.* New York: Oxford University Press, 1969.

Marsh, George Perkins, *Man and Nature.* New York: Charles Scribner & Co., 1864.

———, *The Earth as Modified by Human Action*. New York: Arno Press, 1970.

Martin, P. S., and H. E. Wright, Jr., *Pleistocene Extinction*. New Haven, Conn.: Yale University Press, 1967.

Melosi, Martin V., *Garbage in the Cities*. College Station, Tex.: Texas A & M University Press, 1982.

Muir, John, *Our National Parks*. Madison, Wis.: University of Wisconsin Press, 1981. First published by Houghton Mifflin, 1901.

Murphey, Rhodes, "Man and Nature in China," *Modern Asian Studies*, 1, no. 4 (1967), 313–34.

Nash, Roderick, *Wilderness and the American Mind*. New Haven, Conn.: Yale University Press, 1967.

"Nuclear America" (map). New York: War Resisters League, 1979.

Pearce-Batten, Anthony, "The Future of Renewable Energy," *Focus*, 29, no. 3 (January-February 1979), 1–16.

Rudd, Robert L., *Pesticides and the Living Landscape*. Madison, Wis.: University of Wisconsin Press, 1964.

Rudker, R. G., and E. W. Cecelski, "Resources, Environment and Population: The Nature of Future Limits," *Population Bulletin*, 34, no. 3 (1979).

Runte, Alfred, *National Parks, The American Experience*. Lincoln, Nebr.: University of Nebraska Press, 1979.

Sagan, Carl, "Nuclear War and Climatic Catastrophe: Some Policy Implications," *Foreign Affairs*, 62, no. 2 (Winter 1983/1984), 257–92.

Sauer, Carl O., "The Agency of Man on Earth," in William L. Thomas, ed., *Man's Role Changing the Face of the Earth*, pp. 49–69. Chicago: University of Chicago Press, 1956.

———, *The Early Spanish Main*. Berkeley, Calif.: University of California Press, 1966.

———, "Theme of Plant and Animal Destruction in Economic History," in John Leighly, ed., *Land and Life: a Selection from the Writings of Carl Ortwin Sauer*, pp. 145–154. Berkeley and Los Angeles: University of California Press, 1967.

Schell, Jonathan, *The Fate of the Earth*. New York: Knopf, 1982.

Schlüter, Otto, *Die Siedlungsräume Mitteleuropas in Frühgeschichtlicher Zeit*. Hamburg, 1952.

Schumacher, E. F., *Small Is Beautiful: Economics as If People Mattered*. New York: Harper & Row, Pub., 1973.

Stobough, Robert, and Daniel Yergin, *Energy Future*. New York: Random House, 1979.

Thomas, William, ed., *Man's Role in Changing the Face of the Earth*. Chicago: University of Chicago Press, 1956.

Tindale, N., "Ecology and Primitive Aboriginal Man in Australia," in Allen Keast, R. L. Crocker, and C. S. Christian, eds., *Biogeography and Ecology in Australia*. Den Haag, Netherlands: W. Junk, 1959.

Tuan, Yi-Fu, *China*. London: Longman, 1970.

Turner, Frederick Jackson, "The Significance of the Frontier in American History," *American Historical Association, Annual Report, 1892*, pp. 199–227. Washington, D.C.: U.S. Govt. Printing Office, 1893.

United Nations, *World Map of Desertification at a Scale of 1:25,000,000*. U. N. Conference on Desertification, 1977.

Van Der Heyden, A. A. M., and H. S. Scullard, eds., *Atlas of the Classical World*. London: Nelson, 1959.

Wallace, A. R., *The World of Life, A Manifestation of Creative Power, Directive Mind, and Ultimate Purpose*. New York: Moffat Yard, 1911.

Weir, David, and Mark Schapiro, *Circle of Poison*. San Francisco: Institute for Food and Development, 1981.

Westing, Arthur H., and E. W. Pfeiffer, "The Cratering of Indochina," *Scientific American*, 226, no. 5 (May 1972), 21–29.

White, Lynn, Jr., "The Historic Roots of Our Ecologic Crisis," *Science*, 155 (1967), 1203–7.

Worster, Donald, *Dust Bowl*. New York: Oxford University Press, 1979.

———, *Nature's Economy: A History of Ecological Ideas*, 2nd ed. New York: Cambridge University Press, 1985.

13 FUTURE SCENARIOS

Apart from the fear of a nuclear holocaust, perhaps the greatest concern of many people is the uncertainty about the future availability of resources. In this context, *resources* is a general term referring to all the goods and materials that support human needs and desires. For many people, needs are basic items such as food, water, shelter, and firewood. For those people who are already assured of the necessities of life, their "needs" tend to focus on appliances, vehicles, and a host of other modern conveniences, as well as the electrical energy and fuels to power them.

The term *availability* implies more than just the physical access to a desired good such as firewood or electricity. In a broad sense, it includes the financial ability to obtain existing goods. For example, hungry people with no money may live amid a cluster of grain bins filled with an excess of unsold wheat or rice. But the mere proximity of this resource does not translate into the availability of food.

This topic on the availability of resources involves the ecological perspective of geography because resources are derived either directly or indirectly from the natural environment. In this chapter, the availability of resources is considered primarily as the human geography of the future. The chapter begins with a few general considerations, proceeds with a survey of the views of various experts, and concludes with a series of scenarios that suggest hypothetical futures for the United States.

GENERAL PERSPECTIVES ON THE AVAILABILITY OF RESOURCES

It is very difficult to predict the future quantity of resources for two reasons. One, what is known about the world supply fluctuates. For example, the amount of petroleum that can be used in the future depends partly on what new pools are discovered. Some forecasts made on the basis of known petroleum pools in the past predicted that the world would be without this commodity by 1980. Even with better techniques for estimating probable petroleum resources, predictions are risky.

Furthermore the rate at which existing world resources are being depleted is not known precisely. There are varying estimates about how rapidly groundwater is being depleted, surface water is being contaminated, forests are being cut, and arable land is being lost to erosion, salinization, and desertification. To predict the rate of the depletion of resources for the future is even more difficult.

A second reason why it is difficult to predict the future amount of resources is because people use existing materials of the earth in new ways. Resources do not exist independently of human utilization. In the words of Erich Zimmermann, "Resources are not. They become" (1964, p. 14). For example, although oil existed in the earth, it was not regarded as an energy resource by the American Indians. Likewise, resources may cease to be so defined if substitutes become more economically feasible. In contrast to the situation a few centuries ago, bison herds are not considered a major resource to most inhabitants of the American Great Plains today because alternative sources of food and shelter are available. Also various minerals that are termed resources now may cease to be such in the future if their costs become too high (Table 13-1). Thus a resource base expands and contracts in relation to human needs, its availability, and the feasibility of substitutions.

Optimists declare that, in general terms, resources will not be depleted because technological knowledge will continue to develop new forms. Pessimists insist that even though a variety of goods are being produced

TABLE 13-1. Dates When Prices Must Rise Dramatically to Avoid Exhaustion of Selected Resources

Resources	Year[a]	Year[b]
Coal	2050	3000
Petroleum	1995	2010
Natural gas	2005	2024
Uranium	2005	2030–2070
Aluminum	2025	2038
Chromium	2048	2095
Cobalt	2004	2016
Copper	2053	2094
Iron	2053	2094
Lead	2000	2016
Manganese	2061	2112
Nickel	2014	2032
Phosphate rock	2034	2120
Potash	2104	2368
Sulfur	2010	2036
Tin	2003	2030
Tungsten	2009	2037
Zinc	1993	2065

[a] Based on currently known reserves only.
[b] Based on reserves plus prospective reserves.

Source: Rudker and Cecelski, 1979.

now, ultimately certain finite substances from which these goods are derived will be consumed.

One factor that may help in predicting the availability of resources is the historic record. The progression of resource expansion, as a result of exploration and technological development, has been interspersed with crises. Past resource-related crises have resulted from increased population numbers, cultural resistance to change, external forces such as climatic deterioration, and detrimental social and economic systems. Often the variables are interconnected. The diversity of pressures that have produced particular crises are illustrated in European history.

Western Europe had a sustained period of agricultural improvement, colonization, and population growth by 1300 (Chapter 2). Then climatic deterioration occurred (Parry 1978). England, for example, experienced particularly bad years for agriculture in 1315 and 1316, followed by a series of poor climatic years, which had the effect of contracting the agricultural resource base. In 1348, the Black Death spread through Europe, eliminating one-third of the population. Eventually economic progress was resumed, but not before a period during which the life in Western Europe was devastated.

During the seventeenth century, there were long periods of economic depression in Europe. The economic problems were a product, at least in part, of inflation resulting from the rapid economic growth that followed the exploitation of Middle and South America. European economic conditions were further damaged by protracted religious wars. Also the effects of "the little ice age," a cool period that probably lasted from 1430 to 1850, brought great suffering to Scandinavia, Scotland, Iceland, and New England (Calder 1975, pp. 16–17).

The most severe resource crises in Western cultures during the last 150 years have tended to be economic in nature. Specific crises include the economic slump of the 1840s, the banking and currency problems of the 1890s, and the depression of the 1930s. In each case, accessibility to resources for large segments of the population was disrupted. Notice that the three economic collapses came approximately every 50 years. It has been suggested by the economist Nikolai Kondratieff (1935), and more recently by Jay Forrester (1973), that there is a "long-wave" in economic affairs that is liable to produce massive slumps every half century or so. It remains to be seen whether or not this pattern will be confirmed in the late twentieth century.

Some people hope that because potential problems can be studied, the impact of future crises connected with economic instability, resource unavailability, and rapid population growth can be reduced. They observe that policy makers are able to alter the growth of population, as for example in China (Chapter 3). They note that alternative energy sources that do not depend on nonrenewable fossil fuels can be developed (Chapter 12) and that the history of technological innovations suggests that new technologies will emerge (Chapter 5).

Others are skeptical that policy decisions will relieve future problems in any significant way. They point to many omens existing at the present time. In many less developed countries, population numbers have been rising rapidly (Chapter 3). The more developed nations are not faced with the problems of rapid population increase, but they have an enormous appetite for certain resources. As additional people throughout the world attempt to achieve better living standards by consuming more, a scarcity in currently defined resources may become increasingly critical. Within most societies, social stratification may intensify if the access to resources decreases. Furthermore, the political confrontations and general lack of international cooperation (Chapter 8) seem to indicate that the world economic order, with its unequal distribution of wealth (Chapter 9), will not change much in the immediate future. Some believe that long-wave forces, which defy short-term attempts to manage economic systems, will continue to produce periodic slumps.

Climatic change, a factor over which humans have little control at the present time, may compound any crises created by humans. Geographers, in their desire to avoid the excesses of environmental determinism, have probably paid less attention than they should to the impact of climatic fluctuations on human affairs. The fact is that in most of the resource-related crises in the Western areas of the world, unfavorable climatic fluctuations have been present. This was the case in the fourteenth and seventeenth centuries in Europe. The droughts of the 1890s and 1930s, especially in the North American Great Plains, accompanied the economic depressions of those times. No doubt much of this was coincidental rather than causal, but environmental deterioration aggravated the economic problem.

The role of climatic fluctuations in the future is difficult to assess. It is not necessary to subscribe to the idea of cataclysmic climatic changes to realize that a slow temperature or precipitation trend can be a significant factor in agricultural production. The climatic record shows that temperatures display long periods of being either warmer or cooler than the overall average. Some scientists (Calder 1975, pp. 134–35) suggest that, from a long-term perspective, the present climate of the earth is warmer than usual, and we will be entering a cooling trend that may eventually usher in another ice age. If cooling were to

take place, shorter growing seasons could be expected in parts of North America and Europe. This could have a disastrous impact on the agricultural capacity of these regions, to say nothing of the effect on world grain supplies (Bryson and Murray 1977).

It should be stressed that climatic fluctuations are not fully understood. There is no certainty that they occur in cycles, that such cycles have a high degree of regularity in their timing, or that a cooling trend will occur next. In fact, as already noted (Chapter 12), some observers foresee a warming of the earth's climate caused by the build-up of carbon dioxide in the earth's atmosphere due to the use of fossil fuels and, perhaps, deforestation. A warming of the earth's atmosphere could leave large areas of the Northern Hemisphere drier than at the present time (Figure 13-1). The area of the existing ice sheets (such as Greenland and Antarctica) could be reduced, resulting in a significant rise in sea level, the inundation of many coastal areas, and further changes of climate.

The elements that could converge and result in future world crises are evident. Pressure on resources is heavy, many currencies are weak, international instability is great, and the climatic future is uncer-

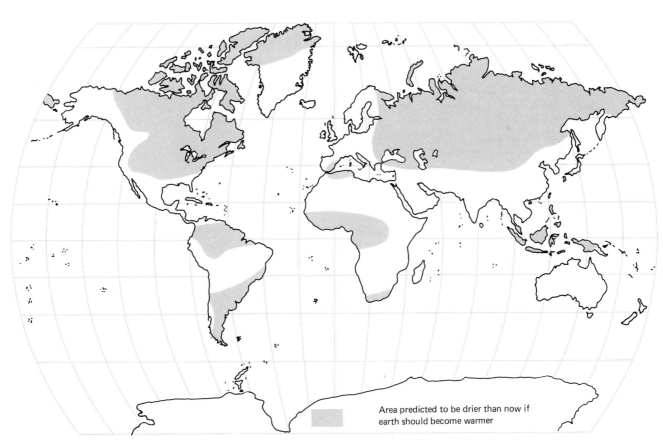

Figure 13-1. Possible Soil Moisture Patterns on a Warmer Earth. If climatic changes produced warmer temperatures, several areas would have less precipitation, drier soils, and probably less agricultural potential. After Kellogg and Schware 1981.

tain. Any one of these elements could set off a chain of events that could result in a prolonged depression. This is not to say, however, that the worst will happen. The views of the future are as varied as the experts who offer them.

VIEWS OF THE FUTURE

Past Views: Franklin, Malthus, and Turner

Benjamin Franklin in *Observations Concerning the Increase of Mankind* (1755) set out the basic propositions of what is now referred to as Malthusian thinking. Franklin suggested that there are no bounds to the reproductive capacity of plants and animals and that, if allowed to, they would fill any available space. Eventually checks on the multiplication of individuals would be imposed by crowding and interfering with each other's means of subsistence. According to Franklin, human beings would go on reproducing until they eventually overtaxed the means of subsistence. Franklin was not alarmed by this prospect because he saw a sparsely populated North America inviting settlement.

Thomas Malthus arrived at his ideas independently. As presented in Chapter 2, Malthus argued in 1798 (in his *Essay on the Principle of Population*) that the potential for population increase is "infinitely greater" than the earth's productive capacity (1976). He was not writing in lightly populated North America where resources seemed limitless, but in England where population growth was already straining the existing resource base. As a country clergyman he saw that births were exceeding deaths in his parish. All around him were the signs of rural poverty: the children displayed stunted growth, family incomes were spent on the bare necessities of life, and the principal food was bread. In short, Malthus was observing a traditional rural society where land was the principal resource and the capacity for producing foodstuffs under the existing system was being overtaxed (James 1979). He concluded that the crisis could only be averted by a reduction in population growth.

The ideas of Malthus were widely discussed in the years after the publication of his essay. This is hardly surprising because his writings appeared in times dominated by war, a run of bad harvests in Britain, and the economic depression that followed the close of the Napoleonic Wars in 1815. Even after these events and conditions ended, his ideas continued to be debated. Whenever subsequent crises have occurred, his ideas have been resurrected and reexamined for their applicability to new times and different societies. Sometimes the Malthusian thesis is restated to read: "Populations have a long-term tendency to make excessive demands on their resource base." Although this more generalized statement includes industrial societies as well as agrarian ones, the importance of constraints on population numbers is still widely debated.

Pessimism was also expressed by the historian Frederick Jackson Turner in his famous 1892 paper, "The Significance of the Frontier in American History." In one sense, his message had a Malthusian tone: Most of the available agricultural land in the United States had been appropriated, and the age of abundance was being replaced by an era of resource scarcity. His thesis, however, was more than an American variant of the Malthusian theme. Turner believed that the American social characteristics and world view—individualism, independence, and democracy—were a product of the frontier, particularly a frontier that had been essentially free. Thus, with the disappearance of frontier lands, he felt the nature of American society would change. He pessimistically wondered, in later works, whether democracy would persist once the land had been completely settled by Euro-Americans (Turner 1920, pp. 244–45).

The severe economic recession of the early 1890s provided a general air of gloom. Turner presented his ideas at a time when there was a general feeling that the United States was "filling up." Because his ideas coincided with the mood of the time, they were widely espoused.

Contemporary Views: Pessimists

As in the 1890s, since the Second World War there has been much pessimism about the future. A general loss of faith in progress has produced a mood of anxiety, an "oppressive anticipation of the future [like] the invisible approach of a dark storm" (Heilbroner 1974, p. 13). Heilbroner sees three threats to the future of humans. One threat is the growth of world population, accompanied by the growing discrepancy between living conditions in the rich and poor nations. The second threat is nuclear war resulting from intense competition among countries. Third, there is the threat of environmental deterioration caused by industrial pollution. Heilbroner doubts that humans can deal with these threats. He thinks that change will only be brought about by catastrophic events leading to the fall of industrial society. The post-industrial society envisioned by him would have fewer resource-dependent industries, more frugal attitudes toward consumption, and tighter social control. Heilbroner's prediction of "convulsive change" is reminiscent of Leslie White's ominous prediction that humans will only realize the need for a new political and economic order in the aftermath of atomic war (White 1949).

Attempts have been made to construct objective models of the future where projections of growth and change are quantified and assumptions stated specif-

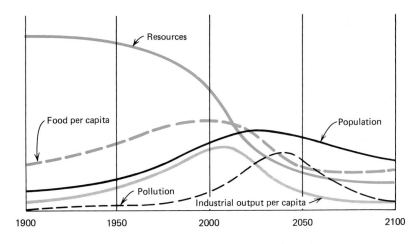

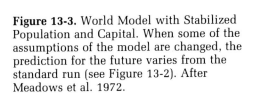

Figure 13-2. World Model, Standard Run. According to the initial assumptions of the model, world production will decline within another 60 years. After Meadows et al. 1972.

ically. A well-known study of this type is the Club of Rome's report, *The Limits to Growth* (Meadows et al. 1972), which predicts the future of economic, ecological, and demographic developments in a finite world. The authors used a model to project interlocking connections among population, industrialization, pollution, food production, and resource depletion. The model emphasizes trends at the global scale only and does not attempt to predict geographic variations or where the limits of growth will be reached first.

The main conclusion of the study is that unless growth trends are slowed down and a condition of ecological and economic stability established, the limits to growth will be reached within 100 years (Meadows et al. 1972). In brief, the world will not be able to withstand exponential growth of population, food production, industrialization, resource usage, and pollution. In the standard run of the model (Figure 13-2), no major changes are assumed in the physical, economic, or social relationships that have governed the world system from 1900 to 1970. Food, industrial output, and population grow exponentially until a diminishing resource base forces a slowdown in industrial growth. Because of natural delays in the system, both population and pollution continue to increase for some time after the peak of industrializa-

tion. Population growth is finally halted by a rise in the death rate due to decreased food and medical services.

In variations of the model, the assumptions are changed to incorporate possible technological breakthroughs. In one variant, the following assumptions are made: (1) resources are fully used, with 75 percent of them being recycled; (2) pollution is reduced to one-fourth its 1970 amount; (3) land yields are doubled; and (4) effective methods of birth control are available to the entire world population. The result is a temporary achievement of a world average income per capita approximately the same as the present U.S. level. Eventually, though, industrial growth is halted, the death rate rises as resources are depleted, pollution accumulates, and food production declines.

In another variant (Figure 13-3), stabilizing people and restricting capital growth are assumed. Once the exponential growth is halted, temporary stability is attained. Levels of population and capital are sufficiently high, however, that they deplete resources rapidly since no resource-conserving technologies have been assumed.

The authors of *The Limits to Growth* concluded that population and capital growth must stop soon, but humankind can still choose the limits rather than

Figure 13-3. World Model with Stabilized Population and Capital. When some of the assumptions of the model are changed, the prediction for the future varies from the standard run (see Figure 13-2). After Meadows et al. 1972.

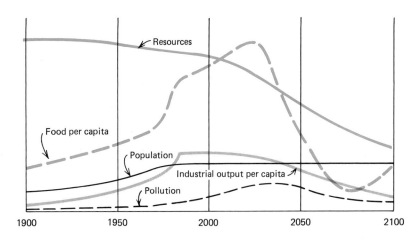

having them imposed by catastrophe (Meadows et al. 1972). These authors believed it would be possible to establish a maintainable system (Figure 13-3) if population and industrial growth are stabilized. Resources will have to be recycled, pollution controlled, and conservation methods adopted. Resources will still be depleted, but at a rate slow enough to allow technological adjustments. *The Limits to Growth* closes on a note of hope, provided action is taken to establish global equilibrium.

More recently, additional pessimistic reports have been issued by various international committees, such as the Independent Commission on International Development Issues (the Brandt Commission) of 1980 and the World Commission on Environment and Development of 1987. These studies vary in their analyses and specific recommendations, but they share the message of escalating environmental damage and increasing economic inequalities. These themes can be amplified by summarizing the findings (published in *Our Common Future*) of the 1987 World Commission.

The World Commission, consisting of representatives from 21 countries, convened in October 1984 and published its report in April 1987. It was observed that during the 900 days the Commission was in session, the per capita gross domestic product of the less developed countries as a whole decreased by 10 percent and an estimated 60 million people, most of them children, died from diarrheal diseases related to malnutrition and unsafe drinking water. Although world food production continued to rise faster than population growth and infant mortality rates generally declined, these benefits were not enjoyed by everyone in the world.

The Commission also found many areas where the natural environment is being degraded rapidly. Each year 6 million hectares of productive dryland deteriorate into worthless desert, more than 11 million hectares of tropical rainforest are destroyed, and species extinction is taking place at an escalating rate. By the end of the century, if these trends persist, there will be little virgin tropical rainforest left other than in Zaire, the western part of Amazonia, and in New Guinea.

Although these crises may appear to be localized, the effects are often felt elsewhere. Dryland degradation, for example, produces refugees who seek survival in other countries. These international refugees, in turn, often affect political and economic relations between countries (Chapters 4 and 8). The reduction of tropical rainforests may produce global climatic changes, which would have significant economic repercussions throughout the world.

Furthermore, the problems cannot be easily compartmentalized as either just ecological or economic. Growing populations combined with the shortage of land in agricultural economies push farming into marginal areas, as in the Sahel region of Africa. When the critical economic needs for all families are cumulated, the total creates severe demands on the existing resources. Likewise, in many poor countries which rely heavily on the exportation of natural resources, there is great pressure to rapidly exploit the environment to earn the necessary capital for basic domestic needs.

As the Commission concludes (p. 5), "Ecology and economy are becoming ever more interwoven—locally, regionally, nationally, and globally—into a seamless net of causes and effects."

Contemporary Views: Optimists

Herman Kahn, chairman of the think-tank at the Hudson Institute until his death in 1983, depicted a very different future. Kahn described himself as a "guarded optimist" and stressed that his predictions were speculative (1982, p. 19). In a series of studies written from the early 1960s to 1982, Kahn envisaged a future world where a stabilized population of 10 billion would be "almost everywhere numerous, rich, and largely in control of the forces of nature" (1982, p. 28).

Kahn believed that the second half of the twentieth century is the crucial phase in what he called the "Great Transition," which first began about two hundred years ago with the start of the Industrial Revolution. This transition will end approximately two hundred years from now with the emergence of a post-industrial world where people will be "mostly well-fed, well-housed, well-clothed, and long-lived" (1979, p. 10).

In Kahn's post-industrial society, primary, secondary, and tertiary activities will be largely automated and will employ few people. Because of technological advancements, many products such as houses and automobiles will be more durable, and industrial production will be reduced because its primary function will be to replace products that deteriorate slowly. A quaternary (communication and information) economy and culture will emerge in which basic survival needs will be taken for granted, leaving more time for leisure, personal development, and protection of the environment.

In Kahn's future world, the gap between the rich and poor countries will be diminished. The currently affluent nations will get richer, as will the presently less developed countries, but the greatest gains will be made by the middle-income countries (i.e., those classed as "intermediate" in Figure 9-8). Countries like Mexico and Brazil, in Kahn's opinion, will enjoy great prosperity in the twenty-first century. In contrast to experts who see an increasing disparity between rich and poor nations as a source of potential economic and political conflict, Kahn saw the gap as an engine of growth. He argued that the abundance of capital, technology, and markets in the more developed countries can be applied to produce rapid progress in the less developed nations. Moreover, the expected high growth rates in the intermediate countries will provide affluent nations with opportunities for investment and trade, which will raise standards of living for both groups. Kahn did not anticipate that the gap between the richest 25 percent and the poorest 30 percent of the world's population will be closed within 100 years, but he did expect it to be substantially reduced (1979, pp. 385–423).

Kahn, believing that human ingenuity can overcome resource depletion and environmental pollution and that changed social values and attitudes will slow the growth of population and industry, ridiculed the idea of physical limits to growth. He criticized the Club of Rome and other neo-Malthusians. He rejected the idea that the earth's resources can be compared to a pie that is quickly consumed. He saw the world's resources as "a process or system for creating and exploiting various kinds of assets and using them in many different ways" (1979, p. 71).

Kahn saw great possibilities for increasing energy supplies from oil and gas through improved techniques of exploration and from other sources such as wood, manure, peat, and coal. In addition, renewable sources of energy including solar, geothermal, and wind power will be more fully utilized, although they will remain secondary to nuclear fission, coal, oil, and gas. With more effective treatment of industrial wastes, the development of a nonpolluting automobile, and systems of mass transportation, technology will provide the answer to pollution problems. Computer networks will overcome the geographic separation of elements in economic systems, which will raise overall efficiency and productivity. Finally, Kahn believed that, by the 1990s, some manufacturing activities (e.g., those in which a vacuum and low gravitation are advantageous) will be conducted in outer space (1982, pp. 65–86).

New strategies for obtaining energy in the future have been proposed by a physicist, Amory Lovins. He rejects what he calls "hard energy paths," which are the continued reliance on coal, petroleum, natural gas, and nuclear fission (1977, p 30). His main objection to hard energy paths is that obtaining the fuel—either from distant oil fields, such as the north slope of Alaska, or from tar sands—will become so expensive that other sectors of the economy will be deprived of capital. Lovins attacks the current policy of centralized energy production. He points out that as power plants become larger, the amount of time that they stand idle rises to as much as 35 percent. Also, the costs of distribution from only a few large production plants make up a large proportion of utility bills. He concludes that, in the future, only the oil-rich nations along the Persian Gulf will be able to afford centralized energy technologies on a large scale.

Lovins suggests "soft energy" alternatives (Figure 13-4). The soft energy path includes conserving already harnessed energy through more efficient utilization and changing from depletable to renewable sources of energy. Lovins claims that the United States could double energy efficiency (the amount of work derived from each unit of energy) by the end of the twentieth century by applying existing technologies. These include insulating buildings and equipment, recovering waste heat in residences and industry, producing more efficient car engines, and developing more systems of mass transit. Americans would use one-third less energy if they were as efficient as the Swedes and West Germans are at the present time.

Soft energy technologies include heating with solar systems, converting farm and forestry wastes into liquid fuels, harnessing wind power, and using other renewable energy sources. These sources are flexible, diverse, and environmentally benign. Furthermore, in contrast to hard energies that encourage centralized locations and monopolistic control, soft energies lend themselves to localized production on a small scale. This makes them suitable for agrarian economies as well as for urbanized societies. Although most soft technologies are regarded as more costly than existing fossil fuels according to economic accounting in the 1980s, it is expected that the increasing costs of hard energies will exceed those of soft energies in the future.

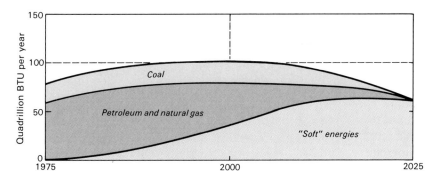

Figure 13-4. The Soft Path to Future U.S. Energy Use. According to Amory Lovins, the "soft" energies could replace the dependence on "hard" energies within a century (see Figure 12-12). After Lovins 1977.

SCENARIOS FOR THE UNITED STATES

It is an interesting exercise to ask what may happen to a modern technological country like the United States under various conditions in the future. The scenarios that follow are not offered as prophesy, and none is likely to be experienced exactly as described here. Readers are invited to project themselves into the situations and ask what would happen to living standards, factors of industrial location, land-use patterns, and social and spatial mobility if some of the projected pressures came into operation. Other scenarios of the future can be constructed using different assumptions.

Scenario A

In scenario A, we start with the assumption that the world monetary system collapses, resulting in a complete loss of confidence in paper money. Although resources and productive capacity still exist, the lack of a financial system prevents their use. The United States is cut off from imported raw materials including oil, iron ore, and nonferrous metals. With the failure of international trade, exports from the United States cease, and the economic system breaks down.

Based on these assumptions, the following conditions might be expected. The existing economy of the United States, along with those of the other more developed countries, would collapse. This would mean a return to an economy based primarily on subsistence agriculture. The United States would be unable to adjust rapidly to the new situation. As a result of famine, disease, exposure, and local civil wars, population would decline quickly. Death rates would be particularly high in large urban places. Major cities, which would cease to function as centers of industry and finance, would be largely abandoned by surviving inhabitants. People would seek refuge in the countryside where they would hope to gain access to the basic necessities of food and water.

Those fleeing to rural areas would not own any land, so they would become landless laborers or, at best, renters of small plots. As the titles of most land are held in one form or another by financial institutions, persons who get control of the remnants of these organizations would become the land barons. Land ownership would become the most important form of wealth and power. The value systems of traditional rural societies would become dominant. Personal activity spaces would shrink greatly. Although patterns of behavior might not differ greatly from those in some parts of the world today, the lives of most Americans would be drastically different from the present.

Scenario B

Elements in scenario A are only likely to develop if there were an extremely rapid collapse of the world economic system. It is more likely that, if such a collapse were to occur, it would be progressive rather than catastrophic. We assume in scenario B, therefore, that a failure of world monetary and trade systems occurs but that the United States has time to make adjustments. There is an opportunity to become self-contained and to develop a domestic economic system that relies solely on raw materials found within the country. Even with conservation, more efficient usage, and substitutions, access to resources is greatly curtailed. The loss of external raw materials, together with the extinction of all export markets and foreign loans, leads to an economic contraction of about 50 percent.

The overall effect, projected from these assumptions, would be to produce a massive economic retrenchment. This would lead to much greater self-sufficiency within regions of the United States because of the high costs of transportation. Many enterprises would be small-scale and oriented to the local community. The high cost of energy would lead to the revival of labor-intensive activities with the products being sold in local and regional markets. In many respects, the patterns of production and consumption would resemble those of the late nineteenth century.

The type of changes can be illustrated by considering farming. Highly specialized farming that now depends on national and international markets would cease. The loss of grain exports would make much of the large-scale farming in the Midwest and Great Plains uneconomical. The general farming of a few generations ago would again become more common. The vineyards, orchards, and horticultural regions of Florida, Texas, and California would be severely hit as transportation costs increase, making it difficult to move produce profitably. Wines and out-of-season fruits and vegetables would only grace the tables of the wealthy. The rest of the populace would drink locally brewed beer and consume the fruits and vegetables of nearby gardens.

Some commentators view aspects of this scenario positively. For example, it does incorporate some of the suggestions of E. F. Schumacher in *Small Is Beautiful: Economics as If People Mattered* (1973). The social costs of travelling to the small and beautiful landscape by the route postulated here, however, would be high. A large number of modern skills and abilities would not be needed. Many Americans, especially younger ones who have become accustomed to having machines do a lot of tasks, would find themselves spending much more time on routine activities, as their grandparents formerly did. It is apparent that the greater concentration on local activities would create a new human geography of American life.

Scenario C

Scenario C assumes that the price of raw materials continues to rise and that no permanent solution to the problem of price inflation is found. Thus the proportion of personal income that can be spent in a discretionary way decreases.

Based on these assumptions, it can be predicted that business opportunities would decrease and unemployment would rise. Increasingly, people would utilize a higher percentage of their take-home pay to meet the costs of travelling to and from work, utility bills, and food. This would result in less spatial mobility, with higher housing densities in areas close to city centers and more reliance on public transport. The high costs of transporting goods could lead to more local production, particularly in the redevelopment of horticulture and dairy zones around cities.

The costs of transportation would make it difficult to deliver goods and services to outlying regions. This would severely damage small towns. Although people in farming areas might produce a higher proportion of their own food, this would not offset the costs of isolation from areas of high population density.

With the decline in discretionary income of the average citizen, most people would spend much of their income on basic needs. Life would resemble characteristics of traditional societies where the average member works full time to provide subsistence for the family. If this happened in the United States, strong social distinctions would develop between a relatively small group who have wealth, leisure, and power and a large majority of the population who work solely to subsist and have very little discretionary income. In short, sustained economic contraction would be accompanied by a movement toward the type of value system characteristic of many traditional societies, where social mobility is severely limited and members are greatly concerned about their place in the social hierarchy.

Some of the societal trends are already apparent. In the last 20 years, as the United States has moved into a period of greater scarcity, the social structure of the country has reinvented some of the characteristics of traditional societies. These have included concern for occupational security and for social status. These trends are apparent from changes of attitude among younger age groups in the United States. In the early 1960s, a time of broad opportunities, college students generally scorned careerism. They flocked into graduate schools to follow academic pursuits, campaigned for political causes, and joined the Peace Corps or Vista. Now there appears to be much more concern about choosing a career, gaining job security, and achieving material well-being.

A movement toward a more structured American society is indicated also by attempts to guarantee group "rights." Initially, the "rights movement" focused on ensuring that groups who had not been participating fully in social and economic opportunities should get their proper share. Now, much human energy is devoted to ensuring that the middle and professional classes have their "rights" affirmed. Nowhere was this more obvious than in the raising of the retirement age through legislation. One generation of professional people, in effect, dealt themselves continued control of positions and jobs at the expense of younger age groups. Allowing the old and venerable to retain power is characteristic of many traditional cultures.

Another aspect of the movement toward a more structured society is the minute defining of jobs and the careful fitting of applicants into specified positions in the socioeconomic order. America was once thought of as the land of opportunity where persons of initiative and talent took jobs and made themselves successful in spite of a lack of formal training. Such hiring practices can only exist in situations where labor is scarce and resources are plentiful. Once the resources become less plentiful, humans compete more forcefully; and in order to reduce potential conflicts, strict rules about training, hiring, and firing are established.

Changes in society, as envisioned in scenario C, would modify the human geography of the United States because social structure is intricately interrelated with other cultural, political, and economic systems and institutions. These factors, as discussed in other chapters, affect the way people behave ecologically and spatially.

Scenario D

Scenario D is optimistic. It is based on the assumption that the country becomes less dependent on conventional energy sources. This is achieved by converting to the soft energies, as proposed by Lovins (1977), and by the widespread use of telecommunications.

Some of the effects of using renewable sources of energy are discussed earlier in this chapter, but they can be summarized by reference to wind and solar energy. If devices that utilize wind and solar power were to become inexpensive and common, then the dependence on centralized power-generating plants would be greatly reduced. This would let consumers, both residential and industrial, choose locations on the basis of other factors and hence allow a greater dispersion of population and activities.

Less dependence on conventional energy sources would also result from changes in the structure of the economy and in the modes of communication. This prediction is based on trends that are already underway. As the United States has shifted toward a post-industrial society, smaller proportions of the work force have jobs in the primary and secondary sectors and more in the tertiary and quaternary sectors (Chapter 10). These changes in production have affected residential patterns. People, in the past, lived near their places of employment, which usually meant sites where resources were located and industries and transportation facilities were agglomerated. Now many economic activities—publishing a magazine, for example—can be performed at any location.

Urban agglomerations are not projected to disappear in this scenario because of the geographic inertia of existing cities and the social advantages of being close to other people. Many people would still choose to be near places offering entertainment and other leisure-time activities requiring large crowds. And, of course, persons working in jobs that provide services requiring direct contact, such as hairdressers and dentists, would live in areas of high population densities.

Scenario D does envision a large proportion of the work force involved with modes of communication that do not depend upon the physical presence of the worker in a particular place. New modes of communication would allow easy access to electronically stored information and personal interaction by electronic means. Brian Berry (1970) has suggested that already we are moving into an age of **telemobility.** He predicted that new systems of communication may be about to alter the structure of many urban areas, thus reducing the need for much human movement within cities and between cities and their hinterlands. As Berry put the matter:

> The revolutionary aspect of electronic environments is not that they reduce the frictions in moving goods and people, but that they move the experience itself to the human nervous system. Traditionally, we have moved the body to the experience; increasingly we will move the experience to the body, and the body can therefore be located where it finds the non-electronic experiences most satisfying. [1970, p. 49]

The geographic implications of the change suggested by Berry are profound. The need for nodal points where humans interact will be reduced for many activities. The amount of spatial interaction requiring the movement of people between places will also decline. For example, the twice-daily commuter flows within metropolises will be greatly reduced, and energy consumed by vehicles will be curtailed.

Those people who choose to live in rural settings can provide most of their financial, retail, educational, and other services through computer networks. In these cases, spatial interaction beween places will consist of electronic pulses, not the movement of persons and their vehicles.

CONCLUSION

These views are a small sample from a vast debate about prospects for the future. Differences in forecasts arise from the various methods of evaluating and projecting trends. Many studies rely on straight-line projections; some extrapolate from cyclical waves. Other differences result from variations in personal and cultural perspectives. The future we see is the present refracted through a lens of values and beliefs (Hughes 1985). For example, Soviet futurists working within a Marxist framework display total confidence in science and technology to solve problems of resource scarcity. They attribute present economic and ecological woes to failings of the capitalist system (Cole 1978).

The future course of humankind is uncharted, but the general direction is being set by current decisions. Many decisions, of course, have important ecological and spatial effects. It is easy to understand the ways personal geographic decisions may affect future activities. For example, most people who interview for a long-term job seriously consider the many implications of moving to a particular site. The same is generally true at the community scale, as demonstrated when citizens debate the advantages and disadvantages of locating a new highway through an urban area. Even at the regional and national level, people usually realize the potential effects of locational decisions, as illustrated by the debates over the selection of nuclear waste dumps.

Today's decisions also have an impact on geographic issues at the world scale. As Willy Brandt, former Chancellor of West Germany, pointed out, problems created by humans can be solved by humans (Independent Commission on International Development Issues 1980, p. 10). Brandt argued that international institutions must be established to confront problems that are now global in extent—population growth, resource depletion, environmental deterioration, misuse of the oceans, financial instability, economic inequality of nations, and the arms race.

The World Commission on Environment and Development (1987) urged international cooperation

---

Telemobility. The transfer of information electronically, which reduces the need for movement of people and the transportation of goods.

through a strengthened United Nations. In *Our Common Future*, the Commission expressed the hope that the distressing trends they have observed can be reversed in the future by much larger international investments in the programs of this supranational organization.

Greater international cooperation will depend on active support by a large population base. Brandt and his international commission of experts concluded that decisions concerning the future of humankind are too important to be left to politicians and experts alone. They emphasized the need for education to increase public knowledge of international affairs, to widen views, and to "foster concern for the fate of other nations" (p. 11). In short, both global awareness and global institutions are needed to solve the economic, social, and ecological problems of the world.

It should be clear, at the end of this book, that geography has an important role to play in broadening horizons. It is stated in the Prologue that geography is worth studying because it gives a global perspective and raises consciousness above the local and national levels—knowledge that is important in a liberal education. More than this, however, geography forms a basis for intelligent decisions whereby humans can exert a decisive influence on the shape of their future.

BIBLIOGRAPHY

Berry, Brian, J. L., "The Geography of the United States in the Year 2000," *Transactions, Institute of British Geographers*, no. 51 (November 1970), pp. 21–53.

Brandt Commission, *Common Crisis North-South: Cooperation for World Recovery*. Cambridge, Mass.: The M.I.T. Press, 1983.

Bryson, Reid A., and Thomas J. Murray, *Climates of Hunger*. Madison, Wis.: University of Wisconsin Press, 1977.

Calder, Nigel, *The Weather Machine*. New York: Viking, 1975.

Cole, Sam, "The Great Futures Debate, 1965–1976," in Christopher Freeman and Marie Jahoda, eds., *World Futures: The Great Debate*, pp. 9–50. London: Martin Robertson, 1978.

Cook, Earl, "The Consumer as Creator: A Criticism of Faith in Limitless Ingenuity," *Energy Exploration and Exploitation*, 1, no. 3 (1982), 189–201.

Ehrlich, Paul R., and John P. Holdren, eds., *The Cassandra Conference: Resources and the Human Predicament*. College Station, Tex.: Texas A & M University Press, 1988.

Forrester, Jay W., *World Dynamics*. Cambridge, Mass.: Wright-Allen Press, 1973.

Franklin, Benjamin, *Observations Concerning the Increase of Mankind*. Boston: S. Kneeland, 1755.

Hall, P., "The Geography of the Fifth Kondratieff Cycle," *New Society*, 55, no. 958 (1981), 535–37.

Heilbroner, Robert L., *An Inquiry into the Human Prospect*. New York: W. W. Norton & Co., Inc., 1974.

Hughes, Barry B., *World Futures: A Critical Analysis of Alternatives*. Baltimore: Johns Hopkins Unversity Press, 1985.

Independent Commission on International Development Issues, *North-South: A Programme for Survival*. London: Pan Books, 1980.

James, Patricia, *Population Malthus: His Life and Times*. London: Routledge & Kegan Paul, 1979.

Kahn, Herman, *World Economic Development: 1979 and Beyond*. Boulder, Colo.: Westview Press, 1979.

———, *The Coming Boom*. New York: Simon & Schuster, 1982.

Kellogg, William W., and Robert Schware, *Climate Change and Society*. Boulder, Colo.: Westview Press, 1981.

Kondratieff, Nikolai D., "The Long Waves in Economic Life," *The Review of Economics and Statistics*, 17, no. 6 (1935), 105–15.

Lovins, Amory B., *World Energy Strategies*. San Francisco: Friends of the Earth, 1975.

———, *Soft Energy Paths*. Harmondsworth, England: Penguin, 1977.

Malthus, Thomas R., *An Essay on the Principle of Population*, ed. by Philip Applemen. New York: W. W. Norton & Co., Inc., 1976.

Meadows, Donella H., et al., *The Limits to Growth: A Report for the Club of Rome's Project on the Predicament of Mankind*. New York: Universe Books, 1972.

Mesarovic, M., and Edward Pestel, *Mankind at the Turning Point. Second Report of the Club of Rome*. New York: E. P. Dutton/Reader's Digest, 1974.

Parry, Martin L., *Climatic Change, Agriculture, and Settlement*. Hamden, Conn.: Archon Books, 1978.

Petersen, William, *Malthus*. Cambridge, Mass.: Harvard University Press, 1979.

Rostow, W. W., *The World Economy: History and Prospect*. Austin, Tex.: University of Texas Press, 1978.

Schumacher, E. F., *Small Is Beautiful: Economics as If People Mattered*. New York: Harper & Row, Pub., 1973.

Simon, J. L., *The Ultimate Resource*. Princeton, N.J.: Princeton University Press, 1981.

Simon, J. L., and Herman Kahn, *The Resourceful Earth: A Response to Global 2000*. Oxford, England: Blackwell, 1984.

Turner, Frederick Jackson, "The Significance of the Frontier in American History," *American Historical Society, Annual Report, 1892*, pp. 199–227. Washington, D.C.: Govt. Printing Office, 1893.

———, *The Frontier in American History*. New York: Henry Holt & Co., 1920.

White, Leslie A., *The Science of Culture*. New York: Grove Press, Inc., 1949.

World Commission on Environment and Development, *Our Common Future*. Oxford and New York: Oxford University Press, 1987.

Zimmermann, Erich W., *Introduction to World Resources*. New York: Harper & Row, Pub., 1964.

GLOSSARY

Absolute location. A position on the earth that is indicated by a fixed grid (or physical features); for example, the site of Chicago is at 41° 49′N, 87° 37′W (see Relative location).

Accessibility. In its geographic sense, the degree to which a place is connected with, and interacts with, other areas.

Acculturation. The modification of a culture through the adoption of new cultural traits from a society with different traditions (see Assimilation).

Activity space. The territory in which a person or group lives and travels.

Age-specific death rate. The ratio consisting of (a) the annual number of deaths for a specific age to (b) the total number of persons of that age (see Death rate, crude).

Agglomeration. The accumulation of persons and economic activities into a relatively small area; sometimes termed aggregation.

Agrarian society. A society based largely on agriculture (hence sometimes called an agricultural society); status and power tend to be determined in relation to land-holdings (see Hunting and gathering society and Industrial society).

Agricultural Revolution. The relatively abrupt change, which first occurred an estimated 10,000 years ago, involving the domestication of plants and animals. Sometimes the term "agricultural revolution" is also applied to later periods of rapid changes in agricultural methods and production.

Animism. The belief that features in the natural environment have sacred significance and power.

Anthropocentric. Interpreting the world from the perspective of human values and experiences.

Apartheid. A policy practiced in the Republic of South Africa that separates officially defined racial groups by designating areas in which each must reside.

Appropriate (or intermediate) technology. The application of relatively unsophisticated procedures and materials that augment, rather than replace, labor.

Arable land. Land that is cultivated or cultivatable; literally meaning "plow land."

Artifacts. The material evidence of human subsistence, shelter, and production (see Sociofacts and Mentifacts).

Assimilation. The process by which nations or communities intermix and become more similar (see Acculturation).

Band society. A type of political organization in which members share resources and territory in an egalitarian manner (see Tribal society, Chiefdom, and State).

Birth rate, crude. The ratio of the number of births per year in a population to the total number of persons in that population. Normally the numerator is expressed in terms of a base of 1000 persons (see Box 2-1).

Boserup thesis. The proposal that intensified use of agricultural land is a result of increasing population density.

Bracero program. The authorized migration from 1940 to 1964 of nearly 5 million Mexicans into the United States to serve as temporary workers.

Buffer state. A country that is regarded as a relatively neutral area because it is located between two, or more, powerful and competing countries.

Built environment. A term that may be used synonymously with cultural landscape but which usually refers to the high density of constructed features in urban places.

Carrying capacity. The theoretical upper limit in the number of persons (or, in other cases, animals) that can subsist adequately on a given area of land under the existing system of technology and land management.

Cartel. A combination of businesses or countries organized to regulate (control) production, pricing, and marketing of goods.

Cartogram. A cartographic representation that shows the amount of a specified phenomenon by the sizes of the areas containing the phenomenon.

Central Business District (CBD). The centrally located core of an urban area containing concentrations of shops, offices, and financial institutions.

Central place. A settlement (village, town, city) that provides goods and services to people in a surrounding trade area.

Centrifugal forces. Factors that destabilize or lead to the break up of an existing unit such as a language, a religion, or a nation (see Centripetal forces).

Centripetal forces. Factors that cohere and bind an existing unit such as a neighborhood, a religion, or a nation (see Centrifugal forces).

Channelized migration. The movement of many migrants along a common route connecting the source area to the destination.

Chiefdom. A type of political organization in which a hereditary ruler allocates resources to other members (see Band society, Tribal society, and State).

Circulation. Movements, usually consisting of short, frequent, and repetitive trips, to and from one's residence.

Circumambulation. Walking around a focal point; illustrated by moving around a sacred object or place as a form of worship.

Civilization. A society that usually has, as a minimum, cities, a written language, a literature, a currency, and a division of labor with elites who control the allocation of resources. The word derives from the Latin word *civitas:* "a city."

Climax vegetation. The stage in which a community of plants becomes stable and begins to perpetuate itself.

Common market. A group of two or more countries that agree (a) to remove tariffs and other restrictions on trade and on the movement of capital and labor between members, and (b) to establish a "common" external tariff on goods imported from outside the single "market" area.

Contagious diffusion. (See Diffusion, contagious.)

Core. When applied to a comparison of national economies, the term refers to the more developed countries around the North Atlantic that industrialized and expanded their trading spheres from the fifteenth to nineteenth centuries (see Periphery and Box 9-1).

Creole language. A language that was originally pidgin but which has become the mother tongue for succeeding generations.

Crude birth rate. (See Birth rate, crude.)

Crude death rate. (See Death rate, crude.)

Cultural convergence. The tendency for societies or cultures to become more similar with time (see Cultural divergence).

Cultural divergence. The tendency for societies or cultures to become less similar with time (see Cultural convergence).

Cultural ecology. The ways different cultures interact with their environments.

Cultural evolution. The successive stages of societies, involving the diversification of cultures as they adapt to particular environments (specific evolution) and the progression of all cultures from hunting and gathering to industrial societies (general evolution).

Cultural landscape. The features constructed by humans that form part of the visible environment (see Natural environment and Built environment).

Culture. The phenomenon that binds people together by shared beliefs and values and by a common image of themselves and the world.

Culture region. An area that is distinguished from other areas on the basis of ethnicity, beliefs, and other aspects of culture (i.e., a type of uniform region).

Death rate, crude. The ratio of the number of deaths per year in a population to the total number of persons in that population. Normally the numerator is expressed in terms of a base of 1000 persons (see Box 2-1).

Decolonization. The process by which a colonial power withdraws from an overseas territory and hands over political control to an independent successor state.

Demographic momentum. The continued effect of a recent history of rapid population change.

Demographic transition model. The generalized decreases in death rates and then birth rates that European populations experienced beginning in the eighteenth century (see Figure 3-5).

Dependency ratio. The ratio consisting of (a) the percentage of population under 15 years and over 64 years to (b) the percentage of that population which is 15–64 years old (see Box 3-2).

Desertification. The spread of aridlike conditions, which may be caused by climatic change, by human activities, or by both.

Devolution. The transfer of some powers from a central government to regional authorities.

Dialect. A distinct linguistic form peculiar to a region or social group but which, nevertheless, can be understood by speakers of other forms of the same language.

Diffusion. The spreading of a phenomenon (such as a group of people, a tool, a disease, an institution, or an idea) over an area of the earth.

Diffusion, contagious. The type of diffusion that spreads by contact among people who are neighbors or are in close proximity (see Diffusion, hierarchical).

Diffusion, hierarchical. The process whereby an idea, technology, or other innovation spreads among settlements of varying sizes, irrespective of their separating distances (see Diffusion, contagious).

Diocese. The territory overseen by a bishop.

Distance decay. The decline in the amount of any phenomenon with increasing distance from a central node (see Box 4-2).

Domesday Book. A record compiled in 1086 which describes landholdings for most of England and from which it is possible to reconstruct information concerning farmland, waste areas, woodlands, urban areas, and population.

Doubling time. The number of years required for a growing population to double in size.

Dual economy. The existence of both a modern economic sector and a traditional sector within the same country, with the former usually being in a few large cities and the latter in the rural areas.

Ecological perspective. An emphasis on the interrelationships between humans and their environments (see Spatial perspective).

Economies of scale, internal. The savings in costs per unit that are achieved by producing large quantities of an item.

Ecosphere. The ecosystem that includes the entire earth (see Ecosystem).

Ecosystem. The complex of interrelationships that function within an environmental setting.

Emigrant. A person who leaves a homeland to settle in another country.

Environmental determinism. The belief that variations in human behavior around the world can be explained by differences in the natural environment (see Possibilism and Box 5-2).

Environmental perception. The way a person or group becomes aware of and comprehends the world (see Perceived environment).

Ethnic group. A term usually applied to a community with cultural characteristics that differ from those of a larger population residing in the same country or general region.

European Economic Community. An organization of Western European countries, commonly called the Common Market (see Box 8-2).

Exclave. A part of a country (or other political unit) that is separated from the main portion by the territory of another country.

Extensive land use. The amount of land that is used for production is large compared to the amounts of labor and capital expended (see Intensive land use).

Fertility rate, total. The number of children that a woman is expected to have during her childbearing years based on the average number of births per woman in a specified population (see Box 3-1).

Formal imperialism. The extension of control by a state over other territories and peoples through political and military power (see Imperialism and Informal imperialism).

Fossil fuels. Earth materials such as peat, lignite, coal, petroleum, and natural gas from which energy can be extracted.

Frontier Thesis. The proposal by Frederick Jackson Turner that American characteristics, such as individualism, independence, and democracy, were a product of readily available land at the edge of settlement (i.e., the frontier).

General evolution. The sequential progression through which all cultures have, or are expected to, develop (see Specific evolution).

Gentrification. The process by which housing in deteriorated inner city areas is taken over by middle or high income groups and is refurbished.

Geographic inertia. The tendency for an activity to retain its location even when the conditions that provided initial advantages change.

Geography. (See Human geography.)

Geostrategy. The study of the political, economic, psychological, and military value of particular portions of earth space.

Gerrymandering. The manipulation of the boundaries of electoral districts for the purpose of maximizing the number of representatives elected from one political party.

Ghetto. A residential area largely occupied by one ethnic group. Originally the term referred to sections of European towns to which Jews were restricted. The term usually implies segregation of a group experiencing discrimination.

Gravity model. A mathematical expression which states that the number of migrants or other persons (or objects) attracted to a place is directly related to the population size of the destination and inversely related to the distance between the origin and destination (see Box 4-3).

Green Revolution. The application of chemical fertilizers and irrigation water to genetically improved seeds to produce high yields of wheat and other grains; a practice that commenced in the 1960s (see Point/Counterpoint, Chapter 9).

Gross National Product (GNP). The total value of goods and services produced (and recorded by monetary transactions) in a country during a year.

Habitat. The environment of an organism or group of organisms.

Hajj. The pilgrimage to Mecca that is prescribed as a religious duty of Moslems.

Hearth area. A place of origin of people, technology, or ideas that subsequently spread to other areas.

Hierarchical diffusion. (See Diffusion, hierarchical.)

Hinterland. A trade area, especially the region situated inland from a seaport.

Human geography. The study of people and their activities from spatial and ecological perspectives.

Hunting and gathering society. A society whose economy is based primarily on hunting wild animals and gathering food and materials from wild plants (see Agrarian society and Industrial society).

Iconography. The images or symbols associated with, for example, national identity or religious affiliation.

Immigrant. A person entering a country for the purpose of living there.

Imperialism. The extension of economic, cultural, or political control by a state or power group over other groups of people (see Formal imperialism and Informal imperialism).

Industrial Revolution. The relatively abrupt change, which first occurred approximately 200 years ago, involving the ways societies utilized energy resources to produce manufactured goods.

Industrial society. A society whose economy depends on manufacturing for the production of many of its needs (see Hunting and gathering society and Agrarian society).

Infant mortality rate. The ratio consisting of (a) the annual number of deaths of infants not over one year old to (b) the total number of live births during that year (see Box 3-1).

Informal imperialism. The extension of economic and political influence by a state over other territories and peoples, but without formal rule; also called neo-imperialism or neo-colonialism (see Imperialism and Formal imperialism).

Information field. An area within which communication among occupants is frequent and influential.

Infrastructure. The basic framework of a system; a term used especially in reference to transportation, utility facilities, and similar installations that support economic production.

Innovation. The introduction of a new idea, technique, or device.

Intensive land use. The amounts of labor and/or capital expended are large compared to the amount of land in production (see Extensive land use).

Internal economies of scale. (See Economies of scale, internal.)

Isogloss. A line on a map showing the areal extent of a linguistic element such as a word, pronunciation, or grammatical characteristic.

Landlocked country. A state that has no ocean frontage and thus is entirely surrounded by land held by other countries.

Language family. A group of languages that are related because they evolved from a common ancient language.

Less developed nations. The group of countries having a wide variety of economic characteristics but generally identified by comparatively low rates of literacy, gross domestic product per capita, and degree of economic diversification when compared to industrialized countries (see More developed nations and Box 9-1).

Life expectancy. The number of years a newborn infant is expected to live (see Box 2-1).

Lingua franca. A language used in common as a second language by people who have different first languages (see Box 6-1).

Linguistic geography. The study of dialects by the mapping of distributions of words, pronunciations, and grammatical characteristics; also called dialectology.

Malthusian. A viewpoint that sees future human population numbers as likely to increase faster than the available food supply (see Box 2-3).

Manifest Destiny. The belief that the westward expansion of the United States during the nineteenth century was an expression of divine will (see Box 7-1).

Map projection. A system for representing the sphere of the earth (or globe) on a flat surface. This necessarily involves some distortion.

Map scale. The ratio of map distance to the corresponding earth distance. For example, 1:30 means one linear unit (such as an inch or a centimeter) on the map represents 30 of those units on the earth. If a second map has a ratio of 1:3,000,000, then comparatively it has a much *smaller* scale (see Box 1-1).

Megalopolis. Originally defined as the nearly continuous urban area stretching from Massachusetts Bay to the Potomac River; the term is often applied to any urbanized area that consists of coalescing large cities.

Mental map. The locational knowledge or mental images that a person has about the positions and characteristics of specific places.

Mentifacts. The world view, values, and beliefs, such as those expressed in religion and art, that hold a society together (see Artifacts and Sociofacts).

Mercantile model. An explanation for the location of cities in North America in terms of long-range trade and wholesaling functions.

Metropolitan area. A region consisting of several urbanized places, usually around a core city, that operates as an economic unit.

Migration chain. The process by which early movers encourage others to move by providing information and communal assistance.

Migration field. The area from which a city or other settlement draws migrants.

Modern society. A society whose members have a high per capita income, low birth and death rates, and access to high quality educational and medical services.

Monoculture. The practice of growing one crop over a large area of land (see Polyculture).

More developed nations. The group of countries that is the richest and most industrialized (see Less developed nations and Box 9-1).

Morphology. The study of form and structure.

Mother tongue. A person's native, or first, language.

Multinational corporation. A business organization with subsidiary companies operating in several countries.

Nation state. A political unit with defined boundaries that encompass a people who share common cultural traits and a sense of identity (see Box 8-1).

Natural environment. The physical elements of the earth, such as landforms, climate, vegetation, and soils (see Cultural landscape).

Natural increase. The difference between the birth rate and death rate for a given population, usually expressed as a percentage (see Box 2-1).

Net reproduction rate. The number of girls who would be born to a hypothetical woman who reproduces at the typical rate in a population as she passes through her childbearing years (usually considered to be ages 15–45) (see Box 3-1).

Nodal region. An area connected to a common place (center or node) by lines of communication (see Uniform region and Box 5-3).

Open fields. Large farm areas that are divided into unenclosed strips for the use of individual farmers.

Overpopulation. A vague but popular term that usually relates the number of people to the resources of an area.

Peasant. A rural dweller who is part of a family unit that practices small-scale agriculture and consumes most of its own production.

Perceived environment. The portion of the total environment that is consciously sensed and which serves as a basis for decision-making (see Environmental perception).

Periphery. When applied to a comparison of national economies, the term has historically referred to all countries other than those identified as belonging to the "core" (see Core and Box 9-1).

Pidgin. A language with simplified grammatical structure that develops from the attempts of people having different languages to communicate.

Plantation. A large agricultural unit that specializes in the growing of a few crops for selling to large, and often foreign, markets (see Box 9-2).

Polyculture. The practice of growing several crops simultaneously within a small area (see Monoculture).

Popular culture. Those aspects of culture which are widely promoted and maintained through mass media.

Population density. The number of individuals residing within a specified area divided by the size of that area. For example, if 164,000 persons live in an area of 2000 square kilometers, the population density of that area is 82 persons per square kilometer.

Population persistence. The degree to which a population continues to reside in one place over a period of time. The persistence is usually expressed as the percentage of remaining population to the total population, and then adjusted for births and deaths.

Population pyramid. A graph showing the percentage of

males and females in each of a set of age classes (see Box 3-3).

Possibilism. The belief that the natural environment provides options for human behavior (see Environmental determinism and Box 5-2).

Post-industrial economy. An economy that has shifted its productive emphasis from manufacturing to service activities.

Primary activities. Economic activities that produce goods by "collecting" materials from the natural environment, such as in hunting, fishing, mining, lumbering, and agriculture (see Secondary and Tertiary activities).

Primate city. The major city that is many times greater in population size and number of economic activities than any other urban place in a given country (see Rank-size rule).

Producers' services. Services that are provided for other businesses rather than directly for consumers.

Pronatalism. A policy that encourages births.

Quaternary activities. Economic activities that produce value by performing communication and information services; sometimes included within the general category of tertiary activities.

Raison d'être. The "reason for being" or justification for the existence of a nation.

Rank-size rule. The regularity in the population sizes of cities in a country or region such that the largest city is twice the size of the second largest place, three times as big as the third-ranked urban center, and four times greater than the fourth largest city.

Received pronunciation. The standard dialect, or "court-correct" form of speech, in Britain.

Region. An area that is differentiated from other areas according to specified criteria (see Box 5-3).

Regional consciousness. A feeling held by the inhabitants of an area that "their territory" is distinctive from other places.

Regional geography. An approach that divides the subject of geography according to areas. For example, the geography of tropical Africa is separated from the geography of the grasslands of Asia (see Topical geography).

Regionalism. A feeling by the inhabitants of an area that "their territory" should be recognized as being a distinct political unit.

Register. A type of speech for a particular social setting or occasion; also called situation dialect.

Relative location. A position on the earth that is indicated in terms of other phenomena. For example, Chicago is situated where rail, water, and highway routes converge (see Absolute location).

Replacement level. The population growth rate at which the size of one generation is the same as that of the previous generation (see Box 3-1 and Zero population growth).

Scatter diagram. A graphic display of points, each of which indicates a pair of values by its position relative to two axes (see Box 3-2).

Secondary activities. Economic activities that produce goods by remaking materials such as through manufacturing and construction (see Primary and Tertiary activities).

Shifting cultivation. A type of agriculture that involves clearing the natural vegetation (e.g., forest) from a small area, cropping it a few years, and then abandoning that area while it reverts to wild vegetation. This type may be subdivided into three subtypes (forest-fallow, bush-fallow, and short-fallow) based on the length of the time the land is not being cultivated.

Site. The internal characteristics of a particular place, such as topography, soil types, buildings, and land use (see Situation).

Situation. The position of a place relative to the locations of external features; for example, a town may be situated in the center of a plain and be located midway between two major cities (see Site).

Sociobiologist. A person who studies the genetic basis of social behavior.

Sociofacts. The institutions, such as family structure and educational system, that bind a society together (see Artifacts and Mentifacts).

Spatial interaction. The exchange that occurs between places which are separated from each other.

Spatial perspective. An emphasis on the locations, patterns, or arrangements of phenomena (see Ecological perspective).

Specific evolution. The process of diversification and development of an individual culture as it adapts to its environment (see General evolution).

State. A type of political organization that occupies a defined area in which lives a people with an independent political identity (see Box 8-1; also see Band society, Tribal society, and Chiefdom).

Stratified society. A society in which subgroups or classes are recognized and ranked.

Subsistence farming. A system of agriculture in which the cultivators, and their families, consume most of their own production.

Telemobility. The transfer of information electronically, which reduces the need for movement of people and the transportation of goods.

Tenant farmer. A cultivator who rents land by paying cash, by sharing the crop, or by providing labor services to the landlord.

Territoriality. The claiming of a specific area by a person or group of people.

Tertiary activities. Economic activities that produce value through the performance of services (see Primary, Secondary, and Quaternary activities).

Three-field system of agriculture. An agricultural practice in which arable land of a community is divided into three open fields with two fields being cultivated and one field, in rotation, left fallow.

Threshold of demand. The minimum number of purchases required to make it feasible to offer a good or service.

Topical geography. An approach that divides geography according to the kinds of subjects (topics). For example, the geography of agriculture is separated from the geography of languages (see Regional geography).

Toponym. The name of a place; a place name.

Total fertility rate. (See Fertility rate, total.)

Trade area. The region around a city from which buyers and sellers come (i.e., the service area), or the region with which a country exports and imports.

Tribal society. A type of political organization composed of associated bands (see Band society, Chiefdom, and State).

Tropical rainforest. A vegetational type consisting of forests growing in warm and wet climates.

Uniform region. An area that is differentiated from other areas by the existence of specified characteristics; a classification of earth space based on the distribution of one or more phenomena (see Box 5-3 and Nodal region).

Urban hierarchy. The ranking of towns, cities, and metropolises by size and function.

Urban majority. A situation in which more than 50 percent of the population of a country or region lives in cities.

Voluntary region. A cultural area that is distinctive because people assemble there to be near others having similar preferences.

World view. The general beliefs held in common by a group which pertain to the universe, the natural environment, and humans.

Zero population growth. A situation in which the number of births and deaths is equal over a sustained period of time (see Box 3-1).

SUBJECT INDEX

AUTHOR INDEX